RETRIEVAL & RE...
Ressourcer...
IN CATHOLIC TH...

The middle years of this century marked a particularly intense time of crisis and change in European society. During this period (1930-1950), a broad intellectual and spiritual movement arose within the European Catholic community, largely in response to the secularism that lay at the core of the crisis. The movement drew inspiration from earlier theologians and philosophers such as Möhler, Newman, Gardeil, Rousselot, and Blondel, as well as from men of letters like Charles Péguy and Paul Claudel.

The group of academic theologians included in the movement extended into Belgium and Germany, in the work of men like Emile Mersch, Dom Odo Casel, Romano Guardini, and Karl Adam. But above all the theological activity during this period centered in France. Led principally by the Jesuits at Fourviére and the Dominicans at Le Saulchoir, the French revival included many of the greatest names in twentieth-century Catholic thought: Henri de Lubac, Jean Daniélou, Yves Congar, Marie-Dominique Chenu, Louis Bouyer, and, in association, Hans Urs von Balthasar.

It is not true — as subsequent folklore has it — that those theologians represented any sort of self-conscious "school": indeed, the differences among them, for example, between Fourviére and Saulchoir, were important. At the same time, most of them were united in the double conviction that theology had to speak to the present situation, and that the condition for doing so faithfully lay in a recovery of the Church's past. In other words, they saw clearly that the first step in what later came to be known as *aggiornamento* had to be *ressourcement* — a rediscovery of the riches of the whole of the Church's two-thousand-year tradition. According to de Lubac, for example, all of his own works as well as the entire *Sources chrétiennes* collection are based on the presupposition that "the renewal of Christian vitality is linked at least partially to a renewed exploration of the periods and of the works where the Christian tradition is expressed with particular intensity."

In sum, for the *ressourcement* theologians theology involved a "return to the sources" of Christian faith, for the purpose of drawing out the meaning and significance of these sources for the critical questions of our time. What these theologians sought was a spiritual and intellectual communion with Christianity in its most vital moments as transmitted to us in its classic texts, a communion that would nourish, invigorate, and rejuvenate twentieth-century Catholicism.

The *ressourcement* movement bore great fruit in the documents of the Second Vatican Council and has deeply influenced the work of Pope John Paul II.

The present series is rooted in this twentieth-century renewal of theology. The series thus understands *ressourcement* as revitalization: a return to the sources, for the purpose of developing a theology that will truly meet the challenges of our time. Some of the features of the series, then, will be a return to classical (patristic-mediaeval) sources and a dialogue with twentieth-century Western culture, particularly in terms of problems associated with the Enlightenment, modernity, and liberalism.

The series will publish out-of-print or as yet untranslated studies by earlier authors associated with the *ressourcement* movement. The series also plans to publish works by contemporary authors sharing in the aim and spirit of this earlier movement. This will include any works in theology, philosophy, history, literature, and the arts that give renewed expression to Catholic sensibility.

The editor of the Ressourcement series, David L. Schindler, is Gagnon Professor of Fundamental Theology and Dean at the John Paul II Institute in Washington, D.C., and editor of the North American edition of *Communio: International Catholic Review*, a federation of journals in thirteen countries founded in Europe in 1972 by Hans Urs von Balthasar, Jean Daniélou, Henri de Lubac, Joseph Ratzinger, and others.

RETRIEVAL & RENEWAL
Ressourcement
IN CATHOLIC THOUGHT

Volumes available

In the Beginning:
A Catholic Understanding of the Story of Creation and the Fall
Cardinal Joseph Ratzinger

Hans Urs von Balthasar: A Theological Style
Angelo Scola

Prayer: The Mission of the Church
Jean Daniélou

The Heroic Face of Innocence:
Three Stories by Georges Bernanos
Georges Bernanos

On Pilgrimage
Dorothy Day

We, the Ordinary People of the Streets
Madeleine Delbrêl

Medieval Exegesis, *volumes 1-2:*
The Four Senses of Scripture
Henri de Lubac

MEDIEVAL EXEGESIS

VOLUME 2

The Four Senses of Scripture

HENRI DE LUBAC, S.J.

Translated by
E. M. Macierowski

WILLIAM B. EERDMANS PUBLISHING COMPANY
GRAND RAPIDS, MICHIGAN

T&T CLARK
EDINBURGH

Originally published as
Exégèse médiévale, 2: Les quatre sens de l'écriture
© 1959 Éditions Montaigne
English translation © 2000 Wm. B. Eerdmans Publishing Co.

Published jointly 2000 by
Wm. B. Eerdmans Publishing Co.
255 Jefferson Ave. S.E., Grand Rapids, Michigan 49503
www.eerdmans.com
and by
T&T Clark Ltd
59 George Street
Edinburgh EH2 2LQ
Scotland
www.tandtclark.co.uk

All rights reserved. No part of this publication may be reproduced, stored in a retrieval system, or transmitted, in any form or by any means, electronic, mechanical, photocopying, recording or otherwise, without the prior permission of the publisher.

Printed in the United States of America

05 04 03 02 01 00   7 6 5 4 3 2 1

Library of Congress Cataloging-in-Publication Data

Lubac, Henri de, 1896-
[Exégèse médiévale. English]
Medieval Exegesis / Henri de Lubac; translated by E. M. Macierowski.
p.   cm.
Includes bibliographical references and index.
Contents: v. 2. The four senses of scripture.
ISBN 0-8028-4146-5 (pbk.: alk. paper)
1. Bible — Criticism, interpretation, etc. — History — Middle Ages, 600-1500.
I. Title.
BS500.L82513 2000
220.6'09'02 — dc21   97-32802
                                                      CIP

British Library Cataloguing-in-Publication Data
A catalogue record for this book is available from the British Library

ISBN 0 567 08760 3

Contents

List of Principal Abbreviations	ix
6. Names and Number of the Biblical Senses	1
7. The Foundation of History	41
8. Allegory, Sense of the Faith	83
9. Mystical Tropology	127
10. Anagogy and Eschatology	179
Notes	227
Index of Names	435

List of Principal Abbreviations

1. Journals

AHDLMA	Archives d'histoire doctrinale et littéraire du moyen âge
ASOC	Analecta sacra ordinis cisterciensis
BALC	Bulletin d'ancienne littérature chrétienne
BLE	Bulletin de littérature ecclésiastique
BTAM	Bulletin de théologie ancienne et médiévale
CCM	Cahiers de civilisation médiévale
COCR	Collectanea ordinis cisterciensis reformati
ETL	Ephemerides theologicae lovanienses
HTR	The Harvard Theological Review
JTS	The Journal of Theological Studies
Med. St.	Mediaeval Studies
NRT	Nouvelle revue théologique
RAM	Revue d'ascétique et de mystique
RB	Revue bénédictine
R. bibl.	Revue biblique
RDSR	Revue des sciences religieuses
REL	Revue des études latines
RHE	Revue d'histoire ecclésiastique
RHEF	Revue de l'histoire de l'Église de France
RHLR	Revue d'histoire et de littérature religieuse
RHPR	Revue d'histoire et de philosophie religieuse
R. Mab.	Revue Mabillon
RMAL	Revue du moyen âge latin

RQH	Revue des questions historiques
RSPT	Revue des sciences philosophiques et théologiques
RSR	Recherches de science religieuse
RTAM	Recherches de théologie ancienne et médiévale
S. Er.	Sacris erudiri
Vig. Chr.	Vigiliae christianae
ZFKT	Zeitschrift für katholische Theologie

2. Anthologies, Collections

An. mar.	Germain Morin, OSB, *Anecdota maredsolana*. 3 tomes (5 vols.). Maredsous, 1893-1903.
ASS	*Acta sanctorum* (Bollandistes).
CCL	*Corpus christianorum,* series latina. Turnholti.
DAFC	A. D'Ales, *Dictionnaire apologétique de la foi catholique.* Paris, 1911-1931.
DB	F. Vigouroux, *Dictionnaire de la Bible.* Paris, 1895-1912.
DBS	F. Pirot, A. Robert, H. Cazelle, *Dictionnaire de la Bible, supplément.* Paris, 1928 ss.
DHGE	A. Baudrillart, R. Aubert, E. Van Cauwenbergh, *Dictionnaire d'histoire et de géographie ecclésiastique.* Paris, 1912 ss.
D. Sp.	M. Viler, F. Cavallera, J. De Guibert, Ch. Baumgartner, M. Ophe-Gaillard . . . , *Dictionnaire de spiritualité, ascétique et mystique, doctrine et histoire.* Paris, 1937 ss.
DTC	A. Vacant, E. Mangenot, E. Amann, *Dictionnaire de théologie catholique.* Paris, 1909-1950.
HLF	*Histoire littéraire de la France,* ouvrage commencé par les Bénédictins et continué par les membres de l'Institut. 3 vols. Paris, 1865-1941.
L. de lite	MGH, *Libelli de lite Imperatorum et Pontificum saec. XI et XII.* 3 vols. Hanover, 1891-7.
Mai	Card. Angelo Mai, *Nova Patrum Bibliotheca.* 10 vols. Rome, 1852-1905.
MBVP	Margarin de la Bigne, *Maxima Bibliotheca veterum Patrum et antiquorum scriptorum ecclesiasticorum.* 27 vols. Lyon, 1677 (tome 13: Ambrose Autpert, *In Apoc.;* tome 17: Raoul of Saint Germer, *In Levit.;* tome 21: Potho of Prüm).

List of Principal Abbreviations

M.D.	Martène et Durand, OSB, *Thesaurus novus anecdotorum*. 5 vols., 1717; *Veterum scriptorum . . . amplissima collectio.* 9 vols., 1724-33.
MGH	*Monumenta Germaniae Historica.* Hanover-Leipzig.
M.W.	Misset and Weale, *Thesaurus hymnologicus.* Tome 1, 1888.
Pez	Bernhard Pez, OSB, *Thesaurus anecdotorum novissimus.* 6 tomes (16 vols.) Vienna, 1721-8.
PG	Migne, *Patrologia graeca.* Paris.
Pitra	Card. J. B. Pitra, *Spicilegium solesmense.* 4 vols. Paris, 1852-8.
PL	Migne, *Patrologia latina.* Paris.
SC	*Sources chrétiennes.* Paris, 1942 ss.
Sp. cas.	*Spicilegium casinense.*
St. ans.	*Studia anselmiana.* Rome, 1933 ss.
St. patr.	*Studia patristica.* Ed. Kurt Aland and F. L. Cross: *Papers presented to the Second International Conference: Patristic Studies held at Christ Church.* Oxford, 1955. 2 vols. Berlin, 1957.
TU	*Texte und Untersuchungen zur Geschichte des altchristlichen Literatur.* Ed. O. von Gebhart and A. Harnack *et al.* Leipzig, 1883 ss.

Clement and Origen (Or.) are cited for the most part according to the editions of the Leipzig-Berlin Corpus: *Die griechischen christlichen Schriftsteller der ersten drei Jahrhunderte;* they are indicated only by the page of the volume containing the work cited. The same is true for certain Latin authors cited according to the editions of the Vienna Corpus: *Corpus scriptorum ecclesiasticorum latinorum.*

3. Certain Frequently Cited Works

Aug., *Conf.*	Saint Augustine, *Confessions.* Ed. P. De Labriolle. 2 vols. Coll. des universités de France. Paris, 1925-6.
Bardenhewer	Otto Bardenhewer, *Geschichte des altkirklichen Literatur.* 5 vols. Freiburg-im-Breisgau. Tome 1 and 2. 2nd ed., 1913 and 1914.
Bardy, *Recherches*	Gustave Bardy, *Recherches sur l'histoire du texte et*

	des versions latines du De Principiis d'Origène. Paris, 1923.
S. Bernard th.	*Saint Bernard théologien, actes du congrès de Dijon* (15-19 Sept. 1953). ASOC, Rome, 1953.
E. de Bruyne	Edgar de Bruyne, *Etudes d'esthétique médiévale*. 3 vols.
Cillier	Remy Ceillier, OSB, *Histoire générale des auteur sacrés et ecclésiastiques*. 17 vols. Paris, 1865-9.
CM	Henri de Lubac, *Corpus mysticum*. 2nd ed. Paris, 1949.
Courcelle	Pierre Courcelle, *Les lettres grecques en Occident, de Macrobe à Cassiodore*. Paris, 1943.
Curtius	Ernst-Robert Curtius, *La littérature européenne et le moyen âge latin*, tr. Jean Bréjoux. Paris, 1957.
Delhaye, ET	Philippe Delhaye, *Le microcosmus de Godefroy de Saint-Victor*, étude théologique. Lille, 1951.
Ebert	A. Ebert, *Histoire générale de la littérature du moyen âge en Occident*. Tr. J. Aymeric and J. Condamin. 3 vols. Paris, 1883-9.
Fontaine	Jacques Fontaine, *Isidore de Séville et la culture classique dans l'Espagne Wisigothique*. 2 vols. Paris, 1959.
Gautier	Léon Gautier, *Œvres poétiques d'Adam de Saint-Victor*. 3rd ed. 1894.
Gerhoh, *Op. in.*	*Gerhohi praepositi reichersbergensis Opera inedita*. I: Tractatus et libeli, cura et studio PP. Damiani ac Odulphi Van den Eynde et P. Angelini Rijmersdad, OFM. Rome, 1955.
Ghellinck, *Mouvement*	Joseph de Ghellinck, *Le mouvement théologique du XIIe siècle*. 2nd ed. Museum lessianum. Bruges-Bruxelles-Paris, 1948.
———, *L'essor*	Id., *L'essor de la littérature latine au XIIe siècle*. 2 vols. Museum lessianum. Bruxelles-Paris, 1946.
———, *Litt. lat.*	Id., *Littérature latine au moyen âge*. 2 vols. Paris, 1939.
Gr. D'Elv., Tr.	*Tractatus Origenis de libris SS. Scripturarum*. Ed. Batiffol. Paris, 1900.
HE	Henri de Lubac, *Histoire et Esprit*. Paris, 1950.
Hugo Métel	(Letters of Hugo Métel in) *Sacrae antiquitatis monumenta*. Tome 2 (1731).

List of Principal Abbreviations

Jerome, *Ep.*	(Ep. 1 to 120:) Saint Jérôme, *Lettres*. Ed. J. Labourt. 6 vols. Coll. des universités de France. Paris, 1949-58.
Keble	John Keble, *On the Mysticism attributed to the Early Fathers of the Church*. 2nd ed. Oxford, 1868.
Labriolle	Pierre de Labriolle, *Histoire de la littérature chrétienne*. 3rd ed., revised by G. Bardy. 2 vols. Paris, 1947.
Laistner	M. L. W. Laistner, *Thought and Letters in Western Europe A.D. 500-900*. New ed. London, 1957.
Leclercq, *L'amour des lettres*	Jean Leclercq, OSB, *L'amour des lettres et le désire de Dieu*. Paris, 1957.
———, *Etudes*	Id., *Etudes sur saint Bernard et le texte de ses écrits*. ASOC, Rome, 1953.
Manitius	Max Manitius, *Geschichte der lateinischen Literatur des Mittelalters*. 3 vols. Munich, 1911-31.
Al. Neckam	Alexander Neckam, *De naturis rerum libri duo, with the Poem of the same Author, De laudibus divinae sapientiae*. Ed. Thomas Wright. London, 1863.
Paré	G. Paré, A. Brunay, P. Tremblay, *La renaissance du XIIe siècle: les écoles et l'enseignement*. Paris-Ottawa, 1933.
Petit, *Prémontrés*	François Petit, *La spiritualité des Prémontrés . . . aux XIIe et XIIIe siècles*. Paris, 1947.
Roger	Maurice Roger, *L'enseignement des Lettres classiques d'Ausone à Alcuin, introduction à l'histoire carolingienne*. Paris, 1905.
Smalley	Beryl Smalley, *The Study of the Bible in the Middle Ages*. 2nd ed. Oxford, 1952.
Spicq, *Esquisse*	C. Spicq, O.P., *Esquisse d'une histoire de l'exégèse latine au moyen âge*. Paris, 1944.

CHAPTER SIX

Names and Number of the Biblical Senses

1. Pauline Allegory

When the analogy between Scripture and man composed of body, soul, and spirit was introduced, the expression "spiritual sense" was found naturally adapted, as has been seen, to designate the third term of this tripartite division. But the term already existed in the fundamental division into two senses. There were immediately certain convergent currents which sometimes replaced it and sometimes combined with it. The two principal ones, both also Pauline, are "allegory" and "mystery"; or "allegorical sense" and "mystical sense."

According to the allegory, that is, the spiritual understanding.[1] This word 'allegory' was imposed by reason of the celebrated passage from the Epistle to the Galatians developing the allegory of Sarah and Hagar. Alluding to the story of Genesis, Saint Paul had written: "These things are said allegorically, *hattina estin allēgoroumena*."[2] It was a recent word then. It had perhaps been formed about sixty years before Jesus Christ, by the grammarian Philodemus of Gadara, to designate that figure of grammar or style "which consists in saying one thing so as to make another be understood by it."[3] One of the first pagan authors who, by an initiative analogous to that of Saint Paul but for a very different end, had borrowed the *tēs allēgorias tropos* [the figure of allegory] or *tropos allēgorikos* [allegorical figure] from the grammarians to apply it to the interpretation of texts, is a Stoic who was writing under Augustus, the Pseudo-Heraclitus of Pontus, author of the *Homērika problēmata*. Longinus also employs it in his treatise *On the Sublime*.[4] Under the verbal form which owes to Saint Paul, one finds the term in the *Geography* of Strabo: "In the histories that Homer recounts, he does not, says Strabo, incessantly invent off the top of his head, but often also allegorizes so as to instruct."[5] It is doubtless to these authors, especially to Heraclitus, that Plutarch alludes when he writes in his treatise *On the Reading of the Poets*: "In Homer one encounters a similar sort of silent teaching, and it always accompanies with useful reasonings those of his tales that have been most severely attacked; to justify them, some have had recourse to what the ancients called *hyponoiai* (hidden meanings, underlying senses, allusions, deep senses) and which today are called *allēgoriai*."[6]

Plutarch designates here the method already inaugurated by the apologists of Homer, such as a Theagenes of Rhegium, or a Stesimbrotus of Thasos, who in fact were looking for edifying or profound "implications" under the salacious letter of certain of his verses, so as to transform them, as a first-century Latin inscription says, into "dutiful incantations" ["pia carmina"]. They had had numerous imitators: "for," says Heraclitus, "if Homer had not spoken in allegories, then he would have advanced all sorts of impieties."[7] The method was quickly adopted by thinkers of various schools who wanted to find in the Poet the source of their "favorite thoughts": an Anaxagoras, a Metrodorus of Lampsacus, a Democritus, a Prodicus of Ceos, a Diogenes of Apollonia, an Antisthenes, a Diogenes. . . . After the apologetic and moral motive, there came into play a motive that can be called both rationalist and utilitarian. It will be considered more and more as a title of honor to have been foretold long ago by "the educator of Greece," as Plato had made Homer be titled by his admirers,[8] one whom a personage of Xenophon proclaimed "the wisest of men,"[9] whom the Pythagorian Aristides Quintilian used to call "the prophet of the All,"[10] and whom the Pseudo-Plutarch had to hail as "the forerunner of all the philosophers."[11] These often mixed motives were tinged with mysticism, for in a society which recognized in antiquity a token of truth, poetry, with all its enigmas, was commonly held to be the primordial and sacred form of knowing. Thus, despite many instances of resistance successively coming from Plato, Epicurus, the grammarians of Alexandria, the New Academy, and from Lucian, all sorts of philosophers — Pythagoreans, Platonists, Cynics, Stoics — rivaled each other in this kind of interpretation. They extended it to all the ancient poets, to all mythology. By them the myths were explicated "piously and philosophically."[12] The Neoplatonists did the same; the late allegorism of a Porphyry, and then of a Sallust, and finally of a Proclus and an Olympiadorus, was an effort to "tie what remained of Hellenic religion, initiations, and mysteries back to the theology of the School."[13]

As to the content of such an exegesis, it was naturally as varied as the doctrines of those who practiced it. It could be of a cosmic, or psychological, or moral, or metaphysical type. Several denominated it "theological." But these diversities did not affect the functional unity of a method by which 'the allegory of the tale' was expounded.[14] It was a method servile on two fronts: not only with regard to the text commented upon — though its arbitrariness was not always as total as a modern is tempted to believe[15] — but also with regard to the superstitions whose true sense it pretended to reveal to the elite,[16] since in authorizing all the kinds of symbols it conciliated, as Lactantius will say, the belief in the "popular gods" with the philosophical idea of the "one natural god."[17] It was a method that it would therefore be quite insufficient to define by any treatments of a merely literary order. It is necessary to call it "physical" or "physiological," following an expression that comes up constantly in the explications of mythologers themselves[18] as well as in the critique instituted by the Christian authors, such as Eusebius,[19] Tertullian,[20] Saint Augustine.[21] It was a naturalistic method, in the sense that it made every historical or personal reality vanish, the sensible individualities of the gods or heroes being transformed within it in regard to the reflection in the nature of things, or in the nature of the soul, or in the nature of the divinity. It was compelled, says Saint Augustine in the course of exposing the theory of Varro, to reduce everything "to natural characteristics."[22] These were "physical interpretations," "interpretations by which [the tales] are shown to signify the nature of things," "certain physiological interpretations, as they say, that is, interpretations of the natural characteristics."[23]

Whether it is a question of just the Homeric poems or of the divine histories as a whole, this allegorical exegesis in the pagan style could then, in the time of the Apostle, be designated chiefly by two names. (The Pythagoreans also used to say, more simply: *exēgēsis*). Dionysius of Halicarnassus uses both terms.[24] *Hyponoia*, which had been the term employed by Plato,[25] Xenophon,[26] Aristotle,[27] and Aristophanes,[28] was again a current expression. It is the term used by the Stoic Cornutus, the teacher of Persius, who under Nero wrote his *Summary of Greek Theology*.[29] It is by this term that Clement of Alexandria will continue to designate the doctrine hidden under the veil of poetry by Orpheus, Lucius, Musaeus, Homer, and Hesiod.[30] Philo of Alexandria will very often use it to characterize his own exegesis of the Bible,[31] an exegesis itself quite different from that which the philosophers practiced upon the data of the fable: although for him the history did not have the same importance nor the same significance as it did for the Christians, we know that he by no means denied it; we also know that, far from rejecting the letter of the Law, on the contrary, he wanted by means of the spiritual explication that he gave of it to "re-value" its practice.[32] Philo also speaks of *allēgoria*,[33] but less frequently, although the title of one of his works is *Nomōn hierōn allēgoria* [*Allegory of the Sacred Laws*]. It falls to him to unite the two words in one and the same expression: the first then designates the objective signification, and the second the procedure thanks to which one extracts that signification from the text under which it is hidden; thus in the *De vita contemplativa* or in the *De praemiis: en tais kath' hyponoian allēgoriais*.[34]

Certain historians at this point place too much confidence in the ancient polemicists, Christian or pagan, notably in Porphyry; or else they allow themselves to be too impressed by secondary — though, it is true, invasive — features. Attentive only to procedures or general conceptions that the Christian writers then, as always, had in common with the men of their time, or concluding too quickly from an unavoidable analogy of vocabulary to an analogy of thought, they believe that they ought to put all of Christian allegory into an essential relation of origin and of nature with the doctrines of the intellectual paganism allegorizing its myths, at the same time as with the exegeses of Philo — whether this is or is not done by the intermediary of certain "Gnostics."[35] Almost every Christian interpretation of the Scriptures comes to appear thereby as a "sort of colony of Greek allegorism" within Christian territory.[36] The Bible itself, through its authentic interpreters being themselves interpreted in that fashion, seems then to become something like a vast myth, dissolved by allegory.

Nevertheless, it is sufficient to read a certain number of texts from the two originators, which here are Tertullian and Origen, to guarantee that, in word and in deed, Christian allegory comes from Saint Paul.[37] If allegory had been enhanced with the resources of the culture inherited from the Greeks, none but he could have made it credible in its essentials.[38]

Against Marcion and the Valentinians, Tertullian took care to establish that the Scriptures contain an "allegorical disposition."[39] In consequence, he applied to biblical exegesis, as one ought to practice it within the Church, the verb "allegorizare," which he coined on the basis of Pauline Greek.[40] Of the Apostle understanding a precept of Deuteronomy from preachers, he writes: "he proved an allegorical law according to us."[41] And he finds it quite natural to speak of the "allegorical arms" of

David.[42] Defending the divine value of the Old Testament against Marcion, he tells him: "I want . . . to bring forward to you the controversy concerning the allegories of the Apostle." The mystery of Hagar and Sarah appeared to him as a "sacrament of the allegory" and, in a passage where he assembles the principal examples of spiritual interpretation that one finds in Saint Paul, he alludes to the Apostle "teaching the Galatians likewise that the two arguments of the sons of Abraham have run together allegorically."[43]

The same usage occurs in Origen, and the same appeal to the Apostle. For him, too, when he has recourse to the "allegorical understanding"[44] or when he calls up the "order of allegory,"[45] the Pauline filiation is direct and in such expressions, as in those of Tertullian, the historical affirmation is included. Often Origen prevails upon the authority of Paul in explicit terms: "Having been imbued through the apostle Paul, we . . .";[46] "we, in accordance with the judgment of the Apostle . . .";[47] "our allegories, which Paul has taught."[48] Let us reread this passage from a homily on Genesis, with regard to the history of Abraham and Abimelech:

> . . . If anyone wants to hear and understand these things according to the letter alone, he ought to have a hearing with the Jews rather than with the Christians. But if he wants to be a Christian and a disciple of Paul, let him hear him saying, "since the law is spiritual." And when he was speaking about Abraham and his wife and sons, let him say that these things are allegorical. And although he had to have such allegories, scarcely would any of us be able to find them easily, but yet he ought to pray that the veil be lifted from his heart, if there is anyone who strives to be converted to the Lord; for "the Lord is spirit"; that he may take away the veil of the letter and open up the light of the spirit, and we may be able to say that "once the face had been unveiled, looking upon the glory of the Lord" etc.[49]

These texts of the homilies are no longer available to us except in translation, and so not every word of them is guaranteed. But they are in perfect agreement with other passages that we still do have in Greek. Moreover, they form one body with the developments that they announce or in which they are inserted. They are indeed not empty formulas. The allegory which the great exegete so often defends against the partisans of the "letter alone," that allegory by which he undertakes — with what success, is another matter — to trace the royal road of the Christian interpretation of the Scriptures, between the negations and the antagonistic or even sometimes allied errors of the Jews and the "heretics," is something he in fact quite consciously borrows from the Apostle. The reproach of abusing it which can be aimed at him does not at all change this basic fact. We have repeated his testimony about it. In the fourth book of the *Periarchōn,* he speaks of allegory once: and this is precisely with regard to the Epistle to the Galatians.[50] On the other hand, when, in the *Contra Celsum,* he treats of the allegory practiced by the Greeks on the histories of their gods, it occurs to him to take up again, along with that word 'allegory', the classical old expression: 'to philosophize in implication';[51] but a little later, in the same book, he writes to the contrary: Whoever will want to pick up the Epistle to the Galatians will see how the reports of Scripture are allegorized: *"tina tropon allēgorēsetai"*;[52] a little further on again, he speaks of the histories that had been consigned to the holy books in view of their allegorical explication, and he cites as an example of this kind of explication several passages from Saint Paul.[53] He writes to the same effect in his commentary on Saint John: "It is necessary for us allegorizing the whole history of Abraham to do spiritually all that he did corporeally . . ."; or again: "Exploring his whole history and understanding that all the things that have been recounted about him are *allēgoroumena,* we are compelled to accomplish them ourselves in spirit"; or again: "Moses knew the anagogic allegories of the histories that he records."[54] And in a homily on Genesis he said: "the mysteries of the Law and the allegories that we have been taught by the Apostle."[55] He is even more explicit in a homily on the Book of Numbers, where the word 'allegory' comes up three times in succession, explicated according to texts of Saint Paul: "Abraham, says Paul, had two sons, etc. Who doubts that these things are true according to the letter? These are certain historical facts. The Apostle none the less adds these things are allegorical. . . . That is to say, that they have their truth according to the letter, but that it is none the less useful, indeed necessary, to receive from them their allegorical signification."[56] The same passage brings the *allegory* of the Epistle to the Galatians together with the *mystery* of the Epistle to the Ephesians: "Paul . . . asserts that these things contain allegorical mysteries, when he says: 'it is a great mystery; I am talking about Christ and the Church.'"[57] On other occasions, again, Origen, using another name to say the same thing, appeals to the same authority, for example in a homily on Exodus: "Let us declare the sort of rule of understanding that Paul the Apostle has left us about these matters";[58] or to the Apostles in general: "But to those who receive the contemplation of the Scriptures according to the sense of the apostles";[59] and in the *Contra Celsum* he explains himself more precisely, one more time, with regard to the facts of the Gospel put in doubt by the adversaries of the faith: "For each of these events it is incumbent upon us to show that it is possible, that it has happened, and that in addition it signifies some tropology."[60] One recent historian, R. L. P. Milburn, is therefore right to say: "Origen, at any rate, chose Saint Paul rather than Philo as the justification for his allegorizings";[61] rather than Philo — and a fortiori, rather than the Stoics or the Platonists. But for him Saint Paul is not a name with which he covers himself; he is, in the very practice of exegesis, a model. Origen, as P. Grelot has well written, "systematically develops the Pauline method of allegory"; in spite of the part borrowed from the Platonic vocabulary, "the spirit, as Origen conceives it, . . . conforms to the Pauline theology."[62]

The same goes for his successors. To define and practice allegory, Saint Hilary has recourse to the Apostle: "The Apostle teaches us to recognize, along with a veneration of the deeds, a pre-formation of the teaching and work of the spirit within them, since the Law is spiritual, while the accomplishments are things that are being allegorized."[63] Saint Ambrose is thinking of him when he writes, in a happy formula which transposes the classic definition: "There is allegory when one thing is being accomplished, another is being prefigured."[64] In the seventy-fifth of his *Diverse Questions*, Saint Augustine rediscovers the expression and the very tone of Origen to comment upon the thought of Saint Paul. The following applies to the resurrection of Lazarus:

> Though we hold with complete faith that Lazarus was revived in accord with Gospel history, nevertheless I do not doubt that he also signifies something in allegory. Nor again, when a fact is allegorized, do people lose faith in the actual accomplishment of the deed: when Paul explains that the allegory of the sons of Abraham is the two Testaments, why should anyone suppose either that Abraham did not exist or that he did not have two sons? So too let us take Lazarus in allegory, etc.[65]

And in the *De utilitate credendi* he says: "What shall I say of the Apostle Paul, who intimates that even the very history of the Exodus was an allegory of the people to come?"[66] And again in the *De Trinitate*: "Where the Apostle calls something 'allegory', he finds it not in the words but in the fact."[67] So numerous will be the texts taking up this distinction of a twofold allegory, even among the moderns, that it would be tedious to detain ourselves with them. It is always the second sort, the allegory "in the fact" or the "allegory of the fact"[68] which is the specifically Christian allegory. (This, of course, does not mean that one is forbidden to recognize that the biblical authors have, like every writer, been able to use the literary figure called "allegory," any more than that one would be forbidden to recall that Jesus often spoke in "parables," or to develop for oneself, with more or less discretion and appropriateness, various allegories starting from the biblical text; one will also encounter among Christian writers of every age many instances where the expression does not designate that specifically Christian allegory.)

Again, when Saint Hilary, for example, speaks of the "allegorical virtues or powers"[69] or Saint Augustine of the "allegorical meanings,"[70] or of the "prophetic allegories";[71] when John Cassian expounds "the character of allegory"[72] and says that the revelation "pertains to the allegory,"[73] with them we are always on entirely Pauline ground. Here Saint Gregory the Great shows himself to be no less Pauline, evoking the "obscurities of the allegories" which are hidden under the letter of the Old Testament and which the "doctors of the New Testament" uncover for us;[74] or distinguishing for one and the same passage the sense "according to the history" from the sense "according to the allegory";[75] or again writing: "We aim through the letter toward the allegory";[76] which he explains in another homily by saying: "The New Testament lay hidden by allegory in the latter of the Old Testament."[77] As with the crowd of writers who will reproduce this language, the equivalence of allegory with the spiritual sense or spiritual understanding, as the preceding chapter has set out, is manifest. Saint Gregory underscores this point again by saying, in formulas that will themselves also constantly be taken up again: "The book of sacred eloquence has been written allegorically on the inside, historically on the outside; inside, in terms of the spiritual understanding, and outside, through the simple sense of the letter."[78] Elsewhere he says the same thing: "Let faith be held in the truth of the history, and let the spiritual understanding be taken of the mysteries of allegory."[79] These formulations, classic in the Christian tradition, were at the service of an equally classic doctrine. The whole Middle Ages will resound with them, as we shall see later on.

The same expression of Paul, Tertullian, Hilary, and Augustine is taken up again by Pseudo-Primasius to comment on the Epistle to the Galatians: "The Apostle gave the rule as to how we ought to allegorize."[80] It was also taken up by Claudius of Turin.[81] Braulio of Saragossa in his turn wanted "to allegorize according to the Apostle."[82] It is in the same sense that Ambrose Autpert, commenting on the Apocalypse, draws attention to the "seal of the allegories."[83] Sedulius Scotus asks Saint Paul for the correct notion of the "allegorical aspects."[84] Paul Alvarus of Cordoba recognizes of him: "Everything he uttered, he uttered allegorically,"[85] etc.

Already among the Greeks Saint John Chrysostom had well noted that Paul, writing to the Galatians, had taken the term 'allegory' to give it a new sense, by catechresis, that is to say: "against normal usage," and he had defined this new sense well: "He means to say this: this history not only declares what is apparent, but it foretells certain other things ['alia'], too; whence it is called allegory."[86] Thus he joins together the explications of Origen and of Tertullian in a perfect fit: Antioch and Alexandria, Greek tradition and Latin tradition, agreed to understand the Apostle and to follow him. Pauline allegory — as the author of a little treatise on Isaiah 6:1-7 also said, though so furiously unjust to Origen — "climbs through the history to the heights, by steps as it were, so as to be not contrary but the more sublime"; Saint Paul, in speaking as he did, "does not at all deny the plainest history, and, drawing the things that have been accomplished to a higher understanding, erects the column in such fashion as not to pull out its lower parts."[87] Saint Jerome had also noted it: what the Epistle to the Galatians designates as 'allegory', said he, is nothing but what Saint Paul elsewhere names 'spiritual understanding'; no one can doubt, for example, that the manna and the rock that he speaks of in his first Epistle to the Corinthians, are to be taken allegorically; it is clear that he was not unaware of the vocabulary of Greek literature; but if he borrowed the word 'allegory', which used to have only a grammatical or literary signification, from thence, this was to enlarge and to transform its import.[88] Saint Jerome's remark will be often reproduced under a scarcely different form — as by Rabanus Maurus[89] or Aimon of Auxerre[90] — and, notwithstanding the persistent ambiguity of the term, no one was deceived by it.[91]

2. Myth and Allegory

We would have rapidly passed over the word *allegoria*, which must occupy our attention once again in Chapter Eight, if it were not necessary, even today, to react against a sort of invincible misunderstanding of the essential meaning that it takes on in the exegetical tradition. This is not without consequences, whether one perceives it or not, for the appraisal of doctrines. Has one not seen, for example, one of the historians who has most closely studied the technical terms of exegesis in the time of the Fathers explain the word without citing either Tertullian or Origen, and, a thing stranger still, almost incredible, omit all reference to Saint Paul on his subject?[1] Some time ago another historian had united helter-skelter, in an impressionistic enumeration, "Essenes, Therapeutes, Philo, Saint Paul, the Stoics, Platonists, Alexandrians," all accused of having practiced the same "allegorical method," a method "which, in the interpretation of texts, substitutes the spiritual sense for the natural sense."[2] An admirer of Richard Simon declared also that he admired "the profound hermeneutics of Origen, with his happy fixed prejudices of allegorism"; this hermeneutic, he thought, constituted a model, because of its "bold adaptations of the old texts to the philosophy of his time," thanks to allegory, which put it at the service "of free speculations for the use of enlightened minds."[3] More recently, a specialist in Byzantine philosophy gave as one of the fundamental principles of Origenism the "reduction of the faith to knowledge with assistance of philosophy," through the middle-man "of the allegorical method."[4] This method, in the eyes of another author, was, in the hands of the Fathers of the Church, a tool that they used to obtain a "timeless super-intelligence" of the whole Bible. Still another, this time taking his point of departure in the late Latin tradition, and chancing to comment on the distich popularized by Nicholas of Lyra, explicated the fate of allegorical exegesis in the following terms: "The scholars of the Middle Ages were interested infinitely more in the derived and philosophical senses of the Bible than in the modest literal sense. . . . They did not hesitate to make the Bible . . . into a sort of code of philosophy and a springboard for ontological meditation. . . . The inspired word became, for the clerics, a pretext for philosophical and entirely spiritual meditations."[5] To believe the first of the authors whom we have just cited on this topic, the sense that Plutarch gives to the word 'allegory' while speaking of the interpreters of Homer will be the sense "common in patristic Greek."[6]

Transmitted indefinitely without serious control, such an idea had begun to be put into circulation by certain Protestant writers, who were reacting, without making the necessary distinction, against the more or less delayed deviations of medieval exegesis and against certain of the fundamental principles of the traditional interpretation in the Church. After having energetically combated it, the Catholic apologists had sometimes ended up by allowing themselves to be intimidated by it. In fact it is the fruit of an indefensible method. Instead of studying Christian allegorism in itself textually, one generally begins by conceiving an idea of allegorism as a sort of unique genus, not to be varied, according to the pagan authors of antiquity as well as according to a literary tradition which maintained itself during the course of the Christian era. Then one decides a priori that the Christian allegorism, applied to Scripture, is merely one species of it, one of the branches rising from this single trunk. One will leave off so as subsequently to introduce, here or there, before the excessively great resistance opposed by the texts (which are generally little cited), some jury-rigging provisions, without perceiving that it was necessary to pass on to a completely different genus. In 1787 — not to go further back — this is how Nathan Morus, who analyzed at length Heraclitus's method of explicating Homer, proceeded to a quick conclusion: the essential characteristics of allegory are found everywhere the same, "in poetry, in works of art, in the dogmas of the philosophers as well as the doctors of our religion."[7] Thus, too, some years later, did I. G. Rosenmüller proceed in his great *History of the Interpretation of the Holy Books in the Christian Church,* one of the most beautiful fruits of "enlightened" Lutheranism. To believe him, the ancient doctors, completely abandoning history, systematically changing the meaning of words, mixing the opinions of the Greeks with the accounts of Moses, putting themselves under the tutelage of Plato, Plutarch, Heraclitus, and Philo, had metamorphosed biblical history into a philosophy; thus, their allegorical exegesis was not only arbitrary, but completely contrary to the purity of our religion.[8] To speak truly, Rosenmüller was a bit embarrassed by the Apostles themselves, particularly by Saint Paul. To be sure, he admitted, Paul did already allegorize from time to time; but can one reasonably suppose that he believed in the value of such a method? Was this not on his part rather a concession to the weakness of the people? A way of being Jewish "with the Jews"? One will easily excuse him for it, concludes Rosenmüller; but it is permissible, or rather recommended, and even more than recommended, not to imitate it.[9] The manifesto of the Epistle to the Galatians, Paul's concession to Jewish weakness! Do not such explications refute themselves?[10]

Nevertheless, how many times since then has the thesis not been taken up again! Let the following assertions of Edwin Hatch, studying "the influence of Greek ideas and customs upon the Christian Church,"[11] serve as an example: "The oldest methods of Christian exegesis were the continuation of methods which were at that time common to the Greeks and Hellenistic Jews; just as the Greek philosophers found their philosophy in Homer, the Christian writers found the Christian theology in Scripture. The reasons brought up for believing that the Old Testament had an allegorical sense were entirely analogous to those that had been given in the case of Homer. The Old Testament was treated in an allegorical manner because a great part of its content became offensive to the Christian consciousness." On reading these placid affirmations, one would truly say that this author had never heard tell of the coming of Jesus Christ, nor of the proclamation of the New Testament. One would say that no trace had reached him of the abrupt change by which the Church took the place of the Synagogue and by which the Christian exegesis had succeeded to the Jewish exegesis within the Church. It is Origen, continues Hatch, who was the principal performer of this work; he did with the Old Testament what Cornutus had done with Greek mythology, and his whole exegesis is nothing but a vast "rationalist expedient." Maintaining then that such a method "has survived the circumstances of its birth and that it has been strengthened by the oppositions that it has encountered," Hatch comes to speak of an "irony of history," because what came at the start, according to him, from a rationalist tendency ended up by being considered as a holy thing, which ought to be protected against the rationalist assaults of the age. This observation, intended to be biting, was suggested to him by reading the chapter that Newman devoted to "the mystical interpretation of Scripture" in his *Essay on the Development of Dogma*. Only, as to his own myth, the historian does not perceive that, if there is in fact an irony, it is he who is tainted by it. For the considerations of Newman, just like those which his friend Keble had long advanced in one of the famous Oxford "tracts,"[12] far from being opposed to, fit quite faithfully with the principal considerations of Origen. One could only be astounded at it, when one knows the familiarity that Newman had acquired with the thought of the Fathers[13] and more precisely the place that the Alexandrian Christians had held in his own spiritual formation: he himself recounts it in his *Apologia*.[14]

Edwin Hatch was writing in 1898. Since then, many analogous judgments have again seen the light of day. There have also been a number of good works well fitted to correct them. Yet one would be unable to say that they have assured the victory of the sounder interpretation. Even by authors who would have seemed experienced in the better scientific methods, we are periodically led into the same rut. Many come to see in the allegory practiced by the Fathers and even already "perhaps" by Saint Paul, nothing but an "adaptation of the Stoic method to the Bible." Struck by the parentage that they discover in literary methods, they think that they find themselves in the presence of a "general scheme of allegorical thought," identical in both cases. The testimony of Porphyry in the text reported by Eusebius then brings them its decisive confirmation.

Myth and Allegory

They think it "revealing." The Christian exegetes would therefore have treated Moses exactly as the Greeks treated Homer. They would have made a "philosopher" out of the Jewish prophet as they did of the Greek epic poet and would have done so in the same sense. What the Hebrew books gave under the form of narratives, would have appeared to them as a veil cast over profound "speculations" which the allegorical method would have permitted them to bring into the clear. It would therefore be possible to establish a parallel between the "logical absurdity and the material absurdity" that Origen speaks of regarding certain biblical texts if they were to be taken literally, and the "absurd immorality" of which the friend of Julian the Apostate, Sallust the Philosopher, speaks regarding the histories of Chronos, Zeus, and the other gods,[15] or again "the odious extravagance" that Plutarch speaks of regarding the dismemberment of Horus or the decapitation of Isis. It is still a quite widely circulated opinion that Origen — upon whom so many others depend — "on his own account scarcely believes in the literal value of the Bible," and without taking too many risks, most of the time, in his commentaries, one brings forth as proof of this opinion a passage from the *Periarchōn* which would be, like Porphyry's testimony, "revealing."[16]

To anyone who will put these lines of the *Periarchōn* back in their context and look at them closely, the revelation will appear less revealing. They are found in the fourth book, which is for the most part a treatise on hermeneutics broadly understood. There Origen states that, according to the letter of Genesis, God had, like a gardener, planted trees in the paradise with his own hands, that he used to walk there at certain hours, that Adam hid himself from him behind the tree, that Cain fled his face, etc.: "What need is there to say more about it? Unless he were completely obtuse, just about anyone can gather many traits of this kind, which are noted as having occurred, but which in reality have not taken place according to the letter."[17] Before and after this passage, Origen brings up divers other examples of varied nature, which hardly allow one to be mistaken about his thought. There would be few, if any, points for a contemporary exegete of sound judgment to criticize. Sometimes, as we have just seen, they are anthropomorphisms: God, in reality, has no shape, he does not work with his hands, man does not meet him during the course of his strolls and does not conceal himself from him by getting behind a tree. (This, however, does not signify — and the remark is of capital importance — that in the thought of Origen such images do not render real events whose actors might be really personal beings.) Sometimes, they are messianic prophecies, whose apparent signification is carnal: the wolf will graze with the lamb, the Messiah will preach material deliverance to the captives and will build a city of God upon this earth; because the incredulous Jews obstinately took these prophecies in their carnal sense, they rejected the true Messiah, who, they say, is a false Messiah, since he had not realized these things.[18] Elsewhere, they are precepts themselves presented also under an imagined form: thus, when the Savior says: "If your right eye scandalizes you, pluck it out," one ought not to believe that he is designating only one of the two eyes, as a culprit deserving correction, considering that the other eye took part in the scandal just as much.[19] Saint John Chrysostom used to have to make the same remark.[20] In the same way, the Apostle's exhortation not to dissimulate one's circumcision ought not be understood in a sense so literal as to be an appeal to shamelessness, or a pointless prohibition of some impossible thing.[21] Sometimes, it is the exterior dramatization of a spiritual fact: it is clear that Jesus could not, from the height of the mountain where Satan had carried him, see "the kingdoms of the whole world"[22] with the eyes of the flesh. If one wanted to find in this last example a generalized rejection of history, it would do just as well to invoke as testimony an analogous remark made by Saint Jerome regarding the words of the prophet Zechariah: "sedens super asinam et pullum," which Saint Matthew had cited: "Literally . . . he was not able to sit on each of the two animals."[23] Finally, there is many another figured expression.

One can, to be sure, dispute the examples that Origen brings up in this book of the *Periarchōn* or in any passage of his commentaries. Doubtless he held as figured this or that detail that we would judge historical, and, on the other hand, he took as historical more than one page where we would most often see only a figure or parable. It is especially regarding the precepts of the old Law that he sometimes too quickly believes in the impossibility of the letter.[24] But on balance, it is probable that the strictly historical part of the Bible for him would be much larger than for us. At first sight, the texts whose "letter" he rejects would appear numerous; but, most often, it is a question not of events, of "episodes," or of entire narratives, but only of certain details, of trifling, very brief elements of redaction, which are, as he says on many occasions, here and there "mingled with the history" and as it were "woven together with it":[25] an idea that he misuses, that leads him to illusory niceties, and which has known far too much success. At bottom, however, the question is chiefly about terminology. Origen habitually uses the expression "letter" *(rhēton, lexis)* in a very strict meaning. Hence he says that "the letter" or "the history" or "the body" is missing, where we, to signify the very same thing,

Myth and Allegory

would say that the text presents a figurative or metaphorical literal sense. Many others do as he did, notably Saint John Chrysostom, who does it in the very same words.[26] The true historians of exegesis know it well; perhaps they have not emphasized the fact enough; in any case, they are rarely consulted. By such language, Origen in no way contests the historical character of the Bible. Besides, in that same fourth book of the *Periarchōn* he himself gives a rough outline of the history of Israel, taking it from the time of Abraham, with a view of showing its importance in the plan of God and the character of prophecy: "The divine letters foretell that a certain people upon the lands have been chosen by God, etc."[27] And again he himself, in this same context, protests in advance against such an error of interpretation: "One should not suspect us of thinking," says he, "that the Scripture does not contain real history, or that the precepts of the Law were not to be fulfilled to the letter, or that what has been written about the Savior has not sensibly taken place.... The truly historical passages are many more numerous than those that are to be taken in a purely spiritual sense."[28] It would be to misunderstand Origen to reject or merely to put in doubt so precise a declaration. No more than the similar declarations of the *Contra Celsum* is it a device aimed at "reassuring opinion." Besides, the homilies and the commentaries easily provide those who are willing to consult them a way to control their veracity.

What is at stake here is important because of the unparalleled influence of Origen upon the development of Christian exegesis. Would it be necessary to admit that a considerable part of this exegesis, that which counts the most in terms of the value of thought, had sold biblical history short? Would it have treated this history exactly as allegorizing pagan philosophy treated mythology? Absolutely not. We find everywhere in him an affirmation of reality — and how energetically he makes it! The very faith of the exegete would seem to hang entirely upon this affirmation. The Living God of Scripture, intervening in the history of human beings, imposes himself on him, without any possible comparison with the gods of myth nor with the impersonal divinity that results from philosophical allegorization. What a distance there is, what an abyss, between Christian thought commenting upon the history of Israel or the Gospel, and the thought of a Pseudo-Heraclitus, a Plotinus, a Sallust and their ilk! "Who then would be so mad," said Heraclitus, for example, to believe that the gods wage war among themselves, "even though Homer related these divine histories only in a physical and allegorical sense?" When the poet evokes the wrath of Apollo, in reality he is not describing "the caprice of a god," but "his own philosophic thought on a physical theory."[29]

And here is Plotinus: "The myths temporally distribute beings that are in reality not separated and separate them from each other . . . ; they make what has never begun begin to be, they divide it, thereby teaching what they can and leaving the trouble of putting it back together again to him who comprehends."[30] And Sallust, the friend of Julian, in this "sort of neoplatonist catechism"[31] which is his little treatise *On the Gods and the World* says: "It is not that these things should never have happened, for they exist from all time; but discourse can express only successively what the understanding sees and grasps all at once."[32]

Like contemporaries of every age, it is clear that the ancients, Christians or not, all participated more or less in the same ambient culture and one and the same mentality. They therefore resembled each other in many things. The parentage of certain exegetical methods from the one to the others, for allegories as for the rest, is undeniable. It is not at all without interest to attempt to render an account of it right down to the smallest details — and there are doubtless many others still to discover or to render precise in this domain. Again, it is desirable that the attention brought to bear on such details, even if they cover a large surface, should not make us lose sight of certain facts of serious importance in other respects. It would therefore be necessary for us to make sure not to misunderstand the diversity of the groups into which they are fitted, nor the fundamental ideas to which they have been subordinated; not to cross at a single bound, without taking due care, from the "procedures" to the "thought." Once certain similarities of allegorical technique have been established between Greek and Christian authors, and consequently, at least generally speaking, certain borrowings of the latter from the former, we shall not be authorized to conclude from that an identity of the two, in the most essential doctrines or attitudes.

Surely there is no need to have deployed all the resources of comparative philology to see that the Fathers of the Church and the thinkers of declining paganism were using one and the same *koinē* — and we understand this to mean not only the language but also many conceptions and many habits of thought. But why does the inventory of these common traits so easily blind us to the more radical difference? How, too, does it come about that one so easily judges as troubling the tiniest convergences of notions, namely expressions, or that one so easily stumbles on peculiarities of terminology? From the fact that the Fathers have not always enunciated, as any good manual would have done, "the rules of a sacred hermeneutic," would it be immediately necessary to conclude, as some have in fact, that they "simply accommodated themselves to the exegesis in use at their time"? As if the rules were not first immanent in the practice and mingled with the doctrine before being extracted from them so as to be codified in manuals![33] Finally, how can good minds confuse the "allegorical" interpretation, for example, of the events of Exodus, or the rites of Leviticus, or the history of David and Solomon, as the Christian tradition everywhere proposes it, with the "exegesis" of the Pythagoreans who see, for example, in Heracles the power of nature; in the Dioscures, the harmony of the universe; in Proteus, the original matter containing in potency all beings in their diverse forms, as unity containing in potency all numerical combinations; in the noise of Apollo's arrows, that which the solar globe produces in its rapid revolution, or in the "misty shadow of Hades' realm," the dark cone which the earth projects in the space on the side opposed to the sun?[34] What page of biblical history has, in the Church at large, ever been interpreted in the manner in which the mythologists used to interpret the story of Saturn devouring his children (Time destroying all that it has engendered)? Or in the manner in which they used to interpret the history of Hera chained and hung in the air by Zeus, with two anvils at her ankles and a golden chain on her hands (a symbol of the formation of the universe with its four elements)? Does one encounter anything in the exegesis of the Fathers like that "allegorical" explication reconciling Tethys with Okeanos, a scene in which certain interpreters of Homer saw an allegory of the concord that ended up reigning in nature between the dry and the wet? Or does one find in their hermeneutics any principle analogous to the Stoic principle reported by Cicero: "It is from a physical doctrine that this crowd of divinities was born, who, clothed in human form, have furnished the poets with a thousand tales and filled the human race with all sorts of superstitions"?[35] When the Pythagoreans explain for us the meaning of Penelope's loom by telling us that its movements back and forth are the movements of thought, or that the threads that circulate between its two spindles are the souls who do not cease to traverse the ether, are they telling us, as do the Fathers of the Church in commenting on Scripture for us, of a history and a symbolic prefiguration? Here it makes little difference whether the interpretation of the myths be "physical," in Stoic fashion, or "moral," "metaphysical," i.e., "theological,"[36] — or "mixed." Under each hypothesis, the difference between this and Christian allegorism is radical. Here too the date or the personality of the Christian exegete is of little importance. The reflections of an Irenaeus or an Origen — as of a John Chrysostom, an Augustine, or a Gregory the Great — upon the Scripture transport us into a completely different region than that to which we are led by the reflections of a Plutarch on the myth of Osiris[37] or a Porphyry on the Cavern of the nymphs.[38] And, regardless of what the abundance or the quality of his "allegorism" had been, what partial borrowing he had been able to make from the procedures or even the ideas of such and such a pagan author, or some interpretation that he had been able to give of such and such a particular text, has any Christian ever undertaken to justify the Bible or the Gospel by saying, as did Theon of Alexandria and others of the sacred texts of Hellenism, that it is necessary to see in them "a mendacious discourse expressing the truth in an image"?[39]

If one wants to find anything like veritable imitators of the ancient mythologists, the Cornutuses and Heraclituses, the Sallusts and Julians, the Procluses and Olympiodoruses, this is not to be achieved by turning to Origens or Gregories, Augustines, Bedes, or Ruperts. It would rather be among a certain number of scholars of the last century, who briskly turned into myths not only the narratives of Genesis but also those of the books of Judges and Kings, and sometimes even those of the Gospels. Such imitators included G. L. Bauer (1802), Lebrecht de Wette (1807), H. Ewald (1843), Th. Nöldeke (1868), Ed. Schrader (1869), J. Wellhausen (1878), E. Stücken (1896), H. Winckler (1902). Such an imitator was D. Fr. Strauss (1835-36). For Bauer, for example, the majority of the alleged facts of the Bible had their parallels in the Greek or Roman fables; for de Wette, the key of myth naturally explained all the alleged miracles of the Bible; for Stücken, the Patriarchs were merely the stars, etc. We recognize there the idea that the histories recorded in the ancient poems or in the ancient sacred collections are fictions enclosing the secrets of science; here, specifically cosmological science. The sole difference — it is big enough, to be sure — is that the majority of scholars that we have just cited hedge in their role of critics; whether they do or do not attribute knowledge to the redactors of the ancient texts, they do not go so far as to take, on their own account, as did their Greco-Roman ancestors, the "secrets" that they disengaged from those "myths."[40]

On the precise subject of allegory, the Catholic scholars themselves have sometimes appealed to definitions which hardly conform to history, and this imperfection of language has contributed not a little to misunderstandings. Thus it is that for E. Dorsch, the "allegorical sense" of Origen supposed at least the neglect of the literal sense.[41] Father A. Vaccari, whose erudition is ordinarily so reliable, declared, at the moment he was choosing the term 'allegory' to define the exegesis of the Alexandrian school and to oppose it to the 'theory' of the Antiochenes, that allegory "denies or at least sets to one side the literal sense of the historical truth of the fact"[42] — which, in this general formulation, is impossible to sustain historically.[43] Others make a distinction between "allegory" and "typology" which expresses a certain truth but which is not founded upon the whole of the texts and, as we have seen in the preceding chapter, does not correspond to the terminology of the ancients. Thus, when it is transported into a historical study, it is almost inevitably exposed to misunderstandings. It is not without some distress that we hear a scholar of merit, an exegete or theologian of note, speak of "symbolism as method of interpretation of a text in classical antiquity and among the Fathers of the Church" without himself distinguishing these two categories, and referring the reader, for his study, to just one author, an unbeliever, who confuses the two.[44] This is also what E. R. Curtius does; but such a thing is less surprising on the part of an historian of literature.[45] A historian of Israel, S. W. Baron, has been able to write that one has not always "accorded sufficient attention to the differences that exist between the Greek methods and the rabbinical methods."[46] How much still more valid is that remark in our case! In reality, under one and the same label, Christian and pagan allegory, if they use a certain number of analogous procedures, are nonetheless two functionally heterogeneous things; they are two opposed methods, proceeding from two opposed doctrines and two frames of mind. They have neither the same foundation, nor the same term. This is what the next two chapters will end up by proving.

Without leaving the most methodically verifiable terrain of historical observation, some twenty years ago Th. Preiss has spoken a few words on this subject that are still to the point:

> However strange the exegesis practiced by the first Christian generations might appear to us today, it nevertheless distinguished itself from that practiced in Hellenistic settings by its sense of history. . . . In a world functionally unaware of history, this exegesis, howsoever fantastic in detail, had defended precisely this historic sense in the name of which we today often, with a certain lack of understanding which perhaps does no great honor to our sense of history, assimilate it to a sort of mythic thought.[47]

3. Mystery

Mystery, mystical sense, mystical interpretation, understanding of the mystery: after *allegory*, it is the second parallel expression. It too is everywhere. "According to the mystic form" is equivalent to "according to allegory."[1] Like 'allegory', 'mystery' has a prophetic resonance. Like 'allegory', and even more so, it carries a strongly objective connotation, more specifically objective than 'spirit'. In other words, if 'mystical' is synonymous with 'spiritual', it is in the most general sense of this word; it is not exactly synonymous with 'spiritual' taken in an individual and subjective acceptation. The mystical sense is the sense related to the mystery, which is a reality, at first hidden in God, and then revealed to human beings at the same time as realized in Jesus Christ. It will therefore be the sense which contains the plenitude of the doctrine: "according to the mystic understanding all these things are related to Christ,"[2] "according to the mystical understanding it is most certainly related to the Church."[3] What the Scripture reports is "done mystically": "it seems to signify something of the mystery."[4] One searches across the holy books for the "mystical understandings of the shadows of the Law,"[5] that is, one looks everywhere within them for the "truth" of these shadows, that Truth which is the Christ.[6] One searches in them for the "mystical character," i.e., one wishes to extract from the text, after having understood it in its letter, the "power, character and mystery, according to the spiritual understanding."[7]

In Latin *mysterium* serves as the double for *sacramentum*. For Saint Augustine, the Bible is essentially the "writing of the mysteries,"[8] and its books are the "books of the divine sacraments."[9] The two words are often simply synonyms. If they are found associated, it is then pure pleonasm. One sees it in the translations of Rufinus, who, conforming to the genius of the Latin language, is accustomed to this procedure of using doublets:[10]

> In his Revelation, John reads the things that have been written in the Law according to the history of the divine mysteries and teaches that certain sacraments are contained within them.[11]
>
> These truths are both useful and divine, but . . . have been covered over with sacraments and wound up in mysteries.[12]

One sees it as well in Saint Hilary, who writes: "the concealed sacraments of wisdom and the hidden mysteries of God";[13] in the *Caroline Books*, which love redundant formulas;[14] in Saint Bernard, who points out the "sacraments of the passion of the Lord" forming a sequel to the "mysteries of the nativity";[15] in his friend William of Saint Thierry, making the soul hearken to the Beloved "revealing the condensations of his mysteries and sacraments";[16] and in many others.[17] At least one can often doubt whether the two expressions thus employed side by side truly carry two distinct meanings. The diffusion of the doublet *sacramentum* is perhaps to be explained originally, in certain cases, by the repugnance felt in some Latin circles for words copied from the Greek. It doubtless also arose from the desire to avoid the usage not only of *mysterium*, but also of its equivalents *sacra, arcana, initia*, with a view to setting off the difference between Christianity and the pagan cults, especially the oriental ones.[18] The Latin version of the Book of Wisdom, a version that goes back to the second century and that has passed as such into our Vulgate, wittingly renders the Septuagint's "mystery" sometimes as *sacrum* and sometimes as *sacramentum*.[19] Tertullian opposes the "divine sacraments" to the "mysteries of the idols."[20] Saint Augustine, mentioning the cults of Osiris and Anubis in the *Confessions*, will oppose in the same way the "sacraments of the Word's humility" with those "sacred sacrileges of proud demons."[21] Nevertheless, in exegesis, one did not feel the same scruples, because *mysterium*, just like *allegoria*, was a Pauline term, and because in this more immediately doctrinal acceptation it had no equivalent in the pagan "mysteries." Thus the two words were soon both used in the vocabulary of Christian writers.

They are sometimes distinguished as the two terms of a relation or as the two poles of an alternating movement. Then *sacramentum* designates rather the exterior component, the "envelope," as Saint Augustine says: "Christ has been preached by the prophets almost everywhere with a wrapping of sacrament."[22] This is the sign or the letter as bearer of the sign: "the signs of things are in the sacraments."[23] Whether thing or person, fact or rite, it is the "type," the correlative of the mystery,[24] just as the "figure" or "image" is the correlative of the "truth":[25] "the sacrament comes before the truth of the thing."[26] It is the *sacrum* rather than the *arcanum*.[27] The mystery is this *arcanum* itself. It is the interior component, the reality hidden under the letter and signified by the sign, the truth that the figure indicates; in other words, the object of faith itself.[28] Doubtless, the exceptions are numerous; so too are the undecided cases: "The mystery of the Law and sacrament of the time," Rabanus Maurus[29] will say, for example; "the hidden sacraments are to be scrutinized diligently," is how Herbert of Losinga will put it.[30] Saint Augustine himself is far from always marking an appreciable difference of sense between the two words; this is so when he writes: "something of the mystery and the sacrament is hidden in the fact itself,"[31] or, regarding certain passages of the Psalms: "they point out a sweet mystery; they hint at a great sacrament."[32] But it is no longer the same when he speaks of the "works of the Law": "those carnally observed sacraments held even those bound who had been subject to the one God by the grace of a sure mystery."[33] When he says again of the letter of the Old Testament that it was "clothed in the terms of carnal sacraments,"[34] it is clear enough that he would not do so well by writing: "of carnal mysteries."[35] The same remark will hold good for Saint Bernard distinguishing the "shell of the sacrament and the soft part of the corn."[36] In short, in the traditional language as in contemporary French, and in the language of exegesis as in that of the liturgy, the sacrament contains the mystery, it relates to the mystery. "Through the grace of the sacrament the fellowship of the mysteries is restored," says Saint Ambrose regarding the pardoned sinner.[37] Consequently, in the relationship between the two Testaments, the *sacramentum* belongs rather to the Old and the *mysterium* to the New. The entire New Testament is a great mystery hidden within this sacrament, or signifies by means of this sacrament which is the Old Testament. "The sacrament of the Old Testament was the New one."[38] But Christ himself, in his incarnation, i.e., in his earthly and temporal appearance *(temporalis dispensatio mediatoris),* will be the *sacrament* of the *mystery* of God *(sacramentum susceptae humanitatis).*[39] In other words, and to speak once more with Saint Augustine, "the reality of the sacrament" will be the "mystery of the reality."[40] Those whose eyes contemplate in Jesus Christ the "concealed features of the Scriptures" see the "hidden realities of the sacraments under the veil of images."[41]

Thence come expressions like "mystic sacraments"[42] or "figured mysteries"[43] along with the varied shadings of their meanings. Thence, too, come the two criss-crossed expressions "mystery of the sacrament" or "mysteries of the sacraments"[44] and — perhaps a bit less frequent — "sacrament of the mystery" or "sacraments of the mysteries."[45] One sometimes finds them used by turns, not far from each other, in the same author.[46] Their respective signification is sometimes subtle and fluid. It shows up well enough in certain cases; for example, in these words of Rabanus Maurus: "the mysteries to be veiled of the divine sacraments,"[47] or: "These things are old and new . . . by which all the mysteries of the sacraments are revealed";[48] and, inversely, in the following expression of Gerhoh of Reichersberg: "salvo altioris mysterii sacramento." One also reads in a homily of Gregory of Elvira: "The mystery of the sacrament . . . is hidden away to the one seeking in the secret of the soul."[49] Mlle Christine Mohrmann cites an analogous example taken from the *De mysteriis* of Saint Ambrose: "Now the time warns us to speak of the mysteries and to

Mystery

publish the very character of the sacraments."[50] Much later, Durandus of Mende will say, "For the mystery is in the sacraments."[51] In the last three texts, it is a question of liturgy and of sacrament almost in the modern sense of the word; but the language of the liturgy here is the same as that of exegesis, and on both sides there is even a partial identity of content. For in part the things of the Old Testament that prefigure those of the New are rites; this is all the figurative part of the Mosaic Law, regarding which Saint Ambrose says once again: "He has stepped beyond the shadow [viz. David] and with the spirit of prophecy has seen the very sacraments of the heavenly mysteries whose type Moses prefigured in the Law";[52] and in return the "sacramenta" of the liturgy, whose mystery is to be uncovered at a fitting time, are not only rites: they contain texts as well, the readings of the Old Testament, chosen in part for their "mystical" content.[53]

Always, according as the allusion looks more directly upon the one or the other of the two terms of which allegory constitutes the living link, one will have one or the other of the two alternate expressions: the typic sense or the mystic sense: "ratio typica" or "ratio mystica" — or again "sacramenti ratio."[54] Saint Gregory says "typic exposition," and "mystery of the typic exposition."[55] The "typic understanding," says the Pseudo-Remigius of Auxerre.[56] One will even speak of Noah, for example, as the "type-creating head of the Church,"[57] or, in the inverse sense, of Saint Paul as "expressing typic utterances for things."[58] Already with Origen — the Origen of Rufinus — it is constantly a question of mystery, of "mystic understanding," of "mystic interpretation," "mystic reason," "mystic place," etc.,[59] and Rufinus clearly indicates to us the import of such expressions when he writes again in his undoubtedly redundant translation: "mystic and dogmatic."[60] Saint Gregory of Nyssa likewise entitles his "allegorical" or "spiritual" commentary on the *Canticle*: a "Mystical Contemplation."[61] Under the pen of Saint Ambrose the expressions "according to the letter" and "according to the spirit" alternate with the expressions "in looks" and "in mystery";[62] he also loves to speak of the "mystic order" and the "mystic interpretation";[63] others will say: "figured interpretation."[64] Saint Gregory the Great professes that the letter ought to lead us "to the mystic understanding,"[65] that it is necessary to place the sacred text "under the mystic understanding,"[66] to make a "mystic interpretation" or representation of it,[67] and that it is in this "mystic understanding" that the mind of the Christian finds its nourishment each day.[68] A blessing of the Mozarabic liturgy calls forth the "omni-valent fullness of the mystic understanding."[69] Following Origen,

Claudius of Turin and others look for a "quid mysticum" under the letter.[70] Paschasius Radbertus discovers the "mystic sacraments of God"[71] in Scripture and Rabanus Maurus sees the text of the Old Testament "related to the mystic and prophetic sacraments."[72] Richard of Saint Victor distinguishes the narration of facts "according to the history" and their interpretation "according to the mystic understanding."[73] Rupert, who makes the same distinction, expresses the second term more precisely: "according to the mystic understanding of the Gospel truth" and he invites us to look into the text for "what it may have of the mystic character."[74] Again Richard wants "to penetrate the depths of the mysteries,"[75] so as to arrive "at the mystic understanding of the divine Scriptures."[76] Others speak more briefly of "Scriptura mystica,"[77] etc. Examples of that sort are countless.

Spirit, mystery, allegory: these then are the three major, practically synonymous vocabulary items. They and their derivatives are frequently intermingled in diverse combinations. To start with, here are a few of the combinations of "mystery" and "spirit." One speaks of the "mystery of the spirit,"[78] of the "sacrament of the spiritual understanding,"[79] of the "mystic significance of the spiritual understanding";[80] one looks for a "spiritual significance according to the mystic sense";[81] one sees that the sacred text "overflows with spiritual mysteries";[82] one comments upon it "according to the spiritual mystery,"[83] "according to a spiritual understanding of the heavenly mystery,"[84] etc. Origen scrutinizes each word "to catch the mystic and spiritual sense";[85] Isidore of Seville posits their equivalence: "in the mystic sense, that is, spiritually";[86] in the same way Beatus writes: "the spiritual sense, which is the mystic understanding in the Church,"[87] and again: "to be understood spiritually in the mystery."[88] The combinations of spirit and allegory are scarcely less varied: "spiritual allegory";[89] "so that by allegorizing we may investigate in the spiritual sense";[90] "allegory is made clear once understood with the spiritual senses";[91] "the spirit of the allegorical understanding," etc. Of the Holy Spirit Rupert said: "The Spirit Who vivifies us through the spiritual sense will give us an allegory"[92] and he posits the following equivalence: "to keep the senses of the allegories" = "to apprehend through the spiritual understanding."[93] Already Rufinus's Origen had laid it down in analogous terms: "now let us see how he may also get an allegorical, that is, a spiritual understanding."[94] And here are the combinations of mystery and allegory: "allegorical mysteries";[95] "to have the sacrament of the allegory,"[96] "the mystic knots of the allegories";[97] "a mystic allegory";[98] "to comment allegorically upon the mystic types,"[99] etc. Saint Gregory

Mystery

writes: "If one . . . wants to discuss the facts through the secrets of allegory, he rises straight from the history into the mystery";[100] one formula, which many will take up again, is dear to him: "the mystery of the allegory,"[101] or "the mysteries of the allegory."[102] "The mystic sacraments of the allegorical matters having been preserved," says Paulinus of Aquilaea;[103] "mystically and allegorically," says Alvarus of Cordoba;[104] "the enclosed sacrament of allegoric contemplation," says Saint Peter Damian;[105] "through allegory it hints at something mystical," says Hugh of Saint Victor,[106] etc.; and again it is the Origen of Rufinus who posited this equivalence: "according to the mystical or allegorical interpretations of the Law."[107] Finally, diverse formulas combine the three words together. Thus, one reads in a homily of Origen translated by Rufinus: "To climb to the mystic and allegorical sense of spiritual understanding."[108] In one and the same sentence, Rupert writes: "According to the spiritual or mystic sense . . . ; for when we get an understanding of the allegory. . . ."[109] In a passage from a homily on Ezekiel, which will be recopied, Saint Gregory the Great takes up the symbolism of the water changed into wine; then too he uses the three words harmoniously unified: "he turns the water into wine for us, when the history itself through the mystery of allegory is transformed into spiritual understanding for us."[110]

There are, then, basically only two senses of Scripture recognized everywhere in the ancient tradition: the one, which consists in the history or the letter; the other, which is more generally named spiritual, or allegorical, or mystical.[111] *The letter signifies one thing, mystic discourse another.*[112] The whole Middle Ages will say it again. "Holy Scripture is understood in two ways, historically and allegorically";[113] "historically" and "with the more sacred mystery."[114] "The scripture of the Law is to be sensed not only historically, but also with the mystical sense, i.e., spiritually."[115] Sometimes one will distinguish, as does Saint Jerome, more simply still: "letter" and "meaning"[116] or "sense."[117] In the assertions and distinctions of this kind it is not at all necessary to see anything which is opposed to the threefold or to the fourfold division. The proof is that one meets them in the writings of the same authors, and we are going to see precisely that it is without any logical incoherence. At Cana it was a question only of wine and water; and Wisdom is said to have "mixed the wine": thus, Saint Bonaventure will say, the fourfold sense is found designated: "the literal sense is like the water; the mystic, tropologic, and anagogic sense is like the wine."[118] To say, with a recent author: "The evolution has gone from a fourfold distinction to a dichotomy, and the trichotomy has served as transitional term,"[119] is to utter an hypothesis that finds no foundation in the facts — no more than the reverse hypothesis. Cassian takes us back, as his predecessors had already, to the fundamental duality, at the very moment where he was trying to develop his doctrine of the four senses; he used to symbolize it either by a word about "Solomon": "Hence too, when Solomon had enumerated the manifold grace of the Church, he added: For all who are in it have been clothed in two ways,"[120] or by the two cherubim of the ark: "All these are protected by the two cherubim, i.e., by the fullness of historical and spiritual science; for 'cherubim' is interpreted as the manyness of science."[121]

But in Scripture itself, one professes that there is no dissociation of the two senses. The spirit does not exist without the letter, nor is the letter devoid of the spirit. Each of the two senses is in the other — like the "wheel within the wheel." Each needs the other. With those two they constitute "the perfect science."[122] To tell the truth, from the start they even constitute really only one. The spiritual sense is also necessary for the completion of the literal sense, which latter is indispensable for founding it; it is therefore the natural term of divine inspiration, and, as Bossuet will say, "pertains to the original, principal plan of the Holy Spirit."[123] *Christus in littera continetur.*[124] *The spirit is not outside the history.* They are given together, inseparably, through the fact of a single inspiration. It is we who, after the event, separate them: "when they are expounded, they are broken."[125] Three verses of Hildebert summarize the tradition on this subject:

The bread means Scripture; to break the bread
Is to expound the Scriptures; Christ gets to be known
When the spiritual sense is opened up.[126]

We separate them, *once the time has come*, on the Savior's order and in imitation of him. For he was the first to separate the fruit;[127] he was the first to crush, so to speak, the letter of the Law, to extract from it for our use the spiritual essence.[128] With his winnowing basket, he has separated the grain from the chaff.[129] By breaking one day the seven loaves that he then had distributed to the crowd, he snapped the seven seals that guarded the mystery of the Word of God.[130] The five loaves that he broke on another occasion were figurations of the five books of Moses, from which he extracted the spiritual content so as to nourish us on it.[131] On the evening of the supper, at that time taking bread into his hands, having blessed it, he broke it: this was done "not only in the mystery, but also in the reading of the Scriptures";[132] "Christ broke this bread; he divided this word" — and the result was the "science of the Scriptures."[133] It is with this same gesture of the breaking of the bread that the disciples of Emmaüs finally had their eyes opened.[134] This gesture of the fraction does not cease to renew us, producing its effect in each of us: "The bread is doubtless being broken in our presence by the Lord, when the mystic depth of the mysteries is opened by interpretation and is made known by his revealing it."[135] As for us, guided by the Spirit that the Lord has left to his Church, today we draw the consequences, fact by fact, text by text, from the work of discernment which he has accomplished once and for all:

> Having commanded that the Law be divided into two parts, the letter and the spirit. . . . For in the evening the Lord's coming was given to us, in which half that part, i.e., the sense or spirit of the Law, according as the Law is spiritual, is offered, tender, sprinkled with oil.[136]

Following the prescriptions of Leviticus, certain animals offered in sacrifice would have to be opened in the middle. We do the same when, in rereading the old texts in the light of the Gospel, we put the letter on one side and the spirit on the other.[137] We do once again as did the Israelites in the desert, who ground the manna under a millstone so as to make delicious tasting bread from it;[138] or as does the miller, who husks the grain to extract its wheat, when we extract the *medulla spiritus* from the *litterae superficies*.[139] This task is necessary, but not always easy: "for the marrow of the barley is covered with a most tenacious dross."[140]

4. Pedagogy and Spirituality

This separation, this "discernment,"[1] this extraction, this construction, if one can put it that way, of the spiritual sense, has given place, as we have seen, to two formulas that one can call, thanks to the precisions advanced above, tripartite and quadripartite. Now it behooves us to see how each of the two is related to the fundamental formula of the twofold sense.

In the formula inspired by the anthropological trichotomy, the psychic sense, an intermediate sense like the soul itself,[2] is a sort of parenthesis. The "tropologies" that it reveals, being themselves without relation with Christ, are heterogeneous with respect to Christian exegesis, though they might be adapted to them. As with Origen and other ancients, particularly Saint Ambrose, they still hold a certain place among our medievals. So with the Pseudo-Bede commenting on Genesis, who sees in Abraham reason and in Sarah the flesh, unless she be taken as virtue; in Lot the manly spirit and in his wife concupiscence, etc.[3] So, too, for Guibert of Nogent, who loves such tropologies;[4] likewise in certain of the Victorine *Miscellanea*;[5] or in Godfrey of Admont, for whom the female ass and the male ass of Palm Sunday figure "the stupid and infatuated soul" and "the mind that, by love for earthly things, allows the image of God within it to be erased."[6] When Rupert writes on a text from the Book of Judges: "In the moral sense, Asha sat upon the ass when his soul presided over the irrational motions of his flesh,"[7] such an exegesis evidently has nothing to do with what he himself says a bit later on about the sacred words: "These sayings taken literally contain many mysteries of spirit and life."[8] It is almost always a question of moral psychology; much more rarely, as we already know, it is about cosmic symbols inherited from ancient Jewish exegesis, such as the symbolism of the High Priest's vestments,[9] which is found explicated in Philo, in Josephus, and already in the Book of Wisdom.[10] At the bottom line, all this is just a negligible survival and never constitutes the framework of the exegetical system. The tripartite scheme is preserved, it is met with frequently, but in the majority of cases it in fact hides another signification: it offered a great pedagogical advantage, felt by preachers. Let us not forget that Christian exegesis was born, first and foremost, in the office of the liturgy, regarding sacred reading that had to be commented upon. That is where it was developed.[11] Our exegetes are often preachers: this is the name given to the best of them following the Apostles.[12] They draw food for their hearers from the two breasts of Scripture. They are themselves compared to these breasts:[13] is not each of them, as Hélinand of Froidmont will say, "a spiritual mother of the divine word"?[14] Even a written systematic commentary, such as that of Paschasius Radbertus on Saint Matthew's Gospel, has its origin in preaching.[15] The bulk of the faithful need a moral teaching rendered sharper and more expressive by a symbolic form and which is accessible to them prior to their being able to be introduced into the depths of doctrine. "Tropology, the speech that converts, is more moving than allegory," Peter Comestor will claim.[16] Thus, morality and allegory seem to belong to the relation between the milk and solid nourishment mentioned by Saint Paul as follows: "'Reasonable and guileless milk' is the moral topos; and 'solid food', the mystical understanding"; this is what Origen says,[17] and more than once he returns to it:

> The food of milk in holy Scriptures is said to be the first moral instruction which is given to beginners, as to little children. For one ought not to hand over immediately to beginning students what pertains to the deep and more secret sacraments; rather, to them are given correction of morals, improvement of discipline, and the first elements of religious converse and simple faith. That is the milk of the Church: beginners get the first elements of little children.[18]

Clement of Alexandria observed, explicitly in his *Paidagogos*, that it requires an effort of moral life to become worthy of receiving the teachings of the Logos.[19] Saint Hilary will say the same thing in commenting upon Psalm 118:

> For [the phrase] "Blessed are those who scrutinize the testimonies of God" is not first, but rather what is first is "Blessed are the blameless in the path." For he is the first to enter the way of truth, once his morals have been strengthened and compounded with the general honesty of probity to constitute a zeal for innocence; then the one following is to scrutinize the testimonies of God and to be ready to investigate them, once his mind has been cleansed and purified. . . .
> Unless the practice of the works of the faith had gone before, an awareness of the teaching will not be reached; and that is to be done by us faithfully so that we may attain knowledge.[20]

Such a pedagogy was entirely natural. It reproduced, mutatis mutandis, the wisdom of the advice given by Seneca, who recommended expounding first the *praecepta*, before going on to the *dogmata*, or the *decreta sapientiae*.[21] In addition, it conformed to the discipline of the Church in preparation for the mysteries. This was the order of initiation. Origen still recalls it; Saint Ambrose does so after him,[22] and Gregory of Elvira too:

> Thus too the Lord ordered him to make a three-room ark as a figure of the Church. For the word of the Law first enters the human catechumen as to the guest-chamber of the body. Then the mystery of the sacrament is put out of sight to the seeker in the secret of his soul as into a cover of linen. Third, it is made to come to the faithful into the upper parts of the house through the steps of the virtues toward the acme of the Holy Spirit.
> Hence too the blessed apostle Paul writing to the Thessalonians

that man is of three forms says: "That your spirit and soul and body may be preserved whole unto the day of the Lord." Hence the flesh of man receives the word of God as guest-chamber; whereas the soul preserves and keeps it safe, and the spirit lifts and raises it.[23]

Mystic things overshadow moral ones, says Saint Ambrose again, but before the fruit of the former could be gathered, the leaves of the former must have come out.[24] Hence its usual sequence: "moralia-mystica."[25] It is only after having searched the "moral place" that one gets to explicate the "riddles of the prophetic Scriptures."[26] Saint Gaudentius of Brescia follows the same order in his homilies: before coming to the promised allegories, he expounded the moral sense for general edification.[27] In the same way Saint Augustine says that one ought to pour the milk of moral exhortation before the wine of the mysteries, and at one time or another, in distinguishing the two explanatory headings that he puts under the general name of allegory, he places the "movement of souls" immediately after the history, before the "law of eternity," that is to say again or almost, morality before mystery.[28] Rabanus compares morality and mystery to the two sorts of bread spoken of in Leviticus, the one common and ordinary, the other made of wheaten flour: one should begin with the first; it is the first which has been made for all.[29] Guibert of Nogent wisely judges that it is not fitting to throw the common faithful immediately "through the huge whirlpools of the mysteries."[30] Hugh of Saint Victor is of the same opinion: "For the word of wisdom advances little by little to attain spiritual things, so as gently to lead the practiced soul to the inner things";[31] in the *Didascalicon*, he recounts the story of a man who tried to penetrate the mysteries of Scripture prematurely, and who did not stand up under its weight, because he had not begun by reading it "with a view to building up his own life."[32] Hervaeus of Bourg Dieu observes that many Psalms "have led us to theology through ethics."[33] Though a dogmatician by inclination, Gerhoh holds pedagogically to the same order: first the moral, then the mystical; Scripture is to be meditated upon for a pure life before being scrutinized for a deepening of the faith.[34] This is the theory of Peter Lombard: "The historical [method of understanding the divine page] is fitting for beginners; the moral, for the advanced; the mystical, for those growing perfect."[35] Alan of Lille will comment in the same spirit upon the three measures of flour under discussion in an episode of Genesis; it is made, he will say, into a loaf cooked under ashes, i.e., a "theological reading": "Three types of men are refreshed by this bread, the big, the middle-sized, and the little. The milk of history is set before the little; the honey of tropology, before the middle-sized; the solid bread of allegory, for those who are bigger."[36] For Alexander Neckam the same pedagogy will command the symbolic explication of natural realities: "Therefore I have decided to raise a preliminary sweat in little works devoted to tropology before I show laborious effort on the peaks of the arduous subtleties of anagogy."[37]

Those were commonplaces. Starting from the same proof, not all, it is true, reasoned in the same way. Some concluded from it merely that in preaching it was necessary to pass more quickly over the "allegory" so as to dwell on the "tropology": such was the position of Guibert of Nogent.[38] But this was only a small number. This pedagogical consideration is sufficient to explain that in the Middle Ages, even among the authors who were aware of the classic formula and who were often faithful to it, *tropologia* sometimes takes a place before *allegoria*. "Milk is given as drink to little ones, not meat."[39] But this milk of "moral instruction" is in reality often already "an evangelical and apostolic milk."[40]

So logic is often stretched in the name of pedagogical utility: *ōpheleia*, as the Greeks used to say. Morality, indeed Christian morality, was placed ahead of the mystery upon which it in fact depended. Good account was rendered of it, for, following Saint Gregory, himself a faithful interpreter of Saint Paul, it was said again and again: "One is not brought into contact with the faith by means of the virtues, but with the virtues by means of faith."[41] The need for rational classification that existed in the Middle Ages as in every epoch, but perhaps more than in the others, called for a new principle of division to justify this stretching or straining. The four senses were grouped into pairs, the first two treating of the things here below, the latter two of the divine and heavenly things; the first two expressing human relations, the latter two the relations of man with God; or again, the first two being chiefly interested in the practical life, the second two, faith and contemplation. Sketched out roughly in a text of the *Miscellanea*,[42] the theory takes on explicit form, without attaining true coherence, in a sermon of the Victorine abbot Absalon, where at great length it is a question of the "quadripartite observance of the Law," that is to say, a question of the history, tropology, allegory, and analogy:

> ... History shows how to act well. Tropology shapes the will. Allegory purifies the heart through faith. Anagogy purifies the inner man by contemplating only things that belong to God. In the history, in addition to the commandment, obedience is found; in tropology, discipline; in allegory, sincerity of faith; in anagogy is found charity. History teaches you how you may live humbly through obedience to

higher things; tropology, how to live in society with your equal and your inferior. Allegory teaches you to believe faithfully; anagogy teaches you to love perseveringly. The first two show the way of justice to one's neighbor; the other two, the cult of piety toward God.

These are the four wings of the cherubim: by two of them they are flying and two they cover their bodies (Ez. 1). For the holy men, who are the cherubim, i.e., those illuminated by the fullness of divine science, cover their bodies with two wings, when they shape our present dealings through history and tropology; they fly with two wings, when allegory and anagogy are lifted up to contemplation through faith and charity.[43]

How artificial this is is obvious. It is a good example of the late "scholasticism" of the fourfold sense worming its way in among the spirituals, at the same time as the combining of the two formulas. But there is another formula, simpler and more frequent, which sticks to the three senses, as was done long ago in the *Periarchōn,* and which is no less integrally Christian. Allegory properly speaking, then, is simply innuendo or implication. It has no need of being made explicit, because Scripture is meditated upon in a climate of faith, without apologetic aim, and less for religious instruction than for the contemplative life. So without having to appear,[44] this allegory confers upon the two senses that follow history their full value: first, to tropology, then to the last sense which does not allow anything else after it — the one that is sometimes called "spiritual understanding," and sometimes "anagogy," or again "theory," "theology," that is to say "contemplation." Such is the most authentic tripartite division, the one that has the favor of spiritual men. It is developed in strict relation with the distinction of the three steps of the spiritual life as they were expounded by William of Saint Thierry, for example, in his celebrated *Golden Letter,* basing himself, as did Origen, upon the tripartite division of man.[45] One will therefore not be surprised to find the principle already in Origen, who was the first great theoretician of spirituality in the Church.[46] It is noteworthy that with Saint Eucher, who depends upon Origen, as we have seen, the third term is named not "allegory," but rather "anagogy" or "higher understanding."[47] In Rupert as well, this third term is closer to anagogy than to allegory: "In spiritual theory, we cross over to things more sublime, leave behind earthly matters, and discuss beatitude and the heavenly things of the future, so that the preliminary meditation of the present life is a shadow of the beatitude to come."[48] Here tropology precedes anagogy, as the active life precedes the contemplative life, or as asceticism ought to sustain mysticism.

Before obtaining the "repose of contemplation," it is necessary to put forth the "effort of good work."[49] Scripture leads "through ethics," then, "to theology," which means "to the fullness of the Gospel" or "to the life-giving spirit," or again "to the holy of holies."[50] Good doctor that he is, Saint Gregory usually puts allegory before tropology; yet he is too great a spiritual not to adopt, on occasion at least, the following scheme, which is that of the ascent of the soul:

> The animals are walking when the holy men in sacred Scripture understand how to live morally. On the other hand, the animals are lifted up from the earth, when the holy men are suspended in contemplation.[51]
>
> In the words [of Scripture] we find as many delicacies as we take diversities of understanding for our advancement, so that sometimes bare history feeds us, sometimes a moral allegory veiled under the text of the letter refreshes us to the marrow, sometimes flashing in the midst of the darkness of the present life as a glint from the light of eternity contemplation holds us in suspense for higher things.[52]

With variations and in a more intellectual context this is again the same scheme that is found in John Scotus, for whom the end of Scripture is to lead us to climb the heights of "theologia": "altitudinem theologiae ascendere."[53]

5. The Doctrinal Formula

We are thus led to correct or at least to fine-tune the results of the comparison sketched out in Chapter Two between the two principal divisions of the scriptural senses. We may speak of one formulation entirely Christian in its structure, and of another with partially secular origins. It would not be necessary, as we now see, to harden such an opposition, nor to assign too harsh a judgment against the second formulation. Though at first less objectively based and encumbered from the start with a content partially received from Philo, it is nonetheless in practice often just as Christian in inspiration as the first, thanks to the explicit or implicit transfiguration of tropology. Less complete and less didactic, it is a better instrument for spiritual initiation. If the classic formula is that of the doctors, of those who have the mission to teach, if it better satisfied minds concerned with synthesis and well-balanced structure, the other is more attractive to the contemplatives. If the one is more expressive of the totality of the Christian mystery in its essential connections and the harmonious complexity of its various aspects, the other perhaps renders rather the mystic impulse by climbing the steps of the ascent of the soul — which are also, from another point of view, the three successive kingdoms of the Law, of Grace, and, in the realm beyond, of the Spirit.[1] The one has more solidity, but the other answers better to the dynamism of the spiritual life. The one is more "noetic," but the other is more "pneumatic." It is natural that in the twelfth century the latter should again be instinctively preferred by three great minds, who were nevertheless not lacking in doctrine: Rupert of Deutz,[2] Bernard of Clairvaux,[3] Richard of Saint Victor.[4]

The classic formulation, that of the fourfold sense, is of basically simpler structure. It neither includes any heterogeneous importation nor any element tacitly understood. It is merely a development from the formula in two terms which is the essential, primitive formula which remains the permanent one. It is, let us remark, not obtained at the cost of adding new elements, tacking them on in series, but, organically, by analysis of the second term and breaking it down into three parts. Here everything comes from the hiatus which had to exist from the first day, between the two comings of Christ. Given this hiatus, the spiritual sense of the Bible, which was an eschatological sense, necessarily had to be subdivided into three. That is to say, even abstracting from certain texts that can be considered as an anticipation, this fourfold sense already exists among the Fathers. It is there at least implicitly. It is even found explicitly in them, but still in a scattered state.[5] On the other hand, right up to the end, its medieval theoreticians will recognize that the formula is reduced entirely to that of the two fundamental senses. Here is the testimony of Nicholas of Lyra at the very moment he has just cited the distich: "The outer Scripture is the literal sense, which is more obvious, since it is signified immediately through the words; the inner Scripture is the mystic or spiritual sense, which is more hidden, since it is designated through the things signified by those words."[6]

In the patristic period, two other expressions — amongst still others — designate the whole second sense. In calling attention to them, we shall conclude by gathering the vocabulary of the fourfold sense and observing its formation. At the same time we shall be able to get some idea of the flexibility of language that characterizes this important epoch. Then, almost as a matter of luck in the circumstances, the deepest, richest, and most solidly constructed doctrine expresses itself almost always without didacticism, without that need for verbal systematization and rigid classification which are generally the product of epigoni, which, to be sure, answer a need, but in which it would be wrong always to see a progress of thought. "He who cares about the truth," Origen used to say, "does not get stuck on verbal questions";[7] and again: "There is no use for superstition about names, if one can pay attention to things."[8] Clement of Alexandria was of the same opinion: "In my view," he said, "he who is looking for the truth must find his terms without premeditation and without troubling himself about them; he should just make himself give the best name that he can for what he means; for things elude the man who is too attached to words and spends too much time on them."[9] Saint Thomas Aquinas will have the extraordinary good sense to share this view: when the foundation in things is clear, he will judge all verbal controversy to be futile[10] and, with an emphasis that is perhaps not superfluous in any epoch, he will restate the principle: "It pertains to the wise not to worry about names."[11]

For some then, the spiritual sense is entirely anagogy: "mystic anagogy," Origen used to say,[12] or again: "the allegories according to anagogy,"[13] or simply: "according to anagogy,"[14] etc. Saint Gregory of Nyssa referred to "the contemplation according to anagogy."[15] This broad use of the word — which, let us note, was not found in Philo — therefore does not specifically characterize, as some have said, the School of Antioch.[16] For others, it is tropology; again, Origen had used the word in this broad sense, and it seems to have had the favor, among others, of Saint Jerome,[17] who writes on a Psalm for example: "The whole [Psalm] pertains to the sacrament of Christ through tropology."[18] Besides, one rarely depends on just one name for anything for long. Everyone would agree with the reflections made by Saint Gregory of Nyssa in the preface to his commentary on the Canticle of Canticles: "This anagogical contemplation [of Scripture], or this tropology, or this allegory, or whatever other name one wants to call it: we shall not dispute how to speak of it, provided that we can usefully think of it. For the great Apostle, in saying that the Law is spiritual, understands by the name 'Law' the historical accounts as well, in such fashion that the whole of Scripture . . . teaches those who scrutinize it, so as to lead them to know the mysteries and pure conduct. . . . In all these names that designate the spiritual understanding, Scripture fundamentally teaches us just one thing: that it is not absolutely necessary to stop at the letter, . . . but to pass on to immaterial contemplation . . . , in accordance with the dictum: 'the letter killeth, but the spirit giveth life.'"[19]

Again, Origen used to speak of 'spiritual explication' or 'discernment',[20] of 'contemplation',[21] of 'mystic contemplation', of 'intellection', etc.[22] He also said: 'to tropologize'[23] or again: 'to be led up to tropology'.[24] He loved the verb *katanoein,* the verbal adjective *katanoēteon,* etc.[25] Didymus the Blind (?) used to use the terms "allegory" and "anagogy" interchangeably.[26] Saint Cyril of Alexandria himself also speaks frequently of anagogy,[27] but just as much of spiritual contemplation, mystic understanding, etc.[28] Saint Jerome is no less eclectic. Aside from "according to tropology," he writes in close succession for the same species of sense in turn: "according to the spirit,"[29] "according to the mystical understandings,"[30] "according to anagogy";[31] he also says: "spiritual contemplation."[32] Though he also uses the term *allegoria* in the sense inherited from Saint Paul,[33] he nevertheless says, for example: "According to anagogy the vineyard of God and garden of apples can be called our soul,"[34] or again: "The ox by anagogy is related to Israel"[35] and, in a way that would appear, in retrospect, particularly paradoxical: "That place . . . can . . . by anagogy be sung of the night of this age,"[36] etc. One naturally finds the same range of vocabulary in the great Carolingian compilers, such as Claudius of Turin,[37] or Rabanus Maurus.[38] One also finds it in Paschasius Radbertus, who writes: "according to the anagogical senses" to designate every mystical sense,[39] as well as in Remigius of Auxerre, who uses at least ten synonymous expressions at random.[40] It is also found in Rupert of Deutz[41] and certain others.

Whatever the words that express it, the twofold biblical sense is already the bearer of the fourfold sense. Thus it happens that all the elements of this fourfold sense were already clearly distinguished even in the time of the Fathers. This is notably the case with Saint Jerome, though there again the vocabulary items do not correspond at every point to the fixed and pre-numbered labels which one day will prevail. Doubtless, even when he does not follow the order that we have studied above (body, soul, spirit), Jerome holds to a tripartite division; thus he cannot hand over to us the four senses in a single defining formula. But to obtain all four of them, we have only, for example, to bring together one sentence from the commentary on Ezekiel and another from the commentary on Amos. The first enumerates the first three senses:

> We can discuss this topic in three ways: . . . either according to the letter . . . , or according to the spiritual understanding . . . , or surely [by] the soul of the believer. . . .[42]

The second, skipping over the third sense or including it together with the second, adds the fourth sense:

> For we ought to understand holy Scripture first according to the letter . . . ; second, according to the allegory, i.e., the spiritual understanding; third, according to the beatitude of those to come.[43]

Here let us retain just this example. How many others one could give, gleaning in the works of the other Fathers, especially Saint Augustine! One will not forget, above all, that all this is already found abundantly in Origen.[44]

One can therefore rightly say, with a theologian of the modern age: "The holy Fathers have most excellently recognized the four senses or methods of expounding God's Scripture."[45] The finding was confirmed by Rosenmüller regarding the *Liber allegoriarum*, which he attributed to Rabanus Maurus: "Along with the more ancient Fathers, he set up . . . the fourfold sense of Scripture."[46] Nevertheless, the tidy, complete, schematized formula is noticeably later. It is customarily assigned to the time of Rabanus Maurus and Amalarius. As one could have gathered in Chapter Two, it should be assigned noticeably further back, to the time of Aldhelm of Sherborne (seventh century) and the Venerable Bede. The established terms for what comes after *historia* or *littera* will be: *allegoria, tropologia, anagoge (anagogia)*. By an appeal to their common matrix, these three last senses will often be said to be contained, as so many subdivisions, under the spiritual or mystical sense. Thus it is that Saint Bonaventure wants to demonstrate a "threefold spiritual sense."[47] The same is done by Nicholas of Lyra, whose prologue to the *Glossa ordinaria* is as explicit as anyone would want:

> The mystic or spiritual sense . . . is in general threefold; since if the things signified by the words are referred to so as to signify the things that are to be believed in the new law, this amounts to the allegorical sense; if they are referred to so as to signify things to be done by us, this is the moral or tropological sense; and if they are referred to so as to signify things that are to be hoped for in the beatitude to come, this is the anagogical sense.[48]

The same goes for Dionysius the Carthusian,[49] and many other moderns starting from the fifteenth century. Sixtus of Sienna proceeds this way in his *Ars interpretandi sanctas Scripturas absolutissima*,[50] etc. Careful to prevent confusion, Stephen Langton already observed that *mystica expositio* is sometimes said, in a restricted sense, of only one of the three that follow the *expositio historica* (according to him, the *anagogica*), but that in other cases it can include all three of them.[51] Sometimes the same holds true for *allegoria*. Several, appealing to the most general acceptation that it used to have long ago,[52] range the last three senses under their general vocabulary term, at the risk of recognizing soon thereafter another, more particular acceptation. Hugh of Saint Victor does so: his role as theoretician of studies inclined him to precisions of this sort.[53] Analogously, the *Speculum de mysteriis Ecclesiae* says: "There is allegory when one fact is understood through another; if the fact is visible, there is simple allegory; if invisible and heavenly, it is called 'anagogy'."[54] Thus, among the great scholastics, Saint Albert the Great says: "Under the allegorical [sense] he includes three items: namely, special allegory, tropological allegory, and special anagogical allegory."[55] This manner of proceeding is also motivated by the desire to reconcile the classic division with the Augustinian text of the *De utilitate credendi* that we have analyzed; a desire which manifests itself at least among certain relatively recent authors, such as Sixtus of Sienna, in a passage which does not reproduce the terminology of the *Ars interpretandi*:

> There are two sorts of explanation for holy Scripture, namely historical and allegorical. The historical, again, is such that one part is analogical, the other aetiological. But there are three sorts of allegorical explanation: the first accommodates the figures of things to the present and keeps the name 'allegorical'; the second [refers] to morals and is called 'tropological'; the third [refers] to the unchangeable eternity and is called 'anagogical'.[56]

But most often, the four senses will be enumerated and defined one after the other without calling up the general sense of which the three last members are merely the species. Such is already the case with Bede,[57] the first author who offers us a developed table, so to speak, of the fourfold sense. Such is also the case with Rabanus Maurus, who copies Bede,[58] then with Guibert of Nogent,[59] in the first Gloss on Genesis,[60] with Honorius,[61] Adam Scotus,[62] John of Salisbury,[63] with Innocent III, etc. This detail of presentation, without importance in and of itself, sometimes gains weight from the fact that one does not care to show explicitly the connection of the diverse senses among themselves. These omissions will contribute not a little to foster the misunderstandings from whence, one day, certain severe judgments will arise. They will obstruct the recognition of the internal unity of the formula, the logic of its structure, and, certain affirmations to the contrary notwithstanding, the truly 'theological' character of its elements.[64]

The Doctrinal Formula

We are now ready to examine more closely, one after the other, each of the four senses and then to study their construction.

CHAPTER SEVEN

The Foundation of History

1. Importance of the Letter

Littera gesta docet: The letter teaches us what was done. This is the first of the biblical senses: the "first signification"[1] is in the text; the "first exposition," in the commentator; the "first understanding," in the reader.[2] Here the word *littera* is doubtless called for by reason of the poetic meter; but it is also conceivable that it was chosen to recall the essential doctrine of the letter and the spirit. In any case, it is synonymous with *historia*, taken broadly. To be sure, certain books of the Bible are more properly called "historical":

> If, however, we use the signification of this term in a broader sense, e.g., to say that "history" is "not only a telling of things accomplished, but the primary signification of any telling that is expressed using words," there is no problem; I think that all the books of both Testaments involve this broader acceptation . . . with regard to the reading in the literal sense.[3]

In the explications of the distich, *historia* is the most frequently occurring alternative. The two words [*littera* and *historia*] are practically interchangeable, and we pass easily from the one to the other. This is why, in the presence of certain texts that we shall call non-historical, especially when their language is figurative, e.g., proverbs, parables, etc., we readily say that they have no literal sense — we shall soon return to this point — no *littera*; whilst, on the other hand, we have no hesitation to speak of the *historia legis.* History, says Isidore of Seville, is "a simple expression that is understood just as it is said"; biblical history is subdivided into two parts: "in relating past deeds and in manifesting the divine precepts."[4] Every passage from the Bible read for the Office is currently designated as *historia,* and in a commentary followed like that of Beatus on the Apocalypse, each portion of the commented text is announced by the same label: *storia.*

An etymology justifies this equivalence by seeming to assimilate history to the letter, i.e., to the exterior and sensible aspect of things, as opposed to their mystic or hidden signification, which is not at all perceived by the senses but only by the understanding: "historîn, meaning 'I see'." Thus, after many others, says Robert of Melun.[5] This is a not too badly deformed use of an etymological explanation taken from classical antiquity. After having been, for the Greeks, at first a synonym for research, inquiry, or description of concrete knowledge (as in "natural history"),[6] history, having become essentially narration, was for a certain number of authors more especially narration "of things at which the narrator was present when they were done" or "of those times that we either saw or were able to see."[7] In that way, it was opposed not only to the fictions of the poets, to "fables," or to "argumenta," i.e., to the report of things that could have happened, but also to the "annales," which were any sort of narration at all, "of those times that our age has not seen."[8] "A historiographer," Conrad of Hirschau will say, is an "eyewitness writer."[9] By adopting such an explanation, which did not distinguish history and historiography, our medieval authors did not hold on to the effort at definition attempted early on by Saint Augustine in the *De ordine.* Augustine had wanted to put under the single name of history "an infinite, multiple thing," comprising both fable and the most distant past as well.[10] The medievals, on the contrary, generally spoke of history in the strict sense only when they could say: "I shall report not things merely heard but those I have seen" or, at very least, "that either I myself have seen or else know by reliable account."[11] As to the word "chronicle," they did not define it only by a law of concision — "the truth of things accomplished, digested briefly according to the law of the chronicle."[12] Rather, it is the name that was habitually applied by them to every history of the past, and not only to "chronographies" in the present sense of the word, or to "annals." Thus it is that Fréculphe of Lisieux (†852), who is a good historian with an extremely wide horizon, declares that he has read all or almost all the "historiographies," before sitting down to compose the two volumes of his own "Chronicles."[13] In the same way again, Ordericus

Vitalis, attempting to write about his own epoch, having himself seen the events he just reported, modestly says that he wanted to issue a simple "historia"[14] that could serve as a document, amongst other such, for future authors of "chronographiae,"[15] whilst Sigebert of Gembloux, when issuing his *Chronica*, expresses his intention in them to follow the "footsteps of our elders," letting himself be guided "through the pathways of the histories."[16] William of Malmsbury likewise gives the title of *Chronicles* to the first three books of his great historical work, in which he treats of the preceding reign, and reserves the title *History* for the report about the contemporary period.[17] Perhaps the case of Otto of Freising is the most significant. While dedicating to the emperor Frederick the report of his *Gesta* Otto tells him: "so I offer your excellency this *history*,"[18] but he quite deliberately presented as a *Chronicon* a universal history that was at the same time a theology of history.[19] It would therefore be twice over to minimize his work to call him, as has sometimes been done, "the chronicler Otto of Freising" — unless it be added that the medieval chronicler, differing in this respect from the chronicler of the patristic age, could have the ambition of performing the task, in the modern sense of the word, of a true historian, and more besides. So he was not only a universal chronicler: he was a writer who strove "to explain history and to present the events in a better order," in short, to compose a veritable "discourse on universal history."[20] In one and the same plan, he combined, so to speak, the *Chronicle* of Eusebius and the *City of God* of Saint Augustine.[21]

The old etymology of *historia* had been recorded by Saint Isidore of Seville, whose *Etymologiae* enjoyed an extreme popularity for centuries: "'History' is derived from the Greek *historein*, i.e., to see and get to know; for no one among the ancients used to write a history, except for one who had been there. . . . For we grasp what happens better with the eyes than we gather it by hearing."[22] It was taken up again on his own account by Hugh of Saint Victor[23] and reproduced again subsequently.[24] Modern philology seems to confirm it[25] — but without, it goes without saying, confirming the deformation that we have seen. But in the other direction — and this second remark has much more importance for us — the letter is found, again to speak generally, assimilated to history: *gesta docet: it teaches what has been done*. Another etymology comes to emphasize this other downslope of the assimilation: "It is derived from *isteron*, i.e., gesturing; for deeds (*gesta*) are denoted in it."[26] In these two etymologies, as we see, the two senses of the word "history," the objective and the subjective, are distinguished and meet up again, pretty much as they do in modern French. To designate, on the one hand, the deeds recounted and, on the other, the report of these deeds, the Latin Middle Ages had, like us, almost nothing but this single word (despite *narratio* and *relatio*) at its disposal; but, then as now, the distinction of meanings was too obvious for the unity of the term to provoke any serious risk of confusion in ordinary use. One author toward the end of the twelfth century gives the two senses as follows: "History is the thing done or the thing seen."[27] A bit later, in a gloss on the *Historia scolastica*, Stephen Langton will propose this definition synthesizing the two components: "History is derived from *ysteron*, which is to see or to gesture; for it reports only about those things that have been done and seen."[28]

Indeed, considered both in its totality and in its letter, Scripture first delivers us facts. "The letter is the deed that the sacred history reports."[29] It recounts a series of events which have really transpired and concerning which it is essential that they should really have transpired. It is neither an exposition of an abstract doctrine, nor a collection of myths, nor a manual of the inner life. It has nothing atemporal about it. "For that people really and temporally attained all these things."[30] Divine revelation has not only taken place in time, in the course of history: it has also a historic form in its own right. It is contained within a *res gesta: a thing that has been accomplished*.[31] It is first of all a fact of history: "The point to chase down in this religion is history."[32] In professing this religion, we are obliged to believe in a whole series of facts that have really come about.[33] God has chosen a people for himself; in this way, he has intervened in the history of men: the first thing to do, then, is to know, according to the book in which the Holy Spirit has recorded it, the sequence of his interventions. Thus it will never be possible to forget history, nor to put it into question again, nor to free oneself of it or spurn it. One must endeavor to receive and preserve its testimony.

The declarations that assure us of it are countless: it is by history and hence by "historical explanation"[34] that everything must begin. "The narration itself first becomes clear according to the letter";[35] "let us first expound the history."[36]

Putting the history of the song everywhere first,

says an elegy of Arator.[37] It is the truth of history that one must first investigate: "to track the truth of history,"[38] "the truth of history is to be pursued. . . ."[39] One must search it out with diligence: "Consider diligently what the text of the history shows,"[40] just as it had itself been writ-

Importance of the Letter

ten diligently.[41] It is this "pure truth of the histories"[42] that one must begin by establishing and proclaiming: "when the truth of the fact has been historically proved";[43] it is this that one must subsequently always maintain. "While the history remains,"[44] "while the truth of the history remains first":[45] these formulas, like so many others, came from Origen-Rufinus. They are taken up again and again,[46] like the almost identical formula of Saint Gregory the Great: "for, in fact, once the truth of the history has been preserved,"[47] or "the truth of the letter having been preserved,"[48] which came from Saint Augustine[49] — and once again from Origen.[50]

To suppress this truth of history in practice, even without intending to deny it, or to dissolve it in fact by too much haste, would be at very least a blunder.[51] It is as if, to take better care of one's soul, one neglected to give to the body everything it needed: by thus killing its own body, the soul would not save itself; the letter of Scripture, which consists in history, is again in this respect comparable to the human body.[52] He who neglects to study it is also like the grammarian who would believe he could neglect the alphabet.[53] Hence, following the forceful pleonasm of Saint Gaudentius of Brescia, the Christian reads the Bible "according to the history of the event."[54] From history he receives reports "according to the reliability of the deeds performed."[55] He begins by explaining the "character of the fact"[56] historically and he knows in advance that, of all that could come later on to make him enter deeper into the divine thought, nothing would ever injure the "truth of the thing performed."[57] On the contrary, it will all merely show off the "character"[58] of the deed to better advantage, and thereby, if need be, to found that character still further. Moreover, he knows that in its own right history often has its own usefulness, its great utility for us.[59] He knows that it possesses a force, a primordial "virtue": "the virtue of history alone," which is other than its "mystic virtue."[60] He knows that it already has its own beauty proper to it alone,[61] that it is already full of great teachings;[62] that it is often "salutary" prior to any allegorical interpretation,[63] bearing "edification": "the very text of history builds us up";[64] "this very thing builds up the reader's moral sense historically";[65] "the letter builds me up . . . ; before I come to the spiritual understanding, I marvel within the letter."[66]

Without wanting to rush things, the Christian habitually searches, therefore, first to "comprehend" this history, in the first place to "possess" it in itself. That, he thinks, is a "necessity." In other words, there is a preliminary attention to the "ratio historiae" — for "history has its own proper character."[67] There is a primary concern about the content of the "order of history";[68] there is a primary historical understanding, "understanding of history," an "understanding of the letter,"[69] a "simple understanding,"[70] "an understanding endorsed in history,"[71] which is important to get prior to pushing the research or development any further. Again, most of these formulas come from Origen, and, like so many others from the same source, they have been copied again and again from century to century.[72] "For whoever desires to investigate the moral and spiritual understanding in the divine Scriptures must first possess an understanding of the history."[73] To acquire this primary understanding, it will not be too much, whenever possible, to have recourse to documents of secular history which could clarify biblical history in some respect: Saint Augustine, like Saint Jerome,[74] had recommended it.[75] Rabanus Maurus manifests care for it: the books of the Jews and even those of the Gentiles will be called to witness many a time, "so that the truth of sacred history may be clear from a comparison of the many books, and the sense of its account may become clearer to the reader."[76] The authors of Chronicles try to facilitate the task for the exegetes by clearing up the points of history that offer difficulty to their intention.[77] Thereby they all show that they truly take this biblical history as something serious and "weighty": "the weight of history," says one of them.[78] They hold it as something "venerable" and "sacred": the two words are dear to Saint Gregory,[79] and they express what everybody believes.[80] No Christian is unaware of it; the sacred character that we venerate in reading the biblical stories is not only that of the text or of the book by reason of its inspiration, "the history of the sacred reading,"[81] the "sacred page"; it is in the first place — always speaking generally — the character of the events that this texts reports: "the sacred history."[82] This is a doubly sacred character, for these events all more or less contribute to prepare the great event upon which hangs the salvation of the world. Thus what Godfrey of Admont says of the history of Rebecca can more or less be said of them all: she is charged with spiritual sense; and yet:

> Even if nothing else could be found in this history but what the bare letter betokens, nevertheless she would be something for us to delight in and something to be embraced with intimate love; since this same Rebecca, about whom the history reports, was doubtless, if we may say so, of the line or matter of that blessed seed from which the Lord Jesus willed to take on the nature of our mortality.[83]

No Christian is unaware of it, and this is one of the traditional objects of admiration: our whole salvation in fact is worked out in the "deepest valley of history."[84] The redemption has not been accomplished in the imagination, but in time and in factual reality. It has been prepared, since the creation of the world, by a sequence of historical events, related in a collection of chronicles whose veracity we cannot put into doubt without putting our patrimony at risk and without damaging our own foundations.[85]

This last word, which is that of Paul Claudel, spontaneously rediscovers the key word of the tradition: in the interpretation of Scripture, history is the universal *foundation*.[86] It was — it would be well to state it one more time, though the illustrious Mosheim, whose verdicts for a long time used to be law, declared exactly the contrary[87] — the key term of Origen, in whom there was such a lively awareness of the opposition of the biblical faith to the wisdom of the pagans. This metaphor of foundation or of foundations had doubtless been suggested to him by the theme that he had to treat at that time, the theme of Noah's construction of the ark. Here is how he expressed himself: "Let us see the reports that are related about [the ark], . . . so that, when we have laid such foundations, we may be able to rise from the text of the history to the . . . sense of spiritual understanding";[88] and again: "The first (exposition) is historical, laid down like a foundation in the lower reaches."[89] In the same homily, Origen found himself led, moreover, to speak of Jesus, "the spiritual Noah," as "the architect of the Church";[90] he commented on the other hand on the texts of Saint Paul that show the foundation of this great spiritual edifice to be either in Jesus himself or in his Apostles;[91] and again he spoke of the "foundation of the faith" which sustains the edifice of each spiritual life within the Church.[92] Ceaselessly recalled and commented on in the same manner,[93] the Pauline texts confer on this word *fundamentum* a dignity[94] that redounds upon the usage that is made of it with regard to history.

Such usage is constant, uninterrupted. Saint Augustine adjures the faithful never to suppress the "fundamentum rei gestae," without which the whole edifice of the "significatio" would be floating "in air";[95] he returns to it on several occasions,[96] and it is quite remarkable that he expresses himself thus in terms that elsewhere serve him to speak of Christ, when he says: "Add on the building, but do not abandon the foundation."[97] Saint Jerome, to whom the paternity of the key word is currently, but incorrectly, attributed,[98] himself calls upon the "foundations of history" more than once;[99] he says, again: "the truth of history, the foundation of spiritual understanding,"[100] "to pile the spiritual building upon the foundations of history."[101] Of Saint Paula he writes: "though she used to love history and to speak of that foundation of truth, she more usually followed the spiritual understanding."[102] The author of the *In Isaiam VI*, translated (?) by Jerome, also says that Saint Paul has built the spiritual understanding "upon the foundation of the history."[103] Saint Gregory takes up the metaphor on his own account; at the threshold of the *Moralia*, he writes: "We are laying down the primary foundation of the history";[104] and later on he observes that "the edifice of doctrine" will be so much the stronger as its foundation is the more carefully laid;[105] still, he seems to prefer the analogous metaphor of a root: "We must first handle the root of history, so as later to be able to satisfy the mind with the fruit of the allegories."[106] Saint Isidore says in his turn: "while the foundation of the history is going on first"[107] and Bede: "once the root of the history has been handed over."[108]

With a series of guarantors like this, it will not be surprising that the two words have done rather well, especially *fundamentum*. It comes up again many times among our Latin medievals. In Alcuin and Adrevald of Fleury-sur-Loire commenting on the blessings of the Patriarchs it shows up in this way: "The foundations of the history are to be laid down first."[109] Notker the Stammerer takes it up with regard to Saint Gregory;[110] Christian of Stavelot proclaims: "history, the foundation of all understanding."[111] Along with Gregory and Bede, Rabanus Maurus wants us to plant "the root of history";[112] for the most part, again, he speaks at least six or seven times about laying the foundations: "First the foundations of history are to be established," and his formulas are more than once the very same as those of Saint Jerome.[113] Angelome of Luxeuil manifests the same need at the beginning of his explication of Genesis[114] as well as of his explication of the Book of Kings;[115] and he is not unmindful of his initial resolve even en route: "We have promised first to lay down the foundations of the history."[116] The necessity for a solid historical *fundamentum* is recalled a bit later by Cardinal Humbert;[117] it is recalled many times by Rupert of Deutz. Rupert is looking for "the sense of the letter" so as to "grasp the certain foundation of history," for he knows that without this foundation the mystical explanation "is permitted to float about."[118] He also compares the letter of the five books of Moses to the five columns that were raised at the entry of the Tabernacle, bearing the capitals of spiritual understanding.[119] Hervaeus of Bourg Dieu is in favor of the "root."[120] Others, such as Raoul of Saint Germer[121] and Petrus Comestor,[122] comparing the four senses of Scripture to the gates at the four sides that open access to the Temple — the Temple which is the Church — see in history the threshold, the *limen*, over which one must necessarily pass. Abelard prefers Gregory's metaphor of the root: "First . . . let us nail down the root, the truth or history of the thing accomplished."[123] In the *Didascalicon,* Hugh of Saint Victor transmits the classical teaching in a series of formulas that themselves are perfectly classic: "the foundation and principle of sacred doctrine is history";[124] or, what comes down to the same thing: "Nor do I think that you can become perfectly keen in allegory unless you had previously been well grounded in history,"[125] etc. Undertaking to compose a *memento* of principles for the use of students, he writes:

> We now have in our hands history to be put in the memory as the first foundation of all doctrine. But since . . . memory rejoices in brevity, and the accomplishments of various times are almost infinite, it behooves us to gather a brief summary of them all, a sort of foundation of the foundation, or first foundation, [a summary] which the mind can easily grasp and the memory retain.[126]

The *fundamentum* comes up again in the *Allegoriae*, where it is said that by the history of Scripture itself "it piles up the foundation of the building almost at the beginning."[127] At the opening of the *Scholastic History*, Petrus Comestor enunciates the principle anew: "History is the foundation."[128] The same goes for John of Kelso in his letter to Adam Scotus,[129] and Adam himself in his Response,[130] as well as for David of Augsbourg in his opusculum on the words "Ad quid venisti."[131] Richard of Saint Victor states that in the eyes of many readers, with whom he is tempted not to disagree, nothing can be solidly founded as a fact of doctrine except "in the soil of the historical sense": without it, all understanding of the Scripture would rest "upon what is empty and void."[132] Arnold of Bonneval sees to it that one does not pull out "the foundation of the letter,"[133] and he protests that in relating many biblical facts to "the inner man" he "is not abolishing any history, which is the foundation of Scripture."[134] Peter of Poitiers himself also wants one always to lay down "the foundation of history."[135] John of Salisbury praises Saint Jerome for being the doctor "most reliable in constructing the foundation of the letter."[136] Henry of Marcy recalls that one can build nothing securely except "on a solid foundation."[137] History, says Stephen Langton, is the "foundation of allegory."[138]

The word comes up again in Alan of Lille.[139] It will pass into the language of the scholastics, with the same signification, set in exactly the same context. Thus in the *Summa de bono* of Ulrich of Strasbourg: "And so one must be zealous for the truth of the literal sense, because without this foundation it is impossible for anyone to become perfect in the spiritual sense."[140] The same goes for Richard of Middleton,[141] and others as well. Dionysius the Carthusian will pick it up: "But the historical or literal sense is the foundation or basis of the other understandings."[142] An anonymous poem of the thirteenth century puts it well:

In holy Scripture there are a type and figure
Rightly to be followed, but one ought not hold in contempt
The report of things accomplished, their text:
Just as the documents ought to bear
The foundations of the typic sense, so ought they deliver
The things by means of words.[143]

And all these authors would be ready to say again about the root or foundation of history what Saint Augustine used to say about the foundation of the faith: "The foundation in a building is usually neglected by the inexperienced. . . . Yet everything that delights you in a tree has risen as a whole from the root."[144]

2. Particularities of Language

From the third to the fifteenth century, then, the same word was used to express the same idea. This will doubtless be enough to brush aside the misapprehension, which was that of so many modern historians and which even today is not so rare, whereby one would see negations of history in a sequence of various expressions all signifying, from various points of view, the refusal to confine oneself merely to the literal sense. But to understand these expressions, a minimum of historical effort is indispensable.

Following the Fathers, our medievals ceaselessly had before their thought the famous text of Saint Paul: "The letter killeth; the spirit giveth life." A modern exegete, confined within his own specialty, can without harm not bother to concern himself with it; the same does not go for those who cannot so easily abstract from the doctrine. But this "letter that killeth" was not the historical reality — neither for them nor for the Fathers nor for Saint Paul: it was "the superseded rule of the letter,"[1] and consequently, when the word was applied to exegesis, it meant the "Judaic" interpretation of the Scriptures.[2] No one would have hesitated to say, along with Origen: "in holy Scriptures we defend both the letter and the spirit";[3] or, with Saint Augustine: "All those things signified something other than they were, but yet they too existed bodily";[4] or, with Bede: "a historical as well as an allegorical science";[5] or, with Rupert: "we take them both up."[6] The spiritual understanding they were looking for was those very events that had taken place long ago, as once more Rupert said it, "in the truth of history."[7] In other words, it was not the "letter" that bothered them, but the "mere letter,"[8] the "mere surface of the letter,"[9] the "property of the letter alone," and those who were aiming like "partisans of the letter" were in fact the "ones understanding according to the letter alone."[10] "A maxim is not to be ground down among those concerned with the mere letter."[11] What they wanted was not at all that one should stop short at the letter, but rather that one might discover and gather the fruit of the spirit hidden under its foliage.[12] Indeed, to stop short at the letter would have been to return to Judaism.[13] As Saint Gaudentius explained, all those "who call upon the Lord" can only in this way separate themselves from those who "are still following a shadow after the advent of the Truth";[14] or, as Saint Jerome used to say, the Christians do not deny history, they do not despise it, but they do not understand it in the same way as the Jews or as the "Judaizers": they would not know how to be among those "who are in love with the history, who follow the Judaic meaning alone, who follow the killing letter and not the life-giving spirit";[15] among those "who follow merely the simple history that killeth."[16] For, in the view of a Christian receiving the Law of Moses, "the carnal observances are extremely bad; the spiritual understandings are extremely good."[17]

There is no room here to examine the various significations that it was possible to draw from the words of Saint Paul and those that were in fact so drawn. We have in view only their repercussions upon the traditional exegesis. Saint Augustine himself, who gave another interpretation in the *De spiritu et littera*, nevertheless recognized the legitimacy of its exegetical acceptation.[18] Even within the limits of the latter, it is clear that the attitude with regard to the "letter" still had to admit of certain nuances, according to which it would have been a question of the letter of history properly speaking or the letter of the law properly speaking, of the "report of the things accomplished" or of the "legal writing."[19] The texts that have just been cited show it already. Nevertheless, in both cases, the fundamental principle was the same: the opposition of the letter that kills and of the spirit that gives life was affirmed as well. For us it is merely a question of not mistaking the habitual sense of this opposition.

When, for example, Saint Cyprian explained that Noah's ark was "none other" than the sacrament of Christ's Church,[20] he would never have dreamed of denying its material reality! When, with regard to certain reports from the Book of Judges, Origen said: "The Jews read these things 'as histories of things done and gone' ['tanquam historias rerum gestarum et praeteritarum'] whilst we, for whom they had been written, apply them to ourselves," none of his hearers would have had to understand that he would have been contesting its primary historicity![21] When Saint Ambrose was writing: "Now it is not the aspect of the lamb, but the truth of Christ's body"[22] about the sacrifice of Abel, this was not to make one believe that only an appearance of lamb had been sacrificed![23] When Saint Jerome, commenting on the Epistle to the Galatians, declared: "The flesh lusts against the spirit, that is, the history and fleshly understanding of Scripture lusts against the allegory and the spiritual teaching,"[24] he did not want to promote an allegory negating the history any more than Saint Paul did! When Saint Augustine taught that many passages of Scripture ought to be taken not "literally" but "figuratively," the three examples that he advanced also showed without any possible doubt that this manner of understanding them presupposed the recognition of their historical sense.[25] When he said again: "Those figures were not the things themselves,"[26] when he spoke of the old Pasch celebrated "like images in the clouds,"[27] or when he alluded to certain "allegorical reports,"[28] one could not be deceived there either. Nor [could one be deceived] when he gave this advice to his hearers regarding the Psalm *In exitu Israel:* "Do not think that the past is being reported to us, but rather that the things to come are being foretold," all the less in that he explained his thought well: "since, even while those miracles were coming about in that people, things present were being performed, albeit not without betokening of things to come."[29] Again, he makes this perfectly clear in more than one other place: we have previously cited a passage from his *Diverse Questions* in which he explains the Pauline aphorism: "For it is not the Old Testament that is eliminated in Christ, but its covering, so that it may be understood through Christ and what was obscure and mysterious without Christ might, so to speak, be laid bare";[30] or the *City of God:* "But no one should think . . . that these things did not happen at all, but are mere figures of speech."[31] In like manner, when Saint Gregory said of the reports of the Book of Kings: "not so much history as prophecy," the sequel showed that he was in no way contesting its reality nor its importance: "the simple, true letter, yet exceedingly high, being accompanied by a deep multiplicity of hidden senses."[32]

Truth to tell, such precisions were not at all necessary for a Christian of the patristic or medieval era, so habituated as he was, in the wake of Saint Paul and the Epistle to the Hebrews, to oppose the most certain realities of the Old Testament to those of the New as "figure," "image," or "shadow" to the "thing itself," the "body," or the "truth." *Per typica ad vera*, Saint Irenaeus already used to say;[33] and, in an identical sense, Origen said: "Let us first see the shadow of the Scripture, to look next for its truth."[34] It is in a language already for a long time fixed, universally received, and consequently not disposed to any equivocation, in which Aimon of Auxerre declares: "All things that were done for them in figure are coming about for us in truth";[35] or in which Rabanus Maurus records: "Here it is apparent how much the truth of the Gospel excels the shadow of the old Law,"[36] or in which, following Origen, he opposes the "true high priest," who is Jesus Christ, to the "image-bearing high priest," who is the Jewish high priest.[37] Gregory of Elvira had treated the Mosaic law as an "image-bearing law," related the "image-bearing affairs" of the history of Israel to the Gospel, and recognized in the former "history of the deed accomplished" an "image-bearing prefiguration" of Jesus Christ.[38] Saint Jerome expressed himself in terms that, if translated literally, would give us a still more paradoxical sense:

> It is therefore said to the leader of the Jews that he should be converted from the Law to the Gospel and, once the *images of the victims* have been left behind, he should betake himself to the truth of spiritual sacrifice.[39]

Rupert finds it quite natural to use the expression "falsus Judaeus" for the Jew of authentic stock who made the mistake of rejecting the Christ,[40] and, in fact, this language came to be classic. For Gerhoh of Reichersberg, the manna that really fell from the sky to nourish the Israelites in the desert was nonetheless "shadow-manna," in contrast with "true manna,"[41] and the victory of David is merely a "figural and mystic victory" in comparison with the "true victory" won by Jesus Christ.[42] "That typic and legal history," is how one preacher will put it.[43]

We shall no longer be sidetracked in the face of many analogous passages, where the letter is declared "useless," or "sterile," or "frivolous," or "unreasonable," or "insipid," or "self-contradictory," such that one does not have recourse to the spiritual understanding: the argument can be weak, it is often abusive, but the result, at least in many cases, is rather to provide a foundation for the letter than to shake it loose: "otherwise the character of the letter cannot stand."[44] Further, there is no reason to suspect any restriction as to the historicity of the facts within figures of speech such as that of Claudius of Turin, for example, showing, according to Origen, the holy Scripture "being of service not so much to historical reports as to the realities and the mystical senses,"[45] or remarking that the history of Abraham first appeared quite strange, but that by taking care to study its allegory one could perceive its being well founded.[46] In all this, let us say it again, there is no equivocation, except for a few moderns too ignorant of the doctrinal tradition of Christianity and its language. In the manner of Jesus himself and of Saint Paul,[47] one unhesitatingly binds together the thing signifying with the thing signified, but from this mystic identification[48] it does not result that one confuses them. The true Noah, the true Moses, the true David, and the true Solomon do not relegate the figurative Noah, the foreshadowed Moses, the imaginal David, or the typic Solomon to the realm of fiction! When the author of the *Meditatio ad Crucifixum* wants to "understand allegorically" Jesus' stretching out of his arms at Calvary, he surely does not mean to throw the historicity of the crucifixion into doubt![49] And yet, as if he had foreseen certain of our gross misunderstandings, Saint Gregory one day took the precaution to say: "In large part we hold the works of the virtues according to the text of the history alone, lest we seem perhaps to empty the truth of the work if we pull these out to hunt down the mysteries."[50]

Under the opposition of the letter and the spirit, or of the shadow and the truth, in its varied and sometimes, for us, paradoxical expressions, there is therefore always the opposition of two peoples, of two ages, of two régimes, of two states of faith, of two "economies," which is affirmed. There are two peoples, two ages, two states, two régimes, two economies, which, however, are opposed to each other in a real contradiction properly speaking only once they have come to coexist, the first not having wished to disappear on the arrival of the one for which its whole task was to prepare, because it had not understood that it was merely the means of getting ready for it. Henceforth, therefore, the two peoples, the Jewish and the Christian, meet face to face. Each of them sucks at one of the two breasts of Scripture: the one is "the letter," Honorius tells us, echoing ten centuries, and the other is "allegory"; but these two breasts are none other than the two Testaments, which are both, today, equally the heritage of the Church, and the second contains within it the whole substance of the first.[51] For, "it is the custom of prophecy — of Scripture — to commence by history," adds Gerhoh, "but so as to make us to pass from it to the mystery."[52] Under the name "letter," in a language that Saint Paul had fixed, the Christian therefore rejects and ought to reject not every "literal sense," but, once again, the "mere letter," or "the naked history,"[53] the letter whose keeping would equivalently be the rejection of the larger meaning.[54] Not that letter of which "the ancient Fathers" perhaps naively did not yet know that it concealed mysteries, but that letter which their unbelieving descendants oppose to these mysteries that have just been accomplished.

If it is a question of practice, the letter that is rejected is that of carnal observances; a letter that the grace of Christ has definitively changed in the spiritual sense and in Christian liberty;[55] a letter of an outdated Testament, which no longer carries the spirit, which no longer promises it; a letter to which he who denies the Gospel, in his blindness, is bound; a letter which no longer has any "hidden virtue," since it has already borne its fruit.[56] It is, in other words, the letter sterilized. This letter kills, because it is itself dead. Since the advent of Jesus Christ, it is, like the body of John the Baptist, decapitated: "John's body is being buried; his head, being put on a dish: the letter is being covered with dirt; the spirit, honored and taken onto the altar."[57] Long ago Origen cried out pathetically, borrowing the words of chaste Susanna: "For if I should consent to you so as to *follow* the letter of the law, it will be death for me!"[58] So it is not necessary "foolishly to defend" that letter, as if Christ had not come.[59] Now it is necessary to accomplish "in the spirit" what the ancients did "in the flesh."[60] As to the literal or historical sense — where, on the other hand, it is found secure — it does not at all go the same for it, although the vocabulary concerning the Law has not failed to overflow a bit onto the vocabulary concerning history: thus, as Saint Jerome remarks, is not the very history of Genesis denominated "Law" by Saint Paul?[61] This sense is quite opposed to the spiritual or allegorical sense as well, but no longer as its antagonist: it is supposed by it, it remains along with it as its correlative.[62] The essential metaphor by which one designates it is not that of a provisional scaffolding, but, as has been seen, that of a permanent foundation. Let us also say that one can get to the spiritual sense usefully only one time "once the business of the letter has been settled";[63] or rather, that if it is necessary to arrive at its fruit, the fruit itself presupposes the leaf in the shelter of which it ripens. The Synagogue is mistaken to content itself with the foliage, i.e., the letter: the Christian culls the fruit of the spirit, hidden beneath this foliage of history and the Law.[64] At that point, explains Saint Jerome, "the friend of the letter" or "of the simple history" no longer enjoys even "the shadow of words," for, once the fruit comes to maturity, the foliage has dried up and perished.[65] Still another image: if the spiritual sense is of gold, the historical sense is of silver, i.e., in itself it is neither without solidity, nor without beauty, nor without value;[66] "the continent external speech shines like silver, and the inner sense sparkles like gold."[67] This gold and this silver, both precious, are united in Scripture[68] — or in the Church who extracts them from the Scripture — as on the neck of the dove of the Canticle.[69]

One might therefore well say — and we shall not fail to do so — that the Latin Middle Ages have, like the age before it and even more than it, made an often intemperate use of allegorism, for which they have brought into play some quite questionable methods. But if one calls forth a "generalized allegorism that sucks out the letter, the historical tissue, and which is the result of some sort of 'mentality',"[70] it ought to be recognized that this allegorism and this mentality do not belong to the Latin Middle Ages. It does not turn into a "biblical docetism." For the Middle Ages the "historical sense is solid" and the "solidity of the history is not violated" by the expression of the spiritual sense.[71] If one is deceived, it is perhaps because of another use of the word *littera*, ill understood by the moderns. Hugh of Saint Victor writes in the *Didascalicon*, for example: "There are certain places in the divine page that cannot be read according to the letter."[72] Origen had already expressed himself in the *Periarchōn* thus: "Not everything in Scripture has a literal sense."[73] So, too, a hundred others. We have alluded to them in a previous chapter. For one who makes the slightest effort, indispensable to the historian, to adopt a past terminology for the moment, there is neither audacity nor paradox.[74] There is merely an objective and banal establishment of a fact that the most historicist of exegetes would have nothing to find fault with (though everybody could argue about some applications). Like Origen, Hugh is simply stating that there are in the Bible a certain number of passages that are not to be taken, as we would say, "literally," but rather "figuratively." Doubtless one can prefer the present terminology. It does have its advantages. Yet if we judge it superior, it is perhaps in part simply because we are used to it: everything that violates what we are used to would easily appear strange, illogical even. It is generally said that the old terminology was at least incoherent, because it confused the figurative sense of a text, which is still a literal sense, with the spiritual sense. That is all there is to it. But are we much more coherent? Is there not verbal incoherence in saying of a text taken in its literal sense that it is not to be taken literally? Is it not a still different incoherence than to oppose, as is currently done today, the typic sense and the figured sense, whilst "typic" and "figured" are in fact the same word under two forms, the one coming from the Greek and the other from its Latin translation? Perfect coherence does not exist in any language, to be sure. In fact, it is necessary to say it again, our ancient authors took "literally" and in a historical sense more passages than do most exegetes of today, even the non-"hypercritical" ones.

When an Angelome of Luxeuil, dedicating to the emperor Lothair the commentary on the Canticle of Canticles proposed for his edification, asked him "not to look for anything historical" in this little book, he was saying nothing so scandalous or naive.[75] Was he wrong not to consider the Canticle as a book of history? Does this booklet composed "in the style of a drama" ["in modum dramatis"] recount the deeds and accomplishments of real persons? Does it not rather present them only "through a sort of history" ["per historiae speciem"]? Further, if a "sort of historical order" ["quasi historicus ordo"] unfolds within it, will the reader not be invited nevertheless to look in it right away not for a primary sense "according to flesh and blood," but a mystical significance?[76] Without speaking of the rabbis, Origen was not the only one in the Christian tradition to believe it. "If these things are not to be understood spiritually, are they not fables?"[77] Angelome was not the only one to say it. Saint Augustine had said it, distinguishing the "kind of speech regarding things that are completely done, as in the books of Kings" and the "kind of speech regarding figurative matters, as in the Canticle of Canticles."[78] The same goes for Aponius, who declares: "there is not a jot of history in this whole Canticle."[79] The same holds for Saint Isidore of Seville, who places the Canticle entirely within the "third kind" of scriptural texts, the one which "is taken only spiritually."[80] The same holds for Ambrose Autpert, who brings together the Canticle with the Apocalypse: in these two books, says he, one must understand that nothing is reported as "done historically"; there are "mystic sacraments," hidden "under the veil of tropical and figurative speech."[81] A little before Angelome, the *Caroline Books* affirmed it anew: "the Canticle of Canticles, in which nothing is to be taken historically but only spiritually."[82] Under an inverted verbal appearance, Rupert judges it in the same way.[83] This book, Saint Bernard will say, is "a contemplative discourse," a "theoricus sermo," and he will cry out: "At the literal level this means nothing to me!"[84] No more than Origen himself, who nonetheless designated its explication of the letter as a "historical understanding,"[85] William of Saint Thierry will have no difficulty speaking of the "historical drama," but he will immediately give as synonyms for it "fable" or "parable," and he too will be of the opinion that the mystic signification is immediate.[86] Richard of Saint

Victor will likewise say that there is no "historia" in this Canticle: "in it everything is 'allegory'; everything in it comes from the condescension of the God full of mercy," "who, to kindle our hearts to the incitement of holy love, descends to words expressive of our base love."[87] Nicholas of Lyra will say: "That whole book proceeds parabolically."[88] Among a hundred others, Louis of Leon will say it again: "All the speech of this book is figured."[89] Today even, good exegetes think so; all those who, whatever be their divergences, reject both the "naturalist" explication and even the "mixed" explication, so as to adopt the "allegorical" explication;[90] in other words, all those who think that the immediate sense of the Canticle concerns the relations of Yahweh and Israel.[91] But when Guibert of Nogent warned his reader that he would say nothing "ad litteram" on Jeremiah, at that point it was no longer a question of the Book, but merely of the commentary. Guibert quite simply left literal exegesis off to one side, so as not to repeat what had been well said by others:

> Yet I do not want you to be surprised that I have said nothing regarding the letter, since what blessed Jerome has explained is quite enough, even more than enough, it is doubtless silly for me to fill in the blanks by repeating the selfsame thing.[92]

In his prologue he had said: "In the fall of the cities, then, let us meditate upon the ruin of minds,"[93] without ever thinking that some day he might be accused — he or those like him — of having denied the historical ruin of cities! In the same way, if such sermonizing immediately interiorizes the report of the wars of Israel, this is nevertheless not to dispute its past reality: it is rather to draw from it the lesson that would seem to him to befit his hearer:

> For if we trust the histories of the ancients, then wars, etc. But I pass by all these things in silence, to speak of wars of vices, etc. If you want to know how Christ dispersed a people of vices. . . .[94]

A sermon is not a course in ancient or even sacred history. Let us therefore not conclude that the preacher would have wanted to deny history — nor even that he participated in the mentality of an age which did not comprehend the value of history.

3. The Biblical Facts

Nor have we noted, at least in a habitual manner, the "contempt of the letter" that Miss Smalley believes is found among almost all the "Christian commentators" of the Bible up to the work of sanitation which would be due to the quite unexpected Latin translations of Aristotle and Maimonides.[1]

Commenting on the proverb: "Take the tarnish off the silver," Bede nicely compares the letter to this tarnish, but only with regard to the "carnal ceremonies" of the Old Law, which no longer have any real value under the New Law,[2] and no Christian, any more in the twentieth century or in the thirteenth century than in the seventh, could judge of it otherwise. Often it is a question of the letter as a "shell" which must be broken in order to reach the core.[3] The image was borrowed from classical literature.[4] But one takes care, at one time or another, to add: "nevertheless the letter is in no way to be despised" ["littera nullatenus tamen est despicienda"]. The "cruder text of the letter" is the indispensable veil which had to cover the face of Moses;[5] it is the clothing of the Word of God.[6] Better still, the shell is already often beautiful and bright, although the core is softer;[7] in any case, one at first keeps it when one intends "to follow the history."[8] The more pejorative word "straw" is also of an ordinarily more particularized usage in which it is justified. For the straw is that which ought to be rejected once the grain has been gathered: "since the grains are in the Catholic" Church.[9] The word has its place, therefore, only by reference to the situation created by the New Testament. If one considers the two Testaments in their historical succession, the comparison is no longer that of straw to the grain, but rather of two different qualities of grain: "hordeum" [barley] and "triticum" [wheat].[10] "The Law is bread . . . ; but it is that barley bread with which the Lord fed the Jews."[11] The "five barley loaves" of the Pentateuch were a healthful food;[12] but those that the Lord now invites to the wedding feast in the Church are no longer delighted "in the rough bread and country food of the letter";[13] the sons are no longer nourished except "on the grain of wheat."[14]

Saint Ambrose used to speak with respect about the simplicity of the history, in which it was nevertheless necessary to know how to discern the sign of admirable mysteries.[15] Commenting on the Epistle to the Galatians, Saint Jerome had said again that contempt for history could only engender a "vain and shadowy" allegory that is "fixed in none of the roots of truth."[16] When Rupert writes: "the not very noble letter,"[17] when he is comparing this "literature of Moses' writing" to a column of brass bearing the golden capital of the spirit;[18] a fortiori when he speaks of the "literal or historical mediocrity of the Scriptures,"[19] one should not accuse him of contempt. In many a detail of the Bible, does not the historical content taken in itself have in fact little grandeur about it? In certain texts, however, it is a question of the "hardness of the letter," which is compared to that of rock.[20] Another expression would even appear, at first sight, more contemptuous: "the worthlessness of the letter," and this "worthlessness" contrasts quite strongly with the "costliness of spiritual understanding."[21] But let us look at it more closely: it is once again a question of the letter being understood "in the Jewish manner," of the letter whose understanding has been systematically evacuated and whose prophetic character one refuses to recognize;[22] it has therefore become "cheap" only after the event, or in the interpretation of it that those who resist the faith present: "as the truth appears, the figure has failed; when the body enters, the shadow has cheapened."[23] One ought to understand that the dignity of the spiritual interpretation rebounds on the letter, in such fashion that its "vilitas" was merely a first appearance.[24] The observances of the Law are like the city of Segor, which was "small and not small": small according to the letter, they were not so according to the spirit.[25] The spirit ennobles the letter that bears it, even when the letter gives merely a history without grandeur, just as a precious liquid ennobles the vessel that contains it: "Holy water within an earthen vessel is the divine wisdom contained in the cheap letter of the Law."[26] "The treasury of the divine senses is contained shut up within the frail vessel of the cheap letter."[27]

Another sort of comparison is more expressive. It is invincibly suggested to us by the employment of the same epithets on both sides, even when it is not explicitly proposed. Origen had said of Christ: "For though he bore the worthless shape of a slave, nevertheless the fullness of divinity was dwelling within him."[28] In invoking the fragility, weakness, and humility of the flesh with which the Word is clothed, in commenting on Saint Paul's dictum: "forma servi," without sugarcoating it, the Christian tradition professes no contempt for the humanity of the Savior;[29] nor does it minimize its essential role: it merely admires the ingenuity of the divine condescension. "For the humble Christ is our milk; the God like unto God is our food; the milk nourishes, the food feeds."[30] Now there is here something more than a comparison; "letter" and "flesh" are not only alike in that they are both likened to a "veil"; for, according to Scripture itself, one can say that "the Word of God has been incarnated in two ways,"[31] since at bottom it is one and the same unique Word of God who descends into the letter of Scripture and into the flesh of our humanity, into this "weak and unbeautiful" flesh, to hide itself there and to manifest itself there all together. In the following chapter we shall see the glorious face of this traditional teaching; here let us take up the humiliated face. It appeared quite natural to Hugh of Saint Victor, after Bruno of Segni,[32] after the Fathers,[33] to bring about the reconciliation of both humiliations of the Word, that of the letter and that of the flesh. In Scripture, says he, "neither do the great things despise the modest, nor again do the modest disdain to be associated with the great, but they adorn each other in a single truth." In other words, the humblest "letter" is in harmonious relation with the most exalted "mystery." Hugh concludes:

> Therefore no one will marvel if, after and amidst the great sacraments of the faith, mention is made of those that seem to be inferior in their own order, since things that are in truth one do not find being together with each other abhorrent. For God himself deigned to be humbled, descending to human things, so as later to lift man up to the divine.[34]

And Gerhoh of Reichersberg: "In this way the sunset-like humility of that Son of man always anticipates the sunrise splendor of the Son of God."[35] Bede said the same thing, meditating upon the crèche of Bethelehem, speaking of the "crèche of holy Scriptures."[36]

Humilitas litterae, like *humilitas Filii hominis*. . . . On both sides, there is the same "dispensation of humility."[37] And is it not normal that, in relation to the magnificence of the Gospel revelation, one esteems as quite "humble" the "earthly" conceptions belonging "to times past"?[38] On the other hand, Saint Jerome goes so far as to speak of the "turpitude of the letter," and there is nothing here more than normal: indeed, what he designates in this manner are certain shameful acts reported by Scripture, such as the coupling of Tamar and Judah.[39] Yet many biblical facts are, already in their letter, on the contrary "magna," i.e., "great." It is in thinking of them that Origen cried out: "What great things have been previously accomplished!"[40] And Saint Bruno of Segni, commenting upon the Apostle's remark on the glory of Moses, said: "So if the understanding of the letter merely glows red, what will the understanding of the spirit do?"[41] It is then a question not of the deeds and accomplishments of our poor humanity, but of the works of God. "The works of God are very great and amazing to all!"[42] A "simple look" at these works is already "delightful," even though the spirit is not truly "nourished" except by hearing them expounded "in the fashion of mysteries."[43] They are, above all, miracles. Then the "deed accomplished" is no longer "humble": it is "illustrious," it is "glorious."[44] It is not at all "worthless" any longer, but rather "marvelous"; "both marvelous in the report and magnificent to understand."[45] These luminous accomplishments, "accomplished in history," proclaim the divine power to all ages.[46] They are the "great things of God," "God's great marvels,"[47] that Saint John used to celebrate in the Apocalypse,[48] the "great things of the divine dispensation which have been exhibited to us in the Fathers."[49] Nevertheless, they are not, as we would say today, supernatural or divine in their substance, and if our sight were not habitually blunted, we would also see all other facts of the same nature as "marvelous and amazing."[50] The role of these extraordinary facts is pedagogical and their principal greatness comes to them from the mystery that they are charged with signifying or of announcing: "They are great indeed, as involving God's mysteries."[51] This reflection was made by Saint Augustine with respect to the miracle of the burning bush; it would also hold good in his eyes for all the miracles of the Gospel. The crescendo starting from sensible "marvels" up to the "marvels in the deep,"[52] or from miracle to mystery, is a constant theme. Saint Gregory makes it his own.[53] "A great miracle on the historical surface signifies an incomparably greater divine work in the spirit":[54] thus speaks Rupert. Gerhoh speaks in the same way: "Let them fill the fields and valleys, and let them cover the mountains, which are God's great works, possible to none beside him; but by these are signified other things greater and more marvelous by far."[55] And Saint Bernard says:

> In the works of God . . . there are . . . both things delightful in external appearance, and much more delightful with inner power; just as He too was externally beautiful in form before the sons of men, but interiorly, as the supereminent brilliance of the eternal light upon the faces of the angels themselves as well. . . .
>
> The surface, considered from outside, is very handsome; but if anyone should crack the nut, he will find inside something more pleasant and much more delightful. . . . Of the signs of the Lord, whose history is quite admirable enough, and whose significance is still more delightful. . . .[56]

The same is true for Isaac of Stella.[57] Here we have the crescendo from the history to the spirit. In the presence of thought like this, how could anyone say that the early Middle Ages did not yet know how to distinguish the supernatural from the miraculous? But on the other hand, let us also note, a thought like this, which marks the distinction so strongly, at the same time shows the union of the two orders: a distinction and a union which here are those of the two senses. Such a thought denotes the care not to exalt either one of the two senses at the expense of the other, but to base each reciprocally upon the other: "For the brightness of the New Testament is such that the brightness of the Old Testament is regarded as darkness; yet each of the two is one Testament, and each is bright and sparkling, if it be understood spiritually."[58] Every analysis of the kind leads us to the same fundamental doctrine.

As counterpoise to the "magnalia Dei" — "great things of God" — or to the "inclyta gesta Dei" — "unnamed accomplishments of God" — the Bible offers us a rich repertory of crimes. But their scandalousness is not capable of shaking the faith in the historicity of the sacred reports. Allegory is not a means to which one would have recourse with a view of getting oneself off the hook; it can, on the contrary, be a means of explaining events from God's point of view, i.e., of corroborating them. There is still a widely enough circulated opinion to the effect that Origen and his successors tried by means of the spiritual sense to "evacuate" the scandal from episodes of the Old Testament "whose literal sense was unedifying."[59] If there is anything correct about this view, it is not in the sense that the majority understand: to evacuate the scandal, our ancient exegetes in no way evacuated the reality of the facts.[60]

Certain of these facts, without having anything reprehensible in themselves, might risk becoming so for us, if we wanted to imitate them to the letter, when the situation has changed and the laws of the Church prohibit them: understanding them allegorically eliminates this temptation. Thus it is for the two wives of Elkanah in the first book of Samuel.[61] More often, it is a question of sins. We are aware of the conclusion the Manichaeans would draw: a book that reports such horrors could not come from a good God. Against them, Saint Augustine had at length taken up the defense of Scripture, which reports nothing without good reasons.[62] Faustus and those like him, said Augustine from the start, often calumniate the ancient Fathers, whose conduct can be explained by the customs of their epoch,[63] or else their praise-worthy designs allow them to be excused to some extent.[64] To judge without excess, it is necessary to take the facts into consideration in all their context. But each time that it is necessary to do so, one ought to agree to recognize their malice.[65] One will therefore avow, for example, that Lot, who wanted to avoid an even graver evil, sinned by error in offering his daughters, or that David, in swearing to kill Nabal, sinned by wrath.[66] By getting rid of Uriah, he "gravely and impiously sinned."[67] In stating such facts, Scripture does not approve of them: it leaves the judgment of them to our conscience enlightened by the divine law.[68] But to grasp its intention, we shall recall that the whole Old Testament has value as prophecy,[69] and in looking for the significance of all that it contains, we will justify Scripture without defending the sins of men.[70]

These principles were not the invention of Augustine. They had been formulated against the Marcionites by Saint Irenaeus, who himself, he says, got them from an old priest.[71] Origen recalled them in almost the same terms, to reply to the objections of Celsus.[72] They will not cease to be applied. Consider, for example, the crime committed by the daughters of Lot upon their father — an example already used by Origen and Irenaeus. It is in itself a disgraceful act, even though the circumstances may have furnished some excuse for it; "it were better to remain sterile than to become mothers in that fashion."[73] Nevertheless, once inserted in Scripture, the account becomes a prophecy.[74] Consider the tricks of Jacob and the homicidal project of Joseph's brothers.[75] Consider the Israelites carrying off the spoils of Egypt: this was at least "a weakness" on their part; so God permitted rather than willed it; but we must marvel that he thus puts to divine use even the weaknesses of his own people, just as he did with the malice of the Egyptians so as mysteriously to signify his designs.[76] Consider the bewildered Psalmist, proffering curses: "In the words like those of one who wants evil things, let us understand the predictions of a prophet."[77] There are again so many other facts about which it is to be admitted that they are "less worthy": they are vessels made of rather gross material; but the Holy Spirit has turned a precious content within them to our intention.[78] The conduct of Solomon was scarcely edifying, and Scripture is silent as to his repentance; David himself bewept his failing; but the faults of both have a rich symbolic import.

As regards that adultery of David, Saint Ambrose had drawn beautiful lessons from an exegesis at first entirely historical. To it he applied the same admirable indulgence as he had shown with regard to Aaron constructing the golden calf.[79] Without excusing it, he showed it to be unique, in the course of so exposed a long life; he emphasizes the repentance; he made those who would have dared to treat the humiliated king without respect to blush. His two *Apologies of David* are a masterpiece of human and Christian sentiment:

> I recognize that the man existed, and that is no surprise; I recognize the common fact, that man sins. He sinned, as kings customarily do; but he did penance, as kings customarily do not....[80]

One could believe that he thus fulfilled the whole program that he had sketched out for himself with regard to Abraham: "Let the Patriarchs instruct thee, not only in their teaching, but also by their erring."[81] Yet this did not satisfy him. Imitating the movement of Origen, he then passed to the "mystery" and showed within this same human drama the symbol of the redemption to come. This had been to find still another new motive for indulgence in it, not by denying the sin, but by taking away from us the right to hold it against the poor sinner king: "How then can sin be imputed in the prefiguration of that mystery, since within that mystery itself there is remission of sins?" Beside the fact that Jesus our Master preaches to us to be gentle with regard to every sinner, David, by confessing his fault, has been admitted to the grace of the mystery, which is a mystery of pardon.[82]

Not all those who will subsequently comment on the same episode will have the emphases of Ambose. But none will seem to be caught up short by the paradox which makes an adultery compounded with a murder into the symbol of the salvific reality. Saint Augustine puts it in vigorous relief.[83] Cases of this sort, according to Saint Gregory, would even be frequent: "Often a thing is a virtue through history, but a sin by signification; just as it is sometimes a sin in the deed itself, but a virtue in what is written by way of prophecy."[84] In the Middle Ages this was a common notion.[85] One sees it illustrated by a history like that of Tamar and Judah, "damnable according to the letter, praiseworthy with respect to its significant understanding."[86] The history of David and Uriah offers a privileged case, since it contains both antitheses indicated by Gregory.[87] Thus in regard to it one gets used to disengaging — despite the opposition that Saint Jerome's good sense had offered to it[88] — one of the most astonishing laws of doctrinal exegesis:[89] an extension of the rhetorical figure called "antiphrasis" or "aetymologia ex contrariis,"[90] which, for example, assigned the name "Sport" to the killjoy "who wants to take a nap whenever there is any fun to do."[91] [There is a] paradoxical application of this law of "inverted significations" to the biblical datum, [a law] which, through Neoplatonism, came from some of the oldest beliefs of humanity; a law which became, in pseudo-Dionysius treating of the knowledge of divine things, the law of "metaphors without likeness";[92] a law which the traditionalist school had wanted to set up again in honor in our days, coloring it with its own proper doctrines.[93] One could have found a first attempt at it in the principle formulated by Saint Gregory as follows: "the baser they are in the literal sense, the more useful in spiritual significance,"[94] as well as an application of the exegesis of these words of Saint Paul: "Adam, who is the form of the One to come"; in fact, says Hervaeus of Bourg Dieu, "with these words the Apostle explains, by way of contrariety, how Adam is the form of Christ."[95] Isidore of Seville observed that in the Bible "bad men are sometimes prefigured by good and the good by the bad."[96] The success borne by Dionysius in the twelfth century gives the law a new popularity and a new significance. Richard of Saint Victor took it for a teaching of the Fathers.[97] For him and his contemporaries, it was allied with the great thesis of negative theology which will be sanctioned, at the beginning of the following century, by the Fourth Lateran Council.[98] Garnier of Rochefort explains it emphatically.[99] John of Salisbury enunciates it in simpler terms: "Sometimes . . . the tracks of the truth are to be followed through the opposition of things";[100] and, in a sermon, Innocent III says: "The panels of history do not always equally answer to the picture of allegory; the significant event sometimes turns out bad and signifies something good, and conversely."[101] The sublime friendship of David and Jonathan escaped this strange law: "This thing both proved faithfulness in the man with respect to history and also pointed out the sacrament in the deed with regard to allegory."[102] But the following relations with Uriah illustrate it admirably:

> What can be called more criminal than that perfect man David, what can be called purer than Uriah? Yet again, by way of the mystery, what is found more sacred than David, what more faithless than Uriah, when the former signifies innocence through the prophetic fault of his life, whereas the latter expresses fault in prophecy through his life of innocence? For the power of sacred eloquence reports transactions so as to express the things to come; it approves them in the deed done so as to contradict them in the mystery; it condemns things accomplished so as mystically to persuade us to do them.[103]

If we enter into the detail of this subtle exegesis, we shall state that it is not determined by all in the same way. Nevertheless, the principle is always the same. In the trail of Saint Augustine,[104] one uses the symbolism of proper names in application: David, whose name signifies "desirable," is the figure of the Church; as to Uriah, Uriah the just, since his name means "the glory of the Living God," one sees in him the figure of the devil, who has usurped this glory for himself.[105] Accordingly Christ comes to steal this Church back from the devil, the Church that the devil took in an illegitimate marriage, and by the sole act of his sacrifice he kills the devil and celebrates his own marriage with his Church.[106] Others see in Uriah the Jewish people, or give both explications,[107] etc. But all this detail is of little importance here. Let us merely recall, with the principle formulated as follows by Remi of Auxerre: "David everywhere signifies Christ,"[108] the attitude adopted by the ancient exegesis, which does not sacrifice any realism: "Let us condemn the accomplished fact in such wise as to embrace the mystery;[109] "So let us hate the sin, but let us not squelch the prophecy."[110]

Let us now consider no longer immoral deeds, but rather certain quite curious accounts, like all those precisions concerning the building of Noah's ark, or the history of Balaam's ass, or that of the sun stopped by Joshua, etc. Origen, as is well known, had not conceived the tiniest doubt as to a place for them. He had not ranged them in the category of texts that had no "corporeal" sense at all, as he had done for the material details of the account of the fall in Genesis, or of the account of the temptation of Jesus in the Gospel. On the contrary, he had sometimes taken meticulous care to justify them most exactly down to the letter. Notably for Noah's ark, he was stimulated, not intimidated by the mockeries of Apelles: he considered everything, weighed everything, calculated everything, and came up with appropriate solutions. One is amazed at the assurance with which a serious historian of high reputation emphatically affirms the contrary on a page worth including in an anthology. For Mr. Lucien Febvre, Origen would have indulged himself "in a thousand pleasantries on the history of the flood, on the ark's holding in the space of a few cubits all the animals of creation, on Sodom and Gomorra, on Lot and his daughters — all this with a liberty, an audacity, a cynicism unsurpassed by Voltaire." In comparison with the "direct attacks" of this "rationalist," of this "profligate," all the "raillery" aimed at the Bible since then would appear "pale." "When one has read these texts," he concludes, "one hesitates to find Rabelais bold; one is inclined to judge him almost timid by comparison." By his "rather strong pleasantries," says Mr. Lucien Febvre again, "this fiery and heterodox Father" leaves far behind him the "poor little giant of fantasy" that the "orthodox" canon of the sixteenth century installs "astride Noah's ark"; he "justifies in advance the objections that the *philosophes* of the eighteenth century were to aim against the Bible."[111] If we point out such an error, it is because the very merit of the historian makes the almost invincible force of prejudice stand out the better.[112] It is also quite gratuitous that one should oppose to the pretended negations of Origen the pretended "scruples" of Saint Augustine, on the ground that Augustine "often affirms that the historical reality of the biblical accounts and descriptions would not be suppressed by the allegorical interpretation that one can draw from it." Thereby, indeed, Augustine merely restates what his great predecessor had already said many times. Nor again should the immorality of adventures, the material difficulties or the strangeness of the miracles discourage him from taking the accounts quite literally, so that he would not believe that he sees an element of internal contradiction in such or such a trait.

In practice, in the case of the ark, Augustine stops at the solutions which, he says, "Origen not inelegantly came up with."[113] Better than many moderns, on that point then our medievals knew what to hold on to. They were still reading both the texts of Origen and those of Saint Augustine. For the "difficult" passages of the Bible, if they had had any scruples, they would have found what to affirm within the knowledge of a unanimous tradition. One of them, Remi of Auxerre, still on the subject of Noah's ark, can well draw attention to this opinion: "Some say that this could not have been done historically, but that it was written for the sake of some signification or mystery."[114] But these "some" can only be objecting from outside, and the response that is appropriate to make to the subversive opinion is borrowed from Origen. Bede had done so already,[115] then Alcuin and Claudius of Turin, commenting on Genesis.[116] So too did Freculphe of Lisieux[117] in his great history. Rabanus Maurus did so as well: it is Origen, says he, who has shown how it was possible that the ark should contain so many things. The *Glossa ordinaria* again did the same.[118] Whatever passage be under examination, one never sees anyone using the fact that it contains a profound mystery as a motive for denying a historical character to the passage in question:

> Though a manifold mystery is contained in the things that have been said, that mystery is not held to be contrary to the literal sense. For profundity is found in many passages of the Scriptures in such wise that many profound mysteries may be contained in it, and yet the literal understanding cannot be removed from it; one arrives the more gracefully at the innermost fruit by as much as the surface of the letter is found to be not only leafy with words but also fruitful with truth.

Even though the spiritual understanding be in agreement with this assertion, the literal sense is still not out of tune: so that, when something mystical is subtly clothed within it, nevertheless it is not denied that it can be taken literally.[119]

For our "spiritual" exegetes, those of the Middle Ages as well as those of patristic times, allegory was therefore not, as it was for the pagan moralists, "a refuge against the shame appropriate to the myths."[120] They did not "reduce the biblical facts to allegories," so as to prevent Christians from having to "blush" at them.[121] They did not attempt to run away from "scandal" in this way.[122] They did not toss upon the letter "a veil to cover its indecency."[123] They did not use a commodious means for "immolating the literal sense without scruple or hesitation" in suppressing "the indecencies, the treacheries, the cruelties, the lies" that would have seemed to them "to lead Christianity to its ruin."[124] On the contrary, all are in agreement, as Saint John Chrysostom had said regarding the fall of David, in thinking that "if the Holy Spirit had perceived no shame in mentioning such histories, we have still less reason to disguise them."[125] More generally, our forefathers were evidently no less exposed than ourselves to the danger of that retrospective illusion which sometimes makes us understand or imagine ancient situations according to our present-day situation; they just happened to fall into it;[126] but their exegesis did not proceed from some conscious or unconscious anxiety, from a shame-based apologetic,[127] and their failings as historians that we have just mentioned did not arise from thence, either. For them, the reality of the history, taken in its totality and right down to its hardest-to-believe and somberest pages, was truly never in danger! Indeed they had rather a tendency to take as historical in the strictest sense a number of accounts which today we would commonly see as history in only a broad sense or even as parable.[128]

4. Conception of History

Assuredly, one will not expect of them the sort of "historical sense" analogous to that which was the glory of the last century. One will not expect of them an immense interest in the human past for its own sake, without any other end than to understand it better and, so to speak, to resuscitate it; nor, a fortiori (though they were not unaware of the "changing of time")[1] that picturesque sentiment regarding differences, that taste for "local color" which has come to us through Romanticism. They could not, like Saint Jerome, explore Palestine at leisure; indeed, the majority doubtless hardly even paid attention to the following reflection, which they could read in one of his prefaces: "He who has seen Judaea with his own eyes, brought together the memory of its cities, observed their names old or new, will understand the Bible better."[2] They were not preoccupied so much with reaching each being in its singularity, but were rather looking for a universal element in it. They shared the conception which was that of the ancients and which would become that of the moderns until a recent epoch. For them, as for Cicero, history was "mistress of life."[3] "The life of predecessors," observes Saint Gregory in the *Moralia*, "serves as a model for successors."[4] History was therefore a moral science, which was studied with a view to improving morals. At least that was its essential goal. Bede recalled this point in the Prologue of his *Ecclesiastical History*,[5] and each historian had to recall it in turn for himself, in response to the objections of sluggish minds who would say: "Good for what?" Among those who do so are, for example, Roger of Wendover,[6] Ariulphe,[7] Otto of Freising,[8] Robert of Mont Saint Michel the continuator of Sigebert,[9] Hugh of Fleury,[10] Richard of Cirencestria[11] or the author of the *Historia compostellana*.[12] John of Salisbury expounds the same conception, both in the prologue of his *Historia pontificalis*[13] and at the commencement of his *Polycraticus*.[14] The author of the *Chronicon aldenburgense majus* adopted it, especially for the history of the Church, dramatizing it under the form of a vision.[15] When Abbo, a monk of Saint-Germain, undertook to recount in verse the siege of Paris by the Normans, it was, he said, through a "desire to preserve the memory of an example useful to those who have been charged with keeping watch over the condition of other cities of the State,"[16] and we have there an echo of the ancient civic morality of Titus Livy. Even Raoul Glaber was incited to write by "this throng of events which would, he thought, be very profitable for men if they were recounted to them, and would become for each of them excellent lessons in prudence."[17] Indeed, whether it were a question of good acts or bad, the history that reports them always draws a salutary lesson from them, teaching people to imitate the good acts and to avoid the rest.[18] Human experience is useful in the conduct of life. The mere consideration of the truth, one chronicler will say later on, would not at all be enough to make history, howsoever erudite it be, to be accepted by serious men.[19] What is true of every history is still more true of sacred history.[20] "Not only Moses, but all the other human authors of the *divina pagina*, in the historical books as well as in the books of morality, apply themselves to make us love virtue and to detest vice";[21] thus we find in the Bible a throng of outstanding examples,[22] and from the very report that it makes concerning the worst crimes there results for our use a "warning to turn to a better life."[23]

Such a conception of history, though compatible with a very wide view of human reality and even with an exacting critique, assuredly presupposes the absence of a certain form of historical curiosity. Only, allegorism plays no role in this shortfall. Or at least it plays only a bit part. Would that non-allegorizing historians had had more of this form of curiosity! In any case, everyone can today without contradiction combine the spirit of Christian allegorism with the taste for the religious past of Israel taken in its most concrete particularity. One would nevertheless avow that such a taste, such a curiosity, would not replace the vistas of the faith. The Bible was not given to Christians merely to satisfy historical curiosity.

Nor will one expect of our ancient authors a "sense of history" analogous to that which exists, or is said to exist, or which is looked for nowadays. It is a theological sense of history, consubstantial with Christian thought, which it would be unfair to deny to them. They doubtless had it more than we do.[24] In often quite commonplace settings, they express it stoutly. But all sense of history supposes precisely that one does not stay at the level of its mere *historia*, i.e., the facts pure and simple, or the pure and simple report of the facts. It supposes that one places oneself, at least at a second time, in another point of view than that of the simple narrator. To explicate the facts — and already somewhat to choose them and to expound them — one thus applies a principle of discernment which can itself be inserted within the facts, but which, as such, pertains to a different sphere and overflows into the observation of the facts. One has recourse to the final causes that the facts would be unable to furnish and which give a retrospective clarification to the whole unfolding of these facts.[25] This is why, if any not merely partial and relative but total, comprehensive, and absolutely valid explication of history is truly possible, this explication can only be theological. Only faith anticipates the future with security. Only an explication founded upon faith can invoke a definitive principle and appeal to ultimate causes.[26] At the same time, it is clear that the word "explication" no longer has the same sense as when it is a question of scientific explications.

Our ancient exegetes did not have any idea, thanks be to God, of that "absolutized History" which is one of the principal idols invented by our age. On the other hand, they did have a sense of biblical history, or even of universal history, because they held on to its principle of discernment in the Mystery of Christ, the absolutely ultimate final cause. The doctrine of the four senses, through which this mystery has found its expression — as we shall see better and better in the course of this study — thus appeared, in the very perspective which it engendered and which kept it alive for a long time, as providing the foundation for the objective sense of history and by that very fact *giving history its proper value*. It disengages its "spiritual energy," which is not dissipated as the facts pass by, but "which endures always."[27] It shows its "force, character, and mystery."[28] As Saint Leander of Seville says, inviting us to lift ourselves above the carnal letter of the Bible, this doctrine makes us extract the sense of the spiritual understanding from the truth of the history: *de historiae veritate intelligentiae spiritalis sensum cape.*[29] For, at the bottom line, it would be of little importance to believe in the historicity of facts if this were just to make oneself uninterested in them[30] — either taking them as simple sensible "props" of an atemporal doctrine — or, again, reading them simply to have a look at the chronicle, to leave them to their scattering and to their relativity — "fluenta historiae"[31] — without recognizing for them a certain order of value, which establishes the necessary "foundation" of something else. Marc Bloch has written that in these centuries of the Middle Ages "exegesis commanded one to recognize (in the Bible) less the picture of events bearing their significance in themselves than the prefiguration of what had to follow them," and this diagnosis can be agreed to — provided, however, that one does not judge that such a "symbolic interpretation" "muddied the understanding of things."[32] On the contrary, it clarified [that understanding], though we do not quite see how any events could "bear their significance," their whole significance "in themselves." One can dispute, if he is not a believer, the principle of intelligibility to which the believer relates himself so as to give a sense to the history of ancient Israel; one can also, within the faith, dispute about the manner in which this principle is applied; but if one entirely gives up finding a certain sense, a certain value, a certain unity, in history, it is still always necessary to have recourse to some principle, some reality, that the event, as such, does not furnish.

The majority of medieval commentators, it is still necessary to recognize, scarcely exercise any "critical sense" such as that which has been developed in the West for several centuries. Not that they had been completely denuded of critical spirit: one credits them with a credulity which many have laughed at. In the ninth century one John the Deacon, for example, offered proof of a meticulous conscientiousness in research and

Conception of History

the use of his sources;[33] thus he hopes that his *Life of Saint Gregory* will always be appreciated by those who love the truth.[34] In the eleventh century one Letald of Micy, who is at once historian and poet but is no less a critic, maps out severe rules for hagiography; he shows himself particularly rigorous for accounts of miracles, for he knows that "nothing which is not true is pleasing to God."[35] An Othloh of Saint Emmeran, writing the Life of Saint Wolfgang, is also himself evidence of an "attempt at historical critique."[36] A certain Rodolphe of Saint Trond (born in 1070), historiographer of the abbots of his monastery, manifests a very exacting and almost combative idea of historical truth, backed up by an austere ideal of impartiality.[37] Raoul Glaber himself knows how to unearth false relics and does not let himself be imposed upon by "frivolous" assurances.[38] Guibert of Nogent methodically expounds principles "which the soundest and most orthodox historical critique can only endorse."[39] Only, even when these principles are professed, still they are not applied, or are but little applied, to the Bible. Not that one would deliberately wish to take them away: but one ill discerns which points of legitimate application [historical criticism] offers for them. In this regard, and to speak very much in broad outline, there is even at first a reaction on the part of the high Middle Ages. Compared to Jerome or even to Saint Augustine, Gregory the Great appeared "extremely uncritical."[40] Bede, who has remarkable gifts as an historian, generally shows himself wiser than the great Carolingian masters will be, and the very effort of these latter will scarcely be sustained until it is taken up again, more than two centuries later, in slightly better conditions. In these texts that we have since then learned to scrutinize endlessly and sometimes almost without hope, the majority see only a "plain simplicity"[41] or what one of them, a disciple of Peter Comestor, easily calls the "ease of history."[42] From their point of view, however, they were not wrong, since they took the text naively, without at almost any time suspecting anything about its prehistory. For them, literary history was, if not nonexistent, at least still circumscribed within quite strictly defined limits, and their idea of the divinity of the Scriptures, not too deep but too strict and too one-sided, did not at all provoke them to look for the trace of the human deficiencies to which our attention is drawn today. Why then, they would say, tarry to explain at length these "unobstructed words of history"?[43] What need was there to explain again this "surface of the history" upon which the light has already spread?[44] "We run through the plain matters so as to spend more time in the obscure."[45] The wise warnings of Junilius the African that Cassiodorus had transmitted have, however, been somewhat forgotten.[46]

As Junilius said, history, like simple doctrine but in contradistinction to prophecy or teaching by proverbs, would appear quite simple on the surface; in reality, it is quite often hard to comprehend.[47] A tradition, which, in the Church, goes back to Origen and Jerome, set apart as "more difficult" only three passages of the Old Testament: the beginning of Genesis, the Canticle of Canticles, the two great visions which frame the prophecy of Ezekiel.[48] Isidore of Seville[49] and Bede[50] have readily spoken of them as well as of many other passages whose explication to them did not seem easy even "according to the text of the history" ["juxta historiae textum"]. Again, it is not certain that it was concern about problems pertaining to criticism that made them express themselves in this way; they rather showed themselves to be much more optimistic.

Doubtless, each of them was ready to say once more with Saint Gregory: "He who neglects to accept the words of the history according to the letter conceals for himself the stolen light of truth."[51] Each would agree with him that the spiritual sense ought, however, to be easier to find, that one will not be embarrassed by ignorance of the narrative or of the "exterior description."[52] No one would have had any difficulty in saying with Guibert: "Unless you openly recognize the letter, you will exercise yourself in vain in trying to search out allegory or morality."[53] It was even a sort of refrain. But very few have thought that this calls for a long, hard effort. Properly "to set the history before one's eyes," as Origen asked,[54] a slight effort of memory ought, they believe, to suffice.[55] "The literal sense is clear enough of itself": what Rupert of Deutz puts thus in a chapter on the prophet Haggai,[56] what Saint Ambrose[57] and Saint Jerome[58] had done long before him, and then Saint Gregory,[59] Paul the Deacon,[60] Bede,[61] Ambrose Autpert,[62] Claudius of Turin,[63] Rabanus Maurus,[64] Aimon of Auxerre,[65] and others[66] have put it regarding more or less numerous reports, has tended to be repeated also with regard to all the chapters of the Bible. "The history is known," "the sense of the history is clear," "these points are obvious according to the history," "the sense with respect to the history is manifest," "it has an easy sense," "the understanding is easy," "the sense of the letter is before one's eyes" . . . ; though it is authorized by a frequent usage by Saint Jerome,[67] the remark shows up a bit too often for our taste. "We regard it as superfluous to expound the rest literally, since they are manifest."[68] Rupert goes so far as to say that every narrative due to a human author is sluggish and "miserably obscure" with comparison to biblical reports: "In holy Scripture," however, "how brief, how clear is every account!"[69] This recalls what were, according to the classical theory, the two essential qualities of narration. In these conditions, although one could dispense with "touching" certain expressions of the history,[70] this, it seemed, was only to pass rapidly over this "letter," so as to have more time to give to the exploration of the "mystery."[71] The latter required above all that one should "scrutinize" the Scriptures,[72] following the recommendation of the Lord: "Since we plainly see the history, let us fully investigate the allegory."[73] Or again, with the Origen of the homilies: "Let us the more quickly relate these things to ourselves."[74] At least, if one put a certain care into reporting its detail, this was "so that its sacrament would be spread out more commodiously."[75] For the rest, one addressed himself most often to hearers or readers to whom the sacred history was familiar; it would have been fastidious and pointless to hold oneself back to recount to them in detail what they already knew quite well.[76] This provides a new motive for keeping things short. "You remember, I believe: for I am speaking to those who know the Law";[77] "Since I am speaking with those who know the matter, it is not necessary for me to elaborate it with many words."[78]

Doubtless again, in principle, all were in agreement with the following declaration of Origen: "It was first necessary to discuss historically the things that are being read, and in this way . . . to seek the spiritual understanding in them."[79] Doubtless, a Berengaud professed that the role of the interpreter was in the first place "to drag the obscurities of the history into the light,"[80] but it was apparent enough that he thought he could do it himself at little cost, for after a few quick remarks concerning Moses' life in Egypt, he hastens to add: "But leaving off these things, let us run back to the spiritual understanding."[81] Doubtless, a Rabanus Maurus and many others would have avowed that the science of Scriptures was full of countless difficulties; they did not hesitate to say that the sacred text defended itself against temerarious reading by a series of obscurities and ambiguities, so that except with a detailed examination one would often run the risk of misunderstanding it.[82] But for them the difficulty resided above all in the "locutiones tropicae," or in the sublimity of certain passages: "words dark owing to the greatness of the mysteries,"[83] and then it was no longer a question of the historical sense alone. They took the opportunity to admire the "magnificent and salutary" art of the Holy Spirit, who knows how to pacify our hunger with the clear passages and to prevent satiety by means of the obscure ones,[84] who made of Scripture both our drink and our solid food, the clear passages being the drink that is effortlessly absorbed, the obscure ones being the bread that one must break, the food that must be chewed.[85] The clarity of the first illuminates us; the difficulty of the second keeps us breathless.[86] Thus, made for all, helpful to all, Scripture is always adapted to all. Without discouraging the simplest minds, it exercises in a thousand ways the ingenuity of the most nimble understandings, which can conquer the hidden truths only at the price of laborious study, and this work preserves them from the temptation of believing such a treasure to be worthless.[87]

These themes were dear to Saint Augustine.[88] They were no less so to Saint Gregory.[89] They have fascinated their spiritual posterity. So right was their inspiration, so propitious were they for the contemplation of the "heaven of the Scriptures," that the premature recourse one took in them scarcely favored, it must be admitted, the application of criticism in the presence of the human difficulties of the text. One supposed, however, in principle that all or almost all that it is possible to draw from the obscure passages is already found in the clear passages:[90] an extension of the principle of the "analogy of faith," which was not made to sharpen research any more! Or again, one compared the letter to a thick black cloud, as a way of saying that, however clear it could be in itself, it covered another sense, and that one mysterious:[91] for if the Scripture was a heaven, this heaven was hidden by the clouds, following the word of the Psalmist: "He who hid the heaven with clouds,"[92] or, according to that of Isaiah: "I shall clothe the heavens with darkness."[93] One thus always came back to the question of the spiritual sense: "for the secrets of the heavenly mysteries are veiled under the gloom of the clouds."[94] There it was again, the teaching of Origen's homilies, taken up again by men of a lesser culture.[95] It was the teaching of Saint Augustine, whose bent for facility in exegesis is well known.[96] It was that of Saint Gregory as well, who had picked up the teaching of his two great predecessors to the point of satiety.[97] Practically, therefore, all the obscurity of the holy books came from their prophetic and allegorical character: "the obscurities, gloom, shadows, darkness of the allegories."[98] Was this not what the Psalmist also said? *Shadowy water in the clouds of the air:* there is nothing more visible than these clouds in the air; and nothing more hidden than that "shadowy water":[99] "a science hidden in prophetic and legal writings."[100] It was therefore allegory that the commentator had to try to set into the light. It was upon it that he had to concentrate his effort.[101]

5. The Word of God

Even if its obscurity had not required the longest attention, allegory would have remained the major preoccupation. For, except in certain rather rare

The Word of God

cases, the exegesis that we are studying was not yet a specialized exegesis; it was at once less and much more: it was a total exegesis; it was not an auxiliary science of theology: it was theology itself — and even more than theology, if the signification of the word is extended as far as spirituality. Thus, if Scripture was a tower, its foundation was history, but its summit or head was the spiritual sense.[1] If it was necessary to take care, in cultivating this science, to subtract nothing from history — "it is necessary for us even according to the history to hang on to all these things that we run over in our allegorical hunt"[2] — it was not less important, on the other side, in hanging on to the truth of the event, not to let its mystical significance escape: "let the truth of accomplishment be held in such fashion that the prophecy of the thing to be accomplished not be emptied out."[3]

To be sure, as Saint Jerome and Saint Augustine have recommended, real care was often taken to examine the context, though, as a consequence of the methods received in the schools for interpreting classical texts, one was generally confined within excessively narrow limits. One wanted to take account not only of the literary context, "the circumstance of the letter,"[4] "the circumstance of the speech,"[5] "the order of the speech,"[6] "the sequence of the words,"[7] or "the circumstance of the Scripture";[8] but also of the historical context: "the circumstance of the things,"[9] "the circumstance of the thing accomplished."[10] In other words, one paid attention to the "order of the history,"[11] to the "ordered report of the accomplishments,"[12] to the "sequence of events."[13] Hugh of Saint Victor even wanted this done on a large scale: "repeating it from start to finish."[14] Sometimes one also had a real concern to determine the intention of the human author, to the extent that the "composition of the speech" or the "composition of the writing" could reveal it;[15] should the need arise, one also knew how to distinguish in one's speech between that which was an affirmation on one's own part and that which was merely a reported opinion.[16] Only, all this work most often had as a bit too immediate an end not to deprive oneself of any detail that could contribute to the mystical understanding. Or else, when one fixed the sense of a passage by clarifying it in terms of a preceding or following passage, this was chiefly by recourse to the idea of the "custom of Scripture,"[17] an idea a bit too large to stick close to a truly historical interpretation. At least in the majority of cases, it was more a question of showing the Holy Spirit's agreement with himself than humanly to comprehend the detail of a text according to its coordinates: "for, when the Truth is speaking, the beginnings ought to agree with the sequel."[18] It was necessary to make one see that "Sacred Scripture is in no part out of tune,"[19] since in its twofold collection and in each of their books it has the same God as author, and one works on it until one can finally say: "All the divine writings stand together at peace with each other."[20] If one does not entirely arrive there by this path, one would then have recourse to "the analogy of faith."[21]

Saint Augustine has well entitled one of his principal commentaries *De Genesi ad litteram* [*On Genesis in the literal sense*] and declared that in it he studied the Holy Book only "according to the faith of the deeds accomplished."[22] But one quickly perceives in his reading that the appellation is to be taken in a rather supple and non-exclusive sense; it is right at the beginning of this work that he posits the principle of spiritual understanding or mystical signification as a principle of faith: "No Christian will dare to say that [the facts reported] are not to be taken figuratively, attending to the words of the Apostle: 'But all these things happened to them in figure' and to what was written in Genesis: 'And they shall be two in one flesh', a great sacrament is commended in Christ and in the Church."[23] When Petrus Comestor, in the prologue to his *Scholastic History*, declared that he wanted to confine himself to a historical resume, "leaving the sea of mysteries to the more experienced,"[24] perhaps for his part he had a little irony for this or that too "clever" a commentator, but in any event his thought did not involve any depreciation in principle with regard to allegory. Certain others have done as he did — there was indeed a need for certain specialists in the "foundation" — but that very thing was rare. For each author who declares, like Christian of Stavelot: "I have striven more for the historical than the spiritual sense,"[25] or later like Hugh of Rouen: "We are treating it more by asking about the history,"[26] how many others there were who generalized the confidence of Saint Jerome in his commentary on Saint Mark: "We do not deny the history, but we prefer the spiritual understand-ing"![27] It happens to them to say it in their turn; thus, Isaac of Stella, addressing his monks: "As for me, I confess, it is the 'mysteries' everywhere that please me the most."[28] Even if the 'mysteries' there are mentioned by way of opposition to 'the moral things', it is clear that in the Abbot's heart they have no less bearing on the simple history. When Hugh Métel praised Saint Bernard for loving to "unearth the spiritual sense underneath the letter,"[29] one can therefore judge that his praise is nothing rare. None of our authors, no more Christian of Stavelot or Hugh of Rouen than the rest, is to the slightest degree "historicist." They would all acquiesce at least in principle to the exhortation of Rabanus Maurus: "So take up the history, and love the spiritual sense pertaining to the grace of Christ in it above all."[30]

For these believers, which they all were, the history or the letter was again merely the threshold giving access to the interior of the Temple of God:

> The temple of God is the whole Church . . . but the threshold of the temple is the historical sense in the Scriptures, since we enter into the temple of God . . . through faith in the history. But the depth of the allegories lies hidden beneath this threshold.[31]

To pick up their habitual metaphor, history could only be the "surface." "History pertains to the fitting report of things, and this is contained in the surface of the letter and is understood just as it is read."[32] In writing these words, Adam Scotus merely brought to expression a judgment already held and known for a long time. Since the epoch of Rufinus[33] and of Pope Gregory,[34] it is constantly a question, in the texts concerning Scripture, of the "simplicity of the letter" or the "surface of the letter,"[35] of the "surface of the narrative,"[36] the "surface of the history,"[37] the "plain of history,"[38] of the "surface of the historical sense," the surface which it is necessary to pass by to penetrate as far as the "height of prophecy,"[39] or the "internal marrow of the mysteries."[40] John of Salisbury specifies it more precisely as the "surface of the history according to the Hebrews."[41] But here again, let us watch out for misunderstanding or exaggeration. Such expressions do not at all signify that the exegete might have wanted to halt the historical understanding of the Bible at the "surface of the words,"[42] though the temptation was sometimes great to unify the two concepts.[43] The letter itself, as letter, had in fact a sort of "inside," since, before passing to the spiritual interpretation, one inquired about the "intention of the letter."[44] Even in profane works, where it was not a question to recognize an allegorical sense, one knew how to distinguish the *superficies verborum* [the surface of the words] and the *intima sententiarum* [the innermost of their judgments].[45] The twelfth century will determine technically, in the study of a given text, three levels of understanding, obtained by three successive explications: "ad litteram," "ad sensum," and "ad sententiam":[46] the first consisted in an analysis of a linguistic order; the second determined the signification of the words; finally, the third, sometimes blocked together with the second,[47] reconstituted the ideological content of the passage. Now this threefold explication, made according to the occasion on a biblical text, was still amenable to the *historia*.[48] In the same way that every profane science, theoretical or practical, howsoever profound it was, was still merely the "surface of the science" as regards the science of the Gospel, the sole provider of the "true wisdom,"[49] so too it was not impossible that, in its own "superficial" order, the historical explication was already profound. One is well aware of it in an exegete of genius, like Origen: who has given a better literal comment upon the scene of the sacrifice of Abraham than he? Kierkegaard himself has perhaps not surpassed him.[50] Such an instance is rare, and our medievals are generally not Origens. But the genius is one thing, and his faith is another. This kind of historical explication, as elaborate as one supposes it, so rich in psychological analysis, so capable at disengaging the religious value from the old biblical texts, had nothing to satisfy the faith of Origen any more than that of anyone else. It is by opposition to the *height of prophecy* that he still belonged to the "surface of the history,"[51] according to the terminology that we shall now try to comprehend. He was still party to what Saint Jerome, translating Origen, used to call the "primary speech of the reading";[52] to what Saint Gregory denominated the "exterior account" or the "exterior description";[53] to what was sometimes in the twelfth century called, though without any pejorative connotation, the "first signification of the words"[54] or the "first signification of the letter."[55]

Now this "first signification," as these men of faith knew well, was not the whole reason why the Bible was given to them. They knew its irreplaceable necessity. But if they "scrutinized" the text, it was to pass beyond that first to the "second signification." In the old Bible, at the end of the reckoning, they did not look for information on "the peculiar character of Israelite piety" or "the characteristic genius of the religion of Israel"; they did not even content themselves with apprehending in it how this religion was "the historic and preparatory stage" for the Christian religion. "The preoccupation with studying the Old Testament as a historical document for the sake of what it teaches us about the history of the Hebrew people" was completely "alien" to them.[56] They were generally lacking, as we have said, "any interest in the past as such," even if it were the biblical past, "in so far as it represents a time dead and gone and which can no longer come back."[57] Thus, of such a kind of research or knowledge as is admired among the most penetrating of our contemporaries, they would still have said, with Beatus of Liebana: "What advantage is it to know many things and understand none of them?"[58] Many of them would have shared the sort of detachment that made Saint Augustine write: "I don't know who the sons of Core were at that time, when they were singing these things; but the spirit ought to give us life, and the letter ought not conceal it";[59] or Saint Gregory about the Book of Job:

"Whoever wrote this was looking into some very inane stuff, even though the author of the book, the Holy Spirit, is faithfully believed."[60] We have indeed the right to think that this was not a point of superiority among them. At least this lack of curiosity — which, let us say it again, did not prevent them from being strongly interested in history from a theological point of view — protected them against all our profane and sometimes perhaps profaning taste for religious history and religious psychology. They knew that "all these things have been written so that they might believe that Jesus is the Christ and the Son of God."[61] If they rise a bit too fast to the absolute for our taste, they at least have the merit of rising there within the faith. In the same way, thought they, as the human authors of the holy Books have died, the events that they have reported have passed away. As such they have played their role, and have played it only once. But the Word of God was expressed through both. It is he who speaks to us still; it is he who reveals himself, "always the same, ever unchangeable and unfailing"; present on every page, "deploying his force from one end to the other," reaching the depth of our souls as the limits of the universe.[62] The men who believed that could not reduce the Bible to a mere historical document, even of divine history. They had learned from Saint Paul that it was made "to instruct, convince, correct, form to justice, and thus set the man of God perfectly in a state to accomplish every good work,"[63] "to restore the forces of our heart and to arm us against temptation."[64] In it they looked for "the light in the night of the present life";[65] or, as Richard of Saint Victor used to say, the "lightning-flash of divine cognition."[66] They ran "to drink at the source of divine cognition," and there to draw "the knowledge of salvation," "a foretaste of the nourishment of the truth," "the food from an eternal word."[67] Through their whole exegesis of all the pages of the ancient Scripture they used to say: "We do not think that this was not said *for us* just because we were not there at the time";[68] for them it was a living Scripture, always animated by the Spirit who was speaking through it: "For the divine Scripture is always speaking and calling, calling and speaking always."[69] In devoting themselves to its study, they felt as though they were leaving the land of bondage already to enter into freedom: they were going before the King[70] and knocking so that he would open up "the gate of the kingdom of heaven."[71]

A similar conviction naturally surged back upon the conception of biblical history and the manner of studying it. Many modern commentators consider the Bible "as a book that interests them, but which does not concern them." Our medievals would not have been able to comprehend this attitude, which has become so general. Historians by temperament or not, they could not, in the presence of the Bible, decide to "play the spectator."[72] Now everything that is amenable to history is still spectacle. From the strictly Christian point of view, it is still figure: *the figures of history*.[73] With history, one is still with the [mere] *appearance*; one has not penetrated into the [inner] *meaning*.[74] The domain of history is still entirely the domain of the relative; it is, as the Epistle to the Hebrews used to say, that "of the shadows."[75] Every kind of explication that confines itself to the history makes us still remain outside: *foris*.[76] When William of Saint Thierry, addressing himself to God, said to him: "the Scripture of thy Truth,"[77] he was thinking of something quite different from the historical inerrancy of the Bible! It was about the Truth of God, about his Word, "God from God, Light from Light," having come to make himself our food.[78] Within the Scripture, God resides; by the Scripture, God makes himself known; the mystery of the Scripture is the very mystery of the Kingdom of God.[79] History, however, is quite insufficient to introduce us into this mystery; it merely opens up for us a first door: the "interior door," the door of the New Testament, is over yonder.[80] Beyond the historical cognition, it is necessary to assimilate the teaching of Scripture "through the understanding of the heart and the imitation of the deed"; it is necessary for us to drink "of the wine of its spiritual sense"; only then "shall that serene dawn of supernal visitation rise upon us."[81] The whole order of history does not yet give us and cannot give us anything but an exterior and distant view of what we too quickly take to be the "Face of God."[82] Only the order of the spirit founded upon history and disengaged from history, will finally allow us to say, with Saint Gregory: *In his Scripture we look, as it were, upon his face*.[83]

CHAPTER EIGHT

Allegory, Sense of the Faith

1. Mysterium requiramus

So now we must pass to the second "mode of explication," to the second "sense" of Scripture: to allegory. Each of the four great doctors invites us, indeed, presses us on to it. "We have drawn the thin lines of history; now let us set our hand to allegory": this is Saint Jerome who is speaking to us.[1] The same, more briefly, goes for Saint Augustine: "We have heard the fact; let us look into the mystery."[2] Saint Ambrose informs us of it: "A higher sense calls us forth,"[3] and he applies the precept of the authority of the Apostle: "For the holy Apostle taught us to look for the secret of the truth in the simplicity of the history."[4] As for Saint Gregory, he gives several notices for it, as though to inculcate an indispensable method in those who are going to read it and re-read it over the centuries: "But since we have briefly discussed the surfaces of the history, let us weigh carefully what lies hidden within them of the mystic understanding";[5] "We believe these facts through history, but now through allegory let us see how they are to be fulfilled";[6] "But if we discuss all these things with a historical treatment, let us also scrutinize them through the mysteries of allegory,"[7] etc. Again, Gregory says: "Thus far let it suffice for us to have gone through the words of the history; let the discussion of the exposition now convert itself to investigate the mysteries of the allegory" — "Hucusque nos verba historiae transcurrisse sufficiat; jam nunc ad indaganda allegoriae mysteria expositionis se sermo convertat."[8] It is therefore always a question of explication, of exegesis — "expositionis sermo"; but within this exegesis it is a question of performing a radical change: "let it convert itself" — "*se convertat*"; a change that we will have nothing more to do with so as to pass subsequently on to the third or to the fourth sense. It is a question of *the* change, which governs everything. Our faith depends on it. It imposes itself; we cannot elude it, if we want to produce a *Christian* exegesis. Gregory indicates it for us using the strongest possible terms: "we are forced," "we are compelled,"[9] "it is necessary," "now the order of exposition *requires* us to lay bare the secrets of the allegories."[10] We do not have the right through "negligence" to deprive ourselves of the many allegories of which history is so full.[11]

Saint Isidore of Seville says it again: "It is necessary . . . that the allegorical sense follow."[12] The same goes for Rabanus Maurus: "The history . . . requires the mystery";[13] he formulates and comments upon this fundamental exigency on various occasions: "For the historical sense is not only not enough for the readers of the divine books, but they must also consider what the prophetic speech intends to intimate."[14] It would be hard to put it more precisely. Beatus of Liebana gives us the reason for this necessity: "The spiritual understanding for the sake of which the history has been repeated follows upon the history that has been presented";[15] and Claudius of Turin, in a more compact formula, says: "This has been done for the sake of the mystery";[16] the Pseudo-Eloi elaborates it in the same terms as Rabanus Maurus, terms that have come from the Fathers.[17] Indeed all these "deeds of the ancients," all these histories of times long ago, would matter little, or at least it would matter little that we should become acquainted with them, unless we knew how to relate them to an order of things that rescues them from the dead past.[18] If it is useful to entrust them to our memory, it is in view of understanding them;[19] for if the Spirit had wanted the history of those two ancient cities, Jerusalem and Babylon, to be preserved for us in the sacred books, it would be to show everyone by means of them two other, more durable cities, which are of concern to us right now.[20] All these historical things *mysticant nobis aliquid:* convey a mystery to us.[21] Once again, beyond the immediate content of the history or the primary sense of the letter, let us look for *the spiritual meaning that is in it.*[22]

The lesson will be repeated everywhere, and the conviction will come to be accepted by everyone. "To remember the deed performed" is fine, but not sufficient: it is also necessary "to sense the inner mystery in the outer fact."[23] It is necessary "to raise our minds," "through the lowliness of historical faith toward the loftiness of spiritual understanding."[24] It is an order: "Let him rise further into the mystery!" cries the Venerable Bede.[25] The same goes for Saint Bruno or an anonymous writer cloaked under his name: "Now that the letter has been treated, let allegory be reached!"[26] And Saint Bruno of Segni writes: "Now that these matters dealing with the letter have been disposed of, let us see what the allegories signify as well."[27] Again, here is Hervaeus of Bourg Dieu: "Now that these points have briefly been said regarding the sense of history, let us search into the mystery."[28] Or, in verse, we have Saint Paulinus of Aquilaea, Othloh of Saint Emmeran, and Adam of Saint Victor:

> For now that the truth of history has fittingly been preserved,
> Let us diligently search out the allegorical senses.[29]

> But let him always note the allegory through the history![30]

> Let the spiritual understanding,
> Covered with the literal branch,
> Advance into public![31]

Or, in formulas from school, there is Hugh of Saint Victor: after the "first instruction of sacred eloquence, which consists in the historical reading," there necessarily ought to come "the second instruction, which is in allegory."[32] Or again the author of the *Rescriptum pro monachis* says: "Just as the truth of the history is most firmly to be preserved, so nevertheless the subtlety of the allegory is also to be investigated."[33]

[It might be objected] that one should not argue from a historic sense clear enough to suffice for everyone. Robert of Melun would reply, making himself the interpreter of all: "By as much as (a doctrine) is the more evident in the literal sense, by so much is it the deeper in the mystical understanding."[34] Nor let one argue from so many beautiful examples given by "the ancient fathers": their lives are like beautiful fruit trees; history shows us their marvelous foliage, but we also need allegory to enable us to appreciate their fertility.[35] Finally, after the milk of the "patent judgment" must come the wine of the "spiritual sense";[36] after the "plodding sequence of the letter," the "prominence of the allegory";[37] after the "weight of history," the "depth of allegory";[38] the latter will reinforce the former: "so that the mystery of allegory may be aided by the words of history."[39] History can satisfy only children — to wit: spiritual children; it merely excites the appetite of the mature mind, which it must placate by allegory.[40] In short, after having *read*, it is necessary for us to *understand*.[41] It is necessary for us to enter the *path of comprehension*.[42] We must enter upon new regions through the "door of intelligence."[43]

Let us immediately, however, clarify that to discover this allegory, one will not find it properly speaking in the text, but in the realities of which the text speaks; not in history as recitation, but in history as event; or, if one wishes, allegory is indeed in the recitation, but one that relates a real event. "The actions speak.... The deeds, if you understand them, are words."[44] Allegory is prophecy inscribed within the facts themselves: "not only in the things said, but also, God disposing all things marvelously, in the deeds themselves."[45] For prophecy produced under divine inspiration can take place "either through doings or through sayings";[46] one meets it "sometimes through the figures of things, sometimes through the riddles of words."[47] Everything that Scripture says of Abraham, for example, is a prophecy in act: "is both deed and prophecy."[48] "Allegory lies hidden within the deeds done."[49] In other words, then, the text acts only as spokesman to lead to the historical realities; the latter are themselves the figures, they themselves contain the mysteries that the exercise of allegory is supposed to extract from them: "the figures of the histories";[50] "to extend the mysteries of history through the exercise of allegory";[51] "History . . . has a spiritual sense in those who have existed before us."[52] In the text it is a question of the "narration of the great sacrament"; in the facts, it is a question of the "sacraments of the deeds."[53] A formula from Isidore brings these two points of view together, by bringing together the two senses of the word 'history': "The history of the sacred law is the deeds and writings without any prefiguration of the things to come."[54]

This is what Saint Paul had already said, as Origen has noted: "the things of which one can doubt only that they have happened in the flesh, the Apostle has spoken as allegorical."[55] Saint Ambrose makes the same remark,[56] as does Saint Augustine: "Where (the Apostle) has used the name allegory, he finds it not in the words but in the deeds";[57] and again: "What shall I say of the Apostle Paul, who signifies that even the history itself of Exodus was an allegory of the Christian people to come."[58] The precision is not at all a specifically "Syrian" trait, as some have said regarding Saint John Chrysostom; it very quickly became a commonplace. Tertullian had given it as follows: "We know what has been prophesied as much by words as by things; the resurrection is preached both by sayings and by doings."[59] Many a time as well Saint Hilary would say: "while the law is spiritual, while its deeds are allegorized";[60] "a thing is done according to its present effect, but a spiritual preformation obtains its order";[61] etc. This is what led him to speak of "mystic history,"[62] just as Saint Gregory of Nyssa spoke about *"understanding the spirit of history*

Mysterium requiramus

without losing its historical reality,"[63] or as Saint Ambrose wrote: "But we have already recounted the mystery of its history."[64] In the chapter that we have just analyzed, Cassian, wanting to explain the word *allegory*, wrote: "those things that have been done in truth are said to have prefigured the form of another sacrament."[65] This is the same idea that Junilius the African, interpreter of Paul of Nisibis, expressed in his *Instituta regularia divinae legis* saying: "A 'type' is a prophecy in things," "things are clarified from things by means of types";[66] or Saint Jerome in this simple formula: "according to typical history."[67] With — or, as is most often the case, without — the word *allegory*, Saint Augustine also said the same thing; he showed Scripture "prophesying even by means of the things done,"[68] the realities of the New Testament figured and announced within prophetic times "not only by speeches but also by actions."[69] "O deeds done," he cried, "but done prophetically! On earth, but heavenly! By humans but divinely!"[70] To make himself more understandable he distinguished between the "parable of the word" and the "parable of the deed."[71] The facts of the Bible, he explained again, in their very reality, "were words, destined to signify something to us,"[72] and in this sense we could say, for example, that the chastisements of the Egyptians recounted in the Book of Exodus were allegorical chastisements.[73] In the same sense Clement of Alexandria said, without distinguishing, that "all our Scripture is in parables,"[74] and Origen had said that "allegorically" the Gentiles were the vices, or that the spiritual man ought to "allegorize" the countries mentioned by the Bible: Judaea, Babylon, Egypt, etc.[75] Saint Gregory does not fail to take up this unanimous teaching in his own terms: "Among the other miracles of prophecy, the books of the prophets have also this to marvel at: that, just as in them things are explained by words, so sometimes words are explained by things, so that not only their sayings but also their doings are prophecies."[76]

All the medievals repeat this. Bede, who speaks of the "things done mystically,"[77] distinguishes the "allegory of deed" from the "allegory of word,"[78] reproduces the definitions of Junilius[79] and puts the "historic prefiguration" of the Old Testament and the "allegorical completion" of the New[80] in correspondence with each other. Rabanus Maurus does so, the one for whom sacred history is also "prophetic history"[81] and who, following Saint Augustine, puts the theory of signifying things in his *Clericalis institutio*.[82] So do Berengaud,[83] Paschasius Radbertus,[84] Claudius of Turin,[85] Remi of Auxerre.[86] So too Saint Peter Damian,[87] Saint Bruno (?),[88] Rupert of Deutz,[89] Godfrey of Admont.[90] Gerhoh of Reichersberg invites one to take "the things that are spoken historically under a higher understanding . . . to allegory";[91] he exposes "the mystery of this fact";[92] he points out the "truth" signified in advance within the "figurative deeds."[93] Analogous precisions are to be read in Adam Scotus,[94] John of Salisbury,[95] Peter Comestor,[96] Peter of Poitiers,[97] etc. Adam of Perseigne defines allegory as "the spiritual signification of the things done."[98] Those who do not discuss it at length nevertheless are not unaware of it; for example, there is Othloh of Saint Emmeran wanting to scrutinize the "mystic sacraments of the things."[99]

For the most part, here is an opportunity to admire the unique privilege of the holy books, which alone transmit to us the report of facts whose allegorical signification is guaranteed by divine authority. Saint Augustine has observed: "Sicut humana consuetudo verbis, ita divina potentia etiam factis loquitur": "Just as human custom speaks with words, so does the divine power speak with deeds as well." Saint Eucher has celebrated this transcendence of the Word of God, "which contains within itself such great things."[100] Thereby, remarked Saint Gregory as well, "even by its very way of speaking it transcends the sciences and doctrines."[101] Hugh of Saint Victor says it again in his didactic works, the *De sacramentis*[102] and the *Didascalicon*.[103] The author of the *Speculum de mysteriis Ecclesiae*, after having enumerated the four traditional senses, concludes: "Therefore holy Scripture is superabundant in the other senses. . . . In the divine page not only do the understanding and words signify things, but the things themselves signify other things."[104] The *Exceptiones allegoricae* of Richard say almost the same thing: "In this respect the divine Scripture is far more excellent than the knowledge of the world: in it not only words, but even things are significant."[105] The same goes for the Pseudo-Hugo who composed the *Questions on Saint Paul*,[106] or John of Salisbury, who himself also neatly contrasts the science of Scripture with that of the profane books: "But in the liberal disciplines, where not things but words are significant, whoever is not content with the literal sense seems to me to err."[107] Garnier of Rochefort passes on the same teaching in entirely scholastic formulations.[108] Stephen Langton, applying himself to a proposition of Hugo, gives it an original and tight spin: "Master Hugo says: The sublimity of the sacred page over the other disciplines is so great that the objects of signification in the other sciences are the means of signification in theology; for what are the things of the names and verbs in the other faculties are themselves names in theology."[109] In short, Scripture is in a way doubly the Word of God, since God speaks to us in it with words about what he has spoken to us in deeds.

Biblical allegory is therefore essentially *allegoria facti*. More precisely, it is *allegoria facti et dicti*. It is, in the Christian sense of the word, *mysterium*. We have seen earlier the equivalence of these two words. John Scotus Erigena explains it in a page on the course of which he distinguishes this allegory or mystery — quite otherwise than is done today in our language — from the simple symbol:

> ... It is to be asked what is the difference between the mysteries of the two Laws ... and symbols. Well, properly, mysteries are things that are handed on according to allegory of deed and word, that is, they are deeds with respect to things done and utterances, since they are narrated. For example, the tabernacle of Moses had both been constructed according to the thing done and uttered and narrated by the text of holy Scripture. Likewise, the sacraments of the legal sacrifices were both done according to history and uttered according to narration. Circumcision, likewise, was both performed in the flesh and narrated in the letter.... And this form of sacraments is reasonably called allegory of word and deed by the holy Fathers.
>
> The other form, which properly got the name 'symbol', is called allegory of word but not of deed, since it is constituted only in the utterances of spiritual doctrine but not in sensible facts. So mysteries are what have both been historically done and literally narrated in both Testaments, whereas symbols are what are said, not done — or, to put it another way, done only by teaching....[110]

In this sense, then, there are indeed symbols in the Bible, just as in other human books. But only the Bible in truth contains mysteries. It alone is to transmit the memory of allegorical deeds, whose reality is divinely guaranteed. *O res gestas, sed prophetice! Gestas in terra, sed caelitus! Per homines, sed divinitus!*[111]

2. Mystery: Future, Interior, Celestial

Nevertheless, this term 'allegory, a sort of alien speech',[1] derived from grammar, this word transcribed from Greek which corresponds to the Latin 'inversio', did not, if one can say so, by itself say much. In popular current usage, as in its original signification, it designates only a "continued metaphor," "making one thing be understood by means of another."[2] The Middle Ages would never stop reading the definition coming from Quintilian: "which points to something in words but something else in sense,"³ or the explanation given by Martianus Capella: "the care of metaphorical words, when either a thing does not discover words appropriate to itself or when we want something to be explained more scintillatingly."⁴ *Allegoria* was one of the fifteen figures enumerated by Isidore of Seville in his *Grammar*,⁵ and it was itself subdivided into seven "subordinate tropes," of which Bede has reproduced the list.⁶ Doubtless, in the application that has been made of this word to Scripture, the sense, as we have seen, has been rendered more precise, following the usage of the Apostle, which had been decisive. The classical explanation has in consequence been modified. Saint Ambrose did it felicitously, thanks to the change of a single word: "there is allegory when one thing is being done, another is being figured."⁷ The formula, as has been seen already, came to be borrowed frequently.⁸ Nevertheless, only a quite generic acceptation, remaining extrinsic and formal, would yet be obtainable in this fashion. Indeed it had been necessary originally for Saint Paul to divert a word, such as it was, from its ordinary acceptation, since for him it was a question of using this word to express an unprecedented, profoundly original thought, the likes of which had never existed before, among the Greeks or even among the Jews. There was no word for it and none could naturally be adapted for it.⁹ The Christian novelty, whose reaction Paul experienced so violently, was radical in a different way than human novelties that let themselves be translated a bit later by an ingenious combination of ancient words and prefabricated concepts! It annexed all things to itself, but at first it was a hapax [legomenon]. Whence came this inevitable inadequacy of language.

Still, a later precision, upon which one could have no doubt, resulted from Pauline usage. Bringing together the allegory of the Epistle to the Galatians with the mystery of the Epistle to the Ephesians, Origen has said: "Paul announces that [haec] which the allegorical mysteries contain by saying 'It is a great mystery; I am speaking about Christ and the Church.'"¹⁰ Haec, that is the whole content of the Bible. Subsequently Saint Hilary said: "The whole task that is contained within the sacred volumes is to announce in words, to express in deeds, and to confirm by examples . . . the coming of our Lord Jesus Christ."¹¹ In his turn, Saint Augustine said, in the *De catechizandis rudibus:* "For all things that we read in holy Scriptures have been written prior to the Lord's coming for no other end than that his coming should be confided and that the Church to come should be presignified";¹² in the *De civitate Dei:* "It is rather to be believed that they have wisely been committed to memory and to writing, that they have been performed, and signify something and that that very something pertains to the prefiguration of the Church";[13] in the *Contra Faustum*, on the entire history of the Hebrew people: "The prophecy of the Christ to come and of his Church is to be examined through and through";[14] in a sermon on the *Psalms:* "The whole mystery of all the Scriptures, Christ and the Church,"[15] etc. Saint Jerome has shown in the Bible the "sacraments to be fulfilled in Christ and the Church,"[16] or again the "bemarrowed sacraments of the Church."[17] Saint Quodvultdeus has written: "All law and prophecy sounds Christ the Lord and the Church,"[18] and: "Figures succeed upon figures, while yet all actions signify Christ and the Church."[19] Saint Isidore of Seville: "But figure exists in a re-presenting of the truth, when we recognize that the things we read, having been pronounced about the patriarchs and prophets in the divine books, have been fulfilled allegorically in Christ and the Church."[20]

Analogous texts in Patristic sources are countless. Whether they bear the word 'allegoria' or the word 'mysterium' spelled out as such, or both, or whether they have neither the one nor the other, the thought is the same. They all come together in the concrete definition of *allegoria* such as one reads, for example, in Bede,[21] or in many others after him:[22] "Allegory exists when the present sacraments of Christ and the Church are signed by means of mystical words or things." The entire Scripture, says Ambrose Autpert, leads us "to contemplate the sacraments of Christ and the Church."[23] Angelome of Luxeuil announces the program of his exegesis in these words: "We shall try to expose the bright sacraments of Christ and the Church."[24] For Aimon of Auxerre, "all the Scripture of the Old Testament invites us to behold the mysteries of Christ and the Church," and again: "The Old Testament, where the mysteries of Christ and the Church have been predicted."[25] For Othloh of Saint Emmeran, all the things that Scripture contains "have been completed in Christ and the holy Church"; to this unique mystery, to this total mystery "the whole history of the Old Testament pertains."[26] For Irimbert of Admont, if the history of Ruth is short — "constrained by the brevity of the speeches" — "nevertheless it is broadened by the immensity of the mysteries."[27] Allegory, repeats Guibert of Nogent, treats "of the mystery of Christ and the Church,"[28] and Honorius: "Allegory, when a thing is set forth about Christ and the Church";[29] and Richard of Saint Victor: "Through allegory we understand how the sacraments of the Church have been foretold by means of the figures of antecedent things."[30] Peter of Poitiers picks up Bede's definition, which twenty others have transmitted to him, with a slight variant: "Allegory is when the hidden mysteries of Christ and the

Church are signified by mystic words or things,"³¹ and in another formula Robert of Melun says nothing different: for him all Scripture has as its object "the incarnation of Christ along with all his sacraments."³² For Peter Lombard, the things of the old Law "announce in veiled manner the sacraments of Christ and the Church."³³ In other words, what the whole Old Testament prefigures is the whole mystery of our redemption.³⁴

It is useless to multiply citations. On the other hand, it is important to observe certain particularities of language so as to avoid false trails. We have already been able to notice: the object of allegory is sometimes said to be Christ, and sometimes the Church, and sometimes both the one and the other. Indeed, if one takes one series of texts, one sees that it relates "to the Lord Savior";³⁵ "let us call everything back to Christ if we want to keep to the path of right understanding."³⁶ If one takes another series, it is a question "of our people, which has been allied within the sacraments of Christ,"³⁷ or of the "future sacraments of the Christian people."³⁸ In the first series, "Christ about to come in the flesh is being foretold," and in the second, "the whole order of his churches."³⁹ Here, or close to it, is what in Christian exegesis has been called, on the one side "Christology from above," and on the other, "Christology from below."⁴⁰ Only these two series are tightly intertwined; for as Saint Paul said, Christ and the Church are just one great mystery: this is the mystery of their union. Now the whole mystery of Scripture, the whole object of *allegoria*, resides in this. This enables one to discover everywhere the "deeper mysteries about Christ and his body."⁴¹ The Church is in truth the "body" of Christ; she is his "flesh"; she forms with him but "one single person": "Christ and the Church is [sic] one person."⁴² Now, "if two in one flesh," asks Saint Augustine, "why not two in one voice?" And consequently, "whether it be head or members that speaks, the one Christ is speaking."⁴³ The inclusion is mutual: "So let Christ speak, since the Church speaks in Christ, and Christ speaks in the Church; and the body in the head, and the head in the body."⁴⁴ In the same sense Aimon of Auxerre explains more precisely that this "body of Christ" of which Saint Paul is speaking in the Epistle to the Colossians, this "truth" and this "body" from the shadows of the old covenant, is at once "Christ and Church."⁴⁵

There are therefore no exceptions to make that might, by separating the applications, destroy the unity of the divine work. "All things are related to Christ by allegorical likeness": the assertion is that of a commentator on the Psalms who lived in the twelfth century;⁴⁶ it could have been by a hundred others. There is truly nothing beyond the "end" marked by

Mystery: Future, Interior, Celestial

Saint Paul: "The end of the Law is Christ."[47] This is how Saint Augustine comments on it:

> Whatever doubt a human being has in mind on hearing God's Scriptures, let him not fall back from Christ; when Christ has been revealed in those words, let him understand that he has understood; but before he come to an understanding of Christ, let him not presume that he has understood.[48]

And Saint Cyril: "Moses guided Israel across the figure and the shadow up to the mystery of Christ."[49] This is what our Middle Ages, always a faithful echo of the Fathers, comments as well, for example, with Saint Peter Damian: "For the end of the Law as to justice is Christ, since whatever the Law says, be it the Old or the New, is undoubtedly related to him";[50] or with Rupert of Deutz: "The wholeness of the Scriptures, in which there are faithful testimonials of Christ."[51] He alone is at once "the goal, the intention, and the sense" of the Law.[52] For, as Saint Ambrose said, "the Law cannot exist without the Word, nor can one be a prophet unless he has prophesied about God's Son."[53] Only, if one considers the whole collection of the texts, it is a question of the whole Christ, inseparable from his Church: "The matter of holy Scripture is the whole Christ, head and members."[54] This was already the first rule of hermeneutics posed by Tyconius the African under the heading: "On the Lord and his body."[55] Here is why we could also say — always speaking in general — with Saint Augustine: "All things that have been written before . . . were also our figures, and in figure they used to happen to them,"[56] or: everything is related "to the prophecy of the Church,"[57] or, with the *Glossa ordinaria:* "There is nothing in divine Scripture that does not pertain to the Church."[58] Doubtless, in detail, the application ought to be made sometimes to the Head and sometimes to the members,[59] sometimes to the one and to the others at once, and sometimes to their relation.[60] Nevertheless, it is always the same, unique Mystery: *The Mystery of Christ, hidden from ages and generations.*[61] Under the diversity of figures, which turns its diverse aspects to account, it is always he who is inculcated in us: "The same mysteries of Christ and of the Church are being repeated multifariously and with many modifications of the figures, but, once repeated, they also bring about something new."[62]

Now all the preceding shows clearly enough that this mystery is entirely concrete. It does not exist in idea. It does not consist in any atemporal truth or object of detached speculation. This mystery is a reality in act, the realization of a Grand Design; it is therefore, in the strongest sense, even something historical, in which personal beings are engaged. He who follows the allegorical sense, Giles of Paris will say, "searches for, finds, and follows Jesus."[63] The object of allegory, by relation to the facts that the Old Testament reports, is therefore a reality to come: this is its most immediately tangible characteristic. *They foretell the things to come.*[64] "All things were signifying that Christ was about to come."[65] "They were done not without signifying the future."[66] "A future allegory about Christ and the Church in the latest times."[67] "Things were signified to be about to come by means of antecedent figures."[68] The mysteries are those of the Word incarnate; of the Word, whose incarnation has to take place within becoming, in the "fullness of time." They are therefore *futura mysteria.*[69] In the whole Jewish Bible "the future mysteries of the Lord are signified."[70] "The future mysteries have been shown to the Fathers by the unfolding of things," says Remi of Auxerre;[71] and Potho of Prüm: Moses has put the "future sacraments of Christ and the Church" that God had revealed to him into his Law.[72] Consequently, in the ancient facts or the ancient institutions that signify them, it is a question of a "certain image of a future thing,"[73] of a "figure and sort of prophecy of future things";[74] to employ a term which was a creation of the Christian language,[75] it is a question of an "allegorical prefiguration,"[76] or of a "mystery of prefiguration."[77] Saint Aldhelm offers us these two very full formulations: "They are declared to have portended the future secrets of the mysteries," and: "The future virginity of the incarnate Word was prefigured by the mystical foreshadowings of the sacraments."[78] "The understanding of the things to come," is how Rupert will say it.[79] Abelard will give this definition: "An exposition is called mystical, when, having been prefigured by it, we teach what had been to be consummated at the time of grace through Christ, or whatever future history is shown to be presignified."[80] Again let us gather the following words of a sacred orator of the twelfth century, who united the two traits that we have just considered:

> Quaedam (Scriptura) sic commendat, ut pariter litteram et mysticum intellectum insinuet, ut in transitu maris Rubri, et manna caelesti, et tabernaculo Dei atque arca testamenti, ubi *futurorum figura,* baptismi vid. *Christi et Ecclesiae* ostensa est praerogativa.

> (Scripture) commends some things in such wise that it hints equally at a literal and a mystical understanding, e.g., in the crossing

Mystery: Future, Interior, Celestial

of the Red Sea, the heavenly manna, the tabernacle of God and the ark of the covenant, where *a figure of things to come*, namely the baptism of *Christ and the Church*, has been shown to be foretold.[81]

There is a perpetual return to this expression "to come," since Origen,[82] or rather, once again, since Saint Paul, who designated the first Adam as "the form of the one to come,"[83] and since the Epistle to the Hebrews speaking of the Law "having a shadow of goods to come."[84] There is an opposition of the *mystery to come* to the *thing done*;[85] of the *things to come* to the *actions performed*;[86] of the *things to be hoped for* to the *things gone by*;[87] of the *thing advancing an image* to the *item to be represented*;[88] of the *truth to come* to the *type*, the *aspect* or the *sacrament*.[89] There is an opposition of the 'then' or *tunc* (past) to the 'now' or *nunc*. An opposition within duration, at the same time as a relation of sign to thing signified. A relation of two Testaments, the one old and the other new, put in evidence by allegory: this Christian allegory to the very idea of which so many historians remain blind, and which Saint Augustine so fittingly called "this form of understanding that comes to us from the Apostles."[90] There is therefore no great interest in informing us that "the opposition of the *gesta* and the *gerenda* is fundamental in the exegesis" of such and such a Christian author:[91] notwithstanding certain subtleties of emphasis, it is present in them all, and there is not the least originality for any one of them in relation to the others; but they all participate, more or less forcefully, in the great originality of Christian allegory. This allegory, applied to the biblical texts, does not, as is still sometimes repeated today, turn up its nose at "the temporal, horizontal dimension"; the "allegorical construction" of the medieval exegetes is not at all "a species of atemporal understanding." Consider as witness again the following affirmation of Honorius, which it will not be necessary to take, as we have just seen, in too superficial a sense: "All these transpired before figuratively and, as though by a finger, pointed out our times."[92] Or this remark of the Cistercian Serlon of Savigny: "For what is read about Elia historically is found spiritually in blessed John and in many of the saints."[93]

Only, as history is not enough to contain the mystery, it is very true that Christian allegory is not contained by the historical dimension. To receive it totally and not to warp it, we must not restrict this reality "to come" which is the New Testament within the bounds of the "superficies historiae," the "surface of the history." It overflows these boundaries. It involves another "dimension." For a mystery, in the Christian sense, is indeed a fact, but it is much more than an ordinary fact. Allegories discover for us a good deal of "mysteria *futura*," but these are also "futura *mysteria*,"[94] and the emphasis can be put in turn on the one or the other element of this pair of words. The "mystery of the dispensation"[95] is a "dispensation of the mystery";[96] this is the "mystical dispensation of Christ."[97] After having seen that it was indeed a question of a historic dispensation, or, as the ancients used to say, of an "economy," albeit in diverse fashion, for the New as well as for the Old Testament,[98] then it is now necessary to add that it is the dispensation of a mystery, which enables us to penetrate into a deep, "interior"[99] and "spiritual"[100] region and which — for many reasons — is realized within the facts only to tie us to the eternal. Walafrid Strabo showed the Christian people introduced by allegory "into the inner cells of spiritual wisdom."[101] Let us see, said Irimbert of Admont while commenting on Ruth, "what the law of the spiritual mystery may contain."[102] Let us say again, with many others, that these "future sacraments of Christ and the Church" contained in the ancient Scripture are identical with the "heavenly sacraments of Christ and the Church,"[103] that are comprehended by a "heavenly understanding."[104] "The Hebrews, knowing nothing of heavenly things.... We, however..."[105] In another style and with different implications, does not a Karl Barth today say something quite analogous when, in the *Römerbrief*, he explains that "every impression of revelation refers to the revelation itself" and that finally "every time bears within itself eternity as its overcoming?"[106]

The Fathers did not fail to draw attention to this capital point. Saint Hilary had said that the Law prefigured "a doctrine and a work of spiritual nature";[107] he had shown that the sacred text, at first "understood simply," had subsequently to be "looked at interiorly," explicated in its "inner causes";[108] he himself constantly had recourse to an "interior understanding,"[109] with a view to disengaging an "aspect of inner understanding," an "inner meaning."[110] In a passage from the *De vera religione* already cited, Saint Augustine had written that there is room to ask "what is the method to interpret allegory, which is believed to have been said through wisdom in the Holy Spirit? Is it sufficient to lead it from the older visible things to the more recent visible things? Or up to the affections and nature of the soul? Or even unto unchangeable eternity?"[111] If indeed the Law of Moses is "to be perceived spiritually," it is by signifying Jesus Christ to us that it leads us "to understand the things within."[112] In virtue of a "spiritual disposition,"[113] it leads us into a "strongbox of inner understanding."[114] The "great mystery of Christ and the Church" is "something great and spiritual."[115] The "mysteries of the heavenly kingdom" are "interior."[116] Therefore, think these medievals of ours, it is necessary for us ourselves "to perceive the inner mystery."[117] To assimilate the "interior sense" of the history, it is necessary for us to pass on to the "interior understanding." It is necessary for us to grasp the "signs of spiritual graces."[118] Is this not what the most usual metaphors suggest? "And what is designated by 'straw' but the surface of the letter? What is meant by the 'barley' if not the inner understanding?"[119] Therefore, by an ascent which will simultaneously be a dive, "let the soul of the reader lift itself to those things that are within, inside the understanding";[120] that it may leave "from the narrows of the letter" to welcome the Savior "in an exalted place."[121] The Christian occupied with meditating upon the Bible is "looking at all things inside," says Gilbert Foliot; he gives as examples the sight of Christ immolated in Abel, the sight of the Church in Noah's ark.[122] This interiority is neither uniquely nor primarily what we today name "the interior life": it is, in the first place, the interiority of the mystery within the very object of the faith. Let us not be afraid of the pleonasm: it is a question of "internal mysteries."[123] If we compare the Scripture to a double-edged sword, this is because, on the one hand, "according to the letter it shapes the outer," and, on the other, "according to the mystical sense it polishes the inner."[124] On the one side there is the letter and on the other side the "interior sense" of this letter.[125] The sense is doubly interior: first, because it is contained within the letter, as the ark of the covenant is contained within the temple;[126] it is not "beside" it, its relation to it is organic and profound: "in the history there is the understanding of the spirit."[127] Then, and this is the point of view that we must develop, because such a sense is related to something interior, to a reality that always bears, in addition to the factual datum, an inside.

Doubtless certain prophetic details have sometimes been able to be realized "literally," in exterior fashion, within sensible facts, as Saint Matthew, most particularly, has shown. Thus it is for the tears of Rachel announcing the massacre of the Innocents,[128] or for the verse of the Psalm announcing the vinegar that the soldiers wanted to make Jesus drink. But even in this case it is appropriate to look still further: "to search for the mystery, to batter the hiding-places, to enter the torn veil of the temple."[129] Doubtless again, more fundamentally, the Incarnation of the Word, announced in so many ways, is real; its whole redemptive work is real. But precisely its reality is of an infinitely deeper nature than that of a simple historical fact, observable from outside, and the reduplicated formulation of a Manegold is not mere redundancy: "by notifying us of the history of the incarnation of his Christ and the mystery of his incarnation."[130] In the same way that the "shadowy and figurative David" was no less real and historical than the "true David" that he was announcing, inversely, in just the same way, the "mystical and spiritual David" is not less real and historical than the "historical David"[131] — but there is much more to him than just the reality falling under the official reports of the historian. All the facts of the Gospel are real, and their factual reality is essential: we will nonetheless say about it, with Saint Augustine, for example, that the glory that once shone upon the face of Moses was "temporal figure," whilst the glory of Jesus is "truth";[132] we shall nonetheless say, with Rabanus Maurus, that the deeds and actions of Joshua, for example, have been recounted to human beings by the Holy Spirit "so that they may learn from the type of the historical Jesus the mystery of the true Jesus."[133] In the case of the "true Jesus," the epithet "historical" is not very strong: on the contrary, it is too weak; for Jesus is essentially "the spiritual performer of the mystery."[134] Hugh of Saint Victor says it all in two words: the object of allegory, that is, the New Testament, consists in *facta mystica*.[135] These are "hidden" facts, which have an inside; and it is this inside which makes of them salvific, absolute, definitive facts. It is through him that they are mysteries and that they live on — the thing is assured, whatever be the manner in which this or that person explains it — in the life of the Church and in eternity: "Spiritual allegory always preaches the ecclesiastical mysteries and the heavenly sacraments."[136] Rupert will therefore call this same reality that the historical letter of the Scriptures has the burden to signify by two consecutive phrases, either "the heavenly mysteries" or "the Gospel teaching"[137] — and indeed this amounts to quite the same thing.[138]

3. The Christian Novelty

The relation of allegory to history is therefore, to be sure, a relation of the after to the before; it is this essentially — but not exclusively. It does not merely make us pass "from things that have been done to those that are being done":[1] it also makes us pass, and does so with the same movement, from things "that are said to have happened historically under the shadow of the law" to those that "come about spiritually in the people of God in the time of grace."[2] It is therefore also of a qualitative order. The "history" of the Old Testament prefigures the "grace" of the Gospel.[3] On this subject one could speak of "infinite qualitative difference": what Richard of Saint Victor expresses, alluding to the table of the Tabernacle which was made of wood and of gold, by comparing the history to the

The Christian Novelty

wood and allegory or the mystical sense to the gold.[4] *For even at that point the kingdom of God exists within us*[5] — this kingdom of God is no other than the Christ. It is absolutely necessary to understand this difference, "so that the depth of the sacrament may appear from the whole."[6] To misunderstand it would be to make out of the allegorical sense, which is a *spiritual* sense, a new literal sense; and this would practically negate the interiority of the Christian mystery. Thereby it would even be deprived of the "interior restoration" that ought to be the fruit of spiritual understanding.[7] This would not be to read Moses as one ought, "to understand the grace of Christ."[8] This would not be to promote "the Synagogue" to the level of the Church: it would rather be to change the Church once again into a synagogue.[9] By merely affirming the succession and not the difference of the times one would suppress the difference at the heart of the legitimate heritage of the "Christian people" regarding the "Jewish people."[10] The prophecies called "historical" (as opposed to the messianic or eschatological prophecies) "have scarcely any success among contemporary exegetes";[11] in most cases, they had no more among the exegetes of the first Middle Ages; not, as today, chiefly on grounds of criticism, but for spiritual reasons. Nevertheless, the temptation to flatten the object of "prophecy" or of "allegory" onto the plane of external history, and to keep it there, is a permanent temptation. By timidity of thought, by spiritual flabbiness, by a spirit of mushiness, or sometimes by fear of appearing to "Platonize," more than one exegesis will have been contaminated with it. One of the following chapters will furnish us examples.[12] But, as a whole, our Middle Ages have not succumbed to it. In the wake of Saint Gregory, it was understood that to look in ancient Scripture for the "incarnate wisdom of God" was essentially "to reduce the sense to its interior features and . . . to examine it . . . according to the spirit."[13] It knew how to "lift itself up to the splendor of the mystery,"[14] the mystery "sparkling as the rays of the sun."[15] Through the mystery of Christ, or, more exactly, within this mystery itself, it knew how to penetrate right to the "depths of God."

Altum intus! The depth within! This is how Christian allegory is accomplished.

If one took account only of certain words, without considering the things, [Christian allegory] would sometimes offer a certain resemblance to philosophical allegory as the ancients often practiced it, as has been seen, regarding their myths and their poems:

The deep man conceals a mystery under a story.[16]

Yet it has required much incomprehension, much polemical spirit, much contempt even in the manner of treating the texts, to come to confuse, in the course of the most recent centuries, two things quite opposed to each other, owing to certain common expressions and analogous customs. We have gone so far as to regard as a simple application to the Bible of pagan exegesis and forms of thought, that which was on the contrary the proper mark of Christian thought and the form in which its unique originality was expressed. For the first, in fact, there is nothing historical, not only in the brute datum, but in the meaning that one draws from it. The first of these two contrasts has already occupied us: we must now devote ourselves to seeing the second better. If Christian allegory differs from pagan allegory by its foundation, it does not differ from it at all *by its terminus*. By the latter no less than by the former, instead of thinning out history or of seeing it at most as a simple "support," it gives it value. If it is indeed, at the bottom line, a dive into the "mystery," it in no way follows that it is, as it has been accused of, a "flight from history."[17]

Let us recall the so expressive previously cited remark of Sallust the Philosopher: "It is not that these things have ever arrived!" In relating the histories of which he made himself the exegete, Sallust "did not allow himself to be misled by incredible fables or absurd miracles"; in all of them he saw only "poetic fictions": this is what his friend and panegyrist Julian tells us.[18] But on the other hand — and this is the aspect that interests us now — what Sallust found signified in these fables was also, in his own words, "things that did not take place at just any moment, but those that endure forever."[19] In other words, they were abstract, atemporal truths; they were ideas about the world, the soul, divinity; speculations of a moral or metaphysical order. Thus Julian himself recognized in the virile attributes of Mercury Quadratus the plenitude and fecundity of reason, or in the peripeties of the myth of Attis the vicissitudes of the soul in search of the divine. Others saw in the labors of Hercules a symbol of the struggle of good against evil, and so on.[20] For a long time, it seems that one had looked no further, to interpret myths like that of Adonis, than for vegetal or agrarian symbolism.[21] It is in this way, remarked Origen, that the subtlest minds of paganism attempted to spiritualize their fables; this is how they treat their "mythic theology."[22] Whether an elementary naturalism or a transcendent spirituality, in either case, it would be merely a question of theories. A scholar of the eighteenth century has nicely defined the essence and the spirit of this pagan allegory, if not the conscious intention of the authors themselves of these myths, by saying of those who delivered themselves over to this game: "They have

The Christian Novelty

shut almost all the secrets of theology, morality, and physics within a realm of fictions."[23]

Now in these words he expressed the exact antithesis of Christian allegory. Here again, the verbal analogy is deceptive; there is no more to rely upon it than upon others, the analogy of the word "sacramentum,"[24] for example, or that of the word "mysticum."[25] In Christian exegesis, there is no longer myth on the one hand; there is no longer naturalistic thought or philosophical abstraction, on the other. What it proposes is to "introduce by figures" the events and the laws of the old Covenant "to the sight of the Truth," which is nothing but "the fullness of the Christ."[26] So thereby one is clearly going, at least in a first step, from history to history — though assuredly not to mere history, or not to what is merely beyond history.[27] One is led by a series of singular facts up to one other singular Fact; one series of divine interventions, whose reality itself is significant, leads to another sort of divine intervention, equally real, but deeper and more decisive. Everything culminates in one great Fact, which, in its unique singularity, has multiple repercussions; which dominates history and which is the bearer of all light as well as of all spiritual fecundity: *the Fact of Christ.* As Cassiodorus puts it, a bit crudely perhaps but forcefully, there is not any one theory or one invention of a philosopher, "which is formed in our hearts with a fantastic imagination"; this is not one idea, itself fitting, happy and fruitful even: this is a reality "which grasps an existing person," a reality inserted at a certain moment in our history and which blossoms in the Church, a "gathering of all the holy faithful, one in heart and soul, the bride of Christ, the Jerusalem of the age to come."[28] If, then, with Cicero, one is willing to call philosophy "every knowledge of the best things and every practice which is related to them," then one could well say that the fruit of Christian allegory is "philosophy." But we can do so only under the proviso that it is "Christian philosophy," or "heavenly" or "divine" philosophy,[29] or the "philosophy of Christ" that our exegetes used to oppose to pagan or secular philosophy as the principle of the only knowledge and the only practice of "the best things," namely: the mystery hidden in Scripture, from whence flows knowledge of Christ and life in Christ. This is "the true philosophy," the life of charity within the Trinitarian life and in the image of the Trinitarian life;[30] this is the wisdom that the "true Plato" teaches from the height of the cross. In a more radical expression, worthy of Origen: this is the Philosophy that Christ is himself, just as he is himself the Kingdom *Ipsa Philosophia Christus. Christ is philosophy itself.*[31]

"The Old Testament is an immense prophecy whose guiding struc tures must be rediscovered, a mysterious land where the royal avenues that lead to Christ are discerned."[32]

Nevertheless reproaches have been directed more than once against the ancient apologists of the Church, especially Origen, Saint Augustine, and Saint Gregory of Nazianzus, for having manifested inconsistency and polemical partiality and for having fallen in "between the straw and the beam," by criticizing an attitude in the philosophers of paganism that they themselves adopted. Some have declared themselves to be surprised by so "paradoxical" a situation: on the one side and the other, in fact, in the nature of its starting point as well as in its point of arrival, allegorical exegesis would be the same, and, at bottom, the Christian would reproach the pagan — as, on the other hand, the pagan would the Christian — only for "the choice of the objects that he subjects to this exegesis." But in reality Christian and pagan exegesis are based, each of them, upon two quite different distinctions which can be retrieved. When Saint Paul and all Christians after him distinguish the letter and the spirit, or the biblical history and mystery of which it is the bearer, or the figure and its fulfillment, or the shadow and the truth, they are not at all inspired, even indirectly, by the Platonic distinction between opinion and true knowledge, to oppose, as did an Antisthenes or a Zeno, an exegesis *kata alētheian* to an exegesis *kata doxan*. This last distinction, between a banal, purely apparent sense, or at least one not going beyond the truth of appearance, and a deep meaning, the only real meaning, was familiar to the Greeks, and one would be right to say also that it commanded the whole exegetic effort among the commentators on Homer. But it does not furnish us a general definition of allegory, holding good for all cases and for all situations. One would not find it in Saint Paul, either in the Epistle to the Romans or in the second Epistle to the Corinthians, nor would one see it even in the author of the Epistle to the Hebrews[33] (despite the bit of "Platonism" that one can point out in him), nor in the cloud of witnesses who comment on or are inspired by these texts. It is not sufficient here to speak, in vague fashion, at once of parables and of the tendency of the Fathers of the Church "always to look for a deep sense hidden under the literal sense in the stories of the holy books."[34] Two senses that get mixed together,[35] or two senses the first of which, quite real in itself albeit external, ought merely to efface itself before the other or transform itself into the other starting from a creative or transfigurative Event, are not mutually exclusive, in the way that appearance and reality, or a "lie" and the truth, exclude each other. Neither, again, does the appearance or the "lie" that Greek mythology speaks of correspond to the "letter" or the "history" of the Christian exegete; the "truth" of the first does not, even from an entirely formal point of view, correspond to the truth of the second — to the "ventura Veritas" ["truth about to come"], to the "futura Veritas" ["truth about to be"] which is Jesus Christ prefigured in the Scripture, the Word of God incarnated for the salvation of human beings. Jesus is "truth," he is "full of truth," because he has made "every shadow and every cloud" to cease: this is a reality that does succeed upon another, that replaces it and takes it over, that justifies it, and at the same time makes it recognize that it has superseded it and made it perish.[36] So, far from constituting even an approximate analogue of the pairs of Greek terms that one might be tempted to assimilate them to, the Christian pairs constitute their antithesis. The union of their two terms in the distinction, which is at the same time the union within the distinction of the two "Testaments" bringing them together, introduces us, so to speak, into a universe of thought that the philosophers, reasoning about and refining their myths, would never have suspected. It is, to summarize everything in a single expression, one of the forms under which the *Christian Newness* appears for us.

On the one side and the other, therefore, the very structure of the symbolism is different. Doubtless the contrast does not strike with full force on every page. In addition to a part of the vocabulary, in addition to usage and the designation of grammatical allegory, the Christian writers, let us repeat, have more than a method in common with the pagan writers. Those of the patristic age, if not those of the Middle Ages, in their controversial writings, love to put in relief certain analogies which might mislead a hasty reader — although even then they speak of it often enough to make the divergences show up.[37] Whether they want to justify the Christian position in the face of those who attack it or try to win the still unfaithful soul over to Christ, this is a tactic common to the apologists of all times.[38] Those of the first centuries often, under diverse aspects, relate the pagan myths with the datum of their faith. Clement of Alexandria, for example, observes that, with regard to their obscurity, the enigmas of the Egyptians are similar to those of the Hebrews and that the Greeks themselves strongly relished this sort of veiled language.[39] However, he used the "poetic psychology" of the fable more boldly to introduce his readers "into the divine dance," that is to say, to lead them to the Mystery of Christ, by "explaining" it to them "by images that are familiar to them."[40] For him, however, as well as for all those who believe they can discern an "aping of the devil" in the myths, the Christian datum, taken in its prophetic announcement or in its realization "in the fullness of time," is always normative, and their very explanations are the negation of the analogy or parallelism, the very idea of which has too often been attributed to them.

Assuredly, whoever should not recognize for himself *the Fact of Christ*, in all its singularity, or should feel some pain at recognizing historically all its causal force, would never succeed at thoroughly comprehending the reverberation of this great Fact in the consciousness of those who were the first to perceive it and to interpret the old Bible accordingly. But every historian can perceive at least something of the extraordinary backwash that it produced; every historian can also see, in the biblical allegorism of the first Christian centuries, the essential role placed by this major datum which is called the "New Testament." He can now ask himself this simple question: where would one find, in the facts of history, or only in the thought or imagination of the Greek allegorists, the irruption of some "new testament" analogous to that of the Christians, an irruption which one day would have turned the ancient exegesis of the Homeric poems upside-down by overturning the very being of their exegete? Where would one find, in Cornutus and the rest, anything even remotely resembling the opposition between the *oldness* of the letter and the *newness* of the spirit? "Christ has been beaten, put on a cross, and this is how He has forced the sources of the New Testament to spurt forth. . . . If he had not been beaten, if the water and the blood had not flowed from his side, we would still be suffering from the thirst for the Word of God," for we would remain chained to the letter of the Old Testament. "The Sun of Justice, our Lord and Savior, has risen; a man has come of whom it was written: Here he is, his name is Orient; now the light of the knowledge of God has spread over the whole world," for the lamp of the Law has been transformed into a brilliant star. . . .[41]

The great writers of the first centuries, those that are called Irenaeus, Clement, or Origen, have left us in the very exercise of their exegesis, many an indication of the intense sentiment of novelty that roused the faithful of Christ and made the sources of an inexhaustible allegory rise up within them. Let us listen to Origen, for example. It is in the following passage which occurs while he is exposing his principles of scriptural interpretation in the course of the *Periarchōn*, which is the most "Greek" and the most controversial of his works, that Origen proudly proclaimed: "This wisdom of ours has nothing in common with the wisdom of this world."[42] He often vigorously denounces "the dogmas of the philosophers, erroneous and shameful dogmas" that he symbolizes by means of the waters of Egypt.[43] He exhorts his hearers not to desire "the deceptive nourishments of philosophy, which turn one away from the truth."[44] He

The Christian Novelty

celebrates him who, by his coming and self-revelation, has made the walls of Jericho to crumble,[45] that is to say, "destroyed the philosophical dogmas right down to their foundation."[46] Though, fallible like every man, it may occur to him at one time or another unduly to maintain such and such a personal idea on the basis of some text of Scripture, for him allegory was not at all a means of "transforming everything into an idea."[47] It was not this "intellectual alchemy" by which, according to a number of historians, he wanted to change the vile matter of the biblical letter into the gold of science, by recovering among the sacred writers the doctrines that the philosophers of Greece had been considered to have borrowed from them long ago.[48] What their exegesis was looking for was not "metaphysical truths";[49] it was the traces of the living, personal, incarnate, vivifying Truth. If everything did not already prove it to us, the passages that have just been cited should suffice to assure us that this allegorist, understood perfectly on this point by a long posterity, did not mean to oppose one philosophy to another or one system to another. Against doctrines of an atemporal and impersonal character, using a method that was appropriate to them, against human and abstract teachings, he did not erect any other doctrine or any other teaching, which would have been of the same character albeit of different content. He rejected the very enterprise of "philosophy," and the form of exegesis that it used, as tangled in idolatry and lies. What he, like Saint Paul, opposed to the "philosophers" was "the foolishness of God," which confounds their wisdom.[50] This wisdom was, once again, a Fact: *the Fact of Christ*. He pointed out this singular Fact, this marvelous reality, the likes of which had never been seen, with all its presuppositions and its consequences; he discerned its proclamation everywhere in Scripture and its flowering in the Church. At the summit of history, the Fact of Christ supposed history, and its radiance transfigured history. In this sense, which is essential, and too much misunderstood, there is no thought more "historical" than the thought of Origen. Now it did nothing in this but express the Christian reality itself, as lived by the Christian community as a whole, but reflected in this great mind with a particular verve (albeit expressed with its particular faults as well, as happens in every human work). So it is not surprising to find it subsequently reproduced, adapted, amplified everywhere, among the commentators of the great patristic epoch, and then among those of the Middle Ages, especially in the West.[51] This immense diffusion cannot be explained merely by the direct or indirect influence of a thinker of genius: it presupposes the everliving action of this very reality at which each Christian generation continued to slake its thirst.

So the Christian exegetes have practiced "allegory" — if one wants to look deeply into the matter — only in a sense quite remote from that of the ancient philosophers. They saw in it, as they do not cease to assure us, a requirement of their faith in Christ. Thus, those among them who, in the first centuries, have criticized pagan allegorism did not commit any "imprudence" by this and did not fall into any "contradiction." They themselves were quite able often to practice "the most intemperate figurative interpretation" upon the Bible; they could also, on the other hand, praise the benefits of allegory in terms strongly analogous to those which the pagan authors had used, and even in a thought sometimes quite near to theirs: but it was essentially not the same sort of allegory that they were talking about.[52] So let us not conclude that, in these centuries, "pagans and Christians agree to recognize the benefits that myth procures for religious philosophy"; or again that, "in the opinion of antiquity both Christian and classical," thanks to a certain number of common characteristics recognized on both sides, "mythic or allegorical expression is found to be naturally adapted to the object of religious philosophy"; or again, that pagans and Christians professed the same doctrine concerning "the prophetic value of myth and allegory." Thus we would not know how to treat pagan exegesis and Christian exegesis, pagan thought and Christian thought in this way without many distinctions and restrictions, nor to lump them together under a common heading that would proclaim "the philosophical unity of mythology." It would be better to maintain "the indisputable originality of Christian allegory" and "the novelty of Pauline allegorism,"[53] whose fundamental principles have always remained present to the Christian consciousness. While looking everywhere in Scripture for prefigurations of all that constitutes Christianity — despite the illusions or insufficiencies of this search — the Christian exegetes have not attempted to harmonize "myth" with "reason" as has rightly enough been said of the "allegorical" interpretations of Homer, that is to say, [to harmonize "myth"] with the dominant sentiments and ideas of a later age.[54] They did not intend to extract an abstract science or wisdom of a "physical," "moral," "metaphysical," or "theological" type from the ancient sacred books considered alone. Their goal was not to construct, in the manner of the "philosophers," a "religious philosophy" thanks to a certain sort of interpretation of the biblical "myth."[55] What they really wanted to construct was, according to a formula that would become popular as has just been seen starting with Saint Gregory the Great, "the edifice of the faith." Because they had a very lively sense of it, a sense indissolubly connected to their faith, they wanted to show, with the instruments that were at their disposal, how all of biblical history bears witness to Christ. They also wanted to show how, in turn, this history, now contemplated in the light of Christ, takes on a completely Christian signification thanks to the "sense of Christ" that Saint Paul spoke about,[56] to "this sense of Christ that no one can receive unless he has rested upon the breast of Jesus."[57]

4. The Edification of the Faith

No more than life in Christ is the knowledge of Christ drawn from Scripture accessible to the natural man, the one who confines himself to mere appearances even in his deepest reflections. Interior and spiritual, the object of allegory is by that very fact a "hidden" object: *mysticus, occultus*. It conceals itself from carnal eyes. Pagans do not perceive it, nor do unbelieving Jews, nor those "carnal" Christians who see in Christ nothing but a human being.[1] It is like a fire hidden in a rock: so long as one holds it in one's hand to observe its surface, it stays cold; but when one strikes it with iron, at that point the spark flashes forth.[2] As it is for Christ, so it is for the Scriptures: with a glance piercing like fire, their secret ought, so to speak, to be wrenched free from them — and it is the same secret: for it is with regard to the written word of God as it is with the incarnate word of God. The letter is his flesh; the spirit is his divinity. Letter and flesh are like milk, the nourishment of children and the weak; spirit and divinity are the bread, the solid nourishment.[3] A bit earlier with regard to history, we have alluded to the twofold and single "humility" of the letter and the flesh: now it is necessary to recognize the twofold and single marvel which hides itself under this humility: that of divinity, and that of the spirit.[4]

"The great Origen" has explained these equivalencies, just as Bossuet indicated again with admiration in his *Panegyric of Saint Paul*.[5] In the West, Saint Ambrose and Saint Augustine have adopted his explanation. The Spaniards Heterius and Beatus,[6] after Bachiarius, have reproduced it. It continues to be transmitted. We find it in Cardinal Humbert, in Rupert, in Saint Bernard, from whom Aelred of Rievaulx[7] and Isaac of Stella[8] received it. The *Glossa ordinaria* confirms it.[9] "The Body of Christ is also understood to be God's Scripture," wrote the author of the *De unitate Ecclesiae conservanda*.[10] One day Claudius of Turin already recalled this traditional teaching to his correspondent Abbot Theodemir, as a well-known truth:

For you know this very well, just as the Word of God clothed with flesh in Mary came into the world — and what was seen in him was other than what was understood of him: for the aspect of flesh in him was patent to all, whereas recognition of his divinity was given to the few and the elect — so too the Word of God, having come to men through the prophets and the lawgiver, was brought forth not without fitting garments. For, just as there his flesh is covered, so here is He covered with the veil of the letter: as the letter is seen as flesh, whilst the hidden spiritual sense within is sensed as divinity.

Such then is what we now find as we search through the book of Leviticus, in which the rites of sacrifices, the diversity of victims, and the ministries of the priests are described; but this is done according to the letter, which, like the flesh of the Word of God, is also a cloak for his divinity, whether they perhaps look upon them worthily or hear them unworthily: yet blessed are those eyes that see the inner object of the divine spirit under the veil of the letter, and blessed are those who have the pure ears of the inner man to hear these things.[11]

If, from the letter of the Scripture to the flesh of the Word incarnate, both the one and the other being conceived as a "garment," there is scarcely more than a comparison — albeit already based upon the very deep relation of Scripture to the Word — from the object of allegory to the divinity of the Word there is more than an analogy: there is, at the endpoint, coincidence. The divinity of the Word of God incarnate is in fact the central object of allegory. It is revealed, however, only to the "eyes of the heart,"[12] to those "inner eyes,"[13] those "spiritual eyes,"[14] those "eyes of the soul,"[15] those "better eyes," that are opposed to the eyes of the flesh[16] and which are in reality the eyes received from God, the eyes "illuminated by the Gospel"[17] or, following a frequent expression, the "eyes of faith."[18] *For faith has her own eyes.*[19] Faith is the light "that makes one see the light of the spirit in the law of the letter"; it is like a lamp lit in the night, penetrating the thick cloud of all the biblical "sacraments" which surround it.[20] We are therefore "to be imbued in the faith through allegory."[21] The truths of the allegory, "mysteries of Christ and the Church," are the "mysteries of the faith" hidden "in the ceremonies of the Law."[22] They are the "sacraments of our faith."[23] Thus again, it is by the footsteps of the faith, "fidei passibus,"[24] that one arrives at a knowledge of them. Everything that allegory discovers is "pertinent to the instruction of the faith";[25] everything in it serves "for the edification of the catholic faith."[26] By allegory one is established "in the revelation of the faith toward a knowledge of the truth," or "in the belief of the unfeigned catholic faith,"[27] "in the fullness of the catholic faith,"[28] or again, "in the belief of the perfect faith," "in the purity of faith."[29] This is our "exercise," which "opens" for us "the mysteries of the faith,"[30] by making us see everywhere the "accumulated mysteries of the faith and truth of the Gospel."[31] In other words, allegory is not only the sense that one could call apologetic; it is also, the doctrinal sense par excellence. The edifice that it builds is "the edifice of doctrine," as Saint Gregory already called it.[32] *The mystic discourse, solid and dogmatic,* Rabanus Maurus[33] used to say, after Origen.[34] By means of the words of Moses God "instructs the holy Church allegorically."[35] One can therefore define the Christian faith as "allegorica doctrina." In fact, "what is allegory but the mystic doctrine of the mysteries?"[36] Its content is exactly "the doctrine of the holy Church."[37] The allegorical sense of Scripture is "the Catholic sense."[38]

This relation of the faith to allegory, as always when it is a question of effecting passage to a higher order, can be understood only as a relation of reciprocal causality.[39] Again, there are two inverse ways of understanding this causality or this reciprocity here, of making the one or the other of the two terms dominant, according as it is a question of the conversion of Jews or Gentiles. This is normally the understanding of Scriptures, that is to say, for one side the discovery of their allegorical sense, which ought to lead the Jew to believe in Christ, as one sees in the case of the Apostles,[40] for example, or in the case of the disciples of Emmaus, or again in the case of the Samaritan woman: having understood Jesus' explanations, "she learned the sacraments of the Law and believed."[41] Thus the apologists who address themselves to the Jews do not fail, for the most part, to apply themselves to make them see the clarity that Christian allegory sheds on the Scriptures. The bishop Saint Avitus did the same, according to what Gregory of Tours says; he had the custom of exhorting them "to understand the readings spiritually once the veil of the mosaic Law had been left behind."[42] The same obtains once again, some years later, for the *Liber allegoriarum contra Simonem Judaeum* by Peter of Cornwall.[43] Peter intends to convince his partner of the Christian significance of ancient Jewish history:

> I have composed two books. In the first I have inserted not all, but the more useful . . . allegories for the largest part of the whole Old Testament, which speak about our Christ . . . and his Church, to the extent that the holy doctors inspired and taught by Christ have explained them. . . . It was decided that the first book should be called

the Book of the allegories of Peter against Simon the Jew regarding the refutation of the Jews.[44]

It assuredly took nerve to toss the Jewish believer in the Bible into the deep end of Christian intelligibility like this, using a method quite remote from what apologists of our own day have called "minimalist method." The marvelous thing is that, in its apparent lack of realism, it seems not always to have been fruitless — though the Jew before whom one deployed one's resources naturally began by bucking: "Wherever you want, you set up allegories and figures!"[45] Certain apologists showed themselves more sober and more careful, e.g., Peter the Venerable, who did not want to base the essentials of his argument on anything except directly prophetic texts;[46] another example is Joachim of Flora, saying to those whom he aimed to convince: "I leave out the allegorical understanding, which you can listen to only with difficulty."[47] But it is not certain that the choice of an "ad litteram" discussion would always have proceeded from a more objective science.[48]

At any event, the Gentile was normally called to the faith by other means, thanks to the direct preaching of the Gospel and to the miracles that accompanied it; only after the event was he able to see his faith confirmed by the multifarious testimonies that are to be discovered in the ancient Scriptures. This is what Berengaud explains in his commentary on the Apocalypse. He finds a symbol for this duality of orientation, from which a convergence results, in the gates that give entry to the heavenly Jerusalem from two opposed points of the compass:

> The southern gate designates the Old Testament; the northern, the New. Those who are said to come in from the south refer to the Jews; those that come in from the north, the Gentiles. The Jews . . . were entering through the southern gate, since, believing that the Messiah was prophesied in many ways in the Old Testament and was prefigured in various ways, their scriptures drew them to take up faith in Christ. Deserting idolatry, however, the Gentiles . . . were wont to enter through the northern gate, since, hearing the teaching of the Gospel and marveling at the powers that were propagated through Christ and his ministers, they ran to accept the faith of Christ.[49]

With Berengaud, Saint Gregory has observed: "Coming to the faith by the Lord's generosity, we learned the Law through the holy Gospel, not the Gospel through the Law"; and it is in Ezekiel that he found the symbolic explication of it. The prophet, according to him, made allusion to the process of the faithful having come from the world of the Gentiles, by mentioning the four animals that represent the four evangelists before mentioning "the wheel within the wheel," which represents the New Testament hidden by allegory under the letter of the Old.[50] "As a confirmation of our faith," Paschasius Radbertus will say in taking up again the symbol explained by Gregory.[51] But for those very ones who came to the Gospel before getting to know Moses, it is far from unprofitable that, by a new gift from God, they should come to see clearly, as the *Caroline Books* say, "that the letter of the Old Testament is full of the mysteries of the grace of the Gospel."[52] It is also far from being unprofitable, and is even quite necessary that the *Ecclesia ex Judaeis* and the *Ecclesia ex Gentibus*, arriving from two opposite points on the horizon, should come to meet each other and finally form just one single Church, in a common interpretation of the two Testaments and of their unity.[53] It is this that Berengaud also points out while bringing the development of his symbol to completion. For all that, continuing to read the Apocalypse through Ezekiel and transforming the hints of the prophet, he supposes that the two groups of pilgrims entering by the two opposite gates had been forbidden to start off again from the gate that they had crossed on their arrival; the lesson that he drew from it is subtle:

> The Jews whom the understanding of the Old Testament led to take up faith in Christ ought not to turn back from whence they had come, namely, to fulfill the observances of the Law in carnal fashion, but ought rather to come forth through the northern gate, namely to betake themselves to meditate upon and scrutinize the teaching of the Gospel, so that they might learn to fulfill spiritually what they used to perform previously in carnal fashion. The Gentiles, on the other hand, who entered through the northern gate, i.e., those who were made sons of the Church through the teaching of the Gospel, ought not to return from whence they came, namely, to regress to studying the errors of the philosophers: but rather, after taking up the faith and teaching of the Gospel, they ought to betake themselves to the southern gate, i.e., to examine the teaching of the Old Testament, so that the faith of Christ might be strengthened within them once they have discovered that Christ had been predicted in it in many ways.[54]

Another symbol again procured the same lesson. It was furnished by the two apostles Peter and John running to the sepulcher on the morning of the resurrection. While Peter served as figure of the Gentiles, John, running ahead of him but entering after him, figured as the Jewish people, who were the first to benefit from the prophetic announcement but who were late in believing. The only thing that interests us here is the feature which a text found in the Victorine *Miscellanea* notes in this connection:

> So John sees the linens first but entered afterward, since, as has been said, the Synagogue took up the prophecy about the one to come.... But Peter enters first and catches sight of the linens later, since the Church of the Gentiles did not come to the faith of Christ through the prophets, but to an understanding of the prophets through the faith of Christ.[55]

To describe this meeting of two opposite movements and to synthesize two long series of interlocking rather than antithetical traditional texts, one could perhaps add that allegory, taken globally or in some of its major themes, leads one to Christ, who is the locus of this accord, by showing the accord between the two Testaments.[56] On the other hand, it is necessary first to believe in Christ and to profess the dogmas that concern him so as to be capable of recognizing him on each page in all the detail of the allegories,[57] detail that faith is, moreover, far from imposing, and so as to give oneself the joy of illustrating the greater allegory through the indefinite multiplication of this detail. Hence we will say, on the one hand, with Othloh of Saint Emmeran: "Any faithful person can readily believe when he considers how much consonance there is between the foretold and the fulfilled, that may also come about in the future,"[58] and in the same way we will hold, with Richard of Saint Victor, that this is a "very solid confirmation of our faith: that the prophets and evangelists so concordantly enunciate the same message";[59] but we shall affirm, on the other hand, with Alexander of Canterbury, that, to penetrate into the cellar where the wines of allegory are tasted, it is necessary to pass through the gate of "correct faith,"[60] and we must avow in the same way with Rupert that, in the luxuriance of its development within the Church, far from constituting a necessary step, allegory is entirely "a fruit of conversion to Christ and of the Christian faith."[61] Once the Gentiles were converted by the Apostles, said Apringius, once the Churches were founded, at that point "the consolation of interpreting the prophetic Scriptures was given."[62] But in reality, let us say it again, there is essentially no point to look for any priority of allegory perceived by relation to faith nor of faith received by relation to the perception of allegory: each mutually conditions the other. It is in one and the same indivisible act — the elements and logical instants of which later theology will analyze — that gives access to the one and to the other under the action of the Spirit of Christ. Finally, whether Christ be recognized by means of prophecy, or prophecy by means of Christ, it always remains that the understanding of prophecy, i.e., the allegory revealed in Christ, has an important place at the basis of the faith of the world, indeed at the basis of the believing universe:

> The Prophets, who were not understood and upon whom the world believing in the Lord were built, have been revealed.[63]

Now the precise significance of the three words that end the first line of our distich can be understood: *quid credas allegoria* ["allegory (teaches) what you should believe"; see Chapter Seven, §1, n. 1]. These three words are the exact equivalent of the Gregorian formula: *"allegory builds up the faith."*[64] The formula is often repeated, whether *ad verbum*: as by Angelome of Luxueil,[65] Guibert of Nogent,[66] and John of Salisbury;[67] or in approximate terms: as by Isidore of Seville,[68] John Scotus,[69] Gerhoh of Reichersberg,[70] or by Hervaeus of Bourg Dieu. "They were promoted to the spiritual sense and through faith came to the Church,"[71] says this last author. "We have crossed the shadows of allegories; the faith has been built up,"[72] says Saint Bernard. "These things have been said for the building up of the faith,"[73] says Aelred of Rievaulx. Hugh of Saint Victor expresses himself many times in analogous fashion: "Allegory informs correct faith,"[74] or: "In history you have the wherewithal to admire God's deeds; in allegory, that to believe his sacraments,"[75] or again: "Meditation according to allegory acts to construct the understanding and the form of faith."[76] The *Glossa ordinaria* on the Apocalypse speaks of the sevenfold Spirit "through whom the faith is disclosed."[77] Gerhoh of Reichersberg says that in the perception of the mysteries of Scripture "the faith is informed";[78] John, "the man of God," says that by assiduous meditation upon the Scriptures "the faith is instructed."[79] Garnier of Rochefort in a sermon evokes the things that are "to be imparted in the faith through allegory."[80] John of Kelso, writing to Adam Scotus, describes the work of the exegete in these terms: "While he lays open the mysteries of the history through the exercise of allegory, he raises the craftsmanship of the mind into the treasure chest of faith."[81] Adam himself gives the allegorical part of his treatise on the Tabernacle the title: "On Christ's Tabernacle, which consists in the faith,"[82] etc.

In the majority of these texts, as verbs like "aedificatur," "informatur," "eruditur" show, it is not merely a question of the first flash of faith. It is also and even more an issue of its taking hold in the mind of the believer, of his progressive illumination, of the objective construction of the doctrinal edifice by the mysteries of allegory. "The instruction of the faith is to be found in allegory,"[83] says Alexander of Canterbury. Through the cultivation of the second of the biblical senses, the faith is affirmed, nourished, deepened, extended. Moreover, as one sees clearly enough, this faith is always the specifically Christian faith: "the things that are to be believed in the new law," will be the comment of Nicholas of Lyra. It is a question of the "faith of the New Testament,"[84] of the "faith of Christ,"[85] of the "faith of the Lord,"[86] of the "faith of the incarnation of the Lord";[87] it is a question of the "faith of the Redeemer,"[88] of the "faith of the Passion of Christ," or of his "Resurrection."[89] It is a matter of the "faith of one who is turned to the Lord,"[90] or again, as, after Origen,[91] Bede, Sedulius Scotus, Rabanus Maurus, and others spoke of the "evangelical faith,"[92] and, as Berengaud, Rupert, and Irimbert said, of the "apostolic faith."[93] It is therefore always a question of "our faith,"[94] of "our Catholic faith,"[95] which is to say, of this "faith of the Church,"[96] in which we share: the only "complete,"[97] "full,"[98] "finished"[99] faith, without prejudice to this faith which ought first to attach itself to the ancient biblical facts, this "faithfulness of the report,"[100] "fidelity of the deeds,"[101] "faithfulness of the history,"[102] "faith regarding the past,"[103] of this faith which constitutes part of the "foundation" of the edifice and which, as the very faith in God, is common to us along with the Jews. Saint Gregory himself is eager to make it more precise: it is necessary that the story of the Holy Spirit "should shine on us through the spiritual understanding, and yet the sense should not depart from fidelity to history."[104] The two acceptations are also found in Saint Isidore of Seville, for whom, on the one hand, "faith" coincides with the "understanding of the sacraments,"[105] and who nevertheless writes, on the other hand, with respect to the Law: "It is necessary to keep the faith historically, and . . . to understand the law spiritually."[106]

There is a certain difference between the habitual language of Saint Gregory and that of Saint Augustine. While Gregory sees in allegory principally "the edification of the faith," Augustine sees in it rather, starting from the faith, the entry into "understanding"; he readily makes the faith line up with the milk of the letter, or of the flesh, and understanding

The Edification of the Faith

line up with the solid nourishment of the spirit or of divinity.[107] Doubtless there was no need to force the contrast. The Gregorian formulation was already to be read in Augustine, albeit in another context,[108] and on his own side Gregory sometimes approaches the Augustinian manner of opposing the Old Testament and the New, or history and allegory, like faith and sight: "If we are intent upon the history, we believe what it has said; if on allegory, we see what it has foretold,"[109] or like faith and understanding: "so that one may have faith in the truth of the history and one may also get a spiritual understanding of the mysteries of allegory."[110] The contrast exists nevertheless.

The passages in which Saint Augustine opposes believing and comprehending, or faith and understanding, are numerous, almost as many as those in which he opposes authority and reason.[111] Though he does not restrict himself to an absolutely fixed vocabulary, the relations of the two senses of Scripture are for him generally those of faith and understanding. In the *De Genesi ad litteram*, the "faith in the things accomplished" is opposed to the "prefigured understanding"[112] and in the *De vera religione*, the "faith in the temporal things" is opposed to the "understanding the eternal ones."[113] In fact, if it is proper to the faith to search, whilst it is proper to the understanding to find,[114] was it not quite fitting to designate the passage from history to allegory, or from the "res gesta" to the finally discovered "mysterium,"[115] or from the Old Testament to the New, as a passage from *fides* to *intellectus?* Were not the rules of Tyconius, that Augustine set great store by, drawn up for "the understanding of the Scriptures"?[116] The principal Augustinian texts concerning the understanding of the faith — we have perhaps not emphasized it sufficiently — are encountered in passages devoted to the interpretation of Scripture. This is notably the case for the classic text from the *Epistle to Consentius*:

> He who understands by true reason what he merely used to believe already is surely to be preferred over him who still desires to understand what he believes; but if he does not even desire to do so and thinks that they are to be understood by merely believing, then he does not know what the faith is for.... Love the understanding intensely, since even the holy Scriptures themselves cannot be useful to you unless you understand them rightly.[117]

This formula: *intellectum valde ama (love the understanding intensely)*, is therefore not a vague and banal appeal to value the things of the understanding: it is a bit of advice for a very precise object. The understanding in question is the understanding of the faith, and the latter renders itself immediately concrete in understanding Scripture. Augustine wants it to be "right"; but by this "right understanding," without which he declares that Scripture remains useless, he does not understand merely avoiding absurdities concerning the letter, since the faith, which precedes understanding, is already supposed to be correct. For him, understanding is not right to the extent that the mind has not rightly penetrated certain great things taught by the letter of Scripture. At that point there is not an underestimation of the faith at all, but a certain restriction of the field that this concept of *fides* covers, and this remark itself ought immediately to be nuanced. For the Augustinian doctrine on the matter is not restricted to the examination of the relation between the two Testaments. It embraces a vaster horizon. Being in itself a vision *(visio, species)*, the understanding of the faith, for Augustine, cannot have attained its fullness by the discovery of the mysteries of Christ under the letter of the Old Testament. Definitive in itself, this fullness is not yet entire; it is not at all complete, in our manner of understanding it. If, indeed, the Mystery of Christ does not allow for a beyond, then the knowledge that we get of it remains still subject to the laws of our present condition. Hence in the New Testament there is a dogmatic datum which we must always try to understand better. It is necessary for us to love this understanding; it is necessary for us to desire it, but what we discover of it is never enough to let us say that we ultimately possess it. Having to look again, it is still a faith. Without distinction from one Testament to the other, we are all, therefore, in this new sense, in the "time of faith" until the day of perfect vision.[118] We must attach ourselves again to the "faithfulness of temporal history," to submit ourselves to the "humility of historical faith."[119] By this "faith in the temporal facts" — which are, in this perspective, now par excellence the facts of the Word incarnate, which the Eternal One has accomplished for us and suffered in the human being that he has assumed in time: we prepare ourselves to "grasp the eternal realities in our turn."[120] "In the things that have arisen he is for us faith, the very one who is truth in things eternal."[121]

For all that, this more complete, more comprehensive perspective does not keep Saint Augustine from making *fides* correspond more especially to the letter of Scripture and from seeing in the passage to the New Testament a first passage to *intellectus*.

Saint Leo at this point brings us a faithful echo of the Augustinian language. He whose turn of mind is so dogmatic, nevertheless speaks much more of understanding than of faith when he explains what the Christian ought to look for in Scripture:

> So that we may venerate the order of events not only by believing but also by understanding them.[122]
>
> So that understanding may keep perspicuous what history has made known.[123]
>
> Now it is necessary for the universal Church to be instructed with greater understanding and enkindled with more fervent hope.[124]

Now, in the medieval tradition, this language is much less frequent. Saint Gregory came after Saint Augustine and Saint Leo. Doubtless one does encounter expressions like "fides historiae"[125] or "fides historica"[126] in their Augustinian acceptation applied to the facts of the Old Testament; but the word there is often taken in an acceptation so little specified that one might as well use it to designate the belief that any fact whatsoever related in a secular document deserves. "To follow the faith of the history" is to rely on a serious reporter.[127] For example, in his *Gesta Friderici*, Otto of Freising speaks of "exact fidelity to history";[128] or again, one of the continuators of Sigebert of Gembloux says: "the trustworthiness of no history is free from corruption."[129] On the other hand, a more rigorous relationship is observed between *fides* in the pregnant, theological sense, and *mysterium* or *allegoria*: "ready belief in the right faith is found in allegory."[130] To pass from history to allegory or from the letter to the mystery or from the shadow to the truth, is without a doubt always to pass to spiritual understanding: but it is also, thereby, "to be converted by the faith,"[131] "to find the order of faith."[132] In the perception of the unity of the two Testaments there is, in the strongest sense of both words, a "fides veritatis."[133]

5. The Gregorian Middle Ages

In this fact of vocabulary we have, it seems, an index of the preponderant influence exercised by Saint Gregory — an influence mingled with that of Origen, who himself also took "spiritual understanding" and "the faith of Christ"[1] as equivalent terms and set the discovery of the "mystery" in relation with "the order of the faith."[2] "The enormous popularity" of Saint Gregory during the Middle Ages has been too readily attributed to the fact that his intellectual level was inferior to that of a Saint Augustine.[3] There have been complaints at seeing in the great pope almost exclusively the author of the *Dialogues*,[4] because this work seems more than any other to bear witness to the abasement of the old Christian culture. Some have used Saint Gregory as a model to sketch that credulous and superstitious "popular Catholicism" that had characterized the centuries of the Middle Ages.[5] At any event, all this involved an undue neglect of the *Moralia* and the *Homilies on Ezekiel*. With respect to these last two works, another historian, though an admirer of Gregory, is astonished "that he had not reserved the discussion of such problems to the little circle of his own monastery."[6] Yet his contemporaries and indeed the whole religious Middle Ages protest in advance against such astonishment.

Indeed, for most of our exegetes, Gregory is the first amongst the masters. From generation to generation, there are disciples who say of him: "our Gregory,"[7] just as the admirers of Vergil used to say: "our Vergil." Some go so far as to say with a hint of tenderness: "Gregory mine."[8] He is the "most wise pope,"[9] the "noble man of eloquence," and "of purest faith in everything," the "venerable and most approved doctor in the catholic faith";[10] he is the "blessed pope and most gentle doctor,"[11] the "marvelous doctor,"[12] "magnificent doctor,"[13] "conspicuous and notable doctor of the Church."[14] But he is not only in general terms "the immense splendor of the human race";[15] he is not only the "consul of God," as his epitaph says, but "the great mirror and tree trunk of God's Church,"[16] the admirable guardian of the universal Church, "just like a type of most luminous Argus," "just like an Argus, with eyes everywhere":[17] he is also, more specifically, the "outstanding homilist";[18] he is the "homilist of the Church" par excellence.[19] He is the "clearest expositor of holy Scripture,"[20] "the most splendid and powerful expositor,"[21] "the subtlest tracker," "the most sagacious tracker of the Word of God,"[22] "a many-sided interpreter of the divine Scriptures, the sharpest tracker of hidden mysteries."[23] He always speaks "most sweetly and fully,"[24] "most truly and most elegantly."[25] He is the true Chrysostom of the West: "Gregory of Rome, the mouth of gold."[26]

And it does not stop there. Gregory is the "outstanding doctor, inspired by divine breath and one made to imbibe from the highest spring," whose thirty-five books of the *Moralia* are, in the words of Saint Odo of Cluny, so many suns.[27] He is the light placed above all the others in the candelabra:[28]

Brighter than gold, and clearer than any glass,
Overcoming all scents with honey-flowing taste.[29]

By means of his allegorical exegesis, taking Scripture as a bow, he has fired deadly arrows against heresy.[30] Expert also in the four senses, like the primordial river with four branches, he has irrigated all of the paradise, i.e., the whole Church.[31] Like a "silvery pillar," like a "golden chariot-seat,"[32] he sustains and embellishes her as a whole. "A man filled with the Holy Spirit," "taught by the Finger of God," he is "the greatest of the apostolic men."[33] Wisdom herself nods to him so as to take her rest in him.[34] He deserves, as few others do after Saint John, the sacred epithet "theologus,"[35] even "most lucid theologian."[36] He is "the most illustrious of the saints and illustrious Fathers."[37] He is the "vessel of election," "the sweet-sounding organ of the Holy Spirit."[38] No one has a "knowledge of the sacred page" like him.[39] While commenting on the Book of Job and certain pages of Ezekiel, "he manifests the secrets of almost the whole of the new and the old Testament."[40] He has decorated the House of the Lord, says Hugh of Saint Victor, by lavishing upon it the beauties and charms of the truth.[41] In many a spot in Scripture, says another Victorine, namely Godfrey, "by the guidance of grace, he found such great depth of mysteries and upbuilding of morals and dug out such marvelous treasures from the earth, that the world can scarcely more admire such treasures having been discovered in the earth than having been contained in it."[42]

Thus everyone admires, along with Paterius, the "honey of Gregorian eloquence."[43] Among the many commentators on the holy books, each or almost every one would be able to say of Gregory, along with Aldhelm and Bede who allude to his role in the conversion of England at the same time as to the etymology of his name: "our instructor and guide,"[44] "our ever-watchful father."[45] Each could call him, with Alcuin, "our doctor,"[46] "our preacher;"[47] or, with Rabanus Maurus, "most agreeable doctor;"[48] or, with Elmer of Canterbury, "sweetest lord, blessed Gregory;"[49] or again, with Eadmer, to mark the solidity of his character and his work: "a stone made perfectly square."[50] Like Notker the Stammerer, each could declare himself eager for the "Roman delights" that the holy pope's writings offer him;[51] like Grimaldus, another monk of Sankt Gall, each could testify to the love and veneration that Gregory inspires in him.[52] Each or almost each would be ready, along with Hugh of Saint Victor, to say that his writings, full of the love of life eternal, are the sweetest and most beautiful of all;[53] with Rupert of Deutz, that they have both a fullness and a sweetness whose combination constitutes their own proper grace;[54] with Adam Scotus, that in his work as a whole "non minus nitide dixit quam profunde sensit," "he spoke no less handsomely than he perceived deeply";[55] along with John of Salisbury[56] or with Hélinand of Froidmont, that his *Moralia* come forth from the very mouth of the Holy Spirit.[57] Each could sing with Peter Damian, addressing himself to Gregory:

> You marvelously solve the mystic
> Riddles of holy Scripture;
> Truth itself teaches you
> Mysteries of contemplation.[58]

Each could associate himself with the marvelous praise of Geoffrey of Auxerre, in whom we hear Saint Bernard: "How many readers in his Books of the Moralities of Job does holy Gregory smite each day, whilst he argues and searches! How many he wounds while he goads them!"[59] Each would be almost ready to make his own, even in the excess called for by circumstance, the elegy that Saint Isidore of Seville bestowed upon him: "provided with the light of knowledge through the grace of the Holy Spirit to such an extent that not only was there not a single doctor of present times his equal, but none was ever in the past, either."[60] Long after the admiring shock produced by the novelty of his work, Honorius declares him in fact "incomparable to all who went before him."[61] Manegold wanted to recognize no other predecessor for him "in the word of truth and the virtue of God" except Saint Paul alone.[62] Later still, calling upon his authority, Stephen of Tournai will say: "you will not be misled by that outstanding doctor, who, just as he was unwilling to mislead, could not be misled."[63]

The influence of Saint Gregory was quite in accord with the admiration that was expressed for him. It was more extensive than an initial inspection might sometimes have led one to believe.[64] It remained more durable than many have realized.[65] Whether it be through a direct reading or through the common tradition issuing forth from him, practically everyone is, as it were, impregnated with his thought. Saint Isidore of Seville incorporates a part of the *Moralia* into his three books of *Sentences.* Saint Bede, having explicated the Canticle of Canticles in six books, adds a seventh book composed of nothing but extracts from the works of Gregory.[66] The great scholar Lupus of Ferrières celebrated the beauty of his speech as well as the merits of his doctrine and his authority in the Church.[67] Along with Augustine and Dionysius, it is Gregory whom Archbishop Adalberon of Reims had young King Robert read to introduce him into the thoughts of the heavenly Jerusalem.[68] Through his *Regula pastoralis,* Gregory, along with Augustine and Rabanus Maurus, is the master of the art of preaching; through his other works he is the principal source of preaching itself, as well as of spirituality.[69] The orators who, in their sermons to the people, scarcely do more than plagiarize him are many: for example, Aelfric the Englishman in the tenth century.

Scholarly circles are far from neglecting him — for example, that of the School of Laon in the twelfth century. Gratian's *Decretal* is packed with his texts. The *Glossa ordinaria*, which owes much to him, propagates his exegeses. The same goes for the *Allegoriae in totam sacram Scripturam*, and the "striking resemblances" that exist between that collection and the *Gregorianum* due to Garnier of Saint Victor have been noted.[70] Gregory's interpretations of the sacred books are so "ingenious," so "elegant"![71] "Each day, without interruption, countless friars, right down to the simplest and least educated, recite, hear, read, and grasp the *Life* of Saint Gregory, his Homilies, his Dialogues": this testimony of Peter the Venerable[72] holds true for several generations.

The *Moralia in Job* in particular, that work "to which all praise is insufficient,"[73] did not cease to be copied, summarized, compiled, adapted, recast in every order imaginable, from the morning after Gregory's death right up to the thirteenth century. It is recounted everywhere how Tajón of Saragossa miraculously received in Saint Peter's basilica the manuscript of it that had been believed lost.[74] It was tabulated; dictionaries were composed from it; *Excerpta, Floscula, Flores* were extracted from it on all sides. It was held an honor to transcribe it in one's own hand, as was the case with the Bible.[75] Also, as was the case with the Bible and for the Lives of certain celebrated saints, people even went so far as to set it to verse.[76] Like the chief classical texts, it was translated into the vernacular language: at the beginning of the tenth century, an Old German version of it was made at Sankt Gall by Notker Labeo; a Spanish version of it existed in the eleventh century; a partial French translation in the twelfth century, etc.[77] Merely with the *Excerptum* of Paterius, the first of all to follow, one has already, in the judgment of Notker the Stammerer, the wherewithal to acquire "universal wisdom."[78] Remarkably, it was in the first half of the seventh century in distant Ireland that one of the oldest abridgments of the *Moralia* was composed: the author of it was Laidcend (†661), a monk of the Saint Carthach group, one of the masters to whom the Irish "Augustine" (author of the *De mirabilibus sacrae Scripturae*) refers.[79] If the head of the Church of Rome had had little immediate effect upon this independent country, the same was not true of the exegete and the doctor.

Everywhere, then, Gregory's explications were carefully collected and classified. Most especially, his allegories. It is these that Notker praises to his old student Solomon of Constance, calling them "Roman candies."[80] John of Salisbury advises his exiled archbishop Thomas Becket "to reflect on the Psalms or to reread the *Moralia* of blessed Gregory."[81]

To acquire self-knowledge, the humanist Hélinand of Froidmont recommends two works above all others: the *De consideratione* of Saint Bernard is the second; the *Moralia*, the first.[82] In a convent of Franconia, one day in a dream a monk heard demons complaining amongst themselves about the harm that such a book caused them:

> He also heard them saying of Gregory's moral books that they were very bad, like cubes or dice that have five or six dots on every face: since, whichever way you roll them, nothing but the best number showed up, just as the greatest number is always thrown on those cubes.[83]

It has been said that, owing to its constant emphasis on the last days, Gregory's work "powerfully contributed to medieval religion" a "somber and anxious turn";[84] to the contrary, a monk of the twelfth century affirmed that in him it poured calm, serenity, courage, and joy.[85] Sensitive to the "mixture of familiar simplicity and of grandeur"[86] from which it emerged, the Middle Ages devoted to its author a cult of "tenderness." This Gregory, so humane, they say, that he wept over the fate of Trajan,[87] appeared, of all the doctors, "the most accessible and the most lovable."[88] So, for centuries, they do not weary of reading him and rereading him:

> He is to be re-read especially and faithfully.[89]

No more do they grow weary of citing him: "the often mentioned and still more often to be mentioned Gregory."[90] His testimony is called for everywhere: "with Gregory as witness," "I have blessed Gregory as witness."[91] In form and content, his writings are regarded as a family estate. How many authors could say, as does Ambrose Autpert in the preface of his commentary on the Apocalypse: "I strive to be so conformed ... to [Gregory's] manner of speaking, that it may be almost impossible to detect where his words leave off and mine begin."[92] Some, like the abbot John of Gorze, even had such frequent recourse to him that, without even half trying, their own discourse turns out to be a tissue of his expressions;[93] the taste for this exquisite work ended by eliminating their taste for every other.[94] Everyone "uses his words"; many a time allusion is made to them, which every reader or every hearer understands immediately.[95] Gregory's images have become common speech. It is also to Gregory, to that "king of Roman eloquence,"[96] to whom, to a great extent, our Middle Ages owe that beautiful chanting, rhythmic, supple, assonant prose, a bit monotonous perhaps, with its swinging gait, its "ingenious antitheses, strengthened by bits of verbal ingenuity,"[97] with its "measured gait of antiphonally corresponding periods,"[98] which has not always been sufficiently admired later on. If many abuse it to the point of affectation by employing a "disingenuous and artificial manner,"[99] the most well-read and most artistic play it with perfection. Others make more or less successful imitations of it.[100] The very ones who imitate him most praise "his style full of gold and of fire," which Bernard of Cluny declares to be immortal:

> Now his golden and fiery style will never die away;
> A golden page will be begotten through his off-shoots.[101]

Finally, from age to age, everyone takes up his exegesis, often right down to the words,[102] in the stereotypical mold of certain phrases,[103] the "Gregorian utterances in which the keys of this craft are most especially found."[104] It seems that what one day came to Saint Odo of Cluny, may come to many others as well. Having seen Saint Gregory in a dream, the future abbot prostrated himself. Then the pope picks him up, takes a pen that he had behind his ear, and offering it to him says: "Take this pen, brother, and write. . . ."[105]

Whether one makes of it, with Saint Gregory, an object of "faith," or prefers, with Saint Augustine, to speak in his turn of "understanding," the allegorical sense is in any case for everyone *the Christian sense of Scripture*.

In principle, as we have seen, it was revealed all at once by Christ. "Our Lord Jesus Christ suddenly emerged in the clear from the thickest forest of allegorical words, in whose dark density he was hitherto concealed."[106] This sudden revelation is not, however, to be confused with the unexpected improvisation hostile to the tradition of Israel that someone like Marcion imagined.[107] It was being prepared for a long time. The ages of the world succeeded each other, from Adam to Noah, from Noah to Moses, from Moses to David, from David to John the Baptist, each marking a stage, and much progress had been made, a lot of successive "spiritualizations" — as well as a lot of repudiations and darkenings in consciences. But as to the essentials, everything changed only in the "fullness of time." Then, as he had promised his disciples, the resurrected Jesus

> has spoken to their heart, taught them all truth through the Holy Spirit, as it was written: Then he revealed unto them the sense, so

they might understand the Scriptures. On the fiftieth day, moreover, by giving them the Holy Spirit he spoke to their heart, and from then on there were not lacking in the Church those in whose minds he also put a knowledge of the Scriptures.[108]

Moses and Elijah, representing the Law and the Prophets, appeared transfigured and glorified only in the glory of the transfigured Jesus. This is what, as one recalls, the miracle of Cana symbolizes:

> ... The water-jar holding nine gallons is every age:
> The water represents the history; the wine betokens allegory.[109]

For each of us, again in principle, the mystery of allegory opens up all at once, too. Starting from the moment when it is gathered within the bosom of the Church, the Old Testament, once renewed, offers, in a sudden blossoming of springtime, the flowers and fruits of the spiritual senses,[110] which henceforth offer themselves to each generation. We fill our jars with water by reading the unfolding of biblical history, but this still does not give us a single drop of wine:[111] everything subsequently must be done through a miraculous power. You will understand the Scripture, said Origen to the Christians who were listening to him, "with Jesus reciting the law to you and revealing it to your hearts";[112] this is nevertheless only at the instant of the "breaking of the bread," at that miraculous instant when the disciples of Emmaüs truly understood, at a single instant, the whole of Scripture and recognized Christ.[113] And Saint Augustine gave fundamentally the same teaching when, in one of his sermons on Saint John, he juxtaposed the two scenes of Emmaüs and of Cana: "How then did he make wine from water? When he revealed to them the sense and explained to them the Scriptures."[114]

The miracle that thus supervenes — this again is what the symbol of Cana brings into sharp focus for us — is none other than the miracle of *conversion*. Just as was the case in the act by which he created the New Testament, Jesus opened the understanding of the Old; in the same way when, in imitation of the Church herself,[115] one turns oneself toward Jesus Christ, each individual, becoming a "new creature," assimilates himself to that new understanding. For it is at that point that he discovers "the true Word." *To go over to Christ* and *to go over to the spiritual understanding* is a single whole.[116] It is always a passing, and it is the same passing. It is a step of faith, because it is the very application of the faith. It is the decisive movement that one accomplishes *revelatis oculis*.[117] It is one and the same illumination. One and the same conversion: the *conversio ad Dominum*.[118] For each one of us, by a twofold unique symbolism, the changing of the water into wine is at the same stroke, jointly, the passing to the understanding of the Scripture and the passing to life in Christ. It takes place during a wedding banquet, because, on Christ's side, to open up the Scriptures is to admit to nuptual union; on our side, to understand them is to accept the espousals.[119] It is to be introduced, like Rebecca, into the tent of the new Isaac.[120] Finally, if we should run the risk of still doubting it, this same symbol of Cana would also remind us that the ingenuity of the exegete, his natural intelligence, his knowledge, his culture, or his imagination — in principle and essentially — has no place in this business: everything definitely arises from the all-powerful Act posited by the Word of God and revealed by his Spirit.

CHAPTER NINE

Mystical Tropology

1. A Twofold Tropology

In passing from history to allegory we passed, as it were, from the letter to the spirit, from the sensible fact to the deep reality, or from the miracle to the mystery. The passage from allegory to tropology involves no such jump. After the historical sense, all those that can still be counted belong to one and the same spiritual sense, "since they have been signified not through the letter but through the spirit of the letter."[1] The "transfer" takes place henceforward within the mystery, in order to explore its successive aspects. Sometimes, from one point of view, we can distinguish things differently and say, with the School of Saint Victor, that in all of Scripture there are two objects to look for: the "cognition of the truth" and the "form of virtue": history and allegory converge on the first; tropology supplies the second.[2] In other words, history and allegory procure "the edification of the faith"; "the edification of morals" comes down to tropology.[3]

So if it is necessary "to scrutinize the Scriptures, this is not only to disengage the mystical sense from it: it is also to draw out its moral sense."[4] In interpreting them, it is necessary "to intertwine the moral with the mystical."[5] What had been written "prophetically" ought to be explained "morally" as well.[6] This "moral exposition" ["moralis expositio"] or "moral explanation" ["moralis explanatio"] is no less indispensable than the foregoing. Understood with its full force, it can, however, come only in third place: it constitutes the "third exposition,"[7] or the "third topic of explanation," as Origen already called it;[8] for, to start from the fact recorded within the narrative, this is the "sacrament of the spiritual understanding" itself which becomes the "most healthful example of virtue"[9] for us. Rectitude of faith is the precondition for purity of mind,[10] and to the extent that this faith is not firm and solid, it would be vain to wish immediately to pass on to morality.[11] "For one is not made to come to faith by the virtues, but rather one is brought to pursue the virtues by means of faith."[12] Let us say again, pushing a popular metaphor a bit far, that the fruits of tropology can come only after the "flowers of allegory."[13] We shall therefore find the tropological sense symbolized, for example, in the third level of the ark such as Noah built it at the Lord's directions,[14] or again, in the steps that led to the door of the sanctuary, once the vestibule of faith had been crossed;[15] more subtly, in the fat of the ram sacrificed following the ritual of Leviticus:

> The ram or the calf is any sentence excerpted from the Old Testament. We peel off, as it were, the skin for this sentence, when, pulling through the historical understanding, we establish it to be true. The flesh is handed over to the sacred fires at the point when allegory understood through the spiritual senses is made clear. We think we offer God the fat and the things that are below it when we scrutinize the morality and those features that depend upon mores with a view to their usefulness to the souls of the faithful and their praise of God himself. Therefore, since in the above treatise we have interpreted the Jacob of history in the allegorical and spiritual sense, we have burned the flesh with the sacred fire, the skin having, as it were, been taken away. Hence it remains for us to move the fat to the divine fire, that is, to advance morality into place by means of the moral and more exalted understanding.[16]

Saint Gregory, one may recall, was shown to be a bit in a hurry to skip over the step of history so as to explain allegory at his leisure. He shows himself no less in a hurry now to skip over the step of allegory to issue forth onto the wide plains of tropology. This will be the third step that we are going to engage in with him:

> We therefore briefly run through the allegorical senses so as to be able more quickly to come to breadth of morality. . . .
> It is enough for us, dearest brothers, to run through these things succinctly to hunt down the mysteries of allegory; now let the mind run back to gaze more broadly at the morality of what has been done.[17]

A Twofold Tropology

But since the allegorical sense of the Old Testament is no other than the New Testament, the moral dimension that the tropological sense is going to liberate will breathe the spirit of the Gospel; and since Christ's deeds in truth, in the depth of the mystery, realize what the facts of biblical history prefigured, when one takes one's point of departure from within these actions of Christ one will no longer have to count three steps but only two, and from history — which is now already more than mere history — one will pass directly to tropology: "Narrating the mysteries of our redemption, Scripture relates what has been done for us historically so as to signify what is to be done by us morally."[18] Or again, "by contemplating what God has done we recognize what is to be done by us."[19]

No more than *allegoria* for the second sense was the word *tropologia* imposed here. In the most general acceptation, a trope was a figure,[20] a mode,[21] or a *turn* of phrase ([Gk.] *tropos*, [Lat.] *conversio*), by which one turns some expression to designate some object other than the one naturally meant. *Tropologia*, accordingly, was a "speech turned around" or "turning" something else "around";[22] it was a "turned" or "turning manner of speech"[23] There was nothing in it that might suggest an idea of moral conversion — any more than there was in *allegoria* anything that would suggest the mystery of Christ. Thus we understand that, within the nascent vocabulary of exegesis, "tropology" at first had been practically synonymous with allegory, as well as with anagogy. The process that little by little needed to distinguish and specialize these three words was almost entirely contingent. *Allegoria* was found to have a right of priority, chiefly because of Saint Paul; it therefore designated, prior to every other distinction, the collection of senses added to *historia*, then, more precisely, the first among them, which in a certain fashion stood at the head of the other two. Anagogy belonged naturally enough to the fourth. All that remained for tropology, then, was the third place; it took it and kept it. It was even more natural that the only figured sense, already designated by this word, would, among the pre-Christian exegetes of the Bible, be found practically to be the moral sense. Then it would be explained as being "a speech turned around toward us, i.e., toward our ways of behaving,"[24] or "a speech turning around, pertaining to the mind's ways of behaving."[25] In the wake of Hugh of Saint Victor,[26] Robert of Melun will amplify it: "Tropologia means speech that turns *(sermo conversivus)*, because *(eo quod)* it designates a deed of such a sort that it is necessary for us to be converted to it with respect to the establishment of moral edification."[27] The logic of this "eo quod," transposing the "conversio" from the realm of discourse to that of moral conversion, was not very rigorous. Others will say more simply, looking right away to the end result: "Tropology is moral speech" or a "moral science."[28] Hence some will then write, as if the grammatical origin of the word had been forgotten: "Tropology is moral speech . . . and it is made either with plain or figurative words."[29] By slightly forcing another signification of the word, which, applied no longer to grammar or to style, but to a human being, one could make it equivalent to a "manner of being or of acting, habit, mores." But one ought not to attach too much importance to these nominal definitions, which do not enter the heart of the matter; they serve at least to distinguish one biblical sense from another; a popular type of this sort, which we borrow from the *Speculum* of the School of Saint Victor, "is called 'allegory' when through one deed another deed is understood . . . . It is 'tropology' when through one deed another thing to be done is pointed out."[30]

In other words, the tropology under consideration in the enumeration of the senses of Scripture is not the "moralis sermo" ["moral speech"] which is uttered "apertis verbis" ["with plain words"]; it is not this "simplex moralitas" ["simple morality"] which immediately flows from "historia" ["history"] when the latter proposes good examples or makes one hate the wicked. Gerhoh of Reichersberg explains this well while distinguishing the wool and the flax provided by the strong woman of the Proverbs:

> It can also be said that some of the examples of the ancient fathers are wool, some are flax. For something like pure, soft wool is found in those of their deeds that are proposed to be imitated just as they have been done and written, e.g., the faith and obedience of Abraham, the piety of Joseph, the meekness of Moses, the humility of David, and the like, in which the simple morality is acceptable even if no allegory is sought. But those that are said by way of allegory, e.g., that Abraham had two sons . . . , and that Jacob had two sisters for wives and their slave girls as concubines, and the like, are to be dried out like raw linen and purified in many ways, so that once the carnal element of the sense of the letter that killeth has been removed, only the life-giving and edifying spirit may be accepted within them.[31]

Describing in verse the great river of Scripture up to its many branches, Godfrey of Saint Victor arrives at its branch of tropology:

Here I marveled at the clearer streams of the Practical,
Whose confederated waters also belong to all,

But though they are more turbulent elsewhere,
Here they are clearer than light-penetrating glass.[32]

After this fervent but banal elegy,[33] one might believe that the tropological sense does not have much to do with spiritual understanding, as it was explained in the preceding chapter. The same impression already occurs from a poem quite a bit earlier, the poem of Paulinus of Aquilaea on Lazarus, in which we read these verses:

If, flying summarily through all theoric things
We bend one back, and succinctly touch morally
Its features, each by each, that have been promulgated through the
   tropical style,
We can competently understand them otherwise. . . .[34]

Indeed some definitions that speak only of something "moral," or "mores," or of things "to do," would also lead one to suppose that this sense is anterior or remains exterior to the mystery. This impression seems to be confirmed by a certain number of texts that oppose "simplex moralitas" to "allegoria,"[35] or the "merely moral sense" to this "higher sense," to this "more sacred sense" in which the "deeper mysteries"[36] are uncovered. Richard of Saint Victor even puts such a distinction into vigorous relief:

> Tropology treats of what anyone can easily grasp. . . . For the situation of tropology is quite different from that of allegory. For what is tropology but moral science, and what is allegory but the mystical doctrine of the mysteries? The honorable elements of morals are inscribed naturally upon the human heart. But surely no one untemerariously presumes upon the depths of the mysteries in their proper sense.[37]

In the economy of the four senses, these ways of speaking suppose the order according to which tropology comes in second place, right after history. For in this case, it can scarcely be considered as constituting part of this spiritual sense proper to the divine Scripture alone, and although some lines lower down he observes that "a useful and observable discipline of mores is imparted from the power of the sacraments," Richard of Saint Victor nonetheless concludes: "Holy Scripture alone uses the allegorical and the anagogical sense mystically; it alone among them all is crowned with this twofold supereminence."[38] But this amounts to the fact, as we know, that there is "a twofold tropology."[39] In distinguishing the one from the other, Honorius says that the one joins the soul with the spirit, so that from their union the "good work" results, and the other unites us to Christ by charity.[40] Thus the one is "natural," but the other is "mystical." The one "moralizes" the biblical datum in the same way that any datum of literature, man, and the universe can be "moralized"; thus in the following reflection contained in the Psalter of Saint Alban (Hildesheim), we find at the top of an image depicting the siege of a fortified town: "What the image shows you *corporaliter*, ought to be reproduced *spiritualiter*; the combats that the design helps you to be present at call up the struggle that you have to sustain against evil."[41] But the other tropology, the one that occupies the third place in the most frequent and the most logical formulation of the four senses — and which even those who make no distinct mention of it did not miss — relates to the spiritual sense proper to Scripture, not only in fact but also by necessity. It contributes to the elaboration of this sense which characterizes Scripture only. It does not precede "the spiritual edifice," but it "adds to it,"[42] or rather it exerts itself within it to complete it. It is within allegory. It constitutes an integral part of the mystery. Coming after the objective aspect of which it is the allegory, it constitutes its subjective aspect. It is, if one can say so, its intussusception, its interiorization; it appropriates it for us. Tropology draws its *exempla* from this *mysterium*.[43] It is this "mystic sense of morality,"[44] this "understanding of spiritual life,"[45] that a practiced eye detects everywhere in the two Testaments. If allegory, starting from the facts of history, envisions the mystical body in its head or in its totality, tropology envisions it in each of its members:

> From history we have heard what we may marvel at; from the head we know what we may believe; now, from the body, we consider what we may hold in living life. For we ought to transform what we read within ourselves.[46]

> We are running across these briefly treated matters with a view to the signification of our head: now for the edification of its body, let us unfold the things to be treated morally, so that we may know how the act that is narrated exteriorly in a work may be actuated interiorly in the mind.[47]

If allegory develops dogma, it develops not just any morality, but Christian anthropology and the spirituality that flows from the dogma. After the *facta mystica* ["mystic deeds that have been done"] given by the allegory, both in immediate dependence and in internal dependence upon them, it indicates the *facienda mystica* ["mystic deeds that are to be done"].[48] After the "mystery of faith" come the "works of faith."[49] After the "mystical faith" comes the "moral grace."[50] It makes us see everywhere in Scripture something that concerns us: "Look, these are your affairs, brothers . . . , your affairs, I say, your affairs!"[51] It therefore fulfills the program twice enunciated by the Apostle, in the Epistle to the Romans: "Whatever things have been written have been written for our instruction,"[52] and in the first Epistle to the Corinthians: "These things were happening to them in a figure, but they have been written down for our reproach into whom the ends of the ages have come down."[53] Therefore, inverting the old Ambrosian image, one can call it with complete truth the fruit, in view of which God first procures the foliation of history and then the flowering of allegory:

> *Early in the morning let us rise to the vineyards,* i.e., rising from the letter to the spirit, from history to the mystical sense, let us approach the Sacred Scriptures; in which the leafy boughs of history grow green, the flower of allegory gives off its scent, the fruit of tropology suffices. And this occurs *early in the morning,* i.e., through the dawning of the spiritual understanding. And in this way *let us see,* i.e., let us be experienced, that is, may you make me be experienced, *if the vineyard has borne fruit,* i.e., whether Scripture has come into me through the allegorical sense. *If the flowers bring forth fruits,* through the moral understanding; since, just as the fruit follows after the flower, so the moral understanding comes to inform us after allegorical interpretation.[54]

So, far from being in its own starting point a "creation of the individual mind," tropology thus understood has its own indispensable place in the concatenation of the scriptural senses. Far from being exterior and inferior to the "deeper sense" of allegory, as it seemed just now, it even marks, in a certain sense, a deepening of it, or even its summit: "We are nourished on history and parables; we grow by means of allegory; we are brought to perfection by morality."[55] Far from constituting a negligible appendix, its procedure is essential to the full understanding of Scripture. After the "transposition of the fundamental data of the Word of God with reference to Christ," ought to come the "assimilation of these data to ourselves through his mediation."[56] At the same time that they symbolize the four times of the mystery of Christ, and for the very same reason, the four animals of Ezekiel symbolize the four times of Christian life. Every allegory is concentrated within the pascal mystery; but we must still say, with Saint Ambrose: "Every year the pasch of Jesus Christ, i.e., the crossing of souls, is celebrated...."[57] In other words, if it is true that nothing is superior to the Mystery of Christ, one ought not forget that this Mystery, which was prefigured in the Old Testament, is realized again, is being actualized, is being completed within the Christian soul. *It is truly being fulfilled within us.*[58] In saying these things, we neither dilute nor misconstrue the unique singularity of the Mystery: we unfold its own internal logic, we make the most of its depth and fruitfulness. We point out, with Saint Bernard, that it reaches right up to us today.[59] Typology, without ever denying it, sometimes leaves this mystery in the shade when it is not entirely faithful to the thought of Saint Paul on the *typoi*.[60] One modern has understood it well: "The public, 'objective' revelation of God in history is also a revelation of his ways with regard to each of us"; borrowing an image from Plato in the *Republic*, "we can say that the Bible depicts the ways of God to man in the 'big letters' of the history of the community."[61] Thereby not everything is said, but, as we shall see, something essential has been. To stop at the objective datum of the mystery would be to mutilate it, to betray it. "The mind understands God's words more truly when it searches for itself within them."[62]

2. Quotidie ["Daily"]

The two great masters of the tropological sense are Origen and Saint Gregory. Following their teaching, which was spread everywhere, everything in Scripture that is susceptible of being allegorized also can and ought to be moralized. We pass from history to tropology through allegory. The latter consisting entirely in the Mystery of Christ, this mystery finds itself interiorized within tropology. "What has preceded historically in the head is consequently also revealed to come about morally in its body."[1] It can sometimes happen (and it is even a matter of some frequency) that the intermediate step is not always explicitly traversed; the mystery, taken in itself, is not expressed; it is nonetheless always presupposed. Thus it is that one author, calling up the events of Israel's captivity in Egypt, writes: "Though those deeds were corporeally performed in Egypt, they are nevertheless now being performed spiritually in us";[2] and another: "that which Scripture commemorates historically about the earth seems to belong morally to hearts."[3] This is evidently possible only by the mediation of the mystery — "in virtue of the cross of Christ"[4] —

Quotidie ["Daily"]

and every believer knows this quite well. This "we" at issue, or this "soul," or this "inner man," is therefore not any one human being or the soul in general, or human nature abstractly considered: it is a question of the Christian people; concrete souls are at stake, Christian souls. Thus the Tabernacle of Moses or the Temple of Solomon, which allegorically is Christ, is also by necessary consequence "our heart."[5] It is "the very mind and consciousness of the faithful":[6] it is Saint Gregory who tells us this. Adam Scotus will explain at length that there are three tabernacles, the third being this little secret of the Holy Spirit, the pure soul.[7]

The pure soul, the holy soul, the faithful soul is such only "within the Church": it is "the soul in the Church," "the ecclesiastical soul," or again "the ecclesiastical person."[8] It is such only by being part of this great Body of which the Christ is the Head. The tropological sense therefore does not only presuppose the Mystery of the Christ, but also that of the Church, which is, as we have seen, inseparable from it. The tropological sense presupposes, or rather, expresses the mystery: for if the souls are Christian only within the Church, the reverse holds: "it is within the souls that the Church is beautiful."[9] The whole life of the Christian flows from the "mystical fecundity of the Church."[10] Everything that the Gospel history contains, says Saint Bernard, can therefore be interpreted "according to tropology, so that what has preceded in the head may consequently also be believed to come about morally in its body."[11] In its body, that is to say: both in the entire Church as well as in each of her members, following this great principle that commands all of Christian life and that we find admirably formulated by Saint Gregory:

> Almighty God, who is neither stretched out in big things nor squeezed in very small ones, speaks about the whole Church all at once just as if he is speaking about just one soul; and it is often the case that nothing prevents what has been said by him of one soul from being understood of the whole Church at once.[12]
>
> ... So once these matters have been gone through by means of figurative exposition, their moral senses can now be inferred, so that, once the figure of the Church is known, which we believe to have been expressed in general fashion, we may also hear what we may specifically gather from these words in single instances.[13]

This is what Pascal had to recall one day to Mlle de Roannez: "Everything that happens to the Church also happens to each Christian in particular."[14]

The scheme is universal. As it applies to the whole configuration of Christian life, so it applies to all of Scripture. To the six days of creation, for example, there correspond the six days or ages of the Church, which will also be followed by a seventh, the day of definitive great repose; but, as Saint Augustine remarks, "each of us has those distinct six days in our good works and right life, too, and after them he ought to hope for rest."[15] There is not one of the symbols of the Church which is not also a symbol of the soul. Nevertheless, it is in the commentary on the Canticle of Canticles that the tradition has pursued this scheme in the most systematic manner and in the manner that speaks to us most immediately. This little book is in fact taken from one end to the other as expressing the heart of the revelation everywhere diffused in the Scriptures: it symbolically celebrates the great mystery of love, the union of God and man prefigured in Israel and realized by the incarnation of the Word; in other words, the wedding of Christ and his Church. There under divine inspiration Solomon, says Saint Bernard, has sung "the praises of Christ and the Church, the grace of holy love, and the sacraments of the eternal marriage."[16] This view of the Christian tradition does not exclude that of the ancient commentators of Israel: it presupposes it, it integrates it by deepening it. It is sometimes said that the Christian tradition presents two different lines of interpretation for this subject: the one ecclesial and the other spiritual; and that the first is readily assigned to Saint Hippolytus, the second to Origen. In fact, the "mystical preaching" of this "divine book"[17] is understood by everyone, in its essentials, in the same manner. According to the needs, the circumstances, the interests of the commentator, the accent can be put on one aspect or another; but there are not two parallel — still less, divergent — lines. Notably for Origen, the Bride of the Canticle is simply the Church. He does not cease repeating: "I the Church, I the bride"; "the Church, which is speaking"; "the Church seems to be described by Christ"; "the Bride, that is, the Church," etc.[18] But at the same time she is "the individual soul," she is each believing soul, that "microcosm of the perfect Church"; just as the City of God, Jerusalem, is at the same time the Church of which Christ is the architect and this city remains what is being built in each of our hearts.[19] More exactly, if the soul can effectively be united to the Word of God, this is because the Church is united to Christ.[20] The like obtains in the case of Aponius, who passes constantly from the Church to the soul regenerated by baptism, to the just soul, to the perfect soul, to the soul united to the Word of God.[21] Likewise for the Middle Ages. One of the tableaux of the *Hortus deliciarum* has as its legend: "Solomon is resting in bed, i.e., in the Church"; and when Adam Scotus undertakes to celebrate the "internal, joyful, pure" union of the soul and God, he makes it quite clear that this union can be realized only by depending on the "profound mystery" into which his Fathers and teachers have been initiated.[22] It is in "the home of the present Church," says Potho of Prüm, a home "created in the image of God," that souls acquire the divine likeness.[23] It is therefore not appropriate to harden the duality that can be observed between the "Christian Socratism" of certain texts commenting on Scripture in an apparently entirely interior sense and the "ecclesiastical" doctrine of certain others.[24] They complete each other without excluding each other and are inscribed in a general framework of interpretation which constitutes part of common knowledge. Neither do the Marian commentaries on the Canticle, beginning from the twelfth century, introduce a third, absolutely new line; they always put the same principle into practice. The application that they will make of it will be, properly speaking, in no way different: it will only be, in the precise sense in which they understand it, "special":[25] "These things are said specifically of blessed Mary, and generally of the perfect Church of the saints." Some, in the wake of Odorannus[26] and Rupert, will attach themselves entirely to the first period of the mystery: to the union of the Word and human nature effected within the womb of the Virgin "in the incarnation of the Word"; upon the "foundation" of the Canticle they will construct an edifice "of the incarnation of the Lord."[27] Others, more and more, will rather celebrate, at the interior of the mystery of the Church or at its summit, the Virgin Mary as realizing the perfection of the Christian soul.[28] To be sure, this is merely a schematic view, intended simply to show that the basic interpretation remains everywhere the same, and that it constitutes simply a case of this mystic tropology in which the third sense of Scripture consists.

"The Church, or any faithful soul";[29] "the universal Church as well as each beloved soul";[30] "the whole Church and each holy soul";[31] "the Church, or the soul loving God":[32] the same sort of remark is encountered in each instance, among extremely diverse authors, regarding scriptural passages that are themselves most diverse. "We can relate this to the Church or to the soul of the holy man," says Saint Jerome commenting on Isaiah;[33] "Each one of us can relate the things that have been said of the Church to himself," Letbert of Saint Ruf will say in commenting on the Psalms;[34] and Saint Gregory again, in Claudius's redaction, commenting on the Canticle, says, "What we have said in general about the Church as a whole, let us now feel specifically about each and every soul";[35] etc.[36] In the one case and in the other, declares Saint Bernard, it is basically a question of the same reality, "except that what is designated by the name 'Church' is not one soul [*anima*] but a unity or rather a unanimity of many."[37] With a professor's precision Adam Scotus insists on: "the Holy Church, or, with respect to the moral sense, the devoted soul."[38] That remark doubles with another, no less frequent, which completes it: in this Christian soul, it is *each day*, it is *today*, that the mystery, by being interiorized, is accomplished. "It existed historically then; today it exists spiritually."[39] *Moraliter, intrinsecus* and *quotidie* are three adverbs that go together.[40] "The present reading," says Hervaeus of Bourg Dieu in a homily, "has been completed historically once in fact, but with respect to the spiritual sense it is being fulfilled every day."[41] Each day, deep within ourselves, Israel departs from Egypt; each day, it is nourished with manna; each day it fulfills the Law; each day it must engage in combat . . . ;[42] each day the promises that had been made to this people under a bodily form are realized spiritually in us.[43] Each day also the Gentiles give themselves over to the worship of their idols; each day the Israelites themselves are unfaithful; each day, in this interior region, the land devours the impious. . . .[44] Each day again, there is the Lord's visit; each day he approaches Jerusalem, coming from Bethphagê.[45] Each day is his advent: "The Lord coming in the flesh has visited us: and, morally, we also discern this come about every day."[46] "Within those who are devoted, he comes every day."[47]

Now everything that came about for the first time in history had no other end than that. All that is accomplished in the Church herself had no other end. Everything is consummated in the inner man.[48] This ought to be said of all the external facts related in the books of the two Testaments; it ought equally to be said of the Mystery of the Christ. History, allegory, tropology, draw an unbroken line from the unique redemptive action: "Whatever is taught either under history or under allegory or else under tropology, is thoroughly taught for the sake of this covenant, namely, our restoration."[49] The mystery is always unique:

> In the blood of Christ the circumcision of all is celebrated, and in his cross all have been crucified, . . . and buried together in his tomb.[50]

> Therefore whatever has been done on Christ's cross, in his tomb, in his resurrection on the third day, in his ascension into heaven, and in his seat at the right of the Father, has been done in such a way that the Christian life that is being lived here would be configured to these things not merely as having mystically been said but also as having been done.[51]

Quotidie ["Daily"]

This is, as we see, pure Pauline mystical doctrine, and one can in fact understand the exegesis of the Apostle himself only in relation with his mystical doctrine. Everything is done to conduct us "to the inner parts,"[52] to make us observe the Law "according to the inner man."[53] The soul is "the temple of God, in which the divine mysteries are celebrated."[54] Everything ought to lead to this intimate wedding: "But what is the preparation of the marriage except the exposition of the holy Scriptures?"[55] To the extent that this term is not attained, even though everything be done, nothing, so to speak, has yet been done, because the mystery has not produced its fruit. As Angelus Silesius will put it in a bold but, in intention, we believe, perfectly orthodox distich:

Scripture is only scripture. My consolation is the Essence,
And may God speak within me his Word of eternity.[56]

To understand it properly, it is first necessary to read its title: "Scripture without the Spirit is nothing." Jean Baruzi has indeed seen that here the poet "above all intends to combat the Protestant point of view,"[57] which would refuse the spiritual interpretation of the Scriptures. Nevertheless it is not entirely a "doctrine of interior illumination" in general that these two verses express; it is the doctrine of the interiorization of the biblical datum: its history and its mystery. Neither this history nor this mystery is denied or forsaken, as it would at least be possible to believe among those who speak of a birth of the *Word* only within the contemplative soul. Angelus Silesius speaks of Jesus Christ. Only after "the coming of our Savior in the flesh" — it is still Angelus Silesius who is speaking — is there his coming "in spirit."[58] After his earthly birth and thanks to it, there must finally be his birth within the soul. Fundamentally, nothing is more traditional. Let us only recall that our Silesian friend expresses himself in the already habitual language of mystical thought — overmuch cut off from the roots that it had in ancient exegesis — and without taking it in a lesser sense than that which his master, the Jesuit Sandaeus, did. "Each day," said Saint Jerome, "the divine Word is born of the virginal soul."[59] The theme, along with its overtones, is common in medieval spirituality. Hélinand of Froidmont, for example, distinguishes the three births of Christ: "the nativity of eternity," "the temporal nativity," "the mystical nativity"; this third birth, he adds, is to last right up to the end of the world: "for Christ is born as often as anyone is becoming a Christian,"[60] and one is never finished with becoming Christian. It is, moreover, not only a question of birth; just as he is born in us and was conceived by us, so, says Aelred of Rivaulx, ought the Lord Jesus to grow in us and to find nourishment in us, "until we all meet the perfect man, the measure of the age of the fullness of Christ."[61] From another point of view, Saint Augustine meant nothing else than this in saying that all that the Christ accomplishes in the life, death, and resurrection of his flesh is "a sacrament of the interior man," all of Christian life being a "configuration" to the mystery of Christ.[62] But Origen had already more precisely called up "the daily birth of our Savior," "the continual coming of the Logos";[63] he had already said in a question that contained even the fine points of the thought picked up by Angelus Silesius: "What good does it do me for the Logos to have come into the world if I myself do not have him?"[64] Again, he already said: after his coming on earth, Jesus must also come into each soul, so as to overturn the idols within it, to conquer Babylon within, the city of the devil: "but if the city of confusion has not fallen within the heart of anyone, to him also Christ has not yet come."[65] Christ must once again be conceived and formed in each soul, so that the "great joy" may be renewed as many times as the angels have announced it of old.[66] Saint Bernard seems to want to comment on these texts when he says in his turn: "for there are those to whom Christ has not yet been born."[67] Speaking more directly of the very words of Scripture, which, in their essence, are the selfsame Word, Paul Claudel will rediscover this great theme of the tradition at the end of a development in which he will show how we must read these words, meditate upon them, make them our own:

> Now . . . it is no longer we who are acting; it is these words, once having been introduced, which act within us, releasing the spirit of which they have been made, the meaning and sonority included within them, and which veritably become spirit and life, and action-producing words. They belong to a place beyond our mental control; there is a certain irresistible force of authority and order in them. But they have ceased to be exterior; they have become ourselves. *And the Word was made flesh and dwelt among us:* one must understand the whole captivating, appropriating power of these two words: *in nobis.*[68]

It is by the tropological sense thus understood that Scripture is fully *for us* the Word of God, this Word which is addressed to each person, *hic et nunc* ["here and now"] as well as to the whole Church, and telling each "that which is of interest to his life."[69] God has spoken but once, and yet

Quotidie ["Daily"]

his Word, at first extended in duration, remains continuous and does not entirely cease to reach us.[70] It is not only "our prophecy":[71] it is our day-to-day guide; it is such not only by the moral teaching of its letter, but in every respect. There is not a page, not a word "of the Old or of the New Testament" that is not the most perfectly straight ruler of human life so as to guide it to the heights of perfection.[72] In this precise sense, Scripture is "for us a complete whole."[73] "In the shadows of the present life, it is the light of the path."[74] For every thing, on every occasion, it indicates to us not only what we should believe and hope for, but also what we have to love or flee.[75] It is our daily nourishment, and if we grasp anything in it today that we did not know yesterday, tomorrow holds something equally surprising in store for us.[76] Upon this abundantly supplied table, the Lord "restores us each day, at his side, in spiritual science,"[77] and we always find on it what belongs to every condition we find ourselves in.[78] In everything, Scripture invites us to conversion of heart.[79] All the wars that it recounts are the wars of the Lord;[80] all the migrations, all the travels it traces are the wanderings and travels of the soul:[81] it is thus from one end to the other the book of spiritual combat[82] at the same time as it is the book of departure and of mystical ascent. With Abraham we abandon our home and we arrive at the oak of Mamre, where God goes to visit us.[83] With the children of Israel we flee "the furnace of Egyptian servitude," we cross the Red Sea, we wander in the desert, our forces are refreshed by a miraculous nourishment, we enter at last into the promised land.[84] With them we again collide with the surrounding peoples; with them we return from the captivity of Babylon and rebuild the temple and the city.... Finally, whatever page I meditate upon, I find in it a means that God offers me, right now, to restore the divine image within me. Thus I myself become Jerusalem, the holy city; I become or become again the temple of the Lord; for me the promise is realized: "I shall dwell in their midst." "God walks with me in the garden, when I read the divine Scriptures...."[85]

All this teaching of the Scripture, all this strength which shapes me to the divine likeness, is summarized in a single word: charity. Many things in the letter itself already recommend it to us; by means of tropology everything tends to it. It is in charity that tropology shows itself to allegory in interior perfection: for the perfection of the Law is charity and it is at the same time the Christ. Saint Augustine took this from Saint Ambrose,[86] who himself got it from Saint Paul. "Charity manifests itself in what you understand in the Scriptures; charity hides itself in what you do not understand."[87] So many books, endowed with such great authority and such great sanctity, "act with us only so that we may love . . .";[88] when we do not see it clearly, this is because the passage that occupies us, whatever be its apparent clarity, is still obscure to our eyes.[89] Saint Gregory draws the consequence, in a formula parallel to that which he employed for allegory: tropology tends "to the upbuilding of charity."[90] In this respect, remarks Rabanus Maurus, it constitutes "the superior understanding."[91] Let us therefore say with Saint Gregory once more: "The astonishing and unspeakable power of sacred eloquence is recognized when the mind is penetrated by the highest love."[92]

But if charity is fulfillment and end, then, to guide us thither, Scripture first presents itself to us as a mirror. Vaguely sketched out in the Epistle of Saint James,[93] the comparison was found developed in Philo's treatise on the contemplative life.[94] Saint Augustine made it his own on several occasions[95] and Saint Gregory exploited it after him.[96] The whole Middle Ages comments upon it. In this mirror we learn to know our nature and our destiny; in it we also see the different stages through which we have passed since creation, the beautiful and the ugly features of our internal face.[97] It shows us the truth of our being by pointing it out in its relation to the Creator.[98] It is a living mirror, a living and efficacious Word, a sword penetrating at the juncture of soul and spirit, which makes our secret thoughts appear and reveals to us our heart.[99] It teaches us to read in the book of experience[100] and makes us, so to speak, our own exegesis. "Here it is not man who explicates Scripture, but rather man uses Scripture to explain himself to himself, so as to surpass himself."[101] "The souls that stick close to the heavenly bridegroom ought to perceive themselves in the mirror of the Scriptures."[102] In return, once acquired by meditation on Scripture, experience permits one to deepen this meditation, though it could never free itself of it. It becomes the path that leads to genuine spiritual understanding.[103] Interior experience and meditation on Scripture accordingly tend to merge in a unique "experience of the Word."[104] Without it, the wisest can indeed explain certain things; but what is essential is still missing to them, because *per experientiam nondum intelligunt*.[105] In this reciprocity, Scripture, which is always primary, is always also last. The superior experience that it communicates to the one who questions it can only be acquired within faith.[106] It is the Scripture that measures us,[107] and which scrutinizes us, and which makes the fountains of living water spring forth in us,[108] and which ends by saying to us, not to deny it to us but showing us the unity of the first Source: "Drink the water from your vessels and from your wells."[109]

> This fountain is the pious mind meditating upon heavenly things:
> Living rivers of doctrine it does not cease to bring forth within itself.
> Hence the living fountain of flowing, dancing water, says Scripture,
> will be unto life for anyone [coming] from out of those [rivers].[110]

3. Monastic Exegesis

Nevertheless, the conditions of Christian life do evolve. Medieval society is no longer ancient society. Christianity no longer knew exactly the same problems as did the age of the Fathers. He who wishes to follow the Gospel is no longer in the same situation in relation to the world as the Christian of the first centuries. This evolution results more from a change of perspective in an exegesis whose principles remain unchanged but which do not cease to search in Scripture for the light for the present life. A breach is being produced, enlarging tropology in relation to allegory, and tropology itself takes on certain new aspects. While the spiritual understanding consisted first and foremost in the passage from the Old Testament to the New, that is to say, in the entry to the Christian faith, it more and more came to consist, in the midst of a believing society, but one where faith coexists with secular manners, in throwing light on the "conversio morum," the passage from the sinful life to the virtuous life, from the mediocre life to the spiritual life, or more precisely, in many cases, from the "world" to "religion"; then it will describe the progress of the monastic life, and the steps of contemplation traversed by the monk faithful to his cell will emphasize the progress realized in the science of the Scriptures. *Nova et vetera*. It is difficult to assign a *terminus a quo* for such an evolution. In the course of a homily on Ezekiel, Origen had distinguished three types of just men, represented by Noah, Daniel, and Job.[1] With more precision and persistence, Saint Augustine had recognized in these three holy personages the figure of three categories of Christians: the chiefs who govern the Church well (Noah), the continent with their holy desires (Daniel), the married folk living in the midst of the trials of this world (Job).[2] Saint Gregory had likewise distinguished the "three orders of the faithful" both under grace and under the law: "the order of preachers is one thing, that of the continent another, and that of good married persons still another."[3] These "three professions" had been described at length by Isidore of Seville.[4] Noah, builder and patron of the ark, had, however, for ever been predestined to symbolize the heads of the Church.[5] In the Middle Ages, where one loves classifications and personifications,[6] the trio is adopted everywhere.[7] It represents, they say, the "three distinct ways of living well" or the "three orders of those believing in Christ."[8] "Having been established by the Glossa ordinaria," the theme will much later take on "imposing proportions in Saint Bonaventure."[9] Peter of Riga dedicates one poem of his *Floridus aspectus* to it, a poem whose verses he uses again in the *Aurora*.[10] Here or there the three "supernumeraries" of Ezekiel are merely replaced or doubled by three personages from the first Book of Kings: Hazael, Jehu, Elisha,[11] or else by Ephraim, Benjamin, and Manasseh, themselves associated with the three Magi,[12] or even by some other symbol.[13] But — this is what we must note — the explanation given for it is sometimes bent in a more exclusively monastic direction or spirit. For example, instead of emphasizing, as did Isidore, that the distinction ought not to harm the fundamental unity of the "universal people of the Church," or that in each of the three orders both good and bad are found; instead of observing with Saint Gregory and Rabanus Maurus that "those in wedlock," who "owing to their office stand in lowest position," can also be the object of the highest contemplative graces,[14] certain authors on the contrary emphasize the fact that the three orders are three "degrees." Thus, for Abbo of Fleury, the order of clerics (which includes the prelates) "is intermediate between the laity and the monks, to the extent that it is superior to the inferior, to that extent it is inferior to the superior."[15] For Rupert of Deutz, the three symbolic personages are also, respectively, the "workers in the field," the "millers in the mill," and the "ones resting in bed" of the Gospel; the first group, or the "order of the wedded," is "lowest"; the second, the "order of those who supervise well," is "intermediate"; the third, the "order of those who are free for contemplation," is "highest."[16] Or again certain authors believe it should be made clear that the "wedded" find a place in the Church only "by concession";[17] others declare that they will be saved "at the last moment" only by a particular effect of God's mercy,[18] or restrict their category by calling them "wedded and penitent."[19] Such restrictions, let us observe, are not encountered in a Robert Puyllen,[20] or again as a rule in a Saint Bernard, who defines the "wedded" as the "faithful licitly possessing earthly things"[21] and who recalls that Noah, Daniel, and Job have an equal need to have recourse to the "fount of mercy."[22] Another indication of the monastic spirit is this: the heads of the Church, who have to unite the active life to the contemplative life,[23] are sometimes replaced in the enumeration by the "contemplatives," who form a more perfect category of monks; which gives the following ascending hierarchy: "wedded — continent — contemplative";[24] or, more simply: "wedded — continent — virgins."[25] Sometimes the threefold distinction is even made entirely within the monastic state: Noah signifies, then, the superiors, or "prelates"; Daniel signifies the assembly of the religious, the "encloistered"; finally, Job, those who have to fulfill an office outside the monastery: they are the "brothers on assignment,"[26] also called "obaedentiales."[27] Or again, the threefold series becomes that of the "prelates," the "penitent," and the "innocent,"[28] etc.

Another parallel fact is no less significant. In the essays on theology of history that multiply in the course of the twelfth century, some divide the duration of the Church of Christ here below, in the same way that of the Old Testament had been divided, into five ages. Now, after the ages of the Apostles, the Martyrs, the Fathers or Doctors, and before that of the Antichrist, they see a privileged age blossoming: the age of the continents and the monks. It is the age of consolation, of the holy life within the Church.[29] For many, "Christian discipline" has the "discipline of the cloister,"[30] just as "Christian philosophy," in its ascetic and vital acceptation, has become the monastic philosophy.[31] In certain expressions, it would even seem that the law "of hermits and cloisters" had succeeded "at the end" the less perfect law "of the Christians," just as the latter had early on succeeded the law "of the Jews" and that "of the philosophers";[32] that, after the "law of nature" came the "law of the letter," then the "law of grace," and finally, in increasing order of perfection, the "law of the Rule."[33] In the same way, a "convert" is no longer a man that has come from error to the truth, from paganism or Judaism to the Gospel: it is the one who renounces the "world" for the "cloister."[34] He has no more to reject idols but rather the "means for acting in the world."[35] The day of his entry into religion is the day of his "conversion."[36] In contemporary language one would scarcely say, as in the ancient formula which nevertheless remains official, "conversion of morals."[37] To become a monk is "to come to conversion,"[38] a formula already ancient;[39] to help those who delay to decide, one speaks to them "about speeding up the conversion."[40] The first thing a cloistered nun ought to do on the day after her conversion is to get her hair cut.[41] The word then became institutionalized, and this new signification is even more felt as the primary analogate, so that the new usage ends up by prevailing.[42] It is the same for the correlative word "vocatio": the "celestial vocation" is no longer the heavenly vocation of every Christian: it is that of the monk, called by God to withdraw "from the vanity of the world."[43] The monastery is therefore the "house of conversion."[44] The saying of the Lord, "Unless ye be converted, ye shall not enter into the kingdom of heaven," is cited to prove that there is no entry, or at least no sure entry to life outside the monastic state.[45] "Flee the world and human beings if you wish to be saved."[46] *Pari passu*, to renounce one's rule, to leave the monastery, is "to apostatize";[47] but on the other hand, Christ has promised to be with those who remain faithful to their observance right up to the end.[48] The monastic profession is the perfection of baptism;[49] it is a second baptism, a second regeneration,[50] which remits all sins.[51] The cloister is so much the place of "spiritual conversion" that, in a twelfth-century collection, in the margin next to a passage from Origen where it is a question of non-spiritual men, a gloss is added: "still in the world."[52]

The texts that were traditionally understood of the Church are therefore now understood, in addition, of the monastic institution. The images of the ship[53] and of the city[54] are applied to it. Babylon and Jerusalem are opposed to each other from now on in a new sense even within Christianity: they are the world and the cloister.[55] Adam Scotus reads into Saint Peter's words on the "house of God," the "chosen nation," the "royal priesthood," and the "chosen people," an allusion to the various people who have vowed themselves to the Lord under the two forms then reigning, namely the "class of clerics regular" and the "class of monks."[56] The blessed mother, of which Mary, mother of Jesus, is the prototype, becomes, in the moral sense, "the holy congregation," whose fruit is still Jesus, because she gives birth to him in the soul of her members.[57] The society united and sanctified by one and the same Spirit gathered under just one head, is that very community of religious governed by their prelate.[58] To leave Egypt for the promised land is again to leave the world for the religious profession,[59] and when a monastery becomes lax, it is Jerusalem that turns back to Egypt.[60] Paradise, which was formerly the Church, is now the cloister;[61] for some, the Church of the Cistercians;[62] for others, that of the Premonstratensians. Adam Scotus, exploiting the symbol to the hilt, exhibits this place of delights rising from a river which is divided into four branches, because there are four sorts of religious distinguished in it:

> "And a river was going out of the place of pleasure to irrigate Paradise. . . ." The place of pleasure is the Church of the Premonstratensians. . . . The river is going out of this place of pleasure by which Paradise is being irrigated, when healthful things are insti-

tuted in the Church of the Premonstratensians, which is our mother, so that the order itself may be repaired. Since its institutions are many, it also establishes these [men] most of all: the penitents, the leaders, the workers, and the contemplatives, and any other such; these are the novices, the functionaries, the prelates, and the encloistered. "The river goes forth," says Scripture, "from the place of pleasure to irrigate Paradise, which thence is divided into four heads. . . ."[63]

Honorius analogously transposes the traditional symbolism of the Canticle of Canticles: the "cells" are the cloisters, and he who has just said good-bye to secular life cries out joyfully: "The king has introduced me into his cells": the faithful soul rests in the shadow of Christ when, far from the annoying heat of secular life, she refreshes herself in the repose of spiritual life; she looks for the Beloved in the desert, that is to say, in the secrecy of cloistered existence, etc.[64] A Cistercian, Geoffrey of Auxerre, also turns the whole datum of the Canticles to the praise of the community of monks, which he sees figured in the Bride: living together in charity, the monks are the peerless, perfect dove.[65] In the same way, for Gerhoh of Reichersberg, Sarah, the free woman whom Christ just married, is at the same time Rachel, symbol of the form of religious life of which he became the promoter.[66] For the author of the *Vitis mystica*, the "new song" of the Apocalypse is no longer simply the song of the Church or of the Christian, compared by Paul to a consecrated virgin: it is the song of the consecrated virgins, the cloistered nuns.[67] Petrus Cellensis judges that Leviticus is par excellence the book of the monk, because he finds described in it all the sacrifices of purification to which he ought to commit himself in his cell.[68] The free man of whom Saint Paul speaks, the new man, the citizen of the city of Christ, bearer of the divine likeness, is, for Henry of Marcy, the monk, faithful to his vocation: "Am I not free? Am I not a monk? . . ."[69] For Arno of Reichersberg, Peter and John running to the tomb on Easter morning no longer signify the Jewish people and the Gentiles, but rather the two great orders which run together in the Church, the monastic and the canonic: John is the monastic order, given to work and contemplation; Peter is the canonical order, given to the ministry of the word; both run equally, albeit in divers ways, to meet the one thing necessary; both are equally beloved of God and love him.[70] Aelred of Rievaulx compares Saint Benedict, the father of the monks, to Saint Paul: for "in Christ Jesus he begot us through the Gospel";[71] Benedict, he says again, is "our Moses": his teaching and his example are the two lifted hands which obtain for us grace and salvation.[72] Finally, the traditional axiom: "there is no salvation outside the Church" becomes for certain people quite naturally "outside the cloister there is no salvation."[73]

All these transfers are, in general, justified by the "liberty of tropology," which, under the safeguard of the analogy of faith, permits Scripture to apply to all sorts of new situations. Nothing is simpler or more legitimate. These transfers, however, are also justified by a more precise theory which tends to give them a more direct sense; a theory which sees in monastic (or canonic) life not only the perfection of Christian life, but the only true Christian life. It is, they say, the form of life which was at the origins of the whole Church. The first monks were the Apostles,[74] themselves preceded and prefigured by the "sons of the prophets" under the Old Testament. The monastic vestment is the same as that the Prophets and Apostles wore.[75] The monastic life is none other than the apostolic life, that is to say, the life that the first Christian community led at Jerusalem gathered round the Twelve,[76] all then being "one heart and one soul":

This is the way for monks, whom a social life binds together.[77]

Testimony for this idea is thought to be found not only in the Acts of the Apostles, but also in Philo: has not the latter described the kind of life of the first disciples of Christ with praise and called their houses monasteries?[78] In addition, they say that the monasteries realize the "form of the apostolic institution."[79] They talk constantly about the "common and apostolic life," of the "regular and apostolic life," of the "apostolic rule,"[80] of the "apostolic profession,"[81] of the "apostolic institution,"[82] about the "discipline of the apostolic observance."[83] Of Saint Benedict they say that he was "the first of the apostolic Fathers" to signify that he is the legislator of the religious life.[84] They want to lead or to restore a life "according to the imitation of the Apostles"[85] or "in the fashion of the primitive Church,"[86] etc. On the other hand, one can discuss and, unfortunately, in defiance of the bull promulgated by Urban II in 1092, even argue about what exactly this "truly apostolic life" was, properly monastic or on the contrary "canonic," just as was disputed between black monks and white at the same period:[87] it is always the case that the Church has not begun with the "secular" life. Monks and canons, who with Arno of Reichersberg were recognized in the cherubim and the seraphim as well as in the two great apostles running together to the tomb or seeing Jesus on the seashore,[88] agreed to proclaim themselves prior to and superior to the clergy remaining in the world.[89] The two great patriarchs, Saint Augustine and Saint Benedict, are not so much the founders of a new kind of life as the "conservers,"[90] the "restorers,"[91] at the very most the "elucidators"[92] of a kind of life whose true "authors"[93] and true "institutors"[94] are the Apostles themselves. Augustine and Benedict are only "particular masters."[95] The one for the canons regular, the other for the monks properly speaking, they have engineered the bed of the two great rivers that flow directly from the revealed teaching of Moses, of Jesus, and of Saint Paul.[96]

None of all this, as we have said, is absolutely new. Well before the twelfth century, Origen had traced a first sketch of monastic life recalling the ideal of the community of Jerusalem;[97] Eusebius had used the word "philosophy" in the sense of ascetic Christian life.[98] Saint Jerome had assigned Saint John the Baptist, the "sons of the prophets," and even the Rechabites to the monks, if not as founders, at least as ancestors and patrons; we might say, as archetypes.[99] Denis the Little, at the moment of translating the story of the discovery of the head of Saint John the Baptist, congratulated himself on the fact that this remarkable relic of the "institutor of the monks" had been found by monks.[100] For Saint Pachomius, to live as a monk was quite simply "to live according to the Scriptures," and the "Rule of Saint Augustine" referred quite naturally to the Acts of the Apostles, whose text it reproduced almost word for word.[101] In speaking of the "monks of the Old Testament," Rupert was authorized by an ancient and common usage.[102] The expression "apostolic life"[103] was itself very ancient, and Cassian has affirmed that the "royal road" of the monastic state is paved with "apostolic and prophetic stones."[104] The assimilation of the monastic profession to a baptism was already made in ancient monasticism[105] and since then it had become classic;[106] at least in the eleventh century it was even doubled with an analogy with confirmation.[107] There is no longer anything quite unusual to want "to abandon the Egypt of this world" or, as Peter Damian and Saint Anselm[108] had done in the previous century, to praise the charms of the "paradise of the cloister,"[109] symbolically to rediscover in it the four rivers of the first paradise,[110] or even to think that all the inhabitants of heaven would be monks, from the moment that it was explained in a reasonable sense.[111] "The bodily paradise," Aelred used to say, "is cloistered repose."[112] Why should we deny him the right to say of his own cloister what his fellow countryman Alexander Neckam would soon say of Paris:

> Is it the case that Paris is a greater Paradise of delights
> because it is more highly praised?[113]

Without missing the essential doctrine nor the respect due to the Apostle, Saint Bernard, in a moment of heartfelt eloquence, was quite able to refer to Clairvaux as the true Jerusalem, "the free woman, our mother," and without missing the faith of the Church either, Odo of Ourscamp, having been created a cardinal, could nostalgically call up "this paradise of pleasure, this garden of delights" from which we have wrested him.[114] But what was at first merely a search for traditional support or an analogical application to the second degree, every now and then hardens and becomes systematized. Whereas a short while ago people were searching merely for authoritative examples, for divine indications, now they want to affirm a historical bond grounding some sort of exclusivity. This is, however, more a tendency of the mediocre than of the true spirituals. A William of Saint Thierry, for example, in no way materializes ideas like those of "conversion" or "newness of life."[115] Nevertheless let us say at least that in certain cases a stronger stress is noticeable; that a certain line of force has been displaced.

Doubtless one is nowhere justified in speaking of "monastic exegesis" better than here. The monks who read Scripture in this new context evidently differ a good deal from the Fathers who, in the course of the first centuries, have constituted the canon of spiritual understanding. They "do not have the same function in the Church, and a new sensibility inspires them."[116] In their hands, it would sometimes seem as though the traditional doctrine is excessively specialized, that it is thinned down, so as to put itself at the service of an ever richer and subtler inner experience, but one which is no longer, one which can no longer be, simply that of the Church herself, that of the whole community of the faithful. A spiritual hothouse culture, [with its] ardent meditation upon liturgical texts rather than upon a Bible directly studied, is an aristocratic exercise, suspension of time within an oasis; while outside — life, the life of the world, the true life of men pursues its course, little by little engendering a new form of exegesis, simpler, more objective, more robust. A late-season fruit, one can believe, and tastiest of all, but one which would no longer hold any promise. Mystical embroidery, analogous to that art of the cloisters that, as André Malraux says, ends up by expressing nothing more than "a sacred secret."[117] Certain phenomena can lend plausibility to such a judgment. Nevertheless, it would be wrong. Let us avoid hardening these rigidifications still more ourselves. Let us not imagine factitious contrasts: it is not possible to be at once at the summit of the spiritual life and aloof from reality.[118] This would be to delude oneself regarding the monks so as to believe their meditation on the Bible to be entirely dependent upon the liturgy.[119] Saint Bernard, for example, reads the holy books "integrally, in the order in which they occur."[120] To whatever family they belong, the elite of these monks is always bathing in the great current of the tradition. They particularize it much less than they prolong it. They always bear in mind the doctrinal foundations that sustain their edifice. The greatest among them have a very lively awareness of the Christian mystery in the solidity of its structure and in the breadth of its rhythm. This can be observed even in the apparently most special case, the "Cistercian novelty" and the work of Saint Bernard.

For whether it be a matter of admiration or of scandal, the same word is upon all lips in the first half of the twelfth century just as at the time of the first Christians: novelty. "What is this new law? This new doctrine? Whence does it arise? Whence comes this new and unheard of presumption?"[121] This is how one adversary expresses his indignation. "At Clairvaux," an enthusiastic voice replies, "the new man is engendered in the newness of life";[122] the "marvelous tabernacle," the "house of God" that Scripture speaks of is this house of Clairvaux, which is not made by the hand of man;[123] from the Old Testament and the shadow of Cluny, from its observances that were like the Jewish law, we have taken flight toward the purity of Cîteaux;[124] this change from black to white, like that of the Ethiopian who would be made a new skin, is truly the work "of the finger of the Most High."[125] Let us now listen to a historian adding his own voice in agreement: "A crowd of nobles, of rich men, and of deep philosophers have hastened to the neighborhood of the first inhabitants of Cîteaux, *pro novitate singularitatis.*"[126]

Now with Saint Bernard the novelty redoubled.[127] It is a new springtime of exegesis, "it is a new language that sings the sacred mysteries"; a new spiritual sense pours forth, like oil from a new press; a new wine flows from new cellars, where the friends of Bernard ask to be introduced.[128] Even further than that of the Fathers and their imitators from what we call exegesis, the Cistercian exegesis, is in fact especially tropological. So as to illuminate a contrast which nevertheless ought not to be forced, one historian was able to write: "chiefly committed to contemplate salvation history in its objective reality, as did Rupert of Deutz in his *De Trinitate*, whereas the Cistercians looked for God chiefly in his invisible image restored in the soul through charity."[129] Faithful to the instruction given by Saint Benedict to look in Scripture for the "most correct norm for human life,"[130] they everywhere interiorized it, "moralized" it; they received its whole history, as one of them put it, "below the house of conscience,"[131] so as to enrich the substance of their treatises *De anima* from it.[132] As still another says, with regard to scenes from the Canticle of Canticles, "They refer to the mysteries of the Church, but we, pursuing the moral interpretation...."[133] Those who hold themselves to the program thus sketched by Gilbert of Stanford will perhaps explore the depths of the soul "capable of eternity":[134] will this not be at the price of a constriction of horizon? Let us take only two examples. While with Rabanus Maurus the four sides of the cross provided matter for a large cosmic symbolism, Saint Bernard, exploiting a certain Augustinian line, sees in it "continence, patience, prudence, and humility."[135] While a long, firm tradition explained the six urns of Cana as the six periods that divide the history of revelation, for Bernard, again, preoccupied above all with spiritual conversion and interior life, these urns do not contain anything more than the water necessary for the "six purgations of the soul": they are "silence, psalmody, vigils, fasting, manual labor, chastity";[136] his new exegesis, developed at least on three occasions, will set a fashion:[137] Adam Scotus will see in the six urns the six types or six degrees of meditation by which the soul passes from the good to the better, until the point that, by the miracle of the water transformed into wine, death is absorbed in victory.[138]

Furthermore, it is not merely by such or such an unprecedented interpretation, it is by his whole manner that Bernard treats Scripture with a new liberty; with an "audacious liberty," says Father Claude Bodard.[139] "With the spirit of freedom going on before," says Bernard himself.[140] He uses it so freely, remarks Geoffrey of Auxerre, "that he seems rather to precede it than to follow it, to lead it where he wanted, himself following the Spirit who is its author."[141] Of him more than any other it therefore seems true to say that he does not properly speaking explicate the Scripture: he applies it; he does not clarify it: he clarifies everything by means of it, and the human heart to start with. We shall soon have to see if this is to the detriment of theological exegesis. Let us recognize from now on that if his method should appear so completely subjective, he first let himself be formed by the Word of God in secret, with the result that there is "an intimate bond between his own mind and the spirit of the Scriptures."[142] As Saint Augustine had done in a few pages of lyric exaltation,[143] but more habitually, he composes centos.[144] He pulls the texts from their context. He appropriates them. The result is admirable. Father Dumontier justly compares such pages of his to the *Magnificat*: "What then did the Blessed Virgin do but to engage in centonization, to pour her own personal sentiments into the molds of the old language of Scripture, and, with the words and verses that she borrowed from it and intermingled with her own language, to form from it the most sumptuous, the most majestic portico opening upon the New Testament?"[145]

4. Bernard, Gregory, and Origen

In the novelty of its themes, is the exegesis of Bernard still traditional? In the freedom of its style, is this tropology still, in the old sense of the word, mystical? Yes, certainly. Saint Bernard is not only mystical in the modern sense, in the sense that he does not rest content with moral analyses but develops a doctrine of union; he is still, or rather already, mystical in the ancient sense, in the sense that his tropology remains rooted in the mystery, and in this respect he is traditional. In other words, no more with Bernard than with the Fathers is tropology cut off from allegory. He "sees all the aspects of spiritual life only in their relation with the great central mystery, without which there would be no meaning."[1] To come back to one of our examples, in the explication of the mystery of Cana, everything that he says of the individual soul he says first of the Church.[2] Thus he proceeds in particular all throughout the sermons on the Canticle: the Church and the soul are inseparable in it: "The Church, or any studious soul."[3] "Thanks be to you, Lord Jesus, to you who have deigned to join us to your beloved Church!"[4] Without didacticism but with his usual freedom, Bernard passes constantly from souls to the Church, or from the Church to souls.[5] His interiorizing contemplation is never, not even in appearance, individualistic. "In terms like those of Saint Leo, Saint Ambrose, and Saint Augustine, he insists on the social aspect of life in the Church and on the solidarity which unites all the members of which Christ is the head."[6] If one wants to find in the twelfth century a purely "spiritual" or "mystical" commentary on the Canticle, in the modern and already almost "separate" sense of these words, Bernard is not the one to read, but rather Richard of Saint Victor. Bernard always takes his inspiration directly from the great sources of the tradition.[7] This first of the great moderns is also truly "the last of the Fathers of the Church." In the same way, in him, spiritual experience is still quite explicitly a function of the datum of the faith as a whole, as it is always an "experience within the Church."[8] He "always remembers the totality of the mysteries."[9] Thereby, howsoever personal his exegesis may be, it is traditional even in its form. The true genius is never eccentric.

Bernard in particular stays very close to the two great initiators of medieval exegesis: Saint Gregory and Origen. Let us express ourselves better: he does not *stay* very close to them, as a conservative mind devoid of initiative might do; he rather brings them nearer, making them live again in himself.

Nevertheless we thought we saw a discreet manifesto against Gregorian allegory in a few phrases from his sermons on the Canticle. Alluding to his preaching at vigils, Bernard says one day:

> Contrary to my plan, our discussion of the sacraments has detained us for a long time. I thought, I should say, one sermon to be enough for this topic, and that we would quickly cross that shadowy and intricate forest of allegories and arrive at the plain of the moral senses in, as it were, a day's journey: but it happened otherwise.[10]

Is there truly in this "a sort of irreverent humor mingled with great poetry"? Does not such a proposal seem like "a burial of allegory," albeit assuredly "not without flowers and coronets"? Should we believe that we are "among these thorny thickets, far from Gregorian allegory, with its fruits so sweet to spoon up, 'allegory's fruit is sweet to grasp'"?[11] Saint Gregory himself has spoken of the "shadiness of the woods" ["opacitas silvarum"] that one finds in penetrating into the allegorical depth of the Scriptures. It is true that this was to praise its coolness, contrasting with the sultry heat of the world.[12] The metaphor comes to him from Saint Augustine, who, with respect to the text of the Psalm, "and he will reveal the woods" ["et revelabit silvas"], has celebrated the "shady spots of the divine books and the little shadows of the mysteries" ["opacitates divinorum librorum et umbracula mysteriorum"], where contemplative souls "walk in freedom."[13] The "shadowy mountain" of the Book of Habakkuk was for Gregory also the mount of the Scriptures, "shadowy through allegories."[14] But if he finds the fruits of this obscure allegory sweet and flavorful, he was then no longer unhappy subsequently to go out upon "the level grass of the moral sense":

> With the generous aid of our Lord Jesus Christ, we have discussed the beginning of a book on Ezekiel the prophet, a beginning shut up within great obscurities and tied up with certain knots of mysteries. Now the things that follow are plainer, and less difficult. So we are speaking with deference to your charity, giving thanks to that same almighty God, since, after so many dark spots of the forest,

we at last have joyfully come out to the fields, in which we may set foot undaunted with the free steps of our speech.[15]

Often enough he even came to show his haste to come from there to this third, "larger," easier sense, that one can treat more freely, and for which the speaker feels that he will have less trouble in making himself understood:

> Therefore we go over the allegorical senses only briefly, so that we can the more quickly come to the breadth of morality. . . .
> Dear brothers, let it suffice for us to have crossed these matters succinctly to track down the mysteries of allegory; now let the mind run more broadly so as to look into the morality of what has been done.[16]

It is clear that Bernard is acquainted with such passages and that he is inspired by them; but it does not seem that this was in the least with any intention of deviating from them or only of increasing their gradient. Nevertheless, the following sermon on the Canticle contains another sentence of which "the beautiful balanced construction," which "makes Gregory's Latin pale," would indicate moreover, in the view of one interpreter, that Saint Bernard "does not find himself comfortable with allegory," which he doubtless accepted because it procures "the faith's handrail," all the while considering it "as a shadow zone" to cross as quickly as possible, an arid stage during which the soul finds no nourishment to its taste:[17]

> We have gone across the shadows of allegories, the time has come to explore moral matters; faith has been built up, let life be provided for; the understanding has been trained, let the action be rehearsed and enriched.[18]

If the sentence is indeed beautiful, it is nonetheless true that its very thought and expressions are classic. We already know from whence these "shadows of allegory" come. From the same source, from Gregory again, comes the formula: "faith has been built up" ["aedificata est fides"]; there is therefore no hidden agenda to look for, as if it were Bernard who invented it. What is more, the image of the "handrailing" would rather badly render the idea of constructive power that this formula presupposes. As to the threefold antithesis of Bernard's sentence, it very effectively marks the succession of the two stages; it even does so with a certain didacticism, but without any pejorative nuance affecting the one side or the other. The explication of the moral sense ought to follow upon the explication of the allegorical sense; but Bernard does not insinuate that he needs to disencumber himself of the first so as to give himself over to the second, as if they were not only distinct, but separate things: he knows quite well that the second is the fruit of the first, because it is already within allegory that "the Spirit of Love" has prepared his manna for us. Finally, we have his own testimony that he is not at all ill at ease in the course of the first stage. He even lingers a bit too long there at the pleasure of his hearers; does he not excuse himself on one occasion in the following terms?

> Some of you, as I have ascertained, are less than pleased that, while the sermon that I have been delivering for so many days already entices you to cleave to astonishment and admiration at the sacraments, it had been supplied with none or at most with a meager amount of the salt of morality. This is quite unusual. . . .[19]

The sequel supplies a precision regarding these famous "shadows of the allegories." Jesus Christ was once held hidden under the letter of the ancient Scriptures, and one could not discover him in them until the hour of his advent;[20] but then:

At sunrise sparkle the higher light's
Law's mysteries full of mist.[21]

Today, that is to say in the whole series of Christian generations, the role of the commentator is precisely to carry this light there, so as to show a "cloud full of light" in Scripture as a whole.[22] This doctrine is perfectly classic. Peter of Riga again will say that he has given his great biblical poem the name *Aurora*, with the desire that "just as Dawn brings an end to night, so too this whole booklet, dispelling the darkness of shadows and the obscurities of the old law, flashes with the lightning of truth."[23] Shadows, darkness, night, thick batches,[24] clouds: such, then, were the words that were used to designate the allegory contained within the texts. *The obscure mysteries of allegory.*[25] "*The mist of the sacrament; Scripture wrapped in mysteries. . . .*"[26] The Gregorian exegesis of the "shadowy mountain" ["mons umbrosus"] was developed by Ambrose Autpert:

> "God will come from Lebanon, and the holy one from the cloudy and thickly covered mountain" (Hab. 3). For the cloudy and thickly covered Mount Lebanon is the height of the divine Scriptures as it was opened up by the figures of the allegories. And our Lord has come from the shadowy and thickly covered mountain, to wit, because he appeared revealed by the allegorical sacraments of the Scriptures when he wanted, in which his predicted advent lay hidden before it appeared. For he who sparkled in the truth of light once the figures of allegories had been removed departed, as it were, from the shadowy and thickly covered dark spots of the woods.[27]

Paulinus of Aquilaea has also spoken of the "thick wood" of allegories.[28] Others were to do it again, both before and after Saint Bernard, such as Richard of Saint Victor.[29] If the abbot of Clairvaux had needed still another patron for so common an expression, he would have found him in Saint Jerome, who said of the ancient Scripture: "it has been wound up with so many obscurities and types of the things to come,"[30] and, in an elegy on Origen's exegesis: "it is investigated with the serene explanation of the clouds of allegory."[31] Bernard therefore shows in his turn, in a formula which is this time proper to himself, how the sacred text — here, the Canticle — concerns allegorically "the secret delights of Christ and his Church." Does not such an expression make one suspect that in the accomplishment of this task Bernard himself found "secret delights"?

> From here on I had but one concern: once the dense mist of these allegories had been discussed, to bring to light the delicate secrets of Christ and the Church. So let us return to investigate the moral dimensions.... And this will be done fittingly if we should assign the same things that have been said regarding Christ and the Church without dilution to the Word and to the soul.[32]

Saint Bernard therefore enjoys the mysteries of Scripture. He repairs thither with ardor: our "intention runs to the mystical."[33] In this respect he is like his contemporary Hugh of Saint Victor, who said: "Let us repair to the pleasant shades of allegory and tropology."[34] There is no longer any exception in the Order of Cîteaux. "For it is quite thankworthy that it is common to the Church" as a whole, says Abbot Gilbert in one of the sermons which continue Bernard's series on the Canticle.[35] We read analogous reflections in a sermon of Guerric, abbot of Igny:

Pardon me, brothers, since I who ought to provide instruction of your morals have paused perhaps more than was necessary in admiring and proclaiming that ineffable mystery. . . . But I know not whether there can be any more effective and sweeter upbuilding of morals than the faithful and pious consideration of this mystery, i.e., the Word incarnate.[36]

That is a frequent theme with Isaac, the abbot of Stella, who, "perfect monk that he is, shows himself decidedly careful about how to construe doctrine."[37] Isaac sometime treats the "mysterium" and the "tropology" together.[38] But when he distinguishes them, his preference is manifest: he does what he can, he says, to meet the expectations of his religious, who always avidly drink up the moral sense, but this is under compulsion; for himself, he pays attention above all to the mystery; it is the contemplation of the mystery which delights him above all.[39]

Let us conclude that if the common man among the auditors, in the cloister as in the world, and in the Middle Ages as in every epoch, manifested a pragmatist tendency, if he were fond of moral applications concerning practical life, if he sometimes failed to awaken his attention by means of certain biting traits — tropology will in the medieval sermon give birth to the satire of customs — the Cistercian preaching in Saint Bernard and his emulators would remain no less entirely faithful to the great doctrinal mysticism which had characterized Patristic exegesis. If it was "monastic," this was by way of addition. "Sticking with the amazement and admiration of the sacraments": the formula is worthy not only of Saint Gregory, but also of Saint Leo.

One day this fidelity expresses itself in the mouth of Bernard by means of the following exclamation, addressed against aberrant methods: "We do not take the divine Scriptures in this way, but neither does God's Church!"[40] This time it was no longer from Saint Gregory that he borrowed his language; it was from Origen.[41] We already know that his sermons on the Canticle carry the mark of Origen. More significant than the abundance of implicit citations, reminiscences or imitations that can be picked up in them is the identity of the fundamental theme in each, right down to their various harmonics. But it is more remarkable still that Bernard shows himself an Origenian even in the effusions in which he is the most personal.

The mysticism of Origen, as Etienne Gilson has written, is "the mysticism of an exegete."[42] This expression is apt. For, at the end of the day, is this so much desired Word of God, viewed from a certain slant, anything else than the meaning to be deciphered from a text? The soul begs for a kiss, when she is in quest of one of these divine meanings which are revealed only in prayer.[43] The search takes on the gait of a long pilgrimage, "to see the glory of Christ and the kingdom, i.e., the perfection of the Word and the kingdom."[44] It also takes on the gait of a hunt:[45] in pursuit of his game, the stalker follows one track, then another, going, coming back, laboring, up until the Lord uncovers for him the explication that satisfies him.[46] "The soul that the love of the Word of God has in its grasp" is first made anxious by the enigmas of the text; "but if she comes to feel that *he* is approaching and receives the sound of his voice from on high," then she takes courage and to the measure that the obscurities are cleared up, to the measure that the meanings of an exalted understanding are proposed to her, she cries out: 'Look: *he* is coming, bounding over the mountains, leaping across the hills!' . . ."[47] Yes, this is indeed the mysticism of an exegete. But is it not equally the exegesis of a mystic? What Origen searches for with such ardor, what he finds with such joy, is it not the Word of God himself, a Speech buried in the letter before being incarnated in the flesh? Is this not truly "the Bridegroom," the Beloved? "The Bridegroom is arriving; here he is!"[48] For the sense of Scripture is not just any thought; it is not an impersonal truth: it is *he. The secret and hidden sense of Christ itself.*[49] Here he is who is appearing behind this wall of the letter. He is living: he watches through the windows, he spies in across the trellis-work. One could believe him to be entirely confined within the text, like the water within the urn of the Samaritan woman: but "he is worth more than the urn," he is the Source from whence it is filled.[50] He overflows every sense, this person of whom the Apostle Paul has said: "We have the sense of the Christ." In pursuing her effort at exegesis, the soul sees him in reality. "Why does my Bridegroom send me kisses through Moses? or send me kisses through the prophets? I am already eager to touch his own mouth: let him come, let him descend."[51] Already, without yet seeing him, she engages in dialogue with the Bridegroom. When she has found him, then she will grasp "what the eye has not seen, what the ear has not heard, which has not risen up to the heart of man." She will be "nourished with the perfection of the Word."[52] She will be introduced into the king's chamber, where all the treasures of wisdom and of science are hidden, and Christ will make himself directly known to her: *Christ leads the soul to understand him.*[53] The discovery of the spiritual sense of Scripture, which is procured through Jesus,[54] is also truly the appearance of Jesus.[55]

Accordingly one understands the soul's emotion, her alternatives of anxiety and joy. The Word hides himself, then lets a glimpse of him be seen, then hides himself again. He bounds over the mountains, only to disappear in the bottoms of the valleys. He comes, approaches, then retires forthwith. He shows himself for an instant only to stir up desire. His furtive visits seem like unkept promises. "But we have to endure these things until we become such that not only does he visit us frequently, but stays with us, following the answer that he gave his disciple: 'If anyone loves Me, he keeps my word, and my Father loves him, and we shall come to him, and we shall establish our home with him!" Then "the winter will have passed," and the trellis-works themselves will be torn apart.[56]

Saint Ambrose and Saint Jerome have read these pages long ago, and if the second retained nothing but its rind,[57] the first, while commenting in his turn upon the words of Scripture, "Behold he is approaching, leaping over the mountains," recovered something of Origen's accent.[58] Saint Gregory also united exegesis and mysticism when he said: "Mouth speaks to mouth, as though to kiss, and to touch the inner understanding with the mind."[59] Quite recently, Rupert again said: "What is apprehending the Beloved except finding the sense of Christ within the Scriptures?"[60] After many others, Bernard now reads Origen's commentary in the translation of Rufinus. He nourishes his own experience with it. Looking everywhere for "spiritual understanding" and "spiritual" fruit,[61] he too is looking for the Word in his Scripture. He in his turn describes the soul's quest and the encounters with the Beloved. For him as for Origen, and as with Gregory, there is a whole "dialectic of presence and absence, of possession and non-possession, of certitude and incertitude, of light and darkness, of faith and eternal life."[62] This is what he calls the "alternations," the "vicissitudes of the Word going and coming back";[63] what Jean Mouroux denominates the "drama of vicissitude," a drama which is the necessary expression of temporal and pilgrim existence, and consequently, "the authentic criterion of a real experience of God."[64] Bernard chants the divine Game better than his predecessors,[65] but like them he chants it — as his friend William of Saint Thierry[66] chants it with him on a calmer note; as a certain number of his disciples, a Gilbert of Hoyland,[67] an Aelred of Rievaulx,[68] a Gilbert of Stanford[69] will soon chant it after him; as a Saint William Firmat chants it.[70] He chants it as a Hugh of Saint Victor, who has more wisdom than dash, explicates it;[71] as the scholar Garnier of Rochefort[72] will also explain it among the Cistercians.

The rhythm of Bernard is more breathless; his sensibility, more throbbing. Even when he was expressing an anxiety and while speaking from experience, Origen had a weightier serenity; his whole gait was slower, let us even say heavier, except in rare passages, and, although we may read no more within his text, we divine that he did not burn with quite the same fire. The analogy is no less profound. With Bernard, the figure of Jesus is rendered more concrete; nevertheless his sensible humanity does not halt the movement traversing it to reach the Word.[73] With him, as with Origen, if Christ is the Bridegroom of the Church, it is the Word that is the bridegroom of the soul. God, taking pity on our wanderings, says he, has left "the shadowy and misty mountain" ("de monte umbroso et condenso"), he has pitched his tent among us in broad daylight — though, from another point of view, one ought to say that he has enveloped himself with shadow — and to those who never tasted flesh he offers his own flesh, but so as to take them across it to taste the spirit.[74] Though Gerhoh of Reichersberg reproached him for not sufficiently engulfing Christ's humanity in the glory of his divinity,[75] Bernard, who celebrated the mystery of Christmas so much, celebrated the mystery of the ascension with no less fervor. *Grande mysterium!* The disciples were led to the understanding of the faith through the resurrection; but it took the ascension to enable their love to be purified.[76] "Do not touch me," says the resurrected Jesus to Magdalen: "Grow unaccustomed to this seducible sense; strive for the word; grow accustomed to faith."[77] From now on we ought no longer know the Lord according to the flesh. The flesh does no good; it is the spirit that giveth life, and the Lord is Spirit.[78]

Even more than with Origen, more than with John Scotus[79] or even than with Rupert,[80] who offers us the same theme,[81] the course of the soul in quest of the Bridegroom with Bernard is distinguished by the exegetical search — not, however, to the point of effecting a dissociation between the one and the other. "If I feel my mind open up to the understanding of the Scriptures, or words of wisdom escape in abundance from the depth of my heart, if a flood of light reveals mysteries to me . . . , then I no longer doubt the arrival of the Bridegroom": this is not Origen who is speaking; it is Bernard.[82] In communicating itself to him, the "Divine Fire" not only makes him "burn with love": it produces in him "an extraordinary expansion of the mind"; then his understanding is flooded with the clarity that comes forth from "the eye of the Bridegroom," and in imitation of Saint Paul, "the greatest of the contemplatives," [his soul] "scrutinizes the mysteries of the Scriptures";[83] in the "caves of rock," emboldened by a purified conscience, she "penetrates the secrets of wisdom."[84] What Bernard gathers is therefore still, as with Origen, a harvest of "spiritual senses," and if he discerns three degrees in the intimacy of the Lord, according to which the soul "athirst for God" is introduced into his "garden," into his "storeroom," or into his "bedchamber," these three degrees are at the same time for him the three sorts of sense that one successively discovers in the text: historical, moral, and mystical. There one recognizes the other division of the senses of Scripture, more "pneumatic" than doctrinal in inspiration, the one that we have just said belongs to the contemplatives. Bernard, like Origen who is his initiator into it, uses it concurrently with the first. It is in the storeroom of the moral sense, he explains, that the fruits gathered in the garden of history begin to be sweet; but he has reserved for him who penetrates into the bedchamber of the mystical sense to taste "the mystery of contemplative vision."[85] Thus it is indeed always "in the Scriptures that the soul finds the one she thirsts for."

The age has not yet come which will see the "secrets of Scripture" put on one side and "devotion" on the other; the age where a Saint Lutgarde, having obtained the favor she had asked for of understanding her Psalter, declares herself dissatisfied with that and, to Christ who says to her "What do you want, then?", replies: "I want your heart."[86] Exegesis and mysticism in Saint Bernard remain interwoven, as they are at the same time for the Benedictine Godfrey of Admont who offers many points of comparison with Bernard, due perhaps to a direct influence of Clairvaux upon Admont and, doubtless, to a common meditation upon Origen;[87] as they will be again with the Cistercians Isaac of Stella,[88] Guerric of Igny,[89] Henry of Marcy.[90] If, then, it is indubitable that the exegesis of Bernard is the exegesis of a mystic, it is no less true that, more essentially, by its very texture, his mysticism is the mysticism of an exegete. To understand things properly, this amounts to saying: if his Christianity is mystical, his mysticism is truly Christian. In any event, what his contemporaries recalled about him above all is the fact that he made the honey of the Scriptures to flow. And this is the primary meaning of the nickname that has been ratified by posterity: he is the *Doctor mellifluus*.[91]

5. *Doctor mellifluus*

Doctor mellifluus. The word was subsequently taken as designating the doctor "with words as sweet as honey." This sweetening was not completely a misconception, as we shall soon see. Nevertheless, the authentic sense is different. Again it is Origen who is at its origin. For in a homily

Doctor mellifluus

on Isaiah that we read in the translation of Saint Jerome he said: "And perchance the subtler letters will be the honeycombs, while the honey is what is understood in them,"[1] and again, commenting on Ezekiel: "the contemplations drawn from the prophets and the Gospels are the honey of the bees."[2] Scripture, he said again, is a hive, the sacred writers are bees, and the Christ, who is their king, is like the queen bee.[3] The honey of the Scriptures, which Origen perhaps already implicitly opposed to "Attic honey," was therefore their nutritious juice, which one extracted from the letter. By means of this nourishment of the soul, Pope Saint Damasus subsequently wrote, "all honeys are overcome." The honeycomb found by Samson in the mouth of the dead lion had been produced, said Saint Quodvultdeus, by the patriarchs and the prophets; they had filled it with the divine language, and the Lord, the Lion of Judah, made his disciples taste it by opening their mind so that they might comprehend the Scriptures.[4] In its general outline, that was an already traditional interpretation, as an analogous passage from Saint Paulinus of Nola testifies.[5] For Saint Augustine,[6] then for Cassiodorus,[7] the liquid honey was the exterior doctrine, "the open teaching of wisdom," or the Old Testament, whilst the comb signified "the mysteries" hidden in the depth of the cells, in other words, the New Testament hidden in the Old. If the grace of the New Testament, prefigured in the Old, was compared to milk and honey, this was because it was at once "sweet and full of nourishment."[8] For Aponius, the honeycomb is also "the law of the Old Testament"; patriarchs and prophets, like bees, constructed it with the juice of heavenly flowers, and now the lips of the doctors of the Church distill it.[9] For Saint Aldhelm, without any other precision, the "honey-flowing swarm" represented the wise man who cultivates, along with the arts, the science of Scripture.[10] For Saint Bede, the milk and honey figure "the Old and the New Testaments in the Church";[11] the honey of the "heavenly understanding" has been pulled free by those bees, the Fathers;[12] or again, the milk was the "training of the little ones" and the honey the "doctrina," that is to say, the nourishment which is suitable to the perfect.[13] Bede again opposed the books of the Platonists to the books of the Apostles, as the poisoned honey of yellow-jackets to the sweet honey of true bees.[14] Like the lips of the Bride, said he, the holy books were a "dripping honeycomb" because from the tiniest passage one could draw long commentaries, so great was the fecundity of their spiritual sense.[15] Saint Ambrose Autpert characterized the exegesis of Tychonius in these words: "he pressed together the many honeys of the spiritual senses."[16] Again, without speaking of the "doctor mellifluus,"

Alcuin gave the definition of it in advance while himself also commenting upon the verse of the Canticle, "thy lips, o Bride, are a dripping honeycomb":

> The honeycomb is the honey in the wax; and the honey in the wax is the spiritual sense of the divine eloquence in the letter. The honey [is] dripping, since nearly each and every sentence has multiple senses. The lips of the bride are the doctors, who show that many various senses are present in the sacred letters.

And, in commenting on the other verse: "there are honey and milk under thy tongue," he took up Bede's explication again, reserving for the honey the "stronger doctrine" or the "doctrine of the perfect."[17] In the *Caroline Books,* by allusion to the words of the Psalm: "like honey from the rock," it said of Christ: "Since he is the stone laid down as foundation for Zion, he satisfies the minds of believers with the honeyed drink of spiritual life."[18] The didactic Rabanus Maurus rendered this already classic analogy more precise in the manner of Cassiodorus:

> The honey that is ready to eat hints at the moral surface of the letter; while the honeycomb, in which the honey is squeezed out from the wax, announces the allegorical discourse in figurative fashion, where, once the veil of the letter has been removed, the smoothness of the spiritual sense is sometimes perceived with labor and delay.[19]

These are precisions retained by Aimon;[20] by Manegold: "By the liquefied honey is understood the open teaching of wisdom, whereas by the honeycomb is meant the hidden wisdom of the teaching, which is enclosed within the abstruser sacraments like honey in the comb."[21] The same obtains with Honorius: "The honeycomb is honey in the wax; honey in the wax is the spiritual understanding lying hidden in the letter; but the honeycomb is dripping, while sweet allegory is flowing from the letter."[22] It is retained in the same way by Hugo: "the history, from which the truth of allegory is expressed like honey from the comb," and by Richard of Saint Victor: "Like the comb containing honey within the wax, there is truth hiding under the allegory."[23] The latter will oppose, somewhat like Bede and Alcuin, the honey, which is "the refreshment of the hardy," to milk, which is the "comfort of the little ones."[24] Othloh of Saint Emmeran wishes that one interpret the signs of the sensible world so as to gather from them "the honeys of great virtue and wisdom."[25] Saint Peter Damian designates Scripture as the "honey of God," because in it man finds the "feast of spiritual understanding."[26] Marbodius writes in his elegy of Saint Florentius of Worcester: "I liked that man's discretion in teaching; though he used to hide the spiritual understanding within the letter, i.e., honey within wax, he knew how to offer wine to the strong and milk to the weak so as to captivate each" — a mixture of foods or of images such as may be permitted to a poet.[27] Saint Bernard himself also says: "The honey in the wax is devotion in the letter; otherwise the letter killeth, if you gulp it down without the seasoning of the spirit";[28] and his disciple Guerric of Igny: "Scrutinizing all things like busy bees, gather ye honey from flowers, spirit from speeches."[29] It is in this sense that Aimon of Bazoches, addressing himself to Bernard to obtain the dispatch of the sermons on the Canticle, wrote to him: "Break the bread of the word; apply the honey's comb that your hands have processed,"[30] or that Geoffrey of Auxerre said after his death: "I am not the one to whom it was said: 'Thy lips are a dripping honeycomb.'"[31] Finally, Gilbert of Hoyland shows us well how we ought to understand the expression "doctor mellifluus" itself; this occurs as he pronounces the elegy of Aelred of Rievaulx, "the second Bernard," on the day after his death: "As the honeycomb is contained in the cells of the hive, so is the heavenly wisdom in the sacraments of the figures.... What a honeycomb, how rich and fecund, has just been transported to the heavenly banquet! I am speaking of the abbot of Rievaulx.... No like honeycomb remains in our apiary.... His word spread a science of honey....."[32]

This honey in the wax was therefore the same thing as the pith [la moëelle] in the bark,[33] or the nut in the shell,[34] or the grain in the ear.[35] *The spiritual marrow within the letter:*[36] this was always essentially the same image — and always the same doctrine. Right at the end of the twelfth century, Alan of Lille will summarize it again in his *Distinctiones:* "The page of the Old Testament is called the comb, properly the honey in the wax, because, like honey, it used to contain within itself the teaching of the Gospel,"[37] and a *Summa* composed by one of his disciples presents itself with the goal "that a sort of honeyed teaching should emerge by our labor, as it were, from various blossoms."[38] In all this for the most part it was not particularly a question of sweetness. Often even the nutritive quality of honey was opposed to the sweetness of milk. Nevertheless, one could never make honey not be sweet; or Homer not already to have commended old Nestor's discourses as "sweeter than honey";[39] or Vergil not to have sung in the *Georgics,*[40] and then in the *Aeneid,*[41] of the "dulcia mella," the "fragrantia mella," the "sweet nectar" of the bees; or Scripture itself not to have made more than one allusion to it. Was it not notably a vision of sweetness, the one about the land "where milk and honey flow"?[42] Nor would it be any more possible that this Scripture should not be sweet for the heart of the Christian: "How sweet in my throat is thy eloquence, beyond honey and comb!"[43] How many times the Fathers have celebrated this sweetness: sweetness of the divine oracles,[44] of the truth that they contain,[45] sweetness of the singing of the psalms,[46] sweetness of the preaching of the Gospel.[47] More precisely, there is a sweetness of spiritual understanding: "dulcedo spiritalis intelligentiae."[48] "It savors in the throat of the heart; it grows sweet in the mouth."[49] A sweetness of scrutinizing the mystical sense of the Scriptures.[50] A sweetness of this marrow.[51] A sweetness of the honey of the Gospel, which allegory substitutes for the bitterness of the Law.[52] "Marvelous and ineffable sweetness."[53] There is, in particular, the sweetness of this song of love, the Canticle of Canticles.

Solomon has sung this book with marvelous sweetness. . . .[54]

This spiritual honeycomb was sweet to the palate of the soul:[55] it gave a foretaste of eternal sweetness.[56] If it allowed itself to be found, it was to be tasted.[57] This book that he almost ate, as it was said in Ezekiel, was a honey sweet to the mouth, sweet to the heart.[58] How much sweeter indeed than honey![59] *For what is sweeter than the Word of God?*[60] A sweetness which was not only that of the words of Christ[61] or of his doctrine,[62] but the very sweetness of Christ.[63] Sweetness of the very Name of Jesus, long ago sung by Saint Paulinus of Nola: "It is nectar in the mouth, a honeycomb upon the tongue!"[64]

Speaking of the Word of God hidden within the manna, Origen said: "the sweetness of honey is found for the faithful."[65] Seeing this Word compared sometimes to bread and sometimes to honey, Saint Ambrose explained that it was a bread by its strength, a honey by its winning sweetness,[66] and this explanation was passed on: "The dominant taste of Scripture," Bruno of Segni will say, for example, "is that of flour mixed with honey; for what is sweeter than honey? And what stronger than bread made of wheat? Scripture is therefore soundly composed of what is *dulcis ad gustandum et fortis ad alendum.*"[67] Saint Jerome likewise compared "the mystery of the Scriptures" both to the *flesh of the fruit* and to the *honey from the rock,* and speaking according to Origen, he boasted of its sweetness.[68] Saint Augustine recalled to Jerome the happy time when, in the sweetness of friendship, he tasted with Rufinus "the honey of sacred Scriptures."[69] Saint Gregory multiplied the words for "sweetness," "smoothness," and "delights."[70] Speaking of Origen, Vincent of Lerins said: "whose speech was so lovely, so milky, so sweet, that to me it looks not so much like words as bits of honey to have flowed from his mouth."[71] In his *Etymologies,* Saint Isidore of Seville, with regard to the definition of euphony, had put honey and smoothness together.[72] An old admirer of the Rule of Saint Benedict said that it contains "dulcia mella," since it contains all the doctrine of both Testaments.[73] In the *Life* of Saint Ambrose Autpert, it is a question of the "honey-flowing smoothness" of the Psalms,[74] and he himself, in a sermon on the Assumption, describes the Virgin arriving at a place "where the honey-flowing organs of the angels sound without ceasing."[75] A letter addressed to Alcuin magnifies the "mellifluous knowledge of holy Scripture."[76] Smaragdus mingles texts of Scripture with his grammar, "so that the beginner can sweetly taste the authority of the art more easily accompanied with the sweetness of heavenly honey." The dialectic of Saint Paul in the Epistle to the Romans and, more precisely, the use of two types of syllogism which are "like two delicious fish," inspires Sedulius Scotus to utter the following exclamations: "O marvelous depth! O flowing honeys sweeter than Hyblean nectar! O novel flavor brought from the paradisiacal springs of the heavenly Jerusalem to the earthborn!"[77]

Moreover, in this Carolingian epoch, the epithet spreads everywhere. The poets make great use of it, as of its synonym "dulcifluus" ["sweet-flowing"];[78]

Casting forth sweet juices from honey-flowing breast,

says Alcuin of the archbishop Ecbert.[79] And Sedulius Scotus writes:

Nor do the sweet-flowing gifts of the river Lech delight us,
And honey-flowing mead flees our dwellings.[80]

A "chorus mellifluus" is sung by Milo of Saint Amand.[81] The voice that made itself heard at the baptism of Jesus, says Paulinus of Aquilaea, proffers "mellifluous utterances."[82] Again, they speak of "honeyed delight,"[83] of "mellifluous love,"[84] of "honeyed flavor,"[85] of "mellifluous voices,"[86] of "mellifluous words,"[87] of "mellifluous commands."[88] They exchange letters "anointed with mellifluous meanings."[89] They compose "melliflua carmina" ["mellifluous songs"]. The name of a friend is a "mellifluous name."[90] In a style that makes one think of the Précieuses, Alcuin speaks of "whoever takes sweeter wounds than any honeycomb in his heart by means of the honey-flowing spear of charity . . .";[91] he calls to witness the "the broadest bay of honeyed breast" of his colleague the bishop Cunibert, a man of many holy friendships.[92] In the poems of Saint Paulinus of Nola on Saint Felix, writes Dungal, "all things, the flowers, the smells, the roses, the sweet-smelling lilies are flowing with honey."[93] Rabanus Maurus thinks that the Lord, in the course of his mortal life, has drawn honey from the rock when he showed his disciples the sweetness of his miracles.[94] A bit later, Saint Peter Damian evokes the "honeyed smoothness" of angelic concerts as well as the "mellifluous sweetness" of the service of God;[95] and when he mentions Saint Paul:

> Paul watered the whole world with mellifluous rains,[96]

the rains of apostolic understanding are also for him rains of sweetness. Fulbert of Chartres was, says he, celebrated "with mellifluous fluency of mouth."[97] The biographer of Saint John Gualbert speaks of his "mellifluous and salvation-bearing writings."[98] A poet of Tegernsee writes to his friend:

> "Hail, fellow-brother, for me always sweet with love,
> Thou art sweeter unto me than the taste of honey in the mouth:
> The fluid knows no bitterness, but love grows sweet and to the heart
> Enters, and joins the other's breast in compact."[99]

A liturgical hymn will magnify the sweet Saint Gregory

> Guiding the rule of the apostolic See
> With mellifluous teaching.[100]

The *Liber confortatorius* of Goscelin evokes memories of childhood: "fatherland flowing with milk, parents with honey, sweet relations, many friends, flattering letters."[101] John of Saint Vincent commends Ambrose Autpert for having explained the holy books with "melliflua suavitate."[102] John of Ford addresses his sermons on the Canticle to a correspondent whose "serene visage and mellifluous elocution" he admires; "your mellifluous lips," he says to him again, "glisten with discussions sweeter than honey": a fine compliment, but scarcely original.[103] For the chronicler of the abbots of Gembloux, "cantum melificare" is to compose a very sweet song.[104] Odo of Cambrai cries out in his prayer: "Your voice, O Jesus, is full of mellifluous charity."[105] Saint Bernard denounces Arnold of Brescia as a man whose language is honey but whose doctrine is venom.[106] Irimbert of Admont takes up the comparison of holy Scripture with the bee that makes its honey with the juice of various flowers: thus, from the diverse sentences of which the holy books are composed there results the "sweetness of the divine Word."[107] Godfrey of Saint Victor speaks of a "celestial and mellifluous song."[108] Aelred of Rievaulx rediscovers the accents of Saint Augustine to say that nothing could ravish his affection, "that had not been honeyed with the honey of the most sweet Jesus," and that, from the day on which for him, from holy Scriptures, "something of the sweetest honeycomb began to flow and the mellifluous name of Christ has won for itself unadulterated affection," he could no longer taste anything else.[109] Egbert of Schönau says to the Lord Jesus: "Thou hast given honey its sweetness, and thou art sweeter than honey."[110] In the *Anticlaudianus*, Alan of Lille observes:

> ... And the ear
> having been seduced by the sweet tune of a mellifluous voice
> seduces the mind. . . .[111]

Attempting to apply to herself the old metaphor of the busy bee, Herrad of Landsberg says that she has composed her *Hortus deliciarum* with juice drawn from the flowers of Scripture and gathered "as though into a single mellifluous honeycomb." Soon Saint Gertrude will contemplate Saint John reclining at supper "upon the mellifluous breast of the Lord"; she will celebrate the "mellifluous presence of the Savior" and, addressing herself to him, will say: "Your voice, full of mellifluous smoothness," etc.[112] In short, there is *sweetness in honey*.[113]

From then on, all the while that allegory was in the letter, the honey in the wax was more particularly the sweetness of this allegory. It was, as Origen said, the "smoothness of Christ's teaching."[114] It was, as Rupert says, the "smoothness of the mysteries."[115] It was the "delights of the heavenly sacraments,"[116] or, as Saint Bonaventure will say, the "loveliness of the mysteries of holy Scripture."[117] It was the "sweetness of spiritual understanding," the "mellifluous smoothness of the hidden mystery," the "honey of mystic sweetness," extracted from the "honeycomb of the letter."[118] It was the "inner sweetness" of the Scriptures.[119] Is it not by obtaining this spiritual understanding of the old books that one learns to know "how the Lord is sweet"?[120] "There are just as many delights," says Gilbert Foliot, "as there are varieties of spiritual understanding."[121] "The divine oracles are very happily compared to a honeycomb," says Hugh of Saint Victor eager to explain, because they are "full of sweetness inside."[122] "Spiritual edification," that is to say, the allegorical interpretation, makes one taste this sweetness.[123] "Spiritual honey of highest sweetness," says Richard of Saint Victor.[124] This honeycomb is, for Irimbert of Admont, "the sweetness of redemption," or "the sweet mystery of the Passion of Christ" hidden in prophecy.[125] "The one who has experienced it," says Rupert again, "knows how sweet is the nourishment of the Scriptures, that is to say, their spiritual sense."[126] A poet of the preceding generation, Williram of Ebersberg (†1084), has sung of this sweetness in his verse paraphrase of the Canticle of Canticles. The citation is a bit long; we give it nevertheless, in memory of the candid avowal that Williram gave us about how he himself was affected on its completion:[127]

> Your lips give liquefied honeycomb throughout the waxy honey.
> And under your tongue there are milk and sweet honeys,
> while the fragrance of incense rises from your vestments.
> As comb lies hidden in wax, so does the full letter
> contain the mysteries of the subtle sense within.
> When the teachers like rich repositories
> Pour them as wines in little vessels of luxuriant doctrine,
> The sweetness of the supernal word from hence gives off its scent to the strong.
> But yet under this tongue that trickles sweet honeys,
> Let not abundance of milk be lacking to the weak senses.
> Let it feed those with histories, these with allegories.
> And while pupils or teachers clinging together
> Surround you, o bride, like handsome vestments,
> A smooth aroma sends me a scent of your benefactions.[128]

The metaphor of the honeycomb — like that of the bee — has for a long time passed from Scripture to its commentator. He who nourishes himself on the Word of God, they say, is comparable to honey; but he who, not content with assimilating its sweetness, distributes it to others by his preaching is like the honeycomb.[129]

How in these conditions could a "doctor mellifluus," while being just the one who brings to light the profound sense of the Scriptures, not have been, at the same time and for the same reasons, the doctor for the words sweet as honey? In a certain fashion Saint Gregory predicted it the day he spoke of the book that becomes like honey in the mouth of him who eats it:

> The book that has filled the innards has become sweet as honey in the mouth, since they themselves who have learned truly to love it in the innards of their heart know how to speak smoothly of almighty God. For holy Scripture is sweet in the mouth of him, the innards of whose life are filled with his commandments, since, for the one within whom they had been imprinted to live, Scripture is smooth to speak.[130]

Addressing Gregory himself, did not Saint Peter Damian sing:

> Your lips drip bits of honey
> sweetening the heart:
> Does your eloquence overcome
> the power of the fragrant aromas?[131]

Did not Hadrian I previously celebrate the "mellifluus doctor" in his predecessor Gregory?[132] Was not the elegy of the writings of the holy pope soon condensed within the expression: "the mellifluous words of Gregory"?[133] Did not Manegold celebrate the "mellifluous pope Gregory"?[134] Did not Saint Columban, writing to Gregory to thank him for his *Pastoralia*, already praise this writing as "sweeter than honey"? And was it not the sweetness at the same time as the solidity of the holy pope's preaching that John the Deacon wanted to set in relief by writing: "he was gathering the seeds of the doctrine . . . that he would later declaim with his throat to honeyed peoples"?[135] From at least as early as the tenth century, in the library of Sankt Gall, did not a book containing the works of Saint Ambrose bear this inscription on its cover:

> Take hold of the honeys redolent of the nectar of Ambrose?[136]

In that same Sankt Gall, did not the biographer of the gentle Notker the Stammerer, after having recalled his affable manners, write: "The tears of those who had seen the man and were survived after him clearly manifested how mellifluous he was in his replies and his addresses, to those inquiring after him"?[137] And now did not Hugh Métel, while pirating his homilies on the Canticle, still write to Bernard: "Your tongue is a honeycomb dripping honey," and again: "he will kiss me with the kiss of his mouth: . . . with the kiss of your mouth: . . . honeyed eloquence proceeding from your pleasant mouth"?[138] Did not Geoffrey of Auxerre, pronouncing the elegy on his but recently departed spiritual father, say, in a reminiscence of Saint Paulinus of Nola: "holy Bernard, for whom Jesus is honey in the mouth"?[139] Did they not also say of him that, by reason of his great sweetness, though "a law of fire" was in his mouth, he had "honey and milk under the tongue"?[140] Toward the same date, did not a letter from Roger mention the "mellifluous mouth" from whence flowed the doctrine of the Savior?[141] Finally, did not Bernard himself speak of the "liquor of smoothness" that flows from the honeycomb?[142]

The better to enter into all the nuances of this term "mellifluous," it would be necessary to examine in detail the commentaries on the various biblical texts where it is a question of honey; to follow the image of "mel in cera" ["honey in the wax"] in certain other applications, above all in that of the incarnate Word, so close to ours;[143] to look more closely at the relations of "mel" and "favus" ["honeycomb"], of which the one is loved for itself because it is itself sweetness, whilst the other is loved only as actual or possible receptacle of the first[144] — or, of which the one is the divine Word and the other the resurrected flesh of Christ, which is united to it for ever.[145] It would also be necessary to consider attentively these four pairs: the pair "tricitus et mel" ["wheat and honey"]; the pair "vinum et mel" ["wine and honey"]; the pair "butyrum et mel" ["butter and honey"],[146] which can, among other significations, be the twofold wisdom, human and divine, but also, again, the humanity and the divinity of the Savior;[147] finally, the pair "lac et mel" ["milk and honey"], which is equally the twofold nature of the God-Man,[148] or the love of God and of neighbor,[149] or else, *per modum unius*, the collection of the joys of the homeland, of the "promised land."[150] It would be necessary to scrutinize the etymologies in the train of Isidore of Seville;[151] to enumerate the divers species of natural honey, according to their origin;[152] then to distinguish "wild honey" and "domestic honey";[153] to define the divers properties of honey, according as it is "purgativum," "conservativum," etc.,[154] without forgetting to observe the mores of the bee,[155] "which is naturally productive of honey,"[156] and which is sometimes Scripture and sometimes its commentator.[157] It would also be necessary to distinguish pure honey and honey mixed with water or with vinegar;[158] the "honey on the tongue" and the "honey under the tongue";[159] the detestable honey, which the Lord in Leviticus forbids to be offered to him in sacrifice, or the one which the lips of the courtesan, according to the Book of Proverbs, distill, and which is the honey of heretics, or of the "sweetness of the flesh,"[160] or of the "applause of flatterers" and the "blandishments of deception"[161] — the simply profane and vain honey, which is that of "philosophy for the worldly," the "honey of secular sweetness" — finally, the sacred honey.[162] It would also be necessary to set out the hierarchy of the four honeys: "honey sweetness," "honey of sweetness," "sweet honey," "sweetened honey," i.e., the Divinity itself, the Word proceeding from the Father, the understanding of Scripture, human wisdom.[163] It would finally be fitting to take up a certain number of late refinements[164] and complications, certain lists of "allegoriae" or certain efforts at synthesis of a scholastic style, such as the two sermons of Peter Comestor[165] and a sermon of Absalon on the Nativity,[166] in which a good number of the traits that we have just indicated are found amassed. But it ought to suffice for our plan, to close this chapter on tropology, by making two general remarks. We shall observe, on the one hand, in the Cistercian school, a sudden inflation of this language of "sweetness," tied to a more pronounced interiorization of the mystery in the soul that meditates on it; and, on the other hand, outside this school, a transfer from the "sweetness" or simply the interest of allegory or of the spiritual sense in general to tropology: a sign of a more pronounced specialization in the attributions of each sense.

Saint Bernard, like Saint Gregory and even more than he, had the words "honey," "smoothness," "delectation," "sweetness" on his lips.[167] Contemplating these "holes of the rock" which symbolize for him the wounds of the crucified Lord, he cries: "What a great multitude of sweetness there is in them!"[168] For his preaching he wants "to elicit something smooth,"[169] etc. After him the same goes for Aelred,[170] Gilbert,[171] Guerric, and Nicholas; the same for Oger as well,[172] for the author of the sermon on Emmaüs,[173] and again for Absalon.[174] Aelred dreams of the happiness of those who gather the "mellifluous speeches" coming from the very mouth of Jesus,[175] and Gilbert praises this same Aelred whose mouth "used to trickle with the sweetness of the divine speech."[176] They all chant in choir: "What sort of honeys drip from the honeycomb of sacred eloquence!"[177] Only, as already in Saint Gregory,[178] this sweetness is above sensible sweetness. For Bernard it is the sweetness of the Truth, which man does not ordinarily savor without a difficult apprenticeship;[179] the sweetness of Wisdom — of the "animated Wisdom," Origen[180] used to say — which is the Word of God, and which only the Spirit reveals and makes one taste.[181] For all of Scripture teaches these men who do not cease to be impregnated with it the "sweet and divine and so to speak honeyed wisdom" as Saint Paul did to the Corinthians. The smoothness of the Bridegroom, says Bernard again, is "the smoothness of the Word"; the embraces of the Bridegroom are "the embraces of the Word," "whose goodness, justice, wisdom, and divinity are one and the same thing in God and one and the same thing with God."[182] When the Word comes to the soul, it is to instruct her in wisdom,[183] and this union of the soul with the Word "has nothing imaginary" about it.[184] So it is not a question of yielding to a movement of easy sensibility at some surface level; the taste of wisdom is a spiritual taste: "To a sound palate, it already tastes good; wisdom herself does the tasting,"[185] and even when "the history" is already sweet in itself, we have still to search "whether even within so sweet a history something still sweeter lies hidden."[186] No more, on the other hand, is it a question of gratifying oneself intellectually in a knowledge of the mysteries of allegory that would remain completely objective, leaving the heart unchanged. This would be an illusory knowledge; for in these sorts of things understanding comprehends nothing if experience is absent:[187] the mystery interiorizes itself within the heart, where it becomes experience[188] — though always passing over in itself "the limits of experience"[189] as well as those of reason. The "virtus mysteriorum," their proper energy, acts within the one who contemplates them in faith:

> This is the taste that the spirit of understanding — i.e., the understanding of the Scriptures and the sacraments of God — produces for us in Christ. Hence, when the Lord appeared to the disciples after his resurrection, "at that point, says the Evangelist, he opened their senses so that they might understand the Scriptures." For when we have begun not only to understand the inner sense of the Scriptures and the power of the mysteries and the sacraments of God, but also, if I may say so, to touch and handle them with a hand of experience . . . , then at last Wisdom accomplishes what is his. . . .[190]

It is in this way that the profound sense of Scripture is truly revealed. It is thus that the "blessed knowledge in which eternal life is contained" is acquired. One will therefore say indifferently, either that this sense is grasped or that it is tasted: here "to taste" means "to understand." The Apostle was precisely "satiated with this taste through this flavor in this wisdom," when he cried out in joy: "To me, the least of all the saints, was given this grace, to announce among the Gentiles the incomparable riches of Christ."[191] The smoothness "above all spices" that one tastes is therefore that of the riches of Christ; the "mellifluous song" that arises from the Scriptures is the song of the Name of Jesus;[192] their "sweet honey" is the "Spirit of the Lord":[193] it pours the joy into us "not only in

Doctor mellifluus

the Spirit, but also of the Spirit himself." *The Spirit before our face is Christ the Lord.*[194] In short, the old doctrine is always affirmed in a lyrical mode and in a renewed experience: "The mystical signification is beautiful and delightful."[195] "Indeed all things are full of the supernal mysteries and they each redound with heavenly sweetness, if at any event they have a careful onlooker."[196] This is the taste of "honeyed wisdom" that Saint Paul communicated to the "perfect" in distributing to them a "pure and full understanding of the spiritual mysteries."[197] The savor and joy of interiorized allegory. *The smoothness of the Spirit.*[198] Mystical tropology.

Saint Bernard and the Cistercians do not have a monopoly on it. Mystical tropology triumphs as well, for example, with a contemporary of Bernard, the Benedictine Godfrey, abbot of Admont in Styria (†1165). With the one as with the other, the same themes drawn from Origen rise up again, and the tones with which the old Germanic abbey of Admont now resounds are often very close to those that drew attention to the young French abbey of Clairvaux. We have already noted many cases of it. Here are some others. Godfrey, too, knows these mysterious visits, as brief as they are sudden, "as though in snatches and in passing,"[199] which are a lasting light for the heart.[200] He who finds himself thus visited rests, as did the Apostle John at the supper, upon the chest of Jesus, which is no other than sacred Scripture.[201] There, in this Heart, life gushes forth; there resides the power of the mysteries; there the life-giving secrets that escape those who are merely doctors are concealed. Only compunction enables one to learn these things.[202] The understanding of the heart receives them so as to make them its nourishment.[203] This sweet, strong food fills it with joy.[204] At such a degree of interiority, allegory is no longer distinct from tropology; mystery and morality are united in a single mystic vision full of sweetness: "Though that sense is allegorical, nevertheless it is also redolent of morality, and the very mysteries of the allegories are not devoid of the sweetness of morality."[205] Godfrey does not cease to sing of this "internal sweetness" of spiritual understanding,[206] a sweetness which arises from the harmony of the two Testaments and which is confused with the "sweetness of the divine wisdom,"[207] and with the "very sweetness of God."[208]

In this epoch one says again, for example, with Rupert in the same sense: "to exhaust the sweetness lying hidden in the Scriptures,"[209] or with Honorius: "The honey is the sweet doctrine of allegory."[210] Irimbert, successor to Godfrey at Admont, puts the sweetness of allegory together with that of morality; he chants the books of Moses, "redolent of the mysteries of eternal enjoyment, incorruption, smoothness."[211] Gilbert Foliot does the same, in greater detail, but with a drier soul.[212] In his explication on Joel, Hugh of Saint Victor (?) shows himself to be equally conservative: after the "moral doctrine," he reserves the "sweetness" for "spiritual upbuilding";[213] he does the same in his more didactic writings.[214] But one will soon read in the *Speculum Ecclesiae* composed by one of his disciples: "the allegorical sense is sharper; the tropological, sweeter."[215] Already, in this pedagogical order where morality came before allegory, the first was often the milk; the second, the solid food; now, is not the milk what is sweet? Also, speaking however less of two senses than of two kinds of words in Scripture, did not Saint Ambrose write: "The mystical speech . . . is like the bread that strengthens the heart of man, as the stronger bread of the word; ethical speech, however, is persuasive, sweet, and softer"?[216] We are now reminded of it in another context. Whatever be the order adopted, a trend is taking shape toward the beginning of the twelfth century, which tends more and more to put usefulness — and charm — on the side of tropology. With the organization of ecclesiastical studies and the differentiation of disciplines, allegory became more theoretical, more impersonal, in a certain way drier, and tropology, on the contrary, more practical, looking more to regulate external activity than to nourish the interior life. In our present categories, we would say that the first becomes the object of theological speculation, whilst the second tends to monopolize preaching: is it necessary always to recall dogma to a believing society? Is it fitting to speculate upon mysteries in the presence of overly uneducated auditors? Would even cultivated hearers, more attracted by the things of nature than previously, put up with an excessively mystical tone? Finally, for the preacher himself, was not the amazement provoked not long ago by thoughts of the faith sometimes now being blunted? Or might he not be afraid to contravene the opinion of the Sage: "Altiora tua ne quaesieris"?

Whatever be the case, the "smoothness" for many becomes an attribute of the moral sense alone. Now one puts the "more hallowed sense" of allegory on one side and the "smoothness of morality" on the other.[217] Hugo of Rouen invites one to taste the "sweetness of morality."[218] Adam Scotus, in the Prologue to the *Allegoriae*, opposes the "savory refreshment" that tropology procures to the "bread of allegory."[219] It is true that Adam rejoins at least in part ancient and Cistercian thought thanks to contemplative anagogy, as we shall see in the following chapter. Alexander of Canterbury does the same: for him, all the casks of the Bridegroom's cellar, which contain the wine of the four senses, are "mellifluae dulcedinis plena," in the same way that for Gilbert Foliot all the senses are full of "delights";[220] nevertheless there is a gradation:

> There is a very sweet drink in history; but still sweeter in allegory; most sweet, however, in morality; but incomparably sweetest by far, the one in anagogy, i.e., in contemplation.[221]

But Peter Lombard quite simply opposes no longer the "milk" but rather the "honey of tropology" to the "solid bread of allegory." Alan of Lille puts the "milk of history," the "honey of tropology," the "solid bread of allegory" in series;[222] or again, distinguishing the threefold element of the milk, he recognizes history in the first, watery portion; allegory in the cheese, which is firm nourishment; and finally, tropology in the butter, which is so soft to the palate.[223] For Giles of Paris, it is also the moral sense that has the sweetness of a honeycomb in the mouth. Thomas of Vercelli will see in the historical sense a "cruder food," in the moral sense a "sweeter food."[224] Peter Comestor or one of his disciples explicates the "milk and honey" of the promised land as being the "ease of history" and the "sweetness of tropology."[225] In another place he remarks: "Tropology is more moving than allegory,"[226] making an echo from one end of the century to the other to the observations of Guibert of Nogent.[227] He himself, as is well known, became part of this group of "masters" who made it their duty to preach and who, without depriving themselves of a sometimes quite complicated allegorical form, preach the moral sense. It is of them that Peter of Riga is thinking in his great poem the *Aurora* which earned him the honor of being set among the rank of mellifluous writers by Everard of Bethune:

> Peter of Riga, the rock whose beginnings Christ watered
> and wove both Laws together with honey-flowing style.[228]

Witness to the teaching and preaching of these Parisian masters at the end of the twelfth or perhaps at the dawn of the thirteenth century, Peter of Riga took up again the old symbol of the lips of the Bride to designate the doctors who expound the Word of God:

> The Church uses the name 'lips' to denote the doctors
> through whom the sweetness of the sacred words trickles down:
> within the aromatic honeycomb lies concealed the honey, while
>   the wax is seen,
> and the moral sense is held enclosed within these words.[229]

CHAPTER TEN

Anagogy and Eschatology

1. A Twofold Anagogy

Let us expand the extent of the mystery still higher.[1] *Let us pursue the peaks of spiritual understanding.*[2] After the long advent of the history of Israel, the object of the historical sense, "at the end of the age and at the evening of the world,"[3] "the Word was made flesh and dwelt amongst us." Then was revealed the mystery that constituted the object of the mystical or spiritual sense. But this mystery could not receive its ultimate fulfillment all at once. It unfolded in three phases, or was elaborated in three successive states. In other words, as was announced in the ancient Scriptures, a threefold advent of Christ may be distinguished[4] — and this requires correspondingly a distinction of a threefold mystic sense. The first advent, "humble and hidden," on our earth, performs the work of redemption, which is pursued in the Church and in her sacraments: this is the object of allegory in the proper sense of the word. The second advent, entirely interior, takes place within the soul of each of the faithful, and is unfolded by tropology. The third and last advent is saved up for the "end of the age," when the Christ will appear in his glory and will come to look for his own to take them away with him: such is the object of anagogy.

As the philologists are wont to observe, the term *anagogia* is a barbarism. It did not usually replace the simple transliteration *anagogē* till rather late. Thus one can scarcely explain it by a confusion made by the Latin translator between the two Greek words *anagōgia* and *anagōgē*.[5] It rather results from a deformation caused by the influence of the other words of the series: historia, allegoria, tropologia. Moreover, it is a matter

179

of little interest. For it is certain that, in the bad Latin of some of our authors, this word *anagōgia*, canonized by association, is intended to translate the Greek term *anagōgē*. The translator takes this word in the meaning that had become normal in the first centuries of our era and that the Neoplatonic school would settle upon: i.e., not in the sense of a "trip" or "passing through" as it had among the ancient Pythagoreans, but in the sense of a "climb" or an "ascent."[6] The etymology bruited about would be explained by its equivalent "sursumductio"; it comes, as they say, "from *ana*, which is sursum" (upward) "and *agōgē*, which is ductio" (leading).[7]

In its most general and most abstract acceptation, then, the anagogical sense is that which leads the thought of the exegete "upwards." Proclus was aware of "anagogic gods," "anagogic powers," "anagogic heroes."[8] Commenting on the *Phaedo,* Olympiodorus describes the "anagogic drive" of the soul.[9] Pseudo-Dionysius often speaks of anagogy.[10] Nevertheless, he was not the one to introduce the word into the language of Christian exegesis. Origen, Gregory of Nyssa, Didymus, Jerome had already made anagogy one of the names of the spiritual sense in general. Already in Cassian and, perhaps a bit less clearly, in Eucherius, anagogy became a specialized term. But it subsequently ended with a certain concordance being established between the Dionysian explanations of *anagōgē* and the definition of the fourth sense of the Bible. Were not the commentators on the *Celestial Hierarchy* at the same time commentators of Scripture or theoreticians of hermeneutics? Did not Dionysius himself speak of "anagogic Scriptures"?[11] Further, it was a sham concordism, for "the anagogy of Dionysius develops in a metaphysical order and within a play of symbols, where history, including sacred history, is completely eliminated and scorned."[12] Nevertheless, at least during the period we are studying, those who read it easily made up for what was wanting.

Anagogy is first off, they will say, "a sense of the things above."[13] It leads the mind's consideration "from things visible to those invisible,"[14] or from things below "to the things above,"[15] i.e., to "the divine things."[16] It is this sort of allegory "which lifts the understanding of the mind through visible things to the invisible,"[17] or "through which speech is borne over to the invisible things to come."[18] More concretely, this will be the sense that lets one see in the realities of the earthly Jerusalem those of the heavenly Jerusalem: "for a certain part of the earthly city has been made an image of the heavenly city";[19] "understand that supernal Jerusalem now."[20] Although these things no longer belong to time, nevertheless, for us who trudge and toil through time, they are things yet to come,

A Twofold Anagogy

objects of desire and of hope. Thus one finds oneself in the presence of an anagogic sense "when through understanding one deed there is another, which is to be desired, namely, the eternal felicity of the blessed."[21] After allegory which built up faith and tropology which built up charity, there is anagogy which builds up hope:

> For what do we call *anagōgē* but the mystical and upwardly directive understanding? In the two previously mentioned there is sought a teaching of customs and of the mysteries. To *anagōgē* belongs an advance insight into the rewards to be hoped for.[22]

To be sure, by showing us the "fulfillment of the prefigurations" already realized in Christ and in his Church, allegory *serves as foundation for* our hope;[23] but it is anagogy which in the proper sense of the term *builds it up*, by constituting its proper object for it. The following definition of a late theoretician, Alonso Tostado, expresses this point:

> The fourth [sense] is the anagogic, namely, when we want to signify through the things designated in Scripture still further something that pertains to the state of the life to come; and it is called 'anagogic', i.e., upward leading, namely, toward heavenly things.[24]

Nevertheless, just as there were two tropologies, there are also two anagogies: the one which fulfills the doctrinal formulation of the fourfold sense; the other, which fulfills the spiritual formulation of the threefold sense. But, contrary to what took place at first for tropology, both the one and the other equally constitute part of the Christian mystery; in both cases, each in its own way, they constitute either the high point or the term. The standpoint of the first anagogy is objective and doctrinal; that of the second pertains to subjective realization; in other words, the one is defined by its object, and the other by the manner of apprehending it. If one wants to distinguish them by verbal contrast, one would say that the first is more a "higher sense"[25] and the second a "higher contemplation."[26] Or again, the first "*declares* the sacraments of the future age,"[27] or "disputes about the life to come,"[28] whereas the second leads "to *beholding* the mysteries of the age to come,"[29] "to *contemplating* the heavenly mysteries."[30] Before all this is what Cassian said: "Anagogy, however, climbing from spiritual mysteries to certain more sublime and more sacred secrets of the heavens."[31] We over-emphasize the opposition; but, as we shall see, it is justified. Let us say that the first of the two anagogies teaches that part of Christian dogmatics called "eschatology" — which itself is further subdivided into two parts, according as the ultimate end of each person or that of the universe as a whole is concerned: from whence derive the texts of a later epoch that come to distinguish no longer three, but rather four advents of the Son of God.[32] As to the second anagogy, it introduces us here and now into the mystic life; at the terminus of its movement, it fulfills that "theology" which is made etymologically the equivalent of "theoria" and which is the contemplation of God.[33] In modern terms, the one is speculative; the other, contemplative. Let us start with the first.

Jewish prophecy, that of the ancient prophets as well as that of the apocalypses, was eschatological. It proclaimed a final order of things that was to be substituted for the present order — or disorder — and the closer the time of the Messiah approached, the more this final order was conceived at the same time as transcendent: a heavenly dwelling and a heavenly temple would replace the holy city and its temple.[34] The facts would run counter to this expectation. Once the Messiah came and his work was accomplished and he was himself resurrected, time continued its course upon an unchanged earth. The hour "of the universal restoration that God had spoken of through the mouth of his holy prophets"[35] had not struck in the way it had been expected. A gap opened up between the first and the last coming. In that gap the Church would unfold its existence for an indeterminate period.

Nothing would be seen there any more except "through a mirror and in an enigma."[36] At the death of Jesus only the outer veil was torn, not the inner: that of the temple, not that of the sanctuary. The whole mystery of salvation had undoubtedly been revealed; but it would not fully be grasped, and the end of time would not take place until the conquering Lamb had completed the breaking of the seals of the Book.[37] Moreover, it was revealed only to faith; so "when the perfect should have come," it would at last become accessible to another sort of knowledge. After the "mirror" and the "enigma" would be the "face to face." For some, this would be life eternal; for the others, the punishment of Gehenna.[38]

It would seem necessary, then, to conceive the New Testament as truth with respect to the Old, but as mere "image" with respect to the ultimate reality still to come. "Through the Gospel we see on earth prefigurations of the heavenly mysteries."[39] It has not itself brought beatitude, but only its promise: it merely prepared for it.[40] "Dawn and foggy enough to boot was Christ's whole life upon the earth."[41] The resurrection of Jesus Christ was the pledge and exemplar of our own future resurrection:[42] then only, death being at last vanquished, shall we enjoy the whole "truth" whose "figure"[43] the Son of God had brought upon the earth. The "shadow of the Christ" in which we live would be followed by perfect light; the "temporal Gospel," by the "eternal Gospel."[44] Meanwhile, just as the Hebrew people have prefigured the Christian people, so the Church on earth by the unfolding of her liturgy bears the standard as the forerunner of the solemnities of the age to come.[45] As the Passover of the Jews was celebrated in days gone by as a figure of our Passover, so is ours celebrated now a figure of the Passover to come[46] — *donec veniat quod perfectum est* ["until that which is perfect is come"].

This perspective found its expression in one word, an adverb: *interim;* an "adverb of time for which there is no modern equivalent in religious language."[47] It is a beautiful notion and necessary, but incomplete, not yet entirely taking account of the deepest reality of dogma. Notwithstanding the gap opened by the first coming and the still unchanged conditions of our knowledge, notwithstanding the sorely felt distance between the *nunc* ["now"] of the earth and the *tunc* ["then"] of eternity,[48] it is in fact the very reality of salvation which henceforth is inserted in history and immediately offered to us. By faith, the believer is not wrested from the "night" which indiscriminately covers the whole of present existence;[49] but he can paradoxically say "night is illuminated as day," "night, the illumination of my delights."[50] He already holds "the substance of the things that he hopes for"; he has already, albeit still secretly, penetrated into the kingdom. Allegory and anagogy ought to be considered in a more perfectly interior relationship. This is what the primitive Christian community did. From the first instant, it has had "an intense awareness of being at once the Israel of God and the heavenly kingdom anticipated on earth."[51] Saint Paul, writing to the Galatians, identified the Church, such as it already existed in its visible state, with "our Mother, the Jerusalem above": she was free, he affirms, and, from her freedom, her children were already free.[52] Paul knew only Hagar and Sarah: there is no personality between the two of them. His thought steps over the gap in a single bound; it denies it, not admitting that a real separation corresponded to the appearance. The Epistle to the Hebrews proceeds the same way: "You have had access," proclaims the epistle, "to the mountain of Zion, the city of the living God, the Jerusalem above."[53] This new turn, an effect of a profound and victorious view of faith, owed nothing to the illusions of the first period concerning an immediate return of Christ in glory. Right now, on earth, with her discipline and her rule of faith, with her magisterium and her apostolic succession, in her precarious and militant condition, the Church of Christ was already "the heavenly Church."[54] Her members, though still living in the flesh, were already citizens of heaven.[55] They were "the new people in the new Jerusalem."[56] "The heavenly fatherland, which we call the Catholic Church."[57] The patristic tradition on this subject is taken up again by Saint Gregory in a formula that comes to him from Saint Augustine: "Et ipsa civitas, sc. Sancta Ecclesia, quae regnatura in caelo adhuc laborat in terra."[58] This is a theme endlessly repeated, but it will suffice, for the Middle Ages, to borrow an expression from Saint Peter Damian:

> For Jerusalem was the royal city where a most renowned temple had been constructed for God; but after that [city] came which was the true temple of God, and the heavenly Jerusalem began to reveal the mysteries, the earthly one was destroyed where the heavenly one appeared.[59]

In this deeper perspective pointing out the mystical identity of the Church of heaven and that of the earth, of the New Testament and of the eternal testament, anagogy would naturally team up with allegory: it supplied the doctrinal sense of Scripture in its fullness. In the *De principiis*, then, Origen expressed allegory and anagogy simultaneously in the unique term "spiritalis explanatio" *(pneumatikē dihēgēsis)*.[60] In the later tradition, anagogy either remains implicit — unless it should sometime be allegory — or else comes to double before passing on to tropology, which then would be found to occupy the fourth level. This occurs more than once in Paschasius Radbertus,[61] or in Adam Scotus.[62] Though apparently illogical, it betokens a higher logic: here too the gap is filled in. Faith is victorious.

Finally, a much larger number of other texts simply stick to the spiritual understanding without having to choose any ordering among its three phases, which they do not distinguish. So they do not unfurl their full importance unless they reproduce the whole movement which took the author of the Epistle to the Galatians as well as that of the Epistle to the Hebrews to the goal in a single bound: "They serve as a shadow and an image of the heavenly things."[63] The temporal things of the Old Testament, contemplated in the light of Christ, ought to carry us over to the eternal things of the New Testament, to those "things above" that the Christian ought to look for and to taste so as to rejoin the resurrected Christ from now on.[64] This is what Irenaeus expresses forcefully in a series of antitheses, only the first of which have we previously cited:

A Twofold Anagogy

"Through the typic to the true, from the temporal to the eternal, through the fleshly to the spiritual, and through the earthly to the heavenly."[65] There is also what Origen expresses in a text that seems to us much more "significant" of Christian thought itself that of any mentality peculiar to the Alexandrine doctor: "It is not necessary to believe that historical realities are figures of other historical realities, and bodily things figures of other bodily things; but bodily things are figures of spiritual ones, and historical things of intelligible ones."[66] These "spiritual and intelligible things" are not, as some have believed, "ideas" or "speculative truths";[67] they are, as Origen himself says, "the inheritance of the eternal life to come," which the Christ has acquired for us.[68] The same thought is found in Saint Jerome: "We ought to climb from the letter to the spirit, from earthly to heavenly things."[69] The same thought again is to be found in Saint Gregory Nazianzen:

> As for us, let us receive the Law with the spirit of the Gospel and not according to the letter; in perfection, and not imperfectly; eternally, and not with a lapse. Let us take as head not the Jerusalem below, but the mother City above; not the one that at this very hour armies are trampling underfoot, but that which the angels glorify.[70]

Again, without slipping, any more than Origen, into a realm of ideas or theories, without suppressing, any more than he, every temporal relation, he said: "From the flesh and the things of time, let us pass on to things spiritual and eternal."[71] And it is always the same thought that we find in Saint Augustine;[72] in Saint Leo or one of his imitators;[73] in Saint Gregory the Great. The last-mentioned invites us to pass, by means of the Law and the Prophets, "a sacramentis temporalibus ad aeterna."[74] Again, says he, Scripture is a letter that comes to us from eternity, to make us aspire to eternity.[75] The same teaching is delivered to us by the Middle Ages. We find it summarized, for example, in this verse of Othloh of Saint Emmeran's poem on "spiritual doctrine":

> . . . Et quae sint sursum capias per mystica rerum.[76]

This is what Saint Thomas Aquinas will also say while commenting on the Epistle to the Hebrews: "For the Lord wanted to lead us by the hand to intelligible and spiritual things."[77]

It is therefore quite right to speak, not only for Origen alone, but for the whole of Christian thought, of an "ascending dialectic." But under two conditions. The first condition is to understand that this dialectic does not at all substitute for the investigation of a "temporal development," but follows on it and gives it its meaning: for a temporal development is not self-sufficient; it must indeed finally lead to results if it truly advances, and time must ultimately lead to what no longer belongs to time. The history of salvation draws our attention, but it cannot arrest it: it carries it on to salvation itself. In other words, one ought to avoid confusing the passage of time to eternity, which is always at the horizon of Christian thought, with escape into the atemporal. To assign to history, as indeed one must, a term that no longer belongs to history is quite a different thing than to deny history, or at least its role, its value, its fruitfulness; it is just the opposite. No longer being "historical," the "heavenly" and "spiritual" things are, in relation to us who have to live in time, "future things."[78] They are "the mystery to come."[79] For us they constitute part of the "age to come."[80] The Christian ought, following Saint Paul, to consider "not the things that are seen but those that are not seen, i.e., not fleshly things but spiritual ones, not things present but those to come."[81] *Caelestia mysteria ventura* ["the heavenly mysteries to come"]. In other words, the doctrinal and spiritual exegesis practiced by the great Christian tradition could be defined neither by the establishment of a simple "historical progression" nor by a pure "vertical symbolism."[82] There is nothing else to match it. The second condition required for speaking of an "ascending dialectic" is closely akin to the first. The texts themselves impose it on us. It will have to consist in not conceiving such a dialectic as an effort to leave the plane of things and to escape to some sort of personal engagements in "attaining the Idea": for the "things above," the "heavenly Jerusalem," the "spiritual goods," "eternal Life," the company of the resurrected Christ sitting at the right of God, are not for any Christian, however large a dose of "Platonism" that he has digested, "Ideas" in the current meaning of the term. They are, in a sense quite other than the Platonic Idea, Reality itself.[83]

In the very formulas that we have just cited, it is truly *the whole* of the Christian mystery that is expressed, advancing forthwith to its term. In them, consequently, it is no longer the anagogy that remains implicit as happened in a number of other texts: now it is the allegory and the tropology. Both are contained within the anagogy, as the first and the second coming of Christ are included within the last. This was already seen in the case of allegory, thanks to the identity of the Church in its twofold condition, earthly and heavenly. This is no less true for tropology. For it is in each of the members of his mystical body that Christ, at the end of time, completes the work of the Father.[84] The true typology, as we have seen, is mystical. In fact, the moral life gets its Christian value and is fruitful for eternity only if it proceeds from Christ, whose mystery is interiorized within the soul. Thus the goal and the path to it are interwoven, so to speak, with the same material. They are not at all heterogeneous. That, it seems, is what Saint Ambrose wanted to say in one of those pithy sentences full of deep symbolism that clearly show that he is not merely the Ciceronian moralist he is sometimes thought to be: "Sicut enim spei nostrae octava perfectio est, ita octava summa virtutum est."[85] Between virtuous activity on earth and its blossoming forth in the realm above, the correspondence is perfect; more than correspondence: substantial identity. One "octave" answers to the other: or rather it is the same octave: *octava, summa virtutum est*. The difference exists only for us, so long as our knowledge remains imperfect. The moral sense and the anagogic sense are in continuity with each other; the object they aim at is of the same structure. As Saint Jerome says, the Mystery of Christ "is being fulfilled daily in believers and will be fulfilled perfectly when this corruptible has put on incorruption."[86] The joys of the eternal realm are, as Saint Gregory says, "the secret joys of the interior life."[87] Or, as Saint Peter Damian says, the heavenly temple dedicated under the eternal reign of the true Solomon is not decorated "with the brightness of sparkling gems, but shines with the elegance of spiritual virtues."[88] While accomplishing the Lord's command one does not merit nor merely prepare for, but rather one is already building the tower of the heavenly Jerusalem.[89] Taking up the thought of Saint Ambrose, the cosmologist Alexander Neckam will explain that the octave of beatitude brings the perfection of its consonance to the septet of the virtues, just as the eighth sphere in our material universe brings its completion to the harmony of the heavens.[90] Thus anagogy realizes the perfection both of allegory and of tropology, achieving their synthesis. It is neither "objective" like the first, nor "subjective" like the second. Above and beyond this division, it realizes their unity. It integrates the whole and final meaning. It sees, in eternity, the fusion of the mystery and the mystic. In other words, the eschatological reality attained by anagogy is the eternal reality within which every other has its consummation. In its final state, it is that "new testament, which is the kingdom of heaven."[91] It constitutes "the fullness of Christ."[92]

2. Exegesis and Contemplation

But the meaning of anagogy is not its very own reality. A gloss on Genesis defines it as "the spiritual understanding through which one treats of the highest heavenly affairs and we are led to the higher things."[1] Two formulas are juxtaposed here; but the first does not *ipso facto* entail the second. Doctrinal anagogy can indeed, as Rabanus Maurus says, be "mystic, dogmatic, and solid speech,"[2] but for all that this speech does not establish him who holds it or who hears within the mysteries of the future age. It is one thing to theorize about the final ends, and quite another to be carried off in ecstasy. In the one case, it is close to allegory, which it brings to fulfillment; in the other, it completes the movement of mystical tropology.[3] This suggests a late division influenced by the pseudo-Dionysius, which was just grafted on to the etymological explanation of *Zion*. The Mount Zion of Palestine, which prefigures the Church of Christ, is therefore also a figure for the Christian soul. Now "Zion is interpreted as *speculatio*." Only this last term signifies two quite distinct things, according to whether it is derived from *speculum* or from *specula*. In the first instance, it is a matter of a knowledge "in a mirror," something enigmatic, by means of similitudes; the soul will remain within the clouds of faith. In the second instance, on the other hand, the mind will be established in an elevated region where, having no further need of signs, disencumbered of every image, with a clarity that encroaches upon eternal vision, it will contemplate its "infinite and superessential" divine origin.[4] That is effectively anagogical contemplation, if at least one can call it eschatological. It is the kiss of eternity.[5] What one must envisage here is a knowledge of "mystic" order in the modern sense of the word.

In its highest degree, it marks the third term of the triad that we have named a spiritual or contemplative formula. It is real or practical anagogy as opposed to the still abstract theoretic anagogy. Thus one can say either that this contemplation is the end toward which the understanding of Scripture is tending, or, the other way around, that the understanding of Scripture is its end, according as one first considers Scripture in its letter and in the plurality of its teachings or as one immediately looks to its final essence, which is the Word of God. Saint Augustine has often taken up the first point of view, on several occasions distinguishing the Gospel and him who has given us the Gospel:

> The fruit of faith [is] understanding, so that we may arrive at eternal life, where the Gospel would not be read to us, but he who

has given us the Gospel now would appear with all the pages of the reading and the voice of reader and commentator removed.[6]

... For will there be discussion like this in thy house, as though it should instruct the ignorant or remind the forgetful? Or again, will the Gospel be recited in the heavenly homeland, where God's Word himself is to be the object of contemplation?[7]

The just and the saints, again he would say, would enjoy the Word of God "without reading, without letters."[8] What need is there to read or to seek the truth from without, once one has joined up with Wisdom herself, who fills the heart and the mind of those who possess her?[9] Similarly, Origen opposed to him who has to read and meditated upon Scripture here below the one who, like the angels, "has within him a source of gushing water revealed by the Word himself and Wisdom herself."[10] John Scotus Erigena, inspired by a Greek tradition that goes back as far as Origen,[11] stresses even more the oneness, inscribed in the language, of the Logos, the "Word"; he also puts himself in a perspective at the other end from that of Augustine:[12] for him, in the same way as here below the search for the truth is merged with the effort to interpret Scripture, the joy above consists in the full understanding of the Word of God.[13] Rupert sides with Augustine's opinion when he compares the Scriptures to those luminaries which are the sun and the moon, creatures by means of which we raise our mind to the invisible Creator: what shall we do in the heavenly Jerusalem, where the Word will directly be our light, "in himself and in the heart of the Father"?[14] But on other occasions he prefers the point of view of John Scotus, for example, when he says that "to comprehend the mysteries of Scripture in mind and in life is already to reign in the kingdom of God,"[15] and again: "What then is holy Scripture to us but the true land of promise?"[16] The representatives of each of these two tendencies would seem to have an heir in modern times in the person of Jean-Jacques Olier, a true mystic poet, untouched by the spirit of modern rationalism, a man for whom the divine Word is no other than the Gospel, but "the living Gospel, the Gospel fulfilled," constituting together with all the saints "a perfect volume," "lying upon the simple leaf of God's essence"; the "divine Gospel" that "we shall be reading forever in heaven. . . ."[17]

As is clear enough from these examples, though the two points of view are complete reciprocals, they are perfectly commensurate with each other, without any remainder. The "science of the Scriptures" is nothing, as Paschasius Radbertus says, in comparison with the light to come;[18] and yet, as a sermon of Innocent III says, "The violent tear into the kingdom of heaven, i.e., they understand the mysteries of the Scriptures."[19] This means that the full understanding of the Scriptures amounts to the suppression of the Scriptures as such.[20] One can also say — and this is another way of reconciling the two points of view — that there is a parallelism between the degrees of contemplation and the hierarchy of the senses of Scripture. One of the festal homilies of Godfrey of Admont explains this point. In an enumeration which had become completely standard since Saint Jerome and Saint Augustine,[21] Godfrey distinguishes three sorts of "visions"; "corporis, spiritus et mentis," to which he makes three of the "senses" of Scripture correspond: "litteralis, spiritalis, intellectualis," and in Saint Paul he points out that which attains at once the third kind of vision and the third sense of Scripture, the day when he was lifted up to the third heaven.[22] On this summit, says Hervaeus of Bourg Dieu, the divine things are contemplated no longer "through a spiritually or corporally figurative meaning" but rather "by means of the pure, sharp understanding of the mind";[23] this he calls, using an Augustinian expression, the "contuitus mentis" [a connatural "intuition of the mind"]. As for the rest, the details and nuances of the enumerations matter little: here we have only to keep the picture as a whole in mind. In any case, as Ambrose Autpert said commenting on this threefold degree of understanding or vision, "the mind is then lifted up *(sublevatur)* by a breath of eternity," "to root up the divine mysteries."[24] This same expression, "mentis sublevatio" ["lifting up of the mind"], is found in Richard of Saint Victor.[25] For Hugo, who also sees in anagogy the real ascent of the soul, the relations of tropology and of anagogy are those of the active life and of the contemplative life.[26] The same goes for Adam Scotus, for whom tropology is the nourishment of those who work, while those whose desire has reached toward the heavenly things are made drunk by "the wine of anagogy."[27] As for Peter Lombard, he distinguishes allegory and anagogy — in a sermon — pretty much as we have distinguished the two anagogies: by the first, "the intellect is nourished"; but the second "pours itself out upon the mind, so that it carried off to the house of God."[28]

Concrete (or as one would say today: existential) anagogy is therefore the point of junction (it would even be necessary to say: fusion) at the summit of a pyramid: fusion between the understanding of Scripture and mystical contemplation.[29] The movement of unification interior to each is also the movement that unifies them among themselves: "(The perfect) have depth of understanding in the contemplation of spiritual things."[30] Accordingly this is clearly not the full liberty of the mind, which can only be eschatological, but the first spring of this liberty.[31] It is Christian ecstasy at the end of a process whose starting point was the letter of the holy books. One of those who explained it most clearly is a Benedictine monk of the twelfth century, Alexander of Canterbury. His text is found embedded in the book called *On the Similes of Saint Anselm*. It constitutes the 104th chapter, which develops the "simile of the cell." We have already cited it in part. Here we shall supply a fuller citation, because it constitutes a good example of an explanation of the four senses. Here Alexander is commenting on the verse of Canticles 1:4: "Introduxit me in cellam vinariam." This mystic cave where the Spouse, who is the king of kings, introduces his wife the soul, is holy Scripture, and the deeper one penetrates it, the more good wine one finds there:

> ... In this room there are four large jars full of honeyed sweetness; these are their names: simple history, allegory, morality, anagogy, i.e., the understanding tending toward the things above. These jars are ordered as we have said above: for in the first place, in holy Scripture, there is simple history at the front door; then comes allegory; after that morality; and lastly, as though in a niche, there is anagogy or contemplation. History is a very sweet drink; but there is an even sweeter one in allegory; a very sweet one is found in morality; but incomparably sweeter by far is the one in anagogy.
>
> The drink contained in the first jar, namely history, is designated by the simple deeds and examples of the saints: when we are intent on them, we somehow make our souls drink with great sweetness. In the second jar, namely allegory, there is instruction in the faith; for through allegory we are educated to the faith and in the inner man we are imbued with the taste of a wonderful sweetness. In the third jar, morality, there is the establishment of customs; for we establish our customs through morality and, as it were, refreshed by a drink of marvelous sweetness, we appear joyful and amiable to our neighbors. The drink that is contained in the fourth jar, the one that stands in the niche, i.e., in anagogy, is the sweetest passion of divine love: when our soul is refreshed by its ineffable sweetness, it is somehow united to the highest divinity itself.
>
> So when this innkeeper introduces guests into his room, namely holy Scripture, as we have said above, he offers them something to drink; for he usually gives the simpler folk uneducated in the faith

and its love a drink from the first jar, history; he gives those of greater capacity a draft of allegory; those still more perfect he serves with morality; but he offers the most perfect a drink of anagogy, or contemplation. It should be known, however, that whosoever shall drink from the fourth jar, the one that stands in the niche, i.e., of anagogy, howsoever little he shall have tasted of it, shall immediately become drunk because of the marvelous sweetness of that drink, with that drunkenness to which the bridegroom in the Canticles invites his guests: "Eat, friends, and drink and get drunk, o dearest ones," etc.

... Now that room has a door in it; and in that door there is a key through which it is shut to those without faith and open to the faithful. The doorway of this room, i.e., of holy Scripture, is orthodoxy; and its key, humility. . . .[32]

Nevertheless the fully concrete anagogy, total anagogy, is reserved for the "fatherland."[33] Mystical contemplation is not yet vision. To mark both its grandeur and its limits, Berengaud borrows a symbol from the Apocalypse. He saw the angel conduct the prophet in four stages, across history, the moral level, and spiritual understanding, right into a place where the heavenly mysteries began to be uncovered. Then the prophet found himself at the edge of a great torrent — and the angel abandoned him there:

And he was not able to cross the torrent, since there is no one who is able to investigate the depth of the divine and heavenly mysteries as it is. . . . Behold: the angel is leading the prophet right up to the determined place, and did not lead him across, since Almighty God guides his saints to the point of contemplating the secret and hidden mysteries of his divinity but never leads them across; since human frailty is unable to comprehend those inscrutable divine mysteries.[34]

This is what Ambrose Autpert, inspired also by the Apocalypse, calls "the half-hour's silence": an incomplete silence, an interrupted life, since here below "contemplation is never brought to perfection, even though it be most ardently undertaken."[35] And this is what Rupert of Deutz expresses another way saying that by this higher understanding of the Scriptures we progress as explorers right up to the Land of the Living — but we do not establish our abode there.[36]

"O Jerusalem, city of the Great King, city filled with joy by an impetuous river, you are oblivious of weight and measure, and no longer do you know number, since all those who share in your delicacies become merely one. But we, subjected in all things to the law of changes and of numbers, when shall we arrive at this unity, O Lord, in the sight of thy glory?"[37]

So however high anagogy leads, it always leaves something to look for and always with greater fervor, because it still does not uncover the Face of God. The motive principle of the understanding of the faith, for Augustine as for all the medievals who follow him, is none other than the understanding of the Scriptures:

Always seek his face; so that discovery may not bring an end to this quest, whereby love is meant, but, as love increases, let the quest for what has been discovered increase as well.[38]

Saint Gregory translates this very same idea in his own inimitable way in his third homily on Ezekiel. There he explains what is meant by the face and wings of the four "living creatures" perceived by the prophet in his first vision. Both the former and the latter bear a relation to holy Scripture, but they symbolize two quite different modes of grasping it: "For what is meant by the face except awareness, and what is meant by the wings except flight?"[39] On the one hand, there is the awareness, the *notitia:* clear and precise knowledge, an object of teaching, which was the concern of history or even of allegory: Gregory does not distinguish here the three from the four senses; definitions, explanations, all that tends to build up the faith properly speaking is included. On the other hand, there is the *volatus:* flight, impulse, no longer intellectual representation but spiritual movement, anagogy; all that lifts the mind toward contemplation: "So the face pertains to faith, the wing to contemplation." Objectively transmitted by the "word of preaching," the awareness constitutes a rule for the understanding of the believer; but this rule assures him who sincerely wills to live it the freedom of flight: "it crosses over to the freedom of the contemplative life." And Gregory takes up this expression that so enchants him, again and again: "they fly with the wing of contemplation" — "they fly off to higher things by means of the contemplative life" — "wherever they fly with the wing of contemplation," etc.[40] Elsewhere he calls this flight the "volatus allegoriae":[41] with him the vocabulary is not fixed. He assigns it "the excellence of the Word"[42] as its object, or rather its aim. The "airy" region where it transports us in this way[43] is not subject to the vicissitudes of the science of exegesis or even of theology: without spurning such science, indeed while using it, it transcends it. The notitia is transcended by the volatus, just as intelligence is transcended by the "heart."[44]

Howsoever high its "flight" may lead, this contemplative anagogy did not pretend to lead beyond the faith. On the other hand, in anagogy as previously in mystical tropology, of which it is the extension, the flowering, or the translation into other nuances of thought, the objective data of the biblical revelation and of the Christian mystery were allied with the congenital gifts of a mind made in the image and likeness of God: with what Saint Bernard felt obliged to call "the 'soul-in-law' to the Word."[45] In the previous chapter we have noted the place held by the "treatise on the soul" in Cistercian exegesis, for example. The confluence of these two sources, natural and revealed, was sketched out as far back as the work of Origen, particularly in that beautiful topic of the wells which enriches several of his homilies on Genesis and on Numbers.[46] It was a delicate balance. Augustinism constituted a favorable climate for its flowering: just as it united the symbolic sense to the historical one, it spontaneously associated the Church and the soul, the intimate quest for the Word and the collective hope of the City of God; within the objective supernatural revelation it exhibited a deep knowledge of the interior man. "By the unfolding of events and of stories," said Saint Gregory once again, "we are led step by step, as it were, to eternity."[47] But when, laden with an insufficiently transformed Neoplatonism, the thought of Dionysius was introduced into the West, the risk of a disturbance in equilibrium arose, at the expense of supernatural historicity and of the eschatological component. This risk came to a head in the work of John Scotus. It was reinforced by the second Dionysian wave in the course of the twelfth century. This Dionysian anagogy, whereby one passes from the order of visions to that of pure contemplation or from symbolic theology to mystical theology,[48] is neither first nor foremost the end time of an exegesis: it is, as it were, the last spurt of a sort of cosmic energy raising each nature according to its hierarchic order in the graduated series of illuminations.[49] It makes the mind, as Hugh of Saint Victor says commenting on the *Celestial Hierarchy*, penetrate "into the contemplation of higher things,"[50] but these "higher things" would at the same time scarcely appear any longer as "the last things." By anagogy, said Cassian, "speech is carried over to the invisible things to come."[51] This was, as we have seen, the language of the Epistle to the Hebrews and that of Origen; it was also to be that of many others. In the tradition influenced by Dionysius, however, a dissociation tended to develop between the *invisibilia* and the *futura*, as between the mystic life and the meditation on Scripture. No longer aware of a certain order of personal intimacy between the two liberties, the divine and the human, the mysticism formed by Dionysius spontaneously tended toward "the edification of the holy Church."[52] When these traits came to dominate, they profoundly differentiated the mysticism of Dionysius from that of Origen, Augustine, or Gregory. The history of struggles for influence and of attempts at synthesis between these two mystical traditions would be extremely interesting to untangle. Here let us simply recall the explanations that Garnier of Rochefort soon gave us about the purification of the understanding which empties itself of every image so as to climb back to its "superessential" original. They no longer have any more than a very loose connection with Scripture. Now, try as they might to appeal to the authority of the *Soliloquiae*, they in fact came straight from Dionysius.[53]

The progress of the dialectical forms of thought, with its consequences in the new economy of theological wisdom, acted in the same direction. It has been observed that "eschatology occupies almost no place in Abelard's teaching."[54] This is doubtless not an isolated happenstance, for one theologian observes that the "lack of the eschatological sense . . . represents the most crucial defect arising from scholasticism."[55] We can add that this defect — which is otherwise neither constant nor irremediable — comes about precisely from the fact that theology then no longer has the form of an exegesis. But a state of mind was created that affected exegesis itself and the theory of the four senses, affecting everything, especially the definition of anagogy. This last, says Peter Comestor, "deals with God and the things above the heavens,"[56] as if it were a question of intemporal objects. "Anagogy," Ockham will say later, "is an explanation whereby the invisible things of God are seen to be understood through those that have been made."[57] In short, two sorts of dissociation are produced. Strained toward the ultimate advent, the one in which the great Christian hope is expressed, that which was scriptural anagogy tends to become, on the one hand, a process of natural mysticism, and, on the other, a chapter of natural theology.

But if we now confine our consideration to the limits of the twelfth and thirteenth centuries that we have assigned as the terminus for the first part of this work, we shall see at play there, under the sign of Dionysius, the meeting of mystical exegesis, in the ancient sense of the word, and of mystical contemplation, in the modern sense of the word. The meeting occurs at the endpoint: and this point is anagogy. In language quite close to that of Gregory, Rupert said: our light is Scripture, "so that in it or by it we can weight carefully at any time, not what or how God is, but what he is not, and that God is to be likened to no creature."[58] Toward the middle of the century, Isaac of Stella, more open to the influence of Dionysius than Saint Bernard ever could have been, taught the same doctrine.[59] A half-century later, Garnier of Rochefort, who is a disciple both of Origen and of Dionysius, as he is (which is almost the same thing) of Saint Gregory and of John Scotus, orchestrates this thought in a description of anagogy which is at the same time a description of ecstasy:

> ... Climbing to the heights by the steps of sure contemplation, the human mind also contemplates anagogically the heavenly secrets by the holy gaze of divine eloquence; and thus starting from two kinds of visions it ascends to all the perfection that had been infused in the minds of theologians and prophets through the grace of divine revelation; in Greek they call this (first) kind of vision *theophanies*, i.e., divine manifestations; the other, whereby it strives to contemplate the most holy heavenly one as he is by the mind's climbing up and going out in nakedness and purity and without covering, is the kind that is called *anagogic*.
>
> But in this last kind of vision the human mind so trembles and shudders that, dizzied by the darkness of its own ignorance, it cannot go forth toward that brightness and glow of truth unless it be directed; but, as it were, blind and guided by hand, it advances whither it does not see and begins to be melted through the vision and the visitation of the Beloved, so that it neither conceives what it ought or want to about God nor is able to utter what it conceives, when it strives to investigate that bit of the heavenly kingdom beyond still surrounded by veils and the yet uncircumscribed dimension of the divine glow, and, though still investigating, fails. Thunderstruck, the mind clings fast in contemplation; it becomes numb with agitation; speaking, it is rendered utterly silent; and the copiousness that poverty had made copious returns the poverty; in advancing it falls short in wondrous way, and then advances the more once it has reached its shortfall.[60]

In this sermon on Saint John the Baptist, where Garnier wants to show us the superiority of "theology" over "prophecy," i.e., of the New Testament over the Old, and finally of negative cognition over symbolic cognition, of the rejection of signs over the use of signs, there is quite a bit of razzle dazzle doubletalk. The tie maintained by this mysticism with scriptural anagogy at least keeps it from following an extravagant orbit outside the norms of the faith.

3. The Unity of the Fourfold Sense

It is in traditional eschatology that the doctrine of the four senses is achieved and finds its unity. For Christianity is a fulfillment, but in this very fulfillment it is a promised hope. Mystical or doctrinal, taught or lived, true anagogy is therefore always eschatological. It stirs up the desire for eternity in us. This is also why the fourth sense is forced to be the last. No more than it could really lack the three others could it be followed by a fifth. Neither is hope ever lacking nor, in our earthly condition, is it ever surpassed even if it already encroaches upon its term.

If Scripture as a whole is in principle to be understood according to the four senses, naturally certain facts and certain objects better lend themselves to it than others. There are certain favored symbols whose complete, didactic exposition is thus naturally found rather among the late authors. Let us listen to Saint Thomas Aquinas, for example, on "fiat lux."

> For when I say "fiat lux" with reference to the literal meaning of corporeal light, this pertains to the literal sense. If "fiat lux" be understood to mean 'Let Christ be born in the Church', this pertains to the allegorical sense. If "fiat lux" be said as meaning 'Let us be led into glory through Christ', this pertains to the anagogic sense. And if "fiat lux" be taken to mean 'Through Christ let us be illumined in understanding and enkindled in emotion', this pertains to the moral sense.[1]

Or, much later, there is his confrere J. M. de Turre on David killing Goliath:

> Intended historically [this] is understood of the killing of Goliath by his own sword by the boy David. Allegorically, it signifies Christ conquering the devil with the same cross that the latter had prepared for him. Tropologically, it denotes the war of the just against the devil tempting the flesh; for when the flesh is curbed and kept in check, the [devil's] head is cut off, when his first attacks are rendered defeated and fruitless. And anagogically, the victory of Christ on the day of

judgment is implied, when death the final enemy is finally destroyed.[2]

Understanding the words of Ecclesiasticus "he who has created me has rested in my tent *(tabernaculum)* [Ecclus. 24:12] as direct prophecy, Saint Bonaventure comments upon them as follows:

> According to the literal understanding, it applies to the Virgin Mary, in whose tabernacle the Lord rested bodily. According to the allegorical, it applies to the Church Militant, in whose tabernacle the Lord rests sacramentally. According to the moral, it applies to the faithful soul, in whose tabernacle the Lord rests spiritually. According to the anagogic understanding, it applies to the heavenly court, in whose tabernacle he rests sempiternally.[3]

The symbol of marriage is one of the richest. Honorius explains it by doubling each sense; this permits him to make a place in the same tabulation for varieties of the senses that are rarely found together. The following text is in the prologue to his explication of Canticles:

> This book treats of marriage, which comes about in four ways, namely, historically, allegorically, tropologically, anagogically. . . .
> With respect to history, marriages come about in two ways: either by intermingling of the flesh, or by mere betrothal. . . .
> With respect to allegory, too, marriage comes about in two ways: one, whereby the Word of God joined flesh together with himself, i.e., whereby God assumed the human nature, which, exalted at the right hand of the Father, he has set on the throne of glory; the other, whereby Christ the God-man has associated the universal Church, i.e., the whole multitude of the faithful, with himself through commingling his own body with it. . . .
> With respect to tropology, also, marriage comes about in two ways: in the one, whereby the soul is linked to Christ through love; in the other, whereby the soul, because it is a power inferior to the spirit of the interior man which is its superior man, is conjoined with it through the consent of the divine law. . . .
> Nonetheless do marriages come about in two ways with respect to anagogy: the one, that whereby Christ, rising from the dead, ascends the heavens as a new man and associates the multitude of the angels with himself; the other, that whereby even after the res-

The Unity of the Fourfold Sense

urrection he has linked the whole Church to his glory in the vision of deity.[4]

But the most privileged symbol of all is that of Jerusalem. In it we have much more than an example; for in this single name of Jerusalem the whole history of the people of Israel is summed up, and in it also is contained the whole substance of the Old Testament; and along with it is the whole Church of Christ, the whole Christian soul, the whole city of God — and the whole mystery of the "Virgo singularis"[5] as well — so much so that the explication of Jerusalem condenses "in nuce" ["in a nutshell"] as it were, the total explication of Scripture and the total exposition of the Christian mystery. So it is not surprising that the Christian tradition, summoned to do so by Scripture itself, was very soon attached to it. In Didymus the Blind's commentary on Zechariah, recently discovered in the sands of Egypt and translated by Father Doutreleau, one reads: "Jerusalem has often received a threefold allegorical interpretation: it is either the soul established in virtue, or the Church glorious, which has neither spot nor wrinkle . . . , or the heavenly city of the living God."[6] As a matter of fact these various acceptations are found in Origen,[7] along with a feeling of the continuity of the one for the other and a frequent predominance of the eschatological Jerusalem, which turned out to draw upon him certain scarcely deserved reproaches on the part of Saint Jerome regarding his second manner.[8] Also well-known is the breadth of the Augustinian vision as it unfolds in the *De Civitate Dei:* the allegory of Jerusalem is its basis: "that Jerusalem to whose peace we are running. . . ."[9] The four senses of the City are already stock phrases in Cassian.[10] One finds them again in Bede,[11] Rabanus Maurus,[12] Sedulius Scotus,[13] Guibert of Nogent,[14] Honorius,[15] and in a great number of others. The *Speculum Ecclesiae* recalls them,[16] as do the *Miscellanea,*[17] John Béleth,[18] Stephen Langton,[19] etc. From then on Jerusalem will be the typical exemplar illustrating the fourfold sense: in Nicholas of Lyra it immediately follows our distich.[20] The whole fourth book of the *De claustro animae* of Hugo of Fouilloy is a treatise in forty-three chapters on the fourfold Jerusalem: five chapters for the history, fourteen for the mystical and the moral senses more or less intermingled, twenty-four for anagogy alone: it is a long description of the heavenly city, where all the problems concerning the last things are tackled.[21] Indeed, the name of Jerusalem is applied especially to the anagogic Jerusalem. When one wants to emphasize the differences of situation more than the identity of essence, the word "Zion" is preferred, to designate the Church on earth, the *Ecclesia quae nunc est.* "Zion," then, is a "speculatio," the view in a glass darkly, whereas Jerusalem is the "vision of peace."[22] Mystic city, happy city.[23] City at whose breast "all is consummated into the One."[24] Is there any need to cite the celebrated hymn:

> Caelestis urbs, Jerusalem, beata pacis visio . . .

or the description that ends the great poem of Saint Odo of Cluny?[25] Rather let us reread a sequence of the eleventh century, chanted during the octave of the dedication:

> This is great Jerusalem, that supernal city
> Woven all about with pure gold, with gems that sparkle throughout the widths of its wall.
> This is the heavenly court, the fatherland of the angels,
> The Church, both stable rock and eternal palace,
> Which is called the high-set city Jerusalem, which vision of peace
> Is constructed from living stones, the souls of the blessed. . . .[26]

Or certain verses of Bernard de Morval's *De contemptu mundi*, a poem in which some have been wont to see merely an expression of medieval terrors in expectation of coming disasters and in an obsession about eternal punishments:

> Fatherland of light unaware of trouble, knowing no contention . . .
> Splendid Fatherland, and flowery earth free from thorns. . . .
>
> City of Zion, good city, harmonious Fatherland, Fatherland of light, . . .
> Golden City of Zion, milk-rich Fatherland, beautiful for the citizen,
> You overwhelm every heart, you build so high as to block off for all both heart and mouth,
> I know not, I know not what jubilation, what sort of light belongs to you,
> What convivial joys, what special glory. . . .
>
> Peerless city of Zion, mystic mansion founded in Heaven . . .
> That beauty of yours overwhelms every heart, O Zion, O Peace![27]

The Unity of the Fourfold Sense

In a beautiful poem in prose, a disciple of Saint Gregory and of John of Fécamp also sings of the divine city and its king.[28] Aimé of Monte-Cassino described its splendors.[29] The same goes for Godfrey of Saint Victor,[30] etc. The praise of this heavenly Jerusalem re-echoes everywhere: our mother, mother of freedom, city in which one hears the "chorus of freedom."[31] The spiritual Middle Ages is indeed the heir of Saint Augustine, who said of her: "When I speak of her, I do not want to stop."[32] And our funeral liturgies still end with the supreme wish: "Deducant te angeli in civitatem sanctam, Jerusalem!" ["May the angels lead thee into the holy city Jerusalem!"]

But what most texts do not show at all or what they ordinarily show less, the fuller and more didactic they are in exposing the four senses, is the secret soul of the theory. This is the dynamic unity of these four senses, their reciprocal interiority. We speak, as indeed we must, of diverse senses: one exegete explains such and such a sense; someone else, still another; to distinguish them from each other, one superimposes them, juxtaposes them, or opposes them; one enumerates them and parades them in succession as if they were so many independent entities. This is an unavoidable flattening arising from language, which did not deceive the ancients — any more than a good Thomist would take the principles of the being of which he asserts the real distinction as so many "things." Just as one ancient author says of the four degrees of contemplation, so ought we to say of these four senses that they are interlinked like the rings of a priceless chain: *concatenati sunt ad invicem*.[33] Let us recall once more the "wheel within the wheel" of Ezekiel, commented on by Saint Gregory, the full meaning of which will soon become clear to us. Each of them possesses a propulsive force such that the one leads to the other "through increments of understanding, as it were by certain steps of the mind." "The word of history" is brought to completion by "the sense of allegory," and, in their turn, "the senses of allegory" of themselves incline "to the exercise of morality."[34] We pass by means of a natural and necessary movement "from history to allegory, and from allegory to morality."[35] Allegory is in truth *the truth* of history; the latter, just by itself, would be incapable of bringing itself intelligibly to fulfillment; allegory fulfills history by giving it its sense.[36] The mystery that allegory uncovers merely makes it open up a new cycle; in its first season, it is merely an "exordium";[37] to be fully itself, it must be brought to fulfillment in two ways. First it is interiorized and produces its fruit in the spiritual life, which is treated by tropology; then this spiritual life has to blossom forth in the sun of the kingdom; in this [spiritual life consists] the end of time which constitutes the object of anagogy: for that which we realize now in Christ through deliberated will is the very same thing which, freed of every obstacle and all obscurity, will become the essence of eternal life.[38]

This development is first of all temporal. In time history precedes the mystery; it is "prefiguration": "Do not things to be done spiritually follow upon those done corporeally?"[39] For us, eternal life is future life: for us, the spiritual world is a world to come.[40] But the succession in time is not all. There is a development from the one sense to the other which can be called logical. The object of the second sense by its relation to the object of the first constitutes a repetition, an internal advance, a more admirable "recapitulation." Isaac of Stella has noted the fact in striking terms:

> ... Wherever something has been said or done marvelously, it is recapitulated and commemorated still more marvelously in the sacrament. *Therefore all things together are made to revolve from the start again.* For all things that were before are figures of those that are later, which begin now to be revealed in their own times; and these are themselves envelopes *(involucra)* for and exemplars of the things to come. And just as these things are more true and more manifest than those before, so too those that are to come [are truer and more manifest] than these, so that all vanity, every living human being, may always be crossing over in image and vanity till it arrive at the naked, manifest, and stable face of the truth.[41]

The term *involucrum* nicely indicates the relation of the historical sense precisely as historical to the allegorical. For the latter gives us the Christ, who is the "fat of the grain," the "grain of wheat": now "no grain can come to maturity unless it shall have lurked within the straw."[42] "To arrive at the future, first it is necessary to pass through the present." The most "allegoristic" of these old authors of ours are not those who insist the least upon the need for temporal ripenings. But among the three last senses, the bond is more interior still. The New Testament is homogeneous, and that is why these new relations could no longer be expressed very happily by the word "allegory," though it would still be a question of the mystical or spiritual sense. The history of Abraham, or that of David, was "allegorical": that of Jesus was not.[43] Everything is being produced right now, everything is living on and buckled up inside one and the same mystery: *Christ is substantially always the same; Christ signifies himself.*[44] The passage from one sense to the other is more precisely a passage from the one into the other, a coming-to-be of the one by means of

The Unity of the Fourfold Sense

the other.[45] *Christ is a metaphor for the Church*. . . .[46] The Church will turn out to be the fullness of Christ, and — let us restate that beautiful expression of Saint Ambrose — "it is in souls that the Church is beautiful."

Temporal succession, logical development — it is still living development. The fourfold sense unfolds organically. "From the root of history, allegory produces spiritual fruits," which are garnered for eternity.[47] Thus "quite a play of correspondences ties together the aspects and the stages of the plan of salvation which unfolds here below eventually to be consummated beyond history."[48] Each sense leads to the other as its end.[49] So they are several, but they constitute a unity. A unity of source, and a unity of convergence: by means of these, says Richard of Saint Victor, *Scripture tells us many things transformed into one*.[50] This is a mystic identity. So too for anagogy and tropology: the soul, says Saint Bonaventure, "by entering into itself enters into the supernal Jerusalem";[51] and Raoul of Saint Germer likewise said: "But Jerusalem, i.e., the vision of peace, has to be our soul, the city which God may deign to dwell in."[52] Again the same holds true for allegory and anagogy: the Church of time, as we have seen, is no other than that of eternity,[53] though it be in quite a different state: "not yet in fact, but nevertheless in hope. . . ."[54] "Heaven is the holy Church."[55] History itself in its relative exteriority participates in this mystic identity: for, as Rupert explains again, the salutary facts, and even those that are such only at a distance under the aspect of preparations, are no longer without "reason" that the Father is without the Word, and "just as the eternal Father does nothing without the coeternal Son, so too none of those things that have been done corporeally for the salvation of men, whether in the Law or in the Gospel, can be devoid of a spiritual understanding."[56] Subsequently the identity is affirmed in a still better manner: it is the "mystery" which is the "exemplar,"[57] this is its substance, "this is the very thing to be borne in his heart."[58] In the mystery, nothing suffers separation. Through each of its phases the coming of Christ "is something indivisible."[59] If the traditional understanding of Scripture perfectly assures, within the history of our salvation, this "junction of the event and the sense,"[60] which, for every reflective mind, is one of the major preoccupations, it is by Christ and in Christ that the understanding assures that junction at each of its stages. It is always pointing to the mystery of Christ in its indivisibility. This is the selfsame unparalleled mystery which is again the mystery of ourselves and the mystery of our eternity. Each phrase of Scripture has several senses; but at a still profounder level, all these phrases of Scripture never have just one single sense.[61] Its every "letter" contains a unique treasure, "our treasure."[62] There the "vision of the image" ["visio imaginis"] is different on each occasion; but its "intention of the mind" ["intentio mentis"] is always the same.[63] Each phrase, in its aim, joins all the others together; they all converge upon that unique Home from whence, secretly, they originated.

Mysterium Christi. Only this unique mystery possesses infinite depths, and the mind of each of the faithful has varying capacities for comprehending it. From this there results for every spiritual understanding, as we have seen more especially for anagogy, an incurable character of incompleteness. But, as the Gregorian term *volatus* for anagogy has already indicated, this fatal incompleteness is to be considered above all in its positive and dynamic aspect. The Word of God does not cease to create and to hollow out within the one who readies himself for it the capacity to receive it, with the result that the faithful understanding can increase indefinitely. By allegory the old text can always let more novelty shine through;[64] the new mystery can always be more interiorized and introduce eternity more deeply into the heart. As one saint put it, namely Gregory of Nyssa,[65] just as the knowledge of God is itself always going "from commencements to commencements," so too the understanding of Scripture: "Since (God) is already beginning to open up for us the greatest abyss of the sacraments as though from the start."[66] Thence we are called to be "transformed from glory unto glory, as by the Spirit of the Lord."[67] That is what Origen had taught with respect to the manna. In his conference on *spiritual science,* John Cassian repeated it for the West: "According to the measure that our mind is renewed by meditation upon the Scriptures, the face of the Scriptures itself begins to be renewed, and the beauty of a more sacred meaning begins to increase, so to speak, according to the measure of our progress."[68] Saint Gregory's *Moralia* propagated the same teaching[69] and the *Sentences* of Isidore of Seville echoed them: "Scripture may vary like manna for the understanding of each reader . . . and though (the Lord's speech) may be diversified for the understanding of each, yet it remains one in itself."[70] In the last century again, Mgr. Gerbet said the same thing: "The symbol has a somehow expansive signification, which stretches along with the understanding of the reader."[71] A philosopher called it to our mind just yesterday: "Scripture differentiates its answers according to the level of the understanding one has; and the value of these answers, one may suspect, varies with the quality of the questioning."[72] Provided that these remarks be taken without any subjectivism, there is a marvelous correspondence between them and those of Rabanus Maurus: "To the extent that anyone advances on high, to that extent the sacred speeches speak of higher things."[73]

No one has put the matter better, at once more poetically and more

The Unity of the Fourfold Sense

precisely, than Saint Gregory. It is to him that Rabanus Maurus is especially indebted, after Isidore, after Smaragdus,[74] and in succession with so many others. Scripture, says Gregory, "advances with those who read it." Containing God's revelation about himself, it is, so to speak, extendable — or penetrable — to infinity. Thus Gregory applies to it a law of religious consciousness that he expresses elsewhere with regard to the meeting of the two travelers and the resurrected Jesus on the road to Emmaus. One might believe, he explains in this latter passage, that Jesus at first concealed his true identity, so as not to be recognized at all; but this way of understanding his going about incognito would be superficial and hardly worthy of him who is the Truth: "Therefore the simple Truth does nothing through duplicity, but he showed himself to them in body such as he was with them in mind."[75] This explanation will be retained through the Middle Ages.[76] It had also been advanced at length by Origen with regard to the Gospel account of the Transfiguration.[77] It is to this law that Gregory returns in the seventh of his homilies on Ezekiel, while commenting on the great inaugural vision of the Prophet. In his eyes it constitutes one of the foundations of Christian exegesis, and he grounds this law itself on the following truth: that it is the selfsame God who gives the Scripture and who makes it possible to grasp it, and that what would appear to Gregory as two successive acts is in fact but one. For God is not subject to the exteriority of our temporal sequences. Consequently, there would be reciprocal priority or causality between the objective sense and its interpretation each time it should come from the Spirit. There is nothing in this like the idea of new dogmas held in reserve from the time that the Spirit had been given to the Church as a sort of revelation to come. One ought not to imagine the sacred text as harboring completely formed sequences of meaning more or less ready to allow themselves to be discovered. The Spirit communicates to it a virtuality without limits: hence it involves infinitely possible degrees of depth. No more than it is the case that the world is created once and for all, is this true of that other world, Scripture: the Spirit is still "creating" it each day so to speak to the extent that he "is working" it.[78] By a marvelous and rigorous proportion, he "expands" it to the measure that he expands the understanding of the one who receives it.[79] For, as Origen had already said, "Our soul, which had previously been contracted, is being stretched out so as to be able to hold the wisdom of God."[80] The *volatus* of the contemplative soul, howsoever far it lead the soul within the heaven of the Scriptures, will never make it hit a boundary: for the space and the flight are supplied at once, in due measure. This is an audacious view, but, if it be well understood, involving an audacity which is exactly that of the faith itself. It is also a view at times likely to dizzy our perhaps too-human good sense, at any rate to baffle the positivist mentalities of our age.

This is what Saint Gregory, after Origen and after Cassian, restated with a new depth. He saw all this signified in the fact that the chariot contemplated in the vision by Ezekiel followed in its own motion the movements of the Spirit of Life that was within its wheels. His explanation confirms with complete rigor the related symbol of the twofold abyss: *deep is calling unto deep.* Is this like something that Harnack thought of, when, faithful to a banality that dates back to Melanchthon[81] and which one is pained to see rehashed by Catholic historians, he reckons that the great pope had lowered the spirituality of the patristic age to the level of coarse minds?[82] Is this also what one of the masters of the *Aufklärung* ["Enlightenment"], J. Brücker, was alluding to when he wrote that all the teaching and all the piety of "this teacher of little judgment" may practically be reduced to the "superstitions of an external worship"?[83] Is it by reason of such passages that so many other historians point out to us the faith of this man "deeply rooted in the fear of hell,"[84] setting the centuries of the Middle Ages ablaze with his gloomy flame? Again, is it such traits as these that caused Ebert himself, in his otherwise solid history of literature of the Middle Ages, to have neglected the homilies on Ezekiel as "having no particular interest for us"?[85] Well, let us learn to show ourselves a bit more equitable. This puny, sick pontiff overburdened with affairs and concerns, speaking to a wretched people in a half-ruined town at whose gates the enemy would soon be camping,[86] not only showed off the radiant but still distant vision of the heavenly Jerusalem in the face of his hearers; in his contemplative faith he was able to summon enough energy serenely to fathom — with a freedom of mind that one day was to provoke the admiration of Saint Bernard[87] — the most exalted, indeed the most mysterious subject: that of the living contact of our understanding with the truth of the God who reveals himself to us. And the word of this good shepherd was so persuasive that by extraordinary miracle his flock did not cease to follow him from church to church, but was reborn to hope, like those bones that the Prophet saw brought back to life through the breath of the Spirit.[88]

"From there minds . . . grow wide in themselves, whence they admit the light of truth to themselves as though through the narrows."[89] Doubtless the primary idea that guides Gregory in his explanation is derived from Origen.[90] The first lines of the symbol that he exploits are already found sketched out in Saint Ambrose.[91] But the symbol itself, as he understood it, is entirely his own. In this seventh homily, he expounds it in terms of such power and such beauty that it is necessary to cite at least a part of it in the text itself:

> *Wherever the spirit was going, while it goes there, the wheels were lifted in equal measure, following it.*
>
> For where the spirit of the reader tends, thither are the divine utterances also lifted up, since just as you may have sought by seeing or feeling something high in them, these same sacred utterances grow with you and ascend with you to things still higher. For in one and the same sentence of Scripture, one person is nourished by history alone, another seeks out the typic sense, and yet another seeks contemplative understanding through the type. And it often comes about that in one and the same sentence all three can be found together at once.[92]
>
> Therefore the sayings of the sacred utterance grow along with the spirit of the readers. . . .
>
> Let us see how the wheels follow the spirit, who is called the spirit of life and is said to be in the wheels. To the extent that one advances on high, to that extent do the sacred utterances tell him of still higher things. The wheels go, they stand, they are made to rise, since the sacred reading[93] that is sought is found to be such as the one by whom it is sought becomes. For you have advanced to the active life: it stays with you. Through God's grace you have arrived at the contemplative life: it flies with you.
>
> For us in the darkness of the present life this Scripture has become the light of the journey. Yet we know that it is also obscure for us unless the Truth should illuminate it for our minds. For the created light does not shine for us unless it be illuminated by the uncreated Light. Therefore, since almighty God himself has both created the sayings of the holy Testaments for our salvation, and has opened them up, the spirit of life was in the wheels.[94]

4. Questions of Method

Except for citing certain filiations for a passage or for distinguishing certain nuances, we have proceeded up till now as if the doctrine of the fourfold or the threefold sense, once constituted, formed a whole which never underwent any notable evolution for the whole length of the Middle Ages. In our exposition we have even been constantly mingling features borrowed from the earlier period, using numerous patristic texts, clarifying one set of texts by means of others without always taking care to be sure that there was a real filiation among them, and without each time ascertaining to whom the paternity of this or that exegesis ought to be assigned. Accordingly we have quite neglected the fine points, and perhaps have even suppressed certain points of opposition. We seem to have presented a sort of mosaic of doubtful objectivity and, at any event, of drifting chronology. If there is an offense against method in all this, the offense was premeditated. At the very least, let us say that we are aware of the paradox.[1]

Doubtless nothing human is ever completely stable. Profound transformations can be effected under the permanence of the formulas, in sooth complete upheavals, and, even where nothing seems to budge because no burning crisis or abrupt innovation is occurring, often "it is the basis of thought that is changed like a sun in movement."[2] We shall soon have occasion to acknowledge it in our subject as well. Only, in wanting to retrace the details of these changes as soon as possible, it seems to us that one would risk never getting hold of the doctrine in its essence. A too sketchy historical method would ill permit one to disengage the real continuity beneath its metamorphoses as to the individual variations of all those who have expressed one or another aspect of it. In our view the doctrine is functionally one. In its most general outline, across many centuries it has remained self-identical, though more or less deeply understood (sometimes ill understood), more or less completely explained, and more or less subtly analyzed. As is all too clear, not all the elements that integrate it have been equally reflected by everyone. Each author receives it and exploits it as one or the other among them modestly put it, using an expression of Saint Jerome that made a fortune,[3] "according to the capacity of his little mind" or "to the extent of the thinness, to the measure, to the capability, with regard to the simplicity of his little mind"[4] or "his little knowledge."[5] Each generation, each individual genius or each family of minds almost undetectably changes the accent of the doctrine. To be sure, it experiences dormant periods, mechanical repetitions, subsidences, unhealthy overgrowths, and its life is sometimes almost smothered under the mass of devices that were intended to assist it. On the other hand, it goes without saying that the perspective of a theoretician, of a professor, or of a debater is not that of a preacher, a moralist, or a pure spiritual. In preaching itself, an abbot addressing his monks will not speak — the remark is one of Saint Bernard's[6] — exactly like a pastor exhorting his parishioners. Neither the one nor the other will speak as the author of a strict "exposition" would write. The situation determines the nature of the exegesis: thus, preaching to the people on a Psalm, Saint Augustine sidesteps a problem that came up, as being too technical: "here is not the place to discuss this matter."[7] It is natural to find less science and more tropology in a homily than in a commentary; a master addressing novices tends to "moralize," even if he is a good historian and is able to handle doctrinal allegory, and we would get three quite different ideas of Origen if he left us only scholia, or only commentaries, or only homilies.

In exegetical literature, then, as well as in biblical literature, there are different literary genres. This simple finding is of very great importance and of very rich application, when it is a question of an epoch where this literature that we call exegetic consitutes the largest part of sacred literature. There have always been a certain number of more or less specialized disciplines in Scripture studies. If we see them only rarely associated in reality, they are nevertheless not incompatible in principle; they were not judged such by their practitioners. The scope of the resulting diversities ought not to be exaggerated, even if it is true that they result not only from varied competencies or needs but also from diverse preferences and inclinations of mind. Even less ought one to allow oneself to be hypnotized by them. To be sure it is the role of the historian to analyze and illuminate evolutions and divergences. But one would blind oneself to what is essential if one did not first try to grasp, even at the price of a certain sketchiness, the reality from and within which the evolutions and divergences arise. History lives on particularities, differences, oppositions; flatness of surface is its death. The very variety of all this shifting detail sometimes runs the risk of disguising certain great constants, certain unities maintained at a deep level.

These last observations seem to us to hold good in general for the whole history of ideas, but much more still for the history of traditions, at least to the extent to which these traditions have deep roots. Now — without explicitly fighting against it, it sometimes happens that one forgets it — "the force of tradition"[8] is therefore something very real, that the resources of philology and literary history are not enough to appreciate. Further, the testimonies of a tradition lived in the faith cannot be studied entirely as if they constituted merely a sequence of individual thinkers. Each of them, even if he retains the influence of his predecessors in many things (and much more than he believes), does not ultimately want to build only upon himself. All those of first rank, on the contrary, build from one and the same foundation, which they accept in its totality even if they assimilate it only partially or superficially. By that very fact, they find themselves really possessing in common certain ideas that are nevertheless not possessed in totality by any one among them.[9] The philosopher does not stick only to his own thought: the believer adheres to a whole spiritual universe, to which he knows that his own thought, as expressed, is never adequate; he communes across the centuries with all those who have connected themselves with his selfsame universe; aided by them, he works with them toward a Truth which he knows he is not even capable of conceiving as a whole; he nourishes himself on works that that Truth has already called into being; he reads "the Fathers," who are for him precisely his own Fathers; in the new situation in which he finds himself, he extends the furrow that they had begun to plow. With his own proper individuality, having to respond to often quite new problems, he is, in his particular place, the witness of a tradition that perpetuates itself beyond him. Without ever entirely making it explicit from the ground up, he is always presupposing it, and presupposes it as a whole. Provided that the discernment that is required in each case is applied to it, there is nothing arbitrary in using some of these witnesses to comment on the others. In some cases it will even be indispensable to bring their separate testimonies to a focus, so as to allow the common foundation that was doubtless never fully clarified to appear.[10] Let us go even to extreme cases. Two authors can crash into each other, contradict each other, fight each other, each presenting a different expression — and one that he thinks incompatible with the other one — for the selfsame principle which they both live; they pay attention only to their points of disagreement: we have to disengage what unites them as well. It is no less important to recall that a doctrine does not exist only where it is laid out in didactic and scholarly fashion: it is also present *in actu* where it inspires thought; it can be there in a much more organic and much more powerful way than in some formula whose verbal balance and clarity leave nothing to be desired. Finally, how can one comprehend certain minor texts, how can one not risk an unjust and unintelligent contempt for them, except by reuniting them to the tradition which, perhaps unbeknownst to their author, carries him on, and which one can recognize in them, rediscover through them, but without getting stuck in them.

These points are admitted, *mutatis mutandis*, for certain types of concrete thought, for example, for primitive mythologies. It is admitted that they constitute a complete interpretation of existence. Each is a complete cycle, present as a whole within the least of its elements, and to understand each element, even if it presents itself in isolation, it must be put into its place within this cycle. It is also admitted that the smallest "hierophany" constitutes part of a "coherent system" which can be entirely called up by "any of its material supports," and that this system "maintains its consistency in spite of all degradation," even after those who transmit disjointed fragments of the system have ceased to perceive it. We recall that to interpret any primitive symbol correctly one must always call upon the "global experience of the sacred," which, prior to any one symbol, includes them all and is never exhausted by any one of them.[11] Only in this way does that which might to an incompetent observer seem to be merely pitiable superstition reveal a depth that balks analysis and provokes admiration. Shall we refuse the benefit of this sort of explanation on behalf of archaic man, *mutatis mutandis* again, to the mental syntheses that the history of the Christian faith offers for our consideration? Will the believers themselves be incapable of furnishing, so as to understand those who have lived the same faith in other periods of thought, the effort of imagination that the scholars of this age furnish with a view to reconstituting sympathetically — an essential condition for understanding — the mental universe of ancient civilizations, or even to rediscovering the cosmic vision illuminated by the first lightning bolts that pierced the animal night? Could they be satisfied with stating flat-footedly that they have made progress in theology as well as in exegesis and that, without condemning the ancients, who did what they could, they, for their part, do not have to go back to baby diapers? Even if none of it were still alive or ought to come to life again, the past deserves less disdainful treatment than that. In any case, for the historian of doctrines, even if he does not at all share the faith that he is studying, the internal logic of the Christian mystery ought not to be a hollow word. Here it is entirely a question of the Christian mystery. For it is about a collection of conceptions that are straining to express that mystery. They deal with its substance and its rhythm, although in their letter they evidently contain a number of transitory elements, today obsolete; well, let's admit it: a lot of junk. To have disregarded it, so to speak, from the opening move, means that more than one historian, more than one scholar, believer or unbeliever, has totally missed the range of this doctrine of the four senses. A certain historical positivism leads one methodically to kill the object of one's study, with one's eyes closed.

Besides, here we are speaking only of a very general doctrine or methodology. We are always considering only a collection of principles of hermeneutics and of reflections on Scripture. As to exegesis itself,[12] taken in the strict, specialized meaning of the word, which has become dominant; as to its practice, at the level of science or scientific consciousness which is manifest in it; as to the progress or regress of critical sense and to the history of the various sorts of preparatory stages that have arisen in this domain on the way to modern science — these are subjects that go outside our scope in more than one respect. There is incomparably greater change in these areas than in ours. The advantage that we have over the ancients in them is much more obvious. But for the study of such issues we can only refer to works like those of Miss Beryl Smalley, Father C. Spicq, Father A. Vaccari, Berhard Bischoff, Mr. L. W. Laistner, Father Robert E. McNally, etc.

Nevertheless a few remarks might help to prevent misunderstandings.

First, we shall not forget that a greater or lesser critical spirit or knowledge of languages, a greater or lesser eagerness to associate with the rabbis, or a greater or lesser interest in the ancient phase of salvation history in no way prejudices an author's greater or lesser "allegorism." We must watch out for artificial antinomies. By means of an a priori that is above all lacking in historical spirit, it comes about that one naively attributes to the ancients generally the idea of a disjunction between science and allegory, or between history and symbolism — an idea that exists only in a certain recent state of mind — and one is then surprised how it is that from a "non-sequitur," and from a "sort of contradiction," grammarians, linguists, philologists, historians of ability, men who show themselves capable "of collating manuscripts," could nevertheless still be interested in something other than the literal sense of the Bible. How, they ask, could such men have been able still to believe "that there is a hidden sense in the Bible, surpassing the investigations of grammar and philology"? How could they seriously sustain "the legitimacy of the allegorical sense"?[13] Such infantilism in minds that otherwise appear seriously adult! How perplexing is human nature! But they fail to perceive that they are themselves the victims of a prejudice and that by interjecting partly subjective criteria in this way they shut the door to understanding the thought that they are studying.

Meanwhile, the great example of Origen already stands as evidence of it: this "prince of the critics" is at the same time the "allegoricus interpretes" par excellence, as Saint Jerome calls him; with the same genius and the same fervor, he has constructed the monument of his *Hexapla* and that of his allegorical commentaries.[14] The fecundity of his spiritual elaboration, however one judges it, ought not make us forget the veneration he had for the letter of Scripture, nor his efforts to elucidate the historical sense.[15] Saint Augustine, who is just as much an "allegorist" as Origen, is no less indissolubly the great theoretician of the theology of history. Saint Jerome, who had formed, in his enthusiasm, the plan to translate into Latin the entire works of Origen, imitated the great Alexandrian both in his scientific zeal and in his abundant, nay superabundant, practice of allegorical exegesis, and even his "palinode on Origen"[16] had to change nothing as to his usual practices in this domain.[17] He remained faithful to allegorism to the end, both to its most controversial procedures and to its best grounded principles, to the point that — as his latest historian informs us — "those who did not have a taste for allegory were reluctant to read the commentaries of Jerome."[18] From time to time he confined himself to literal explication, but that was in self-defense: as soon as he had the liberty to do so, he "fell back," as Zöckler put it, "into the labyrinth of tropology";[19] he himself would have preferred to say that after having eaten dust like a serpent despite himself he finally began to climb "the summits of spiritual understanding."[20] In his second commentary on Abadias, when he has just criticized the inexperienced allegorism of the writing of his youth, he writes:

> Since . . . we have interpreted historically and have set up our skiff amidst broken crags, we spread the sails of spiritual understanding, so that, with the Lord blowing and unlocking his mysteries, we may joyfully reach port.[21]

In his eyes as in the eyes of the other Fathers, the Mosaic Law was fully justified only by the reality to come of which it was the symbolic announcement: thus, with the Apostle, he proclaimed it "spiritual," and concluded that "everything that the Jews accomplished carnally" was or ought to be "accomplished spiritually" by the Christians.[22] Many a time he repeats that the Law and the Prophets are to be understood not "according to the letter that killeth," but "according to the spirit that giveth life."[23] Cassiodorus, himself also an allegorist, was, to the extent possible, very interested in comparing the diverse versions of the Bible: one would have quite astounded him if one had told him that this attitude of his was self-contradictory. Saint Bede the Venerable is doubtless the most scientific mind of the high Middle Ages, interested at once in criticism, history, and natural science; yet it is he who coined the definitive formula for the fourfold sense. One can also recall, for example, that Saint Bernard, who not only practiced spiritual exegesis with extreme liberty, but who went so far as to proclaim, with a view to defining his goal and his method:

"Nor do I care less to explain the words than to touch souls,"[24] did not show himself any the less careful about exactitude in literal explanation, as the following passage from the letter *Explanationem* published by Dom Jean Leclercq attests:

> I have caught us deviating in several places by wandering from the truth of the literal level, while we have been too intent upon discovering moral senses. . . . The remaining places are, as best I can judge, correct, and the erroneous passages can easily be corrected.[25]

Analogous examples will present themselves subsequently. Here let us take just one last, more modest instance. The letter of the anonymous Victorine, *De modo et ordine legendi sacram Scripturam*, puts just as much emphasis on advocating spiritual understanding as the sole end of scriptural studies as it does on recommending, as the first step, three and even four "historical" readings of the whole Bible. History, says our anonymous author, ought to be "et *perscrutanda* et *pertranseunda*": in which he does scarcely anything else than to repeat very ancient counsels. This brief writing, which seems to offer no great difficulties of interpretation, is also seen to be cited by some — who oppose it and so the Victorines — as a monument of allegoristic aberration; by others — who, on the contrary, link it to Saint Victor — as evidence of growing literalism, according as they retain one phrase or another, nay one word or another, which is alone judged significant.[26]

These few examples recall to us, contrary to a modern prejudice, a permanent truth: interest in the letter and a taste for the spirit are not perforce meant to be divorced from each other; the sense of history and the mystic urge are in no way incompatible. On the other hand — the fact is only too certain, and the history of modern exegesis in the Church prior to the scientific renewal of the nineteenth century offers too many instances of it as well — literalism is an entirely different thing from criticism, the rejection of all "allegory" is not a guarantee of solidity in history, and one can be a shabby scholar and spiritually undernourished to boot.

Nor again will one forget, if one does not want to set up artificial oppositions everywhere, that there have always been certain writings that, owing to their very character or the particular end they have in view, contain exclusively or at least predominantly a literal exegesis. This applies to certain glosses or scholia: there is not much allegory, as we have already alluded, in Origen's scholia. There is none at all in Saint Augustine's *Locutiones in Heptateuchum,* which constitute a sequence of linguistic and grammatical remarks.[27] In drafting his short glosses on Porphyry and Boethius, Abelard did not at all mean to explicate their philosophy;[28] those who did as much for the biblical text did not mean to uncover the deeper sense of it either. The same holds for certain manuals, like the celebrated *Scholastic History* as well. It does not follow that the authors of such writings ought to be included among the "literalists." The same will be said for the redactors of chronicles: a certain Fréculphe of Lisieux in the ninth century announces his plan to restrict himself in his *Chronicle* to a short summary of the *historiae veritas*;[29] the same goes in the twelfth century for Godfrey of Viterbo in his *Pantheon*;[30] in the chapters of his *Chronicon* where he summarizes the history of the Bible, Otto of Freising does not, at least habitually, give himself over to allegory or morality; he informs the reader of the fact that his specialty is *historia*, not dogmatic or spiritual exposition: "Let no one expect judgments or moralities from us: for we intend to pursue history ... not in the fashion of one disputing but in the order appropriate to one who discusses the matter";[31] this did not keep this genial Cistercian from being the friend of Saint Bernard and from tasting the mystic exegesis of Clairvaux.[32]

The same remark holds good in the other direction. In seventh-century Ireland, for example, a certain Aileran the Wise, writing a "mystic interpretation" and a "moral interpretation" of the genealogy of the Savior, nevertheless neither denies the historical reality of the ancestors of the Word made flesh nor underrates it.[33] For reasons of convenience, Guibert of Nogent decided to stick to the moral sense in his commentaries: no more does this decision signify that he rejects the literal or the allegorical sense, or even that he challenges their importance. His explanations are very clean: he knows full well, on the one hand, that a precise knowledge of the literal sense is indispensable for fruitful research into the other senses,[34] and, on the other hand, if he omits allegory, it is not because it embarrasses him: it is only because, in a pastoral perspective, he judges tropology to be more useful for the task at hand.[35] As to critical spirit, without having applied it to the data of the sacred text, he has on other occasions shown that he was sufficiently provided with it, earning the nickname "the skeptical Guibert de Nogent."[36] One will not ask for any more from Honorius than what he promises the reader in the title of his opusculum "De decem plagis Aegypti spiritualiter."[37] The case of Peter Comestor is analogous: in assigning himself as his proper task the exposition of the "rivulus historicus" ["the brook of history"], Peter neither denies nor undervalues the allegorical or moral sense; it is not even certain that in proceeding in this way he gave in, as perhaps Aileran or Guibert may have, to his natural bent; at any event, he was so far from wishing to repudiate or even to consent to allow the doctrine of the fourfold sense to be blurred that he in fact offered a precise exposition of it in his preface[38] and he himself constantly applied it in his sermons. Here again, we are simply in the presence of a case of specialization.[39]

Just as many authors can divide up the task among themselves, it also happens that one and the same author in different works by turns focuses upon one or another sort of exegesis, upon exposition using one or another of the senses. Sometimes the reason for this is the occasion. Thus, Saint Jerome first composes a purely historical explication of certain chapters of Isaiah, because such was the express wish of the bishop Amabilis: later on, integrating it into his large commentary, he doubled it with a spiritual explication.[40] Rabanus Maurus complies in the same way with the instructions of King Lothair who solicited it: the latter ordered from him "a literal commentary on the beginning of Genesis, a spiritual commentary on the chapters of Jeremiah omitted by Jerome, a moral commentary on the continuation of Ezekiel."[41] In the same way again, when Saint Bernard and William of Saint Thierry, co-patients in the infirmary at Clairvaux, conversed together about the Canticle of Canticles, Bernard's oral commentary is more restricted and specialized than the one he later addressed to his monks and edited: at the express request of William that the remedies of the body should lead one to think of the remedies of the soul, he discusses the Groom and the Bride "morally only, with the mysteries of the Scripture left out." William, who informs us of the fact, explains: "since I wanted it so and had asked him to do it that way,"[42] and himself, in the preface of his *Expositio altera in Canticum,* speaks of his own plan to restrict himself just to the moral sense, without dealing with the profound mysteries concerning Christ and the Church: "holding ourselves in, and pacing ourselves within our proper courses."[43]

5. The Apostolic Preaching

One major case calls for some explanation. This is that of the commentaries on the Pauline Epistles. In a very large measure, we can say that they are all literal commentaries. Would their authors be growing cool towards allegory? Absolutely not. There is nothing more literal, for example, than Cassiodorus's *Complexiones* on the Epistles of the Apostles, and nothing more allegorical that his *Expositio* on the Psalter. Here there is neither contradiction nor mystery. Cassiodorus knows that Paul taught the Romans "by means of the truth brought to light from the New and Old Testament."[1] He knows what all Christians before him know and what all after him will know still: the twelve apostles, to whom we owe, directly or indirectly, the writings of the "New Testament," were, at the same time, the first *expositores* of the ancient Scripture: "the twelve apostles, through whom the Scripture of the New Testament was preserved and the mysteries of the Old revealed."[2] "Instructed by the Truth" in person, they have, by preaching the Gospel, attested that the Christ had accomplished this Scripture.[3] They were the first "preachers of the New Testament": this means, as Saint Gregory explains it, that they were the first, their eyes fixed upon the Christ, to disengage the "heavenly mystery" till then hidden under the shadow of allegories.[4] One does not cease, after him, to tell it and retell it.[5] Just as the stags first entering into thick forests use their antlers to open a passage for the other animals that follow them, so the apostles have set up avenues for us across the mysteries of the ancient Scripture, so that each generation could penetrate into it and find its nourishment there:

> For stags entering amid the thicknesses of the forests are accustomed to separate the branches by means of their horns and to open up a field to pasture both themselves and other animals, just as the holy apostles disclosed the dark shadows and hidden mysteries of the Scriptures in which they themselves were pastured and in which they pastured others.[6] So, when Richard of Saint Victor wanted to lead some "Judaizers" to understand the sense of the prophecies, he told them: "Let him who cannot understand the voice of the prophet at least heed the sense of the expositor; let him who does not understand the sense of the oracular prophet trust the judgment of the evangelist's exposition."[7]

We must rediscover the force and dignity, in part lost, of this term "preaching" in the traditional language. It does not only designate some "oratorical genre" or some sort of "moral teaching." The "word of preaching" is the white horse of the Apocalypse.[8] Those who have received the "grace of preaching"[9] from God in the footsteps of the Twelve are not only men who attempt to cite the Bible in their discourses with a view to giving them "force and effectiveness," or who draw upon the holy Letters for "pious reflections," "lessons," and "examples" appropriate for "illustrating the divine truth."[10] They are "the preachers of the Truth."[11] With Saint Paul they can say: "The word of the faith which we are preaching."[12] They raise the "ferment of the faith."[13] They spread the divine fire.[14] In space and time they extend the same "sound of the apostolic preaching": "every order of preachers is collected together in the union of the apostles."[15] They proclaim the name of Jesus Christ everywhere.[16] They announce "the mysteries of God." Scripture has been delivered over to them.[17] Through them it penetrates into every place;[18] through them the Church unceasingly engenders Christ.[19] Charged with inviting humanity to the Wedding Feast of the Lamb,[20] with "binding the members to the Head,"[21] they communicate "the fullness of the Gospel."[22] As to the spiritual sense, they are "the kings of the earth."[23] The function they accomplish is thus not a derived function. Preaching, says Saint Gregory, is "the thunder of God."[24] The "ministry of preaching" or "the office of preaching," to speak as did Gregory again,[25] is not the mere popularization of a doctrinal teaching existing in a more abstract form, which would be prior and superior to it: it is, under its own form, the highest, the doctrinal teaching itself. This was true of the first Christian preaching, that of the apostles; this is equally true of the preaching of those who succeed them in the Church: the Fathers, the Doctors, and our present-day pastors. "The successors of the apostles, the holy preachers."[26] "The apostolic Doctors."[27] When, in the ninth century, Alcuin wanted simultaneously to exalt the power and not only the sacred but the properly Christian character of the restored empire, he shows Charlemagne holding two swords, the one outside, the other inside: the second was "the sword of preaching." With the council of Frankfurt, Alcuin declared Charles "king and priest," using a formula borrowed from the titles of the emperors of Byzantium, but specifying that his priesthood consisted in "the ministry of teaching"; or rather, joining the biblical image of the trumpet to that of the sword, he wrote, using his master as the model for the ideal portrait of the emperor: "the sword of triumphal power is swinging in his right hand and the trumpet of Catholic preaching is resounding on his tongue."[28]

Such was the grandeur of "praedicatio" everywhere recognized in days of yore. An anonymous treatise of the thirteenth century says it again: "Preaching is an instrument by which God's Church is constructed."[29] Now this "praedicatio," which is more especially the deed of the New Testament, forms a body with the "expositio" of the Old. "The apostolic net, woven together from the twofold web of the New Testament and the Old."[30] In this sense it is, as Saint Gregory loves to say, a "nova praedicatio," the "vera praedicatio," entrusted to "novi praedicatores," to a "novus ordo praedicatorum."[31] The Lord himself wanted to prepare his apostles to "preach the Gospel," i.e., to "unveil and explain the Scriptures": these two expressions, or other similar ones, are given as synonyms.[32] "Apostoli enim et prophetae novi Testamenti, qui exponunt Scripturas."[33] They draw the fire, that is to say, the light of the faith, from the pits where the patriarchs and the prophets had hidden it, that is, from the deep obscurity of the Scriptures.[34] The Old Testament was "opened" once and for all by the Christ: it is still necessary now for the "doctors of the Church," or the "catholic doctors," or the "evangelical doctors,"[35] or "spiritual doctors,"[36] thanks to the "inspiration of the Holy Spirit," to manifest its content in their "expositions."[37] For them and through them, "In the whole text of the Old Testament, the mysteries of Christ shine forth."[38] Such was the essential object of the great miracle of Pentecost, before the external gift of tongues: the disciples there were filled with the Spirit; they themselves became like a book written within and decorated without: "Since their hearts have both been filled up inside with the understanding of the Scriptures and various tongues were being heard outside."[39] Now the miracle is being perpetuated from generation to generation. For, taken to its source, its permanent source, the essential element of the Christian teaching consists always in unfolding the Scripture, as Jesus did, by relating it all to Jesus. It consists in making the most of the two Testaments, the one by means of the other, by showing the New within the Old. This is the ferment that makes the whole dough of Scripture to rise.[40] This is *the virtue and the power of the Gospel preaching.*[41]

Such was the thought of Saint Irenaeus when he claimed for himself the "tradition" or the "preaching of the apostles."[42] Such too was that of Origen: "while the holy apostles are removing the surface of the letter."[43] The Christians, he said again, are those "who receive the understanding of the Scriptures according to the sense of the apostles";[44] those who are taught by their "mystic contemplation of the Law and the Prophets."[45] Such will be thought of our medievals. For Saint Paulinus of Aquilaea, the "apostolic sense" of the Scripture is its allegorical sense.[46] "The Evangelists reveal the hidden things among the secrets": thus speaks John of Ford;[47] and Thomas of Perseigne, by allusion to the word of Jesus on the teaching that he gave in private so that his disciples would then preach it on the roof-tops: "The preachers . . . teach in secret the hidden matters of the Scriptures which are spoken in the open so as to nourish the sons of the Church."[48] Rupert proclaims it in his own strange and beautiful way: "The true Isaac, i.e., the Lord Jesus Christ, took to his own wedlock, i.e., for the use of the Gospel preaching, the Mother of us all, holy Scripture, according to which we are reborn for God."[49] And again, Innocent III, comparing the preaching of the Gospel to the river that watered Paradise according to Saint Gregory:[50]

> The river . . . is the Gospel preaching which proceeds from the Lord Jesus Christ, who is the fountain of life, in whose light we shall see light, from whom all true pleasure emanates in a general way. . . . This (water) has flowed down at such length and breadth as to have filled the whole world. . . . It irrigates paradise, i.e., it fecundates the Church. . . .[51]

Here we recognize, under one of its most common expressions, the fundamental idea that we have explained in Chapter Five: the "preaching of the Gospel," or "of the faith of the Church,"[52] which continues the preaching of the apostles, is strictly correlative with the preaching of Jesus Christ. Now the latter is the New Testament, which delivers to us the spiritual sense of the Old, rendered manifest in Jesus Christ: "the mystery of the Savior made clear by the apostolic preaching."[53] The "dispensers of the New Testament" are therefore, as Saint Augustine says, identically the same as the "expositors of the Old Testament."[54] They draw from their treasury things new and old, preaching the same unique mystery of the two Testaments.[55] They preach the New Testament, "where the obscurity of the Old is revealed."[56] They can be called indifferently "expositores," or "praedicatores," or "doctores," because in this "explication" of the Old Testament, "preaching" Jesus Christ, they dispense the "doctrine" of the New Testament.[57] Jesus breaks the loaves in the presence of his disciples and gives them to them so that they might distribute them to the crowd, "since he laid open the sacraments of prophecy for the holy doctors, so they would preach them through the whole world."[58] They are the seat where the Lord resides. They are the door which gives access to the house, the house of his Word.[59] They are the mouth of the Lord.[60] They are the eyes of the Church, the body of Christ;[61] they are his lips, throat,[62] teeth, cheeks,[63] breasts;[64] they are his neck.[65] All these metaphors, borrowed from the Canticle of Canticles,[66] designate an aspect of their role in the explication of the Scriptures. Thus, with regard to the lips:

> The preachers of the Church are well said to be the lips of the bride, since she speaks to peoples through them and through them little children are raised, while the hidden features of divine Scrip-

ture are, like what is concealed in the heart, made manifest through them.[67]

Or indeed, with respect to the teeth:

> As food is subjected to the action of the teeth, so too the word of God, who is the bread of life treated in the apostolic tradition, which is being compared with the teeth, seems to be submitted to all the organs of the body of the Church.[68]

Or yet again, if the Church is a temple, they are its windows, the ones who "pour forth the light of preaching within the people of the faithful."[69] Renewing, so to speak, the miracle of Cana, these doctors of the New Testament pour out for their hearers "the wine of evangelical preaching."[70] Like Abraham's servants, they dig and dig out again the pits of understanding:

> By "the servants of Abraham" understand the holy doctors
> who draw the mystic words from the Scriptures.[71]

It is at their word that the Church conceives and gives birth to her spiritual children.[72] The "river of holy preaching" transmits to each Christian generation the doctrine that came from the apostles, that is to say, to speak as did Abelard, that she "opens up Scripture by giving out its evangelical understanding."[73] If "deep calls unto deep," if "the Old Testament announces the New," and if "the New cites the Old and bears testimony to it," this comes about, following the Psalm, "in the voice of the waterfalls," that is to say, in preaching.[74] The storm clouds and winds that the Lord calls forth, according to another Psalm, are likewise the preachers of the doctrine, and if they are called "winds," it is, as Saint Augustine explains, "because of the spirit."[75] An exegetical index from the beginning of the thirteenth century, a work of an English Cistercian, says it yet again:

> The heavens [means] holy Scripture, as where [it says]: "The heavens will be rolled up like a book"; and again: "Stretching out the heavens like a tent."
> The rolling up of the book is the hiding of the mysteries of holy Scripture, or the withdrawal of preaching. The stretching out of the book or the heavens is the revelation of holy Scripture or its mysteries.[76]

In other words, Christian preaching is an exegesis, and indeed an "allegorical" exegesis.[77]

Now, by a disposition of providence, Saint Paul, the last of the apostles to be called, came to eclipse all the rest by his preaching. He is, says Saint Gregory, the "the true preacher of wisdom."[78] He is, antonomastically, the "praedicator inclytus," the "egregius praedicator": Gregory particularly loved to award him this last title,[79] and the whole tradition followed him.[80] "So great a preacher," the *Caroline Books* say of Paul. In his Epistles, did he not himself use this term many times, many times lay claim to this title?[81] At the same time Paul is "the outstanding doctor" — for some, this appellation even takes the place of a name;[82] he is the "marvelous doctor,"[83] the "special doctor,"[84] the "perfect doctor of the Gospel," and the "great and marvelous catechizer of the world."[85] He is the "outstanding explainer,"[86] the one who "penetrated the deep, obscure passages of holy Scripture":[87] "for he explained the sacraments of the Law and the Gospel more clearly than the other apostles."[88] "The Apostle explains the depth of the prophets."[89] There is scarcely a page in his Epistles that does not draw its sense from the treasury of the Law and the prophets.[90] "It was incorporated using the old instrument."[91] While he was still Saul, "he persecuted the spiritual understanding";[92] but in the revelation of the Lord Jesus that the Holy Spirit made to him, "all the mysteries of the Law and of the Gospel were manifested to him":

> The ethereal light that with its surrounding brilliance deprives one
>   of sight
> Gives him spiritual insight.[93]

"By a singular grace, the Lord has opened up his understanding that he might comprehend the Scriptures."[94] In the train of Christ, then, he has broken the bread, that is to say, he has "divided the word," disengaging the spirit from the ancient letter, without adding to it anything extraneous:

> Moses said that Abraham had two sons . . . ; Paul said: these are the two Testaments. He divided the word and uncovered the mystery. So blessed is he who collects what Christ has divided.[95]

It is Paul who drew the honeycomb from the mouth of the dead lion, to give it as nourishment to the Gentiles.[96] The first of all the doctors, he taught the Christians and their pastors to walk according to the spirit.[97]

He is therefore par excellence "the Apostle of the New Testament,"[98] "the minister of the New Testament, not through the letter, but through the Spirit."[99] It is he whose preaching shows "all the mysteries consummated in Jesus Christ."[100] This amounts to saying that just as he is "the Apostle" par excellence, so is he the allegorist par excellence.

We shall not be surprised, then, that a certain Atto of Vercelli, for example, writing in the tenth century, does not allegorize each verse of Saint Paul on his own account. Nor is this unusual. Rabanus Maurus does not do so either, in his *Enarrationes in Epistolas Pauli*.[101] Nor will Saint Bruno do so. Not even the author of the books mistakenly entitled *Allegoriae in Epistolas Pauli*.[102] Nor, to tell the truth, does any commentator upon the Apostle in any century. In this, all resemble Cassiodorus. It is enough for Atto to form his own allegorical doctrine, as Richard of Saint Victor will say, to the measure of that of Paul.[103] This he does following the example of the earlier tradition that he, like Claudius of Turin and Rabanus Maurus, exploits fully.[104] He shows how it is the Apostle himself who "allegorizes" not only to establish a certain number of more or less exotic agreements, but to manifest "the accord of the Law and the Gospel."[105] He adds a no less traditional remark, that the Apostle thus indicates to us by a few examples how we ought in our turn to "allegorize."[106] There is no difference here between the commentaries of Atto of Vercelli and the explication of the Epistle to the Hebrews that had been attributed to him but which in fact is that of Claudius of Turin.[107] In the footsteps of Saint Paul, said Claudius, we can render an account "of the figures and of the truth of Christ":[108] for, as the Epistle to the Hebrews teaches most especially, all that the Jewish people had received from God had been given to it with a symbolic intention; in the Old Testament everything was "figure," everything was "shadow," "exemplar," and "sign."[109]

Florus of Lyon showed the same thing in the previous century: how the preaching of the great Apostle had unveiled the mystery hidden in the Scriptures.[110] This is also what was proclaimed in 796 by the council held around Saint Paulinus of Aquilaea to condemn the errors of Felix of Urgel: "The blessed Apostle . . . discussed the enigmas of the law in many words of disputations,"[111] and the allegorical sense rejected by Felix was called the "apostolic sense" by Paulinus.[112] Alvarus of Cordoba, on the subject of Paul, recognized: "All that he uttered, he uttered allegorically, and he taught by understanding everything mystically."[113] Sedulius Scotus, following in the footsteps of Origen, showed how the Apostle in the Epistle to the Romans addressed those who knew the Law, that is to say, those who knew "what oldness of letter and newness of spirit is in the Law."[114] Some years before Atto, Remi of Auxerre compared Paul to Benjamin, the lastborn of Jacob's sons, with respect to the sack in which the silver cup had been deposited:

> Silver cup: splendor of the divine speeches. . . . He used to have a silver cup, i.e., divine science, but it lay hidden within a sack, i.e., within the vileness[115] of the letter of the law. But the steward came and tore apart the sack: Ananias came, sent by Christ, and dispersed the grossness, i.e., the blindness, of the letter of the law. Soon the cup shone forth again, since Paul immediately began to act boldly in the synagogues, preaching Christ and translating the letter that killeth into the spiritual understanding.[116]

The author of the *De divinis officiis* recently attributed to Alcuin commented on the miracle of Cana, where the water of the letter had been changed into the wine of the spirit, as follows: At the banquet Paul took the part of the *architriclinus* ["chief steward"]; he was the one who was the first to serve the miraculous wine to humanity that was invited to the wedding.[117] Here is a designation that became traditional, which later made Isaac of Stella say: "Hear the doctor of the Gentiles; hear one of the ministers who know from whence the wine came and how it came to be good."[118] Thus too, by allusion to two other passages of the Gospel, the *Caroline Books*, after the Fathers, make us see in Paul either the innkeeper in the parable of the Good Samaritan, that innkeeper "to whom the Redeemer paid with the twofold science, i.e., the two Testaments";[119] or again, the door key, in emulation of Peter: "when the Son of God had bestowed the keys of the kingdom of heaven upon the one, and the key to open up the words of the law upon the other."[120] Here is how Odo of Canterbury will explain it: ". . . after Paul mentions the history, he immediately follows it up by explaining the mystery of this affair."[121] Thus Godfrey of Saint Victor:

> Now he lays open mystical matters with serene speech.[122]

At all events, Peter Cellensis, in a very expressive phrase, put it this way: "O how good and pleasant it is to sit at Paul's table. *And this refreshment is allegorical.*"[123] Saint Hildegard repeats the same thing, using a more complicated symbolism, which at least has the advantage of showing that Paul does not allegorize the Scripture on his own account but interprets it in light of the Fact of Christ:

> ... Just as the wheel carries the wagon, and the wagon every sort of load, so Paul's doctrine bears the law of Christ, since the new law is woven from the old law, in which Moses included circumcision and oblations, all of which the Holy Spirit has renewed into a new holiness, and which Paul, with new fire, has cemented together within the humble chain of the necklace of justice.[124]

For a long time it has been remarked that the Pauline corpus comprises fourteen Epistles. This number is that of the Decalogue united to the four Gospels, and a symbolic intention is meant to be seen in it:

> The Church ... rightly ... holds [the number] of the Epistles of blessed Paul [to be] not more than fourteen, so that even from the very number of the Epistles she might show that the outstanding doctor had rooted up the secrets of the Law and the Gospel.[125]

Analogous conclusions are drawn still more subtly from the fact that Paul wrote ten letters to the churches, that he wrote four to disciples, and that the Epistle to the Hebrews is set to one side, in the last place.[126] Is it still necessary to recall the theme, so famous, of Paul's mill? Suger put it in four verses just below the symbolic stained glass window in the basilica of Saint-Denis:

> By working the millstone, Paul, you lift the flour from the bran:
>   You make known the inmost features of Mosaic law;
> From so many grains is made the true bread without bran,
>   and our perpetual and angelic food.[127]

A picturesque capital at Vézelay reproduces the same scene: Paul gathers his flour at the exit of the mill in which the prophets have come to process the wheat. The theme is treated again in a miniature of the *Hortus deliciarum*. It is carved on the portal of Saint-Trophime d'Arles, where one sees a statue of the Apostle pointing with his finger to a banderolle with this inscription:

> The Law of Moses conceals what Paul's speech reveals:
> Now the grains given at Sinai have, through him, been made into
>   flour.[128]

In fact — it is Rupert who explains it, and his explication is that of everyone — "in the stalk of the holy letter is the germ, i.e., the seed of spiritual understanding," and it is "from the stalk of that letter" that the Christians ought to eat the "flour of spiritual understanding."[129] And is it not Saint Jerome who said, in addressing the Apostle, more especially charged than anyone else with preparing this flour: "You have changed the sacrifices by means of the religion of such a Gospel"?[130] Under these circumstances how can one be surprised that Saint Bernard on several occasions expressly has recourse to Paul's exegesis, that he appeals to this "Paul, the vessel of election, the aromatic vessel,"[131] to this "mouth of Paul, the great and unfailing fountain"?[132] Along with the whole tradition from which we have just cited a few witnesses, he recognized a fact which our best exegetes have recognized even today. Paul, writes Father Stanislas Lyonnet, did not claim to deduce the New Testament from the Old: "it was never in this way that he conceived scriptural proof; but rather he recognized the beginnings, the germ, or better, the prefiguration of this revelation of the Christ in the Old Testament, whose authentic import, or, if one prefers, whose 'full' sense he reveals."[133] And, more briefly, we already find Father Lagrange saying: "We must always keep repeating that the genius of Saint Paul, the illuminations that he received from God, never showed up better than in the concord that he perceived between the two Testaments."[134]

Notes

Notes to Chapter Six
§1. Pauline Allegory

1. *Juxta allegoriam, id est, intelligentiam spiritalem:* Jerome, *In Amos* (PL, XXV, 1025 D).

2. Gal. 4:21. Marius Victorinus, *In Gal.:* "We have interpreted as through an allegory" — "Sic utique nos interpretati sumus, quasi per allegoriam" (PL, XVII, 1185 C). Aug., *Civ. Dei,* Bk. XV, c. ii: Things "which are in allegory" — "Quae sunt in allegoria" (XLI, 438); *De Trin.,* Bk. XV, c. ix, n. 15 (Agaësse, 460). Tertullian, *Adv. Marc.,* Bk. V, c. iv (Kroymann, 581). Theodoret, *III, in loc.* (PG, LXXXII, 489 D); etc.

3. Cicero, *Orat.,* c. xxvii. See Chapter 8.2 below.

4. C. ix (B. Weiske, 1809, 30).

5. *Geogr.,* Bk. I, c. ii, n. 7: *pros epistēmēn allēgorōn* (Meineke, 23).

6. C. iv (Didot, I, 22; tr. Bétolaud, I, 43-4: "On rencontre chez Homère un pareil genre d'enseignement muet, et il accompagne toujours de raisonnements utiles celles de ses fictions que l'on a le plus sévérement attaquées; pour les justifier, quelques-uns ont recoursà ce que les anciens nommaient des *hyponoiai* [sens cachés, sens sous-jacents, allusions, sens profonds] et que l'on nomme aujourd'hui des *allēgoriai.*") Cf. *On Isis and Osiris,* c. xxxii (Didot, I, 444).

7. *Panta gar ēsebēsen, ei mēden ēllēgorēsen* (Fr. Oelmann, 1).

8. *Rep.,* Bk. X, 606 e.

9. Nicephorus, in the *Symposium,* 3, 6.

10. 3, 26. Cf. A. Delatte, *Et. sur la litt. pythagoricienne* (1915), 116.

11. *De vita et poesi Homeri,* c. vi. Similarly, Macrobius will judge that Vergil knew all the sciences. Cf. Felix Buffière, *Les mythes d'Homère et la pensée grecque* (1956).

12. Plutarch, *Isis et Os.,* 355: *hosiōs kai philosophōs.*

13. L. Duchesne, *L'Église au VI s.,* 158. Proclus, *Th. plat.,* Bk. IV: *tēs mythōn hyponoias.*

14. *hē tou mythou allēgoria:* Olympiodorus, Comm. on the *Phaedo* (W. Norvin,

3). Maximus of Tyre, *Diss.* 10: who has thought about the gods better, the poets or the philosophers? (Fr. Dübner, 1842, 35-7).

15. On the "mystic elements of the Odyssey," for example, cf. the explications of Gabriel Bermain, *Essai sur les origines de certain thèmes odysséens et sur la genèse de l'Odyssée* (1954), 625-36. M. J. Carcopino, *De Pythagore aux Apôtres* (1956), p. 202, has spoken of the "secret accord, a sort of preestablished harmony which prevailed between the storytelling of the *Odyssey* and the key tendency of Pythagoreanism" — "accord secret, la sorte d'harmonie préétablie qui avait prévalu entre l'affabulation de l'*Odyssée* et la tendance maîtresse du pythagorisme." For the myths in general, we shall read the reflections of Étienne Borne, *Le problème du mal* (1958), c. ii: "Les fausses confidences de la mythologie."

16. Thus Maximus of Tyre: "Our weakness constrains us to call 'god' whatever is most beautiful among us; the essential point is that symbols may make us recognize the divine. That a Phidias should by his art awaken in us the memory of the gods, and that on the other hand the sacred animals could do so for the Egyptians, I admit. The diversity of symbols does not disturb me" — "Notre infirmité nous contraint d'appeler dieu ce qu'il y a de plus beau parmi nous; l'essentiel est que les symboles nous fassent reconnaître le divin. Qu'un Phidias réveille en nous par son art le souvenir des dieux, et que d'autre part les animaux sacrés y poussent les Égyptiens, j'y consens. La diversité des symboles ne m'indigne pas" (cited by E. De Faye, *Origène*, II, 162). Cf. Plato, *Timaeus*, 51 e.

17. "dii populares" — "unus naturalis deus": *Div. inst.*, Bk. I, c. v (Brandt, 16).

18. Thus Menander the grammarian: [literally: "a 'nature-talk' hidden as an 'under-thought'"] — *physiologia enkekrymmenē kath' hyponoian* (Spengel, 338). Balbus: Cicero, *De nat. deorum*, Bk. II, c. xxiii, n. 60 (Mayor, II, 22). Diogenes of Babylon following Velleius: *ibid.*, Bk. I, c. xv, n. 41. Varro (following Aug., *Civ. Dei*). Heraclitus: "and he allegorizes the riddling whole about nature" — *holon te to peri physeōs ainigmatōdes allēgorei* (Oelmann, 37); "when Homer theologized these things physically through allegory" — *Homērou physikōs tauta di' allēgorias theologēsantos* (79); etc.

19. *Praep. ev.*, Bk. IV, c. i, n. 4: "the rather physical allegory of the tales" — *tēs tōn mythōn physikōteras allēgorias* (162).

20. *Ad nat.*, Bk. II, n. 17: "physiologically to interpret through allegorical argumentation" — "physiologice per allegoricam argumentationem interpretari" (Borleffs, 61); *Adv. Marc.*, Bk. I, c. xiii: "he flees off to an interpretation of natural things" — "ad interpretationem naturalium refugit" (Kroymann, 307).

21. *Civ. Dei*, Bk. VII, c. xxvii, n. 2 (PL, XLI, 217); Bk. VI, c. viii (186). Analogous considerations in K. Rahner, *Ecrits théol.*, I, 30-1.

22. "ad naturales rationes": Bk. VII, c. xxxiii: "Whose sacred things Varro now strives to relate to natural characteristics, as it were" — "Quorum sacra Varro dum quasi ad naturales rationes referre conatur" (PL, XLI, 221).

23. "interpretationes physicae" — "interpretationes quibus ostendantur (fabulae) rerum significare naturam" — "physiologicas quasdam, sicut aiunt, id est naturalium rationum interpretationes": Varro in Aug., *Civ. Dei*, Bk. VII, c. v (PL, LXI, 198); Bk. VI, c. viii (186).

24. *Ars rhet.*, 9 (Us.-Rad., 323); *Ant. rom.*, 2, 20 (Jacoby, I, 181).

25. *Rep.*, Bk. II, 378 d.

26. *Symposium*, III, 5-6.

27. *Eth. Nic.*, Bk. IV, viii, 6.

28. *Frogs*, v. 1425.

29. *peri tēs Hekatēs hyponoian* (C. Lang, 74). Cf. 45, 64, 73, 75. [Trans. note: See the *Oxford Classical Dictionary*, s.v. Cornutus.]

30. *Strom.*, Bk. V, 24: "they provide many philosophical accounts through a hidden meaning" — *di' hyponoias polla philosophousi* (Stählin, 2, 240). Cf. Or., *C. Cels.*, Bk. IV, c. xxxviii: "to philosophize in a hidden meaning" — *en hyponoiāi philosophein* (309).

31. *De Abr.* (Mangey, II, 14; II, 18). *De migr. Abr.* (I, 450). *De Cher.* (I, 142). *Quis rer.* (I, 544). *Quod deter.* (I, 211, 223). *De congr.* (I, 544). *De agric.*, (I, 97); etc. Mr. René Cadiou translates: "explication suggérée" (*La Migr. d'Abr.*, 92; SC, 47, 49).

32. *De spec. leg.* (M., II, 275). *De vita cont.* (Conybeare, 64-5). *De plant. Noe* (M., I, 335); etc. The same in Josephus, *Ant. jud.* (Niese, I, 7).

33. Thus, *Spec. leg.* (M., II, 147). *De Josue* (II, 46). *De vita cont.* (Conybeare, 118-9).

34. [In English translation the order of the Greek terms is reversed: 'in the allegories taken according to implication'.] *exhēgēsis . . . di' hyponoiōn en allēgoriais* (Conybeare, 118-9). *De praem.*, 65 (M., II, 148).

35. As, amongst others, R. H. Malden thinks, "St. Ambrose as an Interpreter of Holy Scripture," JTS 16 (1914-5), 510. One will note that the expression does not figure in the fragments of Heracleon preserved by Origen.

36. Jean Pépin, *Mythe et allégorie, les origines grecques et les contestations judéo-chrétiennes* (1958), 215: "this sort of first colony of Greek allegorism in Semitic territory" — "cette sorte de première colonie de l'allégorisme grec en territoire sémitique"; the second will be in Christian territory.

37. Pépin, *op. cit.*, 459: Paul "doit être considéré comme le garant et l'initateur" of it. We shall see later on what is missing from this avowal of paternity.

38. On the precise sense of allegory expounded in Gal. 4:22-30: St. Lyonnet, *Mél. A. Robert*, 497, note 1. In this text one grasps nicely, along with the new idea, the survival of the method that will give it its name.

39. "allegorica dispositio": *Adv. Valentinianos*, c. 1 (177).

40. *Adv. Marc.*, Bk. IV, c. xvii (476).

41. "legem allegoricam secundum nos probavit": *Op. cit.*, Bk. V, c. vii (595).

42. "arma allegorica": *Adv. Judaeos*, c. viii (PL, II, 621 C).

43. "Volo . . . tibi de allegoriis Apostoli controversiam nectere" — "allegoriae sacramentum" — "docens proinde et Galatas duo argumenta filiorum Abrahae allegorice cucurrisse": *Adv. Marc.*, Bk. V, c. xviii (639); c. iv (541); Bk. III, c. v (383).

44. "allegorica intelligentia": *In Gen.*, h. 5, n. 5 (64).

45. "allegoriae ordo": *In Gen.*, h. 6, n. 3 (69). *In Num.*, h. 14, n. 4: "After this [i.e., the historical explanation] it seems appropriate to touch on a few points about allegory, too" — "Post haec (= following the 'explanatio historiae') conveniens videtur aliqua etiam de allegoria contingere" (126).

46. "Nos imbuti per apostolum Paulum . . .": *In Gen.*, h. 3, n. 4: "we say that, just as many other things came about in figure and image of the truth to come, so too that carnal circumcision. . . . So listen to how Paul, the doctor of the Gentiles . . . teaches the Church of Christ" — "dicimus quia, sicut multa alia in figura et in

imagine futurae veritatis fiebant, ita et circumcisio illa carnalis etc. Audite ergo quomodo Paulus doctor gentium. . . . Christi Ecclesiam docet" (43).

47. "nos, secundum Apostoli sententiam . . .": *In Gen.*, h. 1, n. 17 (22).

48. "allegorias nostras, quas Paulus docuit": *In Gen.*, h. 3, n. 5 (45).

49. ". . . Si quis haec secundum litteram solum audire vult et intelligere, magis cum Judaeis quam cum Christianis debet habere auditorium. Si autem vult christianus esse et Pauli discipulus, audiat eum dicentem, 'quia lex spiritalis est.' Et cum de Abraham atque uxore ejus ac filiis loqueretur, pronuntiat haec esse allegorica. Et licet cujusmodi allegorias habere debeat, haud facile quis nostrum invenire possit, orare tamen debet ut a corde ejus auferatur velamen, si quis est qui conetur converti ad Dominum; 'Dominus' enim 'spiritus est'; ut ipse auferat velamen litterae et aperiat lucem spiritus, et possimus dicere, quia 'revelata facie gloriam Domini speculantes . . .' etc.": *In Gen.*, h. 6, n. 1 (66). Cf. *Rom.*, VII, 114; Gal. 4:24; 2 Cor. 3:17-8.

50. Bk. IV, c. ii, n. 6: Paul is writing to the Galatians, who do not understand that there are allegories in the things that have been written — *allēgorias en tois gegrammenois einai* (316-7).

51. *en hyponoiāi philosophein:* Bk. IV, c. xxxviii (309-10). Cf. Clement, *Strom.*, Bk. V, c. iv, 24 (Stählin, 340).

52. Bk. IV, c. xliv (317).

53. Bk. IV, c. lxix (321-2). Cf. *In Jo.*, Bk. XX, c. x (339).

54. Bk. XX, c. x (337, 339). Cf. c. xxvi (376). Bk. VI, c. iv: *tas kata anagōgēn allēgorias tōn anagegrammenōn par' hautōi historiōn* (111).

55. "mysteria legis et allegorias, quas ab Apostolo edocti sumus": H. 10, n. 1 (94). Cf. h. 6, n. 1 (66), etc.

56. H. 11, n. 1 (77-8). *In Matt.*, t. X, n. 14 (Klostermann, 17). Cf. *In Ez.*, h. 1, n. 3: "When you hear about the capitivity of the people, believe indeed that it truly happened according to the faith of the history, but that it preceded as a sign of another thing and signified a subsequent mystery" — "Cum audieris de populi captivitate, crede quidem vere accidisse eam juxta historiae fidem, sed in signum rei alterius praecessisse et subsequens significasse mysterium" (325). *In Gen.*, h. 7, n. 2: "he calls the things about which there can be no doubt that they were accomplished according to the flesh 'allegories' " — "de quibus non potest dubitari quin secundum carnem gesta sint, haec ille dicit allegorica" (72).

57. "Haec quod allegorica mysteria contineant, Paulus . . . pronuntiat, dicens: mysterium magnum est, ego dico in Christo et in Ecclesia": *In Num.*, h. 11, n. 1 (77).

58. "Nobis qualem tradidit de his Paulus Apostolus intelligentiae regulam indicamus": H. 5, n. 1 (184). H. 9, n. 1 (235). On Origen and St. Paul: HE, c. ii.

59. "His vero qui secundum apostolorum sensum theoriam Scripturarum recipiunt": *Periarch.*, Bk. II, c. xi, n. 3 (186). Leo XIII, speaking about the traditional allegory in the Church in the encyclical *Providentissimus*, will say the same thing: "The Church has taken this sort of interpretation from the Apostles" — "Talem enim interpretandi rationem ab Apostolis Ecclesia accepit."

60. Bk. V, c. lvi; GCS, 3, 59-60 (Koetschau). Cf. *In Jud.*, h. 9, n. 2: "Great mysteries are pointed out in almost all the accomplishments of the ancients" — "In omnibus pene veterum gestis mysteria designantur ingentia" (250).

61. *Early Christian Interpretations of History* (1954), 45; cf. 42.

62. "développe de façon systématique le procédé paulinien de l'allégorie" — "l'esprit tel que le conçoit Origène est . . . conforme à la théologie paulinienne": In the *Introd. à la Bible*, by A. Robert and A. Feuillet (1957), 187.

63. "Docet nos Apostolus, cum veneratione gestorum, praeformationem in his doctrinae atque operis spiritalis agnoscere, cum lex spiritalis est, cum gesta allegorumena sunt": *In ps. CXXXIV*, n. 18 (705). Cf. Jerome (?), *In Is.*, VI, 1-7: "while explaining the sacraments of Adam and Eve, he did not deny their creation" — "exponens sacramenta Adae et Evae, non negavit plasmationem eorum" (*An. mar.*, 3, 104-5).

64. "Allegoria est cum aliud *geritur*, aliud figuratur": *De Abraham*, Bk. I, c. i, n. 28 (PL, XIV, 432 C). Again, Ps.-Hugo, *Speculum*, c. viii (PL, CLXXVII, 375 A); etc.

65. "Quanquam secundum evangelicam historiam ressuscitatum Lazarum plena fide teneamus: tamen et in allegoria significare aliquid non dubito. Neque cum res factae allegorizantur, gestae rei fidem amittunt. Sicut duorum filiorum Abrahae allegoriam Paulus exponit duo esse Testamenta: numquid ideo aut Abraham non fuit, aut illos filios non habuit? Unde et in allegoria accipiamus Lazarum, etc.": *De div. quaest.* 83, q. 65 (PL, LX, 59). Cf. *In ps. XXXIII, s.* 1, n. 3 (CCL, 38, 275; Dekkers).

66. "Quid ego de Apostolo Paulo dicam, qui etiam ipsam Exodi historiam futurae plebis allegoriam fuisse significat . . . ?": C. iii, n. 8, on 1 Cor. 10:1-11 (Pegon, 221).

67. "Ubi allegoriam nominavit Apostolus, non in verbis eam reperit, sed in facto": Bk. XV, c. ix, n. 1: ". . . when he showed that the two Testaments are to be understood from the two [sons] of Abraham, the one from the slave-girl, the other from the free, which was not only said, but also done" — ". . . cum e duobus Abrahae, uno de ancilla, altero de libera, quod non solum dictum sed etiam factum fuit, duo testamenta intelligenda monstravit" (PL, XLII, 1069).

68. "in facto" — "allegoria facti": For example, Bede, *De schem. et tropis*, c. xii (PL, XC, 185 CD). John Scotus, *In Jo.*, fragm. 3 (CXXII, 344-5); etc.

69. "allegoricae virtutes": *Tract. sup. psalmos, instr. ps.*, c. v (5-6).

70. "significationes allegoricae": *De Civ. Dei*, Bk. XV, c. xxvii, n. 1 (PL, XL, 473).

71. "allegoriae propheticae": *Gen. litt.*, Bk. I, c. xvii, n. 34 (PL, XXXVI, 259). *S.* 33, n. 1: "So we also discern the two Testaments, old and new, which the Apostle says are also figured allegorically in the sons of Abraham" — "Ita etiam duo Testamenta discernimus, vetus et novum, quae in allegoria dicit Apostolus etiam in Abrahae filiis figurari" (XXXVIII, 207).

72. "ratio allegoriae": *Coll.* 14, c. viii (SC, 54, Pichery, 189-92).

73. *Ibid.*: "For the revelation pertains to the allegory, through which the things that the historical narrative covers are disclosed by the spiritual sense and exposition" — "Revelatio namque ad allegoriam pertinet, per quam ea quae tegit historica narratio, spiritali sensu et expositione reserantur."

74. "allegoriarum caligines": *Mor.*, Bk. XVIII, c. xxxviii, n. 59 (PL, LXXVII, 71 A); c. xxxix, n. 60: "obscured by the darkness of the allegories" — "allegoriarum tenebris obscura" (71 C).

75. "juxta historiam" — "juxta allegoriam": *Op. cit.*, Bk. XX, c. xxxiv, n. 66 (LXXVI, 178 AB), etc.

76. "Per litteram ad allegoriam tendimus": *In Ex.*, Bk. II, h. 3, n. 18 (LXXVI, 968 A).

77. "In Testamenti veteris littera Testamentum novum latuit per allegoriam": Bk. I, h. 6, n. 12 (834 A).

78. "Liber sacri eloquii intus scriptus est per allegoriam, foris per historiam; intus per spiritalem intellectum, foris autem per sensum litterae simplicem": Bk. I, h. 9, n. 30 (883 B).

79. "Fides habeatur in veritate historiae, et spiritalis intelligentia capiatur de mysteriis allegoriae": Bk. II, h. 1, n. 3 (936-7). Cf. *Mor.*, Bk. XIX, c. xvii, n. 26 (114 AB).

80. "Dedit regulam Apostolus, quomodo allegorizare debemus": *In Gal.* IV (PL, LXVIII, 596 D).

81. *In Gal.* IV (PL, CIV, 888 A).

82. "secundum Apostolum allegorizare": *Ep.* 44 (J. Madoz, 200; cf. 203).

83. "allegoriarum sigilla": *In Ap.*, Bk. V (516 H).

84. "allegoricae rationes": *In Gal.* (PL, CIII, 190 AB).

85. "Omnia quae protulit, allegorice protulit": *Ep.* 4, n. 16 (PL, CXXI, 436 C).

86. "praeter usum" — "Hoc autem vult significare: haec historia non hoc solum declarat quod apparet, verum et alia quaedam praedicat; unde et allegoria dicta est . . .": *In Gal.* IV, n. 24 (PG, LXI, 662).

87. "quasi quibusdam gradibus per historiam ad excelsa conscendit, ut sublimior sit, non contraria" — "apertissimam historiam nequaquam negat, et ea quae gesta sunt ad excelsiorem intelligentiam trahens sic erigit culmen, ut fundamenta non subtrahat": *An. mar.*, Bk. III, iii, 104-5. Theodore of Mopsuestia, *In Gal.* IV, 24: "For the Apostle does not abolish the history nor does he spin out things previously done" — "Apostolus enim non interimit historiam neque evolvit res dudum factas" (Swete, 1, 73). On the injustice of the quarrel made here to Origen: Huet, *Origeniana* (PG, XVII, 1073-4).

88. *In Gal.*, Bk. II: "Allegory properly belongs to the art of grammar. . . . From this and other things it is clear that Paul was not unaware of secular literature, and what here he called 'allegory' elsewhere he called the 'spiritual understanding'. And at 'We know that the Law is spiritual' it stands for allegory or something allegorically figured. And elsewhere . . . there is no one who doubts that the manna here . . . and the rock . . . are to be taken allegorically" — "Allegoria proprie de arte grammatica est etc. Ex quibus et aliis evidens est Paulum non ignorasse litteras saeculares, et quam hic allegoriam dixit, alibi vocasse intelligentiam spiritalem. Ut ibi: 'Scimus quod lex spiritalis est' (*Rom.* VII, 14), pro eo quod est allegoria, sive allegorice figurata. Et alibi . . . (*I Cor.* X, 34). Manna hic . . . et petra ipsa . . . quod allegorice accipienda sint, nemo est qui dubitet" (PL, XXVI, 389-90).

89. *In Gal.* (PL, CXII, 330 CD).

90. *In Gal.*: "Blessed Paul has the custom of calling the spiritual understanding allegory. Allegory, however, pertains properly to the grammarians; for it is a figure of speech by which something other than what is said is signified" — "Hanc habet consuetudinem beatus Paulus, ut spiritualem intelligentiam alle-

goriam appellet. Allegoria autem proprie ad grammaticos pertinet, est enim tropus quo aliud significatur quod dicitur . . ." (PL, CXVII, 687 C); etc.

91. Cf. Süheylâ Bayran, *Symbolisme médiévale* (1957), 2: "A côté du sens (ancien) qu'il conserve toujours, (le mot) allégorie désigne encore autre chose dans la littérature chrétienne. L'Église reconnaît que l'Écriture sainte contient une allégorie différente de celle des rhéteurs, puisqu'elle ressort non des mots, mais des choses exprimées par les mots. . . . Car, pour les chrétiens, les faits racontés dans la Bible . . . ont été préordonnés par Dieu de telle façon qu'ils préfigurent . . . des événements futurs. . . ." Roger Arnaldez, *Grammaire et théol. chez Ibn Hazm de Cordue* (1956), 10: — "Les Pères de l'Église, Or. en particulier, verront dans l'A.T. la figure du Nouveau, et à côté du sens littéral qui s'adressait à des hommes d'une race et d'un temp, ils feront surgir, conformément à l'esprit paulinien, un sens spirituel, vérité éternelle pour tous les hommes. Et cette interprétation en figures sera commandée par les valeurs que le christianisme affirme, au terme d'une évolution de Judaïsme dirigée par Dieu lui-même." (It is clear, in addition, that this "eternal truth" is that of the Christian mystery and the "values" affirmed are all based upon the faith in Jesus Christ.) One should wish to encounter such comprehensive texts more usually among authors who speak ex professo about patristic exegesis.

Notes to Chapter Six
§2. Myth and Allegory

1. H. N. Bate, "Some Technical Terms of Greek Exegesis," JTS 24 (1920). Only one allusion is made to St. Paul regarding a text of Chrysostom.

2. Ad. Franck, "De la philosophie d'Or. par M. J. Denis," *Journal des savants* (1884), 181.

3. Henri Margival, "Richard Simon . . . ," c. iv (RHLR [1897], 232).

4. Basil Tatakin, *La philosophie byzantine,* in E. Bréhier, *Histoire de la philosophie,* 2 fasc. suppl. (1949), 11.

5. "Les savants du moyen âge s'intéressèrent bientôt infiniment davantage aux sens dérivés et philosophiques de la Bible qu'au modeste sens littéral. . . . Ils n'hésitèrent pas à faire de la Bible . . . une sorte de code de philosophie et un tremplin pour la méditation ontologique. . . . La parole inspirée devenait, pour les clercs, le prétexte à des méditations philosophiques et toutes spirituelles": Alain Guy, *La pensée de Fray Luis de Leon* (1943), 209.

6. Bate, *loc. cit.,* 10.

7. "in carminibus, operibus artis, dogmatibus philosophorum, aeque ac religionis nostrae doctorum": Sam. Fr. Nathan Morus, *Dissertationes theol. et philosophicae* (Lipsiae, 1787), 12: "Ostenditur quibus causis allegoriam interpretatio nitatur" (370-93).

8. *Hist. interpretationis librorum in Ecclesia christiana, inde ab apostolorum aetate usque ad Or.,* P. I (Hildurghusae, 1795), 25-35.

9. *Ibid.,* 32: "I have not dared to determine whether the writers of the New Testament approved this method of interpretation and regarded it as true, or accommodated themselves to the minds of their popular audiences through a sort

of wise management" — "Utrum vero scriptores novi T. hanc interpretandi rationem approbaverint et pro vera habuerint, an vero per sapientem quamdam *oikonomian* ingeniis popularium suorum se accommodaverint, id equidem definire non ausim." Many think that this was "because of the feeble-mindedness of those to whom they were writing. . . . This does not seem to be a shrinking-back from the truth. . . . Paul particularly did it. . . . Whatever be the case, it is not right for us to imitate the Apostles in this. . . . Nevertheless the Apostles may easily be excused . . ." — "propter ingenii imbecillitatem eorum ad quos scribebant. . . . Hoc a vero non abhorrere videtur. . . . Hoc fecit praesertim Paulus. . . . Quicquid sit, nobis in hoc non licet imitari Apostolos. . . . Facile tamen excusantur Apostoli. . . ."

10. F. W. Farber, *History of Interpretation* . . . (Brampton Lectures), XXIII, will again attempt to eliminate the testimony of St. Paul, writing of Gal. 4:21-27: "It may be merely intended as an *argumentum ad hominem;* it does not seem to be more than a passing illustration; it is not at all essential to the general argument; it has not a particle of *demonstrative* force; in any case it leaves untouched the actual history." Cited by K. J. Woollcombe, *Essays on Typology* (1956), 55. Remarks not without justice in their particularity, but which stand quite outside the thought of Paul, and which in any case treat what is essential by pretermission.

11. *The Influence of Greek Ideas and Usages upon the Christian Church* (7th ed., 1898), lect. 3: Greek and Christian Exegesis (50-85).

12. *Tracts for the Time,* 89th volume. This work, very weighty, is too little known.

13. *The Arians of the Fourth Century,* appendix, note 1: "In all ages of the Church, her teachers have shown a disinclination to confine themselves to the mere literal interpretation of Scripture. . . . The formal connexion of this mode of interpretation (the mystical sense) with Christian theology is noticed by Porphyry, who speaks of Origen and others as borrowing it from heathen philosophy, both in explanation of the Old Testament and in defence of their own doctrine. It may almost be laid down as an historical fact, that the mystical interpretation and orthodoxy will stand or fall together" (1833; ed. of 1876, 104-5). *An Essay on the Development of Christian Doctrine,* p. II, ch. VII, 4: *Scripture and Its Mystical Interpretation* (ed. of 1894, 338-46).

14. Ch. 1 (ed. of 1908, London, 26-8; trans. Michelin Delimoges, 2nd ed., 1939, 55-71).

15. Jean Pépin, "A propos de l'hist. de l'exégèse allég., l'absurdité signe de l'allégorie," *St. patr.,* I, 397. "Le 'challenge' Homère-Moïse aux premiers siècles chrét.," RDSR (1955), 105-22. *Mythe et allégorie* (1958), 370, 464; a bit more nuanced judgment on "la typologie de S. Paul," 250, note 13 *bis*.

16. *Mythe et all.,* 270 and 462. Already Mgr Freppel, *Origène,* 2 (2nd ed., 1875), 158, said, curiously enough, of Porphyry speaking about Origen: "Porphyry himself was aware of it" — "Porphyre lui-même s'en est aperçu." This was scarcely just a blunder with him. On the contrary, for example, E. Vacherot, *H. crit. de l'Ec. d'Alexandrie,* I (1846), 286: "This doctor sees only a perpetual allegory in the sacred text" — "Ce docteur ne voit dans le texte sacré qu'une perpétuelle allégorie."

17. *Periarch.,* Bk. IV, c. iii, 4. 1: "And what more ought one to say, those not entirely being able to bring together very many features of this kind, some recorded

as having happened, but not having come into being according to the letter" — *Kai tí dei pleiō legein, tōn mē pany ambleōn myria hosa toiauta dynamenōn synagogein, anagegrammena men hōs gegonota, ou gegenēmena de kata tēn lexin?* (324). It is necessary, we believe, to let the neuter *toiauta* to have a very general sense: "features of this kind," and not to translate it as "episodes" (as does Pépin, 462). There is no reason, either, to force the *myria*, which is also found a bit further on, in the affirmation of certainly historical passages (c. III, n. 4; 329), and in several other spots Or. says merely: *tines, tina* (nonnulla) (314, 321, 328). A late author will write in the same sense: "[Scripture says] some things only mystically, as when it says that God breathed the spirit of life into the face of Adam, whereas [God] has neither a mouth to breathe from nor hands to work with" — "Quaedam (Scriptura dicit) tantum mystice, ut cum Deum dicit insufflasse in faciem Adae spiraculum vitae, qui tamen os ad spirandum non habet nec manus ad operandum," Ps.-Aug. (12th cent.), *De assumpt.*, c. i (PL, XL, 1143).

18. Bk. IV, c. ii, n. 1 (306-7). Cf. Irenaeus, *Demonstr.*, c. lxi (Froidevaux, SC, 62, 126-7). Fragment of the 12th cent. (? Landgraf, *Biblica*, 37, 408). Aimon, *In Zach.*, c. xiv: "according to the tradition of the Hebrews they think all these things are to be fulfilled literally in the coming of the Messiah. But now we must look into what the spiritual understanding of the doctors of the Church holds" — "haec juxta Hebraeorum traditionem ad litteram, quae omnia illi putant in adventu Christi implenda. Videndum nunc quid spiritualis doctorum Ecclesiae intelligentia contineat" (PL, CXVII, 271 AB).

19. Bk. IV, c. iii, n. 3 (327-8). Cf. Chromatius, *In Matt.*, tr. 4, n. 1-2: "You are the salt of the earth . . . let us follow . . . the power of the Lord's saying with the spiritual understanding" — "Vos estis sal terrae. . . . Dominici dicti virtutem spiritali intellegentia . . . assequamur"; tr. 5, c. iv, n. 5-6: "Let your loins be girded and your lamps lit; it is to be understood that the Lord commanded this not in a bodily sense but for a spiritual reason" — "Sint lumbi vestri praecincti et lucernae ardentes; quod utique Dominum praecepisse non corporali sensu sed ratione spiritali intellegendum est" (CCL, IX, 402, 408).

20. *In Matt.*, h. 17 (PG, LVII, 258).

21. Bk. IV, c. iii, n. 3 (328). Cf. 1 Cor. 7:18. *In Matt.*, t. 13, c. xxv (247).

22. Bk. IV, c. iii, n. 1 (324).

23. "Secundum litteram . . . super utrumque animal sedere non quiverit . . .": *In Matt.*, Bk. III (PL, XXVI, 147 B). Cf. Zech. 9:9; Matt. 21:5.

24. For the facts, certain cases are unclear; thus the fragment *In ps. L* preserved in the Philokalia, regarding David and Uriah (PG, XII, 1453); but the passage *In Ez.* h. 10 (PL, XXV, 760 BC) does not seem to permit any doubt.

25. *Periarch.*, Bk. IV, c. ii, n. 9: "the Word of God managed to arrange some things like obstacles and stumbling-blocks and impossibilities in the midst of the Law and the history" — *ōikonomēse tina hoionei skandala kai proskommata kai adynata dia mesou enkatatachthēnai tōi nomōi kai tēi historiāi ho tou theou Logos* (320-1). C. iii, n. 1: "put down/compose" — . . . *synkatathesthai* (324). C. iii, n. 3: "some are woven together with the past history" — . . . *prosyphantai tina tēi ge[n]omenēi historiāi* . . . (327-9); n. 2: on the law of the sabbath (326).

26. Only he says *rhēma* instead of *rhēton. In ps. IX* regarding Prov. 5:19, "that thy source should be for thee alone": "for this is of great inhumanity, if you un-

derstand the subject and whilst you do not avoid the word, you pursue the thought" — *touto gar, an to keimenon noēsēis, kai mē phygēis men to rhēma, diōkē[i?]s de to noēma, kai pollēs apanthrōpias esti* . . . (PG, LX, 126). *In ps. XLVI*, n. 1: When the psalm invites one to clap one's hands, this cannot oblige one in a material sense: "But once one gets to be higher than the history, one may justly take the psalm more anagogically" — *Dikaiōs d' an tis ton psalmon kata anagōgēn mãllon eklaboi, tēs historias anōteros genomenos* (LV, 208). This is also what Jerome says in language closer to ours, *In Hab.* Bk. II, c. iii: "The history itself is frequently woven metaphorically" — "Frequenter historia ipsa metaphorice texitur" (PL, XXV, 1328 C).

27. "Gentem quamdam praedicant super terras divinae litterae electam esse a Deo, etc.": Bk. IV, c. iii, n. 6 (331-2).

28. Bk. IV, c. iii, n. 3: *pollōi gar pleiona esti ta kata tēn historian alētheuomena tōn prosyphathentōn gymnōn pneumatikōn* (329). *Ibid.*: "it is to be said that the truth of the history clearly assists us concerning some things" — *lekteon hoti saphōs hēmīn paristatai peri tinōn to tēs historias einai alēthes*. N. 5: He who examines things closely will sometimes be in difficulty, not knowing whether he ought to take such and such a text literally or not (331).

29. *Quaest. hom.* (Oelmann, 25, 58; cf. 26, 36, etc.). On Heraclitus: Hermaniuk, *op. cit.*, 402-6.

30. "Les mythes distribuent dans le temps et séparent les uns des autres des êtres qui en réalité ne sont pas séparés . . . ; ils font naître ce qui n'a jamais commencé, ils le divisent, enseignant ainsi ce qu'ils peuvent et laissant à qui comprend le soin de recomposer": *Ennead,* III, c. v, n. 9 (tr. R. Arnou, modified).

31. E. Bréhier, *H. de la phil.*, I, 467. He "addresses the common people with the pretense of basing himself solely upon the common meaning and myths known by everyone" — "s'adresse aux gens du commun avec la prétention de s'appuyer uniquement sur le sens commun et sur les mythes connus de tous."

32. C. iv (tr. Formey). Father Claude Mondésert cites this text in *Clément d'Alexandrie, introduction à l'ét. de sa pensée relig. à partir de l'Écriture* (1944), p. 144, note 1. The Christian allegory of Clement is neither a simple use nor a simple completion of pagan allegory. The fact that Clement agrees with the pagan writers on the advantages of symbolic thought does not mean, however, that he refuses "d'opposer l'allégorisme païen et l'allégorisme chrétien."

33. Cf. M. Heidegger, *Essais et conf.*: "that a thought remains behind what it thinks characterizes what it has from a creator" — "qu'une pensée reste en arrière de ce qu'elle pense, caractérise ce qu'elle a de créateur" (tr. Préau, 142).

34. Cf. A. Delatte, *Études sur la litt. pythagoricienne* (1915). Franz Cumont, *Recherches sur le symbolisme funéraire des Romains* (1942), 186-9.

35. *De nat. deorum*, Bk. II, c. xxiv, n. 63: "from a . . . physical account a great multitude of gods has flowed, who, clothed with human looks, have supplied tales for the poets and filled the life of human beings with every superstition" — "ex ratione . . . physica magna fluit multitudo deorum, qui induti specie humana fabulas poetis suppeditaverunt, hominum autem vitam superstitione omni referserunt." *Ibid.*: "A fine physical account has been enclosed within immoral tales" — "Physica ratio non inelegans inclusa est in impias fabulas."

36. *De nat. deorum*, Bk. I, c. xliii, n. 119, regarding the mysteries, Cicero ob-

serves: "When these things are explained and called back to account, it is the nature of things rather than that of gods that comes to be known" — "Quibus explicatis ad rationemque revocatis, rerum magis natura cognoscitur quam deorum." This is almost St. Augustine's phrasing in *Civ. Dei*, Bk. VI, c. viii, n. 1, on Varro's "theologia naturalis": it is not a true "theologia," but a "physiologia" (PL, XLI, 186). Cf. Athenagoras, *Supplicatio,* c. xxii (Bardy, SC, 3, 127-8). *Hom. clem.*, VI, c. xx: "Ceux qui ont voulu expliquer les faits et gestes des dieux par des allégories . . . ne se sont pas rendu compte qu'en appliqant aux dieux leurs interprétations naturalistes entortillées, ils ont supprimé l'existence de ces dieux et, par allégorie, fait évanouir leurs personnes dans les éléments du monde" (tr. Siouville, 196). See pp. 3-4 above. Julian, *Orat.* 4, 143 B: "Il y a des dieux apparentés au soleil . . . ; ils deviennent multiples dans le monde, mais dans la région du soleil ils sont une unité" (Hertlein, 1, 185; tr. P. Nautin, *R. de philologie,* 21, 228). Macrobius, *Saturn.*, Bk. I, c. xviii-xxiv (Fr. Eyssenhardt, 104-28).

37. C. xx: "Si de telles fictions débitées sur le compte d'une nature bienheureuse et impérissable . . . sont crues et racontées comme des faits véritables qui se seraient passés, je n'ai pas besoin de te dire, Cléa, qu'il faut, suivant l'expression d'Eschyle, les rejeter en crachant et se rincer la bouche" (tr. M. Meunier, 75-6).

38. The cavern is the world; the nymphs are the souls; the stone jars are their bodies; the two gates are Cancer and Capricorn, etc. Cf. *Odyss.* V, 102 ss.

39. *Progymnasmata,* 3: *Mythos esti logos pseudes eikonizōn alētheian* (Spengel, 72); classic definition. Julian, *Disc.* 8 (252). Macrobius, *Somnium Scipionis,* Bk. I, c. ii: "ipsa veritas per quaedam composita et ficta profertur," "narratio fabulosa" (Fr. Eyssenhardt, 481).

40. M. Lepin, "Mystère (sens)," in F. Vigouroux, DB, V, 1376-1424.

41. *De insp. S. Script.* (1912), 256.

42. *Inst. biblicae* (1927), 256: "Theory differs from allegory, because the latter either denies or at least prescinds from the literal sense or the historical truth of a fact, whereas theory always necessarily presupposes it. Just as allegory is characteristic of the Alexandrians, so is theory the characteristic token of the Antiochenes" — "Theoria differt ab allegoria, quod haec sensum litteralem seu veritatem facti historicam vel denegat vel saltem ab ea praescindit: theoria e contrario illam semper necessario praesupponit. Ut allegoria propria es Alexandrinorum, ita Antiochenorum propria quasi tessera est theoria." And *Scritti di erudizione . . .* , II (1958).

43. More than once, when Origen takes the word *allēgoria* in its sense of denying the letter, it is to reject it; thus *In Matt.*, t. XV, c. xv (391); *In Jo.*, Bk. XIII, c. ix (233); c. x (234-5); Bk. XX, c. xx (352); c. xxxvi (376).

44. Cf. C. Spicq, *Esquisse,* 16, note 9.

45. *Le moyen āge latin et la litt. europ.*, Fr. tr. (1956), 375.

46. *Hist. d'Israël,* Fr. tr., 2 (1957), 1193.

47. "Quelque étrange que puisse nous paraître aujourd'hui l'exégèse pratiquée par les premières générations chrétiennes, elle se distinguait pourtant de celle pratiquée dans les milieux hellénistiques par son sens de l'histoire. . . . Dans un monde foncièrement étranger à l'histoire, cette exégèse, quoique fantaisiste dans le détail, a précisément défendu ce sens historique au nom

duquel nous l'assimilons souvent aujourd'hui, avec une certaine incompréhension qui ne fait peut-être pas grand honneur à notre sens de l'histoire, à un mode de pensée mythique": "La mystique de l'imitation du Christ et de l'unité chez Ignace d'Antioche," RHPR (1938), 223-4.

Notes to Chapter Six
§3. Mystery

1. "Secundum mysticam formam" — "secundum allegoriam": Or., *In Jud.*, h. 6, n. 1 (498).

2. "juxta mysticum intellectum haec omnia referuntur ad Christum": Peter Damian, *Op.* 37, dub. 4 (PL, CVL, 624 D). For Eusebius of Caesaraea, *Dem. ev.*, Bk. III, c. vii, the teaching concerning the divinity of Christ is "more mystical" than that which concerns his humanity (PG, XXII, 248 B).

3. "juxta mysticum intellectum certissime ad Ecclesiam refertur": Autpert, *In Ap.*, Bk. V (531 E).

4. "mystice factum": "videtur quiddam significare mysterii": Or., *In Jer.*, h. 11 (PL, XXV, 676 A).

5. "mysticos legalium umbrarum intellectus": John Scotus, *H. in Prol. Jo.* (PL, CXXII, 296 D). Prosper, *In ps. CII:* "mystico intellectu" (LI, 290 B); etc.

6. *Ibid.:* "that the truth of the symbols of the Law has been fulfilled in him" — "legalium symbolorum veritatem in Ipso esse impletam"; "He is . . . the truth of the symbols of the Law" — "Ipse est . . . veritas symbolorum legalium."

7. "ratio mystica" — "vim, rationem atque mysterium, secundum spiritalem intelligentiam": Gregory of Elvira, *Tr.* 7 (B.-W., 76); etc.

8. "mysteriorum scriptura": *C. Julianum,* Bk. VI, c. vii, n. 20 (PL, XLIV, 834).

9. "divinorum sacramentorum libri": *De ut. cred.*, c. xvii, n. 35 (Pegon, 296).

10. Thus, *In Cant. prol.*, to translate, it seems, a single word: "caritatem vel dilectionem," "caritatis dilectionisque." Cf. G. Bardy, *Recherches* (1923), 119; Hélène Pétré, *Caritas* . . . (1948), 85-6; Jean Scherer, *Le commentaire d'Or. sur Rom.* II,5–V,7 (1957), 88 (intelligere et considerare, exigua et parva, volunt et confidunt).

11. "Joannes in Revelatione sua, ea quae in lege secundum historiam scripta sunt, adducit ad mysteria divina et sacramenta quaedam in iis edocet contineri": *In Num.*, h. 20, n. 1 (187).

12. "Haec vera et utilia et divina sunt, sed . . . obtecta sacramentis et involuta mysteriis": *In Jos.*, h. 20, n. 4 (422).

13. "sacramenta absconsa sapientiae et occulta Dei mysteria": *In ps. CXVIII* (PL, IX, 514 A).

14. Bk. I, c. xv: "they beam with excellent mysteries and shine with sacraments" — "excellentibus radiant mysteriis et rutilant sacramentis" (PL, XCVIII, 1037 B); Bk. II, c. xxvi: "which overflow with so many mysteries and abound with sacraments" — "quae tot redundet mysteriis et exuberet sacramentis" (1092 D). Cf. Bk. I, c. xii: it "would have prefigured with typic sacraments and hinted at with speechless mysteries" — "typicis praefiguraverit sacramentis et tacitis innuerit mysteriis" (1033 B).

15. "sacramenta dominicae passionis" — "mysteria nativitatis": *In nat. Dom.*,

s. 1, n. 8 (PL, CLXXXIII, 119 C). *In f. omn. sanct.*, s. 3, n. 4: "Your charity ... desires to hear the sacrament of this altar and to know the sacred, secret mystery" — "Desiderat . . . caritas vestra audire sacramentum altaris hujus et sacrum secretumque nosse mysterium" (471 A).

16. "revelantis condensa mysteriorum et sacramentorum suorum": *In Cant.*, n. 115 (M. M. Davy, 146). *Disp. adv. Ab.*, c. ix: "according to the rite of the mystery and the manner of the sacrament" — "secundum ritum mysterii et modum sacramenti" (PL, CLXXX, 208 C).

17. Willibald, *V. s. Bonif.*, c. ii, n. 1, on the disciples of the saint reading the Bible: "They used to meditate continually upon the hidden points of the sacraments and the concealed issues of the mysteries" — "Sacramentorum arcana mysteriorumque abdita jugiter meditabantur" (MGH, *Scr.*, II, 336).

18. Chr. Mohrmann, *Latin vulgaire, latin des chrétiens, latin médiéval* (1955), 31. *Idem:* "*Sacramentum* dans les plus anciens textes chrétiens," HTR 47 (1954), 141-52. Certain indications also in M. Verheijen, "*Musterion, sacramentum* et la Synagogue," RSR 45 (1957), 321-37.

19. Jean Doignon, "'Sacrum', 'sacramentum', 'sacrificium' dans la traduction lat. du 'Livre de la Sagesse,'" REL 34 (1957), 240-53.

20. "sacramenta divina" — "idolorum mysteria": Cited by Mohrmann, HTR 47, 144.

21. "sacramenta humilitatis Verbi" — "sacra sacrilega superborum daemoniorum": Bk. VIII, c. ii, n. 4 (1, 179).

22. "Pene ubique Christus aliquo involucro sacramenti praedicatus est a prophetis": *In ps. XXX*, s. 2, n. 9 (CCL, 38, 209).

23. "rerum signa sunt in sacramentis": Aug., *In ps. LXV*, n. 17 (CCL, 39). Just as with Cyprian, the biblical *sacramentum* was most often prefiguration: J. B. Ponkens, BALC 2, 275-88.

24. *typos* is translated by: imago, figura, figuratio, species, forma, similitudo, sacramentum, etc. It is frequent in Justin, Ps.-Barnabus, Irenaeus.

25. "figura" — "imago" — "veritas": Gregory of Elvira, *Tr.* 5: "[the history bears] the image of the figure; there will neither be truth without figure, nor figure without truth" — "figurae imaginem (historia gerit); nec veritas sine figura, nec figura sine veritate constabit." Cf. E. Auerbach, *Figura, Archiv. romanicum*, XXII (1938), 436-89.

26. "praevenit sacramentum rei veritatem": Or., *In Ez.*, h. 11, n. 3 (PG, XIII, 749 D).

27. Aug., *ep.* 139: "on the variety of signs that are called sacraments when they pertain to divine things" — "de varietate signorum quae, cum ad res divinas pertinent, sacramenta appellantur" (PL, XXXIII, 327). Guerric, *Innat. apost.*, s. 3, n. 2: "The shadows are the obscure meanings of the old sacraments" — "Umbrae sunt obscurae significationes veterum sacramentorum" (CLXXX, 184 C).

28. CM, c. ii. Cf. Ambrose, *In Luc.*, Bk. VII, n. 73: "This is the simple history of the truth. . . . If it were considered in a higher fashion, it signifies the mysteries to be admired" — "Haec simplicis historia veritatis est. . . . Quae si altius consideretur, admiranda signat mysteria" (Tissot, SC, 52, 33). Filaster, *Haer.* 136: "The Law of Moses . . . containing the mystery of Christ" — "Lex Moysi . . .

Christi mysterium continens" (CCL, IX, 301). With St. Leo the usage is rather the inverse (PL, LIV, 290 A, 311 B).

29. "Legis mysterium et temporis sacramentum": *De laud. s. crucis*, Bk. II, c. xix (PL, CVII, 284 C).

30. "latentia sacramenta diligenter perscrutanda sunt": *S. in Pent.* (G.-S., II, 258).

31. "aliquid in ipso facto mysterii et sacramenti latet": *In Jo.*, tr. 8, n. 3 (CCL, 36, 83); *s.* 83, n. 5: "magnum mysterium, admirabile sacramentum" (PL, XXXVIII, 516); *s.* 252, n. 1: "in mysteriis et sacramentis" (XXXVIII, 1171); *s.* 123, n. 3 (682), etc. Cf. C. Couturier, "'Sacramentum' et 'mysterium' dans l'œuvre de S. Aug." (H. Rondet, etc., *Études aug.*, 1953, 161-332).

32. "indicant dulce mysterium, insinuant magnum sacramentum": *In ps. LXVI*, n. 1 (CCL, XXX, 529). *In ps. LXXX*, n. 1: "something posited mystically and signified in sacred fashion" — "mystice aliquid positum et sacrate significatum" (XXXIX, 1120).

33. "carnaliter observata illa sacramenta, etiam eos obstrictos tenuerunt, certi mysterii gratia, qui uni Deo subditi erant": *In ps. VI*, n. 2 (CCL, XXXVIII, 28).

34. "vestita terminibus carnalium sacramentorum": *In Jo.*, tr. 25, n. 5 (CCL, XXXVI, 246).

35. "carnalium mysteriorum": One also says: "corporalia sacramenta," but not so easily: "corporalia mysteria" though Aug. says it once (*C. Faustum*, Bk. XII, c. xx; PL, XLII, 265), but by opposition to the "perspicua contemplatio veritatis" of the heavens. Cf. Peter Lombard, *In ps. LXXV* (CXCI, 702 AC). Regarding the Eucharist, Aug. says: "mysterii altitudinem" (*Ep.*, 54, 8; XXXVIII, 203); he would scarcely have written "sacramenti."

36. "cortex sacramenti et adeps frumenti": *In Cant.*, s. 33, n. 3 (PL, CLXXXIII, 952 C); *De div.*, s. 22, n. 8 (600 A). Or for Serlon of Savigny saying of the Eucharist: "Tunc . . . sine sacramento eo perenniter perfruemur" (Tissier, 6, 129).

37. "Per gratiam sacramenti, mysteriorum consortio restituitur": *In Luc.*, Bk. VII, n. 232, commentary on the prodigal son (SC, 52, 95).

38. "Sacramentum veteris Testamenti, erat novum": *Civ. Dei*, Bk. IV, c. xxxiii (PL, XLI, 139).

39. William of Saint Thierry, *In Cant.*, n. 126 and 130 (Davy, 158, 162); etc.

40. "res sacramenti" — "mysterium rei": Cf. Aug., *In ps. LXVII*, n. 26: "Even the heading contains the mystery of this thing" — "Cujus rei mysterium continet etiam titulus" (CCL, 39, 889)

41. "abscondita Scripturarum" — "res sacramentorum sub velamine imaginum latentes": Petrus Comestor, *s. ad sacerd.* (PL, CLXXI, 773 AB).

42. "mystica sacramenta": Autpert, *In Ap.*, Bk. VII (567 A). Paulinus of Aquilaea (PL, XCIX, 158 AB). Paschasius, *In Matt.* (CXX, 183 A). Peter Damian (CXLIV, 331 C). Quodvult., *De prom.* P. I, c. xvii, n. 24: "that a mystic sacrament of the Lord's future passion is accomplished" — "mysticum quoddam futurae passionis dominicae geri sacramentum" (LI, 747 A).

43. "figurata mysteria": Aug., *In ps. CIII*, s. 2, n. 1 (CCL, 40, 1492).

44. "sacramenti mysterium" — "sacramentorum mysteria": See CM, Note A (343-50). In addition: Aponius, *In Cant.*, Bk. V (96); Bk. XII (248). Isidore, *De ill. eccl. scr.*, c. xl, n. 54 (PL, LXXXIII, 1102 B). Rabanus, *In Eccli.*, Bk. IX and X (CIX,

1082 C, 1105 D); *In Paral.*, Bk. IV, c. xxxii (518 D); *De univ.*, Bk. V, c. 1 (CXI, 106 B); h. 53 (CX, 247 B). Claudius of Turin, *In Gen.*, Bk. II (L, 972 D). Paschasius, *In Matt.*, Bk. II, c. iii (CXX, 172 A, 173 A, 174 D). Atto of Vercelli, *ep.* 5 (CXXXIV, 110 D). Ps.-Atto, *In Hebr.* (CXXXIV, 767 D). Ps.-Remigius, *In ps.* (CXXXI, 136 A). Damian, *op.* 6, c. 1 (CXLV, 122 D). Hugh, *De arca mor.*, Bk. IV, c. ix (CLXXVI, 680 B). Henri of Marcy, *De per. civ. Dei*, tr. 6 (CCIV, 299 CD, 300 A, 300 C). William of Saint Thierry, *Adv. Ab.*, c. ix (CLXXX, 280 C). Garnier, *s.* 3 (CCV, 591 C). Martin of Leon, *s.* 2 (CCVIII, 40 A). St. Leo (LIV, 697 D).

45. "mysterii sacramentum" — "mysteriorum sacramenta": *Ibid.* Add: Maximus of Turin, h. 13 (PL, LVII, 249 C). Isidore (LXXXIII, 379 C). Ildefonsus, *De cogn. bapt.*, c. ii (XCVI, 112-3). *Idem* (?), *s.* 2 *de assumpt.* (252-3). Leidradus: "a sacrament of so great a mystery" — "tanti mysterii sacramentum" (XCIX, 858 A). Alcuin, *Div. off.*, c. ix (CI, 1186 B). Sedulius Scotus (CIII, 151 D, 152 A). Rabanus, *De laud.*, Bk. I (CVII, 193 D, 221 A); *In Gen.*, Bk. III (568 B). Paschasius, *In Matt.* (CXX, 144 B, 174 D). Hincmar, *De una . . . trin.* (CXXV, 608 B). Odo of Canterbury: "Open up for us the sacrament of this mystery" — "Aperi nobis sacramentum hujus mysterii" (Leclercq, *St. ans.*, 31, 125). Philip of Harvengt, *V. s. Amandi*, c. viii, n. 72: "after the sacraments of the heavenly mystery have been taken" — "post suscepta caelestis sacramenta mysterii" (PL, CCIII, 1274 B). Pontificale Romanum, *De alt. consecr.:* [the altar] on which the sacrament of the saving mystery of the Lord's passion has been shown" — altare "in quo salutaris mysterii sacramentum dominicae passionis ostensum est." Bachiarius (Morin, BALC, 4, 122, 124). Arnold of St. Emmeran (MGH, *Script.*, 4, 555).

46. Thus in Apringius, *In Ap.*: "to discuss the two forms of the history of the divine Law by means of the twofold mystery of the sacrament" — "biformem divinae legis historiam duplici sacramenti mysterio disserendam" (Vega, 1); "sacramento mysterii" (9, 29). Or Beatus, *In Ap.* (36, 53, 72, 75).

47. "divinorum sacramentorum velanda mysteria": PL, CIX, 518 D.

48. "Haec sunt nova et vetera . . . quibus cuncta sacramentorum mysteria revelantur": *De univ.*, Bk. V, c. 1 (PL, CXI, 106 B). Cf. Ambrose, *Apol. David.*, c. xii, n. 59: "He does not empty the sacraments of the Old Testament and yet teaches that the Gospel mysteries are to be preferred" — "Et veteris Testamenti sacramenta non evacuat, et evangelica docet mysteria praeferenda" (XIV, 875 B).

49. "Ad competentem in secreto animae . . . mysterium sacramenti absconditur": *Tract. in SS. Scripturaram*, 12 (*Op. omnia*, Vega, I, 131).

50. "Nunc de mysteriis dicere tempus admonet atque ipsam rationem sacramentorum edere": HTR 47 (1954), 152. Cf. Botte, SC, 34 and 108.

51. "Mysterium enim est in sacramentis": *Rationale*, Bk. I, c. xxix (Lyon, 1551, 26 r).

52. "Supergressus est umbram (David) et spiritu prophetico ipsa vidit mysteriorum sacramenta caelestium, quorum typum Moyses praefiguravit in Lege": *Apol. David*, c. xii, n. 58 (PL, XIV, 874 C).

53. On this unity of language: CM, *loc. cit.*, HE.

54. Hilary, *Tr. myst.*, Bk. I, n. 31 (SC, 19, 126).

55. "typica expositio," "mysterium typicae expositionis": *In Ez.* (PL, LXXVI, 921 B); *Mor.* (9 A).

56. "Typicus intellectus": *In ps. praeambula* (PL, CXXXI, 139 A).

57. "caput Ecclesiae typicans": *Ep. Joannis de Varennis:* "The happy dove which, bringing an olive branch to the ark of the Lord, announced peace by means of the green leaves to the highest patriarch Noah, serving as type for the head of the Church" — "Columba laetabunda, quae ad arcam Domini ramum ferens olivae, virentibus foliis pacem nuntiavit patriarchae summo Noe, caput Ecclesiae typicanti" (Martène, *Ampl. coll.,* VII, 519).

58. "typicans oracula rebus": *Acta s. Cassiani:* "The other was Paul . . ." — "Alter erat Paulus . . ." (Du Cange, *Glossarium med. et inf. lat.,* nouv. Tirage, VIII, 1938, 220).

59. *In Gen.,* h. 2, n. 5: "The Spirit of God announces figures of the great sacraments both through Moses and through Paul" — "Spiritus Dei et per Moysen et per Paulum ingentium sacramentorum figuras enuntiat" (PG, XII, 171 A). *In Lev.,* h. 7, n. 1: "To the extent that it looks to the understanding" — "Quantum autem ad intelligentiam spectat" (477 A); h. 5, n. 3: "if they should have been able to penetrate their secrets by knowledge and mystical understanding" — "si scientia et intellectu mystico potuerint eorum secreta penetrare" (452 B); h. 9, n. 9: "let us see what they contain regarding their mystic character" — "quid haec secundum rationem mysticam contineant videamus" (521 B). *In Jud.,* h. 6, n. 1: "related to the mystic and prophetic sacraments" — "refertum mysticis et propheticis sacramentis" (974 C). *In Gen.,* h. 4, n. 2: "the whole mystical [deed] that he does is as a whole full of sacraments" — "totum quod agit mysticum, totum sacramentis repletum est" (185 A, etc.).

60. Or., *In Jos.,* h. 9, n. 7 (351), etc. Rufinus himself, *De ben.,* Bk. II (PL, XXI, 314 C); *In Gen.,* h. 17, n. 1 (PG, XII, 253 C).

61. PG, XLIV, 765 A.

62. "juxta litteram": "juxta spiritum": "in specie": "in mysterio" [Trans. note: Here *species* is being taken in its literal, etymological sense, denoting the objective counterpart for the verb *specto,* 'look at'; cf. Lewis and Short, *A Latin Dictionary,* s. vv. *specto* and *species* II. A., pp. 1736-7.]: *In Luc.* (PL, XV, 1731 B, 1731 C, etc.).

63. "mysticus ordo" — "mystica interpretatio": *In Luc.* (PL, XV, 1735 C, 1622 A, etc.). Eucherius, *Introd.,* Bk. I, *De epist. Jo.:* "But more here, using a mystic interpretation, understand the Trinity itself" — "Plures tamen hic ipsam, interpretatione mystica, intelligunt Trinitatem" (137-8).

64. "figurata interpretatio": Richard (PL, CXLI, 282 B).

65. "ad intellectum mysticum": *In Ez.,* Bk. II, h. 3, n. 18: "for the mystic understanding of the innermost contemplation" — "ad intellectum mysticum intimae contemplationis" (PL, LXXVI, 968 B).

66. "sub intellectu mystico": n. 17 (967 C). Prosper, *In ps.* (PL, LI, 290 B, 333 C). Bede (XCI, 298, 306).

67. "mystica interpretatio" — "designatio": *Mor.,* Bk. VI, c. i, n. 2 (PL, LXXV, 729 B; 730 BC), etc.

68. *Mor.,* Bk. XVI, c. xix, n. 24: "while it is nourished on the mystical understandings, it is being lifted to contemplate daily the things above . . . ; while the studious mind is being refreshed through mystic understanding" — "dum mysticis intelligentiis pascitur, ad superna quotidie contemplanda sublevatur . . . ; dum per intellectum mysticum studiosa mens reficitur . . ." (PL, LXXV, 1132 D). Gregory writes again: "typica expositio, significatio, investigatio,

interpretatio, intelligentia" (PL, LXXV, 9 A, 123 B, 513 C; LXXVI, 1045 C, etc.); "figuralis intellectus" (LXXV, 577 D).

69. "mysticae intelligentiae omnimoda plenitudo": *Lib. Mozarab. sacram.*, Pentecost (Férotin, 343).

70. *In Matt.* (PL, CXX, 183 A).

71. "mystica Dei sacramenta": *In Jud.*, Bk. I, h. 13 (PL, CVIII, 1138 B); copied from Origen.

72. "refertum mysticis et propheticis sacramentis": Claudius, *In Reg.*, Bk. III (PL, L, 1140 CD).

73. "juxta historiam" — "juxta intellectum mysticum": *Tr. in Act.* XII, 1 (PL, CXLI, 277 C).

74. "juxta mysticum evangelicae veritatis intellectum" — "quid mystice rationis habeat": *In Ap.*, Bk. IX, c. xv (PL, CLXIX, 1109 AB); *In Ex.*, Bk. I, c. xxviii (CLXVII, 596 D).

75. "mysteriorum profunda penetrare": a frequent formula: PL, CXCVI, 1309 B, etc.

76. "ad mysticam divinarum Scripturarum intelligentiam": PL, CXVI, 1305 B.

77. Potho of Prüm, *De magna domo Sapientiae* (515 D).

78. "spiritus mysterium": Aug., *Ep.* 196, c. iii, n. 13 (PL, XXXIII, 897). Rupert, *In Deut.*, Bk. I, c. xix (CLXVII, 938 A).

79. "spiritualis intelligentiae sacramentum": Peter Damian, *op.* 48, c. ii (PL, CXLV, 718 A). *Idem* (CXLIV, 331 D; CXLV, 1047 A).

80. "mystica significatio spiritualis intelligentiae": Baldwin of Canterbury, *L. de sacr. alt.* (PL, CCIV, 645 B).

81. "spiritalem significationem juxta mysticum sensum": Rabanus, *Ep.* 37 (MGH, *Ep.* 5, 473). Rupert: "The Christian people possesses Scripture in such fashion that it also may obtain the spiritual mysteries along with the history" — "Populus christianus sic sanctam possidet Scripturam, ut cum historia spiritualia quoque obtineat mysteria" (PL, CLXVII, 930 B).

82. "spiritualibus redundare mysteriis": Peter Damian, *op.* 60, c. xxvii (PL, CXLV, 854 A). Bede, *In Sam.* (XCI, 534 A): "spirituale et mysticum" (500 A).

83. "secundum mysterium spirituale": Or., *In Matt.*, ser. 27 (45).

84. "secundum spiritalem caelestis mysterii intellectum": Gaudentius, *Tr.* 9, n. 1 (75).

85. "ad mysticum et spiritualem recipiendum sensum": *In Lev.*, h. 3, n. 8 (315); *In Gen.*, h. 7, n. 6: "intelligentia spiritualis et mystica" (76). Sicard, *Mitrale*, Bk. VI, c. v: "discerning the mysteries of the Scriptures and understanding them spiritually" — "Scripturarum mysteria discernentes et spiritualiter intelligentes" (PL, CCXIII, 261 B). Potho of Prüm (493 H).

86. "mystico sensu, id est, spiritualiter": *De fide*, c. xx, n. 1 (PL, LXXXIII, 528 C).

87. "sensus spiritualis, quod est in Ecclesia mystica intelligentia": *In Ap.* (Florez, 1780, 175).

88. "in mysterio spirtualiter intelligendus . . .": *Ibid.*, p. 501.

89. "spiritualis allegoria": Greg., *In Ez.*, Bk. I, h. 3 (PL, LXXVI, 807 C). Rabanus, *In Ez.*, Bk. I (CX, 510 D). Sedulius Scotus, *In Gal.* V: "'The flesh lusts against the spirit', i.e., the carnal understanding of the Scripture against the spiri-

tual allegory" — "Caro concupiscit adversus spiritum hoc est, Scripturae carneus intellectus adversus allegoriam spiritualem" (CIII, 192 D).

90. "ut allegorizando spirituali sensu perscrutemur": Luke of Mont Cornillon, *In Cant. mor.* (PL, CCIII, 511 C).

91. "allegoria spiritualibus sensibus intellecta dilucidatur": *Ibid.*

92. "allegoricae intelligentiae spiritus" — "Spiritus dabit allegoriam, qui nos per sensum spiritualem vivificat": Rupert (PL, CLXVIII, 1279 A).

93. "allegoriarum sensus retinere" = "per spiritualem intelligentiam apprehendere": Rupert (PL, CLXVII, 935 AB).

94. "nunc autem videamus quomodo et allegoricum, id est, spiritalem recipiat intellectum": *In Num.*, h. 11, n. 2 (80).

95. "allegorica mysteria": Or., *In Num.*, h. 11, n. 11 (77).

96. "allegoriae habere sacramentum": Tertullian, *Adv. Marc.*, Bk. V, c. iv (581).

97. "mysticos allegoriarum nodos": Greg., *Moral.* (PL, LXXV, 966 B).

98. "mysticam allegoriam": Alhelmus, *De metris et aenigm.* (MGH, *A. ant.*, XV, Ehwald, 69).

99. "typos mysticos allegorice commentari": Ermenric of Ellwangen, *Ep. ad Grim.* (MGH, *Ep.* 5, 575). Paschasius, *In Threnos Jer.:* "According to the mystic senses of the allegories" — "Juxta mysticos allegoriarum sensus" (PL, CXX, 1089 B).

100. *In Ez.*, Bk. I, h. 6, n. 3: "Si quis . . . facta velit per allegoriae arcana discutere, protinus ab historia in mysterium surgit" (PL, LXXVI, 929 C). Didymus, *Fr. in Job* (PG, XXXIX, 1144 C).

101. "allegoriae mysterium": *Mor.* (PL, LXXVI, 83 D, 171 C, 172 B, 762 B, etc.). Peter Damian (CXLIV, 415 D, 884 A).

102. "allegoriae mysteria": *In ev.*, h. 40, n. 3 (PL, LXXVI, 1304 C). Angelome, *In Cant.:* "allegoriarum mysteria" (CXV, 554 A). Odo, *Epist. Mor.* (CXXXIII, 353 D). Abelard, *Intr. ad theol.*, Bk. II, c. i: "ad allegoriarum mysteria discutienda" (CLXXVIII, 1040 D). *Rescriptum pro monachis*, n. 67: "if any sacraments of the allegories be hidden within them" — "si qua in eis allegoriarum sacramenta lateant" (*St. ans.*, 41, 108).

103. "Salvis allegoricarum rerum mysticis sacramentis": *Conc. Foroj.*, c. xiv (PL, XCIX, 302 A). *C. Fel. Urg.*, Bk. I, c. xix: "not a mystery wrapped in the dark leaves of allegories as in prophecy" — "non quasi in prophetia umbrosis obvolutum allegoriarum mysterium foliis" (XCIX, 371 B).

104. "mystice atque allegorice": *Ep.* 4, n. 17 (Madoz, 131).

105. "arcanum allegoricae theoriae sacramentum": *Op.* 11, c. xvi (PL, CXLV, 245 D). Disciple of Peter Damian: "they might often cover [it] under the type of allegories or under a secret mystery of some sort" — "sub allegoriarum typo sive sub cujuslibet mysterio saepe tegerent arcano" (989 A). Or., *In Gen.*, h. 10, n. 1: "The things that are being read are mystical; they are to be expounded in allegorical sacraments" — "Quae leguntur mystica sunt, in allegoricis exponenda sunt sacramentis" (93).

106. "mysticum aliquid per allegoriam insinuet": *Did.*, Bk. V, c. ii (PL, CLXXVI, 790 B). Petrus Cellensis, *L. de panibus*, c. ii (CII, 937 A).

107. "secundum mysticas vel allegoricas legis interpretationes": *In Jud.*, h. 5, n. 6 (496). Hervaeus, *In Hebr.*, V: "An utterance susceptible of interpretation, i.e.,

Notes to Pages 25-26

one having many expositions of sacraments and allegories" — "Sermo interpretabilis, id est multas habens expositiones sacramentorum et allegoriarum" (PL, CLXXXI, 1567 D).

108. "Ascendere ad spiritualis intelligentiae mysticum et allegoricum sensum": *In Gen.*, h. 2, n. 1 (PG, XII, 161 A).

109. "Juxta sensum spiritualem vel mysticum . . . ; cum enim intelligentiam suscipiamus allegoriae . . .": PL, CLXVII, 1433 C.

110. "Aquam nobis in vinum vertit, quando ipsa historia per allegoriae mysterium in spiritualem nobis intelligentiam commutatur": *In Ez.*, Bk. I, h. 6, n. 7 (PL, LXXVI, 831 BC); copied by Beatus, *In Ap.* (261; cf. 268).

111. Cf. Passaglia, *De imm. conc.* 113: "If we speak properly, it is subject to the divine letters by reason of no other sense than what we call the literal and the spiritual" — "Si proprie loquimur non alterius ratione sensus divinis litteris subest, nisi quem litteralem et spiritalem nuncupamus."

112. *Aliud littera, aliud mysticus sermo significat:* Jerome, *Ep.* 18, c. xii (I, 66).

113. "Sacra Scriptura duobus modis intelligitur, historice et allegorice": Honorius, *Elucid.*, Bk. II, c. xxvii (PL, CLXXII, 1154 B). Cf. Greg., *In Ez.*, Bk. II, h. 3, n. 18 (LXXVI, 968 A). Othloh, *V. S. Wolfkangi:* "He not only penetrated the surface of the historical sense, but also investigated the innermost marrow of the mysteries" — "Non solum historici sensus superficiem penetravit, verum etiam intimas mysteriorum medullas investigavit" (MGH, *Scr.*, 4, 528).

114. "historialiter" — "sacratiori mysterio": Rabanus, *In Esther* (PL, CIX, 637 C).

115. "Legis scriptura non solum historialiter, sed etiam mystico sensu, id est, spiritaliter sentienda est": Isidore, *De fide*, Bk. I, c. xx, n. 1 (PL, LXXXIII, 528 C).

116. "litteram" — "significationem": Bruno of Segni, *In Gen.*, c. i (PL, CLXIV, 152 B).

117. "sensum": Jerome, *In Is. prol.:* "ut cuncta quaeramus in sensu" (PL, XXIV, 20 B) = to relate everything to Christ by the spiritual understanding — "licet sit pulchritudo etiam juxta litteram scire quae legas, tamen vis decoris omnis in sensu est" (*An. mar.*, III, i, 55).

118. "sensus litteralis est velut aqua; sensus mysticus, tropologicus et anagogicus est sicut vinum": *Prothema sec.* (*Quar.*, IX, 731).

119. "L'évolution est allée de la quadruple distinction à la dichotomie, et la trichotomie a servi de terme de transition": P. C. Boeren, *La vie et les œuvres de Guiard de Laon* (1956), 165.

120. "Unde etiam Salomon, cum Ecclesiae multiformem gratiam enumerasset, adjecit: Omnes enim qui apud eam sunt vestiti sunt duplicibus": *Coll.* 14, c. viii (PL, XLIX, 962 B).

121. "Haec autem omnia, duobus cherubim, id est, historicae et spiritualis scientiae plenitudine, proteguntur; cherubim enim interpretatur scientiae multitudo": *Coll.* 14, c. x (971 B).

122. Rabanus, *In Ez.*, Bk. XVII: "so that you have the spiritual understanding within the history, and the truth of the history within the tropology, each of which needs the other, and if one should be lacking, perfect knowledge would be missing" — "ut et in historia spiritalem habeas intelligentiam, et in tropologia

historiae veritatem, quorum utrumque altero indiget, et si unum defuerit, perfecta caret scientia" (PL, CX, 978 C); Bk. XVIII (1024 B); etc.

123. "du dessein primitif et principal du Saint-Esprit": *Instruction contre la traduction du N.T. de Richard Simon* (*Œuvres*, Bausset, II, 686; cf. 571). Pierius, S.J., *In Gen.*, XV, 5 *disp. prima*, n. 25 (Rome, 1595): "Both senses, the literal as well as the mystical, have been intended by God principally, each in its own genus. . . . Though, if there should be a comparison between them, I do not deny that the mystic and spiritual sense has been intended by God very much more" — "Uterque sensus, tam litteralis quam mysticus, in suo quisque genere principaliter a Deo intentus est. . . . Quanquam, si sit inter eos comparatio, haud inficior, impendio magis esse intentum a Deo mysticum et spiritualem."

124. Hervaeus, *In I Cor.* (PL, CLXXXI, 824 C).

125. "haec, cum exponuntur, franguntur": Aug., *s.* 130, n. 1 (PL, XXXVIII, 725). Abbaud (CLXVI, 1343 BC). Hervaeus (CLXXXI, 504 C). *Sent. divinitatis*, tr. 5 (Geyer, 134); etc.

126. "Panis significat Scripturam; frangere panem
    Est exponere Scripturas; cognoscitur inde
    Christus, cum sensus aperitur spiritualis." (PL, CLXXI, 1278 B)

127. Tertullian, *Adv. Marc.*, Bk. IV, c. xi: [Christ] "used to separate them and show that they were together. . . . As the fruit is separated from the seed, . . . so too is the Gospel separated from the Law" — "Quae separabat (Christus) et in uno ostendebat fuisse. . . . Sicut fructus separatur a semine, . . . sic et evangelium separatur a lege . . ." (452).

128. Rabanus, *In Reg.*, Bk. IV: "Our Lord and Redeemer . . . crushed . . . the very letter of the Mosaic Law which that people of the Law used to echo diligently, and he taught us to understand within it the spiritual sense" — "Dominus noster ac Redemptor . . . ipsam litteram legis mosaicae, quam ille populus legalis assidue resonabat . . . contrivit, ac sensum spiritalem in ea intelligere nos docuit" (PL, CIX, 252 C). Honorius, *Sp. Eccl.* (CLXXII, 934 C). Cf. Baldwin of Canterbury, *De sacr. alt.* (204, 761-2), etc.

129. Jerome, *In Is.*: "the straws, which, having been separated from the wheat by the winnowing-fan of the Lord" — "paleas quae ventilabro Domini a tritico separatae . . ." (PL, XXIV, 651 BC). Werner, *Defl.*, Bk. II: "History is a doctrinal threshing-floor in which good discoursers using the whips of diligence and the threshing-fan of inquiry separate the grain from the straw" — "Historia est doctrinalis area, in qua boni discursores flagellis diligentiae et ventilabro inquisitionis granum a paleis separant" (CLVII, 1137 B).

130. Paschasius, *In Matt.*, Bk. VII (PL, CXX, 549 AB).

131. Bruno of Segni, *In Ex.* (PL, CLXIV, 314 B). Garnier, *s.* 9 (CCV, 632 B). Durandus of Mende, *Rationale*, Bk. VI, c. cxlii, n. 2 (423); n. 2; etc.

132. "non solum in mysterio, sed etiam, in Scripturarum lectione": Rupert, *In Eccl.* (PL, CLXVIII, 1230-1). Ps.-Yvo, *s.* 5, *De conven. vet. et novi sacrificii* (CLXII, 559 BC); etc.

133. "fregit hunc panem Christus, divisit hoc verbum": Ambrose, *In Luc.*, Bk. VI, n. 91 (SC, 45, 262); n. 63 (250); n. 86 (260). Rupert, *loc. cit.*, (1231 A); etc. Honorius, *Sp. Eccl.* (CLXXII, 895 C).

Notes to Page 27

134. Bruno of Segni. Master Simon, *Tr. de sacram.* (H. Weisweiler, 3). Master Hermann (PL, CLXXVIII, 1742-3). Bonav., *Feria 2 post Pascha* (Q., 9, 286); etc.

135. "Panis coram nobis procul dubio a Domino frangitur, quando mysteriorum profunditas mystica interpretatione aperitur, ipsoque revelante cognoscitur": Richard, *De erudit. hom. int.*, Bk. I, c. xx (PL, CXCVI, 1264 B). *Vitis myst.*, c. xxxii, n. 118 (184, 706 C).

136. "Legem in duas partes dividi praecepti, in litteram videlicet et spiritum.... In vespera enim nobis datus est Salvatoris adventus, in quo pars illa dimidia, hoc est, sensus vel spiritus legis, secundum quod lex spiritalis est, offeratur oleo conspersa tenera": Or., *In Lev.*, h. 4, n. 10: "when the letter of the Law is broken through them and the spiritual food hidden within is drawn forth from it" — "cum legis per eos littera frangitur et cibus ex ea latens intrinsecus spiritalis elicitur" (331); h. 1, n. 4: one "who pulls off the veil of the letter from the word of God and exposes what is inside, which are the spiritual members of understanding" — "qui de verbo Dei abstrahit velamen litterae et interna ejus, quae sunt spiritalia intelligentiae membra, denudat" (409 C); *In Gen.*, h. 12, n. 5 (111-2).

137. Or., *In Lev.*, h. 2, n. 2: "'And broken in the middle' — For the middles were broken when the letter was separated from the spirit" — "Et medio fracta. Frangebantur enim media, cum littera separabatur a spiritu" (292). Irimbert, *In Jud.:* "at the high-point of spiritual understanding in holy Scripture the spirit is removed from the letter that killeth" — "acumine spiritalis intelligentiae in sacra Scriptura spiritus a littera occidente sequestratur" (Pez, 4, 157; cf. 156).

138. Luke of Mont Cornillon, *In Cant. mor.* (PL, CCXIII, 503 CD).

139. Peter Damian, *In Jud.*, c. iv (PL, CXLV, 1082 D); 1031 A: "Just as the finest wheat flour is ground between two millstones, so that the bran may be separated from the white winter wheat of the flour, so is holy Church pressed together between two mill-stones, namely of the Law and of the Gospel, so that the surface of the letter may be distinguished from the marrow of the spirit" — "Sicut simila inter molam utramque conteritur, ut a farinae siligine cantabrum separetur, ita velut inter duas, legis scilicet et evangelii molas sancta Ecclesia stringitur, ut litterae superficies a medulla spiritus discernatur." Bede, *In Esdram:* "Once the shell of the letter has been peeled off, to find something deeper and more holy in the marrow of the spiritual sense" — "Detecta cortice litterae, altius aliud et sacratius in medulla sensus spiritalis invenire" (XCI, 808 B). Jerome, *ep.* 58, c. ix (3, 83). Cf. Rupert, *In Ap.*, Bk. IX, c. xiv (169, 1102 D); etc.

140. "hordei enim medulla tenacissima palea tegitur": Bede, *In Marc.* VIII (PL, XCII, 206 D). Godfrey, *Microc.*, Bk. III, c. cxlix: "he drew such marrow ... from the most tenacious straws of the Old" Testament — from "tam tenacissimis paleis veteris ... talem medullam eruit" (166).

Notes to Chapter Six
§4. Pedagogy and Spirituality

1. Or., *In Lev.*, Bk. IV, n. 8: "And if we were to have such an understanding, we would be able by means of spiritual interpretation to discern each of the

things written in the Law" — "Et nos si haberemus talem intellectum, possemus singula quae scribuntur in lege, spirituali interpretatione discernere" (328).

2. Cf. Or., *In Jo.*, t. XXXII, c. xviii: "L'âme est quelque chose d'intermédiaire," [Greek:] *meson ti* (455).

3. *In Gen.* (PL, XCI, 328 C, 240-1, 243 D, 246 A). Cf. Ambrose, *De Abraham*, II.

4. *Mor. in Gen.*: "Per duos angelos sensualitas et imaginatio accipitur": "By 'the two angels' is meant sensuality and imagination"; "old Isaac is the failure of the soul's spiritual strength" — "Isaac senectus, animae est a spirituali robore defectus" (PL, CLVI, 146 D, 206 A); etc. *Trop. in Lam. Jer.* (451 AB).

5. Bk. I, tit. CLVIII: "If we want to understand the 'woman' mystically as sensuality and the 'man' contrary-wise as reason" — "Si per sensualitatem mystice mulierem intelligere volumus et per rationem virum contrarium" (on Ecclus. 42; PL, CLXXVII, 556 B).

6. *H. dom.*, II (PL, CLXXIV, 27-8).

7. "Moraliter Axa super asinam sedit cum irrationabilibus carnis suae motibus anima praesidet": *In* c. iii (PL, CLXVII, 1025 C).

8. "Haec ad litteram dicta, magna spiritus et vitae continent mysteria": *In* c. vi (1031 D).

9. Rupert, *Div. off.*, Bk. I, c. xviii (PL, CLXX, 21-2).

10. See Chapter 3 above.

11. Cf. Hilary, *Tr. myst.*, Bk. II, n. 11: "For the reading of the divine Scriptures" — "Lectioni divinarum Scripturarum . . ." (SC, 19, 156).

12. Ps.-Remigius, *In ps. LVIII*: "Praedicatores, ut Ambrosius, Augustinus, Hieronymus et alii multi" (PL, CXXXI, 437 B). See Chapter 10.5 below.

13. Greg., *In Cant.* (PL, LXXIX, 485 A). Aponius, *In Cant.*, Bk. VI (114); Bk. XII (235). Honorius, *In Cant.*: "The 'nipples' of the Church are the two Testaments from which her preachers suck the milk of mystical understanding; and these preachers are also called 'nipples', since they furnish the uneducated with the milk of doctrine" — "Ubera Ecclesiae sunt duo Testamenta, de quibus sugunt praedicatores lac mysticae intelligentiae; qui praedicatores dicuntur ubera, quia rudibus praebent lac doctrinae" (CLXXII, 466 D).

14. "divini verbi mater spiritualis": *In Purif., s.* 1 (PL, CCXII, 543 BC).

15. Paschasius explains in the prologue that he had received the order to preach on the Gospels at the solemn feasts (PL, CXX, 31 BC).

16. "Tropologia, sermo conversivus, magis movet quam allegoria": *Hist. sc[h]ola[s]t. theologicae disciplianae* (PL, CXCVIII, 1055).

17. "Rationabile et sine dolo lac, moralis locus; et solidus cibus, mysticus intellectus": *In Ez.*, h. 7, n. 10 (399). *In Num.*, 27, n. 1 (255-8); etc. Origen also often distinguishes two classes of Christians; sometimes three, following 1 Cor. 12:8-9 (fides, scientia, sapientia): *C. Cels.*, Bk. VI, c. xiii (2, 83); perhaps in relation with the trichotomy.

18. "Lactis cibus esse dicitur in Scripturis sanctis, prima haec moralis institutio, quae incipientibus velut parvulis traditur. Non enim in initiis statim discipulis de profundis et secretioribus tradendum est sacramentis, sed morum correptio, emendatio disciplinae, religiosae conversationis et simplicis fidei prima eis elementa traduntur. Istud est Ecclesiae lac, haec incipientibus parvulorum prima sunt elementa": *In Jud.*, h. 5, n. 6 (496). Cf. *Fr. in Luc.* 68 (267).

19. Bk. I, c. ii and vi (91-4, 104-21).

20. "Non enim primum: 'Beati scrutantes testimonia Dei,' sed primum: 'Beati immaculati in via.' Primus enim est, confirmatis moribus et in innocentiae studium ex communi probitate honestate compositis, viam veritatis ingredi; sequens deinde est scrutari Dei testimonia, et expurgato emundatoque animo ad investiganda adesse. . . . Nisi fidelium operum usus praecesserit, doctrinae cognitio non apprehendetur; et agendum a nobis antea fideliter est, ut scientiam consequamur": *In ps. CXVIII*, s. 1, n. 1; s. 2, n. 10 (PL, IX, 504 AB, 516 A).

21. *Ep.* 95: "[The commands] are overt, but the decrees of wisdom are covert" — "aperta sunt (praecepta), decreta vero sapientiae in abdito" (O. Heuse, 441).

22. *De mysteriis*, Bk. I, n. 1-2: "We have had daily discourse about morality. . . . Now they warn it is time to speak about the mysteries and to publish the very meaning of the sacraments" — "De moralibus quotidianum sermonem habuimus. . . . Nunc de mysteriis dicere tempus admonent, atque ipsam rationem sacramentorum edere" (B. Botte, SC, 25, 108; cf. *De sacram.*, Bk. I, n. 2: 54).

23. "Sic et Dominus praecepit ut tricameratam arcam in figuram Ecclesiae faceret. Primum enim catechumenum hominem quasi ad hospitium corporis sermo legis ingreditur. Deinde ad competentem in secreto animae quasi in pergulam lini mysterium sacramenti absconditur. Tertio ad fidelem in superiora domus per virtutum gradus ad culmen Sancti Spiritus pervenitur. Unde et beatus Paulus apostolus triformem hominem esse ad Thessalonicenses scribens dicit: 'Ut integer spiritus vester et anima et corpus sine querela in diem Domini reservetur'. Caro ergo hominis verbum Dei quasi hospitem recipit, anima vero conservat et tutat, spiritus extollit et elevat": *Tr.* 12 (135).

24. *In ps. I*, n. 41: "The fruit is inner. . . . The fruit is in the mystical affairs, the foliage in the moral" — "Fructus interior est. . . . In mysticis fructus est, in moralibus folium" (Petchenig, 35-6). Cf. *In ps. CXVIII expos.*, s. 1, n. 2 (PL, XV, 1199-1200).

25. *In ps. I*, n. 41-2 (PL, XIV, 943-4); *In Luc.*: "historiam — mores — mysterium" (15, 1603 C). (But *ibid.*: 1787 AC, 1792 B, 1793 A).

26. "moralem locum" — "propheticarum Scripturarum aenigmata": *De Abraham*, Bk. II, c. i (PL, XIV, 455 AB).

27. *Tr.* 8: "But these things having been said morally for the general edification, I now go on to the promised allegories of the Gospel reading itself. And, though I do not think myself fit to explain the mysteries of Christ . . ." — "Sed his pro communi aedificatione moraliter dictis, jam venio ad promissas allegorias ipsius evangelicae lectionis. Et licet ad explanationem mysteriorum Christi idoneum me esse non arbitrer, etc." (Glueck, 65).

28. "motus animarum" — "lex aeternitatis": *De vera rel.*, c. 1, n. 99 (Pegon, 168).

29. *In Lev.*, Bk. VII, c. ii: "If you have the science of the secrets, if you can knowledgeably and carefully discuss the faith of God, the mystery of Christ, and the unity of the Holy Spirit, you may offer the Lord bread and flour; if however you use common warnings to the people and know only how to deal with the moral topic which pertains to all, you will know that you have obtained the common bread" — "Si habes scientiam secretorum, si de fide Dei, de mysterio Christi, de sancti Spiritus unitate potes scienter cauteque disserere, panes et simila offeres

Domino; si vero communibus uteris ad populum monitis, et moralem scis tantummodo locum tractare qui ad omnes pertinet, communem te obtulisse noveris panem" (PL, CVIII, 518 B).

30. "per immensas mysteriorum voragines": *Tropologiae in Os. et Am., in fine* (PL, CLVI, 487 A). Aelred of Rievaulx observes that the tropology is more accessible and more useful: "solet magis et prodesse et placere," *S. de temp.* 25 (PL, CXCV, 353 B).

31. "Paulatim namque promovet se sermo sapientiae ad spiritualia contingenda, ut exercitatum animum ad interiora subducat": *In Eccl.*, h. 16 (PL, CLXXV, 226 A).

32. "ad aedificationem vitae suae": Bk. V, c. vii (PL, CLXXVI, 795 B).

33. "per ethicam nos duxerunt ad theologiam": *In Gal.* (PL, CLXXXI, 1164 B). But, *In Hebr.* V: "For the 'milk' is the brief hint of the faith and the ready observance of morals; the 'solid food', however, is the explanation of the faith itself and perfect establishment of life" — "Lac quippe est brevis insinuatio fidei et facilis observantia morum; solidus autem cibus est ratio ipsius fidei et perfecta institutio vitae" (1568 C).

34. *In ps. CXVIII:* "The divine testimonies are to be scrutinized in the Scriptures, first the moral ones, then the mystical; life is shaped in the former; faith, in the latter, in such wise that life may be spotless and faith unfeigned." — "Scrutanda sunt in Scripturis veritatis divina testimonia, primitus moralia, deinde mystica; in illis vita, in istis fides informatur, ut et vita sit immaculata, et fides non ficta" (PL, CXCIV, 731 C).

35. "Historicus (modus divinam paginam intelligendi) incipientibus, moralis proficientibus, mysticus perficientibus congruit": Hauréau, *loc. cit.*

36. "lectio theologica" — "Hoc pane reficiuntur tres viri, sc. majores, mediocres et minores. Minoribus proponuntur lac historiae, mediocribus mel tropologiae, majoribus solidus panis allegoriae": *S.* 4 (PL, CCX, 209 CD). Cf. Gen. 18:6.

37. "In opusculis igitur tropologiae deservientibus praesudare decrevi, antequam arduarum subtilitatum anagoges apicibus operosam exhibeam diligentiam": *De nat. rerum*, Bk. I (2).

38. *Liber quo ord. Trop. in Os. et Am., proem.* (PL, CLVI, 339 C); despite what he seems to say in the text cited on p. 412. In this [he is a] disciple of Gregory: We are speaking, the latter used to say, to the faithful, whom one can in a few words remind of the allegory, so as to have the time to preach to them the "morality" that they need, and it is good that this "morality" should come in the last place, "since those things are more usually better recollected which happen to be heard later on" — "quia ea plerumque solent melius recoli, quae contingit postmodum audiri": *In ev.*, Bk. II, h. 40, n. 1 (PL, LXXVI, 1302 AB).

39. "Parvulis lac potus datur, non esca": Bernard, *In Cant.*, s. 76, n. 9 (PL, CLXXXIII, 1154 C).

40. "moralis institutio": Rabanus, *In Jud.*, Bk. I, c. xii (PL, XVIII, 1137 C).

41. "Non virtutibus ad fidem, sed fide pertingitur ad virtutes" — ". . . ut beatus papa Gregorius exposuit": Bede, *In Act.* (PL, XCII, 906 B). Rabanus, *In Ez.*, Bk. XV (CX, 932 CD).

42. Bk. I, tit. XIII: "and these four things are generally distinct in all of

Scripture: commandments and prohibitions, promises and threats. The first two of these pertain to the shaping of life; the latter two, to instruction in faith" — "et sunt quatuor ista generaliter discreta in omni Scriptura: praeceptiones et prohibitiones, promissiones et comminationes. Quorum duo prima ad vitae informationem pertinent, duo subsequentia ad fidei instructionem" (PL, CLXXVII, 484 D).

43. "quadripartita legis observatio" — "Historia viam bene operandi demonstrat. Tropologia voluntatem informat. Allegoria per fidem cor mundat. Anagoge interiorem hominem sola ea quae Dei sunt contemplando purificat. In historia, praeter praeceptum invenitur oboedientia; in tropologia, disciplina; in allegoria, fidei sinceritas; in anagoge invenitur caritas. Docet te historia qualiter per obedientiam ad superiorem vivas humiliter; tropologia, quomodo ad parem vel ad inferiorem socialiter. Allegoria docet te credere fideliter; anagoge docet te amare perseveranter. Et duo prima ostendunt viam justitiae ad proximum; reliqua duo, cultum pietatis ad Deum. Haec sunt quatuor alae cherubim, quarum duabus volant, et duabus tegunt corpora sua (Ez., 1). Sancti enim viri, qui sunt cherubim, id est plenitudine divinae scientiae illuminati, duabus alis tegunt corpora, quando per historiam et tropologiam praesentem informant conversationem; duabus alis volant, quando allegoria et anagoge per fidem et caritatem sursum eriguntur ad contemplationem": *S.* 16, *in Purif.* (PL, CCXI, 100 AB).

44. It sometimes does appear; thus, in the doubly concordist formulation of Alexander of Canterbury: "For the simpler and uncultivated in the faith and in the love of the faith . . . ought to drink of the history; the more capable, of allegory; those more perfect still, of morality; and the most perfect should drink in anagogy, i.e., contemplation" — "Simpliciores namque et rudes in fide ac ejus amore . . . solet potare de historia; capaciores vero, de allegoria; perfectiores autem, de moralitate; perfectissimos autem de anagogen, id est de contemplatione": *Bk. de simil.*, c. cxciv (PL, CLIX, 708 B).

45. *Ep. ad fr. de Monte Dei*, Bk. I, c. v, n. 12 (PL, CLXXXIV, 315-6; tr. Déchanet, 50-2); c. xii, n. 35-9 (330-3); c. xiv, n. 42 (335 BC); Bk. II, c. ii, n. 3-4 (339-40); c. iii, n. 22-3 (352 BC).

46. On the relation of the spiritual life to meditation upon Scripture, see, among others: *In Gen.*, h. 10, n. 2 (95). On the three "animae profectum differentiae," or the three degrees of penetration of the soul by Christ: *In Num.*, h. 9, n. 9 (354-6).

47. "superior intellectus": *Formulae* (Wotke, 4). See Chapter 3.3 above.

48. "In spirituali theoria, ad sublimiora transimus, terrena dimittimus, de futurorum beatitudine et caelestibus disputamus, ut praesentis vitae praemeditatio umbra sit futurae beatitudinis": *In Eccl.* (PL, CLXVIII, 1230 CD). Nevertheless, *In Soph.*, Bk. II (668 D). See Chapter 2 above. Cf. G. Foliot, *In Cant.*, c. viii: "The history is feeding us now, and the moral allegory is refreshing us; sometimes contemplation of higher things holds us" — "Modo nos pascit historia, reficit moralis allegoria, aliquando suspendit contemplatio ad altiora" (CCII, 1298 C).

49. "requies contemplationis" — "labor boni operis": Peter Damian, *op.* 60, c. xxvi (PL, CXLV, 854 B). Cf. Or., *In Jo.*, Bk. I, c. xvi (20).

50. "per ethicam" — "ad theologiam" — "ad evangelicam plenitudinem" — "ad spiritum vivificantem" — "ad sancta sanctorum": Jerome, *Ep.* 121, n. 10 (Hilberg, 3, 50); *In Ez.* (PL, XXV, 382 A; cf. 446 D).

51. "Ambulant animalia, cum sancti viri in Scriptura sacra intelligunt quemadmodum moraliter vivant. — Elevatur vero a terra animalia, cum sancti viri se in contemplatione suspendunt": *In Ez.*, Bk. I, h. 7, n. 8 (PL, LXXVI, 843 C); Bk. II, h. 2, n. 1 (948-9); h. 9, n. 5 (1045 C).

52. "In (Scripturae) verbis tot delicias invenimus, quot ad profectum nostrum intelligentiae diversitates accipimus, ut modo nuda nos pascat historia, modo sub textu litterae velata medullitus nos reficiat moralis allegoria, modo ad altiora suspendat contemplatio, in praesentis vitae tenebris jam de lumine aeternitatis intermicans": *Mor.*, Bk. XVI, c. xix, n. 24 (PL, LXXV, 1132 B). See Chapter 3 above.

53. *In Jo.*, fr. 2 (PL, CXXII, 336 C); fr. 3 (340 B); cf. fr. 1 (312 AD).

Notes to Chapter Six
§5. The Doctrinal Formula

1. Cf., among the Greeks, Andrew of Caesaraea, *On the Ap., prol.* (PL, CVI, 217).

2. It will be noted that the expression "theoria spiritualis" adopted by Rupert comes less from Alexandria than from Antioch. The criss-crossing influences are very complex. We are perforce schematizing.

3. The sequence: "the garden, the storage room, the bedchamber" — "hortum, cellarium, cubiculum" is at once that of the three scriptural senses and that of the three stages of contemplation (PL, CLXXXIII, 714-5, 885 D). See Chapter 9.4 below.

4. *Benj. major*, c. iv, associating explication of Scripture and the contemplative process: "For what do we call sacred Scripture if not 'Rachel's bedchamber', in which we do not hesitate to hide the divine wisdom under the decent veil of allegories? As often as Rachel is sought in such a bedchamber, so often is spiritual understanding being hunted in the sacred reading" — "Quid enim Scripturam sacram, nisi Rachel cubiculum dicimus, in qua sapientiam divinam sub decenti allegoriarum velamine latitare non dubitamus? In tali cubiculo Rachel toties quaeritur, quoties in lectione sacra spiritualis intelligentia indagatur" (PL, CXCVI, 4 A).

5. See Chapter 3 above. Dominic of the Trinity, *Biblioth. theol.*, II (1667), 461: "It is manifestly gathered from the holy Fathers, who, though they may not have marked out this division, nevertheless did clearly enough hand down the very reality that is signified by the division: especially Augustine" — "Colligitur manifeste ex sanctis Patribus, qui, licet hanc divisionem non assignaverint, nihilominus rem ipsam, quae per divisionem significatur, satis expresse tradiderunt; praesertim Augustinus."

6. "Scriptura exterior est sensus litteralis, qui est patentior, quia per voces immediate significatur; Scriptura vero interior est sensus mysticus, vel spiritualis, qui est latentior, quia per res significatas vocibus designatur": *Op. cit.* (PL, CXIII, 29 A).

Notes to Page 35

7. *Periarch.*, Bk. IV, c. iii, n. 15 (347): he adds: "he aims more at the matter signified than the manner of words it is signified by; especially in such great and such difficult things" — "et hoc magis quod significatur, quam qualibus verbis significetur, intendat; praecipue in tam magnis et tam difficilibus rebus. . . ."

8. *In Jo.* XIX, 15 (315). Cf. Gregory Thaumaturgus, *Elogy of Origen*, c. i: "these admirable men . . . put the words in second place; they want to tackle the things themselves" (PG, X, 1052 B).

9. *Strom.*, Bk. II, c. iii, n. 2 (SC, 38, 34). It does not seem, then, that Clement and Origen had, as Wolfson, 63-4, believes, made "varied efforts to establish a fixed vocabulary."

10. I *Sent.*, d. 2, q. 2, a. 2: "For when there is agreement about things, controversy about the words is held to be futile, as Master [Peter Lombard] says" — "Cum enim de rebus constat, frustra in verbis habetur controversia, ut dicit Magister." It goes without saying that things are quite different when unsound inferences might result from equivocal or ill-analyzed language.

11. "Sapientis est non curare de nominibus": I *Sent.*, d. 3, q. 1, a. 1; *Prima*, q. 54, a. 4, ad 2m.

12. *anagōgē mystikē: Periarch.*, Bk. III, c. vi, n. 21 (331); Bk. IV, c. iii, 4. 6 (333).

13. *tas kata anagōgēn allēgorias: In Jo.*, VI, 2 (111). Cf. *In Matt.*, XV, 7.

14. *kata tēn anagōgēn: Sel. in Ez.* (PG, XIII, 813 C; cf. 822 C); *Sel. in Thren.* (608 D); *C. Cels.*, Bk. IV, c. xxi (1, 290); *In ps. III* (PG, XII, 1125 C); *In Jo.* (240), *In Matt.* (369); *In Jer.*, Bk. XIX, n. 15 (176); etc. *In Jo.*, Bk. X, c. xxxix: *anagein* (216).

15. *hē de kata anagōgēn theōria: In Cant.*, h. 5 (PG, XLIV, 864 C). Cf. Chrysost., *In Ps. XXXIV*, n. 1: *epi tēs anagōgēs tou hyiou tou Abraam* (LV, 209).

16. Cf. H. Hoepel, *Tr. de inspir. S. Scripturae*, 2nd ed. (1929), p. 146, note 2: "Among the Fathers of the school of Antioch, 'anagogy' signifies an interpretation that goes beyond the literal sense, i.e., a hunt for the spiritual or typic sense" — "Apud Patres scholae Antiochenae, *anagōgē* sive *anagōgia* significat interpretationem quae excedit sensum litteralem, id est, indagationem sensus spiritualis sive typici." On the comparison of the Antiochene and Alexandrian terminology, see H. de Lubac, "'Typologie' et 'allégorisme'," RSR 34 (1947), especially 200-208; Jacques Guillet, "Les exégèses d'Al. et d'Ant., conflit ou malentendu?" RSR 34, 257-302.

17. PL, XXIV, 72 B, 80 A, 87 BC, 105 A, 115 C, 135 D, 137 A, 151 D, 153 C, 158 D, 186 B, 196 B, 215 D, 239 D, 250 C, 252 B, 259 C, 260 D, 267 A, 315 B, 317 C, 340 D, 343 B, 373 A, 398 D, 520 C, 550 AB, 639 C, 666 B, 684 C, 708 D, 743 A, 809 C, 867 C. PL, XXV, 519 BC, 1328 D, 1418 A. *In Jonam*, SC, p. 66. *Ep.*, 16, 110; Hilberg, t. III, 12, 276. For a much later example: PL, CLVII, 358 B, 398 D. Cf. Sidonius Apollinaris, *Ep.*, IX, 3, to Faustus: "dictandi istud in vobis tropologicum genus, ac figuratum."

18. "Totus per tropologiam ad Christi pertinet sacramentum": *Excerpta de psalt., prol.*, c. viii (*An. mar.*, III, 1, 21). Sometimes, however, the *tropologia* is the sense intermediate between the *littera* and the *sublimis sacraque intelligentia* which makes for knowing the *mystica: In Ez.*, Bk. V, c. xvi (PL, XXV, 147-8).

19. *In Cant., proem. ad Olymp.* (PG, XLIV, 756-7). Cf. *Life of Moses* (376 D, 398 C, 400 D; Daniélou, SC, 1, 2nd ed., 1955). H. 5 (44, 864 C).

NOTES TO PAGES 35-36

20. *pneumatikē diēgēsis, dianoia: Sel. in Thren.* (PG, XIV, 609 A, 612-6, 616 C, 652 B). *C. Cels.* Bk. VII, c. xx (2, 171); etc.

21. *theōria: Sel. in Jer.* I, 13 (PG, XIII, 545 A).

22. *mystikē theōria, noēsis: Periarch.,* Bk. IV, c. ii (318), etc.

23. *tropologein: In Matt.,* t. XII, c. xli (163): it is a question of looking for the spiritual sense after the literal one. Cf. *C. Cels.,* Bk. II, c. xxxvii: "in a tropology of explication" — *en tropologiāi diēgēseōs* (162); Bk. V, c. lvi: *tropologia* (2, 60).

24. *anagesthai epi tropologian: C. Cels.,* Bk. IV, c. xliv (1, 317); c. xlix: "histories written as though for the goal of tropology" — *tais historiais hōs skopōi tropologias gegrammenais,* which is well translated: "they have been written so as to be explained by allegories" — "scriptae sunt ut allegoriis explicarentur" (321-2; PG, XI, 1108 B).

25. Ex. and ref. in HE, 123-5. [Trans. note: In classical Greek, *katanoein* means to 'remark' or 'observe' (Liddell and Scott); Lampe's *Patristic Greek Lexicon* renders it 'contemplate'; the citations mention *noēsis* and words of the same root, but without the *kata-* prefix.]

26. *In ep. prim. Petri,* 3, 6 (Zoepfl, 28, 29).

27. PG, LXIX, 776-7, etc.

28. *In Jo.,* Bk. III (PG, LXXIII, 460 AB, 501 D, 513 C, 616 B); *C. Jul.,* Bk. IX (LXXVI, 969 B, 993 B); Bk. X (1029 C, 1032 B), etc. Cf. St. Maximus, *Scholia in Dionysii ep.* 9: over and above history "allegory and anagogy must also necessarily be admitted" (PG, IV, 568 D).

29. "juxta tropologiam" — "juxta spiritum": PL, XXIV, 20 B, 153 C, 159 A, 184 C, 186 A, 362 A, 494 B, 517 A, 517 C, 631 C, 692 B, 724 B, 877 D. PL, XXV, 35 A, 256 B, 402 A, 1390 C, 1536 B. *Ep.,* t. III, 132; t. VI, 118; Hilberg, III, 43 and 360. *An. mar.,* III, 2, 21, 68, 348; III, 4, 30 and 32; etc.

30. "juxta mysticos intellectus": PL, XXIV, 106 A, 197 C, 239 A, 822 D. PL, XXV, 89 B, 134 C, 1553 C. *Ep.,* I, 597; II, 24 and 83. *An. mar.,* III, iii, 80; etc. And the numerous "mysteria," "sacramenta," etc.

31. "juxta anagogen": PL, XXIV, 49 B, 50 A, 55 A, 130 B, 141 B, 205 D, 240 D, 246 C, 265 B, 271 A, 304-5, 318 C, 344 D, 499 A, 535 C, 669 B, 689 A, 691 D, 701 C. PL, XXV, 61 CD, 1343 C, 1488 C. *In Jon.* (SC, 82). *Ep.* 120, c. ii (6, 139); etc.

32. "spiritualis theoria": *Ep.* 120, 9-12 (6-162).

33. Thus PL, XXIV, 200 A: "et juxta historiam, et juxta allegoriam"; 315 D; XXV, 1027 D, 1063 D, 1418 A; XXVI, 413 A; etc.

34. "Juxta anagogen vinea Dei et pomorum paradisus, anima nostra appellari potest": PL, XXIV, 31 BC.

35. "Bos juxta anagogen refertur ad Israël": PL, XXIV, 27 A.

36. "Locus iste ... potest ... juxta anagogen de saeculi hujus nocte cantari": *In ps. CIII* (*An. Mar.,* II, 1, 75).

37. Let us point out these two forms in his work: "juxta litteram — haec in prophetia" [letter vs. prophecy], *In Gen.,* Bk. III (PL, L, 1044 A and B); "Juxta historiam — juxta translationem" [history vs. transference], *In Reg.,* Bk. IV, (50, 1196 A).

38. Often synonymous expressions: "juxta allegoriam," "juxta anagogen," "juxta mysticos intellectus," "juxta spiritualem sensum," "tropologicōs," etc.

39. "secundum anagicos sensus": *In Matt.* (PL, CXX, 382 C), etc.

40. PL, CXVII.
41. PL, CLXX, 385 D; etc.
42. "Possumus tripliciter locum istum disserere: . . . vel juxta litteram . . . , vel juxta spiritualem intelligentiam . . . , vel certe anima credentis . . .": *In Ez.*, Bk. X, c. xxxiii (PL, XXV, 318 D).
43. "Debemus enim Scripturam sanctam primum secundum litteram intelligere . . . ; secundo juxta allegoriam, id est, intelligentiam spiritalem; tertio secundum futurorum beatitudinem": *In Amos,* Bk. II, c. iv, 6 (PL, XXV, 1027 D).
44. A page of the *C. Cels.*, Bk. VI, c. ix, itself gives, it seems, the four senses in succession regarding four expressions from Plato. See the Conclusion in Volume 4.
45. "Sancti Patres optime quatuor sensus, sive modos exponendi Scripturam Dei, agnoverunt": J. M. de Turre, *op. cit.*, III, 22.
46. "Quadruplicem Scripturae sensum . . . cum antiquioribus Patribus statuit": *Hist. interpretationis librorum sacrorum in Ecclesia christiana,* V (1814), 129.
47. "triplex sensus spiritualis": *De reduct. artium ad theol.*, n. 5 (Q., V, 321).
48. "Sensus mysticus, seu spiritualis . . . est triplex in generali; quia si res significatae per voces referantur ad significandum ea quae sunt in nova lege credenda, sic accipitur sensus allegoricus; si autem referantur ad significandum ea quae per nos sunt agenda, sic est sensus moralis vel tropologicus; si autem referantur ad significandum ea quae sunt speranda in beatitudine futura, sic est sensus anagogicus": PL, CXIII, 28 CD.
49. *Op. omnia,* V, 389 (in Pesch, 198). Cf. Philothaeus Achillinis, *Somnium Viridarii,* c. lxxxiv (Goldast, *Monarchiae S. Romani Imperii,* t. I, 88).
50. *Ars Int . . . , Fr. Sixto Senensi dominicano, theologo profundissimo* (Coloniae, 1577), 4-14. Cf. C. Chauvin, *Leçons d'introd. générale aux div. Ecritures* (1908), 446: "In the thought of the scholastics who have chiseled out this adage, the three words allegoria, moralis, anagogia, designate one and the same scriptural sense, namely the typic or spiritual sense, as opposed to the literal sense" — "Dans la pensée des scolastiques qui ont buriné cet adage, les trois mots allegoria, moralis, anagogia, désignent un seul et même sens scripturaire, le sens typique ou spirituel, par opposition au sens littéral."
51. B. Smalley, AHDLMA 5 (1931), 169; M. B. de Vaux Saint-Cyr, RSPT 39, 229.
52. Cf. again Ambrose, *Ep.* 33, n. 2: "You know that sometimes when Scripture utters an allegory, it related some things to the aspect of the Synagogue and others to that of the Church; some to the soul and others to the mystery of the Word, others again to the various species and qualities of souls; he who judges by the spirit discerns these things" — "Non ignoras quod interdum Scriptura, cum allegoriam dicit, alia ad speciem Synagogae, alia ad Ecclesiae refert; alia ad animam, alia ad Verbi mysterium alia ad diversas species et qualitates animarum; quae discernit, qui dijudicat spiritu" (PL, XVI, 1072 A).
53. *De scripturis:* "allegory . . . which is subdivided into simple allegory and anagogy" — "allegoria . . . quae subdivid[it]ur in simplicem allegoriam et anagogen" (PL, CLXXV, 11-2).
54. "Allegoria est, quando per factum intelligitur aliud factum; si visibile, simplex allegoria est; si invisibile et caeleste, anagoge dicitur": c. viii (PL, CLXXVII, 375 A).

55. "Sub allegorico [sensu] comprehendit tres: allegoricum scilicet specialem, et tropologicum, et anagogicum specialem": *Summa theologiae, Prima,* tr. I, q. 5, m. 4, ad 11m.

56. "Sacrae Scripturae duplex explanatio, vid. historica et allegorica. Rursus historica alia est analogica, alia aetiologica. Allegorica vero triplex: prima figuras rerum ad praesentia accommodat, et retinet nomen allegoricae; secunda ad mores, et dicitur tropologica; tertia ad incommutabilem aeternitatem, et dicitur anagogica": *Bibl. sancta,* Bk. III, c. iii. Cf. Vasquez, *In primam,* q. 1, a. 10, disp. 16, c. ii. J. Bonfrère, *In totam Script. sacram Praeloquia* (1625), c. xx, sect. 1.

57. *De tab. et vasis ejus,* Bk. I, c. vi (PL, CXI, 410 BD).

58. *In Ex.,* Bk. III, c. xi (PL, CVIII, 147-8).

59. *Bk. quo ordine* (PL, CLVI, 25-6).

60. Cited by the author of the *Girum cœli* (J. Leclercq, AHDLMA 13, 321).

61. *Exp. in Cant., prol.* (PL, CLXXII, 349 AC).

62. *Allegoriae* (PL, CXII, 849); *Trip. tab.* (CXCVIII, 697 AB). Cf. *De triplici genere contemplationis, ep. Adami* (CXCVIII, 792 D).

63. *Polycr.,* Bk. VII, c. xii (PL, CXCIX, 666 AB).

64. *Bk. de quadripartita specie nuptiarum:* "according to the four theological understandings: historical, allegorical, tropological, and anagogical" — "juxta quatuor theologicos intellectus: historicum, allegoricum, tropologicum et anagogicum" (PL, CCXVII, 923 A).

Notes to Chapter Seven
§1. Importance of the Letter

1. "prima significatio": Hugh (see note 3 below); *De sacr. prol.*, c. iv: "The history is the report of the things accomplished, a report that is contained within the first signification of the letter" — "Historia est rerum gestarum narratio, quae in prima significatione litterae continetur" (PL, CLXXVI, 185 A). *De trib. max. circ.*: "per primam litterae significationem expressa" (*Speculum* 18, 491). [Trans. note: *Littera gesta docet.* Father de Lubac is alluding to the distich that he quoted in the very first paragraph of his introduction to the work as a whole. Here is Mark Sebanc's English translation from Volume I, p. 1: "The letter teaches events, allegory what you should believe,/Morality teaches what you should do, anagogy what mark you should be aiming for" and the Latin original quoted on p. 271, note 1:

"Littera gesta docet, quid credas allegoria,
Moralis quid agas, quo tendas anagogia."

2. "prima expositio" — "primus intellectus": Or., *In Gen.*, h. 2, n. 6 (37); *De princ.*, Bk. IV, c. ii, n. 6 (315).

3. "Si tamen hujus vocabuli significatione largius utimur, nullum est inconveniens ut sc. 'historiam' esse dicamus 'non tantum rerum gestarum narrationem, sed illam primam significationem cujuslibet narrationis, quae secundum proprietatem verborum exprimitur'; secundum quam acceptionem omnes utriusque Testamenti libros . . . ad hanc lectionem secundum litteralem sensum pertinere puto": Hugh, *Did.*, Bk. VI, c. iii (PL, CLXXVI, 801 A); *De script.*, c. iii: "It is usually taken in a broader sense, so that the sense which is related to things in the first place on the basis of the signification of the words is called 'history'" — "Solet largius accipi, ut dicatur historia sensus qui primo loco ex significatione verborum habetur ad res" (CLXXV, 12 A). Cf. *Reportatio* of Laurent (Lottin, RTAM 25, 276). Alexander of Hales, *Summa*, tr. intr., q. 1, a. 4, 1 ad 2m: "The 'historical' is spoken of in two ways, with respect to the thing itself and with respect to a likeness of a thing: with respect to the thing, as in the things actually accomplished; with respect to a likeness of a thing, as in the parables" — "Historicum dicitur dupliciter, secundum rem et secundum rei similitudinem; secundum rem, sicut in rebus gestis; secundum similitudinem, sicut in parabolis" (Q., 1, 12).

4. "simplex locutio, quae ita ut dicitur intelligitur" — "in relatione praeteritorum gestorum et in manifestis divinisque praeceptis": L. *de variis quaest.*, c. ix, n. 4 (Vega-Anspach, 30); c. liii, n. 1: "Concerning the animals that . . . were forbidden to be eaten by the faithful . . . through the express provision of the law" — "De animalibus quae per legis historiam . . . ab esu fidelium prohibentur" (161).

5. "historin, id est video": *Sent.*, Bk. I, P. I, c. vi: "History is derived from the Greek *historin*, meaning 'I see'. . . . Hence history is not unfittingly spoken of as from *historin*. . . . But the mystical or hidden sense of things is so called, because it is subject to the comprehension of the understanding alone and is far removed from every cognition of the sense" — "Historia autem dicitur a graeco quod est

historin, id est video. . . . Propter quod non incongrue historia est dicta, quasi ab historin. . . . Rerum vero significatio mystica, id est occulta appellatur, eo quod solius intellectus comprehensioni subjecta est, et ab omni sensus cognitione remota" (Martin, 171).

6. Cf. Pierre Louis, "Le mot *historia* chez Aristote," *Rev. de philologie* 29 (1955), 39-44.

7. "rerum quibus gerendis interfuerit qui narret" — "eorum temporum quae vel vidimus vel videre potuimus": Gellius, 5, 18 following Verrius Flaccus. Servius, *In Aen.*, I, 373: "derived from *historein*, i.e., 'seeing'" — "dicta *apo tou historein*, id est videre." Cf. P. Scheller, *De hellenistica historiae conscribendae arte* (1911), 9-14. Isidore, *loc. cit.*, takes the formula from Gellius.

8. "eorum temporum quae aetas nostra non vidit": Isidore, *Etym.*, Bk. I, c. xliv, n. 3-5 (PL, LXXXII, 124 AB).

9. "Historiographus . . . rei visae scriptor": *Dial. sup. auctores* (Schepps, 24).

10. *De ord.*, Bk. II, c. xii, n. 37 (R. Jolivet, 428).

11. "neque enim audita, sed quae vidi narraturus sum" — "quae vel ipse viderim vel probatorum veridica relatione cognoverim": Létald of Micy, *Mirac. S. Maximini*, c. x, n. 34 (PL, CXXXIX, 814 C); prol. n. 2 (796 B). Cf. Eginhard, *V. Caroli magni* proem. (CMGH, *Script.*, 2, 443).

12. "secundum legem chronicae rerum gestarum breviter digesta veritas": *Chronicle of Sigebert, continuatio Gemblacensis* (PL, CLX, 259 A). Not all the "chronicles," however, have the dry brevity, for example, of the "Chronicon ex chronicis" of Florentius of Worcester (†1117-8).

13. *Chronica,* t. I, Bk. I, c. i (PL, CVI, 919 C); t. II, Bk. IV, c. xvi: "historiographers, whose intention was to present these things in letters to future generations" — "historiographi, quorum intentio fuit ut litteris haec ad futuram posteritatem porrigerent" (1218 B).

14. *Eccl. hist., prol.:* "I propose to explore and communicate the modern events of the Christians. Hence I should like the present work to be called an Ecclesiastical History. . . . I work out the things I have seen in our time or have learned to have happened from neighboring regions. [Later on will come one who] will perhaps draw from my notes and those of others like mine what he may fittingly insert in his own chronography or account for the information of those to come" — "Modernos christianorum eventus rimari et propalare satago. Unde praesens opusculum Eccl. Historiam appellari affecto. . . . Ea quae nostro tempore vidi, vel a vicinis regionibus accidisse comperi, elaboro. [Later on will come one who] forsitan de meis aliorumque mei similium schedulis hauriet quod chronographiae narrationique suae dignanter ad notitiam futurorum inseret" (PL, CLXXXVIII, 16 AB).

15. Bk. IX, c. xx: "that there will doubtless be certain latecomers who will avidly scrutinize the likes of me from the chronographers of this generation" — "Mei nimirum similes autumno quosdam esse futuros, qui generationis hujus ordinis a chronographis avide perscrutabuntur" (716 C); etc. On Ordericus: H. Wolter, S.J., *Orderi[c]us Vitalis, ein Beitrag zur Kluniazensischen Geschichtsschreibung* (1955).

16. "vestigia majorum" — "per semitas historiarum": PL, CLX, 58 D.

17. *Hist. novella, prol.:* "I have not neglected to entrust to writing many of the

accomplishments of your father of happy memory and . . . to these writings, in three books, I have given the name *Chronicles*. Now the mind of your grace wishes that what has happened in Anglia . . . in modern time should be handed on to posterity" — "Pleraque gestorum præcellentis memoriae patris vestri stylo apponere non neglexi et . . . in tribus libellis quibus Chronica dedi vocabulum. Nunc ea quae moderno tempore . . . acciderunt in Anglia ut mandentur posteris, desiderat animus vestræ serenitatis etc." (Stubbs, 2, 525).

18. "hanc ergo tuae nobilitati offero historiam": *Gesta Frid. imp., proem.* (MGH, *Scr.*, XX, 352).

19. Cf. Ekkehardus Uraugiensis († v. 1130): *Chronicon universale* (PL, CLIV). In the 13th century, Matthew Paris will be called "historiographus et chronographus magnus."

20. Paul Rousset, RHEF 36 (1950), with regard to R. Glaber; "this attitude . . . is that of the majority of the Chroniclers. . . . Contrary to the traditional opinion, we believe that the universal Chronicler is also an historian who is even, in his own way, a philosopher of history" — "cette attitude . . . est celle de la plupart des chroniqueurs. . . . Contrairement à l'opinion traditionnelle, nous croyons que le chroniqueur universel est aussi un historien, qui'il est même, à sa manière, un philosophe de l'histoire." *Idem,* "La conception de l'hist. à l'ép. féodale," *Mél. L. Halphen* (1951), 623-33. M.-D. Chenu, "Hist. et allégorie au XII s.," *Festgabe Lorz* (1957), 59-60.

21. Cf. Ch. H. Haskins, *The Renaissance of the Twelfth Century* (1927), 24-30. It is therefore too little, we think, to say with Marc Bloch, *La société féodale* (1939), 142: "The makers of chronicles . . . did not have a deliberately narrow scope" — "Les fabricants de chroniques . . . n'avaient pas l'horizon volontairement étroit."

22. "Dicta autem graece historia *apo tou historein,* id est, a videre et cognoscere; apud veteres enim nemo conscribebat historiam, nisi is qui interfuisset. . . . Melius enim oculis quae fiunt deprehendimus, quam quae auditione colligimus": *Etym.*, Bk. I, c. xli, n. 1 (PL, LXXXII, 122 BC). *Sp. Eccl.,* c. viii (CLXXVII, 375 A). Guibert of Nogent refers to this definition when he writes, *Gesta Dei per Fr.,* Bk. IV, c. 1: "If one were to reproach me for not having seen it myself, he would at least not reproach me for not having heard it"; he has interrogated "those who have seen and who know" (CLVI, 729 C). Liutprand of Cremona (†972?) has been invited to write the history of the Europe of his time "as one who is not doubtful by merely hearing, but is sure by vision" — "sicut is qui non auditu dubius, sed visione certus": *Antapodosis,* Bk. I, c. I (CXXXVI, 7900 D).

23. *De script.,* c. iii (PL, CLXXV, 12 A).

24. Sicard of Cremona, *Mitrale,* Bk. I, c. xiii: "History is derived from *historin,* i.e., 'to see', since it is the job of historiographers to expound the things accomplished with regard to the first signification of the words" — "Dicitur autem historia ab historin, quod est videre, quia historiographiorum est res gesta[s] secundum primam vocum significationem exponere" (PL, CCXII, 47 AB). The last words adjoin the tendentious explication of Robert of Melun, which does not interest us here.

25. F. Muller, "De 'historiae' vocabulo et notione" (*Mnemosyne,* nov. ser., 54, 1926, 238): ". . . that the sense and character of 'history' has arisen from the employment of witnesses accepting only things that they had seen or heard as

known for certain" — "historiae sensum atque rationem ex testium munere ortam esse, ea solum quae vidissent quaeque audivissent tanquam certo cognita accipientium." Nevertheless, 235-6: of the historian: "was he the one who sees . . . a thing, or the one who has completely seen through a thing and knows it?" — "fuitne is qui rem . . . vidit, an potius is qui rem penitus perspectam habet eamque novit?" [Trans. note: See also Lampe, *A Patristic Greek Lexicon*, s.v. *historia*, 678-9. For a range of Indo-European vocabulary items of the same root, consider the English 'wit' and 'wisdom'; German 'wissen'; Sanskrit 'vedanta'; Greek 'eidō' (not used in the present tense); Latin 'video'.]

26. "Dicitur ab isteron, quod est gesticulatio; in ea enim gesta denotantur": Langton, *In Gen.* (Smalley, AHDLMA 4, 168).

27. "Est autem historia res gesta, res visa": *Alterc. Syn. et Ecol.* (J. Châtillon, RTAM 23, 52).

28. "Historia dicitur ab ysteron, quod est videre vel gesticulare; narrat enim tantum de iis quae gesta sunt et visa": G. Lacombe, AHDLMA 5, 43.

29. "Littera est factum, quod sancta narrat historia": John Scotus, *In Jo.*, fr. 2 (PL, CXXII, 320 B). Aug., *Doct. chr.*, Bk. III, c. xxviii, n. 44: "narratione historica" (Combès-Farges, 46).

30. "Haec omnia temporaliter atque realiter iste populus adeptus est": Gerhoh, *In Cant. Moysi*, I (PL, CXCIV, 1052 B).

31. Hilary, *Tr. myst.*, Bk. I, n. 26: "History bespeaks the thing accomplished" — "Rem gestam historia loquitur"; 22: "A thing is being accomplished" — "Geritur quidem res"; 29: "the spiritual order has been preserved in the events" — "spiritalis ordo conservatus in gestis est" (SC, 118, 112, 122).

32. "hujus religionis sectandae caput est historia": Aug., *De vera rel.*, c. vii, n. 13 (Pegon, 42).

33. Aug., *s.* 2, c. iv, n. 6 (PL, XXXVIII, 29-30); *Civ. Dei*, Bk. XIII, c. xxi (XLI, 394-5); *In ps. XXXIII*, *s.* 1, n. 2: "and it is very true that it happened, . . . and although the title of the Psalm was so written in mystery, it was nevertheless presented about a thing that was accomplished" — "et verissimum est, quia contigit, . . . et quamvis titulus psalmi in mysterio sic scriptus sit, tamen ductus est de re quae gesta est" (XXXVI, 300). Cf. Bachiarius, *Prof. fidei*, c. 6: "And not eliminating the trustworthiness of the history, we believe that everything we read has been accomplished" — "Nec evacuantes historiae fidem, credimus universa gesta esse quae legimus" (XX, 1033 B).

34. "historica explanatio": Jerome (PL, XXIV, 129 A, 249 A, 250 B, 281 B); etc.

35. "Ipsa prius narratio juxta litteram patefiat": Greg., *In Ez.*, Bk. II, h. 10, n. 2 (PL, LXXVI, 1058 CD). Or., *In Ex.*, h. 10, n. 2: "For it was first necessary to discuss historically the things that are read" — "Oportebat enim prius secundum historiam discutere quae leguntur"; *In Num.*, h. 5, n. 1; h. 9, n. 5 (25, 60); *In Matt.*, t. X, n. 14 (17), etc. Cf. Chrysost., *In psalmos, proem.*

36. "primum exponamus historiam": Rabanus, *In Ez.* (PL, CX, 648 A). John of Salisbury, *Polycr.*, Bk. VII, c. x: "Cum vero primum sit excutiendus sensus historicus" (CXCIX, 659 A).

37. "Historiam prius praeponens cantus ubique": *Poetae lat. m. aevi*, VI, 176.

38. "historiae indagare veritatem": Rabanus, *In Judith* (PL, CIX, 543 C). Or.,

De princ., Bk. IV, c. iii, n. 4 (329). Rupert, *In Os.*, Bk. III: "how it stands with the truth of history" — "qualiter veritas historiae consistat" (CLXVIII, 123 B).

39. "historiae veritas prosequenda est...": Rabanus, *In Ez.*, Bk. IX; Bk. XIII: "haec juxta historiae veritatem" (PL, CX, 732 D, 858 A).

40. "Considera diligenter quid indicet historiae textus": Or., *In Num.*, h. 25, n. 6 (769-70); *In Lev.*, h. 14, n. 1: "The history has been reported to us, and though its narration may seem obvious, nevertheless, its inner sense will scarcely be clear to us unless we follow out more diligently the content of what is there according to the letter" — "Historia nobis recitata est, cujus quamvis videatur aperta narratio, tamen, nisi diligentius continentiam ejus quae est secundum litteram consequamur, interior nobis sensus haud facile patebit.... Videamus ergo primo quid sibi velit historia quam proposuimus.... Haec est historiae continentia" (478-9). Rabanus, *In Lev.*, Bk. V, c. xi: "Sed diligentius haec secundum historiam intenda sunt"; *In Num.*, Bk. IV, c. vi (PL, CVIII, 436 B, 801 A).

41. Hilary, *Tr. myst.*, Bk. I, c. xxv: "They have all been written... so diligently" — "Omnia ita diligenter... scripta sunt" (116).

42. "pura veritas historiarum": Rabanus, *Cler. inst.*, Bk. III, c. i (PL, CVII, 377 B).

43. "veritate facti historialiter approbata": Gaudentius of Brescia, *Tr.* 9 (79): "Let us first explain the character of the fact itself" — "explanemus primum facti ipsius rationem" (86). Berengaud, *In Ap.*: "Understand spiritually the deeds you have read historically to have been done at first" — "Intellige spiritualiter ea quae primo tempore historialiter facta legisti," "understand spiritually what you have learned was done by the patriarchs" — "intellige spiritualiter quae a patriarchis facta cognovisti" (PL, XVII, 813 C, 822 C).

44. "Manente historia": Or., *In Num.*, h. 11, n. 2 (78). Rabanus, *In Num.*, Bk. II, c. xxii (PL, CVIII, 697 D).

45. "manente prius historiae veritate": *In Gal.* (PG, XIV, 1297 A); *De princ.*, Bk. IV, c. iii, n. 4: "It is evidently being decided by us that the truth of history both can and must be preserved in as many cases as possible" — "Evidenter a nobis decernitur in quam plurimis servari et posse et oportere historiae veritatem" (329).

46. Ps.-Primasius, *In Gal.* (PL, LXVIII, 536 D). Sedulius Scotus (CIII, 190 B). Claudius of Turin, *In Gal.* (CIV, 888 A); etc. Angelome, *To Leoticus:* "If we are not ... so that history may inculcate the truth of the facts and the reliability of the report" — "Nisi sumus... ut historia veritatem factorum ac fidem relationis inculcet" (MGH, *Ep.* 5, 622).

47. "servata quippe veritate historiae": *Mor.* (PL, LXXV, 545 A, cf. 729 B); "the truth of the history having been preserved" — "servata veritate historiae" (LXXVI, 112 B); *In Ez.*, Bk. I, h. 12, n. 1 (919 B); *In ev.*, Bk. II, h. 40, n. 1: "the truth of the history... within the words of sacred eloquence is to be preserved first" — "in verbis sacri eloquii... prius servanda est veritas historiae" (1302 A).

48. "litterae veritate servata": *Mor.* (PL, LXXV, 772 A).

49. *Civ. Dei*, Bk. XVII, c. iii, n. 2: "in so far as the truth of the history is first preserved" — "servata prius dumtaxat historiae veritate" (PL, XLI, 526). Richard, *De vinculis S. Petri:* "History is also to be embraced venerably according to the letter with due faith; yet... it does not seem unfitting if, the truth of the history having been preserved, we show how it can as a whole be understood spiritually" —

"digna prorsus fide historia est etiam juxta litteram venerabiliter amplectenda; verumtamen . . . non videtur incongruum si historiae veritate servata, quomodo spiritualiter tota possit intelligi demonstramus" (CXCI, 278-9).

50. *De princ.,* Bk. IV, c. iii, n. 4: "that it is both possible and necessary for the truth of history to be saved" — "servari et posse et oportere historiae veritatem" (329). Cf. Hervaeus, *In Is.,* Bk. V: "In holy Scripture even those things that can be taken historically are often to be understood spiritually, so that faith may be had in the truth of the history, and spiritual understanding may be taken of the mysteries of allegory; just as we believe that those things that are now reported of the king of the Assyrians and Hezekiah were truly done according to the history of that time, but yet prefigured others that were to be done in the New Testament" — "In Scriptura sacra et ea quae accipi secundum historiam possunt, plerumque spiritaliter intelligenda sunt, ut fides habeatur in veritate historiae, et spiritalis intelligentia capiatur de mysteriis allegoriae; sicut ea quae nunc de rege Assyriorum et Ezechia narrantur, veraciter quidem secundum historiam tunc temporis facta esse credimus, sed tamen alia, quae Novo Testamento facienda erant praefigurasse" (PL, CLXXXI, 335 D).

51. Jerome, *Ep.* 73, n. 10 (4, 26). Hilary, *In ps. CXXIV,* n. 13 (PL, IX, 758-9).

52. Heterius and Beatus, *Ad Elip.,* Bk. I, c. civ: "It is as though we completely kill our body and do not give it what it needs. . . . The soul will not be safe when it has unnaturally killed its own body. . . . The letter is like a man's body: the letter is the history itself" — "Tale est tanquam si corpus nostrum omnino occidimus et non damus ei quae necessaria sunt. . . . Jam non erit anima salva, quae corpus suum occidit contra naturam. . . . Littera est sicut corpus hominis: quae littera est ipsa historia" (PL, XCVI, 958 A).

53. Hugh, *Did.,* Bk. VI, n. 3 (PL, CLXXVI, 799-800).

54. "juxta historiam gesti": *Tr.* 9, n. 1 (75); *Tr.* 8: "knowing the true history of the deed, as was necessary" — "veram gesti historiam, ut oportuit, cognoscentes" (66).

55. "juxta fidem rerum gestarum": John Scotus, *In Jo.,* fr. 2 (PL, CXXII, 332 B); etc.

56. "ratio facti": Gaudentius, *Tr.* 8: "But before we reveal the spiritual knowledge, let us expound the character of the fact historically" — "Sed priusquam spiritalem scientiam revelemus, rationem facti historialiter exponamus" (64).

57. "veritas rei gestae": Paschasius, *In Matt.,* Bk. V: "that the figures of the allegories do nothing to diminish faith in the truth of the thing accomplished" — "allegoriarum figuras, de veritate rei gestae nihil ad fidem minuere" (PL, CXX, 338 D); "Henceforward that allegory of things that we spoke of is always prefigured mystically in such fashion that it is rightly believed that it takes away none of the deeds accomplished, since, taken typically, they do not cancel the truth of the deeds done" — "Porro allegoria rerum illa de qua diximus semper ita mystice figuratur, ut de rebus gestis nihil subtrahere jure credatur, quia non rerum factarum typice auferunt veritatem," etc. (339 C). Or., *In Jos.,* h. 11, n. 1: "These historically accomplished deeds" — "Haec secundum historiam quidem gesta," etc. (363).

58. Or., *In Gen.,* h. 2, n. 2: "to the extent that it pertains to the character of the history" — "quantum ad historiae pertinet rationem" (29-30).

Notes to Pages 45-46

59. Or., *De princ.*, Bk. IV, c. ii, n. 6: "Therefore, what great usefulness is to be found in this first so-called historical understanding!" — "Quanta igitur sit utilitas in hoc primo quem diximus historiali intellectu" (315); n. 5 and 8 (314, 321). *In Num.*, n. 28, n. 1: "These can be necessary to see and useful even as regards the letter" — "Possunt haec necessaria videri et utilia etiam secundum litteram" (281); *Sel. in Num.*: "This history is very usefulness even with respect to the literal sense" — "Etiam secundum litteralem sensum haec historia magnas habet utilitates" (PG, XII, 578 C); *C. Cels.*, Bk. I, c. xviii; Bk. IV, c. l (1, 69-70, 323). Rabanus, *In Num.*, Bk. III, c. ii: "You see how great the usefulness of even history itself is in the law of God" — "Vides quanta sit etiam historiae ipsius utilitas in lege Dei" (CVIII, 775 A).

60. "solius historiae virtus" — "virtus mystica": Greg., *Mor.*, Bk. XXII, c. xiii, n. 26: "but now, following the power of the history alone" — "sed nunc, solius historiae virtutem sequentes" (PL, LXXVI, 228 C); cf. c. xxiv, n. 56: "the opinions of blessed Job full of mystic power" — "beati Job plenas mystica virtute sententias" (250 A).

61. Jerome, *In ps. LXVII* (*An. mar.*, III, 1, 55).

62. Rabanus, *In Lev.*, Bk. VII, c. vi: "The letter, too, has no little instruction to offer" — "Habet autem et littera non parvam instructionem" (PL, CVIII, 533 B).

63. Hervaeus (?), *Exp. myst. l. Tobiae* (Morin, RB 24, 37-8).

64. "ipse nos aedificat textus historiae": Or., *In Lev.*, h. 3, n. 2: "So in this chapter he himself sufficiently . . ." — "Sufficienter ergo in hoc capite ipse . . ." (302-3); h. 3, n. 6: "This law ought to edify its hearers even regarding the letter" — "Quae lex etiam secundum litteram aedificare debet audientes" (311); *In Num.*, h. 20, n. 1: "But the very text of the history first builds us up" — "Sed nos primo ipse historiae textus aedificet" (186).

65. "juxta historiam, moralem sensum legentis haec ipsa res aedificat": Rupert, *In Ex.*, Bk. IV, c. xxxiv (PL, CLXVII, 734 D). Rabanus, *In Num.*, Bk. II, c. xxii: "What need is there to look for allegory in this, when even the letter is edifying?" — "Quid opus est in his allegoriam quaerere, cum aedificat etiam littera?" (CVIII, 697 A). Petrus Comestor, *s.* 4, on David and Abishag (III *Reg.* I): "On this point we are edified regarding the letter. . . . In this we are edified as to the letter in three ways. . . ." — "In quo aedificamur juxta litteram. . . . In quo ad litteram ad tria aedificamur" (CXCVIII, 1731 BC).

66. "aedificat enim me littera . . . ; antequam veniam ad spiritualem intelligentiam, miror in littera": *Brev. in ps.* (PL, XXVI, 1160 C). "On the surface of the letter the Book of Tobias is wholesome" — "Liber Tobiae in superficie litterae est salubris etc.": Richard, *L. except.*, P. II, Bk. IX, c. ii (Châtillon, 358) following Bede (PL, XCI, 923 CD) and the Gloss (CXIII, 725 BC).

67. Or., *Sel. in Ez.*, c. xxviii: "historia propriam rationem habet, — *tou echein tēn historian ton idion logon*" (PG, XIII, 821-2 C). [Trans. note: Here the Latin 'ratio' and its underlying Greek 'logos' (which de Lubac renders into French as 'raison') are translated 'character', to emphasize the objectively given basis for thinking or speaking about the event itself.]

68. "ordo historiae": Or., *De princ.*, Bk. IV, c. ii, n. 5, 6, 9 (314, 315, 321). *In Num.*, h. 5, n. 1: "If you have understood what the order of history contains" — "Si intellexisti quid historiae ordo contineat" (25).

69. "historiae intelligentia" — "intellectus litterae": Or., *In Num.*, h. 5, n. 1: "Let us first understand what is being related according to the letter, and then, with the Lord's help, let us ascend from an understanding of the letter to the spiritual understanding" — "Primo intelligamus ea quae secundum litteram referentur, et ita, praestante Domino, ab intellectu litterae ascendemus ad intelligentiam spiritalem" (24-5). Philip of Harvengt, *Ep.* 1 (PL, CCIII, 12 CD and 15 D).

70. "simplex intellectus": Ambrose, *De ben. patr.*, c. vii, n. 32: "The simple understanding involves the following" — "Simplex quidem intellectus hoc habet" (PL, XIV, 684 B).

71. "intellectus signatus in historia": Manegold, *In ps. LII* (PL, XCIII, 762 D).

72. Luke of Mont Cornillon, *In Cant. mor.* (PL, CCXIII, 498 C).

73. "Quisquis enim moralem et spiritalem intelligentiam in divinis Scripturis investigare desiderat, necesse est ut historiae intelligentiam prius possideat": Berengaud, *In Ap.*, v. 7 (PL, XVII, 960 D).

74. *In Is.*, Bk. V, c. xxiii (PL, XXIV, 201 D); Bk. II, c. v (83 A), etc.

75. Aug., *Doct. chr.*, Bk. II, c. xxviii, n. 42-4 (Combès-Farges, 504-6). Jerome, *In Dan.*, XI, 5 (25, 559).

76. "ut ex multorum librorum collatione veritas sacrae historiae pateat, et sensus narrationis ejus lectori lucidior fiat": *In I Mach., prol.*: "I want your holiness to know that I have stitched the work itself together partly from the divine history, partly from the tradition of Josephus the historian of the Jews, and partly from the histories of other nations, so that in this book mention might be made not only of the Jewish nation and its princes, but also likewise of the other nations, etc." — "Volo sanctitatem tuam scire quod ipsum opus ideo partim de divina historia, partim de Josephi Judaeorum historici traditione, partim vero de aliarum gentium historiis contexui, ut, quia non tantum gentis Judaeae ac principum ejus, sed et aliarum gentium similiter in ipso libro mentio fit, etc." (PL, CIX, 1128 B). Cf. Rupert (CLXVII, 445 B), etc.

77. Thus Fréculphe of Lisieux, *Chron.*: "Jussisti ut perscrutando diligenter volumina anitquorum seu hagiographorum, sive etiam gentilium scriptorum, quaecumque pertinet ad historiae veritatem breviter ac lucide colligere desudarem. . . . Quaestiones etiam difficiles . . . enodare non negligere, quantum attinet ad historiae veritatem" (PL, CVI, 917 BC).

78. "historiae gravitas": Peter of London, *Remediarium conversorum, prol.* (Wasselynck, 399).

79. Greg., *Mor.*: "Nevertheless we earnestly entreat him who lifts his mind to the spiritual understanding that he should not fall off from his veneration of the history" — "Haec tamen magnopere petimus, ut qui ad spiritalem intelligentiam mentem sublevat, a veneratione historiae non recedat" (PL, LXXV, 554 C).

80. Rupert, *In Job*: "But there are still mysteries of allegory to be tracked down with the things said in the veneration of the sacred history" — "Sed his dictis in veneratione sacrae historiae, mysteria jam indaganda sunt allegoriae" (PL, CLXVIII, 1089 C).

81. "sacrae lectionis historia": Greg., *In Ez.*, Bk. I, h. 6, n. 7: "He orders the jars to be filled with water, since first our hearts are to be filled through the history of

the sacred reading" — "Impleri hydrias aqua jubet, quia prius per sacrae lectionis historiam corda nostra replenda sunt" (PL, LXXVI, 831 B).

82. "sacra pagina" — "sacra historia": Greg., *Mor.*, Bk. II, c. xxvii, n. 46 (SC, 32, p. 214); *In Ez.*, Bk. II, h. 1, n. 12 (PL, LXXVI, 955 B).

83. "Si autem in hac historia nihil aliud posset inveniri quam quod nuda sonat littera, diligenda tamen nobis, et intimo amore esset amplectenda, quia nimirum haec eadem Rebecca, de qua narrat historia, quaedam, ut ita dicamus, linea vel materia fuit beati illius seminis, de quo Dominus Jesus naturam voluit assumere nostrae mortalitatis": *In Script.*, h. 1 (PL, CLXXIV, 1059 BC).

84. "profundisssima vallis historiae": Cf. John Scotus, *H. in Prol. Jo.* (PL, CXXII, 291 B). Aug., *In Jo.*, tr. 15, n. 10: "Jesus came . . . to the depths of this dwelling place of ours" — "Venit Jesus . . . ad profunditatem hujus habitationis nostrae" (CCL, 36, 154).

85. Paul Claudel, *Introduction au Livre de Ruth* (1938), 22; 21: the literal sense "is the very foundation" — "est le fondement même."

86. Cf. H. Goldhazen, *op. cit.*, 153: "For, generally speaking, as Hetius shows, the Fathers used to believe that the literal sense had been previously laid down as foundation" — "Generatim enim loquendo, uti demonstrat Huetius, Patres litteralem sensum tanquam fundamentum ante positum credebant."

87. He wrote in 1753, *De rebus christianorum ante Constantinum magnum Commentarii* (3rd cent., n. 28; 633), that Origen had at first refused to consider the grammatical and historical sense as the foundation of the mystical senses. More than one historian still depends upon Mosheim without knowing it.

88. "Videamus quae de (arca) secundum litteram referantur, . . . ut, cum hujuscemodi fundamenta jecerimus, ab historiae textu possimus ascendere ad spiritalis intelligentiae . . . sensum": *In Gen.*, h. 2, n. 1 (26); n. 3: "spiritalis aedificatio" (30).

89. "Prima (expositio) historica est, veluti fundamentum quoddam in inferioribus posita": *Ibid.*, n. 6 (36).

90. *Ibid.*, n. 3 (31).

91. 1 Cor. 3:11; Eph. 2:20.

92. "fundamentum fidei": *In Jos.*, h. 4, n. 3 (311).

93. E.g., at the beginning of our tradition, Greg., *Mor.*, Bk. XVIII, c. xxvi, n. 39 (PL, LXXVI, 588); Bk. XXVIII, c. v, n. 14-20 (455-60); *In Ez.*, Bk. II, h. 1, n. 5 (939 C). And toward the end: Hugh of Fouilloy, *De claustro animae*, Bk. III, c. xv: "In building the house of the Lord, first the foundation is laid, which, unless the earth be overturned and tossed up, is found firm: Let us not build upon earth, but upon rock; the rock was Christ" — "In aedificanda domo Domini, in primis fundamentum ponitur, quod nonnisi eversa et ejecta terra firmum reperitur, ne aedificemus super terram, sed supra petram; petra autem erat Christus" (CLXXVI, 1116 AB). Cf. Aug., *In ps. XXIX*, 9-10 (CCL 38, 180-2), etc.

94. Or., *In Jos.*, h. 9, n. 1: "So blessed are those who have built religious and holy structures upon such a noble foundation. But in this structure of the Church . . ." — "Beati ergo qui supra istud tam nobile fundamentum aedificia religiosa et sancta construxerint. Sed in hoc aedificio Ecclesiae" (347); etc.

95. *S.* 2, c. vi, n. 7: "But above all, brothers, in the name of the Lord we both admonish and command to the utmost of our power this: that when you hear the

sacrament of the Scripture telling what has happened, you first believe that what has been read has in fact happened exactly as it was read; lest, once the foundation of the accomplished fact has been removed, you attempt to build, as it were, in air" — "Ante omnia tamen, fratres, hoc in nomine Domini et admonemus, quantum possumus, et praecipimus, ut quando auditis exponi sacramentum Scripturae narrantis quae gesta sunt, prius illud quod lectum est credatis sic gestum, quomodo lectum est; ne, substracto fundamento rei gestae, quasi in aere quaeratis aedificare" (PL, XXXVIII, 30). Conceding a bit to the common prejudice, H. I. Marrou attributes this text to the influence of the school of Antioch as opposed to that of Alexandria: *S. Aug. et la fin de la culture antique* (1949), 493.

96. *S.* 8, n. 1: "Once the solidity of the facts has been established in the first place as a foundation, we ought to look into its significance; lest, after the foundation be removed, we seem to want to build on air" — "Prius in fundamento posita rerum gestarum firmitate, significantiam debemus inquirere; ne substracto fundamento, in aere velle aedificare videamur" (PL, XXXVIII, 67). *S. Frangipane*, 1, n. 2 (Morin, 170-1).

97. "Adde aedificium, noli tamen relinquere fundamentum": *In Jo.*, tr. 98, n. 7 (CCL, 36, 580). Cf. *Ep.* 93, c. viii (XXXIII, 334).

98. Thus Freppel, *Origène*, 2 (2nd ed., 1875), 163. At the least we can go further back than him; thus A. C., in *Corn. a Lap.* 21 (1875), XV; Paré, 223, note: "The fundamental role of history is already affirmed by St. Jerome, cf. 129, and in a more concealed fashion, by St. Augustine" — "Le rôle fondamental de l'historia est dejà affirmé par S. Jérôme, cf. 129, et d'une façon plus voilée, par saint Augustin": Spicq, 19-20; R. Baron, 1 1-2; De Bruyne, II, 305.

99. "historiae fundamenta": *In Jonam* (Antin, SC, 43, 54). *In Amos*, Bk. III, c. ix (PL, XXV, 1090 B). *In Ez.* (229 B, 244 C, 283 A, 412 A). *In Is.* (XXV, 229 B). Cf. *De ben. Jacob* (XXIII, 1308).

100. "historiae veritas, fundamentum intelligentiae spiritalis": *Ep.* 129, n. 6 (III, 173).

101. "super fundamenta historiae spirituale extruere aedificium": *In Is.* (PL, XXIV, 205 C).

102. "cum amaret historiam et illud veritatis diceret fundamentum, magis sequebatur intelligentiam spiritualem": *Ep.* 108, n. 26 (PL, XXII, 902). In *Ep.* 58, c. ix, the "fundamentum" is the science of Scriptures: text cited by Benedict XV in his encyclical *Sp. Paracletus*.

103. "super fundamentum historiae": *An. mar.*, III, 3, 105.

104. *Mor., ep. miss.*, c. iii: "Primum quidem fundamentum historiae ponimus" (SC, 118).

105. *Mor.*, Bk. XXIII, c. i, n. 1: "so that . . . the building of the doctrine may rise so much the stronger by as much as the foundation is more zealously put in mind from the considered origin of the cause" — "ut . . . tanto robustius surgat doctrinae aedificium quanto ex considerata causae origine studiosius ponitur in mente fundamentum" (PL, LXXVI, 249 B). Curious inversion of the metaphor, *In I Reg. proem.*, n. 5, where the "solidum fundamentum" of the historical and moral senses comes from allegory, because "in salute fidelium fides operibus prior est" (LXXIX, 22 C).

106. "Debemus prius historiae radicem figere, ut valeamus mentem post-

modum de allegoriarum fructu satiare": *Mor., Praef.,* n. 21 (SC, 141); Bk. VI, c. i, n. 2: "so that it may sprout the spiritual fruits of allegory, which the truth of history nevertheless produces from the root" — "ut spiritales fructus allegoriae germinet, quos tamen ex radice historiae veritas producit" (PL, LXXV, 730 C). *In Ez.,* Bk. I, h. 2, n. 1: "historiae radicem figat" (LXXVI, 795 C). *In ev.,* Bk. II, h. 40, n. 1: "Tunc namque allegoriae fructus suaviter carpitis, cum prius per historiam in veritatis radice solidatur" (1302 A). With regard to the faith, Paulinus of Aquilaea will unite the two images, *Libellus sacr. c. Elip.:* "super fidei fundamentum firmiter radicatum" (XCIX, 154 C; cf. B).

107. "praecedente historiae fundamento": *Myst. exp. sacr., praef.* (PL, LXXXIII, 208 B); *De eccl. off.,* Bk. I, c. l, h. 2: "The former old law is the root; the latter, new one is like fruit growing from the root" — "Illa lex vetus radix est, haec nova velut fructus ex radice" (745 C).

108. "transmissa historiae radice": *In Sam.,* Bk. III, c. iii: "let us climb to seize the sweet-smelling fruits of spiritual allegory" — "ad carpenda allegoriae spiritualis odorifera poma scandamus" (PL, XCI, 624 B).

109. "Prius historiae fundamenta ponenda sunt": Alcuin (PL, C, 559 A). Adrevald (XX, 715 B).

110. *Notatio* (PL, CXXXI, 996 D).

111. "historia, fundamentum omnis intelligentiae": *In Matt.* (PL, CVI, 1262 C).

112. *Cler. inst.,* Bk. II, c. liii, as Isidore (PL, CVII, 365 C); *In Ez.,* Bk. I, c. i: "to show the truth more solidly, let him first plant the root of history and afterwards, through signs and allegories, bring forth the fruits of the spirit" — "quatenus ad veritatem solidius oste[a]ndendam, ante historiae radicem figat, et post fructus spiritus per signa et allegorias proferat" (CX, 498 D).

113. "Primum historiae fundamenta jacienda sunt": *In Ez.,* Bk. XIII (PL, CX, 867 A); Bk. I (498 D); Bk. VII (685 B); Bk. XI (801 A); *In Num.,* Bk. II, c. xix (CVIII, 685 D); *In Par.,* Bk. IV, c. xxvii (CIX, 514 B); *In Gen.* (CVII, 655 A), Bk. IV, c. xiv (654-5).

114. *In Gen.:* "The foundations of the history are to be laid down first" — "Prius historiae fundamenta ponenda sunt" (PL, CXV, 232 C).

115. *In I Reg., praef.:* "prius fundamenta ipsius historiae" (CXV, 248 B).

116. "Polliciti sumus prius fundamenta historiae ponere": *In I Reg.,* c. i (CXV, 248 C).

117. *Adv. Graec. calumnias,* c. xxxviii (PL, CXLIII, 955 A).

118. "fluitare permittitur": *In Gen.,* Bk. I, c. xxvi: "Here we are seeking the sense of the letter, so that we may hold on to the sure foundation of history" — "Hic nos litterae sensum quaerimus, ut certum historiae fundamentum teneamus" (PL, CLXVII, 221 C). *In Matt., prol.* (CLXVIII, 1307). *In Cant., prol.:* "Non ignoro quantum vel quale susceperim negotium, sc. historiae sive rei gestae aliquod ponere fundamentum et super illud magnum, quod sub istis vocibus continetur, superaedificare mysterium. Tunc enim expositio mystica firmius stat, neque fluitare permittitur, si super historiam certi temporis vel rei demonstrabilis rationaliter superaedificata continetur" (PL, CLXVII, 838).

119. PL, CLXVII, 716 A.

120. *In Is.,* Bk. I: "to show the truth more solidly, let him first plant the root of history and afterwards, through signs and allegories, bring forth the fruits of the

Spirit" — "ad veritatem solidius ostendendam, ante historiae radicem figat et post fructus Spiritus per signa et allegorias proferat" (PL, CLXXXI, 17 A).

121. *In Lev.*, Bk. X, c. i: "But the threshold of the Temple is the historical sense in the Scriptures" — "Limen vero templi, sensus historicus est in Scripturis" (MBVP, 17, 142 D).

122. Ps.-Hildebert, *s.* 60 (PL, CLXXI, 634-5).

123. "Primo . . . rei gestae veritatem quasi historiam figamus radicem": *Exp. in Hexaem.* (PL, CLXXVIII, 731 D); "juxta radicem historiae" (770 B).

124. "fundamentum et principium doctrinae sacrae, historia est": *Didasc.*, Bk. VI, c. iii (PL, CLXXVI, 801 C).

125. "Neque ego te perfecte subtilem posse fieri puto in allegoria, nisi prius fundatus fueris in historia": *Ibid.* (799 C); c. iv: "primum fundamento posito" (802 B); "jam historiae fundamenta in te locata sunt" (803 C; cf. 804-5).

126. "Historiam nunc in manibus habemus, quasi fundamentum omnis doctrinae primum in memoria collocandum. Sed quia . . . memoria brevitate gaudet, gesta autem temporum infinita pene sunt, oportet nos ex omnibus brevem quamdam summam colligere, quasi fundamentum fundamenti, id est primum fundamentum, quam facile possit animus comprehendere et memoria retinere": *De trib. max. circ.* (W. M. Green, *Speculum* 18, 491).

127. "quasi inchoando fundamentum aedificii jactat": PL, CXII, 849-50.

128. "Historia fundamentum est": PL, CXCVIII, 1054.

129. Adam Scotus, *De trip. tab.* (PL, CXCVIII, 627 A).

130. *Ibid.* (631 D).

131. C. xiv: "Lean often upon the divine eloquence of holy Scripture; this must be your first foundation" — "Saepe divino sacrae Scripturae eloquio incumbe; hoc tuum primum esse debet fundamentum etc." (PL, CLXXXIV, 1194 D).

132. "super vacuum et inane": *In vis. Ez., prol.*: "To many the divine Scriptures grow much sweeter when they can perceive something fitting in them regarding the literal understanding. At that point, as it seems to them, the structure of the spiritual understanding is more firmly established, when it is aptly founded in something solid belonging to the historical sense. For who can found anything solid or establish it firmly on something empty and void?" — "Multis divinae Scripturae multo amplius dulcescunt, quando congruum in eis aliquem secundum litteram intellectum percipere possunt. Et tunc, ut eis videtur, spiritualis intelligentiae structura firmius statuitur, quando in historici sensus solido apte fundatur. Super vacuum enim et inane quis possit solidum aliquid fundare, vel firmiter statuere?" (PL, CXCVI, 527 AB). See Chapter 15 below.

133. *Tr. de operibus:* "The things that are found in the Scripture persuade us to understand these things spiritually, although they do not remove the foundation of the letter" — "Quae in hac Scriptura inveniuntur, nos haec spiritaliter intelligere persuadent, licet fundamentum litterae non avellant" (PL, CLXXXIX, 1523 D).

134. *Hexaem.:* "But in that we relate many things to morals, and, enumerating the affections of the inner man, we stay longer in that part which stands out, we in no way abolish the history, which is the foundation of Scripture; nor do we do violence to the letter by twisting its proper character in some other direction" — "Quod autem ad mores multa referimus et interioris hominis affectiones enu-

merantes, in illa diutius parte quae praestat moramur, nequaquam abolemus historiam, quae Scripturae fundamentum est; nec vim facimus litterae, proprietatem ejus in sensum alium retorquentes" (PL, CLXXXIX, 1529 C).

135. *Alleg. sup. tab. Moysi, prol.:* "if the foundation of history has not been laid down . . . the whole edifice of spiritual understanding changes" — "non supposito historiae fundamento . . . totum spiritualis intelligentiae aedificium mutat" (2).

136. "in construendo litterae fundamento probatissimum": *Ep.* 143 (PL, CXCIX, 125 C).

137. *De peregr. civ. Dei,* tr. 1: "We have introduced these matters about laying down the history of the old Testament, so that we may build securely on a solid foundation" — "Haec de historia veteris Testamenti ponenda duximus, ut solido fundamento secure superaedificemus" (PL, CCIV, 256 D).

138. "fundamentum allegoriae": Smalley, *Speculum* 6, 63. Cf. Joachim of Flora, *Sup. quat. ev.:* "The book of the generation. . . . At the beginning of this reading of the holy Gospel, it behooves us to lay down for its exposition a foundation strong enough to sustain the fabric of its whole understanding" — "Liber generationis. . . . In exordio sacrae hujus lectionis evangelicae, tale nos oportet in expositione ipsius jacere fundamentum, quod valeat totius intelligentiae fabricam sustinere" (Buon., 33; cf. 49).

139. *S.* 4, *de Pascha* (PL, CCX, 209 C).

140. "Et ideo studere veritati sensus litteralis adeo necessarium est, quod sine hoc fundamento impossibile est quemquam perfectum fieri in sensu spirituali": Daguillon, p. 56.

141. *In I Sent., prol.* (14).

142. "Sensus vero historicus seu litteralis est fundamentum seu basis intellectuum aliorum": *Op. omnia,* t. V, 389.

143. "Sunt in Scriptura sacra typus atque figura
Jure sequenda, sed non est vilis habenda
Rerum gestarum narratio, textus earum:
Ut fundamenta typici sensus documenta
Debent portare, res vocibus insinuare."

Wattenbach, *SB d. Münch. Akad d. Wissenschaften, hist.-philos. Klasse* (1873), 701 (in Glunz, 1937, 185).

144. "Fundamentum solet in aedificio ab imperitis contemni. . . . Totum tamen quidquid te delectat in arbore, de radice surrexit": *In Jo.,* tr. 40, n. 8 (CCL, 36, 354).

Notes to Chapter Seven
§2. Particularities of Language

1. Rom. 7:6.
2. Ambrose, *In ps. XXXVI,* n. 80 (PL, XIV, 1007-8), etc. See Chapter 5 above.
3. "et litteram et spiritum in Scripturis sanctis defendimus": *In Lev.,* h. 14, n. 2 (480). Cf. Pamphilus, *Apol. for Origen* (PG, XVII, 595).

4. "Aliud quam erant illa omnia significaverunt, sed tamen etiam ipsa corporaliter fuerunt": *Gen. litt.*, Bk. VIII, c. iv, n. 8 (PL, XXXIV, 375); inversely, *In ps. III*, n. 1: "Though they can be taken historically . . . , nevertheless spiritually . . ." — "Quanquam historice possit accipi . . . , tamen spiritaliter . . ." (CCL, 38, 7).

5. "historicam simul et allegoricam scientiam": *Sup. Par. Sal.*, Bk. I, c. ix (PL, XCI, 968 B).

6. "utrumque suscipimus": PL, CLXVII, 1433 C: "For since we take up both, namely the truth of history and the understanding of allegory, we truly have a wheel within a wheel" — "Cum enim utrumque, sc. veritatem historiae et intelligentiam suscipiamus allegoriae, rotam veraciter habemus in medio rotae."

7. "in veritate historiae": *In Ex.*, Bk. II, c. xxxii: "Just as this was done in the truth of history, so too has it been done through Christ in the fullness of spiritual grace till now and is being done continuously" — "Hoc sicut in veritate historiae factum est, ita veraciter in abundantia spiritalis gratiae per Christum hactenus factum est et fit jugiter" (PL, CLXVII, 640-1; cf. 1489 BC).

8. "littera" — "littera sola": Or., *In Gen.*, h. 6, n. 1: "If someone wants to hear and understand these things according to the letter alone" — "Si quis haec secundum litteram solam audire vult et intelligere" (66); *In Ex.*, h. 7, n. 3: "If we follow the history alone" — "Si historiam solam sequamur" (208); *In Lev.*, h. 4, n. 5: "If he thinks of them only according to the letter" — "Si hos tantum secundum litteram putat" (321); *De Princ.*, Bk. IV, c. iii, n. 4: The Holy Spirit "has deigned to give us the divine scriptures not so that we can be edified from the letter alone or in everything stemming from it" — "(Sp. sanctus) nobis scripturas divinas donare dignatus est, non ut ex sola littera vel in omnibus ex ea aedificari possimus . . ." (328). *In ps. XXXVI*, h. 3, n 6 (PG, XII, 1341 B).

9. "sola superficies litterae": Hervaeus, *In Jo.*, Bk. VII (PL, CLXXXI, 506 A).

10. "proprietas tantummodo litterae" — "litterae sectatores" — "secundum solam litteram intelligentes": *In Jos.*, h. 6, n. 1: "If the law is to be understood according to the letter alone . . ." — "Quod si secundum litteram solam intelligenda sit lex" (323), etc. Aug., *In ps. LXVII*, n. 9 (CCL, 39, 874). Ambrose, *In Luc.* (PL, XV, 1676 B). Candidus of Fulda, *De pass. Dom.*, c. xix (CVI, 100 A). Raoul of Saint Germain, *In Lev.*, Bk. X, c. i (143 D). Maurice of Sully (CLXXI, 172 C).

11. "Non in his solius litterae conterenda est sententia": Or., *In Num.*, h. 17, n. 4 (159). Othloh, *L. de cursu sp.*, c. xviii: "So I have said this for the sake of certain simple folk who are friends of the letter alone and not of the spiritual understanding" — "Haec igitur propter quosdam simplices et litterae solius, non autem intelligentiae spiritualis amicos dixi" (PL, CXXXIII, 206 B).

12. Jerome, *In Ez.*, XLVII, 12 (PL, XXV, 475 C). Rabanus Maurus, *In Lev.*, Bk. IV, c. iv: "Hence we must not aim at the letter alone but at the fruit of the spirit" — "Unde non nos oportet ad solam intendere litteram, sed ad fructum spiritus etc." (CVIII, 388 C). Hervaeus, *In Is.*, Bk. VII: "Hence it is clear that that wisdom is to be followed which exists not in the leaves and the flower of words, but in the pith and fruits of the senses" — "Unde patet eam sectandam esse sapientiam, quae non est in foliis et flore verborum, sed in medullis et fructibus sensuum" (CLXXXI, 505 D); Bk. VIII: "Blind men tapping on holy Scriptures like a wall, seeking only their words and the leaves, not the fruit or the sense which is held within the letters" — "Scripturas sacras quasi parietem caeci palpantes verba

tantum earum et folia, non fructum vel sensum qui tenetur in litteris quaerentes" (536 B). *Glossa in Job.*, according to Bede: "History excels allegory as much as apples excel leaves" — "Quantum pomi foliis, tantum historia allegoriae praecellit" (CXIII, 725 B). Cf. Isidore, *L. de var. q.*, c. ii (8). Irenaeus, *Adv. Haer.*, Bk. IV, c. iv, n. 2: the vine shoot and the grape cluster (PG, VII, 982 A).

13. Greg., *In Ez.*, Bk. I, h. 6, n. 3: "That Gentile people has in mind precepts that the Jewish people could not have while it regarded the mere letter in those precepts" — "Ille gentilis populus praecepta tenet in mente, quae Judaicus populus habere non potuit, dum solam in eis litteram attendit" (PL, LXXVI, 830 A), etc.

14. "post adventum Veritatis adhuc umbram sequuntur": *In Ex.*, tr. 2: "Therefore as often as we receive salvation from the extinct Egyptians by calling upon the Lord, let us learn to eat the Passover not like the stupid Jews, who, after the coming of the Truth, follow a shadow. . . . For, as the Apostle says, the Law is spiritual, and our Passover, the Christ, has been sacrificed" — "Quotquot igitur invocantes Dominum salutem recipimus extinctis Aegyptiis, discamus manducare pascham non sicut insipientes Judaei, qui post adventum Veritatis umbram sequuntur. . . . Lex enim spiritalis est, ut ait Apostolus, et pascha nostrum immolatus est Christus" (25).

15. "qui amant historiam, qui solam judaicam sequuntur sententiam, qui sequuntur occidentem litteram et non vivificantem spiritum": *In Marc. (An. mar.*, III, 2, 348). *Ibid.*, 350-1, on the transfiguration: "For if you follow the letter Judaically, what advantage is it for you to read . . . ? If, however, you understand spiritually . . ." — "Si enim litteram judaice sequaris, quid tibi prodest legere, etc.? Sin autem spiritaliter intelligas . . ."; 417-8, *In Pascha*: "You have the Scriptures, but not the understanding of the Scriptures. . . . You grasp the pages, but we grasp the sense of the pages. You fold together the skins of dead animals; we possess the life-giving spirit" — "Vos habetis Scripturas, et non intelligentiam Scripturarum. . . . Vos tenetis paginas, nos sensum paginarum. Vos complicatis membranas animalium mortuorum, nos possidemus spiritum vivificantem." *In Ez.*: "The Jews having the letter of the law and we the spirit" — "Habentibus Judaeis legis litteram et nobis spiritum" (PL, XXV, 480 D). Same theme in Aug., see Chapter 5.3 above.

16. "simplicem tantum et occidentem sequuntur historiam": *In Jer.* (PL, XXIV, 766 D). Cf. *In Is.* (335 A).

17. "observantiae carnales valde malae sunt, intelligentiae spirituales valde bonae sunt": Serlon of Savigny, *s.* 2 *in Pent.* (Tissier, 6, 108).

18. The interpretation given by Aug., outside the exegetical context, in the *De sp. et littera* (PL, XLIV, 199-246) is well known, but he himself recognized the legitimacy of the exegetical sense when he says, c. iv, n. 6: "So the Apostle's saying 'The letter killeth' is not to be understood *only* in that way" — "Non ergo *solo* illo modo intelligendum est quod ait Apostolus, Littera occidet" (203). Cf. Aimon, *In I Cor.*: "It is to be understood in two ways. The letter of the Mosaic law kills a man in bodily fashion, by commanding and not helping. . . . In the other way. Before the coming of the Lord. . . ." — "Duobus modis est intelligendum. Littera legis mosaicae occidit hominem corporaliter, jubendo et non juvando. . . . Aliter. Ante Domini Adventum etc." (CXVII, 617-8).

19. "narratio rerum gestarum" — "scriptura legalis": Or., *De princ.*, Bk. IV, c. ii, n. 8 (320-1).

20. *Ep.* 75, n. 15 (Hartel, 2, 820). Cf. Richard: "What, pray, were the sacrifices if not a figure of the passion and death of Christ, and thereby sacraments of the same?" — "Quid, quaeso, fuerunt sacrificia, nisi passionis Christi et mortis figura, eo ipso ejusdem sacramenta?" (PL, CXCVI, 670 C).

21. *In Jud.*, h. 2, n. 5 (478). *In Gen.*, h. 10, n. 2: "Do you think that these are fables and that the Holy Spirit reports histories in the Scriptures?" — "Haec fabulas putatis esse, et historias narrare in Scripturis Spiritum sanctum?"; n. 4: "In these things histories are not reported but mysteries are involved" — "In his non historiae narrantur sed mysteria contexuntur" (XCV, 98); etc. From generation to generation, for two centuries, historians have skipped over an erroneous interpretation of such texts, which could have been avoided with a slightly more attentive reading. See, e.g., Lumper, X, 127.

22. "Jam non species agni, sed est veritas corporis Christi": *De Cain et Abel*, Bk. II, c. vi, n. 19 (PL, XIV, 350 D). Or *In Luc.*: "he who was merely able to build God a temple in species or to figure Christ's Church in mystery" — "qui tantum meruit ut vel in specie templu[m] Deo conderet, vel in mysterio Christi Ecclesiam figuraret" (XV, 1731 C).

23. Or Rabanus, *In Paral.*, Bk. II, c. xxiv: "They have been transferred from the tribe of Judah and the figural observance of the law and the ceremonies to the truth of the Gospel and the cult of the New Testament" — "De gente Judaea et figurali legis ac caeremoniarum observantia, ad veritatem evangelii et novi Testamenti translati sunt cultum" (PL, CIX, 392 C); Bk. III, c. iv: "Transferring the very words of sacred eloquence from history to allegory and from shadow into truth" — "Ipsa enim verba sacri eloquii ab historia ad allegoriam et ab umbra in veritatem transferentes" (457 C).

24. "Caro concupiscit adversus spiritum, id est, historia et Scripturae carneus intellectus, contra allegoriam et spiritualem doctrinam": *In Gal.*, Bk. III, c. xv, v. 17: "Spirit is against the flesh, i.e., the truth of the shadow opposes the higher things to the cast-offs, eternal things to the brief" — "Spiritus autem adversus carnem, id est, sublimiora dejectis, aeterna brevibus, umbrae veritas refragatur" (PL, XXVI, 413 AB).

25. *De ut. cred.*, c. iii, n. 5: "(Scripture is handed on) allegorically when it is taught that certain things that have been written are not to be taken literally but are to be understood figuratively" — "Secundum allegoriam (traditur Scriptura) cum docetur non ad litteram esse accipienda quaedam quae scripta sunt, sed figurate intelligenda" (Pegon, 218). Cf. n. 8 (222-5) for the three examples: sign of Jonah, 1 Cor. 10:1-11, Gal. 4:22-6.

26. "Figurae istae non res ipsae fuerunt": *C. Maximinum*, Bk. II, c. xxv, n. 9 (PL, XLII, 811).

27. "per umbrarum imaginaria": *Doct. chr.*, Bk. II, c. xli, n. 62: "Let them therefore remember those who used to celebrate the Pasch at that time through the appearances of shadows" — "Meminerint ergo eorum qui pascha illo tempore per umbra[ru]m imaginaria celebrabant" (C. F., 334). Cf. St. Columban, *Instr.* 6, c. ii: "umbra imaginativae vitae" (Walker, 88).

28. "allegoricae narrationes": *C. Faust.*, Bk. XXII, c. xcv: "these allegorical re-

ports of the deeds accomplished" — "has autem rerum gestarum allegoricas narrationes" (PL, XLII, 463).

29. "Ne arbitremini nobis narrari praeterita, sed potius futura praedici" — "quia illa quoque miracula cum in illo populo fierent, praesentia quidem, sed non sine futurorum significatione gerebantur": *In ps. CXIII*, n. 1 (PL, XXXVII, 1476); Gloss, *In ps.* (CXIII, 1034 D). Cf. *In ps. CVII*, n. 2 (CCL, 40, 1584).

30. "Evacuatur namque in Christo, non Vetus Testamentum, sed velamen ejus, ut per Christum intelligatur, et quasi denudetur quod sine Christo obscurum atque adopertum est": C. iii, n. 9 (Pegon, 228).

31. "Non tamen quisquam putare debet . . . haec [omnino] gesta non esse, sed solas esse verborum figuras": *Civ. Dei*, Bk. XV, c. xxvii, n. 1 (PL, XLI, 473). [Trans. note: The text of de Lubac prints "animo" ("in the mind") instead of the received reading "omnino" ("at all").]

32. "non tam historia quam prophetia" — "simplex veraque littera, sed alta nimis et multiplicitate occultorum sensuum profunda": *In I Reg. proem.*, n. 4 (PL, LXXIX, 20 C). Prosper, *In ps. CXIII*, 1-3: "Things to come are hinted at through prophetic eloquence more than things past are repeated" — "Per propheticum eloquium magis futura indicantur quam praeterita retexuntur" (LI, 326 A).

33. *Adv. Haer.*, Bk. IV, c. xiv, n. 3 (PG, VII, 1012 A).

34. *In Lev.*, h. 8, n. 5 (401-2); h. 9, n. 2, citing Heb. 7:27 and Ps. 109:4: "This whole topic of the Apostle shows that the things that have been written in the law are the models and forms of things living and true" — "Omnis hic locus Apostoli, exemplaria et formas ostendit esse rerum vivarum et verarum, illa quae in lege scripta sunt" (419). *In Jos.*, h. 26, n. 3: "a figure and image of the true altar" — "figura et imago veri altaris" (461); h. 13, n. 1 (371), etc. Jerome, *Ad Aug.*: "The truth has been made through Jesus Christ to stand in for the shadows and images of the Old Testament" — "Pro umbris et imaginibus veteris Testamenti, Veritas per Jesum Christum facta est" (Aug., *Ep.* 75, c. iv, n. 14; PL, XXXIII, 258). Gaudentius, *In Ex.*, tr. 1: "For Christ the Truth has come; he has distributed for us now in truth the goods that he had done before the Jews in shadowy fashion" — "Veritas enim Christus advenit, bona quae ante Judaeis fecit umbraliter, nobis nunc in veritate largitus est" (20-1). Filaster, *Hacr.* 119, n. 4: "What is celebrated by way of shadow in the Law" — "Quod in lege per umbram celebratur" (CCL, 9, 283). When one reads in Or., *In Jos.*, h. 17, n. 2 (402): "the truth is deformed in the shadow of the Law" — "in umbra legis veritas deformatur," each of these four words runs the risk of being misunderstood by a modern.

35. "Omnia quae facta sunt illis in figura, nobis eveniunt in veritate": *In I Cor.* (PL, CXVII, 558 C).

36. Rabanus, *In Ex.*, Bk. III, c. ii: "Hic apparet quantum praecellat umbrae veteris Legis veritas Evangelii" (PL, CVIII, 126 D).

37. "pontifex verus" — "pontifex imaginarius": *In Jos.*, Bk. III, c. xiv (PL, CVIII, 1110 B). Or., *In Jos.*, h. 26, n. 3 (463).

38. "lex imaginaria" — "res imaginariae" — "historia rei gestae" — "imaginalis praefiguratio": *Tr.* 10, 2, 11 (109, 114, 13, 117).

39. "Dicitur ergo ad principem Judaeorum, ut convertatur de Lege ad Evangelium, et *victimarum imaginibus* derelictis, transferat se ad spiritalis sacrificii veritatem": *In Is.* (PL, XXIV, 275 B); *id.*: Hervaeus, *In Is.* (CLXXXI, 220 C).

40. *In Ex.*, Bk. II, c. xxii: "Whoever is still a wanderer and not yet in the household of the faith, whether he be pagan, or heretic, or even a false Jew" — "Quisquis adhuc peregrinus et nondum domesticus fidei est, sive ille paganus, sive sit haereticus, aut certo falsus Judaeus" (PL, CLXVII, 630 D).

41. "manna umbratricum" — "manna verum": "He gave the shadow-manna only to the Jews, but he gives the true manna . . . to all flesh" — "Solis Judaeis dedit manna umbraticum, sed omni carni . . . manna verum dat" (PL, CXCIV, 904 C). Peter Comestor: "a shadowy gate" — "porta umbratilis" (CLXXI, 743 A). Rupert, *In Ex.*: "a typic and shadowy dwelling-place" — "typicum et umbraticum tabernaculum" (CLXVII, 718 B). Cf. St. Leo, s. 58, c. 1, opposing "sign-sheep" — "ovis significativa" and "true sheep" — "ovis vera" (LIV, 332 D).

42. "victoria figuralis et mystica" — "victoria vera": PL, CXCIV, 955 B, 997 C: "therefore, since holy Scripture as a whole is a book of wars of the Lord" — "cum ergo sacra Scriptura tota sit liber bellorum Domini." *Exp. sup. canonem*, regarding Abel and the Patriarchs: "if you wanted to understand only the figurative features" — "si sola figuralia volueris intelligere" (*Op. in.*, I, 55).

43. "Typica illa et legalis historia": Absalon, s. 24 (PL, CCXI, 143 D).

44. "aliter non potest litterae ratio stare": Petrus Alphonsus, *Dial.* (PL, CLVII, 553 A; cf. C). Peter Damian, *Ep.*, Bk. II, ep. 13 (CXLIV, 280 AB). Raoul of Saint Germain, *In Lev.*, Bk. X, c. 1 (143 DE). Garnier, s. 26 (PL, CCV, 741 A); etc. The argument comes from Origen and Augustine, *Civ. Dei*, Bk. XV, c. xxvii, n. 1 (XLI, 473); *Spec., praef.* (XXXIV, 887-9); etc.

45. "non tam historicis narrationibus, quam rebus et sensibus mysticis servientem": *In Gen.*, Bk. III (PL, L, 1025 CD). Or., *In Gen.*, h. 15, n. 1: "and serving not so much for historical reports as for the things themselves and their mystic senses" — "neque tantum historicis narrationibus quantum rebus et sensibus mysticis servientes" (127); *In Jos.*, h. 8, n. 5: "You see that the things that follow pertain more to the truth of the mystery than to that of the history" — "Vides quia haec quae sequuntur, magis ad mysterii quam ad historiae pertinent veritatem" (340). Irimbert, *In Jud.*, Bk. II: "For while holy Scripture reports the history of past affairs, it is also weaving the prophecy of things to come" — "Sancta enim Scriptura, dum quasi rerum praeteritarum narrat historiam, rerum futurarum texit prophetiam" (Pez, 4, 363).

46. *In Reg.*, Bk. II: "What seems marvelous in the history. . . . But those who diligently pay attention to the allegory . . ." — "Quod mirum videtur in historia. . . . Sed qui diligenter ad allegoriam intendunt . . ." (PL, L, 1094 A); *In Gen.*, Bk. III: "Then he removed the shadows and images with which the history of the law was covered" — "Tunc amovit umbras et imagines, quibus legis operiebatur historia" (992 C). John Scotus, *In Jo.*, fr. 1: "The Law . . . is nothing other than a sort of shadow and symbol of the New Testament" — "Lex . . . nihil aliud est, nisi umbra quaedam et symbolum novi Testamenti" (CXXII, 300 A); etc.

47. Ps.-Hugo, *In Gal.*, q. 42: "in such contexts the verb *esse* ('to be') stands for *significare* ('to mean')" — "hoc verbum esse, in hujusmodi locis, ponitur pro significare" (PL, CLXXV, 564 B).

48. The monk of Farne, *Med. ad crucifixum*: "Thou art Adam. . . . Thou art Jacob. . . . Thou art Moses. . . . Thou art illustrious Jonathan . . ." — "Tu es Adam. . . .

Tu es Jacob.... Tu es Moyses.... Tu es illustris Jonathas..." (H. Farmer, *St. ans.*, 41, 159-65).

49. *Ibid.*, c. xlii: "I shall be able to take the arms or outstretched hands of Christ allegorically as the Law or the Prophets" — "Allegorice igitur brachia vel manus Christi expansas, Legem vel Prophetas accipere potero" (183).

50. "Virtutum opera ex magna parte juxta solius historiae textum tenemus, ne si haec ad indaganda mysteria trahimus, veritatem fortasse operis vacuare videamur...": *Mor.*, Bk. XX, c. xli, n. 19 (PL, LXXVI, 188 A). Cf. Joachim of Flora, *Concordia*, Bk. 5, c. lxiii: "significativum David" (fol. 93, 3).

51. "By the breasts are meant the two Testaments of the Church, by which her sons are nourished on the milk of the letter and of allegory. The Jewish people... sucked on the one; the Christian people is sucking on the other: the former [sucked on] the letter, we [suck on] the allegory" — "Per ubera Ecclesiae duo Testamenta accipiuntur, per quae filii ejus lacte litterae et allegoriae nutriuntur. Unum ... suxit populus judaicus, aliud sugit populus christianus; ille litteram, nos allegoriam" (PL, CLXXII, 893 D). One will note the past tense: "suxit."

52. *In ps.:* "It is the custom of prophecy to begin with history for a while, but then it crosses over to mystery" — "Mos est prophetiae ab historia incipere interdum, sed inde transit ad mysterium" (PL, CXCIII, 669 C).

53. Cf. St. Maximus, *Scholia in Dion, ep.* 9 (PG, IV, 568 D).

54. Greg., *Mor.*, Bk. XXI, c. 1, n. 1: "So many of the judgments of [sacred eloquence] are pregnant with the conception of allegories that whoever is taken as holding them to the history alone is deprived of understanding them through his own lack of care" — "Multa quippe ejus (sacri eloquii) sententiae tanta allegoriarum conceptione sunt gravida, ut quisquis eas ad solam tenere historiam actitur, earum notitia per suam incuriam privetur" (PL, LXXVI, 187 B). Cf. *Brev. in ps. LXXX:* "I ask you, who follow merely the letter" — "Requiro te, qui tantum litteram sequeris" (XXVI, 1060 A). Peter of Blois, *C. perf. Jud.*, c. xxv (CCVII, 855 B); etc.

55. Bede, *Hexaem.*, Bk. IV: "With these words (Gal. 4:30) he obviously shows that he is teaching that neither Scripture nor the writers of the Old Testament are to be driven from the precincts of the Church as the slave-girl and her son; but he says that the carnal observance of that Testament is to cease after the grace and freedom of the Gospel have shone in through Christ, and is to be fulfilled faithfully once changed by the inheritors of the New Testament into the spiritual sense" — "Quibus verbis (Gal. 4:30) patenter ostendit quia non Scripturam neque scriptores Testamenti veteris quasi ancillam et filium ejus de finibus Ecclesiae pellendos esse docet; sed carnalem ejusdem Testamenti observantiam, postquam per Christum gratia et libertas Evangelii illuxit, dicit esse cessaturam, atque in spiritalem sensum immutatam ab haeredibus novi Testamenti fideliter implendam" (PL, XCI, 188 C). Peter of Blois (CCVII, 855 D).

56. Isidore: "Every earthly activity has a hidden power for understanding the grace of Christ, which ... has been revealed by the New Testament" — "Omnis terrena operatio habet occultam virtutem intelligendae gratiae Christi, quae ... novo Testamento revelata est"; but the Jews keep a superseded Law (PL, LXXXIII, 225 AB).

57. "Corpus Joannis sepelitur, caput in disco collocatur: littera humo tegitur,

spiritus in altari honoratur et sumitur": *Comm. de Mc.,* VI, 28-29, first half of the 5th cent. (PL, XXX, 608 C).

58. "Si enim hoc consensero vobis, ut legis litteram *sequar,* mors mihi erit!": *In Lev.,* h. 1, n. 1 (280-1).

59. Paul the Deacon, *De temp.,* h. 77: "Unaware of the dispensation of the Savior Lord, they most stupidly used to defend the letter of the Law" — "Legis litteram stultissime defendebant, ignorantes dispensationem Domini Salvatoris" (PL, XCV, 1231 B).

60. Richard, *De sacrificio David proph.:* "So let us taste nothing carnally in the carnal sacrifices of the Jews, but let us discuss spiritually the flesh they taste according to the letter" — "In carnalibus igitur Judaeorum sacrificiis nihil carnaliter sapiamus, sed quae juxta litteram carnem sapiunt, spiritualiter discutiamus" (PL, CXCVI, 1033 D).

61. *In Gal.,* IV, 21 (PL, XXVI, 387 D).

62. Odo, *Epit. mor.,* Bk. XX: "But we must also keep to the history throughout all the things we run through in our investigation of allegory" — "Sed haec quae allegoriae indagatione transcurrimus, oportet ut per omnia etiam juxta historiam teneamus" (PL, CXXXIII, 353 B). (Following Greg.)

63. "peracto litterae negotio": Richard (?), *In Nahum,* n. 60 (PL, XCVI, 933 D).

64. Rabanus, *In Lev.,* Bk. IV, c. v: "to the fruit of the spirit, which just as [ordinary fruit] is kept under the leaf, so [spiritual fruit] is kept under the letter of the vine of the Law" — "ad fructum spiritus, qui quemadmodum sub folio, ita sub littera legalis vineae custoditur" (PL, CVIII, 388 C). Bruno of Segni, *In Matt.,* Bk. IV, c. xxi: The Synagogue "which is stuck in its lack of faith and, shaded by the leaves of loquacity, does not bear the fruit of spiritual understanding" — "(Synagoga) quae in sua infidelitate perdurat, et loquacitatis foliis obumbrata, spiritualis intelligentiae fructum non reddit" (CLXV, 246 B). Cf. Jerome, *In Ez.* (XXV, 475 C).

65. *In Is.,* Bk. IX: "Let the Jews and the friends of merely simple history answer, who do not look for fruits on the tree but merely for leaves and the shadow of words that quickly dry out and perish" — "Respondeant Judaei et amici simplicis tantum historiae, qui fructus non quaerunt in arbore, sed folia tantum umbramque verborum, quae cito arescit et deperit" (PL, XXIV, 335 A).

66. Jerome: "So the outer ornament of the words is designated by the name of silver, whereas the more hidden mysteries are contained in the buried works of gold" — "Exterior itaque verborum ornatus in argenti nomine demonstratur, occultiora vero mysteria in reconditis auri muneribus continentur" (*An. Mar.,* III, 1, 55, note 5). Cited by B. Bischoff, *S. Er.,* VI, 263: "What does the color of silver mean except the eloquence of the divine history? By the form of gold, however, he is pointing to the threefold spiritual sense, namely, tropological, anagogical, allegorical" — "Quid argenti color, nisi eloquentiam divinae historiae significat? Per auri autem formam, sensum triplicem spiritalem indicat, id est, tropologiam, anagogen, allegoriam."

67. "exterior sermo castus nitet quasi argentum, et interior sensus rutilat velut aurum": Rupert, *In Matt.,* Bk. XI (PL, CLXVIII, 1557 A).

68. Paulinus of Aquilaea, *Libellus sacros. c. Elip.,* c. viii (PL, XCIX, 159 B).

69. Rupert, *In Cant.,* Bk. I: "Gold on the back, i.e., on the posterior parts of the dove, is the inner sense of holy Scripture; the silver is the outer sense" — "Aurum

in dorso, vel in posterioribus columbae, interior est sensus sacrae Scripturae; argentum vero, sermo exterior" (PL, CLXVIII, 853 D); cf. *In Ap.*, c. x (CLXIX, 1011 A). Jerome, *In ps. LXI.* (*An. mar.*, III, 1, 55).

70. "allégorisme généralisé qui évacue la lettre, le tissu historique, et qui est le fruit d'une mentalité": *Esquisse*, 28, note 2.

71. "sensus historicus solidus est" — "soliditas historiae non violatur": Prudentius of Troyes, *Sup. aedif. Prudentii* (Pitra, 3, 423). Prudentius, *Psychom.*, v. 821-44.

72. "Sunt quaedam loca in divina pagina, quae secundum litteram legi non possunt": Bk. VI, c. iii (PL, CLXXVI, 801 B).

73. Bk. IV, c. iii, n. 5 (p. 331). Cf. *In Matt.*, t. XV, c. ii: "So let anyone who wants to look at the letter and not understand the intention of the words sell his own bodily garment and buy a sword" — "Si quis ergo litteram volens aspicere et non intellegens voluntatem verborum *(mē enidōn tōi boulēmati tōn lelegmenōn)*, vendiderit vestimentum suum corporale et emerit gladium" (352).

74. Cf. J. Quasten, *Initiation aux Pères de l'Égl.*, tr. J. Laporte, II (1957), 113-4. [Trans. note: The 1983 Christian Classics reprint of the 1953 English original, entitled *Patrology*, reads as follows (II, 93): "He goes so far as to affirm that in Scripture 'all has a spiritual meaning, but not everything has a literal meaning' (*De princ.* 4,3,5). We have here the point of departure for all the exaggerations of medieval allegorism. Thus it is by reason of the Philonian impact on his thought that Origen occasionally denies the reality of the letter, in a manner indefensible...."] There we do not see Philonian influence, and, on the other hand, if it is true that Origen and the Middle Ages have sometimes misused the principle posited here, the principle itself seemed to impose itself on everyone, as, in fact, everyone recognized it; if one has regard for Origen's terminology, one will see that even the most historicist historian does not deny what he advances when he says that not everything in the Bible has a literal sense.

75. He extends neither his remark nor his advice to "the entire Scripture," as R. Baron writes in *Science et sagesse chez H. de SV*, 101.

76. Or., *In Cant.*, h. 1, n. 2 (O. Rousseau, SC, 37, 64-5); comm. Bk. I and II (89, 90, 108, 134).

77. "Haec si non spiritaliter intelligantur, nonne fabulae sunt?": P. Jouon, *Le Cant. des cantiques* (1909), 8: "For the ancient ecclesiastical writers, the Canticle of Canticles is a pure allegory" — "Pour les anciens écrivains ecclésiastiques, le Cantique des cantiques est une pure allégorie."

78. "genus locutionis rerum omnino gestarum sicut in Regnorum libris" — "genus locutionis figuratarum rerum, sicut in Cantico canticorum": *Gen. litt.*, Bk. VIII, c. 1, n. 2 (PL, XXXIV, 371); *Speculum, De Cant.*: "Since the whole [book] commends the sacred loves of Christ and the Church is figured speech and speaks forth with the height of prophecy" — "Cum totus (liber) amores sanctos Christi et Ecclesiae figurata locutione commendet, et prophetiae pronuntiet altitudine" (XXXIV, 925).

79. "nihil historiae in toto hoc cantico": *In Cant.*, Bk. II (36). Angelome knew Aponius's commentary.

80. "tertium genus" — "tantum spiritualiter accipitur": *Diff.*, Bk. II, n. 155: "If these things be sensed according to the sound of the words or the action of the

deed, bodily luxury rather than the power of the sacraments is what one comes away with" — "quae si juxta sonum verborum vel efficientiam operis sentiantur, corporalis magis luxuria quam virtus sacramentorum accipitur" (PL, LXXXIII, 94-5). *L. de var. q.* c. ix, n. 4: "once the history is taken away, there is nothing with regard to the letter and all things are to be taken spiritually" — "remota historia, nihil secundum litteram sed spiritaliter cuncta sunt accipienda" (31).

81. "historialiter factum" — "mystica sacramenta" — "sub velamine locutionis tropicae figurataeque": *In Ap.*, Bk. VII (567 AB); *praef.* (405 G). The same goes for Aimon on the Ap.: *In Ap., praef.* (PL, CXVII, 938 C).

82. "Cantica canticorum, in quibus nil historialiter, sed tantum spiritaliter accipiendum est": Bk. I, c. xvii (PL, XCVIII, 1045 A).

83. *In Cant., prol.* (PL, CLXVIII, 839-40).

84. "Nihil mihi et litterae huic!": *In Cant., s.* 73, n. 2 (1134 D).

85. "historica intelligentia": *In Cant.*, Bk. I (93).

86. *Exp. alt. in Cant.*: "This can be the drift of the proposed historical drama, fable or parable . . ." — "Propositi vero dramatis historialis, fabulae seu parabolae, hoc potest esse argumentum . . ." (PL, CLXXX, 476 D); "Thus, to give men a canticle of spiritual love, the holy Spirit exteriorly clothed his whole inner spiritual or divine task with images of carnal love" — "Ideo Spiritus sanctus, Canticum amoris spiritualis traditurus hominibus, totum spirituale vel divinum ejus interius negotium exterius vestivit carnalis amoris imaginibus etc." (481 A).

87. "qui, ut cor nostrum ad instigationem sacri amoris accenderet, usque ad turpis amoris nostri verba descendit": *In Cant., prol.* (PL, CXCVI, 405 C). Cf. Luke of Mont-Cornillon, *In Cant.*, Bk. II (CCIII, 301 A); etc.

88. "Totus iste liber procedit parabolice": *Postilla sup. Cant.*, c. i (col. 1827).

89. "Tota hujus libri oratio figurata est": *In Cant.* (*Opera*, Salamanca, II, 1895, 15).

90. We are using the distinctions of Father Joüon, *op. cit.*, 21-58.

91. Thus D. Buzy, "Un chef-d'œuvre de poésie pure," *Mél. Lagrange* (1940), 147, 151-2. Thus A. Robert, A. Feuillet, A. M. Tournay, etc. For the contrary: R. J. Dubarle (1954), J. P. Audet (1955).

92. "Caeterum, ad litteram nihil me dixisse nolo mireris, quia quod beatus Hieronymus satis superque elucidasse in promptu est, idipsum repetendo schedulas implere supervacaneum procul dubio mihi est": *Trop. in Jer., Epil. ad S. Norbert* (PL, CLVI, 488 C).

93. "In defectu ergo urbium, ruinas meditemur animorum": PL, CLVI, 450 D.

94. "Si enim veterum credimus historiis, bella, etc. Sed haec omnia sub silentio praetereo, bella vitiorum locuturus, etc. Si vis scire qualiter Christus gentem vitiorum dissipavit . . .": Absalon, *s.* 12 (PL, CCXI, 76-7).

Notes to Chapter Seven
§3. The Biblical Facts

1. *History,* 295.

2. "Aufer rubiginem de argento": *Sup. Par. Sal.*, Bk. III, c. xxv: "Take away the surface of the sacred eloquence, and you will find the purest sense hidden with

the subtlety (= under the baseness?) of the letter, and that spiritual mysteries lay hidden under the prefiguration of the carnal ceremonies" — "Aufer litterae superficiem de sacro eloquio, et invenies sensum purissimum subtilitate (= sub vilitate?) litterae reconditum, et sub carnalium figuris caeremoniarum spiritualia latuisse mysteria" (PL, XCI, 1011 D).

3. Jerome, *Ep.* 58, n. 9 (3, 83); cited by Alvarus, *Ep.* 4, n. 13 (Madoz, 128), etc. Alan of Lille, *Eluc. in Cant.* (PL, CCX, 102 D).

4. Cf. Plautus, *Curc.* 55: The fellow "who wants the kernel to be outside the nut cracks the shell" — "e nuce nucleum qui esse vult frangit nucem."

5. "grossior textus litterae": Rupert: "Since Moses' face shines everywhere from his conversation with God, and for that reason it was necessary to veil with figurative words his own sense, which is what is understood by 'face', but then there is in the creation of a world of such splendor as all the sons of Israel could scarcely have borne it, unless he had wrapped it in the grosser text of the letter like an infant in swaddling clothes" — "Facies Moysi cum ubique ex collocutione Dei splendida sit, et idcirco figurativis cum vocibus sensum suum qui per faciem intelligitur velare oportuerit, tum vero in creatione mundi tanti splendoris est, quantum ferre nequaquam potuissent universi filii Israël, nisi illum grossiori textu litterae, quasi pannis infantiae, obvolvisset" (PL, CLXVII, 197 BC).

6. Ambrose, *In Luc.*, Bk. VII, n. 12 (Tissot, SC, 52, 13). Cf. Or., *In Matt.*, t. XII, c. xxxviii: "the words and letter of the Gospels with which Jesus has been clothed" — "sermones et littera evangeliorum, quibus Jesus est indutus" (154), etc.

7. Jerome, *Ep.* 58, n. 9: "Everything that we read in the divine books is shiny and bright on the outward part, but is still sweeter in the meat" — "Totum quod legimus in divinis libris, nitet quidem et fulget etiam in cortice, sed dulcius in medulla est" (538).

8. Remi, *In Gen.*, c. xxx: "For where we follow the history, we send away the outer shell; but where, fleeing the history, we stand on allegory, we open the bran [reading 'cantabrum' instead of 'canebrem'] of spiritual understanding as though the husk had been peeled off" — "Ubi enim historiam sequimur, corticem dimittimus; ubi vero, historiam fugientes, allegoriae insistimus, quasi cortice subtracto canebrem spiritalis intelligentiae operimus" (PL, CXXXI, 108 CD).

9. "quia grana sunt in Catholica": Aug., *In ps. CXIX*, n. 9 (CCL, 40, 1785). Cf. Irenaeus, *Adv. Haer.*, Bk. IV, c. iv, n. 3 (PG, VII, 982-3).

10. Aug., s. 130, n. 1 (PL, XXXVIII, 725). Greg., *Mor.*, Bk. IX, c. xxxi, n. 47 (LXXV, 884 AC). Rupert, *De div. off.*, Bk. X, c. xxiv (CLXX, 287 BC). It fell to Jerome to take "palea" ["straw"] in a larger, non-pejorative sense, when he recognized its nutritive qualities; *In Is.*, Bk. IV, c. xi: "In the holy Scriptures I think the 'straw' is understood as the simple words; the 'wheat-flour', however, is the inner meat, the sense which is found within the letter; and it frequently happens that worldly men, ignorant of the mysteries, are nourished by the simple reading of Scriptures" — "Paleas puto in Scripturis sanctis verba simplicia intelligi; triticum autem et interiorem medullam, sensum qui invenitur in littera; et frequenter evenit ut homines saeculi, mystica nescientes, simplici Scripturarum lectione pascantur" (XXIV, 148 BC). *Idem* in Rupert, *In Is.* (CLXVII, 1322 A), Franco, *De gratia Dei*, Bk. X (CLXVI, 774). Cf. *Miscell.*, Bk. IV, tit. 30 (CLXVII, 712-3); etc.

11. "Lex, panis . . . ; sed panis iste, hordaeus, quo Dominus Judaeos pavit":

Aelred, *S. ined.* 17: "... the Jews, who, like beasts of burden, are nourished on the letter of the Law as on cheap barley" — "Judaeos qui more jumentorum littera legis quasi vili hordeo pascebantur" (Talbot, 118).

12. "quinque panes hordaeacei": Aug., *In Jo.*, tr. 14, n. 5-6 (PL, XXXV, 1504-5). Paul the Deacon (XCV, 1155 B).

13. "in grosso pane litterae et rusticano cibo": Bruno of Segni (MBVP, 6, 785 F).

14. "de medulla tritici": Hilduin (L. Bourgain, *La chaire chrétienne au XII s.*, 1879, 384).

15. *In Luc.*: "This is the simple history of the truth, which, if it be considered more deeply signifies marvelous mysteries" — "Haec simplicis historia veritatis est, quae si altius consideretur, admiranda signat mysteria" (PL, XV, 1731 C).

16. "vana et umbratica, et nullis veritatis fixa radicibus": *In Gal.*, Bk. III (PL, XXVI, 423 AB).

17. "non valde nobilis littera": *In Ex.*, Bk. IV, c. xv (PL, CLXVII, 716 A).

18. "litteratura Scripturae Moysi": *Ibid.*

19. "litteralis sive historica Scripturarum mediocritas": *In Ez.*, Bk. II, c. xxiv (CLXVII, 1485 BC).

20. Henry of Marcy, *De per. civ. Dei*, tr. 9: "Here the spiritual understanding, by a likeness drawn from the hardness of the letter as by some new-found humor" — "Hic spiritualis intellectus ex duritia litterae tracta similitudine quasi quodam humore reperto ..." (PL, CCIV, 322 A).

21. "vilitas litterae" — "vilitas" — "pretiositas spiritalis intelligentiae": Or., *In Num.*, h. 12, n. 1: "Hence the cheapness of the letter sends us back to the preciousness of the spiritual understanding" — "Unde vilitas litterae ad pretiositatem nos spiritalis remittit intelligentiae" (93). *Idem:* Rabanus, *In Num.* (PL, CVIII, 715 C).

22. "more judaico": Greg., *In I Reg.*, Bk. III, c. iv, n. 5: "Now if these things are weighed, in Jewish fashion, according to the cheapness of the letter, not only are they to be despised, they are not even worthy of hearing. He understands these things fittingly who, by as much as he hears more worthless things through the letter, understands them to be more useful through their spiritual signification. For the Holy Spirit, by whose inspiration this whole sacred history is being written, would never have promised things so cheap if he did not signify great and very precious mysteries within the secrecy of this cheapness" — "Haec profecto, si more judaico secundum litterae vilitatem pensantur, non solum despicienda sunt, sed nec auditu digna. Quae profecto digne accipit qui quo viliora per litteram sonum audit, eo ea per spiritalem significationem utiliora esse intelligit. Nam Spiritus sanctus quo inspirante tota haec sacra historia scribitur, numquam tam vilia promeret, si in hujus vilitatis arcano magna quaedam et pretiosa valde mysteria non signaret" (PL, LXXIX, 184 BC); cf. *proem.*, n. 4 (20 A).

23. "apparente veritate, defecit figura; ingredienti corpore, viluit umbra": Aelred, *S. in.*, 3, *in Epiph.*: "The wine has failed ... and the vessel of the letter has stayed behind" — "Defecit ergo vinum ... et vas illud litterae remansit" (Talbot, 34). Hervaeus, *In Is.*, Bk. III: "In the valley of the giants, who are the Scribes and Pharisees, i.e., in the worthlessness of the letter" — "In valle gigantum, qui sunt scribae et Pharisaei, i.e., in vilitate litterae" (PL, CLXXXI, 184 B). See Chapter 12.3 below.

24. Luke of Mont Cornillon, *In Cant. mor.*: "Although the Scripture of the prophets has been covered with the hard shell of the exterior letter, it is nevertheless not to be looked down upon, since the precious spiritual understanding lies hidden inside" — "Scriptura prophetarum, quamvis duro cortice exterioris litterae sit circumspecta, nullatenus tamen est despicienda, quia intus latet pretiosa et spiritualis intelligentia" (PL, CCIII, 562 A). Rupert, *In Ap.*, c. x: "and the things that have been conquered from the treasures of the Scriptures with laborious zeal will not seem despicable" — "et quae de Scripturarum thesauris laborioso fuerint studio conquisita, non vilia videbuntur" (CLXIX, 1011 B). *Misc.*, Bk. IV, tit. 30: "Sacred Scripture, having a cheapness in the aspect of the letter while retaining sweetness in the depth of the spiritual understanding, is the 'bread under the ash'" — "Sacra Scriptura vilitatem habens in specie litterae et dulcedinem servans in profunditate spirtualis intelligentiae, panis est sub cinere" (CLXXVII, 712 CD).

25. Or., *In Gen.*, h. 5, n. 5 (63).

26. "Aqua sancta in vase fictili, divina est sapientia in vili littera legis comprehensa": Rabanus, *In Num.*, Bk. I, c. ix (PL, CVIII, 621 A).

27. "Divinorum sensuum thesaurus intra fragile vasculum vilis litterae continetur inclusus": Or., *De princ.*, Bk. IV, c. iii, n. 14 (345). Jerome: "hordeum litterae" (PL, VXX, 960 A); vilis intelligentia secundum litteram" (XXVI, 376); "humilitas litterae" (XXV, 1083), etc.

28. "Quamvis enim vilem servi gesserit formam, plenitudo tamen in eo divinitatis habitabat": *In Lev.*, h. 2, n. 3 (294). *In Jos.*, h. 2, n. 3: "The letter of the Law has been laid upon the ground and lies there face down" — "Legis littera humi posita est et deorsum jacet" (298).

29. Greg., *Mor.*, Bk. II, n. 58: "He took on the humility of the flesh" — "humilitatem carnis suscepit" (SC, 32, 224); Bk. XXVII, c. xii, n. 21: "the sacraments of lordly humility" — "humilitatis dominicae sacramenta" (PL, LXXVI, 412 B); etc. *In Ez.*, Bk. I, h. 9, n. 31: "humanitatis ejus infirma" (884 B); Bk. II, h. 1, n. 9 (941 D). Apringius, *In Ap.* (Vega, 5). Angelome, *In Reg.*, Bk. III, c. iv: "Our Redeemer arrived by descending from the high excellence of heavenly glory to the lowliness of flesh" — "Redemptor quippe noster ab alta excellentia gloriae caelestis usque ad carnis humilitatem descendendo pervenit" (CXV, 403 D). Cf. Leo (LIV, 259 BC, 269 D, 353 D, 397 B, 1066 D).

30. "Humilis enim Christus, lac nostrum est; qualis Deo Deus, cibus noster est; lac nutrit, cibus pascit": William of Saint Thierry, *Exp. alt. in Cant.* (PL, CLXXX, 488 C). Gregory of Elvira, *Tr.* 19: "Jesus . . . was seen in filthy clothing. . . . For like a cloak He took on man's flesh guilty of sins. . . . He was seen in the filthy clothing of the flesh" — "Jesus . . . in sordibus vestimentis est visus. . . . Carnem etenim hominis obnoxiam peccatis sicut vestimentum adsumpsit. . . . In sordidis vestimentis carnis est visus" (202-3). Cf. P. Adnès, "L'humilité du Verbe incarné d'après S. Aug.," RAM 28, 208-23; 31, 28-46. T. Van Bavel, "L'humanité du Christ comme *lac parvulorum* et comme *via* dans la spiritualité de S. Aug.," *Augustiniana* 7 (1957), 245-81. J. M. Déchanet, *Les fondements et les bases de la spirit. Bernardine* (1953), 11-2. Aug., *Conf.*, Bk. 7, c. xx, on the "fundamentum humilitatis, quod est Christus Jesus" I, 170.

31. John Scotus, *In Jo.*, fr. 1 (PL, CXXII, 307 B). Cf. HE, 337-40, 375.

32. *In Lev.*, c. vii: "For just as at one time the word and the wisdom of God was concealed in the flesh, so even now would it not appear unless the pelt and skin of the letter were taken away" — "Sicut enim quondam verbum et sapientia Dei latebat in carne, sic et modo, nisi subtracta pelle et litterae velamine non apparet" (PL, CLXIV, 402 D); *In Ex.* (255 CD). Hesychius, *In Lev.*, Bk. II (PG, XCIII, 879 B). Greg., *In ev.*, Bk. II, h. 22, n. 8 (PL, LXXVI, 1180 A); etc.

33. Thus Ambrose, *In Luc.*, Bk. VII, n. 12 (Tissot, SC, 52, 13).

34. "neque magna modica descipiunt, neque rursus modica magnis associari indignata sunt, sed ornant se invicem in una veritate" — "Nemo igitur miretur si, post magna et inter magna fidei sacramenta, eorum quae in suo ordine inferiora videntur mentio fit, quia se non abhorrent simul, quae in veritate unum sunt. Nam ipse Deus humiliari dignatus est, ad humana descendens, ut hominem postmodum ad divina sublevaret": *De sacram.*, Bk. II, prol. (PL, CLXXVI, 363-4); *De script.*, c. v (CLXXV, 14-5). Bernard, *In Cant.*, s. 33, n. 3: between the "cortex sacramenti" and the "adeps frumenti," there is the same relation as between the "forma servi" and the "imago Dei" (CLXXXIII, 952 D).

35. "Sic orientalem splendorem Filii Dei praecedit semper quasi occidentalis humilitas ejusdem Filii hominis": *In ps. LXVII* (PL, CXCIV, 168 C).

36. *In Luc.* (PL, XCII, 334 D).

37. "dispensatio humilitatis": Aug., *C. Faust.*, Bk. XII, c. xlvi (PL, XLII, 279).

38. Hilary, *In ps. CXXVI*, n. 2 (614-5).

39. *In Amos.*, Bk. I, c. ii: "If he should follow the baseness of the letter and not ascend to the dignity of the spiritual understanding" — "Si turpitudinem sequatur litterae et non ascendat ad decorem intelligentiae spiritalis" (PL, XXV, 1003 D).

40. "Quanta ante gesta sunt!": *In Jos.*, h. 4, n. 2 (309).

41. "Si ergo litterae intelligentia tantum rutilat, quid faciet intelligentia spiritus?": *In Ex.*, c. xxxiv (PL, CLXIV, 376 A; on 1 Cor. 3).

42. "Magna valde et stupenda sunt universis opera Dei!": *De van. mundi*, Bk. III (PL, CLXXVI, 726 A).

43. "mysterialiter": Gerhoh, *In ps. LXXVII* (PL, CXCIV, 482 CD).

44. "res gesta" — "humilis" — "clara" — "gloriosa": Gerhoh, *Exp. in Cant. Moys.*, 1: "The deed accomplished of the glorious magnificence of the Lord is clear: for the water has been divided" — "Clara est gloriosae magnificentiae Domini res gesta: quia divisa est aqua etc." (PL, CXCIV, 1017 B).

45. "vilis" — "mirabilis" — "et narratione mirabilis, et intellectu magnifica": Or., *In Num.*, h. 22, n. 3 (206).

46. "secundum historiam gesta": Or., *In Jos.*, h. 11, n. 1: "These historical accomplishments foretell to all ages the miracles of the divine power, nor do those things in which the light of the accomplishments sparkles need interpretation from outside" — "Haec secundum historiam quidem gesta, miracula divinae virtutis universis saeculis praedicant, nec interpretatione extrinsecus indigent, in quibus gestorum lumen coruscat. Quid tamen in iis spiritalis intellectus contineat, requiramus" (362).

47. "magnalia Dei" — "magna Dei mirabilia": Aug., *In ps. XCVIII*, n. 1 (CCL, 39, 1378); 105, n. 6 and 22 (40, 1558, 1562). Alvarus, *Ep.* 18, n. 3: "For God's great miracles that have been inserted in the Law never fall out of our heart, nor do

those terrible deeds with which he struck Egypt with unheard-of power" — "Numquam enim ex corde nostro excidunt magna Dei mirabilia, quae legi existant inserta; vel terribilia illa, quibus Aegyptum percussit potentia inaudita" (PL, CXXI, 494-5).

48. *Ap.* XV, 3: "Magna et mirabilia sunt opera tua, Domine." Autpert, *In Ap.*, Bk. VI (571 C).

49. "divinae dispensationis magnalia quae nobis in Patribus exhibita sunt": John of Salisbury, *Hist. pont., prol.* (M. Chibnall, 1).

50. "mira et stupenda": Aug., *In Jo.*, tr. 6, n. 1 (PL, XXXV, 1503).

51. "Magna quidem sunt, tanquam involucra mysteriorum Dei": Aug., *s.* 7, n. 1 (PL, XXXVIII, 63). Cassiodorus, *In ps. CXIII* (LXX, 811 A).

52. "mirabilia" — "mirabilia in profundo": Ps.-John of Rouen, *s.* 5, *ad sacerdotes:* "God's hidden mysteries" — "mysteria occulta Dei," "God's marvels in the deep" — "mirabilia Dei in profundo," "marvels . . . perceptible by the eyes of the heart" — "mirabilia . . . oculis cordis perceptibilia" (PL, CXLVII, 232 B).

53. Greg., *In Ez.*, Bk. II, h. 8, n. 10 (PL, LXXVI, 1034 AB). Taio of Saragossa, *Sent.*, Bk. II, c. xviii (LXXX, 802-3). Cf. Leo, *s.* 35, c. 1 (LIV, 250 A).

54. "Magnum in superficie historica miraculum, incomparabiliter majus in spiritu significat opus divinum": Rupert, *In Reg.*, Bk. V, c. xxxvi (PL, CLXVII, 1269 A).

55. "Impleat campos, valles, et operiat montes, quae sunt magna Dei opera, nulli praeter ipsum possibilia; sed alia per haec significantur longe his majora et mirabiliora": *In ps. CXLVI*, 16 (PL, CXCIV, 980 D).

56. "In operibus Dei . . . sunt . . . et exteriori specie delectabilia, et interiori virtute multo delectabiliora; quemadmodum et Ipse exterius quidem speciosus erat forma prae filiis hominum, interius autem tanquam candor lucis aeternae etiam ipsis supereminens vultibus angelorum. . . . Superficies ipsa, tanquam a foris considerata, decora est valde; at si quis fregerit nucem, intus inveniet quod jucundius sit, et multo amplius delectabile. . . . Signorum Domini, cujus et historia satis admirabilis, et significatio amplius delectabilis . . .": *Dom. prima post oct. Epiph.*, *s.* 2, n. 1-2 (PL, CLXXXIII, 157 CD, 158 BC).

57. PL, CXCIV, 1719 B.

58. "Tanta est enim claritas Novi Testamenti, ut Veteris Testamenti claritas pro tenebris habeatur; utrumque tamen Testamentum unum est, et utrumque clarum et splendidum est, si spiritualiter intelligatur": Bruno of Segni, *In ps. LXXIII* (PL, CLXIV, 982 D).

59. J. Daniélou, "Or. Exégète de la Bible," *St. patr.*, I, 288.

60. Already in the last century John Keble had protested against such an opinion. Sometimes, said he, it occurred to the Fathers to sacrifice the letter, when the sense appeared to them physically or historically impossible; but "it is not as easy to meet with a passage where the same solution is applied to any narrative, merely on the ground of its apparent immorality; which yet, with our modern notions, would seem to be the most tempting ground of all" (74).

61. Bede, *In Sam. proph. alleg. exp., prol.*: "If . . . in Jewish fashion we care to follow only the figures of the letter, what do we acquire by reading or hearing among . . . the countless wanderings of this life of spiritual doctrine, when, once, for example, the book of blessed Samuel has been opened, we find that one man

Elkanah had two wives; particularly we to whom, by custom of ecclesiastical life, it is proposed that we should be far from wifely embrace and remain celibate? If we do not know how to exculpate the allegorical sense even of these and similar sayings, who refreshes us by lively interior chastising, educating, and consoling?" — "Si . . . solas litterae figuras sequi Judaico more curamus, quid inter . . . innumeros vitae hujus errores spiritualis doctrinae legentes vel audientes acquirimus, dum aperto libro, v.g. beati Samuelis, Elcanam virum unum duas uxores habuisse reperimus; nos maxime quibus, ecclesiasticae vitae consuetudine, longe fieri ab uxoris complexu et caelibes manere propositum est? Si non etiam de his et hujusmodi dictis allegoricum noverimus exsculpere sensum, qui nos vivaciter interius castigando, erudiendo, consolando reficit?" (PL, XCI, 499-500).

62. *C. Faust.*, Bk. XXII, c. xxvi (PL, XLII, 418).

63. *Ibid.*, c. xxiii (XLII, 417); regarding Abraham, c. xx-xl (420-5).

64. Thus, regarding Lot: *C. mendac.*, c. ix, n. 20 (PL, XL, 530); c. xiv, n. 40 (539); on the daughters of Lot: *C. Faust.*, Bk. XXII, c. xlii-iii (XLII, 426); on Lot himself: c. xliv (426-7).

65. *C. Faust.*, Bk. XXII, c. xxxiv: "Because if it were necessary for those things to be understood, we would recognize man's sin" — "Quod si ista necesse esset intelligi, peccatum hominis agnosceremus" (PL, XLII, 422); etc.

66. *C. mend.*, c. ix, n. 21 (531).

67. "graviter sc[a]elerateque peccavit": *C. Faust.*, Bk. XXII, c. lxxxvii (PL, XLII, 459).

68. *In Hept.*, Bk. VII, q. 49: "Scripture neither approved nor disapproved of this, but leaves it to be estimated and weighed once justice and God's law have been consulted" — "neque approbavit hoc Scriptura neque reprobavit, sed justitia et lege Dei consulta aestimandum pensandumque dimisit" (XXXIV, 812); *C. Faust.*, Bk. XXII, c. lxv: "He lets us judge such deeds; he does not require us to praise them" — "Talia facta . . . judicanda nobis permittit, non laudanda praescribit" (XLII, 439); c. lxix (440-1); c. xlv: "those things have been reported, not praised, in the business of the daughters of Lot" — "in illa re gesta de opere filiarum Loth narrata ista sunt, non laudata" (427); c. lx (438).

69. This is the argument of the *C. Faust.* and of the *Adv. Legis et Prophet.* Cf. A. M. La Bonnardière, *St. patr.*, I, 378-9. In the case of the ruse of Jacob, it must be admitted that Aug. has pushed a bit far to excuse it: *Civ. Dei*, Bk. XVI, c. xxxvii (PL, XLI, 515); *C. Mend.*, c. x, n. 24 (XL, 533-6). Already in Origen, *In Jo.*, Bk. X, c. v (175).

70. *C. Faust.*, Bk. XXII, c. xlv: "But we are defending not the sins of men, but the holy Scriptures" — "Nos tamen Scripturas sanctas, non hominum peccata defendimus" (PL, XLII, 427); "God therefore . . . reported these things; he did not do them; he warned us what to watch out for, he did not propose these things to be done" — "Deus ergo . . . prodidit quippe ista, non fecit; et cavenda admonuit, non imitanda proposuit," etc.

71. *Adv. Haer.*, Bk. IV, c. xxxi, n. 1: "Reporting such things as these about the ancients, the priest refreshed us and said: As to the crimes for which the Scriptures themselves berate the patriarchs and prophets, it is not necessary for us to upbraid them, nor to become like Ham, etc. And as for those that the Scriptures do not blame, but which are simply laid down, it is not necessary for us to become

accusers . . . but merely to search out the prefiguration" — "Talia quaedam enarrans de antiquis presbyter, reficiebat nos et dicebat: De eis delictis, de quibus ipsae Scripturae increpabant, patriarchas et propheta[s], nos non oportet exprob[r]are eis, neque fieri similes Cham etc. De quibus autem Scripturae non increpant, sed simpliciter sunt positae, nos non debere fieri accusatores . . . , sed typum quaerere . . ." (PG, VII, 1068 AB); excuse for the daughters of Lot: n. 1-2 (1068-9).

72. *C. Cels.*, Bk. IV, c. xlv: Lot "can be excused in a way"; one will admire "the sincerity of the Scripture, which does not dissimulate even dishonorable actions"; here, Scripture neither praises nor blames; it is necessary, however, to draw a tropology from it; c. xlvi, in the same way for Jacob and Esau (318-9), etc. David's fault is recalled, *In Ez.*, IV, 10 (PL, XXV, 760 B). The history of Lot is again reported, *In Gen.*, h. 5, n. 3 (60), "famosissima fabula"; it is not less held as very real.

73. Aug., *In ps. LIX*, n. 10: the girls "did not treat their father rightly" — "non legitime usae sunt patre" (PL, XXXVI, 720).

74. Claudius, *In Gen.*, Bk. II: "Nor yet do we justify this deed of Lot or of his daughters because it signified something that foretold certain persons' future perversity: for the daughters intended to do one thing, and God, who permitted it to be done so that he might thence point something out to signify things to come, intended quite another. In like fashion, when that deed is reported in holy Scripture, it is prophecy; but when it is considered in the life of those who committed it, it is a disgrace" — "Nec ideo tamen hoc factum vel ipsius Loth vel filiarum ejus justificamus, quia significavit aliquid quod futuram quorumdam perversitatem praenuntiaret: aliud enim illae ut hoc facerent intenderunt, aliud Deus, qui hoc fieri permisit ut etiam aliquid inde monstraret pro significatione futurorum. Proinde, illud factum, cum in sancta Scriptura narratur, prophetia est; cum vero in illorum vita qui hoc commiserunt consideratur, flagitium est" (PL, L, 965 D).

75. Cf. Ambrose, *De Josepho*, c. iii, n. 12: "invidia per figuram, pietas per affectum" (PL, XIV, 646 A). He goes too far in excuse; one would, however, be able to say, with J. J. Ampère, *H. litt. de la Fr. avant le XII s.*, I (1839), 387, that Ambrose "ne voit qu'une figure là où l'Écriture a mis un fait."

76. Aug., *In ps. CIV*, n. 28: "They were permitted rather than commanded to do those things by the one who was looking into their heart and examining their desires. . . . Just as God has divinely used the iniquity of the Egyptians, so has he done with the infirmity of [the Jews] to prefigure and foretell what was necessary for those deeds" — "Magis . . . ab illo qui cor eorum videbat et cupiditates examinabat, permissi sunt facere ista, quam jussi. . . . Sicut autem Aegyptiorum iniquitate, sic istorum infirmitate ad id quod opus erat illis factis figurandum et praenuntiandum divine usus est Deus" (CCL, 40, 1548). *C. Faust.*, Bk. XXII, c. lxxi and xci (PL, XLII; 445, 461-2). See p. 418, n. 21, in Volume 1, above.

77. "In verbis quasi mala optantis, intellegamus praedicta prophetantis": *In ps. CVIII*, n. 7 (CCL, 40, 1589).

78. "minus digna": Bernard, *Dom. prima post oct. Epiph.*, s. 2, n. 1: "The mystical signification is fitting and delightful in the works of those [fathers of the Old Testament]; but if those works were considered by themselves, they would sometimes be found less worthy, e.g., the deeds of Jacob, the adultery of David, and many others of the sort. The foods are precious, but the vessels not nearly so pre-

cious" — "In operibus eorum (Patrum V. T.) decora et delectabilis est significatio mystica; ipsa tamen si per se considerentur, invenientur aliquando minus digna, ut sunt facta Jacob, adulterium David et multa similia. Pretiosa quidem sunt fercula, sed vasa non adeo pretiosa" (PL, CLXXXIII, 158 B).

79. *Ep.* 66, n. 3: "We can neither excuse so great a priest nor dare to condemn him" — "neque excusare tantum sacerdotem possumus, neque condemnare audemus" (PL, XVI, 1225 C). Cf. *De Jacob*, Bk. II, n. 5, on the parents of Jacob and Esau: "Nor are we to leave the parents unexcused because they put the younger son before the elder" — "Sed nec parentes nobis inexcusati relinquendi sunt, quod juniorum filium seniori praetulerint" (XIV, 616 D).

80. "Agnosco hominem fuisse, et nihil mirum; agnosco commune, ut homo peccet. Peccavit, quod solent reges; sed paenitentiam egit, quod non solent reges . . .": *Apol. David alt.*, c. iii, n. 7 (PL, XIV, 889-90). Cf. *Apol. proph. David*, c. xi, n. 44: "Do not marvel at a man and think him to be made equal to the angels most of his life; nay rather consider him who spends his time from youth amid wealth, honors, and command, having been put amidst many temptations, to have given place to error just once" — "Non miraris hominem, et angelis adaequandum judicas, plurimum vitae suae, imo a pueritia in divitiis, honoribus, imperiis demorantem, in multis tentationibus positum, semel tantum locum errori dedisse" (XIV, 853 C). Cf. P. Lombard, *In ps. L* (CXCI, 483-4). The same indulgent respect is shown in Ambrose regarding Peter's denial: *In Luc.*, Bk. X, n. 78-92 (SC, 182-7) as in Origen for the daughters of Lot (*In Gen.*, n. 5, n. 4-6, 61-3); cf. Alcuin, *In Gen interr.* (C, 542-3).

81. "Instruant te Patriarchae, non solum docentes, sed etiam errantes": *De Abr.*, Bk. I, c. vi, n. 58 (PL, XIV, 442 A).

82. "Quomodo igitur in typo ejus mysterii peccatum imputari potest, cum in ipso mysterio sit remissio peccatorum?": *Apol. Dav.*, c. xvii, n. 81: "Jesus Himself, the end of the shadow and the Law, came as master of humility, to teach the proud in sense and the inflated with swelling of the heart to move over toward mildness and simplicity. How then, etc.? Unless perchance David himself confessed his own inquiry and the sin of what had been admitted, so that he too might belong to the remission of sin and the grace of the mystery" — "Ipse Jesus, umbrae finis et legis, advenit, humilitatis magister, docere superbos sensu, et tumore cordis inflatos, ad mansuetudinem et simplicitatem esse migrandum. Quodmodo, etc.? Nisi forte ideo ipse David iniquitatem suam peccatumque confessus est ejus admissi, ut et ipse ad remissionem peccati et gratiam mysterii pertineret" (PL, XIV, 882 CD). C. 1, n. 3: "quem Deus justificavit, ne tu dijudices" (853 A); c. iii, n. 10 and 14 (855 D, 857 AB), etc. Cf. Greg., *In I Reg.*, *proem.*, n. 5: "Si ergo aliquid indecens etiam in planioris historiae explanatione lector inspexerit, tanto benignius veniam dare poterit, quanto rationabilius agnoscit quia, dum a plano quod cernitur, ad illa sublimia ultra non tendimus, facile cavillamus, etc." (LXXXIX, 22 B). Cf. Rupert (CLXIX, 1305-7).

83. *C. Faust.*, Bk. XXII, c. lxxxvii (PL, XLII, 459).

84. *Mor.*, Bk. IV, *praef.*, c. ii (PL, LXXV, 634 BC).

85. "Saepe res quaelibet per historiam virtus est, per significationem culpa; sicut aliquando culpa in facto, in scripto prophetiae virtus": Claudius, *Q. triginta sup. libros Reg.*: "Nor ought it seem absurd to you that the deeds of the reprobate,

performed badly, should signify some good; or again that the good works of the just should be laid down as signifying their opposites; for read the *Moralia* of the holy pope Gregory, where he expounded how blessed Job cursed his day saying: 'Let the day on which I was born perish', and you will see that it was quite customary in the Scriptures, etc." — "Nec tibi absurdum videri debet ut male reproborum acta, boni aliquid significent; aut rursum bona justorum opera, in contraria significatione ponantur; lege enim Moralia sancti papae Gregorii, ubi exposuit quodmodo beatus Job maledixit diei suo, dicens: Pereat dies in qua natus sum, et videbis quia usitatissimum est in Scripturis, etc." (PL, CIV, 689 B).

86. "exsecrabilis juxta litteram, laudabilis juxta significativam intelligentiam": Autpert, *In Ap.*, Bk. III (434 C). On the other hand, the history of Lot is detestable both in its signification and in its letter *(ibid.).*

87. Cf. Greg., *Mor.*, Bk. XXXIII, c. xii, n. 23 (PL, LXXVI, 687 B).

88. As to Zedekiah, *In Ez.*, Bk. III, c. xii: "For neither can an impious king serve as a prefiguration of him who is the model of all piety" — "Neque enim rex impius in figuram potest praecedere illius, qui totius pietatis exemplum est" (PL, XXV, 102 D).

89. Rupert, *In Reg.*, Bk. III, c. xxxiv: "Though the deed accomplished be on the surface a cause of damnation, in the mystery it is nevertheless a prophecy of virtue" — "Res gesta, etsi in superficie causa damnationis, in mysterio tamen est prophetia virtutis" (PL, CLXVII, 1135 D). *Glossa in II Reg.*, xi (CXIII, 572 A).

90. Isidore, *Aetym.*, Bk. I, c. xxxvii, n. 24 (PL, LXXXII, 115-6). Nearly the same idea in Autpert, *In Ap.*, Bk. X: "Much baser in its nature than the sapphire, . . . the Chalcedonian stone is yet in the mystical senses found to be very precious itself" — "Chalcedonius lapis . . . , multo vilior est in natura sua quam saphirus, sed in mysticis sensibus valde invenitur et ipse pretiosus" (641 F).

91. "Jocus" — person "qui nullius jocosae jucunditatis vult meridiari deliciis": Alan of Lille, *De planctu nat.* (PL, CCX, 459 D). Hélinand, *s.* 2: "Lucifer . . . who, though he be as a whole full of darkness, is nevertheless called 'Lucifer' by antiphrasis, in the same way as a forest clearing is so named from shining, since it does not shine at all" — "Lucifer . . . qui cum totus sit tenebrosus, tamen per antiphrasin dictus est Lucifer, sicut lucus a lucendo quia minime lucet" (CCXII, 486 D).

92. *Hier. cael.*, c. II, n. 2-3: "La révélation sacrée se fait selon deux modes. . . . L'autre, recourant à des figurations dissemblables, pousse la fiction jusqu'au comble de l'invraissemblable et de l'absurde" (tr. M. De Gandillac, SC, 58, 77). On this Plotinian law of *enantiôsis* or *heterotês*: F. Buffière, *Les mythes d'Homère et la pensée grecque,* 36 and 56.

93. Thus René Guénon and Frithjof Schuon.

94. "quo viliora per litterae sensum, eo per spiritalem significationem utiliora": *In I Reg.*, Bk. III, c. iv, n. 5 (PL, LXXIX, 184 B).

95. "Adam, qui est forma futuri" — "his verbis declarat Apostolus qualiter Adam forma Christi sit a contrario": *In Rom.* (PL, CLXXXI, 664 B).

96. "et per bonos homines mali et per malos nonnumquam praefigurantur boni": *L. de var. quaest.*, c. viii, n. 5 (23).

97. *De vinculis S. Petri:* "[Scripture] itself, as we are instructed by the teaching authority of the Fathers, sometimes signifies a virtue worthy of praise according

to the mystical understanding by means of what it reports done blamably according to the history" — "Ipsa (Scriptura), sicut Patrum magisterio edocemur, nonnumquam per hoc quod vituperabiliter juxta historiam gestum narrat, virtutem laude dignam juxta mysticum intellectum significat" (PL, CXLI, 277 C). Father Jean Châtillon has restored to Richard this text attributed to Fulbert of Chartres: RMAL 5 (1949), 364; 6 (1950), 287-98.

98. Richard, *In Ap.*, Bk. I, c. i (PL, CXCVI, 689 AD). Hugh, *In Hier. cael.*, Bk. III (CLXXV, 971-2; 977-9). Potho of Prüm, *De statu domus Dei*, Bk. IV, c. iv: "De dissimilibus similitudinibus" (503 F).

99. *S.* 31 (PL, CCV, 765-6); etc.

100. "Interdum ... per antithesim rerum sequenda sunt veritatis vestigia": *Polycr.*, Bk. II, c. xvi (PL, CXCIX, 432 D). Garnier, *s.* 29: "There are those who [prefigure] certain things, some negatively; others positively" — "Aliqui (figurant) aliqua, quaedam remotive, quaedam positive" (CCV, 765-6); etc.

101. "Tabulae historiae non semper aeque respondent picturae allegoriae; significans quandoque fit malum et significat bonum, et e converso": *S.* 24 (PL, CCXVII, 561 D). We have conjecturally re-established a corrupt text.

102. "Quae res et fidelitatem probavit secundum historiam in viro, et sacramentum juxta allegoriam ostendit in facto": Angelome, *In Reg.*, Bk. II, c. ix (PL, CXV, 359 AB).

103. "Quid ergo perfecto isto David scelestius, quid Uria mundius dici potest? Sed rursus per mysterium quid David sacratius, quid Uria infidelius invenitur, quando et ille per vitae culpam propheticam signat innocentiam, et iste per vitae innocentiam in prophetia exprimit culpam? Virtus namque sacri eloquii sic transacta narrat, ut ventura exprimat; sic in facta re approbat, ut in mysterio contradicat; sic gesta damnat, ut haec mystice gerenda persuadeat": Claudius, *In Reg.*, Bk. II (PL, L, 1091 AB); Bk. III (1161 CD); Bk. II: "Something is very often a virtue historically and a fault by signification; as when, etc." — "Plerumque quaedam res per historiam virtus est, per significationem culpa; sicut aliquando etc."; the "saepe" of Gregory here becomes "plerumque." Rabanus, *In Reg.*, Bk. II, c. xi (CIX, 101 B). Angelome, *In Reg.* (115, 362 D). Rupert, *De div. off.*, Bk. XI, c. i: David "committing a grave sin according to the deed performed, but presignifying a great mystery" — "grave quidem committens piaculum secundum rem gestam, sed grande praesignans mysterium" (CLXX, 294 BD). Richard (CXLI, 277 C). In the reverse sense, Bernard: "The angel Gabriel was sent to Mary, i.e., the preacher of the divine word to the sinner" — "Missus est angelus Gabriel ad Mariam, id est praedicator divini verbi ad peccatorem etc." (Leclercq, *Etudes*, 57).

104. *C. Faust.*, Bk. XXII, c. lxxxvii (PL, XLII, 458-9).

105. Autpert, *In Ap.* (473-4). Honorius, *In ps. L* (PL, CLXXII, 283 BD). Gerhoh, *In ps. L*, 1-2 (CXCIII, 1602-3). John of Salisbury, *Polycr.*, Bk. II, c. xvi (CXCIX, 433 B). Peter Comestor (Smalley, 258).

106. Primasius, *Sup. Ap.*, Bk. II (PL, LXVIII, 824 BC). Analogous explication for the daughters of Lot (825 C).

107. Absalon, *s.* 37 (PL, 211, 217 D); *s.* 49 (279-80). Two explications already in Angelome, *In Reg.* (CXV, 361-3).

108. "David ubique Christum significat": *In ps.* (Vaccari, *Biblica*, 26, 74).

109. "Rem gestam sic damnemus, ut mysterium amplectemur": Rupert, *In Reg.* (PL, CLXVII, 1135 D).

110. "Oderimus ergo peccatum, sed prophetiam non exstinguamus": Angelome, *In Reg.* (PL, CXV, 363 A); following Augustine (XLII, 459).

111. *Le problème de l'incroyance au XVI s., la religion de Rabelais* (1942), 174-6 and 340-1.

112. Mr. Lucien Febvre thinks that he has read all this "dans un magnifique in-folio dépourve de toute clandestinité," the Latin edition of Origen procured in 1512 by Jacques Merlin. He had spent too much care in feeling the weight, in measuring and describing the magnificent in-folio volume, to have had time in addition to flip through its pages. On the other hand, he had perhaps read in the *J. des savants* (1884), 181, these lines of Ad. Franck: "L'histoire du déluge, l'arche de Noé, qui, dans l'espace de quelques coudées, renfermait tous les animaux de la création, la destruction de Sodome et de Gomorrhe, Loth et ses filles, lui suggèrent (à Origen) des plaisanteries qui n'ont certainement pas été dépassées par celles de Bayle et de Voltaire." As for Franck, he had doubtless read E. Vacherot, *H. crit. de l'Ec. d'Alex.*, I (1846), 283: "A le voir (Or.) sourire ou s'indigner tour à tour, à propos de certaines histoires ridicules ou étranges de l'A. T., on le prendrait pour un ennemie, de la religion nouvelle, si on ne savait qu'il n'insiste tant sur l'absurdité du texte pris dans le sens littéral, que pour en faire resortir la profonde vérité métaphysique. Sauf les intentions, c'est la critique de Celse et de Porphyre." As to Vacherot . . .

113. "Origenes non ineleganter adstruxit": *Civ. Dei*, Bk. XV, c. xxvii, n. 1-5 (PL, XLI, 473-6). *Q. in Hept.*, Bk. I, a. 4 (XXXIV, 549). Or., *In Gen.*, h. 2 (SC, 7, 90-109).

114. "Dicunt quidam hoc historialiter fieri non potuisse, sed propter aliquam significationem vel mysterium hoc scriptum esse": *In Gen.*, c. vii, n. 20 (PL, CXXXI, 76 D).

115. *Hexaem.*, Bk. II (PL, XCI, 91-2).

116. PL, L, 927 AC; C, 529 A.

117. *Chron.*, t. I, Bk. I, c. xxi (PL, CVI, 930 BD).

118. *In Gen.*, VI (PL, CXIII, 106-8).

119. "Etsi in his quae dicta sunt mysterium multiplex continetur, illud tamen litterali sensui contrarium non habetur. Sic enim plerisque in locis Scripturarum profunditas invenitur haberi, ut constet in ea multa et profunda mysteria contineri; nec tamen ab ea litteralem intelligentiam removeri; et eo gratius ad fructum intimum pervenitur, quo, non solum verbis frondosa, sed et veritate fructuosa litterae superficies invenitur. . . . Cui assertioni, etsi intellectus congruit spiritualis, non tamen est absonus litteralis: ut, cum in ea mysticum aliquid subtiliter vestigetur, tamen juxta litteram posse accipi non negetur": Philip of Harvengt, *Ep.* 1 (PL, CCIII, 12 CD, 15 D).

120. J. Pépin, *Mythe et all.*, 472, note 213: "Cette conception de l'allégorie comme un *refuge* contre la honte propre aux mythes est classique; aussi bien chez les païens qui s'en font gloire, que chez les chrétiens qui la leur reprochent."

121. Cf. Tatian, *Disc. aux Grecs*, c. xxi (PG, VI, 853 B). *Hom. Clément.*, X, c. xviii, discourse of Peter: "Ceux des Egyptiens qui gardent encore les principes de la droite raison, rougissant de ces turpitudes manifestes, tentent de les ramener à des allégories" (tr. Siouville, 238). Or., *C. Cels.*, Bk. I, c. xviii (2, 69-70).

122. They say often that Origen would suppress the historicity of many a fact he judged morally too "scandalous." One such assertion seems to come from a false reading of *Periarch.*, Bk. IV, c. ii, n. 9 (321), where the word "scandal" does in fact figure ([Gk] *skandala,* [Lat] *offendicula*); but the sense is not that of shocking immorality: it is a question of the stumbling block (trap, obstacle) that certain internal incoherences present in the text might constitute in the case where one might want to understand it entirely literally. R. L. P. Milburn, *Early Christian Interpretation of History,* 46, says it quite well: "the scandal of difficulties and inconsistencies in Scripture." Cf. 42: "He aimed not so much to depreciate the events of biblical history, as to proclaim that their significance was richer and fuller than an uncomprehending analysis would allow."

123. Cf. Greg. Naz., *Disc.* 4 (PG, XXXV, 656 C); *Elegy of Basil* (Boulenger, 66). Theodoret, *Gr. aff. curatio,* Bk. III (PG, LXXXIII, 876 AB). Lactantius, *Div. inst.,* Bk. I, c. xxi (Brandt, 84).

124. André Lavertujon, *La Chronique de Sulpice Sévère,* I (1896), with regard to Origen. The same year, in a manner no less absurd, Alfred Maury reproached the exegesis of the Middle Ages from the opposite direction: "tout l'enseignement figuré, que le christianisme avait reçu de l'Orient, ne devint plus, mal compris, qu'une source de récits incroyables, de fables singulières, colportées par l'ignorance ou la crédulité." *Croyances et légendes du moyen age* (nouv. éd., 1896), 138; whence "tants de légendes nées de la confusion du sens littéral et matériel avec le sens figuré ou spirituel." In one case as in the other, the generalization is entirely abusive.

125. *In Matt.,* h. 26, n. 6 (PG, LVII, 341).

126. Thus Origen, *In Gen.,* h. 12, n. 2, regarding Rebecca (108).

127. On three occasions, R. P. C. Hanson, *Allegory and Event,* 138, 140, 263, cites Origen, *In Jos.* 4. 11, to show that Origen habitually denies the facts because of an apologetic concern; but this is a misconception.

128. Thus for the parable of Lazarus and the rich man; Aelred, *De anima,* Bk. III: "Though blessed Gregory sculpted out of these things something of allegorical significance, nevertheless that is far from indicating that the rich man should be believed not to have truly existed, when the evangelist says: 'Jesus said to his disciples' and did not add: 'this parable'" — "Licet ex his beatus Gregorius aliquid allegoricae significationis exsculpserit, divitem illum populum interpretatus Judaeorum, pauperem Lazarum populum nationum, abest tamen ut dives ille non vere fuisse credatur, cum dicat evangelista: Dixit Jesus discipulis suis, nec addidit: parabolam hanc" (Talbot, 141-2). Cf. Rupert, *De victoria Verbi Dei,* Bk. VI, c. xxix (PL, CLXXIX, 1358 BD).

Notes to Chapter Seven
§4. Conception of History

1. Otto of Freising, *Chronica, praef.,* etc.

2. "In the way that those who have seen Athens understand the histories of the Greek more, and those who sail from Troas through Leucate and Acroceraunia to Sicily and thence to the mouth of the Tiber understand the third book

Notes to Page 70

of Vergil: so will he more clearly interpret holy Scripture who has contemplated Judaea with his eyes, and has come to know the memory of those ancient cities, or the names, whether the same or changed" — "Quomodo Graecorum historias magis intelligunt qui Athenas viderint, et tertium Virgilii librum qui a Troade per Leucaten et Acroceraunia ad Siciliam, et inde ad ostia Tiberis navigarent: ita sanctam Scripturam lucidius interpretabitur, qui Judaeam oculis contemplatus sit, et antiquarum urbium memoriam earumque vel eadem vocabula, vel mutata cognoverit" *Praef. in Paral.* (PL, XXIX, 401 A).

3. *De orat.*, Bk. II, c. ix.

4. Bk. XXIII, c. xix, n. 34 (PL, LXXVI, 271 C).

5. *Praef.*: "For if the history relates good things of the good, let the careful listener be provoked to imitate the good; if it recalls bad things about the wicked, nevertheless the religious and pious listener . . . etc." — "Sive enim historia de bonis bona referat, ad imitandum bonum auditor sollicitus instigatur, seu mala commemoret de pravis, nihilominus religiosus ac pius auditor, etc." (PL, XCV, 21 A).

6. *Chronica, sive Flores Historiarum, prol.*: "What shall we say against lazy hearers who say disparagingly: 'What need is there . . . to entrust the diverse cases of men to writing . . . ?' They should know that the good morals and lives of predecessors are set down to be imitated by their successors, whilst the examples of the wicked . . . are described so as rather to be avoided" — "Quid contra auditores pigros dicemus, qui obtrectando dicunt: quid necesse est . . . diversos hominum casus litteris mandare . . . ? Noverint isti bonos mores et vitas praecedentium, ad imitationem subsequentium proponi, malorum vero exempla . . . ut potius evitentur describi etc. Hoc omnes divinae paginae scriptores faciunt . . ." (H. D. Coxe, 1841, I, 1-2).

7. *Chronicon Centulense, praef.* (PL, CLXXIV, 1213 AB).

8. *Gesta Friderici, proem.*: "This, I think, was the intention of all who have written down the deeds accomplished before us: to extol the famous deeds of brave men so as to move the minds of human beings to virtue, but either to suppress the dark deeds of the wicked with silence or, if they be dragged to light, to set them out as an error [taking 'pro mendo' as two words] so as to frighten off the minds of those same mortals" — "Omnium qui ante nos res gestas scripserunt, haec, ut arbitror, fuit intentio virorum fortium clara facinora ob movendos hominum ad virtutem animos extollere, ignavorum vero obscura facta vel silentio supprimere vel si ad lucem trahantur, ad terrendas eorumdem mortalium mentes promendo ponere" (MGH, *Scr.*, XX, 351).

9. "For this reason, though others may not be missing, too" — "Hac de causa, licet aliae non desint etc." (PL, CLX, 421 CD).

10. *Hist. eccl.*, letter to the princess *Adele* (PL, CLXIII, 821 AB, 822 A).

11. *Speculum historiale de gestis regum Angliae, proem.*: "so that later men, summoned to the incentives of the virtues by the examples of these princes, might strive to imitate the ones whom they admired" — ". . . quatenus dictorum exemplis principum posteri ad incitamenta virtutum provocati, eos quos mirarentur imitari studerent" (J. Y. B. Mayor, 1, 1863, 3).

12. *Prol.*, citing Rom. 15:2 (PL, CLXX, 889-91).

13. *Prol.*: The historians have written "so that . . . they may make men more

careful in the honor of the Lord and in the cultivation of justice . . . as it were by the proposed examples of reward or punishment" — "ut . . . quasi propositis exemplis praemii vel penae, reddant homines in timore Domini et cultu justitiae cautiores" (Chibnall, 3).

14. Bk. I, *prol.*: "The examples of our betters, which are virtue's incentives and provocations, would not correct or preserve anyone at all, unless the pious care of writers and triumphant diligence of leisure had transmitted them to posterity" — "Exempla majorum quae sunt incitamenta et fomenta virtutis nullum omnino corrigerent aut servarent, nisi pia sollicitudo scriptorum et triumphatrix inertiae diligentia eadem ad posteros transmisisset" (PL, CXCIX, 385 A).

15. *Prol.* (PL, CLXXIV, 1511-4).

16. *Bella Parisiacae urbis, proem.* (*P. lat. m. aevi*, IV, 77).

17. *Historiae, praef.* (PL, CXLII, 613 AB).

18. Fréculphe, *Chron.*, t. II, *praef.*: "In these [books] . . . my lord Charles could look as in a mirror to consider what to do or what to avoid" — "In his (libris) velut in speculo . . . dominus meus Carolus inspicere quid agendum vel quid vitandum sit poterit" (PL, CVI, 116 C).

19. *Annales rerum Danicarum,* 1046-1534 (J. Langebek, II, 1773, 554).

20. Godfrey of Admont, *In Script.*, h. 12: "Though all sacred Scripture instructs and teaches the morals and the life of men" — "licet omnis sacra Scriptura mores et vitam hominum instruat et doceat" (PL, CLXXIV, 1110 C).

21. Robert of Melun, *prol.* (PL, CLX, 421 BC).

22. *V. s. Galli*, Bk. I: "Noah's continence and Abraham's faith were being reported along with the examples of the patriarchs as well as the signs of Moses, once all those deeds of the Law had been rendered into a remedy for souls" — "Continentia Noe et fides Abraham, cum exemplis patriarcha[r]um nec non et mosaicis signis recitabantur, legalibus illis gestis ad animarum medelam cunctis redactis" (MGH, *Scr.*, II, 14). Alexander of Canterbury: "In the history there are the simple accomplishments of the saints and examples, etc." — "In historia sunt simplicia gesta sanctorum et exempla, etc." (*L. de S. Ans. similit.*, c. cxciv; PL, CLIX, 708 A).

23. "admonitio ad melioris vitae conversationem": Othloh, *De cursu sp.* (PL, CXLVI, 192 C, 202 B); *De admon. cl. et laic.*, c. v (254 D); etc. Other texts in Rousset, *Mél. L. Halphen,* 624-5.

24. Cf. Et. Gilson, *L'esprit de la philosophie méd.* II (1944), 365-6: "If the absence of our history were equivalent to the absence of all history, one could be assured that the Middle Ages does not have one. One could as easily prove, by the same method, that it had no poetry" — "Si l'absence de notre histoire équivaut à l'absence de toute histoire, on peut être assuré que le moyen âge n'en a aucune. On prouverait aussi facilement d'ailleurs, par la même méthode, qu'il n'a eu aucune poésie" — or any philosophy.

25. Cf. Henri Niel, S.J., "Le sens de l'histoire," RSR 46 (1958), 60-77. "The work of unification performed by the historian is of a teleological order. . . . The historian tries to understand the facts and not just to lay them out. To understand a fact is to know its signification by substituting it everywhere it was an expression. The intelligible sense of history is a function of the type of ends in function of which the historian has tried to understand the past" — "Le travail

d'unification opéré par l'historien est d'ordre téléologique. . . . L'historien cherche à comprendre les faits et pas seulement à les expliquer. Comprendre un fait, c'est connaître sa signification en le replaçant dans le tout dont il est l'expression. . . . Le sens intelligible de l'histoire est fonction du type de fins en fonction desquelles l'historien a tenté de comprendre le passé."

26. H. Niel, *Ibid.*, 69: The philosophers of history "present themselves as the heirs of Christianity. . . . K. Löwith on this subject remarks that in the course of the 19th century the eschatological current was principally represented by atheistic philosophers. In this regard they spoke of Christian truths gone mad, but without sufficiently noting in what respect they were mad. Nevertheless, carried away by its excesses, this historic movement was itself, as it were, put into question. One after the other, Kierkegaard, Jaspers, Heidegger announced the impossibility of any philosophy of history. They pointed out the impossibility for man to rise from his condition and to embrace the totality of the historical process from the point of view of God" — "se donnent comme les héritiers du christianisme. . . . K. Löwith remarque à ce sujet qu'au cours du XIX siècle le courant eschatologique était principalement représenté par des philosophies athées. On a parlé à ce propos de vérités chrétiennes devenues folles, mais sans assez marquer en quoi elles étaient folles. Cependant, emporté par son excès, ce mouvement historique s'est comme remis en question lui-même. Tour à tour Kierkegaard, Jaspers, Heidegger ont dénoncé l'impossibilité de toute philosophie de l'histoire. On a relevé l'impossibilité pour l'homme de sortir de sa condition et d'embrasser du point de vue de Dieu la totalité du devenir historique." Cf. Karl Jaspers, *Origine et sens de l'histoire* (tr. H. Naef), 6: "I should like to try to sketch out the pattern of a conception of the totality of history. In so doing, I am relying on a thesis that depends upon faith" — "Je voudrais essayer d'esquisser le schéma d'une conception d'ensemble de l'histoire. Ce faisant, je m'appuie sur une thèse qui relève de la foi. . . ." For R. Niebuhr also, "all philosophy of history is a decoy" — "toute philosophie de l'histoire est un leurre": G.-P. Vignaux, *La théologie de l'hist. chez Reinhold Niebuhr* (1957), 34.

27. Cf. Maximus the Confessor, *Q. ad Thal.* 17 (PG, XC, 304 B).

28. Gregory of Elvira, *Tr.* 7: "so that I may discuss the power, character, and mystery of that reading according to the spiritual understanding" — "ut vim, rationem atque mysterium lectionis istius secundum spiritalem intelligentiam disseram" (76); cf. *Tr.* 13: "But we show that the power and spiritual character of all the deeds pertained to the prefiguration of the New Testament" — "Nos vero, vim omnium gestorum et rationem spiritalem ad novi Testamenti figuram pertinuisse monstramus" (141), etc.

29. *Regula sive lib. de inst. virg.*, c. vii: "So that the Old Testament should not be read carnally" — "Ut carnaliter non legi debeat vetus Testamentum" (PL, LXXII, 884 AC). Cf. Isidore, *De fide*, Bk. II, c. xx (83, 528-9).

30. Cf. Cyril of Alexandria on "those who reject the history in the inspired Scriptures as a frivolity, because they did not push as far as the spiritual understanding" (PG, LXX, 192 A).

31. Hervaeus, *In Is.*, Bk. I (PL, CLXXXI, 77 D).

32. "l'exégèse commandait de reconnaître (dans la Bible) moins le tableau d'événements, portant leur sens en eux-mêmes, que la préfiguration de ce qui

devait les suivre" — "interprétation symbolique" — "brouillait l'intelligence des réalités": *La société féodale* (1939), 144.

33. Especially for his *Vita s. Gregorii.* Cf. A. Lapotre, "Le Souper de Jean Diacre," *Mél. d'archéol. et d'hist.*, XXI (1901), 368-9, 374, 378-9. Nevertheless H. I. Marrou (*ibid.*, 48, 1931, 168) mistrusts certain excessively precise details.

34. *Praef.:* "though . . . I presume that I shall be perpetually favored by all who look upon the truth" — "quamquam . . . cunctis veritatem tuentibus me perpetuo placiturum fore praesumam" (PL, LXXV, 62 C).

35. *V. s. Juliani, ep. dedic.*, n. 2: "I should have said it is a deed calling for reverence rather than rejoicing, since things that must be recited in the sight of the Truth are to be spoken and written with the gravity of great reverence, lest what is thought of a source for God's being pleased should rather provoke him to wrath; for nothing pleases him except what is true. . . . Hence the things the Truth has done are to be spoken of with truth; since if any of the Fathers is said to have performed a miracle, it is not the man but God who works it" — "Quod opus reverendum potius quam jucundum dixerim, quia cum magnae reverentiae gravitate dicenda et scribenda sunt quae in conspectu veritatis recitari debent, ne unde Deus placari creditur, inde amplius ad iracundiam provocetur; nihil enim ei placet, nisi quod verum est. . . . Dicenda ergo cum veritate sunt quae veritas gessit; quia si aliquis Patrum aliquod dicitur fecesse miraculum, non illud homo, sed Deus operatur . . ." (PL, CXXXVII, 781-2); n. 3-4 (782-4). Perhaps even more than the first, it is the second Middle Age, and even a more recent epoch which was indeed avid for and credulous of the marvelous. In any case, history was not then, as has been written recently, "merely a collection of *mirabilia*."

Widrici, *Vita S. Gerardi* (v. 1040), *praef.:* — "Nemini autem veniat in scrupulum, quasi hic aliquid inscribatur impostura figmenti commentatum, quia Omnipotentis fideles in supernae laudationis gloria indefesse intenti, non egent adulatoria hominum laude praedicari, et in re tali melius censeo probabiliter reticere, quam quicquam mendacii fuco coloratum praeferre" (MGH, *Scr.*, IV, 490).

36. G. Schnurer, *L'Egl. et la civil. au m. âge*, II (tr. G. Castella, 1935), 222.

37. *Gesta abb. Trud.*, Bk. IV, c. xi: "Let no one vex me, let no one pull me down, if one truth, my soul's fear of lying, God's threat through holy Scripture, should itself compel me to speak the truth. . . . It is the duty of the historiographer neither by flattery nor love nor hate to depart from the pathway of the truth" — "Nemo me mordeat, nemo mihi detrahat, si veritatem loqui ipsa una compellat veritas, ipse animae meae timor de mendacia, ipsa Dei per sanctam Scripturam comminatio. . . . Historiographi debitum est nec assentatione nec amore nec odio nec timore a veritatis tramite declinare" (MGH, *Scr.*, X, 250). Also Adam of Brême, *Gesta Hammab. Eccl. Pontif.* (Manitius, II, 410).

38. *Historiae*, Bk. IV, c. iii (PL, CXLII, 673-4).

39. "que la critique historique la plus saine et la plus orthodoxe ne peut qu'approuver": Ghellinck, *Litt. lat.*, II, 97-9. Cf. Georges Bourgin: Guibert de Nogent, *Hist. de sa vie* (1907), intr. At the threshold of the 13th cent., the *Miracula sancti Gileberti* (1201) will satisfy "certain of the requirements of modern criticism": R. Roreville, *Le Livre de S. Gilbert de Sempringham* (1943), xlviii.

40. Dudden, *St. Gregory the Great*, II, 286.

41. "plana simplicitas": Paul the Deacon, h. 95: "But this is the plain simplicity of the history, so that the deep profundity of the senses may lie hidden within it" — "Sed haec historiae sic est plana simplicitas, ut in ea sensuum lateat alta profunditas" (PL, XCV, 1274 A).

42. "facilitas historiae": Gloss on the Sentences (RTAM, 1931, 355). Augustine, *In ps. CIII*, n. 7: "He restored it to ease, if you take it literally. . . . A marvelous ease" — "ad facilitatem redegit, si ad litteram accipias. . . . Mira facilitas" (CCL, 40, 1479).

43. "aperta historiae verba": Greg., *Mor., ep. miss.*, c. iii: "Sometimes we neglect to explain the plain words of the history lest we come upon the obscure ones too late" — "Aliquando vero exponere aperta historiae verba negligimus, ne tardius ad obscura veniamus" (PL, LXXV, 515 C). Cf. Leo, regarding the Passion account: *s.* 52, c. i; 66, c. i (LIV, 313-4, 364 C); *s.* 69, c. iii: "Hold the order of accomplishments as manifest as if you were to come into contact with all things that belong to the body by touch" — "Rerum gestarum ordinem tam habetote manifestum, quam si omnia corporis et attingeretis et tactu" (377).

44. "facies historiae": Rupert, *In Gen.*, Bk. V, c. vii: "The very face of the present history is now smiling with light serene" — "Ipsa facies praesentis historiae jam sereno lumine arridet" (PL, CLXVII, 372 D).

45. "Plana transcurrimus, ut in obscuris immoremur": Bruno of Segni, *In Is.* (*Sp. cas.*, 3, 4).

46. *Inst.*, c. x, he reports him among the authors "whom I have collected with persistent curiosity" — "quos sedula curiositate collegi" (PL, LXX, 1122 D). He had perhaps met Junilius: Courcelle, 317.

47. *De part. div. legis*, Bk. I, c. iii, *De historia:* history "has this in common with simple doctrine, that both appear plainly on the surface, though they are often hard to understand: for the others [viz. prophecy and proverbs] do not" — "Habet commune cum simplici doctrina, quod utraque superficie plane videntur, cum sint intellectu plerumque difficiles: nam aliae (= prophetia et proverbia) contra" (PL, LXVIII, 17 B); c. vi: "They seem easy on the surface, though they are very often hard to look into or to understand" — "superficie faciles videntur, cum sint inspectione aut intellectu plerumque difficiles" (19 D).

48. Thus Abelard, *In Hexaem., praef.* (PL, CLXXVIII, 731 A). Cf. Bruno of Segni (CLXIV, 147 D).

49. "All the things belonging to the Law . . . are so immense that they cannot easily be explicated even according to the text of the history" — "Omnia legis . . . tam immensa sunt, ut nec juxta historiae textum explicari facile possunt" (PL, LXXXIII, 287 B).

50. *Quaest. sup. Ex., prol.* (PL, XCIII, 364 D).

51. "Qui verba accipere historiae juxta litteram negligit, ablatum sibi veritatis lumen abscondit": *Mor., ep. miss.*, c. iv (PL, LXXV, 514 D).

52. *In Ez.*, Bk. II, h. 9, n. 1: "So once these matters of the exterior narrative have been discussed, let the conversation (which must, thanks to God's assistance, now be easier by as much as ignorance of the exterior description does not constrict us) go back to the spiritual understanding" — "His itaque de exteriori narratione discussis, ad spiritalem intellectum sermo redeat, qui tanto jam esse,

largiente Deo, facilior debet, quanto nos exterioris descriptionis ignorantia non angustat" (PL, LXXVI, 1042 B).

53. "Nisi litteram patenter agnoscas, frustra te in studio allegoriae exquirendae vel moralitatis exerces": *Proem. ad tropol.* (PL, CLVI, 339 D).

54. Cf. Or., *In Lev.*, h. 14, n. 1: "The history has been reported to us, but although its recitation may seem obvious, nevertheless, unless we follow more diligently what it literally contains, the inner sense will scarcely be plain to us. . . . Therefore let us first see what the history we are proposing means, and, though it may seem plain, let us try to set it before our eyes still more clearly" — "Historia nobis recitata est, cujus quamvis videatur aperta narratio, tamen, nisi diligentius continentiam ejus quae est secundum litteram consequamur, interior nobis sensus haud facile patebit. . . . Videamus ergo primo quid sibi velit historia quam proponimus, et, quamvis plana videatur, tamen adhuc evidentius eam tentemus sub oculis ponere" (478).

55. Rupert, *In Jonam*, c. ii: "A very memorable accomplishment does not need exposition, but it is always to be remembered" — "Res gesta valde memorabilis expositione non indiget, sed hoc semper memoriter tenendum est" (PL, CLXVIII, 431 B).

56. "Per se satis patet litteralis sensus": *In Aggaeum* (PL, CLXVIII, 690 D). *In Ex.:* "The literal description is right before your eyes; we can offer no clearer explanation than that" — "Descriptio litteralis est in promptu, qua planiorem descriptionem explicare non possumus" (CLXVII, 720 C): for what is there to add to the description that the chapter commented by Rupert gives of the high priest's vestments?

57. "The expression is clear at the literal level" — "Sermo manifestus est secundum litteram"; "It is clear according to the letter how the ark was able to be opened" — "Liquet quemadmodum arca potuerit aperiri secundum litteram" (PL, XIV, 348 D, 396 A).

58. *In ps. CIII (An. mar.,* III, 1, 75), etc. Cf. note 13.

59. *Mor.*, Bk. XVI, c. iv, n. 4: "But since the things subjoined are quite obvious according to the history, they are not to be expounded according to the letter" — "Ea vero quae subjuncta sunt, quia valde juxta historiam patent, exponenda ad litteram non sunt" (PL, LXXV, 1122 C).

60. *H. de temp.* 102: "But since the things that are related to the letter are sufficiently clear of themselves, let us go on to hunt up the mystery" — "Sed quoniam ea quae sunt ad litteram satis patent per se, ad indagandum mysterium ascendamus" (PL, XCV, 1302 A).

61. PL, XCI, 844 B, 845 D, 884 A, 952 D, 963 B, 988 D, 994 D, 1239 D; XCII, 259 A, 377 B, 501 B, 511 D.

62. *S. de lect. ev.,* n. 14 (PL, LXXXIX, 1302 B).

63. *In Ref.* 1: "The sense of the letter is quite clear" — "Patet sane litterae sensus" (PL, L, 1076 D).

64. PL, CVIII, 719 B, 823 D, 834 D, 952 A, 1039 D; CX, 607 B, 744 A, 781 D, 777 C; CIX, 1139 C; CXI, 702 B, 705 D, 719 D); etc.

65. *In Zach.:* "The things that are obvious enough of themselves need no explanation" — "Quae per se satis aperta sunt, nec egent expositione" (PL, CXVII, 230 D); "The history is clear" — "Historia patet" (973 D).

66. Ps.-Remi, *In ps. LII* (CXXXI, 406 C). Honorius (CXCIV, 579 A, 639 D). Gerhoh (449 C). Petrus Cellensis (CCII, 960 C); etc.

67. *In Is.:* This "does not need exposition" — Hoc "expositione non indiget" (PL, XXIV, 156 C); "This matter does not need interpretation" — "Quae res interpretatione non indiget" (601 A). *In Jer.:* "In many cases the manifest history is interwoven" — "In plerisque manifesta historia texitur" (XXIV, 679 A); "Since they seem clear according to the letter" — "Cum juxta litteram videantur perspicua" (747 D). *In Dan.* (XXV, 512 D). *In Ez.:* "the interpretation is easy according to the letter" — "juxta litteram, facilis interpretatio"; "it is clear according to the letter" — "juxta litteram perspicuum est" (217 D, etc.). *In Matt.:* "The sense is manifest according to the letter; let us extend the sacraments of the spiritual interpretation" — "Juxta litteram manifestus est sensus; spiritalis interpretationis sacramenta pandamus" (XXVI, 100 C); etc.

68. "Reliqua, quia sunt manifesta, secundum litteram exponere superfluum ducimus": Hervaeus, *In Is.*, Bk. I (PL, CLXXXI, 31 A). Anonymous sermon: "Since these deeds of the Lord recalled by the words of the Evangelist are clear enough literally, since they were just as they sound, the mystical sense is to be unfolded briefly" — "Quia haec facta Domini verbis evangelistae commemorata ad litteram satis patent, quoniam ita fuerunt ut sonant, mysticus sensus pro brevitate pandendus est" (CLXXI, 505 A).

69. "Narratio omnis in sancta Scriptura, quam est brevis, et quam dilucida!": *De Sp. sancto*, Bk. VII, c. xii (PL, CLXVII, 1767 D). Not all admitted this sort of apologetic, however: cf. Alvarus.

70. Greg., *In Ez.*, Bk. I, h. 12, n. 15: "so that we may go over it, just touching it according the consideration of the letter" — "ut juxta considerationem litterae tangendo transeamus" (PL, LXXVI, 924 B). Rabanus Maurus, *idem* (CX, 585 A). Angelome, *In Reg. praef. apol.:* "First we strove to touch on the historical signification, which draws out the deeds" — "Studuimus primum historicam significationem, quae gesta depromit, tangere" (CXV, 246 CD). Peter of Poitiers, *Alleg. sup. tab.:* "the sequence of the history is to be touched on briefly" — "breviter series historiae tangenda est" (2); "meanwhile it is necessary to stick with the history briefly, for there to be something upon which the spiritual sense may be built" — "interdum breviter historiae insistere oportet, ut sit super quo spiritualis sensus innitatur" (82). Petrus Cellensis, *s.* 37: "that we may briefly touch upon the letter" — "ut litteram breviter tangamus" (CCII, 752 C).

71. Jerome, *In Ez.*, XXI, 1: "We have briefly spoken of what may appear to us historically; now let us take up the high points of the tropology" — "Quid nobis videatur juxta historiam breviter diximus: nunc tropologiae summa carpamus" (PL, XXIV, 260). Greg., *In Ez.*, Bk. II, h. 8, n. 1: "The words of the Prophet ... need reading rather than explaining" — "Prophetae verba ... lectione magis indigent quam expositione" (LXXVI, 1027 A); h. 10, n. 3: "We run across these words of the letter briefly, so that we may inquire after the mystical senses in them without excessive brevity" — "Haec de verbis litterae sub brevitate transcurrimus, ut in eis sensus mysticos non breviter exquiramus" (1059 AB).

72. Cf. John 5:39. Berengaud, *In Ap.*, V. 7: "no one can see through the depth of the divine ... mysteries as it really is" — "profunditatem divinorum ... mysteriorum nullus, sicuti est, perscrutari potest" (PL, XVII, 961 A). Beatus, *In Ap.:*

"The doctors of the New Testament were led to the point that they scrutinized certain of the allegories hidden in the darkness of the Old Testament" — "Testamenti novi doctores ad hoc usque perducti sunt, ut occulta quaeque allegoriarum in caligine veteris Testamenti scrutarentur" (Florez, 554). Claudius, *In Reg.*, Bk. I: "If we should scrutinize the mysteries" — "Si mysteria perscrutamur" (PL, L, 1069 B).

73. "Quia plane videmus historiam, plene investigemus allegoriam": Innocent III, s. 24 (PL, CCXVII, 561 D).

74. "Citius haec referamus ad nos": *In Lev.*, h. 15, n. 2 (487).

75. "ut et sacramentum ejus commodius pandatur": Petrus Cellensis, s. 16 (PL, CCII, 692 D).

76. Claudius, 30 *quaest. sup. libros Reg., praef.*: "To me it seems superfluous to have to mingle mere questions of the letter amid the spiritual flowers of allegory" — "Superfluum mihi visum est, ut nudas litterae quaestiones inter spirituales permiscere debuissem allegoriae flores" (PL, CIV, 809 D). Richard, s. 63: "Since the history is known and I am speaking to those who know the Law, and it is tedious and seems superfluous to repeat the whole history again, let us attend to the things that pertain to the spiritual understanding, now that we have foregone the report of the history" — "Quia nota est historia, et scientibus legem loquor, longumque est superfluum videtur totam historiam replicare, historiae narratione praetermissa, iis quae ad spiritalem intellectum pertinent attendamus" (CLXXVII, 1092-3). Rupert, *In Gen.*, Bk. VIII: "one ought not to dwell on what is obvious" — "manifestis immorandum non est" (CXLVII, 523 B).

77. "Meministis, credo: scientibus enim legem loquor": Bernard, *In f. SS. Petri et Pauli*, s. 3, n. 6 (PL, CLXXXIII, 414 D); *In oct. Paschae*, s. 1, n. 5: "Let them to whom the history of the Old Testament is well-known recall it" — "Recolant quibus nota est historia V. Testamenti" (244 B).

78. "Quia rem scientibus loquor, non mihi multis elaborandum est verbis": Peter Damian, *Exp. libri Gen.*, c. xxvi (PL, CXLV, 853 B). Cassiodorus, *In ps. LXXIX*: "If anyone should try to repeat the usual things, he will offend learned men and those soundly educated in the hearing of Christ" — "Doctis viris et in auditorio Christi salubriter eruditis, si quis usitata repetere conetur, offendit" (LXX, 579 B).

79. "Oportebat prius secundum historiam discutere quae leguntur, et sic . . . spiritalem in his intelligentiam quaerere": *In Ex.*, h. 10, n. 2 (247).

80. *In Ap.*, v. 7: "For the commentator . . . either manifests the obscurities of the history by explaining them . . ." — "Expositor namque . . . aut obscuritates historiae exponendo manifestat" (PL, XVII, 968 B).

81. "Sed ista praetermittentes, ad spiritalem intelligentiam recurramus": *In Ap.*, v. 3 (PL, XVII, 826 B).

82. Rabanus, *Cler. inst.*, Bk. III, c. iii: "Sed multis et multiplicibus obscuritatibus et ambiguitatibus decipiuntur, qui temere legunt, aliud pro alio sentientes, quibusdam autem locis quid vel falso suspicuntur, cum non inveniunt, ita obscure dicta quaedam, densissimam caliginem obducunt" (PL, CVII, 380 B).

83. "Verba tenebrosa propter mysteriorum magnitudinem": Beatus, *In Ap.* (Florez, 388): "The obscure speech of holy Scripture is an involved book, which has been involved with a profundity of judgments, so that it may not easily be penetrated by the sense of everyone" — "Liber autem involutus est Scripturae

sacrae eloquium obscurum, qui profunditate sententiarum est involutus, ut non facile sensu omnium penetretur" (385-86). Rabanus, *loc. cit.*: "I do not doubt that it was all divinely foreseen, to overcome pride by labor and to restore the understanding from the contempt to which easily investigated topics frequently grow worthless. For in the divine books there are very many places that are difficult by reason of tropological expressions, and also many of the affairs are great in magnitude; and so it is necessary for them to be investigated with sagacity both of sense and of thought and for the things understood to be venerated proportionate to their dignity" — "Quod totum provisum esse divinitus non dubito, ad edomandam labore superbiam, et intellectum a fastidio renovandum, cui facile investigata plerumque vilescunt. Sunt enim in divinis libris plurima loca tropicis locutionibus difficilia, sunt quoque multa rerum magnitudine eximia; atque ideo necesse est ut et sensus et ingenii sagacitate investigentur, et pro sui dignitate intellecta venerentur" (PL, CVII, 380 C).

84. Rabanus, *ibid.*: "The Holy Spirit has so magnificently and healthfully treated the holy Scriptures, that he has attended to hunger with the more obvious passages, but has turned back satiety with the obscurer ones" — "Magnifice ergo et salubriter Spiritus sanctus ita Scripturas sanctas medicavit, ut locis apertioribus fami occurreret, obscurioribus autem fastidia detergeret." *Idem*, in Rathier of Verona, *Phrenesis, proem.* (PL, CXXXVI, 375 A), etc.

85. Autpert, *In Ap.*, Bk. V: "Holy Scripture is sometimes food, and sometimes drink. For in the more obscure matters that can in no way be understood unless they be cleared of knots, it is food; for whatever is explained so as to be understood is, as it were chewed so as to be swallowed. In the clearer matters, however, it is drink; for we swallow drink without chewing" — "Sancta autem Scriptura aliquando cibus, aliquando vero potus est. In rebus enim obscurioribus, quae intelligi nullatenus possunt nisi enodentur cibus est; quidquid enim exponitur ut intelligatur, quasi manditur ut glutiatur. In rebus vero apertioribus, potus est; potum enim non mandendo glutimus" (518 D); Bk. IX (611 H). Paschasius, *In Lam.*, Bk. IV (PL, CXX, 1208 A). Remi of Auxerre, *In Os.*, c. vii (CXVII, 58 D). Aimon, *In Apoc.* (CXVII, 1065-6); *In Is.*, c. iii, 30, 49, 55 (CXVI, 736 D, 867 AB, 966 B, 1001 A). *Miscell.*, Bk. I, tit. 161 (CLXXVII, 558 CD); Bk. III, tit. 66 (672 C). Hervaeus, *In Is.*, Bks. I and VII (CLXXX, 77 BC, 505 BC). Langton, (Smalley, *Speculum* 6, 69); etc. Cf. Bernard (PL, CLXXXIII, 455 C). Berno of Reichenau transposes the theme, *V. s. Udalrici, prol.*: "Let me put together so much material in a moderate sermon, so that approaching from either side, once the measured amount of love has been spread out, both the little ones are able find milk to suck and the strong food to eat" — "talem moderato sermone materiam componam, ut ex utraque parte ad se venientes, media caritate constrata, et parvuli lac quod sugant, et fortes valeant invenire cibum quem comedant" (CXLII, 1184 C).

86. Beatus, *In Ap.*, Bk. III: "The very obscurity of God's speeches is useful, since the word exercises one so as to be stretched out with exhaustion and thus forced to grasp what he cannot grasp when at ease" — "Magnae vero utilitatis est ipsa obscuritas eloquiorum Dei, quia exercet verbum ut fatigatione dilatetur, et extensus capiat quod capere non possit otiosus" (267). Manegold, *In ps. X:* "Some of the sons of men are so exercised by some obscure places of God's Scriptures that they hunt about as though with eyes closed; but are so illuminated by other

obvious passages of the Scriptures, that they see" — "Qui filii hominum quibusdam obscuris locis Scripturarum quasi clausis oculis Dei exercentur, ut quaerant; quibusdam vero manifestis Scripturarum locis illuminantur, ut videant" (PL, XCIII, 545 D); etc.

87. Isidore, *Sent.*, Bk. I, c. xviii, n. 5-6 (PL, LXXXIII, 576-7). Rupert, *In Ap.*, c. x: "At that point, too, the brilliant minds of many will be exercised in many ways, and the things that have been won with laborious zeal from the treasuries of the Scriptures will not seem worthless" — "Tunc et praeclara ingenia multorum multipliciter exercebuntur, et quae de Scripturarum thesauris laborioso fuerint studio conquisita, non vilia videbuntur" (CLXIX, 1011 B). Hugh Métel, *ep.* 5 (333); etc.

88. *Doctr. chr.*, Bk. II, c. vi, n. 7: "to overcome pride by work and to call the intellect back from the disgust to which easily investigated matters frequently seem worthless" — "ad edomandum labore superbiam, et intellectum a fastidio revocandum, cui facile investigata plerumque vilescunt" (Combès-Farges, 244); Bk. IV, c. viii, n. 22 (458). *De cat. rud.*, c. ix, n. 13 (50-1). *De Trin.*, Bk. XV, c. xvii, n. 27: "But to train us, the divine word has not made those things readily available to be sought into with greater zeal, but rather those that are to be scrutinized in secret and to be drawn forth from their secrecy" — "Ut autem nos exerceret sermo divinus, non res in promptu sitas sed in abdito scrutandas et ex abdito eruendas majore studio fecit inquiri" (Agaësse, 500). *C. Faust.*, Bk. XII, c. xiv: "though by as much as these things are brought forth from more hidden places, by so much the more sweetly are they contemplated" — "quae, quamvis tanto suavius contemplentur, quanto ex abditioribus locis enucleantur" (262). *In ps. CIII, s.* 2, n. 1: "What is sought for with greater difficulty is usually sweeter on being found" — "Quod difficilius quaeritur, solet dulcius inveniri" (CCL, 40, 1492). *In ps. CXL*, n. 1: For in holy Scriptures there are deep mysteries, which are hidden lest they seem cheap, are sought to train us, and are opened to feed us" — "Sunt enim in Scripturis sanctis profunda mysteria, quae ad hoc absconduntur ne vilescant, ad hoc quaeruntur ut exerceant, ad hoc aperiuntur ut pascant" (PL, XXXVII, 1815); etc.

89. *In Ez.*, Bk. I, h. 8, n. 1 (PL, LXXVI, 829 AB); h. 10, n. 3 (886-7). *Mor.*, Bk. I, c. xxi, n. 29 (LXXV, 540 BC); Bk. VI, c. v, n. 6 (732); etc.

90. Rabanus, *Cler. inst.*, Bk. III, c. iii: "But almost nothing is dug out from those obscurities that is not found most fully expressed elsewhere" — "Nihil autem fere de illis obscuritatibus eruitur, quod non plenissime dictum alibi reperiatur" (PL, CVII, 380 C).

91. Rabanus, *In Ex.*, Bk. II, c. x: "The letter of the Law is designated by the cloud and everything that was dark in the withdrawal of God; the spiritual sense is shown by the mountain and everything that was brilliant there" — "Per caliginem et omne quidquid tenebrosum in decessu Dei erat, littera legis designatur; per montem vero et omne quidquid ibi splendidum fuit, sensus spiritualis demonstratur" (PL, CVIII, 89 D).

92. "Qui operit caelum nubibus": Ps. 146:8. Cf. Ps. 17:12: "He set the darkness as his hiding-place" — "Posuit tenebras latibulum suum."

93. "Induam caelos tenebris": Isa. 50:3. Peter of Poitiers, *Allegoriae* (Moore-Corbett, 10).

94. "sub caligine quippe litterae, caelestium mysteriorum secreta velantur": Aelred, *s. de oner.* 3 (PL, CXCV, 376 A).

Notes to Pages 76-77

95. Even in his homilies Origen alluded more than once to the difficulties of the letter. Thus *In Num.*, h. 13, n. 3 (110-11); *In Jos.*, h. 25, n. 4 (456); *In Reg.*, h. 1, n. 2 (3-4).

96. *De doct. chr.*, Bk. II, c. vi, n. 7-8 (Combès-Farges, 244-6). *S.* 51, n. 5 (PL, XXXVIII, 336); *In ps. XVIII*, n. 2, n. 4 (CCL, 38, 108); *In ps. CXXVI*, n. 11 (40, 1865); *In ps. CXLVI*, n. 13: ". . . the Scriptures healthfully covering the understanding with certain mysteries, so that the little ones might be trained" — "Scripturas mysticis quibusdam rebus salubriter tegentes intelligentiam, ut parvuli exerceantur" (40, 2132); n. 15: "What is 'he who covers the heavens with clouds'? — he who covers Scripture with figures and sacraments. . . . Therefore he covers the heavens with clouds so as to prepare rain for the earth." — "Quid est, qui cooperit caelum nubibus? — Qui contegit Scripturam figuris et sacramentis. . . . Ad hoc ergo ille cooperit caelum nubibus, ut paret terrae pluviam" (2132-3).

97. *In Ez.*, Bk. I, h. 9, n. 29 (PL, LXXVI, 882-3). *Reg. past.*, 3, c. xxiv (LXXVII, 94 CD).

98. "allegoriarum obscuritates, caligines, umbrae, tenebrae": PL, LXXVI, 71 A, 71 C, 523 C, 967 CD.

99. *Tenebrosa aqua in nubibus aeris:* Greg., *Mor.*, Bk. XVII, n. 36 (PL, LXXVI, 27 A). *In Ez.*, h. 6, n. 1 (829 A). Beatus, *In Ap.*, Bk. III: "The Gospel . . . lies hidden within the Law, as the Psalm writer says: 'There is dark water in the clouds of the air, since in the prophets knowledge is obscure" — "Evangelium intra legem . . . occultum jacebat, sicut Psalmigraphus ait: Tenebrosa aqua in nubibus aeris, quia obscura est scientia in prophetis" (267). Honorius, *In ps. CII*, 3: "'Thou who coverest its higher parts' i.e., the surface of the Scriptures 'with the waters', which means 'Thou coverest the letter with waters' i.e., with deep and obscure allegory" — "Qui tegis aquis superiora ejus, id est, superficiem Scripturae, quod est litteram tegis aquis, id est profunda et obscura allegoria" (CXCIV, 622 B). Richard (?), *In Nahum* (XCVII, 745 BD). Peter of Poitiers, *All. sup. tab. Moys.:* "For of old the water, i.e., the doctrine, was dark in the clouds of the air, i.e., in the prophets who rained down on us with the drops of sacred preaching. For at that point all things were covered over with enigmas and the darkness of figures" — "Olim enim tenebrosa erat aqua, id est doctrina, in nubibus aeris, id est in prophetis qui nos compluunt guttis sacrae praedicationis. Tunc enim omnia erant operta aenigmatibus et tenebris figurarum etc." (10). Cf. Or., *In ps. XVII*, 12 (PG, XII, 1227 D).

100. "occulta scientia in propheticis atque legalibus scripturis": Rupert, *In Cant.*, Bk. V (PL, CLXVIII, 922 D).

101. Hervaeus, *In Is.*, Bk. I: "It is the task of the few to know the strong and hidden things; but that of the many to sense the uncovered parts of the history" — "Paucorum quippe est fortia et occulta cognoscere, multorum vero historiae aperta sentire" (PL, CLXXXI, 77 C).

Notes to Chapter Seven
§5. The Word of God

1. Rabanus, *In Paral.*, Bk. IV, c. xxvii (PL, CIX, 514 B). *In Ez.*, Bk. XII: "For the moment let it suffice to have said these things strictly in accordance with the sim-

ple sense; now let us catch, with the same brevity, such high points of the spiritual understanding as the difficulty of the explanation allows" [reading 'patitur' for 'petitur'] — "Haec interim juxta simplicem sensum strictim dixisse sufficiat; nunc eadem brevitate, quantum explanationis p[a]titur difficultas, spiritalis intelligentiae summa quaeque carpamus" (CX, 826 B).

2. "haec quae allegorica indagione transcurrimus, oportet ut per omnia etiam juxta historiam teneamus": Greg., *Mor.,* Bk. XX, c. xxvii, n. 56 (PL, LXXVI, 171 B).

3. "ita teneatur rei gestae veritas, ut non evacuetur rei gerendae prophetia": *Ibid.,* Bk. XXXV, c. xx, n. 48: "if the good things we know of the life of the saints lack truth, they are nothing; if they do not hold mysteries, they are insignificant" — "bona enim, quae de sanctorum vita cognoscimus, si veritate carent, nulla sunt; si mysteria non habent, minima" (LXXVI, 779-80). Odo of Cluny, *Epit. mor., in fine* (CXXIII, 512 D).

4. "circumstantia litterae": Richard (CXCVI, 265, 614 B, 635 A). Innocent III (CCVII, 757), etc. Cf. Spicq, *Esquisse,* pp. 240-1; J. Daguillon, Ulrich of Strasbourg, *Summa de bono* (1930), 59.

5. "circumstantia sermonis": Aug., *Doct. chr.,* Bk. III, c. iv, n. 8 (C. F., 350). Cf. A. A. Gilmore, *Augustine and the Critical Method* (résumé in BTAM 6, 219-20). Primasius, *In I Cor.:* "Solent circumstantia scripturae illuminare sententia" (LXVIII, 546 B). Rabanus, *Cler. inst.,* Bk. III, c. xii: "the very circumstances of the speech, whereby the writers' intention is known" — "circumstania ipsa sermonis, qua cognoscitur scriptorum intentio" (CVII, 388 C); cf. c. xi: if many senses conforming to the faith are possible, "textus ipse sermonis a praecedentibus et consequentibus partibus, quae ambiguitatem illam in medio posuerunt, restat consulendus, ut videamus cuinam sententiae de pluribus quae se ostendunt, ferat suffragium, eamque sibi contexi patiatur" (387-8).

6. "ordo locutionis": Greg., *In Ez.,* Bk. I, h. 9, n. 3: "We must notice the order of the speech and the work" — "Notandus est nobis ordo locutionis et operis" (PL, LXXVI, 871 A).

7. "verborum consequentia": Jerome, *In Is.,* Bk. I: "For what is the sequence of the words and what is the order and sense of the argument, so that we may say . . . ?" — "Quae est enim verborum consequentia, et qui ordo rationis ac sensus, ut dicamus . . . ?" (PL, XXIV, 55 B).

8. "Scripturae circumstantia": Ps.-Hugo, *In Rom.* (PL, CLXXV, 443 A). Paschasius, *In Matt.,* Bk. XI, c. xxiv: "If the whole situation of the reading is considered and a comparison of the evangelists has been made, too much difficulty may arise . . ." — "Si omnis circumstantia lectionis consideretur, et evangelistarum collatio facta fuerit, nimis difficultas nascitur . . ." (CXX, 818 B).

9. "circumstantia rerum": Bede, *De tab.* (PL, XCI, 394 D). Rabanus, *In Ex.,* Bk. III, c. vi (CVIII, 136 D).

10. "circumstantia rei gestae": Hugo, *In Cant. B. M.* (PL, CLXXV, 413 D); "causa circumstans" (413 B).

11. "ordo historiae": Rabanus (PL, CVIII, 686 C; CX, 802 D, 811 C). Claudius (CIV, 836 A).

12. "ordinata narratio gestorum": Agobard, *Ad cler. et mon. lugd.,* c. vi (PL, CIV, 101 B).

13. "consequentia rerum": Or., *In Jos.,* h. 25, n. 1 (453).

14. "a principio repetens usque ad finem": PL, CLXXVI, 799 B. Cf. Abelard, *In Rom.*, c. x (CLXXVIII, 924 C).

15. "contextio sermonis" — "contextio Scripturae": To know exactly what the "writer wanted to be felt" — "scriptor sentiri voluerit": Aug., *Gen. litt.*, I, c. xix, n. 38 (PL, XXXIV, 260-1); cf. c. xxi, n. 41 (262).

16. Guibert of Nogent (PL, CLVI, 435 A); cf. *De vita sua*, Bk. II, c. i (893 B).

17. "consuetudo Scripturae": Cf. Origen, *In Matt.*, t. XII, c. xxxiv: *kata tina synētheian tēs graphēs* (146). Richard, *De vinculis S. Petri:* "We learn the custom of holy Scripture by often going over it again" — "Morem Scripturae sacrae saepius eam retractando cognoscimus" (PL, CXLI, 277 C).

18. "convenire enim debent praecedentia consequentibus quando Veritas loquitur": Aug., *In Jo.*, tr. 70, n. 1: "The words of the holy Gospel . . . are thus correctly understood if they are found to be in harmony with what has gone on above" — "Verba sancti evangelii . . . ita recte intelliguntur, si cum superioribus reperiuntur habere concordiam etc." (CCL, 36, 502). Cf. Or., *In Ez.*, h. 1, n. 4: "Comparing spiritual things with things spiritual, I shall know that all that were written are speeches of the same God" — "Spiritualibus spiritalia comparans, cognoscam universa quae scripta sunt, ejusdem esse Dei sermones" (PG, XIII, 673 A); *In Rom.*, Bk. III, c. vii: "He who faithfully and integrally gathers the sense of the sacred volumes must show how the things that seem to be contrary are not truly contrary" — "Qui fideliter et integre sacrorum voluminum colligit sensum, debet ostendere quomodo ea quae videntur esse contraria, non sunt vere contraria" (XIV, 942 B).

19. "Scriptura sacra in nulla parte discordat": Aug., *s.* 82, c. vi, n. 9 (PL, XXXVIII, 510). Cf. Or., *In Jos.*, h. 16, n. 3: "Do you think Scripture contains things contrary to itself?" — "Putasne contraria sibi Scriptura contineat?" (396).

20. "Omnia divina scripta inter se pacata consistunt": Aug., *s.* 1, n. 4 (PL, XXXVIII, 25). *In ps. CIII*, *s.* 1, n. 5: "Let us see, too, what another prophet — but not another Spirit — may say about this; for they are not mutually discordant" — "Videamus et de isto quid dicat alius propheta, sed non alius Spiritus; non enim discordant inter se" (36, 1339).

21. See Chapter 17.4 below.

22. "secundum fidem rerum gestarum": Bk. I, c. i, n. 1 (PL, XXXIV, 247); c. xvii (239). On the "rei gestae proprietas" which did not preclude the "figura rerum futurarum": again *Doct. Chr.*, III, c. xxiii, n. 33 (Combès-Farges, 382).

23. "Non esse accipienda figuraliter (facta narrata), nullus christianus dicere audebit, attendens Apostolum dicentem: Omnia autem haec in figura contingebant illis, et illud quod in Genesi scriptum est: Et erunt duo in carne sua, magnum sacramentum commendatur in Christo et in Ecclesia": Bk. I, c. i, n. 1 (XXXIV, 247).

24. "pelagus mysteriorum peritioribus relinquens": PL, CXCVIII, 1054.

25. "Studui plus historicum sensum quam spiritualem": *In Matt.* (PL, CVI, 1262 D). On the occasion, he nevertheless gives a spiritual interpretation (thus 1267 AB) and furnishes the theory of the four senses (1285 D).

26. "Magis historiam exquirendo tractamus": *Tr. in Hex., prol., ad Arnulfum lexov.* (Fr. Lecomte, AHDLMA, 25, 235).

27. "Non historiam denegamus, sed spiritalem intelligentiam praeferimus": *In Marc.*, IX, 1-7 (*An. mar.*, III, 2, 348).

28. *S.* 11 (PL, CXCIV, 1729 D); cf. 1690 D; 1806 B; *s.* 9: "an inner mystery delights me more than an exterior miracle, howsoever great" — "me magis delectat interius mysterium, quam exterius tam magnum miraculum" (1719 B).

29. In Bernard, *Ep.* 479, n. 2 (PL, CLXXXII, 688 B).

30. "Accipite ergo historiam, et sensum spiritualem ad gratiam Christi pertinentem super omnia in illa amate": *In Paral., prol.* (PL, CIX, 280 B).

31. "Templum quippe Dei, omnis Ecclesia est . . . limen vero templi, sensus historicus est in Scripturis, quia per fidem historiae . . . intramus in templum Dei. Sub hoc autem limine, allegoriarum latet profunditas": Raoul of Saint Germain, *In Lev.*, Bk. X, c. i (142 D).

32. "Historia ad aptam rerum narrationem pertinet, quae in superficie litterae continetur, sicque intelligitur sicut legitur": Adam Scot, *Trip. tab.*, P. II, c. viii, n. 92 (PL, CXCVIII, 697 B). Same sentence in *Alleg. in univ. Script.* (CXII, 849 B).

33. Or., *In Jos.*, h. 20, n. 5: "while the holy apostles . . . are removing the surface of the letter" — "sanctis apostolis . . . removentibus superficiem litterae" (424). *In ps.* XXXVI, h. 5, n. 5: "If I go beyond the letter, if I step over the surface of the history and arrive at the spiritual sense" — "Si transeam litteram, si transgrediar historiae superficiem, et perveniam ad sensum spiritalem" (PG, XII, 1364 D).

34. *Mor.*, Bk. XVIII, c. i, n. 1 (PL, LXXVI, 37 D); c. xxxix, n. 60: "'He also scrutinized the depths of the rivers.' — Judaea had the looks of these rivers, while, keeping the surface of the letter, she did not know their depths" — "Profunda quoque fluviorum scrutatus est. — Horum fluminum Judaea speciem tenuit dum, litterae superficiem servans, eorum profunda nescivit" (71 B). Bk. XX, c. iv, n. 8: "we have briefly discussed the surface of the history" — "superficiem historiae sub brevitate discussimus" (139 A); c. ix, n. 20: "There are some who venerate only the surface of the letter in the sacred volumes and do not take any care of the spiritual understanding" — "Sunt nonnulli qui in sacris voluminibus solam litterae superficiem venerantur, nec quidquam de spiritali intellectu custodiunt" (149 C). Bk. XXXV, c. xiv, 24: "which we run over touching surface according to the history alone" — "quae superficie tenus juxta solam historiam contingendo transcurrimus" (762 B).

35. "simplicitas litterae" — "superficies litterae": Bede, *In Tob.* (PL, XCI, 923 D). Berengaud, *In Ap.* (XVII, 801 C). Rabanus, *In I Mach.* (CXI, 1170 D). Peter Damian (CXLV, 1031 A, 1082 D). Rupert (CLXVII, 720 C). Hervaeus, *In Is.* (CLXXXI, 506 A). John of Salisbury, *Polycr.*, Bk. VII, c. xii (CXCIX, 666 A). Cf. Rupert: "he beheld only the exterior letter" — "solam exteriorem litteram intuitus est" (CLXVII, 390 B).

36. "superficies narrationis": Hugh, *In Eccl., praef.* (PL, CLXXV, 115 B).

37. "superficies historiae": Angelome (PL, CXV, 247 B). Peter Comestor, *s.* 8: "The time when this promise was made can be determined from the surface of the history" — "Quo autem tempore facta sit haec promissio, ex superficie historiae potest perpendi" (CXCVIII, 1742 B).

38. "planities historiae": Greg., *In I Reg., proem.*, n. 5 (PL, LXXIX, 22 A).

Notes to Pages 79-80

39. "historici sensus superficies" — "altitudo prophetiae": Peter Lombard, *In ps. CVII*, following Aug. (PL, CXCI, 983 D).

40. "interna mysteriorum medulla": Othloh, *Vita s. Wolgangi episc.*, c. iii: "he penetrated not only the surface of the historical sense" — "non solum historici sensus superficiem penetravit" (PL, CXLVI, 397 A).

41. "superficies historiae secundum Hebraeos": *Polycr.*, Bk. VII, c. xxii (PL, CXCIX, 697 B).

42. "superficies verborum": Othloh, *L. de cursu sp.*, c. iii: "'In his Law we meditate day and night', so that one lingers not only on the history and the surface of the words, but also scrutinizes the mystic sacraments of the things that are found especially in the reading of the Old Testament" — "In lege ejus meditamur die ac nocte, ita ut non solum in historia et superficie verborum immoretur, sed etiam mystica rerum sacramenta scrutetur, quae maxime in Veteris Testamenti lectione reperiuntur" (PL, CXLVI, D).

43. This what Peter Comestor will do, *s.* 10 and 30 (PL, CXCVIII, 1749 BD, 1788 D); and perhaps John of Salisbury, *Polycr.*, Bk. V, c. vi; Bk. VII, c. xxii (CXCIX, 550 D, 697 B).

44. "intentio litterae": Greg., *Mor.*, Bk. XXIII, c. vii, n. 14: "To the extent that he looks to the intention of the letter" — "Quantum ad intentionem litterae spectat" (PL, LXXVI, 259 D).

45. It is Othloh who writes, speaking of his own work: "that they not be intent upon merely the surface of the words . . . , but rather upon the innermost judgments" — "ne solummodo superficiem verborum . . . , sed potius intendant intima sententiarum": *Dial. de trib. q.*, epilogue (PL, CXXXIII, 134 B).

46. Cf. G. Paré, 116-8. For Greg. sensus and sententia were the same thing: "for 'sententia' is so called from 'sense'" — "sententia quippe a sensu vocata est, etc." (PL, LXXVI, 269 CD). Nevertheless, the distinction was already ancient; Agobard, *L. adv. Fredeg.*, c. xi: "Ex quibus patet subtilitatem sacrae Scripturae non secundum philosophos in disertitudine esse verborum, in quo nulla est sapientia, sed in potentia et astutia sensuum, atque in virtute sententiarum" (CIV, 167 AB).

47. Cf. Conrad of Hirschau, *Dial. sup. auctores* (end of 12th cent.), 27: "Explanation is taken in four ways: with regard to the letter, the sense, the allegory, and the morality. It is taken as to the letter when one says how the bare letter is to be understood; it is taken as to the sense, when one says what is being said refers to, etc." — "Explanatio quadrifaria accipitur: ad litteram, ad sensum, ad allegoriam, ad moralitatem. Ad litteram, ubi dicitur quomodo nuda littera intelligenda sit; ad sensum, ubi dicitur ad quid refert quod dicitur, etc." (Cited by De Bruyne, II, 325.)

48. Hugh, *Did.*, Bk. VI, c. viii: "An exposition contains three things: the letter, the sense, and the judgment. . . . The sense and the judgment are not found together in every narrative. But every narrative must have at least two . . ." — "Expositio tria continet: litteram, sensum, sententiam. . . . Sensus et sententia non in omni narratione simul inveniuntur. Omnis autem narratio ad minimum duo habere debet . . ." (PL, CLXXVI, 806 D). Cf. *De mod. dicendi et medit.* (Compilation of texts from Augustine, Alcuin, and Hugh), n. 10 (CLXXVI, 879 CD). Absalon, *s.* 25 (CCXI, 150 B).

49. "superficies scientiae" — "vera sapientia": Peter Comestor, *s.* 31 (PL, CXCVIII, 1794 BD).

50. Or., *In Gen.*, h. 8 (SC, tr. Doutreleau, 162-73).
51. "superficies historiae": Aug., *In ps. CVII*, n. 2 (CCL, 40, 1584).
52. "primus lectionis sermo": *In Jer.*, h. 14 (PL, XXV, 687 A).
53. *In Ez.*, Bk. I, h. 9, n. 1 (PL, LXV, 1042 B).
54. "prima significatio vocum": *Spec. de myst. Eccl.*, c. viii (PL, CLXXVII, 375 A).
55. "prima significatio litterae": Richard, *Lib. except.*, P. I, Bk. II, c. iii: "The history is the narrative of the events, and this is contained in the primary signification of the letter" — "Historia est rerum gestarum narratio, quae in prima significatione litterae continetur" (J. Châtillon, 115).
56. Leclercq, *L'amour des lettres*, 81: "ce qu'on demande à l'A.T. ce sont des lumières sur des problèmes religieux, non sur des problèmes d'histoire, fût-ce d'histoire des religions."
57. *Idem*, "L'humanisme bénédictin du VIII au XII s.," *St. ans.*, 20, 12: it is not this lack of interest, then, that made the monks not to have practiced historical science in the sense understood by the term today, nor a lack of critical intelligence, "for they were capable of demonstrating it when it was necessary" — "car ils étaient capables d'en faire preuve quand il fallait."
58. "Quid prodest multa scire, et nulla intelligere": *In Ap.* (Florez, 1780, 469).
59. "Fuerunt nescio qui filii Core illo tempore, quando ista cantabantur; sed spiritus nos vivificare debet, non littera velare": *In ps. XLV*, n. 1 (CCL, 38, 517).
60. "Quis haec scripserit, valde supervacua quaeritur, cum tamen auctor libri Spiritus sanctus fideliter credatur": *Mor., praef.*, c. i, n. 2 (PL, LXXV, 517 A). At the least this detachment left the way open for critique.
61. Cf. John 20:31.
62. "semper idem, semper incommutabile atque indeficiens": Aug., *In ps. CIII*, s. 1, n. 8 (PL, XXXVI, 1341). Cf. *Sap.* VIII, 1.
63. 2 Tim. 3:16-7.
64. Ps.-Hugo, *In reg. S. Aug.*, c. iv (PL, CLXXVI, 894 A).
65. Greg., *Reg. past.*, P. III, c. xxiv: "so they may ponder how holy Scripture has been set like a lamp for us in the night of the present life" — "ut perpendant quo Scriptura sacra in nocte vitae praesentis quasi quadam nobis lucerna sit posita" (PL, LXXVII, 94 A). *Mor.*, Bk. XXVI, c. xvi, n. 26 (LXXVI, 362-3). *Ep.*, Bk. V, 46: "And what is holy Scripture if not a letter of almighty God to his creature?" — "Quid est autem Scriptura sacra, nisi quaedam epistola omnipotentis Dei ad creaturam suam?" (*Reg. Gr.*, I, 345). Other Gregorian images: Bernard de Vrégille, *D. Sp.*, f. 25, 174.
66. "fulgorem divinae cognitionis": *In Ap.*, Bk. VII, c. v (PL, CXCVI, 867 CD).
67. Ps.-Ambrose, *s.* 27, n. 6: "when we accept the food of perennial eloquence from the divine Scriptures" — "cum de divinis Scripturis cibum eloquii perennis accipimus" (PL, XVII, 662 A). Bede, *De Tab.*, Bk. I, c. vi: "The divine Scripture, by which the holy Church is unceasingly revived" — "Divina Scriptura, qua Ecclesia sancta sine cessatione reficitur" (XCI, 408 C).
68. "Non putemus hoc *nobis* non ideo dictum, quia tunc ibi non fuimus": Aug., *In Jo.*, tr. 30, n. 7 (CCL, 35, 292).
69. "Semper enim divina Scriptura loquitur et clamat, semper clamat et loquitur": Ps.-Ambrose, *s.* 52, n. 1 (PL, XVII, 709 D, 710 A).

70. Bernard, *In Epiph.*, s. 2, n. 2: "You are departing from the sense of the flesh to the understanding of the mind, from the slavery of the concupiscence of the flesh to the freedom of spiritual understanding. You are departing from your land and your family and your father's house, and you are seeing King Solomon" — "Egredimini de sensu carnis ad intellectum mentis, de servitute carnalis concupiscentiae ad libertatem spiritualis intelligentiae. Egredimini de terra vestra et de cognatione vestra et de domo patris vestri, et videte regem Salomonem" (PL, CLXXXIII, 148 B).

71. Rabanus, *In Ez.*, Bk. XIV: "The name 'door' cannot unfittingly be understood as the knowledge of holy Scripture, which, when it reveals understanding to us, opens the doorway of the heavenly kingdom" — "Potest etiam portae nomine Scripturae sacrae scientia non inconvenienter intelligi, quae, dum nobis intellectum aperit, caelestis regni januam pandit" (PL, CX, 894 B).

72. Cf. Karl Barth, *Dogmatique*, Fr. tr., vol. I, t. II, 1, pp. 73 and 118: To understand the Scripture, it is necessary to stop "playing the spectator."

73. *figurae historiarum:* Aelred, *s. de oner.* 28 (PL, CXCV, 478 B).

74. *significatio:* Petrus Cellensis (PL, CCI, 860 D).

75. Heb. 10:1.

76. Rupert, *In Ap.*, Bk. IV: "It is a book written inside and out, since holy Scripture is both to be read with historical or literal tenor and also to be understood in the spiritual sense" — "Intus et foris scriptus est liber, quia nimirum sancta Scriptura et historiali sive litterali tenore legenda et spirituali sensu intelligenda est" (PL, CLXIX, 925 C); etc.

77. "Scriptura Veritatis tuae": *Medit.* 2 (PL, CLXXX, 209 A); *med.* 12 (242 C).

78. Cf. Alcuin, *In ps. CXXVII:* "'Around thy table'. The table of Christ is holy Scripture, whereby we are nourished, whereby we understand what to love, what to desire, and to whom we have lifted our eyes" — "In circuitu mensae tuae. Mensa Christi, Scriptura sancta est, unde pascimur, unde intelligimus, quid amemus, quid desideremus, ad quem habeamus oculos levatos" (PL, C, 630 CD). *L. de virt.*: "The reading of the holy Scriptures is the knowledge of divine beatitude" — "Sanctarum lectio Scripturarum, divinae est cognitio beatitudinis" (CL, 616 C).

79. Godfrey of Admont, *H. dom.* 23: "By the 'mystery of the kingdom of God' is meant the mystery of holy Scripture, which is not unfittingly likened to the kingdom of God: since God is truly present in holy Scripture, God may truly be known from holy Scripture" — "Per mysterium regni Dei mysterium sacrae Scripturae accipitur, quae regno Dei non incongrue assimilatur, cum in sancta Scriptura vere Deus sit, ex sancta Scriptura vere Deus agnoscatur" (PL, CLXXIV, 154 D).

80. Rabanus, *In Ez.*, Bk. XVI: "So for us let the inner door be the New Testament, and the outer door the Old Testament; since the latter opens up the spiritual understanding, and the former preserved the letter in the history of the holy eloquence for still uncultivated minds" — "Sit itaque nobis porta interior Testamentum novum, porta vero exterior Testmentum vetus; quia et hoc spiritalem intellectum aperit, et illud rudibus adhuc mentibus in historia sacri eloquii litteram custodivit" (PL, CX, 949 D). Rupert, *In Ez.*, Bk. II (CLXVII, 1489 BC).

81. "per intelligentiam cordis et imitationem operis" — "serenum illud

supernae visitationis mane super nos orietur": Godfrey of Admont, *De decem oneribus Isaiae*, c. viii (PL, CLXXIV, 1196 D).

82. Gerhoh, *In ps. XXX* (PL, CXCIII, 1306-7).

83. *In Scriptura ejus quasi os ejus intuemur: Mor.*, Bk. XVI, c. xxxv, n. 43: "The minds of the just stand before God almighty through their intention, and in his Scripture they look, as it were, into his face" — "Justorum mentes per intentionem suam omnipotenti Deo assistunt, atque in Scriptura ejus quasi os ejus intuentur" (PL, LXXV, 1142 D). M. A. Gelin writes, with regard to the Book of Ezekiel: "The bits on Tyre are the most famous, owing to the information they supply about international commerce" — "Les morceaux sur Tyr sont les plus célèbres, à cause des renseignements qu'ils donnent sur le commerce international." (Robert-Feuillet, *Introd. à la Bible*, I, 545). This is a statement of a fact. But this fact presupposes among our contemporaries a certain scale of values quite different than that of the men of the Middle Ages.

Notes to Chapter Eight
§1. Mysterium requiramus

1. "Tenues historiae lineas duximus: nunc allegoriae imprimamus manum": PL, XXV, 1063 D. *Ep.* 52, c. 10: for it is necessary to understand Scripture "as our Lord also understood it" — "ut Dominus quoque noster intellexit" (2, 186). Chromatius, *In Matt.*, tr. 15, c. iii, n. 1: "But since we have spoken regarding the letter, we ought to turn to what also is to be thought according to the spiritual understanding" — "Sed quia id secundum litteram diximus, quid etiam secundum spiritalem intelligentiam sentiendum sit debemus advertere" (CCL, 9, 437).

2. "Factum audivimus: mysterium requiramus": *In Jo.*, tr. 50, n. 6 (PL, XXXV, 1760). Ambrose, *Apol. David alt.*, c. xi, n. 57: "sed jam mysterium requiramus" (XIV, 910 B).

3. "Altior sensus provocat nos": *De Noe et arca*, c. xi, n. 38 (PL, XIV, 377 C). Jerome, *In Is.* (XXIV, 246 B).

4. "Docuit enim nos Apostolus sanctus in simplicitate historiae secretum quaerere veritatis": *In Luc.*, Bk. III, c. xxviii (PL, XV, 1600 C).

5. "Sed quia superficies historiae sub brevitate discussimus, quid in his de intellectu mystico lateat perpendamus": *Mor.*, Bk. XX, c. iii, n. 8 (PL, LXXVI, 139 A).

6. "Haec per historiam facta credimus, sed per allegoriam jam qualiter sint implenda videamus": *Op. cit.*, Bk. I, c. xi, n. 15 (LXXV, 533 D).

7. "Si vero cuncta haec juxta historiam tractando discurrimus, per allegoriae quoque mysteria perscrutemur": Bk. XXII, c. iv, n. 7 (LXXVI, 215 D).

8. Bk. II, c. xix, n. 33 (SC, 206; PL, LXXV, 572 B).

9. "cogimur," "compellimur": Bk. XXXV, c. xiv, n. 24: "Though all these things have been spoken truly with respect to their history . . . , we are forced to go back to the mystery of allegory. . . . We are compelled to investigate in the mysteries of allegory even those earlier matters that we run over just touching their surface with respect to their merely historical dimension" — "Licet cuncta haec juxta historiam veraciter dicta sint . . . , cogimur ut ad allegoriae mysterium re cur ramus. . . . Compellimur ut priora quoque, quae superficie tenus juxta solam historiam contingendo transcurrimus, in allegoriae mysteriis indagemus" (PL, LXXVI, 762 B).

10. "necesse est," "nunc ordo expositionis *exigit* ut . . . allegoriarum jam secreta pandamus": Bk. XX, c. v, n. 14: "Necesse est ut expositionis sermo ad spiritalem intelligentiam recurrat" (LXXXVI, 145 A); etc.

11. *Mor.*, Bk. XXI, c. i, n. 1: "Multae quippe ejus sententiae tanta allegoriarum conceptione sunt gravida, ut quisquis eas ad solam tenere historiam nititur, earum notiita per suam incuriam privetur" (LXXVI, 187 B). Cf. Leo, s. 66, c. 1: once the "ordo facti" is known, one must look for the "ratio" (LIV, 364 D).

12. "Necesse est . . . ut allegoricus sensus sequatur": *Myst. exp. sacram, praef.* (PL, LXXXIII, 207 B).

13. "Historia . . . mysterium requirit": *In Reg.*, Bk. I, c. xxv (PL, CIX, 64 B). Cf. *In Ex.*, Bk. III, c. xii: "Videamus ips[a] verba historiae, quo per haec altius atque apertius ad sensum allegoriae pervenire queamus" (CVIII, 158 A).

14. "Neque enim solummodo sufficit lectoribus divinorum librorum sensus

historicus, sed etiam diligenter eis est considerandum quid per allegoriam eis propheticus sermo innuere velit": *In Ex.*, Bk. II, *praef.* (PL, CVIII, 55 C).

15. "Praemissam historiam spiritualis sequitur intellectus, cujus causa historia replicata est": *In Ap.* (Florez, 342). Cf. Greg., *In Reg.*, Bk. III, c. i, n. 22: "it is written to this end: that the understanding of the allegory may be brought forth within the truth of the letter" — "ad hoc scribitur ut in veritate litterae intellectus proferantur allegoriae" (PL, LXXIX, 155 A); c. ii, n. 19 (168 C).

16. "Hoc mysterii gratia factum est": *In Reg.*, Bk. III (PL, L, 1136 C). Cassiodorus, *In ps. CXII:* "Et licet haec historia referatur in veteri Testamento, aliis tamen hic verbis et similitudinibus indicatur, ut evidenter adverteremus, antiqua illa facta spirituali intelligentia salutis nostrae indicia nuntiasse" (LXX, 812 A).

17. H. 13 (PL, LXXXVII, 649 CD).

18. Bede, *Q sup. Jos.*, c. x: "Et haec quidem veteris historiae referunt gesta; sed inspiciendum est quid in narratione mysticae intelligentiae referatur" (PL, XCIII, 420 C). Rabanus Maurus, *In Deut.*, Bk. III, c. xxv; *In Jos.*, Bk. II, c. 1 (CVIII, 948 D, 1037 C). Following Origen, *In Jos.*, h. 9, n. 7 (351).

19. Adam Scotus, *s.* 35, c. x: "Quid sibi volunt haec? Quae utilitas quod breviter referuntur ad memoriam, nisi exponantur breviter ad intelligentiam?" (PL, CXCVIII, 325 D).

20. Cf. Aug. *In ps. LXIV*, n. 2: "Quid ergo istae urbes certis temporibus conditae sunt, ut manifestaretur figura duarum civitatum olim caeptarum et usque in finem in isto saeculo mansurarum, sed in fine separandarum" (PL, XXXVI, 773). *In ps. LIX*, n. 1 (714).

21. [Trans. note: the use of the active Latin verb *mysticare* is quite untranslatable into English. Literal (but still inadequate) renderings might include: "they en-mystery us something," or "they mysticate something to us."] Gerhoh, *In ps. XXVI:* "These unctions convey a mystery to us" — "Quae unctiones mysticant nobis aliquid" (PL, CXCIII, 1174 D); *In ps. XXXVII:* "they convey to us the matter at hand at a mystical level" — "praesentem rem nobis mysticat" (1366 C). Hermann of Werden, *Hortus delic.:* "By expressing the mystery of the Church" — "Ecclesiam mystificando," "the letter betokens him at a mystical level" — "littera mystificat illum" (Pitra, II, 146, 171).

22. *quae sit in ea spiritalis ratio:* Origen, *In Lev.*, h. 14, n. 1 (316). Gregory of Elvira, *Tr.* 6: "though they were performed in the flesh, . . . they portended an image of their mystical significance" — "licet secundum carnem gesta sint, . . . mysticae rationis imaginem portendebant" (58).

23. "Rem gestam memoriter tenere" — "in exteriori facto mysterium intus persentire": Gerhoh, *In Cant. Moysi* I (PL, CXCIV, 1019 A).

24. "per humilitatem historicae fidei, ad celsitudinem spiritualis intelligentiae": Manegold, *In ps. VIII* (PL, XCIII, 526 D).

25. "Protinus in mysterium surgat!": PL, XCIII, 2330 C. Beatus, *In Ap.*: "Protinus ab historia in mysterium surgit" (268). Gerhoh: "Ab historia . . . ad mysterium" (PL, CXCIV, 669 C).

26. "Littera pertractata, allegoria attingatur!": *In ps. LXXVII* (PL, CLII, 1043 A).

27. "His ad litteram dispositis, quid etiam allegoriae significent videamus": *In Pentat.* (PL, CLXIV, 150 A). Bede, *In Tob.*: "etiam allegoricae" (XCI, 923 C).

28. "His juxta sensum historiae breviter dictis, mysterium inquiramus": *In Is.*, Bk. V (PL, CLXXXI, 363 D).

29. Salva namque veritate decenter historiae,
Requiramus diligenter sensus allegoricos.
                    On Lazarus, str. 41 (*P. lat. m. aevi*, VI, 215)

30. "Sed per historiam semper notet allegoriam!": *De doctr. spir.*, c. xii (PL, CXLVI, 271 B).

31. Spiritalis intellectus,
Litterali fronde tectus,
Prodeat in publicum!
                    Prose for Pentecost (L. Gauthier, 61)

32. "prima eruditio sacri eloquii quae in historica consistit lectione" — "secunda eruditio quae in allegoria est": *De sacram.*, Bk. I, *prol.* (PL, CLXXVI, 183-4); Hugh explains why, passing from history to allegory, "he will have changed the reading" — "lectionem mutaverit"; this is the "se sermo convertat" of Gregory.

33. "Sicut firmissime servanda est veritas historiae, ita nihilominus investiganda est et subtilitas allegoriae": N. 67 (Foreville-Leclercq, *St. ans.*, 41, 108).

34. "Quanto in litterali sensu (doctrina) est evidentior, tanto in mystico intellectu est profundior": *Sent. praef.* (Martin, 32).

35. Greg., *Mor.*, Bk. XXIII, c. i, n. 2: "But since the ancient fathers, like fruit trees, are not only handsome to look at but also useful through their productiveness, their life is to be weighted so that, while we marvel at what verdure there is in the history, we may be led to discover also what productiveness there is in the allegory" — "Quia vero antiqui patres, fructigeris arboribus similes, non solum pulchri sunt per speciem, sed etiam utiles per ubertatem, eorum vita pensanda est, ut cum miramur quae sit viriditas in historia, inveniamur et quanta sit ubertas in allegoria" (PL, LXXVI, 251 A).

36. "apertae sententiae" — "sensus spiritualis": Hervaeus, *In Is.*, Bk. VII (PL, CLXXXI, 505 A).

37. "consequentia litterae" — "eminentia allegoriae": Godfrey of Admont, *H. dom.* 3 (PL, CLXXIV, 32 A).

38. "historiae gravitas" — "allegoriae profunditas": Peter of London, *Remediarium conversorum, prol.* (Wasselynck, 399).

39. "ut verbis historiae mysterium suffragetur allegoriae": Berengoz of Trèves, *De mat. ligni dominici* (PL, CLX, 1002 B).

40. Petrus Cellensis, *L. de panibus*, c. ii (PL, CCII, 937 A). Odo of Cluny, *Occupatio*, Bk. VI, v. 749 (Swoboda, 141): *Historia et parvos alit, allegoria vegetos*. Alan of Lille, *Anticlaudianus* (210, 529). Cf. Greg., *Mor., ep. miss.*, c. iv: "Divinus etenim sermo sicut mysteriis prudentes exercet, sic plerumque superficie simplices refovet. Habet in publico unde parvulos nutriat, servat in secreto unde mentes sublimium in admiratione suspendat," and the famous comparison: "Quasi quidam quippe est fluvius, ut ita dixerim, planus et altus, in quo et agnus ambulet, et elephas natet" (SC, 120-1). The "sensus puerilis" of the "littera," of which Robert of Melun speaks, *loc. cit.*, is not "a puerile sense" but rather the sense that a (spiritual) child can understand.

41. Claudius, *In Gen.*, Bk. I: "We read how the creation of heaven and earth was founded historically from the beginning, but let us understand how it be taken spiritually in the Church by her doctors" — "Creatura caeli et terrae quomodo historialiter ab exordio principii condita sit, legimus, sed qualiter in Ecclesia spiritualiter a doctoribus accipiatur, intelligamus" (PL, L, 894 B).

42. *via comprehensionis:* Richard: "He opens up for us the path of comprehension to track down the mystery" — "Ad investigandum mysterium comprehensionis viam nobis aperit, etc." (PL, CXLI, 281 B).

43. Rupert, *In Is.*, Bk. II, c. i: "Nunc ergo per hanc intelligentiae januam ingressi praesentis capituli spatia" (PL, CLXVII, 1312 C).

44. "Opera loquuntur. . . . Facta, si intelligas, verba sunt": Aug., *s.* 95, n. 3 (PL, XXXVIII, 582).

45. "non tantum dictis, sed, Deo cuncta mirabiliter disponente, etiam factis": *Altercatio* (B. Blumenkranz, RMAL 10, 96).

46. "aut per facta aut per dicta": Remi of Auxerre, *Sup. psalterium, praef.* (Vaccari, *Biblica*, 26, 66); "through deeds, as we read that the ark floated in the waves" — "per facta, sicut arcam legimus enatasse in fluctibus." Cf. Chrys., *In Paen.*, h. 6, n. 4-5 (PG, XLIX, 320-1), *In Matt.*, h. 66, n. 2 (LVIII, 627); *In Rom.*, h. 1 (LX, 397).

47. "aliquando per rerum figuras, aliquando per verborum aenigmata": G. Crispin, *Disput.* (Blumenkranz, 50).

48. "et factum est, et prophetia est": Aug., *s.* 2, n. 7 (PL, XXXVIII, 30-1).

49. "In rebus gestis latet allegoria": Herbert of Losinga, *In dom. palm.* (G.-S., 2, 120). Richard is looking for the "mysteria rerum gestarum": *L. except.*, VII, *prol.* (Châtillon, 98).

50. "figurae historiarum": Aelred, *De oner., s.* 28 (PL, CXCV, 478 A).

51. "per allegoriae exercitium mysteria historiae pandere": Cf. John of Kelso, to Adam Scotus, c. vii (PL, CXCVIII, 627 A).

52. "Historia . . . spiritalem sensum habet in iis qui ante nos exstiterunt": Or., *Sel. in Ez.*, c. xxviii (PG, XIII, 821-2 C).

53. "magni sacramenti narratio" — "sacramenta gestorum": Paschasius, *In Matt.* (PL, CXX, 878 B, 713 B).

54. "Historia sacra legis non sine aliqua praefiguratione futurorum *gesta atque conscripta est*": *Myst. exp. sacr., praef.* (PL, LXXXIII, 207 B). Cf. *L. de variis q.*, c. l, n. 6: "While sacred Scripture reports events historically, it mystically hints at things to come" — "Dum sacra Scriptura secundum historiam transacta narrat, futura mystice indicat" (146).

55. *In Gen.*, h. 7, n. 2 (71-2). *In Jud.*, h. 9, n. 2: "In almost all the deeds of the ancients great mysteries are betokened" — "In omnibus pene veterum gestis mysteria designantur ingentia" (520). *In Jo.*, Bk. X, c. xviii (189). *In Lev.*, h. 3, n. 1: "though the deed is done by way of mystery" — "licet per mysterium res agatur" (300), etc. Clement, *Strom.*, Bk. VI, c. xv (2, 95).

56. *De Abr.*, Bk. I, n. 28 (PL, XIV, 432 C).

57. "Ubi allegoriam nominavit (Apostolus), non in verbis eam reperit, sed in factis": *De Trin.*, Bk. XV, c. ix, n. 15 (Agaësse, 460). *In ps. LXVIII, s.* 2, n. 6: "We ought to look for the mystery in the deed itself, not merely in the utterance" — "In ipso facto, non solum in dicto, mysterium requirere debemus" (36, 858). *Ep.*

137, n. 3: "And so much of the depth of wisdom lies hidden not only in the words with which those things are said, but also in the things that are to be understood" — "Tantaque non solum in verbis, quibus ista dicta sunt, verum etiam in rebus quae intelligendae sunt, latet altitudo sapientiae" (XXXIII, 516).

58. "Quid ego de Apostolo Paulo dicam, qui etiam ipsam Exodi historiam futurae christianae plebis allegoriam fuisse significat?": *De ut. cred.*, c. iii, n. 8 on 1 Cor. 10:1-11 (Pegon, 221).

59. "Scimus autem sicut et vocibus, ita et rebus prophetatum; tam dictis quam et factis praedicatur resurrectio": *De carnis res.*, c. xxviii (65).

60. "Cum lex spiritalis est, cum gesta ejus allegorumena sunt": *In ps. CXXXIV*, n. 18 (705). *In ps. CXVIII, Sin*, n. 4: "Haec enim (the Mosaic laws), ut saepe admonuimus, plus significant quam agunt, dum gesta ipsa motionem nobis aeternae dispositionis insinuant" (537).

61. "geritur quidem res secundum praesentem effectum, sed spiritalis praeformatio ordinem suum obtinet": *Tr. myst.*, Bk. I, n. 22 (SC, 19, 112).

62. "Mystica historia" (PL, X, 680 D).

63. *C. Eunom.*, Bk. XII (PG, XLV, 940 A). *Life of Moses* (Daniélou, SC, 1 *bis*, 72), etc. Cyril of Jerusalem, *1st cat. mystag.*, c. ii (*Quasten*, 72).

64. "Sed jam mysterium ipsius recenseamus historiae": *Ap. David alt.* c. vi, n. 34 (PL, XIV, 900 B).

65. "ea quae in veritate gesta sunt, alterius sacramenti formam praefigurasse dicuntur": Coll. 14, n. 8 (Pichery, SC, 54, 190).

66. "Typus prophetia est in rebus" — "typis res declarantur ex rebus": Bk. II, c. xvi (Kihn, 510).

67. "juxta typicam historiam": *In Is.* (PL, XXIV, 608 A).

68. "etiam rebus gestis prophetans": *Civ. Dei*, Bk. XVII, c. viii, n. 2 (PL, XLI, 541); cf. Bk. XV, c. xxvii, n. 1 (473).

69. "non tantum sermonibus sed et actionibus": *C. Faust.*, Bk. VI, c. iv (PL, XLII, 230); Bk. XXII, c. vi (404).

70. "O res gestas, sed prophetice gestas! In terra, sed caelitus! Per homines sed divinitus!": *Civ. Dei*, Bk. XVI, c. xxxvii (PL, XLI, 516).

71. "parabola verbi" vs. "parabola rei gestae": *In Jo.*, tr. 122, n. 7 (CCL, 36, 671).

72. S. 77, c. v, n. 7: "Factum quidem est, et ita ut narratur impletum. Sed tamen ipsa, quae a Domino facta sunt, aliquid significantia erant, quasi verba, si dici potest, visibilia et aliquid significantia" (PL, XXXVIII, 486). Cf. *Gen. litt.*, Bk. VIII, c. vii, n. 13: "caeterae quoque primitus ad proprietatem litterae accipere, non in eis figuratam locutionem putare, sed res ipsa quae ita narratur et esse et aliquid etiam figurare" (XXXIV, 378).

73. *In ps. LXXVII*, n. 26 (PL, XXXVI, 999).

74. *Strom.*, Bk. V, c. iv (St., 2, 341).

75. *Sel. in Thren.*, Bk. X (PG, XIII, 623-4). *In Jer.*, h. 21, n. 1 (PG, XIII, 535 C).

76. "Inter caetera prophetiae miracula, hoc quoque mirandum habent libri prophetarum, quod sicut in eis verbis res, ita nonnumquam verba rebus exponuntur, ut eorum non solum dicta, sed etiam res gestae prophetiae sint": *In Ez.*, Bk. I, h. 11, n. 1 (PL, LXXVI, 905 D). Cf. *Mor.*, Bk. XVIII, c. xlvi, n. 74 (82 A).

77. "mystice gesta": *Sup. Acta exp.* (PL, XCII, 937 C); etc.

78. "allegoria facti" — "allegoria verbi": *De schem. et tropis,* c. xii (PL, XC, 185 CD).
79. *Q. sup. Gen.* (PL, XCIII, 330 B).
80. "historica praefiguratio" — "allegorica completio": *In Sam.,* Bk. III, c. iii (PL, LXVIII, 596 D).
81. "historia prophetica": *In Ez.,* Bk. XII, init. (PL, CX, 811 D).
82. *Cler. inst.,* Bk. III, c. viii: "Sunt autem signa propria vel translata. . . . Translata sunt, cum et ipsae res quas proprie verbis significamus, ad aliquid aliud significandum usurpantur" (PL, CVII, 384 D). *In Jud.,* Bk. II, c. xv (108, 1185 A).
83. *In Ap.,* v. 3 (PL, XVII, 832 D).
84. *In Matt.,* Bk. I, c. i: "Si vero mysterium figurandae rei in ipso facto consideramus" (PL, CXX, 66 D); Bk. XII: "Mysteria in ipso facto . . . commendant"; "ut et mysterium monstretur in facto" (915-6, 987 C).
85. *In Reg.,* Bk. II (PL, L, 1081 D).
86. *In Gen.:* "Haec quae tradita sunt de David ad litteram . . . et de Christo spiritualiter pertinent" (PL, CXXXI, 126 C).
87. PL, CXLV, 180 A.
88. *In ps. LXXVII* (PL, CLII, 1030 B).
89. "Regni Christi filii sui (David) mystica factis praesignaverat, dictis cecinerat; de factis ejus mysticis vel passionibus figurativis, suo loco pro posse diximus" (PL, CLXVII, 1539 D). Cf. *In Ap.,* Bk. V: Fidem "quam . . . praesignaverunt factis mysticis" (CLXIX, 994 A).
90. *In Script.,* h. 14: "mystica narratio" (PL, CLXXIV, 116 C).
91. "sub altiori intellectu . . . ad allegoriam, quae dicta sunt secundum historiam": PL, CXCIII, 721 B.
92. "hujus facti mysterium": *In Cant. Moysi* I (PL, CXCIV, 1018 B; cf. 1019 A).
93. "facta figurativa": PL, CXCIII, 693 C.
94. *Trip. tab.* (PL, CXCVIII, 697 AB).
95. *Polycr.,* Bk. VII, c. xii: "At in liberalibus disciplinis, ubi non res sed dumtaxat verba significant, quisquis pro sensu litterae contentus non est, aberrare mihi videtur" (Webb, 144).
96. *Hist. scol.* (PL, CXCVIII, 1054).
97. *Allegoriae* . . . : "Sciendum est quod quandoque voce significantur res in sacra Scriptura, quandoque re res" (Moore-Corbett, 100).
98. "rerum gestarum spiritalis significatio": *Ep.* 30 (Bouvet, 213).
99. "mystica rerum sacramenta": *L. de Cursu sp.,* c. iii (PL, CXLVI, 146 D).
100. *L. formularum, praef.:* "Nec mirandum quod sermo divinus, prophetarum apostolorumque ore prolatus, ab usitato illo hominibus scribendi modo multum recesserit, facilia in promptu habens, magna in interioribus suis continens" (Wotke, 3).
101. "scientias atque doctrinas ipso etiam locutionis suae modo transcendit": *Mor.,* Bk. XX, c. i, n. 1 (PL, LXXVI, 135 C).
102. *De sacram., prol.,* c. v: "Hence it appears how much the divine Scripture excels all other writings not only in its matter, but also in its method of treatment, subtlety, and depth . . ." — "Unde apparet quantum divina Scriptura caeteris omnibus scripturis non solum in materia sua, sed etiam in modo tractandi, subtilitate et profunditate praecellat etc." (PL, CLXXVI, 185 BC).

103. Bk. V, c. iii: "In the divine eloquence not only words but even things have meaning, which is not the usual way in other writings" — "In divino eloquio non tantum verba sed etiam res significare habent, qui modus non adeo in aliis scripturis inveniri solet etc." (CLXXVI, 790-1).

104. "Igitur sacra Scriptura caeteris in sensibus superabundat. . . . In divina pagina non solum intellectus et verba res significant, sed ipsae res alias res significant": C. viii (PL, CLXXVII, 375 C); cf. 375 A: "we shall understand the historical through the signification of words; and allegory and tropology through the signification of things" — "per vocum significationem, historialem; per rerum autem significationem, intelligemus allegoriam et tropologiam."

105. "In hoc valde excellentior est divina Scriptura scientia saeculi, quod in ea non solum voces, sed et res significativae sunt": Bk. II, c. iii (PL, CLXXVII, 205 B).

106. *In Gal.*, q. 43 (PL, CLXXV, 564 BC).

107. "At in liberalibus disciplinis, ubi non res sed dumtaxat verba significant, quisquis pro sensu litterae contentus non est, aberrare mihi videtur": *Polycr.*, Bk. VII, c. xii (PL, CXCIX, 666 C).

108. *S.* 22: "Theology excels the other arts in this: that they signify words without things or things without words, whilst in theology not only words but even things are significant" — "Caeteras siquidem artes in hoc theologia praecellit, quod voces sine rebus, vel res sine vocibus significant; in ista vero non tantum voces sed etiam res significativae sunt" (PL, CCV, 712 D).

109. "Dicit magister Hugo: tanta est sublimitas sacrae paginae super alias disciplinas, quod significata aliarum sunt significantia in theologia; illa enim quae sunt res nominum et verborum in aliis facultatibus, sunt nomina in theologia": *Ms.* (Smalley, 199, note).

110. ". . . Quaerendum quid inter mysteria distat utriusque legis . . . et symbola. Mysteria itaque proprie sunt, quae juxta allegoriam et facti et dicti traduntur, hoc est, et secundum res gestas facta sunt et dicta, quia narrantur. Verbi gratia, mosaicum tabernaculum et secundum rem gestam erat constructum, et textu sanctae Scripturae dictum atque narratum. Similiter sacramenta legalium hostiarum et secundum historiam facta sunt, et dicta sunt secundum narrationem. Circumcisio similiter et facta est in carne, et narrata est in littera. . . . Et haec forma sacramentorum allegoria facti et dicti a sanctis Patribus rationabiliter vocitatur.

"Altera forma est, quae proprie symboli nomen accepit, et allegoria dicti, non autem facti appellatur, quoniam in dictis solummodo spiritualis doctrinae, non autem in factis sensibilibus constituitur. Mysteria itaque sunt, quae in utroque Testamento et secundum historiam facta sunt, et secundum litteram narrata; symbola vero, quae solummodo non facta sed quasi facta sola doctrina dicuntur. . . ." *In Jo.*, fr. 3 (PL, CXXII, 344-5).

111. *In Gen.*, Bk. II (PL, L, 989 C; Claudius, following Aug.). Cf. Odo of Cluny, *Occupatio*, Bk. IV, v. 543: "Jam Pater hunc verbis promiserat atque figuris" (Swoboda, 84).

Notes to Chapter Eight
§2. Mystery: Future, Interior, Celestial

1. 'allegoria, quasi alienum eloquium': An old definition, still recalled by Sicard of Cremona, *Mitrale*, Bk. I, c. xiii (PL, CCXIII, 47 A).

2. Heraclitus, *On the Life and Thought of Homer*, 70.

3. "quae aliquid verbis aliud sensu ostendit": *Inst. orat.* 8, 6, n. 6: metaphor "transfers" from one word to another, takes place "aut quia necesse est, aut quia significantius est, aut quia decentius"; n. 14: "(translationis) usus continuus . . . in allegorias exit," etc.

4. "translatorum cura verborum, cum res aut sua non invenit verba aut cum volumus splendidius aliquid explicari": *De nuptiis Philologiae et Mercurii*, Bk. V (A. Dick, 251): "ergo aut inopiae aut decoris causa transferuntur. . . . In hoc genere transferendi etiam allegoriam poetae praecipue nexuerunt. . . ." Cf. the definition of metaphor by Augustine, *C. mendac.*, c. x, n. 24: "de re propria ad rem non propriam verbi alicujus usurpata translatio" (PL, XL, 533).

5. *Etymol.*, Bk. I, *De gramm.*, c. xxxvii (PL, LXXXII, 112-7).

6. *Irony, antiphrasis, aenigma, charientism, paraemia, sarcasm, asteism* (Halm, 616-7). E. de Bruyne, I, 159.

7. "allegoria est, cum aliud *geritur*, aliud figuratur": *De Abrah.*, Bk. I, c. i, n. 28 (PL, XIV, 432 C).

8. Thus Ps.-Hugo, *Speculum*, c. viii: "Allegory is when one fact is understood by means of another" — "Allegoria est, quando per factum intelligitur aliud factum"; "allegory, a sort of 'alien talk', when an other thing is understood not by means of words but through the thing done, as by the crossing of the Red Sea is understood the crossing through baptism to paradise" — "allegoria, quasi alieniloquium, quando non per voces sed per rem factam alia res intelligitur, ut per transitum maris Rubri transitus intelligitur per baptismum ad paradisum" (PL, CLXXVII, 375 A). Richard, *L. except.*, Bk. I, Bk. II, c. iii (Châtillon, 115). See Chapter 6.1 above.

9. This what Bonfrère remarked, *In totam Scr. sacram praeloquia*, c. xx, sect. 2: "by reason of the lack of any other word appropriate for that particular sense" — "ob defectum vocis alterius propriae isti particulari sensui" (Migne, *Scr. s. cursus compl.*, I, 247).

10. "Haec quod allegorica mysteria contineant, Paulus . . . pronuntiat dicens: Mysterium magnum est, ego dico in Christo et in Ecclesia": *In Num.*, h. 11, n. 1 (77). Gal. 4:13; Eph. 5:32. Cf. Rolf Gögler, "Die christologische und heilstheologische Grundlage der Bibel-exegese des Origenes," *Tübing. Theol. Quartalschrift*, 1956.

11. "Omne autem opus, quod sacris voluminibus continetur, adventum Domini nostri Jesu Christi . . . et dictis nuntiat et factis exprimit et confirmat exemplis": *Tr. myst.*, Bk. I, n. 1 (SC, 19, 72). *Instr. Psalm*, n. 5 (6); etc.

12. "Neque enim ob aliud ante adventum Domini scripta sunt omnia quae in sanctis Scripturis legimus, nisi ut illius commendaretur adventus, et futura praesignaretur Ecclesia": *De cat. rud.*, c. iii, n. 6 (Combès-Farges, 30); c. xix, n. 33 (102-4). Taken up again by Claudius, *In Gen.*, Bk. II (PL, L, 981 C) and Rabanus, *De eccl. disc.*, Bk. I (CXII, 1194 B).

13. "Magis credendum est, et sapienter esse memoriae litterisque mandata, et gesta esse, et significare aliquid, et ipsum aliquid ad praefigurandam Ecclesiam pertinere": Bk. XV, c. xxvii, n. 5 (PL, XLI, 476). *Gen. litt.*, Bk. XII, n. 17 (XXXIV, 459). *Ep.* 140, n. 36 (XXXIII, 554).

14. "Prophetia venturi Christi et Ecclesiae perscrutanda est": Bk. XXII, c. xxiii (PL, XLII, 417).

15. "Totum omnium Scripturarum mysterium, Christum et Ecclesiam": *In ps. LXXIX*, n. 1 (CCL, 39, 1111). *Doct. chr.*, Bk. III, n. 42-4 (C.F., 304-6).

16. "sacramenta in Christo et Ecclesia adimplenda": *In Job* (PL, XXVI, 742 C).

17. "medullata Ecclesiae sacramenta": *In Is.* (PL, XXIV, 550 C). Filastre, *Haer.* 149: "the mysteries of Christianity" — "mysteria christianitatis" (CCL, 9, 311); *haer.* 110 (276). Bachiarius, *Prof. fidei* (PL, XX, 1033 B).

18. "Lex omnis et prophetia, Christum Dominum sonuit et Ecclesiam": *De prom.*, P. III, n. 12 (PL, LI, 817 C).

19. "Figurae succedunt figuris, dum tamen omnes actiones Christum Ecclesiamque significent": *Ibid.*, P. I, c. xxxiii, n. 45 (749 A).

20. "Figura vero est in repraesentatione veritatis, cum ea quae de patriarchis et prophetis in divinis libris . . . patrata legimus, allegorice in Christo et Ecclesia impleta recognoscimus": *L. de var. quaest.*, c. ix, n. 4 (A.-A., 30).

21. *De tab.*, Bk. I, c. vi; c. ix: "the multifarious sacraments of Christ and the Church" — "multifaria Christi et Ecclesiae sacramenta" (PL, XCI, 410, 422). *De schem. et tropis*, c. xii: "history along with the mystical sense of Christ and the Church" — "historia simul et mysticus de Christo et Ecclesia sensus" (XC, 185 D). *In Sam.*, Bk. III, c. iii: "while they desired that the sacraments of the Law be celebrated externally, all the things to be sought within Christ and the Church began to be shown to be understood" — "dum exterius celebrari legis sacramenta desierant, cuncta interius in Christo et in Ecclesia caeperunt quaerenda intelligenda probari" (XCI, 680 D). *Ep.* 6: "By so much the more will you find the sacraments of Christ and the Church introduced within the ancient pages" — "Quanto plura Christi et Ecclesiae sacramenta antiquis indita paginis inveneris" (XCIV, 687 A).

22. "Allegoria est, cum verbis sive rebus mysticis praesentia Christi et Ecclesiae sacramenta signantur": Amalarius, *Eccl. off.*, Bk. I, c. xix (PL, CV, 1030 A); Bk. IV, c. iii (1172-3). Rabanus, *In Ex.* (CVIII, 148). Aimon, *In ps.* (CXVI, 506 CD). Angelome, *In Gen.* (CXV, 232 C). Honorius (CLXXII, 749 A); etc. Cf. Isidore: "sacramenta Christi et Ecclesiae" (LXXXIII, 301 C). Alcuin, *De ben. Patr.* (C, 559 A).

23. "ad contemplanda Christi Ecclesiaeque sacramenta": *In Ap.*, Bk. IV (482 D); Bk. VII (573 A). Claudius, *In Reg.*, Bk. I (PL, L, 1047 C).

24. "Limpida Christi Ecclesiaeque pandere sacramenta conabimur": *In Reg.*, Bk. II, *praef.* (PL, CXV, 331 BC).

25. "omnis Scriptura veteris Testamenti ad mysteria Christi et Ecclesiae contuenda nos invitat" — "Vetus Testamentum, ubi mysteria Christi Ecclesiaeque sunt praedicta": *In Ap.*, Bk. II (PL, CXVII, 1003 C). Ps.-Remi, *In ps. LXXIX* (CXXXI, 567-8).

26. "in Christo et in Ecclesia sancta completa sunt" — "omnis Testamenti

veteris historia pertinet": *L. de cursu sp.*, c. iii; *Dial. de 3 q.*, c. xxxiii (PL, CXLVI, 146 D, 102 A).

27. — "sermonum brevitate constringitur" — "mysteriorum tamen immensitate extenditur, quia cuncta Christi et Ecclesiae sacramenta pleniter eloquitur": *In Ruth, prol.* (Pez, 4, 444). Paulinus of Nola, *Poema* 27, v. 531-2 (PL, LXI, 660 B):

... Brevis ista videtur
Historia, at magna signat mysteria belli.

... That history seems
Short, but it signals the war's great mysteries.

28. "de mysterio Christi et Ecclesiae": PL, CLVI, 339 C; cf. 20 A. Manegold, *In ps. LXXIX:* "totum omnium Scripturarum mysterium, id est Christum et Ecclesiam" (XCIII, 914 D).

29. "Allegoria, cum de Christo et Ecclesia res exponitur": *In Cant.*, c. i (PL, CLXXII, 359 B).

30. "Per allegoriam sacramenta Ecclesiae, quomodo praecedentium rerum figuris praenuntiata sint intelligimus": *In ps. CXXXIV* (PL, CXCVI, 370 A). *In Abd.:* "The mountain . . . allegorically Christ and the Church" — "Mons . . . allegorice Christus et Ecclesia" (CLXXV, 389 D). Cf. Gregory of Tours making Chilperic speak, *H. Francorum,* Bk. VI, c. v: "The ever unbelieving generation which . . . does not understand that the mysteries of the Church are to be figured in their sacrifices" — "Generatio semper incredula, quae . . . non intelligit ecclesiastica mysteria in suis sacrificiis figuranda" (LXXI, 373 C).

31. "Allegoria est, cum verbis sive rebus mysticis occulta Christi et Ecclesiae sacramenta significantur": *Allegoriae* (101-2).

32. "incarnationem Christi cum omnibus sacramentis suis": *Quaest. de ep. Pauli* (Martin, 2).

33. "sacramenta Christi et Ecclesiae sub velamine denuntiabant": PL, CLXXI, 617 D. Absalon, *s.* 29 (CCXI, 177 B); *s.* 22 (134 C).

34. Hilarius, *Instr. psalm,* n. 5 (6). Irimbert, *In Jud.*, Bk. I: "Christus omnem suae humanitatis redemptionem veteri Testamento includit" (Pez, 4, 234-5). *Altercati* (RMAL 10, 103-9); etc.

35. "ad Salvatorem Dominum": Cf. Cassiodorus, *In ps. I:* "and almost all things are referred to the Savior Lord by means of allegorical likenesses" — "et per allegoricas similitudines pene omnia referuntur ad Salvatorem Dominum" (PL, LXX, 34 D). *De psalm. usu* (V. 850), *praef.:* "So, if you examine them with intent mind and arrive at the spiritual understanding, you will find in the Psalms the incarnation and passion as well as the passion and resurrection of the Lord's Word" — "In psalmis itaque invenies, si intenta mente perscruteris et ad spiritualem intellectum perveneris, Domini Verbi incarnationem passionemque et resurrectionem atque ascensionem" (CI, 465 CD).

36. "totum ad Christum revocemus, si volumus iter rectae intelligentiae tenere": Aug., *In ps. XCVI,* n. 2 (CCL, 39, 1354).

37. "de nostro populo, qui in sacramentis Christi confaederatus est": Or., *In Num.*, h. 16, n. 9 (152). Rabanus, *In Num.,* Bk. III, c. vii (PL, CVIII, 744 B); *In Judith,*

ep. dedic.: "a history transferred by us through the allegorical sense to the mystery of the holy Church" — "historiam allegorico sensu ad sanctae Ecclesiae mysterium a nobis translatam" (CIX, 539-40). Isidore devotes Book I of the *De fide cath.* to texts concerning Christ, and Book II to texts concerning the Church (LXXXIII, 449-538).

38. "ventura christiani populi sacramenta": Cassiodorus, *In ps. CIV* (PL, LXX, 753 D).

39. "praenuntiatur Christus venturus in carne" — "omnis ordo ecclesiarum ejus": Paschasius, *De ben. patr., prol.* (RB, 1911, 427).

40. B. Fischer (tr. fr., *La Maison Dieu*, 27), *Le Christ dans les psaumes*. F. Vandenbrouke, *La lecture chrét. du psautier*, S. Er., v, 5-26. The author rightly observes that if the evocation of the mysteries is frequent enough in the "Psalm prayers," it does not suppress the literal sense in them.

41. "profundiora de Christo et ejus corpore mysteria": Paschasius, *In Lam.*, Bk. III (PL, CXX, 1148 D). Ps.-Remi, *In ps.* (CXXXI, 140 D). Luke of Mont Cornillon, *In Cant. mor.* (CCIII, 515 CD); etc. Cf. Aug., *In ps. LVI*, n. 1 (CCL, 39, 694); *In ps. LIX*, n. 1 (754), etc.

42. "Christus et Ecclesia, una persona est": Greg., *Mor.*, Bk. XIV, c. xlix, n. 57 (PL, LXXV, 1068 B).

43. "si duo in carne una" — "cur non duo in voce una?" — "sive caput loquatur, sive membra, unus Christus loquitur": Aug., *In ps. CXL*, n. 3 (CCL, 40, 2027).

44. "Loquatur ergo Christus, quia in Christo loquitur Ecclesia, et in Ecclesia loquitur Christus; et corpus in capite, et caput in corpore": *In ps. XXX*, 2, s. 1, n. 4 (CCL, 38, 193). *C. Faust.*, Bk. XII, c. xxxix: "Since it was predicted 'there will be two in one flesh', hence too in the ark some things are related to Christ, others to the Church, because the whole is Christ" — "Quia praedictum est, erunt duo in carne una, propterea et in arca quaedam ibi ad Christum, quaedam vero ad Ecclesiam referuntur, quod totum Christus est" (PL, XLII, 275).

45. "corpus Christi" — "Christus et Ecclesia": *In Col.* (PL, CXVII, 757 B).

46. "Omnia referuntur ad Christum allegorica similitudine": *In ps.* (PL, CXXXI, 139 A). It comes from above. A slightly different form in Cassiodorus (see p. 318, n. 35, above).

47. "Finis enim legis, Christus est": Rom. 10:4.

48. *In ps. XCVI*, n. 2: "Quidquid dubitationis habet homo in animo auditis Scripturis Dei, a Christo non recedat; cum ei fuerit in illis verbis Christus revelatus, intelligat se intellexisse. Antequam autem perveniat ad Christi intellectum, non se praesumat intellexisse" (CCL, 39, 1354-5).

49. *In ps. LVIII*, 6: "He is in fact the end of the Law and the Prophets" (PG, LXVIII, 112 D).

50. "Finis quippe legis ad justitiam, Christus est, quia quidquid sive vetus sive nova Lex loquitur, ad illum sine dubitatione refertur": *Testimonia de Eccl.* (PL, CXLV, 1141 B).

51. "Universitas Scripturarum, in qua sunt fidelia testimonia Christi": *In proph. min., prol.* (PL, CLXVIII, 9 B).

52. Trans. of Rom. 10:4 by Barth, *Dogmatique*, vol. I, t. II, I, p. 70. Cf. Rabanus Maurus, *In Ruth*, c. xvi: "The intention of the whole Law tends to our Redeemer" — "Totius legis intentio ad redemptorem nostrum tendit" (PL, CVIII, 1223 A).

Paschasius, *In Lam.* Bk. I: ". . . of Jesus Christ, who is the end of the whole Law unto justice; hence all the signs of the books of divine authority are sacraments of the Lord's incarnation and our redemption" — "Jesu Christi, qui est finis totius legis ad justitiam; propterea omnia illa librorum divinae auctoritatis signa, dominicae incarnationis et redemptionis nostrae sunt sacramenta" (CXX, 1101 CD).

53. "lex non potest esse sine Verbo, neque propheta nisi qui de Dei Filio prophetavit": *In Luc.,* Bk. VII, n. 10 (Tissot, SC, 52, 12).

54. "Materia sacrae Scripturae, totus Christus est, caput et membra": *Glossa*. Claudius: "The whole body along with its head is the one Christ" — "Totum cum suo capite corpus, unus est Christus" (PL, CIV, 645 A); "For here the whole Christ is under discussion, in whom are all his members" — "Totus enim Christus hic loquitur, in quo sunt omnia membra ejus" (L, 1100 A). Peter Comestor, *s.* 18: "For just as Christ and the Church are two in one flesh, so often they can be two in one voice" — "Sicut enim Christus et Ecclesia duo sunt in carne una, ita saepenumero possunt esse duo in voce una" (CXCVIII, 1770 A). M. Pontet, *L'exégèse de s. Aug. prédicateur,* 400-11.

55. "De Domino et ejus corpore": Cf. Aug., *Doct. chr.,* Bk. III, c. xxxi, n. 44 (Combès-Farges, 44). Paschasius, *In Lam.,* Bk. III (PL, CXX, 1141 BC). Tyconius stressed the figures of the Church.

56. "Omnia quae ante scripta sunt . . . et figurae nostrae fuerunt, et in figura contingebant eis": *De cat. rud.,* c. iii, n. 6 (PL, XL, 314); *C. Faust.,* Bk. IV, c. ii; Bk. XII, c. xxxvii (XLII, 219, 273), etc. Already Ambrose (Mersch, t. 2, app. 4). Cf. Rabanus, *In Ex., praef.*: "Among the other writings that the Pentateuch contains, the book of Exodus stands preeminent, in which almost all the sacraments by which the present Church is instituted, nourished, and ruled, are figuratively expressed" — "Inter caeteras scripturas quas Pentateuchus continet, merito liber Exodi eminet, in quo pene omnia sacramenta quibus praesens Ecclesia instituitur, nutritur et regitur, figuraliter exprimuntur" (CVIII, 9 A).

57. "ad prophetiam Ecclesiae": *Civ. Dei,* Bk. XV, c. xxvii, n. 1 (PL, XLI, 473).

58. "Nihil est in divina Scriptura quod non pertineat ad Ecclesiam": PL, CXIII, 844. Peter Lombard (CXCI, 59-60). Joannes Monachus, *Ep. ad Adalberon.*: "The divine law of Moses, containing all the sacraments of the Church" — "Divina lex Moysi, omnia Ecclesiae sacramenta continens" (M.D., *Vet. scr.,* 1, 715).

59. See particularly the commentaries on the Psalms. Cf. *Catholicisme,* c. vi. Claudius, *In Reg.,* Bk. II (PL, L, 1100 A). Robert of Basevorn, *Forma praedicandi* (Charland, *Artes praed.,* 294).

60. Heterius and Beatus, *Ad Elip.,* Bk. II, c. lxxviii: "Hence in the Scriptures it is to be noted when both head and body [apply], or when one crosses over from each of the two to each, or from the one to the other. And so, let the careful reader understand what may come to the head and what to the body" — "Proinde notandum est in Scripturis quando et caput et corpus, aut quando ex utroque transeat ad utrumque, aut ab altero ad alterum. Sicque, quid capiti, quid corpori veniat, prudens lector intelligat" (PL, XCVI, 1018 B).

61. *Mysterium Christi, absconditum a saeculis et generationibus:* Or., *In Num.,* h. 12, n. 1 (96); *Col.* I, 26.

62. "Multifarie et multis figurarum modis eadem Christi et Ecclesiae

mysteria repetuntur, sed repetita novi semper aliquid afferunt": Bede, *In Cant.*, Bk. III (PL, XCI, 1133 C). Aug., *In Hept.*, Bk. VI, q. 30: "One must signify in many ways what was to be fulfilled in one" — "Multis modis significandum, quod uno modo implendum fuit" (XXXIV, 792). Claudius, *In Reg.*, Bk. III: "One and the same sacraments of our salvation are prefigured multifariously and in many ways" — "Multifarie multisque modis una eademque nostrae salutis sacramenta praefigurantur" (C, 1145 B). Richard, *L. except.*, P. II, Bk. IV, c. x: "thus the mystery of human redemption has been presignified with many riddles and figures in the Old Testament" — "sic multis aenigmatibus et figuris in V.T. praesignatum est mysterium humanae redemptionis" (Châtillon, 279).

63. See the Introduction, p. 3 of Volume 1.

64. *Ventura praenuntiant:* Raoul of Saint Germer, *In Lev.*, Bk. XV (185 H).

65. "Omnia Christum venturum esse designabant": Ps.-Bede, *In Jo.* (PL, XCII, 704 A). Rabanus, *In Ez.* (CX, 1023 D); etc.

66. "Non sine futurorum significatione gerebantur": Aug., *In ps. CXIII*, n. 1 (CCL, 40, 1635); n. 4: "That prophet even filed down rough hearts and reached without delay to understand future things from things done in the past" — "Propheta iste etiam grossa corda limavit et ad intelligenda de praeteritis rebus gestis futura incunctanter extendit" (1637). *In Hept.*, Bk. VII, q. 48, n. 13: "The Spirit of the Lord has worked the prefiguration and preaching of future things in the times of the prophets" — "praefigurationem praedicationemque futurorum Spiritus Domini propheticis temporibus operatus est" (XXXIV, 815). *Glossa* (CXIII, 1034 D). Peter Lombard, *In ps. CXII:* "Hence not merely past things are being reported here, but future ones are being predicted, since in those accomplishments are signified the ones to come" — "Hic ergo non narrantur praeterita tantum, sed futura praedicantur, quia in illis gestis futura significabantur" (CXII, 1017 D).

67. "Allegoria de Christo et Ecclesia in novissimis temporibus futura": Aug., *C. Maxim.*, Bk. II, c. xxv, n. 9 (PL, XLII, 811); *s.* 10, n. 1: "The divine old books are accustomed not only to communicate the faith of an accomplished deed but also the mystery of the one to come" — "solent divini veteres libri, non solum rei gestae fidem, sed etiam futurae insinuare mysterium" (XXXVIII, 92); *In ps. XXXIII, s.* 1, n. 3: "the things that you see ... have been accomplished in the mystery of things to come" — "illa quae videtis ... in mysterio futurarum rerum gesta esse" (CCL, 38, 275). Ambrose, *De Joseph*, n. 85: "So the deeds of the patriarchs are the mysteries of things to come" — "Gesta igitur patriarcharum, futurorum mysteria sunt" (PL, XIV, 672 B). Autpert, *In Ap.:* "to treat now of the diversity of the sacraments by which both the future dispensation of Christ and the coming salvation of the Church were prepared" — "de sacramentorum nunc diversitate tractare, quibus et futura Christi dispensatio et Ecclesiae praeparabatur ventura salvatio" (482 B).

68. "Figuris praecedentibus res significabantur esse venturae ...": Angelome, *In Gen.* (PL, CXV, 232 C).

69. Bede (PL, XCIII, 424 D). Jerome, *In Is.:* "The spiritual and sublime understanding of present things carries us over to those to come" — "Intelligentia spiritalis atque sublimis de praesentibus nos transfert ad futura" (XXIV, 517 D). *In Daniel:* "that this is the custom of holy Scripture: to send out advance notice in signs of the truth of things to come" — "hunc esse morem Scripturae sanctae, ut futurorum veritatem praemittat in signis" (XXV, 565 D).

70. "futura mysteria Domini signantur": *Glossa, In ps. VII*, 2 (PL, CXIII, 853 A). Cf. Hesychius, *In Lev.*, Bk. I, c. i: "figurae sequentium mysteriorum" (PG, XCIII, 793 D).

71. "Ostensa sunt Patribus futura mysteria, rerum eventibus": *Sup. Psalt.* (Vaccari, *Biblica,* 26, 88).

72. "futura Christi et Ecclesiae sacramenta": *De st. domus Dei*, Bk. II (493 G).

73. "quaedam imago futurae rei": Aug., *De civ. Dei*, Bk. XVII, c. v, n. 2 (PL, XLI, 526); etc.

74. "figura et quaedam prophetia futurorum": Isidore (PL, LXXXIII, 207 B).

75. With Cyprian this is a neologism: Chr. Mohrmann, *Ét. sur le latin des chrétiens,* 25.

76. "allegorica praefiguratio": Claudius, *In Reg.* (PL, L, 1088 A, 1101 D); 30 *Q. sup. Reg.* (CIV, 721 D).

77. "praefigurationis mysterium": Aug., *In ps. LXXII,* n. 3 (PL, XXXVI, 915). Greg., *Mor.*, Bk. XX, c. i, n. 1: "he knows how to utter the past in such fashion that by that very fact he would know how to preach the things to come" — "sic scit praeterita dicere ut eo ipso noverit futura praedicare" (LXXVI, 135 C).

78. "Futura mysteriorum arcana per allegoriam figuraliter portendisse declarantur" — "Futura incarnati Verbi virginitas mysticis sacramentorum obumbrationibus figurabatur": *De metris et aenigm.* (MGH, *A. Ant.*, XV, 67). *De virg.*, c. liv (*ibid.*, 312).

79. "Futurorum intelligentia": *In Gen.* (PL, CLXVII, 537 B).

80. "Mystica dicitur expositio, cum ea praefigurati docemus quae a tempore gratiae per Christum fuerant consummanda, vel quaecumque historia futura praesignari ostenditur": *Exp. in Hexaem.* (PL, CLXXVIII, 770 C).

81. Ps.-Aug., *De assumpt.*, c. i (PL, XL, 1143).

82. *In Num.*, h. 16, n. 1: "There he foretells the mysteries to come" — "Ibi mysteria futura praenuntiat" (138); h. 9, n. 5: "Hence this was a mystery that was to come about later" — "Hoc fuit ergo mysterium, quod postea futurum" (60); etc.

83. Rom. 5:14.

84. "forma futuri" — "umbram habens futurorum bonorum": Heb. 10:1. Hilary, *In ps. CXVIII, s.* 1, n. 5: "that the law is to be dealt with not according to an understanding of the letter, but the shadow of things to come is to be discerned within it according to spiritual teaching" — "non secundum litterae intelligentiam legem esse tractandam, sed secundum spiritalem doctrinam futurorum in ea umbram esse noscendam" (PL, IX, 505 D).

85. *mysterium futurum* vs. *res gesta:* Aug., s. 10, n. 1 (PL, XXXVIII, 92). *In ps. LIX,* n. 1: "not to get acquainted with accomplished deeds . . . but to prefigure those that are to come" — "non propter cognoscendas res gestas . . . sed propter futura praefiguranda" (CCL, 39, 754).

86. *futura* vs. *transacta:* Greg., *Mor.*, Bk. XXXV, c. xvi, n. 41: "inasmuch as, by the dispensation of the Holy Spirit guiding all things marvelously, the things that have been written both relate to us past accomplishments and predict those to come" — "quatenus ea quae scripta sunt, dispensatione sancti Spiritus cuncta mirabiliter ordinante, et transacta nobis referant et futura praedicant" (PL, LXXVI, 772 A).

87. *res expectandae* vs. *res praeteritae:* Gerhoh: "as past these things are remembered here literally, but in the mystery they are still to be expected" — "quae hic memorantur ad litteram quasi praeteritae sed in mysterio adhuc sunt expectandae" (PL, CXCIV, 903 C).

88. *praeferens imaginem* vs. *repraesentandum:* Cf. Peter Damian, *Op.* 12, c. xxviii: "Elisha . . . offering the image of apostolic dignity then that Paul later represented as expressed" — "Eliseus . . . jam tunc apostolicae dignitatis imaginem praeferens, quam Paulus postmodum expressam repraesentat" (PL, CXLV, 281 D). Claudius, *In Reg.*, Bk. II: "so that the truth presented in that may appear evidently whatsoever sort of figure be adumbrated in it" — "ut evidenter appareat quod in illo figura qualiscumque adumbrata sit, in isto veritas praesentata" (L, 1088 A); "how it may outline a figure of things to come in it" — "quomodo in eo figuram delineat futurorum" (*ibid.*).

89. *futura veritas* vs. *typus, species, sacramentum:* Cyprian, *Ep.* 63, 5: "showing the type of the truth to come" — "typum futurae veritatis ostendens." Hilary, *Tr. Myst.*, Bk. I, c. viii: "Aside from an effect of the present thing there is also contained the aspect of the future" — "Praeter rei praesentis effectum futuri quoque species continetur" (SC, 90); c. x: "the figuration of future things is to be examined in these" — "in his futurorum figuratio scrutanda est" (92); c. xxv: "in praeformandis sui praesentibus futurorum effectibus" (116); c. xiii: "the great sacrament of the future is contained in these" events — "magnum in his futuri sacramentum continetur" (100); *In ps. II*, 23: "to signify the future of things to be accomplished" — "gerendorum futura significare," etc. Chromat., *In Matt.*, tr. 5, c. iv, n. 4: "as an example of the truth to come" — "ad futurae veritatis exemplum" (CCL, 9, 408).

90. *Civ. Dei*, Bk. XV, c. ii, on Gal. 4:24: "Haec forma intelligendi de apostolis descendens locum nobis aperit, quemadmodum Scripturae duorum Testamentorum, veteris et novi, accipere debeamus" (PL, XLI, 439). *In Jo.*, tr. 28, n. 9: "All things that were said . . . in the manifold writing of the Law, were a shadow of those to come" — "Omnia quae dicta sunt . . . in multiplici scriptura legis, umbra fuerunt futurorum" (CCL, 36, 282). Ambrose, *In Luc.*, Bk. II, n. 56: "You see that the whole series of the old law was a type of the one to come" — "Vides omnem legis veteris seriem fuisse typum futuri" (SC, 45, 97).

91. Cf. J. P. Brisson, Intr. to the *Tract. Myst. d'Hilaire* (SC, 19, 25).

92. "Haec omnia olim figuraliter praecesserunt, et nostra tempora quasi digito demonstraverunt": *Dom. in Palmis* (PL, CLXXII, 919 C).

93. "Quod enim legitur de Elia historialiter, in beato Joanne et in multis sanctorum invenitur spiritualiter": *S.* 2 *in f. J. Bapt.* (Tissier, 6, 113).

94. Rabanus, *In Num.*, Bk. III, c. vii (PL, CVIII, 737 D). Gerhoh: "We have sought and we have found the literal sense in these words of the text. . . . They are all better and more fittingly discussed and understood spiritually, because they also hint at words of a time to come [words] prophesying more of a mystery to come than reporting the history of the past" — "In his verbis litterae litteralem sensum quaesivimus et invenimus. . . . Melius et competentius omnia ista spiritaliter disseruntur et intelliguntur, quod etiam verba innuunt futuri temporis de futuro magis mysterio prophetantia quam de praeterito historiam narrantia" (CXCIV, 175 CD). Peter Lombard, *In ps. VII:* "The future mysteries of the Lord are

signified through David's acts" — "Per actus David futura mysteria Domini significantur" (CXCI, 111 C); etc. Cf. Or., *In Num.*, h. 11 (77); etc.

95. "dispensationis mysterium": Greg., *Mor.*, Bk. XXXIV, c. vii, n. 14 (PL, LXXXVI, 725 B). Quodvultdeus, *De prom.*, P. II, c. xxxiii, n. 74: "sacramentum divinae dispositionis" (LI, 808 D). Odilon of Cluny, *s.* 1 (CXLII, 993 D). Guibert of Nogent (CLVI, 507 B). Garnier, *s.* 1: "mysterium futurae dispensationis" (CCV, 565 A); etc. Cf. Aug., *C. Faust.*, Bk. XII, c. xlvi: "dispensationem humilitatis ejus" (XLII, 279).

96. "dispensatio mysterii": Rabanus, *In Lev.*, Bk. II, c. xii (PL, CVIII, 337 A). Or., *In Num.*, h. 4, n. 2 (24). Cf. Eph. 3:9.

97. "mystica Christi dispensatio": Or., *In Jos.*, h. 23, n. 3 (444); *De princ.*, Bk. IV, c. ii, n. 2: "dispensationes quaedam mysticae" (309).

98. Cf. Bernon of Reichenau, *De init. adv.*: "the dispensation of the Word to humanity" — "Verbi humanitati dispensatio" (PL, CXLII, 1086 C). Peter Comestor, on the cross: "Vide ergo dispensationem" (CXCVIII, 1739 B); etc.

99. Hilary, *In ps. CXXXIV*, n. 1 (695). Rupert, *In Gen.*, Bk. VI, c. xliii: "Those that are interiorly the most precious mysteries of Christ and the Church" — "Illa quae intrinsecus sunt pretiosissima Christi et Ecclesiae mysteria" (PL, CLXVII, 442 A).

100. Hilary, *Tr. myst.*, Bk. II, c. v: "to understand the significance of spiritual deeds" — "ad cognoscendam spiritalium gestorum significantiam" (SC, 148); *In ps. I*, n. 1: "readying us for a knowledge of the spiritual sacrament" — "ad cognitionem nos sacramenti spiritalis erudiens" (20). Jerome, *In Jer.*: "No one doubts that these things happen spiritually in the Church" — "Haec spiritaliter accidere in Ecclesia nemo dubitat" (PL, XXIV, 730 C). Greg., *In I Reg.*, *proem.*: "The sacred history of the kings is not . . . to be believed to be void of spiritual sacraments" — "Sacra regum historia non . . . spiritalibus sacramentis vacua credenda est" (LXXIX, 18 A); *In Ez.*, Bk. II, h. 6, n. 1: "since the holy teachers teach spiritual and internal things" — "cum doctores sancti spiritalia atque interna doceant" (LXXVI, 998 B). Rupert, *In Nahum*, Bk. II (CLXVIII, 555 B). Gerhoh: "And what had been commanded to do or to offer bodily in the days of the twelve sons of Israel would be fulfilled spiritually by or through them" (the apostles) — "Et quod illis diebus duodecim filiorum Israël jussum est facere vel offerre corporaliter, hoc ab ipsis vel per ipsos (apostolos) implendum fore spiritualiter" (CXCIV, 120-1).

101. "in interiora sapientiae spiritualis cellaria": *De exordiis et increm.*, c. viii (MGH, *Capit.*, 483). Cf. Aponius, *In Cant.*, Bk. III: "all those things that have been celebrated bodily in the Old Testament have been imaged spiritually in the coming of Christ" — "omnia illa quae carnaliter celebrata sunt in V. T. spiritualiter in Christi imaginata esse adventu" (63-4).

102. "quid mysterii spiritalis lex contineat": Pez, 4, 459; cf. 129, 131-2.

103. "futura Christi et Ecclesiae sacramenta" — "caelestia Christi et Ecclesiae sacramenta": Richard, *In Ap.*, Bk. II, c. i (PL, CXCVI, 746 A); Bk. I, c. i: "caeleste sacramentum" (686 D); c. iii (701). Autpert, *In Ap.*, Bk. VII (567 F); etc. Filastre, *Haer.* 148: "caeleste mysterium" (CCL, IX, 311); *haer.* 129: "caelestis gratiae atque arcani salutaris Christi Domini mysteria" (292).

104. "caelestis intelligentia": Prosper, *In ps. CIII*: "For the preachers of the truth, who lift the hearts of their hearers . . . to the height of heavenly understand-

ing" — "Praedicatores enim veritatis qui corda audientium . . . ad sublimitatem caelestis intelligentiae subvehunt" (PL, LI, 289 AB).

105. "Hebraei, caelestia nescientes. . . . Nos autem . . .": Rupert, *In Ex.*, Bk. IV, c. xxiii (PL, CLXVII, 722 BC). Honorius, *In Prov.* (CLXXII, 327 B); Rabanus (CX, 938 C); etc.

106. 2nd ed. (1922), 53, 65. (Tr. H. Bouillard, *Karl Barth*, 1957, t. I, c. i).

107. *In ps. CXXXIV*, n. 18 (705). Cf. Hippolytus, *In Dan.*, Bk. IV, c. xxiv: "What Moses did in days of yore for the tabernacle was merely types and symbols of the spiritual mysteries" — "Ce que fit autrefois Moïse pour le tabernacle, n'était que types et symboles des mystères spirituels" (M. Lefèvre, SC, 14, 309).

108. "simpliciter intellectus" — "inspectus interius": *In Matt.*, Bk. XII, c. xii (PL, IX, 987 CD).

109. "interior intelligentia": *In Matt.*, Bk. II, c. ii (924 C).

110. "interioris intelligentiae ratio" — "interior significantia": *In Matt.*, Bk. XIV, c. iii (997 B); Bk. VII, c. viii (957 A).

111. "qui sit modus interpretandae allegoriae, quae per sapientiam dicta creditur in Spiritu sancto: utrum a visibilius antiquioribus ad visibilia recentiora eam perducere sufficiat, an usque ad animae affectiones atque naturam, an usque ad incommutabilem aeternitatem": *De vera rel.*, c. l, n. 99 (Pegon, 168-70).

112. "spiritualiter sentienda" — "ad interiora intelligenda": Isidore, *De fide cath.*, Bk. II, c. xx, n. 2 (PL, LXXXIII, 528 C). Claudius, *In Reg.*, Bk. I (L, 1059 D); etc.

113. "dispositio spiritalis": Hilary, *Tr. myst.*, Bk. I, c. xxxvii (SC, 134).

114. "arcanum interioris intelligentiae": Rabanus, *In Jud.*, Bk. I, c. xii: "But let us see what the treasure box of inner understanding breathes out as well" — "Sed videamus quid etiam interioris intelligentiae respiret arcanum" (PL, CVIII, 1134 D). Cf. Or., *In Num.*, h. 5, n. 2: "visible works, to be sure, yet works within which there was another, inner mystical and hidden understanding" — "opera visibilia quidem, sed quibus inesset interior alia mystica et occulta intelligentia" (27); h. 20, n. 1: "There are in them certain mystical secrets of the inner understanding" — "Sunt quidem in iis et mystica quaedam atque interioris intelligentiae secreta" (186). Peter Cellensis, *De tab. Moysi* (CCII, 1047 B).

115. "magnum sacramentum Christi et Ecclesiae" — "magnum aliquid et spiritale": Aug., *In Hept.*, Bk. VII, c. xlix, n. 13-4 (PL, XXXIV, 15-6): "ad significationem spiritalium." *De cat. rud.*, c. xix, n. 33: "yet in all these there were signified spiritual mysteries that pertained to Christ and the Church" — "in his tamen omnibus mysteria spiritalia significabantur, quae ad Christum et Ecclesiam pertinerent" (Combès-Farges, 104).

116. "caelestis regni mysteria" — "interiora": Greg., *In Ez.*, Bk. II, h. 1, n. 3 (PL, LXXVI, 1029 C).

117. "interius mysterium percipere": Gerhoh, *In Cant. Moysi* I (PL, CXCIV, 1019 B; cf. A).

118. "spiritualium gratiarum signa": Richard, *In Act.* XII, 1 (PL, CXLI, 292 C, 303 D, 305 B). Werner, *Defl.*, Bk. I (CLVII, 1000 C).

119. "Et quid per paleam nisi superficies litterae designatur? Quid per hordeum nisi interior intelligentia?": Hervaeus, *In Is.*, Bk. IV (PL, CLXXXI, 294 D).

120. "sustollat se animus lectoris ad ea quae intus in intellectu sunt": Paschasius, *De ben. patr.* (RB, 1911, 427). Gerhoh, *In ps. CXLI*: "warning" us "to lift

the sense of the Psalmist from history to spiritual understanding" — "monens ab historia levandum sensum psallentis ad intellectum spiritalem" (PL, CXCIV, 939 D).

121. "de angustiis litterae" — "in sublimi loco": Jerome, *In Matt.*, Bk. IV, c. xxvi, n. 19: "To me the upper room seems to be understood as the spiritual law which, departing from the narrows of the letter, receives the Savior in an exalted place" — "Videtur autem mihi caenaculum lex spiritalis intelligi, quae de angustiis litterae egrediens, in sublimi loco recipit Salvatorem" (PL, XXVI, 193 C).

122. "introspiciens universa": *Hom. inéd.* (Ch. Dumont, COCR, 1957, 119).

123. "interna mysteria": Rabanus, *In Ez.*, Bk. VIII (PL, CX, 690 C). Rupert, *In Job* (CLXVIII, 1103 D); etc.

124. "secundum litteram exterius informat" — "juxta mysticum intellectum interius erudit": Autpert, *In Ap.*, Bk. I (426 D).

125. *Ibid.*, Bk. VII (573 A).

126. Rupert (PL, CLXX, 238 A). Bede, *In Tob.* (XCI, 923 CD).

127. "in historia, spiritus intelligentia": Rupert, *In Ez.*, Bk. II, c. xxviii (PL, CLXVII, 1489 BC).

128. Paschasius, *In Matt.*, Bk. II, c. ii: "He was promising in more hidden fashion something else far in the future [than] what seemed to sound in the letter of an action" — "Quod tunc in littera rei gestae sonare videbatur aliud longe futurum occultius promittebat" (PL, CXX, 143 A).

129. "mysterium requirere, secreta pulsare, velum templi conscissum intrare": Aug., *In ps. LXVIII*, n. 6: "'And they gave me bile to eat and in my thirst they gave me vinegar to drink.' — This was done literally, and the Gospel tells us as much. . . . Nevertheless it is to be taken in such wise that what had previously been predicted . . . was fulfilled, and in that very fact . . . we ought to search for the mystery, to batter the hiding places, to enter the torn veil of the temple, there to see the Sacrament" — "Et dederunt in escam meam fel et in siti mea potaverunt me aceto. — Factum est quidem ad litteram, et evangelium hoc nobis indicat. . . . Verumtamen sic accipiendum (est) et impletum quod hic fuerat ante praedictum . . . , et in ipso facto . . . mysterium requirere debemus, secreta pulsare, velum templi conscissum intrare, videre ibi sacramentum" (PL, XXXVI, 858).

130. "notificando nobis historiam incarnationis Christi sui et mysterium ipsius incarnationis": *In ps. LXXVII* (PL, XCIII, 900 B). Helinand, s. 1: "The faith of the Lord's incarnation along with all his sacraments" — "Fides incarnationis dominicae cum suis omnibus sacramentis" (CCXII, 484 A).

131. "umbratilis et figurativus David" — "verus David" — "mysticus et spiritualis David" — "historialis David": Manegold, *In ps. II* (PL, XCIII, 495 BC).

132. Aug., *In ps. LXIV*, n. 6 (PL, XXXVI, 778).

133. "ut discant ex typo Jesu historici, mysterium veri Jesu": Rabanus, *In Jos. ep. dedic.* (PL, CVIII, 1000 B). Manegold, *In ps. XXVII* (XCIII, 619 C).

134. "operator mysterii spiritalis": Ambrose, *In Luc.*, Bk. XVIIII, c. xv (Tissot, SC, 52, 145).

135. *De sacr., prol.*, c. vi (PL, CLXXVI, 185 C). Cf. C. Spicq, "Agapè, prolégomènes à une ét. de théol. néo-testamentaire" (*St. hellenistica*, 10, 1955), VIII: the cross "is a mystery as well as a historical fact, and a mystery even more than a

fact" — "est un mystère autant qu'un fait historique, et un mystère plus qu'un fait."

136. "Spiritualis allegoria semper praedicat ecclesiastica mysteria et sacramenta caelestia": *In Cant. mor.* (PL, CCXVII, 504 BC).

137. "caelestium mysteria" or "evangelica doctrina": *In Ez.*, Bk. II, c. xxiv (PL, CLXVII, 504 BC).

138. In his critique of Origen's theory of allegory, R. P. C. Hanson, *Allegory and Event* (1959), writes: according to Origen as understood and approved by de Lubac, "the essential reality is not the historical life of Christ, not some timeless philosophical interpretation of Christ's significance, but the life of the Church in the present world"; and he asks in the manner of an objection: "Is the Church really a higher stage after the Incarnation?" (287). As the present work makes superabundantly clear, Origen and his interpreter are not the only ones concerned here. There is simply no justification to oppose, in the manner in which the author does, the fact of the incarnation and the mystery of the Church. The more importance one gives to the former, the more one exalts the grandeur of the latter. The whole mystery of the Church and its whole life are dependent upon the fact of the incarnation. When the author speaks of "the historical life of Christ," he uses an equivocal expression: it is clear indeed that the exterior facts of Christ's earthly existence, taken purely as exterior facts, are over; but, to speak precisely, they were something quite different: they had an inside, and the efficacious mystery of which they were the carriers continues to exist and to bear fruit.

Notes to Chapter Eight
§3. The Christian Novelty

1. "ex illis quae facta sunt usque ad ista quae fiunt": Aug., *De fide rer.*, c. v, n. 10 (Pegon, 332).

2. "quae sub umbra legis historialiter accidisse leguntur" — "spiritualiter eveniunt in populo Dei tempore gratiae": *Gesta Inn. III* (Muratori, 1, 539; cited by du Cange).

3. Peter Lombard, *In ps. LXXVII*: ". . . all these things mystically, so that the grace of the Gospel may be declared under the history of the Old Testament" — "Mystice haec omnia, ut sub historia veteris Testamenti gratia evangelica declaretur" (PL, CXCI, 732 A).

4. *Nonnullae all.* (PL, CXCVI, 199 CD).

5. *Et tunc enim regnum Dei intra nos est:* Rupert, *In Ap.*, Bk. III (PL, CLXIX, 904 B); *In Ez.*, Bk. II, c. vi: "The exterior threshold is the letter; whilst the interior threshold in holy Scripture is the allegory; for, since we incline to allegory through the letter, just as we come from the threshold which is outside to that which is inside" — "Limen exterius, littera; limen vero interius in Scriptura sacra, allegoria est; quia enim per litteram ad allegoriam tendimus, quasi a limine quod est exterius ad hoc quod est interius venimus" (CLXVIII, 1468 A).

6. "ut ex toto appareat profunditas sacramenti": Cf. Paschasius, *In Matt.*, Bk. I, c. i (PL, CXX, 59 A).

7. Hervaeus, *In Is.*: "the fatness of internal restoration from spiritual under-

standing" — "de spiritali intelligentia pinguedinem internae refectionis" (PL, CLXXXI, 505 C).

8. "ad intelligendum Christi gratiam": Rabanus, *In Deut.*, Bk. III, c. xxv (PL, CVIII, 961 C). *L. carol.*, I, c. xx: "that the letter of the Old Testament is full of the mysteries of the grace of the Gospel" — "litteram veteris Testamenti evangelicae gratiae plenam esse mysteriis" (XCVIII, 1052 B).

9. Paschasius, *In Matt.*, Bk. I, c. i: "Since Christ doubtless advanced the Synagogue into the Church and did not change the Church back into the Synagogue" — "Quia nimirum Synagogam Christus provexit in Ecclesiam, et non Ecclesiam rursus mutavit in Synagogam" (PL, CXX, 54 C).

10. Rabanus Maurus, *In Ez.*, Bk. XIII: "All these things can [be taken] not only according to history with reference to an earlier people and the times of the Law, but also be transferred much the more according to allegory to the time of the New Testament and to the Christian people" — "Quae omnia, non tantum juxta historiam ad plebem priorem et legis tempora, sed etiam multo magis secundum allegoriam ad tempus novi Testamenti et ad populum christianum transferri possunt" (PL, CIX, 847 BC).

11. Henri Crouzel, BLE (1957), 81, note 10.

12. See Chapter 16..

13. the "incarnata Dei Sapientia" — "sensum ad interiora reducere et . . . juxta spiritum . . . perscrutari": *Mor.*, Bk. XII, c. iv, n. 5 (PL, LXXV, 988 BD). Rabanus, *In Ez.*, Bk. VIII (CX, 696 D).

14. Or., *In Num.*, h. 5, n. 1: "If you have understood what the order contains historically, climb now to the splendor of the mystery and to the light of the spiritual law; if you have a pure eye of the mind, behold" — "Si intellexisti quod historice ordo contineat, ascende nunc ad splendorem mysterii et legis spiritalis lumen, si purus tibi est mentis oculus, contuere" (25). Jerome, *In Gal.*: "those who climb to higher things and want to sense allegorically what has been written" — "qui ad superiora conscendant et allegorice velint sentire quae scripta sunt" (XXVI, 391 A). Greg., *Mor.*, Bk. XXI, c. i, n. 3: "let him rise to spiritual understanding" — "ad spiritalem intelligentiam consurgat" (LXXVI, 189 B). Rabanus, *In Ez.*, Bk. IV, c. i (CVIII, 189 C).

15. "ad instar solis radiis rutilans": Bruno of Segni, *In Ex.*, c. xxiv (PL, CLXIV, 376 B).

16. "Latet sub fabula mysterium altus": Coluccio Salutati, *De laboribus Herc.* (v. 1400), cited by Marcel Simon, *Hercule et le christianisme* (1955), 176.

17. Cf. Daniel Lys, "A la recherche d'une méthode pour l'exégèse de l'A.T.," *Et. théol. et rel.* (1955), 28 and 36.

18. Julian, *Disc.*, 8, 251-2.

19. *Des dieux et du monde*, c. iv. See Chapter 6.2 above.

20. Examples given by M. Simon, 33 and 77.

21. Or., *Sel. in Ez.*, c. viii: "Qui autem animi solertes sunt, ut gentilium fabulas eorumque profanam theologiam ad sensus spiritales trahant, dicunt Adonim symbolum esse frugum terrae, quae luguntur quidem quando seminantur, resurgunt vero et gaudio implent agricolas dum nascuntur" (PG, XIII, 799 A). We have the Greek text for it (800 A): *"Hoi de peri tōn anagōgēn tōn Hellēnikōn mythōn deinoi kai mythikēs nomizomenēs theologias, phasi ton Adōnin symbolon einai tōn tēs gēs*

karpōn, thrēnoumenōn men hote speirontai, anistamenōn de, kai dia touto chairein poiountōn tous geōrgous hote phyontai." "Those who are skilled at the anagogic interpretation of Greek myths and a theology that is thought to be mythic say that Adonis is a symbol of the fruits of the earth that are mourned when they are sown, but on rising again when they grow and for this very reason make farmers rejoice."

22. *Ibid.* — Aug., as is known, reproaches Varro in the same way for calling theology that which was in fact merely physiology or cosmology. But his essential critique went, like that of Origen, much further, as we have just seen. Cf. Macrobius, *Saturn.*, Bk. I, c. xviii-xxiv: Pretextatus reduces all the gods to the "natura solis" (Eyssenhardt, 104-28).

23. Massion, *Ac. des Inscript.*, 1706 (cited by Lombard, *L'abbé du Bos*, 185). He says of the ancient poets what would have been better said of their interpreters.

24. Cf. Tertullian, *Adv. Marc.*, Bk. I, c. xiii: the lions of Mithra are the "sacramenta" of the dry and burning nature (307).

25. Cf. Aug., *Civ. Dei*, Bk. X, c. xxi: "the tale signifying this mystic feature" — "hoc mysticum significare fabula" (PL, XLI, 299).

26. Cf. Or., *In Jo.*, Bk. VI, c. iii, n. 14-5 (109).

27. Thus it is insufficient to define the contrast between Christianity and paganism in the time of Diocletian, or any other epoch, by saying with F. C. Burkitt that it is "the contrast between an historical account and a philosophical account, or rather . . . between an annalistic and a systematic account" (*Church and Gnosis*, 1932, 127; cf. 138, 139, 145).

28. "quae in cordibus nostris phantastica imaginatione formatur" — "quae personam habet existentem" — "collectio fidelium sanctorum omnium, anima et cor unum, sponsa Christi, Jerusalem futuri saeculi": *In ps. IV* (PL, LXX, 47 C).

29. Adam of Perseigne, *In l. s. Bened.* (COCR 4, 1937). Adam of Brême, *Gesta Pout. Hammal. eccl.* (PL, CXLVI, 459 A). Bernard, *De consid.*, Bk. III, c. iv, n. 15 (CLXXXII, 767 A); *In ps. qui hab.* (CLXXXIII, 206 D); *Vita Bern.*, Bk. VII, c. xiii, n. 19 (CLXXXV, 423 D). Peter the Chanter (CCV, 29 C). Aldhelm (LXXXIX, 133 C); etc.

30. William of Saint Thierry, *De contempl. Deo*, c. xxv (M. M. Davy, 60).

31. H. Rochais, "Ipsa philosophia Christus," *Med. St.* (1951), 244-7.

32. A. Gelin, *Les idées maîtresses de l'A.T.* (1948), 6.

33. Rom. 5:14; 2 Cor. 3:13-7; Heb. 9:6-10.

34. Jean Seznec, *La survivance des dieux antiques* . . . (1941), 79.

35. [In Greek] Chrysostom says *kata diplēn ekdochēn* (PG, LV, 209), expressing a common thought.

36. Cf. Or., *In Jo.*, Bk. XIII, c. xxvi (251); *In Jo.*, fr. 9 (481); *In I Cor.*, fr. 17 (JTS 9, 353), etc.

37. In "S. Aug. et la fonction protreptique de l'allégorie," *Rech. augustiniennes*, I (1958), J. Pépin rightly observes, regarding the *C. Cels.*, Bk. IV, c. 1 (324), that Origen "prend soin de distinguer radicalement l'allégorie chrétienne de l'allégorie païenne; la Bible comporte une signification authentique préalable à toute interprétation, ce qui lui assure une large audience, alors que la substance de la mythologie est inexistante au sens littéral"; and "ce n'est pas autrement qu'Aug. conjurera le risque d'ésoterisme lié à la fonction élective de l'allégorie et conciliera le privilège de l'exégèse subtile avec l'universalisme." The same au-

thor's *Mythe et allég.*, 460: Origen observes against Celsus "qu l'auteur des récits bibliques s'est toujours préoccupé de donner à son œuvre une valeur littérale de bon aloi."

38. Or., *C. Cels.*, Bk. IV, c. xxxviii (309-10); etc. Cf. HE, 30-4: "Origène contre Origène."

39. *Protrept.*, c. xii, 119 (Mondésert, SC, 2, 188-9).

40. *Strom.*, Bk. V, c. iv, n. 19 and 24 (Stählin, 1, 338-41). On Clement's Christian allegorism, aside from the work by Cl. Mondésert cited already, cf. J. Moingt, RSR 37 (1950), 543-5.

41. Or., *In Ex.*, h. 4, n. 2 (253); *In Lev.*, h. 13, n. 1 (468-71).

42. *De princ.*, Bk. IV, c. ii, n. 1: "Nihil commune habet haec nostra sapientia ... cum hujus mundi sapientia" (305).

43. *In Ex.*, h. 4, n. 6: "the wandering and slippery dogmas of the philosophers" — "erratica et lubrica philosophorum dogmata" (178).

44. *In Lev.*, h. 10, n. 2: "Do not touch the stolen loaves of perverse doctrine; do not crave the false foods of philosophy, which lead you away from the truth; fasting from such is pleasing to God" — "Noli contingere panes furtivos perversae doctrinae; non concupiscas fallaces philosophiae cibos, qui te a veritate seducant; tale jejunium Deo placet" (444). *In Gen.*, h. 10, n. 2: "the proud arrogance of Greek eloquence" — "elatam Graecae facundiae arrogantiam" (96).

45. *Sel. in Jer.* 51, 3: they crumble, "Christ abrogating the dogmas of the Gentile idols and freeing those of the Gentiles who have believed" — "abrogante Christo dogmata gentilium idolorum et liberante eos qui e gentibus crediderunt" (PG, XIII, 599 C). *In Jos.*, h. 7, n. 7: on the philosophers and rhetoricians "who all belong to the city of Jericho" — "qui omnes de civitate sunt Hiericho"; "remember that Jesus ordered there to be a curse upon all the gold that was found in Jericho" — "memento quia Jesus anathema esse jussit omne aurum quod in Hiericho fuerit inventum" (334-5); etc. Cf. Richard, *L. except.*, P. II, Bk. IV, c. ii (J. Châtillon, 279).

46. *In Jos.*, h. 7, n. 1: "and he cast down the dogmas of the philosophers right down to their foundations" — "et philosophorum dogmata usque ad fundamenta dejecit" (328). *In Gen.*, h. 11, n. 2 (103; SC, 7, 199); h. 13, n. 3 (116-7; SC, 7, 220); h. 14, n. 3 (123-4; SC, 7, 231). *In Num.*, h. 13, n. 2: "Let the son of the Church ... use the javelins of God's word and draw ... the sword of the spirit; let him destroy ... all the arms of the Gentile dogmas and let him burn ... the pride of their arguments with the fire of truth" — "Ecclesiae filius ... adhibeat jacula verbi Dei et distringat ... gladium spiritus, destruat ... omnes munitiones gentilium dogmatum et elationes argumentorum ... igne veritatis exurat" (109).

47. A. Vaccari, *Scritti di erudizione e di filologia*, II (1958), 352: the allegory of Origen "transforma tutto in idee." This could be admitted, as of all Christian spiritual exegesis, depending on how one understands the word "idea."

48. *Op. cit.*, I (1952), 90-1.

49. E. Vacherot, *H. crit. de l'Ec. d'Alexandrie*, I (1846), 282-3; etc.

50. Or., *In Rom.*, Bk. II, c. xiv (PG, XIV, 919-20); *In Jer.*, h. 16, n. 9 (140); h. 8, n. 7 (61-2). For R. P. C. Hanson, *Allegory and Event* (1959), no one would be able to doubt "that Origen, though a believing, devout and orthodox Christian, was at

the same time a prince of rationalists" (224). What a strange idea! It seems that for this author, every Christian making use of philosophical reason or not sacrificing human liberty to predestination, or not confusing the miracles of Jesus with the prodigies of Apollonius of Tyana, ought to be a rationalist: by this reckoning there would not be a Catholic theologian who is not a rationalist.

51. Thus Rabanus, *In Ex.*, Bk. I, c. xiii, following Isidore, who reproduced Origen, *In Ex.*, h. 4, n. 6 (177); cf. c. xv and xxi (PL, CVIII, 35 A, 37 C, 45 A); etc.

52. Cf. Or., *C. Cels.*, 3, 23, opposing the history of Jesus to the fables of Dionysius, etc. (219-20).

53. J. Pépin, *Mythe et alleg.*, 478-83; cf. however 261. Cf. Aug., *C. Faust.*, Bk. XII, c. xxxix-xi (PL, XLII, 275).

54. Cf. Milburn, *Early Christian Interpretations of History*, 43, on Theages of Rhegium and others: "their attempt to harmonize mythology with reason and to maintain old and honoured truth side by side with the ideas of a newer age." On the contrary, see P. Hartmann, "Or. et la théol. du martyre," ETL 34, 824.

55. Cf. Aug., *C. Faust.*, Bk. XII, c. xl (PL, XLII, 275-6), etc.

56. "sensus Christi": Or., *De princ.*, Bk. IV, c. ii, n. 3 (310-1); *C. Cels.*, Bk. V, c. i (2, 2); etc. 1 Cor. 2:16.

57. Or., *In Jo.*, Bk. I, c. iv (8).

Notes to Chapter Eight
§4. The Edification of the Faith

1. Heterius and Beatus, *Ad Elip.*, Bk. I, c. xcix: "The Jews do not accept these allegories of ours; carnal Christians do not understand them, and hence they do not confess that Christ the man is God" — "Has nostras allegorias Judaei non recipiunt; carnales christiani non intelligunt, et inde Christum hominem esse Deum non confitentur" (PL, XCVI, 956 A).

2. Gregory, *In Ez.*, Bk. II, h. 10, n. 1 (PL, LXXVI, 1058 AC).

3. Cf. Aug., *In ps. CXXX*, n. 9: "Behold, the bread has been prepared for you: but grow up on milk till you are ready for the bread: . . . first believe and hold firm to what Christ has become for you in your weakness" — "Ecce panis paratus est tibi: sed cresce de lacte ut ad panem pervenias: . . . quod tibi factus est Christus ad infirmitatem tuam, hoc primum crede, et fortiter tene" (CCL, 40, 1905); *In ps. CXVII*, n. 22 (1664). Nevertheless *in Jo.*, tr. 98, n. 2: "For them his very flesh is . . . milk; for those, it is food" — "Ipsa vero caro ejus . . . illis est lac, istis cibus" (46, 576).

4. Cf. Or., *In Jer.*, IV, 10: "Let us cross over from the lowliness of the letter to the spiritual understanding" — "Transeamus autem ad spiritalem intellectum ab humilitate litterae" (PL, XXV, 661 B).

5. Or., *In Lev.*, h. 1, n. 1 (280); cf. *In Matt.*, fr. 11 (19). Cf. HE 336-46.

6. *Ad Elip.*, Bk. I, c. cx: "The Scripture is the body of Christ" — "Haec Scriptura, corpus Christi est" (PL, XCVIII, 962 C).

7. *S. ined.* 10, *in annunt., De trib. tunicis Joseph* (Talbot, 86).

8. *S.* 18 (PL, CXCIV, 1750 B).

9. *In Lev. init.* (PL, CXIII, 298 C).

10. "Corpus Christi intelligitur etiam Scriptura Dei": *De unit.* (*L. de lite*, II, 206). *Miscell.*, Bk. I, tit. 85 (PL, CLXXVII, 519 A).

11. "Quod enim optime nosti, sicut novissimis diebus Verbum Dei in Maria carne vestitum processit in mundum — et aliud quidem erat quod videbatur in eo, aliud quod intelligebatur: carnis namque aspectus in eo patebat omnibus, paucis vero et electis dabatur divinitatis agnitio, — ita et cum per prophetas vel legislatorem Verbum Dei profectus (?) ad homines, non absque competentibus profertur indumentibus. Nam, sicut ibi carnis, ita hic litterae velamine tegitur: ut littera quidem aspicitur tanquam caro, latens vero spiritualis intrinsecus sensus tanquam divinitas sentitur.

"Tale ergo est quod et nunc invenimus, librum Levitici perquirentes, in quo sacrificiorum ritus et hostiarum diversitas ac sacerdotum ministeria describuntur; sed haec secundum litteram, quae tanquam caro Verbi Dei est et indumentum divinitatis ejus, digni fortassis vel aspiciant, vel audiant indigni: sed beati sunt illi oculi qui velamen (= sub velamine) litterae objectum intrinsecus divinum spiritum vident, et beati sunt qui ad haec audienda mundas aures interioris hominis deferunt": *In libros inform. litt. et sp. sup. Lev., praef. ad Theod.* (PL, CIV, 617 AB).

12. Eph. 1:18. Jerome, *In Is.*: "with the eyes of our heart" — "oculis cordis nostri" (PL, XXIV, 536 A). Aug., *In ps. CXI*, n. 1: "oculis cordis" (CCL, 40, 1625); *In Jo.*, tr. 39, n. 3 (36, 346); *s.* 88, n. 5 (PL, XXXVIII, 542). Cassian, *Coll.* 14, c. ix (SC, 54, 195). Greg., *In ev.*, h. 23, n. 1 (PL, LXXVI, 1182 C); *Mor.* (520 D). Claudius, *In Reg.*, Bk. III: "quibus hoc divinitus datum est, ut revelatis oculis cordis sui, manifeste cognoscant litteram veteris T. evangelicae gratiae plenam esse mysteri[i]s" (L, 1127 C). William of Saint Thierry, *In Cant.*, n. 12 (M. M. Davy, 42).

13. Aug., *In ps. CXVIII*, *s.* 18, n. 3: "the inner eyes" — "interiores oculos" (CCL, 40, 1724); *s.* 88, n. 5 (PL, XXXVIII, 542). William of Saint Thierry, *In Cant.*, n. 150 (Davy, 182); *De cont. Deo* (PL, CLXXXIV, 367 B, 368 A, 369 D); *Sp. fidei* (CLXXX, 383 B). Peter Lombard, *In ps. XCVIII* (CXCI, 1081 A). Greg.: "the eyes of the mind" — "oculos mentis" (LXXVI, 491 A).

14. Jerome, *In ps. CV* (*An. mar.*, III, 42, 174). Paschasius (PL, CXX, 1521 D). Rupert (CLXVII, 440 A). Peter the Venerable (CLXXXIX, 617 B). Paulinus of Nola, *Carmina*, 31, 226:

> Ergo oculos mentis Christo reseremus et aures.
> So let us lift up the eyes and ears of the mind to Christ.

15. Or., *In Rom.* VIII, 8 (PG, XIV, 1181 A); *In Matt.*, t. XVI, c. xi (508). Absalon, *s.* 13 (PL, CCXI, 85 D). Cf. Plato, *Rep.* 533 D.

16. Or., *In Num.*, h. 17, n. 3 (157). Cf. Dungal, *Adv. Claud.* (PL, CV, 493 B).

17. *Lib. mozar. ord.*, oratio sup. convertente Judaeo: "Pande sui cordis arcanis mysteria veteris Testamenti, ut beatissimus vates te canuisse, evangelio inluminatus, inveniat" (Férotin, 106-7). Or., *In Jo.*, Bk. XIII, c. xlii (268).

18. A frequent expression: Or., *In Gen.*, h. 7, n. 6 (76-7). Chromatius, *In Matt.*, tr. 3 (CCL, 9, 400). Jerome, *Ep.* 108, n. 10 (PL, XXII, 884). Leo, *s.* 27 (LIV, 216 D). Greg., *In Ez.* (LXXVI, 768 C, 858 C, 860 D). Apringius, *In Ap.*: "who, having been converted in divine admiration, gazing with the eyes of faith upon the disposition of the present times or the order of all the things that as a whole . . . are desig-

nated for God" — "qui in divina admiratione conversi, praesentium dispositionem temporum vel cunctarum ordinem rerum quae universa. . . . Deo signata sunt, fidei oculis intuentes" (33; cf. 31). Beatus, *In Ap.* (284). Autpert, *In Ap.*, Bk. III (466 B). Rabanus (CVIII, 1064 C). Angelome: "fidei oculos in Illum ponat" (PL, CXV, 497 A). Rupert (CLXX, 189 C). Bernard, *In ps. XC, s.* 7, n. 14 (CLXXXIII, 208 C; *s.* 17, n. 3 (251 D). Adam Scot, *s.* 5, c. xiii (CXCVIII, 125 C). Petrus Cellensis, *s.* 30 (CCII, 728 C). Potho of Prüm, *De st. domus Dei*, Bk. V, c. i (MBVP, 21, 509 C); etc. Cf. Claudius, *In Reg.*: "fidei oculo" (L, 1053 C). Rupert (CLXVII, 471 C); Gerhoh (*Op. in.*, I, 99, 301). Irimbert, *In Jud.*, Bk. II (Pez, 4, 355). Géraud of Barri, *Gemma eccl.*: "oculata fides" (J. S. Brewer, 1862, 4); etc.

19. "*Habet namque fides oculos suos* . . .": Aug., *Ep.* 120, c. ii, n. 8 (PL, XXXIII, 456); *In ps. CXLV*, n. 19: "omnino habet oculos fides" (CCL, 40, 2120); 3, 53, n. 6: "oculi isti . . . illuminantur fide" (PL, XXXVIII, 366); etc.

20. Rupert (PL, CLXVII, 787 A). Petrus Cellensis, *s.* 86: "So, like a lamp lit in the night, the faith illuminates all the sacraments round about" — "Fides igitur quasi lucerna in nocte accensa, circumlustret nubem omnium sacramentorum" (CCII, 898 B).

21. "in fide per allegoriam imbuendi": Garnier, *s.* 21 (PL, CCV, 706 B).

22. "mysteria fidei" — "in legalibus caeremoniis": Hugh of Saint Victor, *De sacram.*, Bk. X, c. vii (PL, CLXXVI, 341 A). *In Cant. brevis commentatio*, I: "mysteria fidei . . . scrutatur" (CLXXXIV, 407 C).

23. "fidei nostrae sacramenta": Richard, *Nonnullae all.* (PL, CXCVI, 200 A). Greg., In Ez., Bk. II, h. 10: the whole of Christianity = "sanctae fidei sacramenta" (LXXVI, 1063). Cf. Luke of Mont Cornillon, *In Cant. mor.*, on Solomon: "For he could not bring forth such great sacraments of Christ and the Church without the grace of the Holy Spirit" — "Sine enim Spiritus sancti gratia non potuit proferre tanta ac talia Christi et Ecclesiae sacramenta" (CCXIII, 493 C).

24. Autpert, *In Ap.*, Bk. IV: "A mystici legis et prophetarum eloquio, ad cognitionis intellectum fidei passibus veni, et hoc quod intellectu capis, ipsius operis veritate completem inspice" (402 D).

25. "pertinens ad instructionem fidei": Cf. Ockham, *Comp. errorum papae:* "There is allegory, when through one fact another, pertaining to the instruction of faith about Christ and the Church, is prefigured" — "Allegoria est, quando per factum unum figuratur aliud, pertinens ad instructionem fidei de Christo et Ecclesia" (Golast, 2, 957).

26. "ad aedificationem catholicae fidei": John Scotus, *Div. nat.*, Bk. V, c. xl (PL, CXXII, 1021 C). Gerhoh, *In ps. LXIV*, c. clxiv: "doctrinae quae fidei pertinet aedificationem" (CXCIV, 110 A).

27. "in fidei revelatione ad cognitionem veritatis" — "in catholicae fidei non fictae credulitate": Adam Scotus, *De triplici genere cont.* (PL, CXCVIII, 792 D). *Trip. tab., proem.*, 3, c. vi (631 A); c. viii: "the second [tablet] is of Christ, and it consists in the right belief in sound faith" — "secundum [tab.] est Christi, et est in recta sanae fidei credulitate" (632 AB).

28. "in catholicae fidei plenitudine": Apringius, *In Ap.*, c. xix (Vega, 53).

29. "in perfectae fidei credulitate" — "in fidei puritate": *Allegoriae:* "Allegoria vero aliquid in se plus continet, quod per hoc quod locus de rei veritate ad quiddam dat intelligendum de fidei puritate . . ." (PL, CXII, 849 B).

30. *Ibid.*: "through the practice of allegory he opens up the mysteries of the faith" — "per allegoriae exercitium fidei mysteria pandit" (CXII, 850 A).

31. "fidei et veritatis evangelicae congesta mysteria": Bede, *In Sam. alleg. exp.* (PL, LXXVI, 249 B).

32. Greg., *Mor.*, Bk. XXIII, c. i, n. 1: "doctrinae aedificium" (PL, LXXVI, 249 B).

33. *Mysticus sermo, dogmaticus ac solidus: In Num.*, h. 4, c. i (PL, CVIII, 784 D); *In Ez.*, Bk. XVIII (CX, 1033 A).

34. *In Num.*, h. 23, n. 6 (218).

35. *Glossa, In Deut.*, 31, 30 (PL, CXIII, 487 D).

36. "quid allegoria, nisi mystica mysteriorum doctrina?": Peter Damian, *In Jud.*, c. iv (PL, CXLV, 1082 D).

37. Richard, *Nonn. alleg.* (PL, CXCVI, 200 BC). Cf. Nicolas of Lyra: "If the things signified by the words are referred to signify those that are to be believed in the new law, in this way the allegorical sense is at stake" — "Si res significatae per voces referantur ad significandum ea quae sunt in nova lege credenda, sic accipitur sensus allegoricus" (CXIII, 28 D).

38. Cf. Paulinus of Aquilaea to Charlemagne: "Finally, when any Catholic drinking, with the assistance of the hand of the Lord, from the Chalice of holy Scripture with right faith, devout mind, and sound sense, had been satisfied, and has believed our Lord Jesus Christ, etc." — "Denique cum catholicus quicumque, manu Domini tribuente, de sacrae Scripturae calice recta fide, devota mente, sanoque sensu bibens, satiatus fuerit, credideritque Dominum nostrum Jesum Christum etc." (MGH, *Ep.*, 4, 523). Bruno of Segni, *Tr. de sacr. Eccl.* (PL, CLXV, 1094-95); and MBVP, 6, 710 F: "What is it to understand well and in a Catholic manner? First, according to the letter, and subsequently according to spiritual understanding." — "Quid est autem bene et catholice intelligere? — Prius vid. secundum litteram, postea vero secundum spiritualem intelligentiam."

39. Joachim of Flora, *Sup. 4 ev.*: "Hence, since the event was congruous with Scripture and the word that Jesus had preached, they believed the one on the basis of the other" — "Quia ergo res gesta conveniens fuit cum Scriptura et sermone quem praedixerat Jesus, crediderunt alterum per alterum etc." (Buonaiuti, 247).

40. Goscelin, *Lib. conf.*, Bk. III: "Nor were the holy apostles able to understand the resurrection of the Lord until he opened up to them its sense and they understood the Scriptures" — "Nec sancti apostoli poterant intelligere resurrectionem Domini, donec aperuit illis sensum et intelligerent Scripturas" (Talbot, 81). Cf. Or., *In Matt.*, t. XVI, c. x: "they felt that they were blind, not understanding the intention of the Scriptures" — "sentiebant se esse caecos, non intelligentes voluntatem Scripturarum" (505); *De princ.*, Bk. II, c. iv, n. 3: "understanding with the sight of the heart and the sense of the mind" — "visu cordis ac sensu mentis intelligens" (131).

41. "legis sacramenta cognovit, et credidit": Ambrose, *De Isaac*, c. iv, n. 26: "Once she had heard this, the woman bearing the aspect of the Church understood and believed the sacraments of the Law" — "Quibus auditis, mulier illa quae speciem Ecclesiae gerit, legis sacramenta cognovit et credidit" (PL, XIV, 512 C).

42. "ut, relicto velamine legis mosaicae, spiritualiter lecta intelligerent": Gregory of Tours, *H. Francorum*, Bk. V, c. xi (PL, LXXI, 325 B).

43. B. Blumenkranz, RMAL 10, 103-9.

44. "Duos libros conscripsi, primum sc. in quo allegorias pro maxima parte totius veteris Testamenti, quae de Christo nostro . . . et ejus Ecclesia loquuntur; non tamen omnes, sed utiliores . . . inserui, prout eas sancti doctores a Christo inspirati et edocti exposuerunt. . . . Placuit ut liber ille primus vocaretur Liber allegoriarum Petri contra Simonem Judaeum de confutatione Judaeorum": R. W. Hunt, "The Disputation of Peter of Cornwall against Symon the Jew," *Studies in Med. Hist. Presented to Fr. M. Powicke* (1948), 154-5. Cf. 153: "For I have shown that prior to the coming of Christ the whole Old Testament had been a closed book sealed with seven seals, i.e., wound up and covered with obscurities and enigmas. . . . But after the coming of our Christ it was opened and revealed." — "Ostendi enim quod ante adventurm Christi totum V. T. clausum erat et septem sigillis signatum, id est obscuritatibus et aenigmatibus obvolutum et tectum. . . . Post adventum autem Christi nostri apertum est et reseratum." The work, dedicated to Stephen Langton, was completed prior to 1208.

45. "Ubicumque vultis, allegorias et figuras positis!": *Disp. Judaei et Christ* (Blumenkranz, 72). Another (11th c.) *Disputatio:* "Quid ergo allegorizas de Christo, quod non de ipso sed de Isaac et Salomone dici apertissime vides?" (PL, CLXIII, 1058 C).

46. *Tr. c. Judaeos* (PL, CLXXXIX, 507-650); c. 5: "So I pass over the spiritual understanding, which does not belong to you to whom it has not been given to know the mystery of the kingdom of God" — "Ut praetermittam spiritualem intellectum, qui ad vos non pertinet, quibus non est datum nosse mysterium regni Dei" (621 C); "re-read your Hebrew text and, if your Jewish blindness stand not in the way, you will recognize that this is how the sense of its letter holds" — "relegite vestrum hebraicum idioma, et ita se habere sensum litterae illius, si caecitas Judaica non obstiterit, agnoscetis" (617 D). Nevertheless, *prol.*: an appeal to the patriarchs as well as to the prophets, and: "Christ foretold in many various ways by the prophets" — "Christum a prophetis multifarie multisque modis praenuntiatum" (509 CD).

47. "Omitto allegoricum intellectum, quem vos difficile potestis audire": *Adv. Judaeos:* "so I say that Elijah is to be taken as John, the daughter of Zion as the Church, the people of Israel as the Christian people, and Judah as the confessors of the truth. Let me infer only what can be proved according to the letter by the authorities of the Scriptures" — "ut in Helia dicam accipiendum Joannem in filia Sion Ecclesiam, in populo Israël populum christianum, in Juda confessores veritatis. Illud tantum inferam, quod possit probari secundum litteram auc tor i tatibus Scripturarum" (A. Frugoni, 86).

48. Cf. the anonymous treatise, *Adv. Jud.*, explaining the prophecy of the 70 weeks at length "ad litteram," etc. (PL, CCXIII, 747-800).

49. "Porta australis vetus Testamentum, porta vero aquilonaris novum designat. Hi vero qui ab australi parte venire dicuntur, Judaeos; qui autem ab aquilonari, Gentes designant. Judaei . . . per portam australem ingrediebantur, quia cognoscentes in veteri Testamento multipliciter Christum esse prophetatum, diversisque modis praefiguratum, eos ad fidem Christi suscipiendam suae scripturae pertrahebant. Gentiles vero, idololatriam deserentes, . . . per portam aquilonarem ingrediebantur, quia, doctrinam Evangelii audientes, virtutes etiam

quae per Christum et ministros ejus facta sunt admirantes, ad fidem Christi suscipiendam currebant": *In Ap.,* v. 7 (PL, XVII, 948 AB).

50. "Nos ad fidem, Domino largiente, venientes, non per Legem Evangelium, sed per sanctum Evangelium Legem didicimus": *In Ez.,* Bk. I, h. 6, n. 10-2 (PL, LXXVI, 833-4).

51. "Pro confirmatione fidei nostrae": Paschasius, *In Matt.,* Bk. II, c. i (PL, CXX, 118 AB).

52. *L. carolini,* I, c. xxi (PL, XCVIII, 1052 B).

53. Cf. Isidore, *L. de var. q.,* c. xxvii, n. 5: "On the coming together of both peoples in the unity of a mutually congenial faith" — "De convenientia utriusque populi in unitatem fidei sibimet convenientis" (77).

54. "Judaei, quos intelligentia veteris Testamenti ad fidem Christi suscipiendam perducebat, non debebant reverti ea parte, qua venerant, sc. ut observationes legales carnaliter implerent, sed egredi potius per portam aquilonarem, ad Evangelii vid. doctrinam meditandam et perscrutandam se transferre, ut discerent spiritaliter implere quod antea carnaliter facere satagebant. Gentiles vero, qui per portam aquilonarem ingrediebantur, id est, qui per doctrinam Evangelii filii Ecclesiae efficiebantur, non debebant reverti ea parte qua venerant, vid., ut ad errores philosophorum perscrutandos regrederentur: sed potius post susceptionem fidei atque doctrinae evangelicae ad portam meridianam, id est, ad doctrinam veteris Testamenti perscrutandam se transferre, ut, cum invenirent in eo Christum multis modis esse praedictum, roboraretur in eis fides Christi": *In Ap.* (PL, XVII, 948 BD).

55. "Prius ergo Joannes linteamina vidit, postea intravit, quia prius Synagoga, sicut dictum est, in Scripturis prophetiam de venturo accepit.... Petrus autem prius intrat, postea linteamina conspicit, quia Ecclesia gentium non per prophetas ad fidem Christi, sed per fidem Christi ad intelligentiam prophetarum pervenit": *Misc.,* Bk. I, tit. 96 (PL, CLXXVII, 525-6).

56. Cf. Beatus, *In Ap.,* 204.

57. Georges Courtade, "Les Écritures ont-elles un sens plénier?" (RSR, 1950, 497); placing himself within the second hypthesis.

58. "Cum consideratur quanta consonantia sit in praedictis et impletis, quae quoque in futuris fiat, facile potest credere quisque fidelis": *Dial. de trib. q.,* c. xliv (PL, CXLVI, 121 D).

59. "firmissimum argumentum fidei nostrae, quod idem tam concorditer enuntiant prophetae et evangelistae": Richard (PL, CXCVI, 607 B).

60. "recta fides": Ps-Anselm, *L. de similit.,* c. cxciv (PL, CLIX, 708 CD).

61. "conversionis ad Christum et christianae fidei fructus": Rupert, *In Os.,* Bk. II (PL, CLXVIII, 91 C).

62. "datum est solatium propheticarum Scripturarum interpretandarum...": *In Ap.,* c. x (Vega, 39).

63. "Revelati sunt Prophetae, qui non intelligebantur, super quos aedificaretur orbis terrarum credens Domino": Walafrid Strabo, *In ps. XVII* (PL, CXIV, 786 A).

64. *"allegoria fidem aedificat": In ev.,* Bk. II, h. 40, n. 1 (PL, LXXVI, 1302 A). Cf. *Mor.,* Bk. XXVII, c. xli, n. 69 (439 D); *In Ez.,* Bk. I, h. 12, n. 9 (922 A); *In ev.,* h. 38, n. 11 (1289 B); n. 14 (1290 B).

Notes to Pages 113-14

65. PL, CXV, 246 C.

66. PL, CLVI, 26 A.

67. PL, CXCIX, 666 B.

68. *L. de variis q. praef.* (2).

69. *De div. nat.*, Bk. V, c. xl (PL, CXXII, 1021 C). Bede, *In Sam. prol.*: "Quanta in his singulis fidei et veritatis evangelicae congesta mysteria sint" (XCI, 500 B).

70. Gerhoh, *In ps. XVII*, 12 (PL, CXCIII, 865 B).

71. "Promoti sunt ad spiritualem sensum et venerunt per fidem ad Ecclesiam": H. 7 (PL, CLVIII, 628 B).

72. "Transivimus allegoriarum umbras, aedificata est fides": *In Cant.*, s. 17, n. 8 (PL, CLXXXIII, 859 A).

73. "Haec ad aedificationem fidei dicta sint": *S. ined.* (Talbot, 92). Absalon: "to strengthen the faith" — "ad roborandam fidem" (CCXI, 177 B).

74. "allegoria rectam fidem informat": *De sacram. prol.*, c. vi (PL, CLXXVI, 185 D); *De script.*, c. v: "ad fidei aedificationem" (CLXXV, 14 A).

75. "Habes in historia quo Dei facta mireris, in allegoria quo ejus sacramenta credas": *Did.*, Bk. VI, c. iii (PL, CLXXVI, 801 D).

76. "Secundum allegoriam meditatio operatur ad intelligentiam, et fidei formam fabricandam": *De meditando* (PL, CLXXVI, 994 C).

77. "per quem fides aperitur": PL, CXIV, 720 A.

78. "fides informatur": PL, CXCIV, 731 C. Isidore, *op. cit.*, c. i (Vega-Anspach, 5).

79. "fides eruditur": *Tr. de ord. vitae*, c. vii, n. 24 (PL, CLXXXIV, 575 D).

80. "in fide per allegoriam imbuendi": PL, CCV, 708 B.

81. "Dum per allegoriae exercitium mysteria historiae pandit, in arcem fidei fabricam mentis extollit": N. 8 (PL, CXCVIII, 628 A).

82. "De Tabernaculo Christi, quod est in fide": *De trip. tab.*, P. II (PL, CXCVIII, 683 B); s. 38, n. 4: by allegory "the truth of the faith is revealed" — "veritas fidei revelatur" (344 AB).

83. "In allegoria est fidei instructio": Ps.-Ans., *L. de simil.*, c. cxciv (PL, CLIX, 708 A).

84. Honorius (PL, CLXXII, 799 A).

85. Greg., *In Ez.*, Bk. I, h. 9, n. 31 (PL, LXXVI, 884 A). Rabanus (CIX, 988 A). Claudius (L, 1029 C). Rupert (CLXVII, 606 A, 640 A, 692 D, 1147 A, 1157 C; 170, 114 D). Oger, s. 10, n. 11 (CLXXXIV, 926 C). Cf. Tertullian, *Adv. Marc.*, Bk. V, c. xi: "when he had crossed over into the faith of Christ, he will understand that Moses had been preaching about Christ" — "cum transsierit in fidem Christi, intelleget Moysen de Christo praedicasse (612; cf. 515). Chromat., *In Matt.*, tr. 9 (CCL, 9, 417). Or., *In Num.*, h. 17, n. 2 (155-6); *In Jos.*, h. 7, n. 5 (331-2); h. 17, n. 2: "fidem Jesu" (402). Ambrosiaster, *In II Cor.* III, 14-5 (PL, XVII, 287 D).

86. Rabanus (PL, CIX, 338).

87. Bede, *In Sam.* (PL, XCI, 556 B). Rupert (CLXVII, 701 B). Or., *In Cant.*, Bk. III (183).

88. Rabanus (PL, CVIII, 706 D).

89. Rupert, *De div. off.* (PL, CLXX, 234 B); *De trin.* (CLXVII, 617 A, 1127 B).

90. Greg., *In I Reg.*, Bk. IV (PL, LXXIX, 253 D); Bk. VI (468 A). Rabanus, *In Ex.* (CVIII, 186 B).

91. Or., *In Num.*, h. 23, n. 1: "evangelii fidem" (210).

92. Bede, *In Sam.* (PL, XCI, 500 B). Sedulius Scotus (CIII, 242 C). Rabanus, *In Ex.* (CVIII, 186 B). Rupert, *In Is.* (CLXVII, 1361 A); *In Ez.* (1428 D, 1452 C); *In Os.* (CLXVIII, 134 A); *De div. off.* (CLXX, 205 D). Petrus Cellensis: "fidem evangelii," "firmamentum evangelicae fidei" (*Lib. de pan.*, c. iv; CCII, 946 BC); etc. Chromat., *In Matt.*, tr. 11 (CCL, 9, 422).

93. *In Ap.*, v. 3 (PL, XVII, 807 C). Rupert (CLXVII, 535 A, 615 B, 692 D). Irimbert, *In Ruth* (Pez, 4, 456).

94. Cassiodorus, *In ps. CIII*, 24 (PL, LXX, 736 D). Isidore, *De fide cath.*, Bk. II, c. xix (LXXXIII, 528 A). Bede, h. 10, *post Pascha* (CCL, 122, 246). Richard (PL, CXCVI, 607 B). Cf. Or., *In Jos.*, h. 20, n. 2 (419); h. 21, n. 2 (430).

95. Greg., *In I Reg.*, Bk. IV (PL, LXXIX, 272 D). Bruno of Segni, *In Ex.*, c. xvi (CLXIV, 269 C). Cf. Rabanus (CX, 1169 A).

96. Adam Scotus, *s.* 7, c. i: "As to the allegorical sense of the faith of the Church" — "Quantum ad sensum allegoricum de fide Ecclesiae" (PL, CXCVIII, 135 C); etc. Cf. Jerome, *In Ez.*, Bk. XI: "ecclesiastica fides."

97. Rupert, *In Ex.*, c. i: "We shall pluck the letter on the run and, to the extent possible with his assistance and unbroken fidelity, we shall diligently take on the mysteries of Christ the Son of God that have been hidden within it" — "Litteram cursim vellicabimus, et quae intrinsecus consita sunt mysteria Christi Filii Dei, diligenter pro posse, ipso adjuvante, integra fide conabimus" (PL, CLXVII, 567 B).

98. Or., *In Jos.*, h. 16, n. 5 (400).

99. Paulinus of Aquilaea (PL, XCIX, 159 B).

100. "fides relationis": Angelome to Leotricus: "so that the history may establish the truth of the facts and the reliability of the report" — "ut historia veritatem factorum ac fidem redactionis inculcet" (MGH, *Ep.*, V, 622). [Trans. note: Neither Lewis and Short, *Latin Dictionary*, nor Forcellini, *Lexicon totius Latinitatis*, offer any justification for exactly this interpretation, s.v. *redigo* or *redactio*. But cf. Lewis and Short, s.v. *relatio*, II. B. 2. B. 'A report, narration, relation'. De Lubac's parallel text implies that *redactio* is here synonymous with *relatio* in this sense.]

101. "gestorum fides": Hilary, *Tr. myst.*, Bk. I, c. iii and x (SC, 78 and 94). Braulio, *ep.* 44 (Madox, 198). Peter Damian: "juxta fidem rei veraciter contigisse" (PL, CXLV, 897 D). Hugh [of Saint Victor]: "secundum fidem rerum gestarum" (CLXXVI, 184 AB); etc.

102. "historiae fides": Hilary, *op. cit.*, Bk. I, c. xxix (p. 122). Claudius (PL, CIV, 770 D). Remi [of Auxerre] (CXVII, 117 D). Peter Damian, *Opusc.* 6 (CXLV, 108 C). Raoul of Saint Germain, *In Lev.:* "The limit of the temple, however, is the historical sense in the Scriptures, since we enter the temple of God . . . through faith in the history" — "Limes vero templi, sensus historicus est in Scripturis, quia per fidem historiae . . . intramus templum Dei" (142 D). Cf. Or. (?), *In Gen.*, h. 17, n. 6 (PG, XII, 258 C).

103. "erga praeterita fides": Greg., *Mor.*, Bk. XXXV, c. xx, n. 48: "quatenus tanto fixior animus in suo intellectu permaneat, quanto hunc quasi in quodam medio constitutum, et erga futura spes, et erga praeterita fides ligat" (PL, LXXVI, 780 A). Cf. *In I Reg.*, Bk. II, c. i, n. 28 (LXXXIX, 89 D).

104. "per intellectum nobis spiritalem fulgeat, et tamen sensus a fide historiae non recedat": *Mor., ibid.* (779 D). Cf. Chapter 7.1 above.

105. "fides" — "sacramentorum intelligentia": *De fide*, Bk. I, c. xx, n. 2 (PL, LXXXIII, 528-9).

106. "Et historice oportet fidem tenere, et . . . spiritaliter legem intelligere": *Sent.*, Bk. I, c. xix, n. 6 (PL, LXXXIII, 582 A); c. xviii, n. 12 (579).

107. *In Jo.*, tr. 48, n. 1 (CCL, 36, 413); tr. 98, n. 2 (576); cf. *In ps. XXXVII*, n. 11: "He appeared to the eyes of the flesh so that through faith he might heal those to whom he was about to show the truth" — "Apparuit oculis carnis, ut per fidem sanaret eos quibus veritatem fuerat monstraturus etc." (38, 390); *In ps. CXVII*, n. 22 (40, 1664).

108. *S.* 88, n. 1: "But, since things that were not seen were not believed, he used to build up faith for those that were not seen through the temporal things that were seen" — "Sed, quia illa quae non videbantur, non credebantur: per ista, temporalia quae videbantur aedificabat fidem ad illa quae non videbantur" (PL, XXXVIII, 539); but there it was not a question of the facts of the O.T.; Aug. was speaking of the miracles of Jesus. Cf. *Speculum, praef.*: "In this work, however, we are not guiding the infidel or building him up toward the faith" — "Nos autem in hoc opere nec infidelem vel adducimus vel aedificamus ad fidem" (XXXIV, 889).

109. "Si historiae intendimus, quae dixit credimus; si allegoriae, quae praedixit videmus": *Mor.*, Bk. XIX, c. xvii, n. 26 (PL, LXXVI, 114 AB).

110. "ut et fides habeatur in veritate historiae, et spiritalis intelligentia capiatur de mysteriis allegoriae": *In Ez.*, Bk. II, h. 1, n. 3 (PL, LXXVI, 936-7). In Bk. I, h. 10, n. 2: "For whatever is found in holy Scripture is to be published, since its small points contribute to a simple life, and its great ones build up a subtle understanding" — "Quidquid enim in sacra Scriptura invenitur, edendum est, quia et ejus parva simplicem componunt vitam, et ejus magna subtilem aedificant intelligentiam," "intelligentia" is correlative of "vita" and not of "fides" (886 D).

111. J. M. Le Blond, "Les conversions de S. Aug.," *Théologie* 17 (1950), 108-14. *Œuvres de S. Aug.*, 8, *La foi chrétienne*, by J. Pegon (1951), notes 10 and 12 (494, 500). *De fide et symbolo*, c. i, n. 1. Aug. distinguishes the "credentes" and the "intelligentes" or "viri spirituales" (PL, XL, 181). *De vera rel.*, c. xxiv, n. 45: "Authority demands faith and prepares a man for reason; reason leads to understanding and knowledge" — "Auctoritas fidem flagitat, et rationi praeparat hominem; ratio ad intellectum cognitionemque perducit" (Pegon, 84). On the alternate relations of faith and understanding: *In ps. CXVIII, s.* 18, n. 3-4 (CCL, 40, 1724-6).

112. "fides rerum gestarum" — "figuratus intellectus": Bk. I, n. 1 (PL, XXXIV, 241). Cf. *In ps. CXXXI*, n. 2 (CCL, 40, 1911).

113. "fides rerum temporalium" — "aeterna intelligenda": *De vera rel.*, c. xxv, n. 46: "The faith of temporal things, whether past or future, holds more by believing than by understanding" — "Temporalium autem rerum fides, sive praeteritarum, sive futurarum, magis credendo quam intelligendo valet" (Pegon, 86); c. l, n. 99: "and which may be a stable faith, whether historical and temporal or spiritual and eternal . . . and what is advantageous for understanding and obtaining eternal things . . . [is] faith in temporal things" — "et quae sit stabilis fides, sive historica et temporalis, sive spiritualis et aeterna . . . et quid prosit ad intelligenda et obtinenda aeterna . . . fides rerum temporalium" (170).

114. *De Trin.*, Bk. XV, c. ii, n. 2: "Faith seeks; understanding finds" — "Fides quaerit, intellectus invenit" (*Œuvres*, XVI, Agaesse and Moingt, 1955, 422); cf.

s. 272: "But faith desires instruction . . ." — "Sed fides instructionem desiderat etc." (PL, XXXVIII, 1246).

115. *S.* 10, n. 1: "The old divine books customarily not only arrive at faith in the thing done but also at the mystery of the one to come" — "Solent divini veteres libri, non solum rei gestae fidem, sed etiam futurae insinuare mysterium" (PL, XXXVIII, 92). This was the language of Origen, as translated by Jerome; *In Ez.*, h. 1: "to believe that it truly happened according to the fidelity of the history, but . . . signified the subsequent mystery" — "credere quidem vere accidisse eam juxta historiae fidem, sed . . . subsequens significasse mysterium" (XXV, 697 A).

116. *Doc. christ.*, Bk. III, c. xxxvii (Combès-Farges, 322-4).

117. "Qui vera ratione quod jam tantummodo credebat intelligit, profecto praeponendus est ei qui cupit adhuc intelligere quod credit; si autem nec cupit, et ea quae intelligenda sunt credendo tantummodo existimat, cui rei fides prosit ignorat. . . . Intellectum vero valde ama, quia et ipsae Scripturae sanctae, quae magnarum rerum ante intelligentiam suadent fidem, nisi eas recte intelligas, utiles tibi esse non possunt": *Ep.* 120, c. ii, n. 8; c. iii, n. 12 (PL, XXXV, 456, 459). Cf. *Civ. Dei*, Bk. X, c. xv (XLI, 293).

118. "tempus fidei": opposition of the "time of faith" — "tempus fidei" to the "time of sight" — "tempus speciei": *In ps. LXX*, n. 8; 90, s. 2, n. 13; 97, n. 3 (CCL, 39, 647, 1277, 1323). Cf. *In ps. XXXIII*, s. 2, n. 2 (38, 283). [Trans. note: Like the Greek word *eidos*, the corresponding Latin word *species* is related to a verb of seeing; accordingly, in both cases, there is a focus on the "looks" of a thing, whether visible or invisible. Cf. Liddell-Scott-Jones, *Greek Lexicon*, s.vv. *eidos* and **eidō*, with Lewis and Short, *Latin Dictionary*, s.vv. *species* and *specto*; note that since the root is not the same in the two languages, the comparison gives only a semantic analogy, not an etymology. In each of the two languages, however, there is an etymological connection between the noun and the verb in question; here de Lubac is exploiting the original, etymological sense of the Latin noun *species*.]

119. "fides temporalis historiae" — "humilitas historicae fidei": *In ps. VIII*, n. 5 and 8: "they rise . . . through the lowliness of the historical faith that has been accomplished temporally to the height of the understanding of things eternal" — "per humilitatem historicae fidei quae temporaliter gesta est, ad sublimitatem intelligentiae rerum aeternarum . . . erigunt" (CCL, 38, 51-3).

120. *De Trin.*, Bk. IV, c. xviii, n. 24: "But we can be purged so as to have the same temperament as eternal things only by means of temporal ones. . . . Just as the purified rational mind owes contemplation to eternal things, so does the mind in need of purification owe faith to temporal ones. . . . Now then we apply faith to things done temporally for our sake, and through this faith we are cleansed, so that once we have come to the vision, just as truth succeeds upon faith, so may eternity succeed mortality. . . . When our faith by seeing becomes the truth, then will eternity take hold of our changed mortality" — "Purgari autem ut contemperaremur aeternis, non nisi per temporalia possumus. . . . Mens autem rationalis sicut purgata contemplationem debet rebus aeternis, sic purganda, temporalibus fidem. . . . Nunc ergo adhibemus fidem rebus temporaliter gestis propter nos, et per ipsam mundamur, ut cum ad speciem venerimus, quamadmodum succedit fidei veritas, ita mortalitati succedat aeternitas. . . . Cum fides nostra videndo fiet veritas, tunc mortalitatem nostram commutatam tenebit

aeternitas" (Mellet-Camelot, 396-8). Bk. XIV, c. i, n. 3: "I have shown . . . also that a temporal faith about eternal things . . . is necessary. I have also argued that faith about the temporal things that the Eternal One did for us and suffered in the man whom he carried about temporally and advanced to eternal things is helpful for attaining eternal ones" — "etiam de rebus aeternis fidem temporalem . . . necessariam . . . esse monstravi. Fidem quoque de temporalibus rebus, quas pro nobis aeternus fecit et passus est in homine quem temporaliter gessit, atque ad aeterna provexit, ad eamdem aeternorum adeptionem prodesse disserui" (Agaesse-Moingt, 348-50); c. ii, n. 4, commenting on 2 Cor. 5:6-7: "though through this self-same temporal faith he strive for truth and be intent on eternal things" — "licet per eamdem temporalem fidem ad veritatem nitatur et tendat ad aeterna" (350). *In ps. VIII*, n. 5: "those too, not yet capable of the knowledge of eternal and spiritual things, are nourished by the faith of temporal history, which, for our salvation, after the patriarchs and prophets, was administered by the most excellent Power and Wisdom of God also as a sacrament of the man taken up, [a faith] in which there is salvation for every believer" — "illi quoque nondum capaces cognitionis rerum spiritualium atque aeternarum, nutriuntur fide temporalis historiae, quae pro salute nostra post patriarchas et prophetas a[b] excellentissima Dei Virtute atque Sapientia etiam suscepti hominis sacramento administrata est, in qua salus est omni credenti" (PL, XXXVI, 110-1).

121. "Ipse est nobis fides in rebus ortis, qui est veritas in aeternis": Th. Camelot, O.P., "A l'éternel par le temporel," *Rev. des ét. augustin.*, 1956, *Mémorial G. Bardy*, 2, 163-72. Cf. Gerhoh, *In ps. VIII*: "Beginning from the lowliness of faith, i.e., because he was born, suffered, died, and buried" — "Ab humilitate fidei incipiens, id est, quod natus, passus, mortuus et sepultus est" (PL, CXCIII, 747 C).

122. "Ut rerum gestarum ordinem non solum credendo sed etiam intelligendo veneremur": S. 32, c. i (PL, LIV, 238 BC). Cf. *s.* 66, c. i: "Since, then, fullness of understanding has been promised to a sincere faith" — "Quia ergo sincerae fidei promissa est intelligentiae plenitudo" (364 D).

123. "Ut perspicuum habeat intelligentia, quod notum fecit historia": S. 52, c. i (PL, LIV, 314 A).

124. "Nunc universam Ecclesiam majori intelligentia instrui et spe ferventiore oportet accendi": S. 64, c. i (PL, LIV, 358 A).

125. See p. 388, n. 102. Isidore (PL, LXXXIII, 159 B). Alcuin, *Conf. fidei*, Bk. III, c. xxxvi: "historiae fidem non evacuans, credo universa gesta esse, quae scripta sunt, sed juxta doctrinam apostolicam sensum spiritualem in eis intelligere opto" (CI, 1080 A). Rabanus, *In Ex.*, Bk. III, c. iv (CVIII, 132 D). Raoul of Saint Germain, *In Lev.*, Bk. X, c. i (142 D). Isidore, *Sent.*, Bk. I, c. xix, commenting on the 3rd rule of Tyconius: "et historice oportet fidem tenere, et spiritaliter legem intelligere" (PL, LXXXIII, 582 A).

126. Claudius [of Turin], *In Gen.*, Bk. III: "But if anyone requires [to know] how it is true even with regard to historical faith . . ." — "Si autem quisquam exigit, quomodo etiam secundum historicam fidem verum sit . . ." (PL, L, 1048 A); etc.

127. Andrade: "sequique historiae fidem" (*P. lat. aevi car.*, III, 90). Bede, *Ep. 3*: "Haec sunt quae juxta fidem sacrae historiae . . . abbreviare curavi" (PL, XCIV, 671 A).

128. "Exacta fides historiae": Bk. III, *prol.* (MGH, *Scr.*, XX, 416). Jean de Gorze: "fides gestorum"; *Vita Courundi:* "fides dictorum" (MGH, *Scr.*, IV, 236, 437).

129. "nullius historiae fides est incorrupta": *Hist. pont.,* c. i (MGH, *Scr.*, XX, 518).

130. "in allegoria, rectae fidei credulitas": Adam Scotus, *De trip. tab.*, P. III, c. viii (PL, CXCVIII D).

131. Bruno of Segni, *In Num.:* "et per fidem ad Ecclesiam convertentur" (PL, CLXIV, 489 B).

132. Rabanus, *In Ex.*, Bk. II, c. vi: "invenimus ordinem fidei" (PL, CVIII, 77 A).

133. Rabanus, *In Ex.*, Bk. III, c. x: "The Lord is speaking from the midst of the two cherubim, since he educates us to faith in the truth through the words of both Testaments by their consonant voice" — "De medio duorum cherubim loquitur Dominus quia per verba utriusque Testamenti consona voce nos ad fidem veritatis erudit" (PL, CVIII, 145 B); c. xvii (186 C). Claudius, *In Reg.*, Bk. III (L, 1109 B, 1147 C). Odo of Cluny, *Epit. Mor.* I, 33: "Quique enim fide jam veritatis agnoverunt" (CXXXIII, 489 C). Cf. Greg., *In Ez.*, Bk. I, h. 5, n. 2: "ad aeternorum fidem" (LXXVI, 821 D). Peter Lombard, an eclectic, explains the "da mihi intellectum" of Ps. 118 thus: "He asks that understanding be given to him so that his inner eyes may be rendered more serene; this comes about through faith, by which hearts are cleansed, since although no one can believe in God unless he understand something . . . nevertheless he is strengthened by faith so as to understand more" — "Dari ergo sibi intellectum petit, ut magis serenentur oculi interiores; quod fit per fidem, qua mundantur corda quia, licet nemo possit credere in Deum nisi aliquid intelligat . . . tamen fide sanatur ut ampliora intelligat" (CXCI, 1081 AB, after Aug. and Alcuin).

Notes to Chapter Eight
§5. The Gregorian Middle Ages

1. Or., *In Ex.*, h. 7, n. 1: "without the faith of Christ, without the spiritual understanding" — "sine fide Christi, sine intelligentia spiritali" (206).

2. *Ibid.*, n. 3: "but if we tear open the mystery lying hidden within these things, we find the order of faith" — "si vero rimemur in his mysterium latens, invenimus ordinem fidei" (208).

3. Haskins, *The Renaissance of the Twelfth Century*, 80: ". . . for he occupied a lower intellectual level than the severe and classical Augustine and made a wider appeal to credulity in his stories of the miraculous." Cf. E. Delaruelle, *Hist. du cathol. en Fr.*, by A. Latreille, t. I, 264: "Le fait que le Père le plus lu au X siècle est S. Grégoire, donne une idée de la médiocrité de cette culture." ["The fact that the Father most read in the tenth century is Gregory gives some idea of the mediocrity of this culture."] These judgements are, we believe, excessively derogatory, although they contain some truth.

4. In this way, again, M. Hélin, p. 13, wishes "only to mention" the other works, but goes into the *Dialogues* at some length, "where the supernatural is constantly intervening, and where the struggle between God and the evil one un-

folds before the eyes of a terrified humanity" — "où le surnaturel intervient constamment, et où la lutte entre Dieu et le malin se livre sous les yeux d'une humanité épouvantée." Even A. G. Amatucci, who is so admiring, cites in his text nothing except the *Letters* and the *Dialogues,* and only in a note mentions the other works: *Storia della Letteratura latina cristiana* (1929), 356.

5. Thus, Harnack, von Schubert, etc. Cf. H. O. Taylor, *The Med. Mind,* I, 99: "The miraculous is with him a frame of mind; and the allegorical method of understanding Scripture is no longer intended, not to say willful, as with Augustine, but has become persistent unconscious habit." They emphasize certain "deviltries" of some accounts, and fail to observe that, in contrast with a large part of modern mysticism, Gregorian mysticism is a mysticism "without thought of the Devil" (C. Butler, *Western Myst.,* 2nd ed., 1927, 187).

6. P. Batiffol, *S. Grég. le Grand* (1928), 95: "but the fact is there" — "mais le fait est là. . . ."

7. "Gregorius noster": Tajón of Saragossa (PL, LXXXVII, 415 A). Manegold, *Ad Gebeh.* (L. de lite, I, 331-2, 337, 341, 349, 355, 419; and, citing Bernold, 426).

8. "Gregorius meus": Bernard of Morval, *De contemptu mundi,* Bk. III, v. 309 (H. C. Hoskier).

9. "sapientissimus papa": Berno of Reichenau (PL, CXLII, 1058 C).

10. "vir nobilis eloquentiae" — "per omnia purissimae fidei" — "venerabilis et probatissimus in fide catholica doctor": Alcuin, *Adv. Elip.* (PL, CI, 287 D, 279 C, 266 C). Agobard (CIV, 67 CD). Visigothic text of the 8th century: "insigniter eloquens." Godfrey of Admont: "egregii et eximii doctoris" (CLXXIV, 158 C).

11. "papa beatus ac suavissimus doctor": Rabanus Maurus, *In Reg., praef.* (PL, CIX, 9 C).

12. "doctor mirabilis": Paulinus of Aquilaea (PL, XCIX, 464 A); "egregius d." (465 C).

13. "doctor magnificus": Hincmar (PL, CXXV, 436 B).

14. "conspicuus et insignis doctor Ecclesiae": Peter Damian, *Ep.,* Bk. V, 1 (PL, CXLIV, 340 A).

15. "humani generis splendor immensus": *Vita S. Aug.* (PL, CL, 743 D).

16. "magnum Ecclesiae Dei speculum et robur": Edmer (Wilmart, RDSR 15, 207).

17. "velut Argus quidam luminosissimus" — "velut Argus undique oculatus": John the Deacon, *Vita,* Bk. II, c. lv (PL, LXXV, 112 C). Gerhoh, *L. de laude fidei* (Op. in., I, 186).

18. "tractator egregius": Angelome, *In Reg.* (PL, CXV, 389 B); etc.

19. "ecclesiasticus tractator": Autpert, *In Ap.* (645 A).

20. "sacrae Scripturae lucidissimus expositor": Alcuin, *In Eccl.* (PL, C, 669 C; cf. 670 A); *ep.* 81 (263 D).

21. "luculentissimus ac potentissimus expositor": Autpert, *In Ap.* (512 D); "a man of so subtle a mind" — "tam subtilis ingenii vir" (570 B); "tractatorum Ecclesiae egregius" (576 H).

22. "subtilissimus indagator" — sagacissimus verbi Dei indagator": Martin of Leon, s. 32 (PL, CCVIII, 1213 B). Hadrian I, *ad episc. Hisp.* (LXXC, 496 B).

23. "Scripturarum divinarum multimodus interpretator, abditorum mysteri-

orum acerrimus indagator": Tajón, *Ep. ad Eug. Tolet.* (PL, LXXX, 725 B). Sicard, *Cronica* (MGH, *Scr.*, XXXI, 144).

24. "dulcissime et abundantisime": Hincmar, *De regis persona*, c. xvii (PL, CXXV, 845 B).

25. "verissime et elegantissime": John of Salisbury, *Ep.* 143 (PL, CXCIX, 130 A).

26. "Gregorius romanus, os aureum": [Trans. note: The Latin phrase 'os aureum' or 'mouth of gold' is equivalent to the Greek phrase 'chrysos stomos', except for the word order: 'golden mouth'.] MS letter of the 9th cent. (Bischoff, *S. Er.*, 6, 201, note 4). *Ep. paschalis:* "Gregorii papae . . . a nobis in commune suscepti et oris aurei appellatione donati" (PL, CLXXXVII, 915 A; Bischoff, 210, note 1). Hymn of the 10th cent.:

> Magnum decus Ecclesiae,
> O sacerdotum gloria,
> Dum gregi praestat pabulum,
> Tecta pandit mysteria . . . (Gall-Morel, 239).

> "Great embellishment of the Church,
> O glory of priests,
> Whilst he feeds the flock,
> He lays out the covered mysteries."

27. "doctor egregius, divino afflatus spiramine atque de fonte potatus supremo": *Epit., Mor., praef.* (PL, CXXXIII, 107 C), Notker the Stammerer, *De interpr. div. Script.*, c. iii and vi (CXXXI, 996 D, 999 A).

28. Richard, s. 181, *in f. S. Greg.:* "Haec igitur lucerna, beatus vid. Gregorius . . . super candelabrum non in quolibet loco sed a summo posita, tanto longius et latius suos radios diffundit, quanto sublimius posita fuit. Lucet itaque nobis lucerna radiis diversis, radiis eximiis, radiis praeclaris" (PL, CXXXIII, 109 B).

29. "Lucidior auro, vitro quoque clarior omni,
   Mellifluo gustu cuncta redolentia vincens."
   Odo of Cluny, *Ep. Mor. praef. metrica* (PL, CXXXIII, 109 B).

30. Innocent III, s. 13, *in f. D. Gr.:* "With this bow blessed Gregory prepared weapons of death against gainsaying heretics." — "In hoc arcu paravit b. Gregorius vasa mortis adversus haereticos adversantes" (PL, CCXVII, 516 D).

31. *Ibid.:* "His autem fluminibus b. Greg. irrigavit paradisum, id est fecundavit Ecclesiam" (516 A).

32. "columna argentea" — "reclinatorium aureum": Rupert, *In Reg. S. Ben.*, Bk. IV, c. viii (PL, CLXX, 513 A).

33. Anon of the 12th cent.: "chief of the apostles" — "praecipuus apostolorum"; "a man full of the Holy Spirit" — "vir plenus Spiritu sancto" (Leclercq, *St. ans.*, 41, 114). At the time of the quarrel between the monks and the clerics, Servatus of Worcester writes, v. 1190: "Blessed Gregory, who, having been instructed by the finger of God, embellished all the elegance of the cleric, though he shone forth in monastic habit" — "B. Gregorius, qui pene omnem clerici decorem digito Dei doctus expolivit, licet habitu monastico praefulserit" (*ibid.*,

Notes to Page 119

116). Hugh, letter to Burchard, 12th cent.: "B. Greg., Spiritu sancto plenus" (F. Stegmuller, *Mél. de Ghellinck*, II, 744).

34. Rupert: "in quo sine dubio reclinavit seipsa Sapientia" (PL, CLXX, 531 A).

35. Anselm of Havelberg, *Ep. apol.*: "b. Gregorii magni theologi" (PL, CLXXXVIII, 1126 A).

36. "lucidissimus theologus": Thiofridus, *Flores Epitaphii sanct.*, Bk. III, c. iv (PL, CLVII, 377 C, 378 B).

37. Rupert, *In reg. S. Ben.*, Bk. II, c. xiv (PL, CLXX, 509 D).

38. Odorannus, *opusc.* 7 (PL, CXLII, 813 B). *De vita vere apost.*, Bk. III (CLXX, 636 B). Hugh Metel, *ep.* 28: "Fac cantare b. Gregorium, Spiritus sancti organum" (368). Hymn of the 11th cent. (Dreves, *Anal. hymnica*, v, 9, 184, 186).

39. "sacrae paginae scientiam": Guibert of Nogent, *Lib. quo ord.* (PL, CL, 29 C).

40. "pene totius novi ac veteris Testamenti patefacit arcana": Tajón, *Ep. ad Eug.* (PL, LXXX, 726 A).

41. *De vanit. mundi*, Bk. IV: "Gregorius alter, spiritu plenus, et ipse domum vario decore adornavit, ministrans pulchritudines multas et jucunditates veritatis" (PL, CLXXVI, 739 A).

42. "tantam, duce gratia, mysteriorum profunditatem seu morum aedificationem invenit et quasi mirabiles thesauros de hac terra effodit, ut pene plus mirari possit mundus hujusmodi thesauros in hac terra inventos quam contentos": *Microc.*, c. cc (p. 221). Fréculphe, t. II, Bk. V, c. xxiv: "qui Moralia in Job gratia divina inspirante conscripsit etc." (PL, CVI, 1256 C).

43. "gregorianae mel eloquentiae": PL, LXXIX, 682. Cf. Arnold of Saint Emmeran (MGH, *Scr.*, IV, 546). Bruno archbishop (*ibid.*, 596); etc.

44. "praeceptor et paedagogus noster": Aldhelm, *De virg.*, c. xli (MGH, *A. ant.*, XV, 293).

45. "pervigil pater noster": *Ibid.*, c. lv (314). Bede: "Gregorius, vigilantissimus juxta suum nomen nostrae gentis apostolus" (PL, XCII, 304 C).

46. "doctor noster": *Ep.* 140 (PL, C, 380 C).

47. "praedicator noster": *Ep.* 75 (PL, C, 252 B). *Conf. fidei*, p. 3, c. xxxvii-viii: "Pater Gregorius" (CI, 1081 C, 1082 A).

48. "suavissimus doctor": MGH, *Ep. aevi kar.*, III, 402; cf. 400.

49. "benedictus Gregorius, dominus dulcissimus": *Ep.* 6, n. 1 (Leclercq, *St. ans.*, 31, 87).

50. "lapis perfecte quadratus": *Ascripta de ordinat. C. Gregorii* (Wilmart, RDSR 15, 213-4).

51. "romanae deliciae": *De interpr.*, c. ii, regarding passages on the Canticle (PL, CXXXI, 996 C).

52. Pref. to the *Liber sacramentorum* (MGH, *Ep. aevi kar.*, III, 579). Cf. Ekkehart IV, *Confutatio rhetoricae* (Dümmler, *Zeitschrift f. deutsches Alterthum*, 1869, 2, 22).

53. *Did.*, Bk. V, c. vii: "Inter quae (sanctorum dicta) beatissimi Gr. singulariter scripta amplexanda existimo, quae, quia mihi prae caeteris dulcia, et aeternae vitae amore plena visa sunt, nolo silentio praeterire" (PL, CLXXVI, 794 D).

54. *In Ex.*, Bk. I, c. ii: "Blessed Gregory spoke most fully, in accordance with the sweetness of the grace bestowed upon him" — "B. Gr., secundum dulcedinem gratiae sibi collatae, plenissime dixit" (PL, CLXVII, 1421 D). Gilbert of Stanford,

In Cant.: "B. Gr., unus ex praecipuis dilectoribus et desideratoribus ejus (Domini), dulcedinem erga nos benignitatis illius suaviter exprimens" (Leclercq, *St. ans.*, 20, 213, note 59).

55. *S.* 8, c. ix (PL, CXCVIII, 145 A).

56. *Polycr.*, Bk. VIII, c. i: "This [is] Gregory, or rather the Holy Spirit, through Gregory" — "Haec quidem Gregorius, imo per Gregorium Spiritus sanctus" (PL, CXCIX, 712 D).

57. *De cogn. sui,* c. x: "Lege Moralia beati Gr. de ipso sancti Spiritus ore profusa, teste Petro Diacono, qui columbam vidit, etc." (PL, CCXII, 731 A).

58. "Scripturae sacrae mystica
Mire solvis aenigmata,
Theorica mysteria
Te docet ipsa Veritas."

PL, CXLV, 987.

59. "Quantos in libris Moralium Job legentes quotidie sanctus Gregorius percutit, dum discutit et perquirit! Quantos vulnerat dum compungit!": Leclercq, *St. ans.*, 31, 183.

60. "Tantum per gratiam sancti Spiritus scientiae lumine praeditus, ut non modo illi praesentium temporum quisquam doctorum, sed nec in praeteritis quidem illi par fuerit unquam": *De ill. eccl. script.,* c. xxviii (PL, LXXV, 490 CD). Cf. L. Serrano, "La obra 'Morales de San Gregorio' en la litterature hispanogodas," *Revista de archivos, biliothecas y museos,* XXIV (1911), 482-97. Isidore is here conforming to a "topos": cf. Curtius, *Le m. âge latin et la litt. classique,* Fr. tr., pp. 203-5. John of Garlande will say of Alan of Lille: "Virgilio major et Homero certior" (*De triumphis Ecclesiae;* Wright, 74). [Paul] Alvarus of Cordoba, acknowledging Eulogus [of Cordoba] from the first book of his *Memoriale sanctorum,* ranks him above Demosthenes and Cicero, Titus Livy and Quintilian, for eloquence (PL, CXV, 734-5). Notker the Stammerer says that Alcuin "talem grammaticam condidit, ut Donatus, Nicomachus, Domisitheus et noster Priscianus in ejus comparatione nihil esse videantur": *De interpr.,* c. i (PL, CXXXI, 999 C). Orderic on Lanfranc (PL, CLXXXVIII, 527 B). Peter of Poitiers on Peter the Venerable (CLXXXIX, 47-8, 61). Angilbert on Charlemagne (MGH, *Scr.,* II, 394).

61. "incomparabilis omnibus suis praedecessoribus": *De scr. eccl.,* Bk. III, c. xxxii: "Gregorius . . . organum sancti Spiritus, incomparabilis omnibus suis praedecessoribus, multa prae sole praeclara ac prae obrizo auro pretiosa scripsit" (PL, CLXXII, 227 BC).

62. "in verbo veritatis et virtute Dei": *C. Wolf. Col.* (*L. de lite,* I, 308).

63. "Non te fallet ille doctor egregius, qui, sicut fallere noluit, falli non potuit": *Ep. l,* v. 1178-80 (Desilve, 9).

64. In the commentary of Beatus on the Ap. he is the author of passages "where one had believed he discerned the unmistakable mark of Tyconius": H. L. Ramsay, RHLR 7 (1912), 444.

65. See Chapters 14 and 15 below, for the school of St. Victor.

66. PL, XCI, 1223 AB.

67. *De trib. quaest.*: "Sanctus quoque papa Gregorius, bonis omnibus Latini sermonis capacibus suaeque doctrinae pie studiosis plurimum collaturus";

"summe doctum et mire facundum" (PL, CXIX, 662 C, 658 B). *Ep.* 130: "B. Gr., cujus tanta in Ecclesia resplendet auctoritas" (L. Levillain, 2, 208).

68. *Carmen ad Rob. reg.*, v. 215-26 (PL, 779-80).

69. Cf. Leclercq, AHDLMA 15, 137-8.

70. Delhaye, ET, 69 and 280. Thus Dom Wilmart thinks that the author of the *Allegoriae* could be Garnier: *Mém. Lagrange*, 339.

71. Otfrid, *In ev.*, Bk. V, c. xiv, on John 21: "Gregorius ille bonus interpretatus ho[c] ingeniose, atque multum eleganter, per fidem meam, sicut est mos ejus" (J. Schliterus, 1, 1728, 352).

72. *C. Petrobrus* (PL, CLXXXIX, 839 C).

73. Guitmond of Aversa, *Exc. Mor.*, "lettre d'envoi": "pro dignitate libri omnis laus inferior" (Morin, RB 36, 92).

74. On the formation of this legend: G. Madoz, "Tajón de Zaragoza y su viaja a Roma," *Mél. J. de Ghellinck*, I, 345-61. It was rather a question of the homilies on Ez. Cf. Tajón, *Ep. ad Eug.*, 1 (PL, LXXX, 725).

75. *V. s. Rimberti*, c. xv: "Exceptum legentibus utile de libris s. Gregorii fecit et propria manu conscripsit" (MGH, *Scr.*, II, 771).

76. An unknown monk even versified the Life of the saint by John the Deacon (HLF, 13, 596-7), as Paulinus of Périgaux and Fortunatus had done for the Life of St. Martin by Sulpicius Severus, as Walafrid Strabo had wanted to do and as Ermenric of Elwangen had begun to do for the Life of St. Gall. Bertharius, abbot of Monte Cassino in 848, versified Book II of the *Dialogues* (*De miraculis almi Patris Benedicti*, MGH, *P. lat. aevi car.*, III, 394-8); according to the anonymous of Montier-en-Der, Adson did the same.

77. Cf. the thesis (typescr., Lille, 1956) of Father R. Wasselynck: *L'influence des Mor. in Job de S. Gr. le Grand sur la th. morale entre le VII et le XII s.* Manitius, 2, 694-9. HLF, 13, 6-13. There had been a Burgundian transl. of the homilies on Ez. (published by K. Hoffmann, 1881). From the 8th cent. the Anglo-Saxon poet translated extracts from Gregory's work; in the 11th cent., Alfred, king of Wessex, had the *Regula pastoralis* translated. The other authors translated by Notker Labeo were: Boethius, "Cato," Vergil, Terence, Martianus Capella, Aristotle and the Psalms.

78. "omnimodam sapientiam": *De interpr.*, c. i (PL, CXXXI, 995 AB). On this collection: Wilmart, RB 39, 81.

79. Paul Grosjean, S.J., "Sur quelques exégètes irlandais du VII s.," *S. Er.* 7 (1955), 67-98.

80. See above, p. 345, n. 51.

81. *Ep.* 138.

82. *De cogn. sui*, c. x (PL, CCXII, 731 AB).

83. "Audivit etiam eos dicentes de libris *Moralibus* Gregorii, quod pessimi essent, similesque tesseris seu aleis, quae ex omni parte habent sex vel quinque oculos: quia ubicumque revolvuntur, nonnisi optima invenirentur, sicut in illis tesseris maximus numerus semper projicitur": Richalm of Schoenthal (Bl. Richalmi, Spinosae vallis in Franconia abbatis, O. cist.), *Liber revelationum* (*de insidiis et versutiis daemonum adv. homines*, c. lxxviii, *De libris Moralium Gregorii*, Pez, *Th. anecd. nov.*, I, ii, 442; cf. 466-7).

84. Henri Pirenne, *Hist. de l'Europe* (1936), 32.

85. St. Goswin of Anchin, *Vita Gosw.*, c. xii-iv (R. Gibbon, Douai, 1626). Leclercq, *La Maison Dieu*, V, 32-3.

86. Dom B. Capelle, *L'Anglet. chrét. avant les Normands* (1909), 56.

87. The legend is everywhere. Thus, Hugh Métel, *Ep.* 29 (369). John of Salisbury, *Polycr.*, Bk. V, c. viii (PL, CXCIX, 559-60).

88. Bernard de Vrégille, *D. Sp.*, f. 25 (1958), 171.

89. "Hic specialiter atque fideliter est relegendus": Bernard of Morval [Cluny], Bk. III, v. 317 (Hoskier).

90. "saepe dictus saepiusque dicendus Gregorius": Manegold, *Ad Geb.*, c. x (*L. de lite*, I, 332).

91. "teste Gregorio" — "testem beatum Gregorium habeo": Godfrey of Admont, *Microc.*, c. cc (221), etc. Othloh: "Beato Gregorio attestante" (PL, CXLVI, 405; cf. 414 D, 420 D). Absalon (CCXI, 164 A).

92. "Ad cujus (Gregorii) me locutionis instar . . . ita conformari studeo, ut a rarissimis intelligi possit qua sibi concatenatione illius verba misceantur et mea!": 404 G: ". . . cujus verba non solum in his quae de hac Apocalypsi sensit, verum etiam in aliis quae pro confirmando operis mei dogmate occurrunt, proprium in illis expositionis laborem refugiens, adnecto."

93. John of Saint-Arnoul, *V. Joannis abb. Gorz.*, c. lxxxiii: "In his primum Moralia b. Gregorii ordine quam saepissime percurrens, pene cunctas ex eo continentias sententiarum ita memoriae commendavit, ut in communibus exhortationum sive locutionum confabulationibus omnis ejus oratio ex ejusdem libris decurrere videretur" (MGH, *Scr.*, IV, 360).

94. *Ibid.*: "Praeterea Gregorii in Ez. multo usu detrivit, ut pene memoriae commendasse videretur; ad summam ejusdem quaecumque essent beati Gregorii, unice praeter caetera amplexus est" (283 A).

95. Cf. Garnier, *s.* 13: "Natat elephas, — quomodo pertransibit agnus?" (PL, CCV, 664 C). John of Salisbury, *Polycr.*, Bk. VIII, c. xvii (CXCIX, 784 B). [Trans. note: The sequel to this note was out of place; it is added from the French text, p. 548 at the bottom. It runs as follows:] Hugh of Rouen, *Tract in Hexaem., ep. ad Arnulfum lexov.:* "Ibi elephans periculose natat, ibi agnus secure ambulat; ibi caput elephantis demergitur, ibi pes agni supergreditur" (Fr. Lecomte, AHDLMA 25, 235).

96. "Romanae rex eloquentiae": Adson [of Montier-en-Der], *V. S. Basoli prol.* (PL, CXXXVII, 643 C).

97. A. Wilmart, *Le recueil des Pensées du Bx Guigue* (1936), 1 (with regard to Augustine and Gregory).

98. "numerosus periodorum alternatim respondentium incessus": Sixtus of Sienna, *Bibl. sancta*, Bk. IV (2nd ed., 1576, 351).

99. A. Wilmart, RDSR 15, 187.

100. Thus, for example, the following passage from Richard [of Saint-Victor], *In Ap.*, Bk. I, c. vi: "Antiquus hostis bonum quod non potest impedire ac malum quod non valet efficere per suae superbiae complices daemones, hoc conatur perficere per suae pravitatis imitatores homines, etc." (PL, CXCVI, 719-20).

101. "Jam stylus aureus ejus et igneus haud morietur,
Aurea pagina per sua germina suscipietur."

Bk. III, v. 313-4.

102. Leclercq, *L'amour des lettres,* 31: "Almost all the" monastic "vocabulary" of the Middle Ages "comes from St. Gregory." ["Presque tout le vocabulaire" monastique du moyen âge "vient de S. Grégoire."]

103. Thus for facile turns of phrase like "Sunt qui . . . ," or: "Sciendum tamen est quod . . . ," etc. So too for the characteristic trope: "quid per . . . intelligitur, nisi . . . ?" so frequent in exegesis. It is found in Bede, Autpert, Paul the Deacon, Rabanus Maurus, Angelome, Claudius, Odilon, Peter Damian, Bruno of Segni, Robert of Tombelaine, Hervaeus of Bourg Dieu, Elmer of Canterbury, Hugh and Richard [of Saint Victor], Gerhoh, Godfrey of Admont, Adam Scotus, Gilbert Foliot, Letber of Saint Ruf, Petrus Cellensis, Joachim of Flora, etc. The ground for it was laid in Ambrose (PL, XIV, 356 C, 658 C, etc.) and in Origen and Rufinus: *In Jos.,* h. 8, n. 7 (344-5); *In Cant.,* Bk. I (108); see above, Chapter 3.5, n. 23.

104. "gregoriana dicta, in quibus artis hujus potissimum reperiuntur claves": Guibert of Nogent, *De vita sua,* Bk. I, c. xvii (PL, CLVI, 874 B). On the style of Gregory, see the fine page of de Ghellinck, *Litt. lat.,* I, 23-4.

105. Joannes Italus, *V. S. Odonis,* n. 20 (PL, CXXXIII, 52 AD). Nalgod [of Cluny], *V. alt,* n. 13 (90-1). On the influence of Gregory upon Odo: J. Laporte, in *A Cluny,* 138-43.

106. "Dominus noster Jesus Christus ex condensissima allegoricorum verborum silva, in cujus opaca densitate hactenus latuit, subito manifestus erumpit": Aelred, *S. de oner.,* 28 (PL, CXCV, 478 A).

107. V. [H. de Lubac], *Catholicisme,* ch. VIII.

108. "locutus est ad cor eorum, sive docuit eos per Spiritum sanctum omnem veritatem, sicut scriptum est: Tunc apparuit illis sensum ut intelligerent Scripturas. Amplius autem, die quinquagesimo, dando illis Spiritum sanctum locutus est ad cor eorum, et extunc in Ecclesia, non desunt, quorum mentibus insinuet et notitiam Scripturarum": Rupert, *In Os.,* Bk. I (PL, CLXVIII, 47 CD).

109. ". . . Hydria metretas capiens est quaelibet aetas:
Lympha dat historiam, vinum notat allegoriam."

Verses placed under the stained glass window of the wedding at Cana, Canterbury Cathedral (E. Mâle, *L'art rel. du XIII s. en Fr.,* p. 232). On the six urns and the six ages of the world: Origen, *De princ.,* Bk. IV, c. ii, n. 5 (314-5). Aug., *Q. evang.,* Bk. I, n. 41 (PL, XXXV, 1331). Smaragdus, *Collect.:* "Ergo Dominus vinum in gaudia nuptiarum non de nihilo facere voluit, sed hydrias sex impleri aqua praecipiens, hanc mirabiliter convertit in vinum; quia lex mundi aetates sapientiae salutaris largitate donavit, quam tamen ipse veniens sublimioris sensus virtute fecundavit" (CII, 89 B). Bruno of Segni, *In Gen.* 6 (CLXIV, 175 A) and 15 (189 D). Rupert, *In Jo.,* Bk. II (CLXIX, 286 AC); etc.

110. Berengaud, *In Ap.,* v. 1: "Quia in tabernaculo Ecclesiae postea vetus Testamentum flores spiritualium sensuum protulit, ipsique flores fructus bonorum operum ediderunt" (PL, XVII, 785 D).

111. Beatus, *In Ap.* (271).

112. "Jesu vobis recitante legem et revelante cordibus vestris": Or., *In Jos.,* h. 9, n. 9 (355).

113. John of Salisbury, *Polycr.,* Bk. VII, c. xiii: "Sic enim prodest quaerendi studium si aviditas ipsa sciendi referatur ad Christum. Sed nec ipse, nisi in

fractione agnoscitur, quia mens Scripturarum, nisi refectio fidei aut morum detur animae, omnino non videtur" (PL, CXCIX, 667 C). Rupert, *In Deut.*, Bk. I, c. xxvii (167, 945 D).

114. "Quomodo autem fecit de aqua vinum? Cum aperuit eis sensum, et exposuit eis Scripturas": *In Jo.*, tr. 9, n. 5 (CCL, 36, 43).

115. Or., *In Lev.*, h. 1, n. 1: "ut veritatem Verbi sub litterae tegmine coopertam, ad Christum jam Dominum conversa cognoscat Ecclesia" (281).

116. *Transire ad Christum — Transire ad intelligentiam spiritalem:* Jerome, *ep.* 121, c. x: "Nos juxta spiritum transeamus ad Christum" (PL, XXII, 1031). *Tr. in psalmos:* "Si vero conversi fuerimus ad cor, si spiritaliter intellexerimus" (*An. mar.*, III, 2, 95). Ambrose, *In ps. XXXVI*, n. 60: "Transi ad intelligentiam spiritalem, quia lex spiritalis est" (PL, XIV, 1007-8). Aug., *C. adv. legis et proph.*, Bk. II, c. vii, n. 29: "Non autem omnes qui christiani appellantur, ad Christum transeunt, sed quibus aufertur velamen, quod in lectione veteris Testamenti manet" (XLII, 655); *C. Faust.*, Bk. XII, c. xxxix (274).

117. Greg., *In Ez.*, Bk. II, h. 10, n. 1 (PL, LXXVI, 1058 B).

118. Or., *In Ex.*, h. 12, n. 1: "Si enim conversi essemus ad Dominum, sine dubio auferretur velamen" (262-3); *In Lev.*, h. 6, n. 1 (358-9); *C. Cels.*, Bk. V, c. lx (2, 63-4).

119. Othloh, *L. de cursu sp.*, c. xx: "nuptiasque in nobis faciens tales per quas ipse quidem spon[s]us, anima vero nostra efficiatur sponsa, aquam carnalis vitae, quam vel pro necessitate mortalis naturae vel pro mala consuetudine hucusque bibimus, in vinum spiritualis vitae dignetur convertere" (PL, CXLVI, 213 A).

120. Rupert: "In hoc tabernaculum introduxit Isaac Rebeccam, et accepit uxorem id est, apertis illorum sensibus, immisit Christus spiritualem Scripturarum intellectum, et novam sibi instituit Ecclesiam." See Chapter 5.4 above.

Notes to Chapter Nine
§1. A Twofold Tropology

1. "Quia sunt signati per spiritum litterae, non per litteram": Alphonsus Tostatus, *op. cit.*, 84.

2. The "cognitio veritatis" and the "forma virtutis": *Miscell.*, Bk. I, tit. 13: "In omni autem Scriptura aut cognitio veritatis quaerenda est, aut forma virtutis. Primo studio historia et allegoria proponitur; secundo tropologia . . ." (PL, CLXXVII, 484-5). We do not see how this classification would have caused the value of history to increase, as R. Löwe says, "The Jewish Midrashim and Patristic and Scholastic Exegesis of the Bible," *St. Patr.*, I, 504: "This rearrangement caused the stock of the literal sense to appreciate significantly in the 12th century, and has as its natural consequence the reassessment of the importance of Jewish biblical exegesis and its cultivation by the Victorine scholars." Others think that Hugh valued history by distinguishing it more strongly from allegory. These two judgments would scarcely appear concordant.

3. Cf. Abelard (PL, CLXXVIII, 94 C). Richard (CLXXV, 340 C). John of Salisbury, *Polycr.*, Bk. VII, c. xii: "Ab eadem re saepe allegoria fidem, tropologia mores variis modis aedificat" (CXCIX, 666 B). Isidore, *L. de variis q.*, *praef.* (2).

4. Guerric, *s. in Cant.* VIII, 13, n. 2: "non solum ut eruantur mystica, sed ut sugantur moralia" (PL, CLXXXV, 211 B). Absalon, *s.* 29 (CCXI, 177 B).

5. Peter Damian, *s.* 11: "moralia mysticis internectens" (PL, CXLIV, 562 D).

6. Facund[i]us of Hermiane, *Pro def. trium cap.*, Bk. III, c. vi (PL, LXVII, 605 B). [Trans. note: The *Catholic Encyclopedia* spells his name without the "i" included by Lubac.]

7. "Tertia expositio": Or., *In Cant.*, Bk. I (102); Bk. III (206). Cf. *In Ex.*, h. 1, n. 4; h. 2, n. 3 (150, 166); *In Lev.*, h. 2, n. 4 (294). Rufinus, *Ben. Nephtalim* (PL, XXI, 327 A); *Ben Zabulon*: "moralis locus" (318 B).

8. "Tertius explanationis locus": *In Cant.*, Bk. I (90); Bk. II (133).

9. The "spiritualis intelligentiae sacramentum" becomes the "virtutis saluberrimum exemplum": Peter Damian, *s.* 48, (PL, CXLIV, 768 D).

10. Adam Scot., *Trip. tab.*, P. III, c. i: "ut, quemadmodum in nobis per fidem rectam clarificatus est intellectus, et sic per cogitationem devotam in nobis excitetur et accendatur affectus" (PL, CXCVIII, 743 D). *Ep.*, c. viii: "in recta sanae fidei credulitate . . . , in interna defaecatae mentis puritate"; "tertium in puritate animi, de quo tractat tropologia, quod imitemur" (632 AB).

11. Greg., *In ev.*, h. 40, n. 1 (PL, LXXVI, 1302 AB).

12. "Non enim virtutibus venitur ad fidem, sed fide pergitur ad virtutes": Rabanus, *De univ.*, Bk. XIV, c. xxii (PL, CXI, 398 D). After Greg.

13. A frequent expression: Jerome, *In Matt.*, *prol.* (PL, XXVI, 20 C). Bede (XCII, 937 C). Smaragdus (CII, 13 C). Claudius (CIV, 809 D). Angelome (CXV, 554 C). Luke of Mont Cornillon (CCXIII, 496 B); etc.

14. Or., *In Gen.*, h. 2, n. 6 (SC, 7, 106). Rufinus, *Ben. Isachar*: "Sed quoniam instituimus arcam Scripturae divinae, non bicameratam (sicut ad Noe a Domino dictum est) construere, videamus nunc qualiter nobis Isachar etiam tertium aedificet nidum. . . . In hac morali expositione . . ." (PL, XXI, 320 BC).

15. Rabanus, *loc. cit.*: "per fidem ergo venitur ad opera, sed per opera

solidatur in fide. Vestibulum itaque ante gradus est: quia qui prius crediderit, ipse post virtutum gradibus ad portae aditum ascendit" (PL, XCI, 398 D).

16. Luke of Mont Cornillon, *In Cant. Mor.* (CCXIII, 498 CD): "Aries quippe, sive vitula, est quaelibet sententia ex Veteri Testamento excerpta. Cui sententiae quasi pellem detrahimus, cum historicam intelligentiam pertractantes, veram esse sancimus. Caro autem tunc sacris ignibus traditur, cum allegoria spiritualibus sensibus intellecta delucidatur. Adipes vero, et ea quae infra sunt, Deo offerre nos arbitramur, cum moralitatem et illa quae de moribus pendent, ad utilitatem fidelium animarum et laudem ipsius Dei perscrutamur. Quoniam igitur in superiori tractatu historialem Jacob allegorico et spirituali sense interpretati sumus, quasi pelle subtracta, carnes sacro igne concremavimus. Superest ergo ut adipes igni divino admoveamus, id est, ut moralitatem morali et excelsiori intellectu in locum proferamus."

17. Greg., *In ev.*, h. 40, n. 2-3 (PL, LXXVI, 1302 AB, 1304 C): "Sensus ergo allegoricos sub brevitate transcurrimus, ut ad moralitatis latitudinem citius venire valeamus. . . . Haec nos, fratres carissimi, pro indagandis allegoriae mysteriis succincte transcurrisse sufficiat; nunc ad intuendam latius rei gestae moralitatem animus recurrat." Cf. Angelome, *A Leotricus* (MGH, *Ep.*, 5, 622; cf. 625).

18. "Scriptura redemptionis nostrae narrans mysteria, sic refert quae pro nobis historialiter sunt gesta, ut significet quae moraliter a nobis sunt gerenda": Guerric, *De purif. B.M.V.*, s. 4, n. 1 (PL, CLXXXV, 75 D).

19. "Contemplando quid fecerit Deus, quid nobis faciendum sit agnoscimus": Hugh, *Did.*, Bk. VI, c. v (PL, CLXXVI, 805 BC).

20. Cf. Philo, *De conf. ling.*, c. xxxviii, n. 190 (= the figured explications).

21. Aug., *De Trin.*, Bk. XV, c. ix, n. 15 (Agaësse, 458). Isidore, *Etym.*, Bk. I, c. xxxvii, n. 1 (PL, LXXXII, 112 B).

22. "Sermo conversus" or "conversivus": Peter Comestor (PL, CXCVIII, 1055 A); etc.

23. "Conversa" or "conversiva locutio": *Spec. de myst. Eccl.*, c. viii (PL, CLXXVII, 375 A); etc.

24. "Sermo conversus ad nos, id est, ad mores nostros": Alph. Tostat. We are aware of only one exception in the 12th century: Joachim of Flora, *Lib. introd. in Ap.*, fol. 26 *ab*: "tropologia intelligentia est quae pertinet ad doctrinam . . . ; modos sermonum Dei complectitur et discernit."

25. "Sermo conversivus pertinens ad mores animi": Peter Comestor, *loc. cit.*

26. *De trib. max. circ.*: "Unde etiam recte tropologia, id est sermo conversus sive locutio replicata, nomen accepit, quia nimirum alienae narrationis sermonem ad nostram tunc auditionem convertimus, cum facta aliorum legendo ea nobis ad exemplum vivendi conformamus" (W. M. Green, *Speculum* 17, 491). *Spec.*, c. viii: "Tropologia dicitur conversiva locutio, dum quod dicitur ad mores aedificandos convertitur, ut sunt moralia" (PL, CLXXVII, 375 B).

27. "Tropologia idem sonat, quam sermo conversivus, eo quod factum tale designat, ad quod nos secundum moralis aedificationis institutionem necessarium est converti": *Sent.*, Bk. I, P. I, c. vi (Martin, 173).

28. "Tropologia est moralis sermo," or a "moralis scientia": Richard, *Nonn. alleg. tab. faed.* (PL, CXCVI, 200 B).

29. "Tropologia est moralis sermo . . . et fit apertis verbis, aut figuratis": thus Rabanus, *In Ex.*, Bk. III, c. xi (PL, CVIII, 148 A); etc. Sicard of Cremona, *Mitrale*, Bk. I, c. xiii, adds: "et dicitur tropologia conversa locutio, cum quod dicitur ad mores significandos convertitur" (CCXII, 47 B).

30. "Allegoria dicitur, quando per factum intelligitur aliud factum. . . . Tropologia est, quando per factum ostenditur aliud faciendum": *Spec. de myst. Eccl.*, c. viii (PL, CLXXVII, 375 A).

31. L. *de laude fidei* (*Op. in.*, I, 226): "Potest etiam dici quod exempla patrum antiquorum quaedam sunt lana, quaedam linum. Nam quasi lana munda et mollis invenitur in his eorum factis quae simpliciter, ut acta et scripta sunt, imitanda proponuntur, ut est fides et oboedientia Abrahae, pietas Joseph, patientia Job, mansuetudo Moysi, humilitas David et similia, in quibus, etiam si nulla quaeratur allegoria, simplex moralitas placet. Sed ea quae sunt per allegoriam dicta, ut quod Abraham duos filios habuit . . . , et quod Jacob duas sorores habuit uxores earumque ancillas concubinas, et similia, quasi linum viride primo dessicanda et multis modis purganda sunt, ut carnali sensus litterae occidentis detracto, solus in his accepetetur spiritus vivificans et aedificans."

32. *Fons phil.*, v. 485-7 (Delhaye, 52):

Hic miravi Practicae rivos clariores,
Cujus sunt et omnibus socii liquores,
Sed cum sint in aliis turbulentiores,
Perlucenti vitro sunt hic lucidiores. . . .

33. These verses, says Ph. Delhaye, "reveal to us the author's interest in moral theology better than his exegetical conceptions" do: ET, 278.

34. Str. 50:

Quod si cuncta pervolantes summatim theorica
Replicemus, et succincte tangamus moraliter
Singula, quae sunt per stilum promulgata tropicum,
Possumus haec competenter aliter intellegi. . . .

51:

Potest Lazari per mortem peccatoris anima
Unaquaeque designari . . . (*P. lat. m. aevi*, VI, 216).

[Trans. "Through Lazarus's death can each sinful soul be signified."]

35. Gerhoh, *De laude fidei*, on the stories of the Old Testament: "in which, even if no allegory is sought, simple morality is enough" — "in quibus etiam si nulla quaeratur allegoria, simplex moralitas placet" (*Op. in.*, I, 226).

36. The "sensus tantummodo moralis" opposed to this "altior sensus," this "sacratior sensus" in which the "profundiora mysteria" are uncovered: William of Saint Thierry, *Exp. alt. in Cant.*, praef. (PL, CLXXX, 476 A). Gerhoh, *In ps.* (CXCIII, 1268 D; 311 A, 194). Godfrey of Admont, *h. dom.* 60 (CLXXIV, 401 BC).

37. *Nonn. alleg.* (PL, CXCVI, 200 AB): "Tropologia de his agit quae quisque facile capit. . . . Alia est enim conditio tropologiae, et longe alia conditio allegoriae. Quid est enim tropologia, nisi moralis scientia, et quid allegoria, nisi

mystica mysteriorum doctrina? Morum honesta cordi humano naturaliter sunt inscripta. Mysteriorum vero profunda pro certo nemo nisi temere praesumit de sensu proprio."

38. "Ex sacramentorum virtute morum disciplina utilis et observabilis redditur." . . . "Sola Scriptura sacra allegorico et anagogico sensu mystice utitur, sola inter omnes hac gemina supereminentia coronatur": *Ibid.* (200 D).

39. See Chapter 3 above.

40. The "bonum opus": *In Cant.*: "Juxta tropologiam etiam fiunt nuptiae duobus modis: uno quo anima Christo per dilectionem copulatur; alio quo anima, quod est inferior vis interioris hominis spiritui, qui est superior ejus, per consensum divinae legis conjungitur, de quo conjugio spiritalis proles, id est bonum opus gignitur" (PL, CLXXII, 349 BC).

41. E. de Bruyne, I, 282. Cf. Rabanus, *In Ex.,* Bk. I, c. xii (PL, CVIII, 34 D).

42. Carthusian monastery of Salvatorberg: "ubi sensus tropologicus spirituali aedificio adjectus . . ." (J. de Ghellinck, 295).

43. Paschasius, *In Matt.*, Bk. XII: "Omnis ejus opera, aut mysteria sunt rerum praefiguratarum, aut exempla virtutum" (PL, CXX, 910-1). Peter Damian (see above, p. 127, at note number 5). Bernard, *De div., s.* 3: "Sumamus et nos de mysterio ejus moribus nostris exemplum" (CLXXXIII, 684 A). Guerric, *De annunt., s.* 2, *De Verbi incarn. in Maria et in anima fideli,* n. 4: "et ut plenius noveris conceptum virginis non solum esse mysticum, sed et moralem, quod sacramentum est ad redemptionem, exemplum quoque tibi est ad imitationem; ut manifeste evacues in te gratia sacramenti, si non imiteris virtutem exempli" (PL, CLXXXV, 122-3). Cf. Leo, *s.* 25 and 72 (LIV, 212 C, 390 C).

44. The "mysticus moralitatis sensus": Godfrey of Admont, *h.* 30, *in annunt.* 4: "Quidquid enim legimus vel intelligimus, totum ad interioris hominis usum conferre poterimus. Si ergo totam veteris ac novi Testamenti seriem enucleatius perscrutari velimus, mysticum moralitatis sensum inditum ubique invenimus" (PL, CLXXIV, 765 B).

45. The "spiritualis vitae intelligentia": Othloh, *Dial. de trib. q.,* c. xxxiii (PL, CXLVI, 102 A).

46. "Audivimus ex historia, quod miremur; cognovimus ex capite, quod credamus; consideremus nunc ex corpore, quod vivendo teneamus. In nobismetipsis namque debemus transformare quod legimus": Greg., *Mor.,* Bk. I, c. xxiv, n. 33 (SC, 32, pp. 161-2). William of Champeaux, *Liber Florum Mor.* (mimeogr. ed. R. Wasselynck, 1956, 370).

47. "Haec in significationem nostri capitis breviter tractata transcurrimus: nunc in aedificationem ejus corporis, ea moraliter tractanda replicemus ut quod actum foris narratur in opere, sciamus quomodo intus agatur in mente": *Mor.,* Bk. II, c. xxxviii, n. 63 (PL, LXXV, 586 C). Adam Scot., *Trip. tab., ep.,* c. vii: "tam de tabernaculo sanctae Ecclesiae, quod est in allegoria, quam de cordis humani tabernaculo, quod est in tropologia tractare" (CXCVIII, 631 C).

48. Hugo, *De sacr., prol.,* c. vi: "sub eo autem sensu qui est in significatione rerum ad facta mystica continetur allegoria, et sub eo sensu qui est in significatione rerum ad facienda mystica continetur tropologia" (PL, CLXXVI, 185). Garnier, *s.* 34 (CCV, 790 A). [Trans. note: "The mystic deeds that have been done" (facta

mystica) are contrasted with "the mystic deeds that are to be done" (facienda mystica).]

49. The "mysterium fidei" leads to the "opera fidei": Cf. Or., *In Gen.*, h. 8, n. 8: "nisi opera fidei expleveris" (83).

50. "Mystica fides" then "moralis gratia": Ambrose, *De myst.*, c. vii, n. 38 (Botte, SC, 25, 120).

51. "Eia, fratres, res vestras . . . , res vestras, inquam, res vestras!": Aug., s. 8, c. ix, n. 12 (PL, XXXVIII, 72).

52. "Quaecumque scripta sunt, ad nostram doctrinam scripta sunt": Rom. 15:4; cf. 4:23: "Non est autem scriptum tantum propter ipsum . . . sed et propter nos."

53. "Haec autem in figura contingebant illis, scripta sunt autem ad correptionem nostram, in quos fines saeculorum devenerunt": 1 Cor. 10:6, 11.

54. "*Mane surgamus ad vineas*, id est, ad spiritum a littera surgentes, ab historia ad mysticum sensum, accedamus ad sacras Scripturas; in quibus virent frondes historiae, redolet flos allegoriae, satiat fructus tropologiae. Et hoc, *mane*, id est, per diluculum spirtualis intelligentiae. Et sic *videamus*, id est, experiamur, hoc est, me experiri facias, *si floruit vinea*, id est, sacra Scriptura in me per allegoricum sensum. *Si flores fructus parturiunt*, per moralem intellectum; quia, sicut post florem sequitur fructus, sic moralis intellectus post allegoricam interpretationem ad nostri informationem": Alan of Lille, *Elucid. in Cant.* (PL, CCX, 102 CD).

55. "Historia et parabolis nutrimur; allegoria crescimus; moralitate perficimur": Hugo of Rouen, *Dial.*, Bk. VII, c. xi (PL, CXCII, 1243 C). Abelard: "Triplex intelligentia — Diversa praebet fercula. . . . — Alunt parvos historica — Pascunt adultos mystica — Perfectorum ferventi studio — Suscipitur moralis lectio" (CLXXVIII, 1775-6).

56. L. Bouyer, *L'initiation chrét.* (1958), 113-4: "voilà la clé de toutes ces lectures de la vigile pascale." *Idem: Le trône de la Sagesse*, 119.

57. "Quotannis Jesu Christi Pascha celebratur, hoc est, animarum transitus . . .": *Hexaem.*, Bk. I, c. iv, n. 14 (PL, XIV, 129 B).

58. *Vere impletur in nobis:* Or., *In Ex.*, h. 3, n. 3 (170).

59. "Hodie usque ad nos": *In oct. Paschae*, s. 1 (PL, CLXXXIII, 294 BD).

60. 1 Cor. 10:6. Cf. "'Typologie' et 'allegorisme,'" RSR 34 (1947), 219-26, and the study pushed further by G. Martelet, "Sacrements, figures et exhortation en I Cor. x, 1-11," RSR 44 (1956), 323-59 and 515-59.

61. C. H. Dodd, *La Bible aujourd'hui* (Fr. tr. Ledoux, 1957), 161.

62. "Verba Dei tunc mens verius intelligit, cum in eis semetipsam quaerit": Greg., *Mor.*, Bk. XXVIII, c. viii, n. 19 (PL, LXXVI, 459 C). Cf. R. P. C. Hanson, *Allegory and Event, A Study of the Sources and Significance of Origen's Interpretation of Scripture* (1959), 281: "This tendency to dissolve historical events into religious experience has been defended as entirely legitimate by some modern scholars. De Lubac has described it as 'interiorizing history'." All reservations having been made regarding the expression "religious experience," which is susceptible of a wide variety of meanings, this "interiorizing of history" is not only declared legitimate by certain "modern scholars": it has been declared real and necessary by the whole Catholic tradition. It in no way "dissolves" history: it obtains or exhib-

its the fruit of history. Likewise, the "always" and the "every day" that result from the unique Event are not going on "timelessly" (287)! And this Event is not uniquely "unique" in the sense that every event is!

Notes to Chapter Nine
§2. Quotidie ["Daily"]

1. "Quod historice praecessit in capite, consequenter etiam revelatur fieri moraliter in ejus corpore": Bernard, *De div.*, s. 58, n. 2 (PL, CLXXXIII, 682 C).
2. "Licet illa in Aegypto corporaliter gesta sint, spiritualiter tamen nunc geruntur in nobis": Heterius and Beatus, *Ad Elip.*, Bk. I, c. li (PL, XCVI, 924 B).
3. ". . . cordibus moraliter convenire videtur, quod historialiter de terra Scriptura commemorat": Elmer of Cant., *Ep.* 9, n. 2 (Leclercq, *St. ans.*, 31, 97).
4. "In virtute crucis Christi": Or., *In Ex.*, h. 3, n. 3 (170).
5. "Cor nostrum": Cf. Greg., *Mor.*, Bk. XXVIII, c. viii, n. 19 (PL, LXXVI, 459 BC).
6. "Ipsa mens atque conscientia fidelium": *In ev.*, h. 39, n. 7 (PL, LXXVI, 1298 A).
7. *Trip. tab., ep.*, c. viii (PL, CXCVIII, 632 AB); *ibid.*, final letter: "Tropology pertains to the third tabernacle, and it is in the internal purity of the secret consciousness" — "Ad tabernaculum tertium pertinet tropologia, et est in interna secretae conscientiae puritate" (792 D); *s.* 39, c. v: "anima devota" (355 B).
8. "Anima in Ecclesia," "anima ecclesiastica," or "ecclesiastica persona": Gerhoh, *In ps.* (PL, CXCIII, 1121 A, 1114 B, 1179 D, 1665 AB, 1760 D; CXCIV, 300 D, 304 B, 767 D, 769 A, 794 A); etc.
9. Ambrose, *De myst.*, c. vii, n. 39 (SC, 25, 120). Goscelin, *Lib. conf.*, 2: "the universal Church, and the unique bride of all the elect" — "universalis Ecclesia, et unica universorum electorum sponsa" (Talbot, 54).
10. *In Gen.*: "sanctae Ecclesiae mysticam edisce fecunditatem, moralique intellectu, etc." (PL, CVII, 442 C).
11. "Juxta tropologiam, ut quod historice praecessit in capite, consequenter etiam credatur fieri moraliter in ejus corpore": *De div.*, s. 58, n. 2 (PL, CLXXXIII, 682 C). Cf. Bossuet, *Sermon pour le jour des Rameaux:* "Jesus Christ bears us in himself; we are, if I dare to say so, more his body than is his very own. . . . That which comes about in his divine body is the real figuration of what ought to be accomplished in us" — "Jésus-Christ nous porte en lui-même; nous sommes, si je l'ose dire, plus son corps que son propre corps. . . . Ce qui se fait en son divin corps, c'est la figure réelle de ce qui se doit accomplir en nous."
12. "Omnipotens Deus, qui nec in magnis tenditur, nec in minimis angustatur, sic de tota simul Ecclesia loquitur, ac si de una anima loquatur; et saepe quod ab eo de una anima dicitur, nil obstat si de tota simul Ecclesia intelligitur": *In Ez.*, Bk. II, h. 2, n. 15 (PL, LXXVI, 957 BC); picked up by Autpert, *In Ap.*, Bk. X (639 H). Rabanus, *In Ez.*, Bk. XIV (PL, CX, 982 C). Jerome, *In Gal.*, Bk. II, c. iv: "For whatever the Wisdom of God has furnished to the whole human race as to one Son, is always granted in his own time and dispensation to each of the saints" — "Quaecumque enim toto generi humano Sapientia Dei quasi uni Filio

praestitit, haec eadem unicuique sanctorum semper suo ordine et dispensatione largita est" (XXVI, 376 AB). Richard, *In Cant.*, prol.: "The coming of the Lord in this time is awaited from the voice of the Church generally so that each soul . . . may especially catch sight of God's entry into its own heart" — "Sic autem generaliter ex voce Ecclesiae adventus Domini in hoc tempore praestolatur, ut etiam specialiter unaquaeque anima ingressum Dei ad cor suum . . . conspiciat" (CXCVI, 409 D).

13. ". . . His igitur figurata expositione transcursis, jam nunc inferenda sunt quae moraliter sentiuntur, ut, figura Ecclesiae cognita, quam expressam generaliter credimus, audiamus etiam quid ex his verbis in singulis specialiter colligamus": *Mor.*, Bk. XXVI, c. xlii, n. 77 (PL, LXXVI, 394 B). On the solidarity of the two interpretations: William of Saint Thierry, *Exp. alt. in Cant.* (CLXXX, 476 A). Cf. Greg., *Mor.*, Bk. XXIX, c. xiv, n. 26: "If we shift our eyes for a moment from the common and public good, and look at what it is doing hiddenly in each of us" — "Si a bono communi ac publico parumper oculos flectimus et quid in singulis nobis latenter agat intuemur" (LXXVI, 491 C).

14. "Tout ce qui arrive à l'Église, arrive aussi à chaque chrétien en particulier": Brunschvicg, 209.

15. "Habet etiam unusquisque nostrum in bonis operibus et recta vita distinctos istos sex dies, post quos debet quietem sperare": *De Gen. c. Man.*, Bk. I, c. xxv, n. 43 (PL, XXXIV, 193-4).

16. "Christi et Ecclesiae laudes, et sacri amoris gratiam, et aeterni connubii sacramenta": *In Cant.*, s. 1, n. 8 (PL, CLXXXIII, 788 B).

17. Cassiodorus, *In psalt.*, praef.: "quae liber ille divinus mystica praedicatione complectitur" (PL, LXX, 24 A).

18. "Ego Ecclesia, ego sponsa"; "Ecclesia, quae loquitur"; "Videtur autem Ecclesia describi a Christo"; "Sponsa, id est Ecclesia," etc.: *In Cant.*, h. 1, n. 7; h. 2, n. 3; cf. h. 1, n. 2 (SC, 37, 74, 84, 63-4). *In Cant.*, Bk. I (96); Bk. II: "The bride who is speaking takes the person of the Church gathered from among the Gentiles" — "Haec sponsa quae loquitur, Ecclesiae personam tenet ex gentilibus congregatae" (113; cf. 116-9, 142, 155, 160-2); Bk. III (176, 201, 204). "According to the order of the exposition set out, Christ is to be understood as saying this about the Church" — "Secundum propositae expositionis ordinem, Christus haec de Ecclesia loqui intelligendus est" (PG, XIII, 149 B).

19. *In Ex.*, h. 9, n. 3-4 (237-44), etc. Cf. P.V., RB 68, 300.

20. Or., *In Gen.*, h. 10, n. 5 (99). Ambrose, *In ps. CXVIII*, s. 6, n. 8: "The soul of a just person is the bride of the Word" — "Anima justi est sponsa Verbi" (PL, XV, 1270 B); *Ep.* 45, n. 4: "it expresses the mysteries either of the soul and the Word, or of Christ and the Church" — "mysteria exprimit vel animae et Verbi, vel Christi et Ecclesiae" (XVI, 1142 C); etc. Meanwhile, e.g., Bernard, *In Cant.*, s. 75, n. 2: "Christ the bridegroom" — "Christus sponsus" (CLXXXIII, 1145 B). Adam Scot., *Ad viros rel.*, 2.13: "Groom and bride, Christ and the soul" — "Sponsus et sponsa, Christus et anima" (Fr. Petit, 233).

21. *In Cant.* (7, 18, 29, 31, 59, 66, 88-90, 133).

22. "Internam, jucundam et mundam": S. 45, c. vi (PL, CXCVIII, 414 C).

23. *De st. domus Dei*, Bk. II (493 CD).

24. Cf. E. De Bruyne, III, 31-2. The duality noted by the author nonetheless exists.

25. *Tr. de seminibus scripturarum* (on Apoc. 12:1); Fr. Pelster, *Liber floridus* (1950), 350; Joachim of Flora (?). Thus already in Paschasius (PL, CXX, 106 C). Godfrey of Admont, *h. dom.* 4, on the Cant.: "though it can be referred to the holy Church and to each and every faithful soul, it nevertheless also especially belongs to the one through which the salvation of the world appeared to believers" — "licet ad sanctam Ecclesiam et ad unamquamque fidelem animam referri valeat, specialiter tamen et convenit, per quam salus mundi credentibus apparuit" (CLXXIV, 37 AB). Cf. P. Lombard, *In ps. XLIV,* v. 20 (CXCI, 446 D). Alan of Lille, *In Cant.:* "Specialissime" (CCX, 53 B).

26. *Opusc.* 7 (first half of the 11th cent.; PL, CXLII, 814 BC).

27. "De incarnatione Domini." Title of the work: *In cantica cant. de incarnatione Domini commentaria* (PL, CLXVIII); *prol.* (837-8); Bk. I: "Let him kiss me with the kiss of his mouth. What eye has seen this? Into the heart of which human being does this arise? Yet to thee, O Mary, has he revealed himself, the one kissing, the kiss, and the mouth of the one kissing" — "Osculetur me osculo oris sui. Quis oculus hoc vidit? Cujus in cor hominis ascendit? Tibi autem, o Maria, semetipsum revelavit et osculans, et osculum, et os osculantis" (840 A). Petrus Cellensis, *s.* 72: "My dove is one, . . . the virgin of whom I conjoin the marriage of divine and human nature" — "Una est columba mea, . . . virgo de qua divinae et humanae naturae matrimonium conjungo" (CCII, 863 CD). Philip of Harvengt, *Comm. in Cant.,* Bk. I (CCIII, 187-246). Cf. Aug., *In ps. XLIV,* n. 9 (CCL, 38, 495).

28. Thus Honorius, *Sigillum B. Mariae* (PL, CLXXII, 499 D). Cf. *Meditation on the Church,* ch. XI, on the commentaries on the Canticle up to 1200: F. Ohly, *Hohelied-Studien* . . . (1958); cf. RB 68, 299-300.

29. "Ecclesia, vel quaelibet fidelis anima": Nearly so: Greg., *In Ez.,* Bk. II, h. 4, n. 15 (PL, LXXVI, 982 A). Aimon, *In Sophon.* (CXVII, 210 D). *Vitis myst.,* c. iii, n. 10 (CLXXXIV, 643 B). Gerhoh, *De laude fidei* (*Op. in.*, I, 55); etc. Cf. Or., *In Cant.,* Bk. III (CLXXXI, 185, etc.).

30. "Universalis Ecclesia, simul et singularis anima dilecta": Arno of Reichersberg, *Apol.:* "Hence he deigned to call 'bride' both the universal Church as well as any single soul beloved to him and loving him" — "Unde et universam Ecclesiam, simul et singularem quamlibet sibi dilectam seque diligentem animam, sponsam vocare dignatus est" (Wéribert, 8).

31. "Omnis Ecclesia et unaquaeque anima sancta": Bede, *In Cant.* (PL, XCI, 1215 A; cf. 1105 D, 1106 D; 1109 B, 1123 A, 1198 B); *In Luc.* (XCII, 347 B). Raoul of Saint Germer, *In Lev.,* Bk. V, c. 1 (91 H). G. Foliot, *In Cant.* (PL, CCII, 1183 C, 1220 B); *ep.* 212 (pref. to the comm. on Cant.; *Ep.,* t. I, J. A. Gilles, 304).

32. "Ecclesia, seu anima diligens Deum": Bernard, *In Cant.,* s. 29, n. 7 (PL, CLXXXIII, 932 B); etc.

33. "Possumus haec referre ad Ecclesiam, vel ad sancti viri animam": *In Is.,* Bk. XVII, c. lxiv (PL, XXIV, 626 C); *In Ez.,* Bk. XII: "(Hoc) nos ad Christum referimus Ecclesiam et quotidie in sanctis ejus aedificari cernimus" (XXV, 375 C).

34. "Haec quae de Ecclesia dicta sunt, unusquisque nostrum ad se referre potest": *In ps. XLIV* (PL, XXI, 824 D).

35. "Quod generaliter de cuncta Ecclesia diximus, nunc specialiter de

unaquaque anima sentiamus": *In Cant.* (PL, LXXIX, 479 B; cf. 481 C, 488 B). Robert of Tombelaine, *In Cant.* (LXXIX, 498 A, 504 A, 513 D, 540 C, 546 C).

36. Rabanus, *In Ex.:* "Hence not only to the Church of all generally, but also specifically to each of her members" — "Unde non solum omnium generaliter Ecclesiae, verum etiam specialiter unicuique membrorum ejus" (PL, CVIII, 178 A).

37. "Nisi quod Ecclesiae nomine non una anima, sed multarum unitas, vel potius unanimitas designatur": *In Cant.*, s. 61, n. 2 (PL, CLXXXIII, 1071 C).

38. "Sancta Ecclesia, sive anima secundum sensum moralem devota": *Ad viros rel.*, s. 7, s. 5 (Petit, 187, 169); *De trip. tab.*, P. III, c. i; n. 138: "Just as in part I am showing how these things . . . regard all the sons of the holy Church in allegory . . . , so too shall I show how they pertain to them individually in tropology" — "Sicut ex parte ostendi quomodo haec . . . in allegoria ad universos sanctae Ecclesiae spectent filios . . . , sic etiam ostendam quomodo et in tropologia ad singulos pertineant" (PL, CXCVIII, 743 B).

39. "Tunc historialiter, hodie spiritualiter": Adam Scotus, *Trip. tab.*, *proem.*, c. xx (PL, CXCVIII, 622 D).

40. Greg., *In Ez.*, Bk. I, h. 12, n. 21: "We know that that siege by which the city of Jerusalem was destroyed has already happened; but now let us ask about another, inner siege, which is being undertaken every day" — "Illam itaque obsidionem qua Jeresolymorum civitas destructa est, jam factam novimus; sed nunc aliam intrinsecus, quae quotidie agitur, requiramus" (PL, LXXCI, 929 A); n. 33: "si ad historiam . . . , si ad mysterium quod quotidie erga uniuscjusque animam a doctore agitur" (934 B).

41. "Praesens lectio secundum historiam quidem semel opere completa est, sed secundum spiritalem sensum quotidie impletur": Ps.-Anselm, h. 13 (PL, CLVIII, 660 B).

42. Or., *In Ex.*, h. 5, n. 5: "In this way, then, we can even today see the Egyptians dead and lying on the shore" — "Hoc ergo modo possumus etiam hodie Aegyptios videre mortuos et jacentes ad litus" (191); h. 7, n. 2: "For the world is figurally called 'Egypt'" — "Aegyptus namque mundus figuraliter appellatur" (207). Ps.-Remi, *In ps. CXIII*: "For that which was prefigured there once is fulfilled in each believer at the end of the age by means of the Church's daily mournings; for Israel departs from Egypt daily, when one of the faithful spiritually departs from this world; hence Paul. . . ." — "Quod enim semel illic praefiguratum est, hoc in isto fine saeculi quotidianis Ecclesiae fletibus in unoquoque credente completur; quotidie enim exit Israël de Aegypto, cum fidelis spirtualiter exit de hoc mundo; unde Paulus . . ." (PL, CXXXI, 721 A). Peter Damian, *opusc.* 3: "for the commandments of the law are truly fulfilled just when they come about in accordance with the spiritual understanding for which they have been instituted" — "tunc enim mandata legalia veraciter adimplentur, cum juxta spiritualem intelligentiam ad quam instituta sunt, fiunt" (CXLV, 60 B); *op.* 32, c. ii (547 A).

43. Jerome, *In Is.*: "Whatever is promised carnally to the people of Israel we show to have been fulfilled spiritually in us and to be fulfilled today" — "Quidquid populo Israël carnaliter repromittitur, in nobis spirtualiter completum esse monstramus, hodieque compleri" (PL, XXIV, 865 D). Cf. Cassian, *Coll.* 10, c. xi (SC, 42, 50).

44. Or., *In Ex.*, h. 6, n. 6: "Indeed even today the earth swallows up the impious: or does it not seem to you that he who is always thinking about the earth is swallowed up by the earth?" — "Impios quidem et hodie devorat terra: aut non tibi videtur terra devorari ille qui semper de terra cogitat?" (197). Richard, *In ps. II* (PL, CXCVI, 265-6).

45. *S. in dom. palm.* (PL, CLXXXIV, 870 C). Jerome, *In Amos*, Bk. III, c. ix (XXV, 1090 B); *In Zach.* (1514 B). [Cf. Matt. 21:1; Luke 19:21.]

46. "Dominus in carne veniens visitavit nos: quod et moraliter quotidie evenire cernimus": Hugo of Fouilloy, *De claustro an.*, Bk. I, c. xvi (PL, CLXXVI, 1046 AB).

47. "Quotidie in devotis venit": Richard, *In Cant.*, c. xxxii (PL, CXCVI, 495 C). Cf. Garnier, s. 8, citing Gal. 4:19 (CCV, 627 A). Paschasius, *In Matt.* (CXX, 818 D, 819 C); etc.

48. Cf. Bernard, *De adv.*, s. 3, n. 4: the first advent was "to humans" — "ad homines," the second "into humans" — "in homines" (PL, CLXXXIII, 45 AB).

49. "Quidquid vero vel sub historia, vel sub allegoria, sive sub tropologia docetur, causa hujus pacti, id est, nostrae restaurationis edocetur": Garnier, s. 34 (PL, CCV, 790 A).

50. "In sanguine Christi circumcisio universorum celebrata est, et in illius cruce omnes simul crucifixi, . . . et consepulti in ejus sepulcro": Ambrose, *Ep.* 72 (PL, XVI, 1246 A).

51. "Quidquid igitur gestum est in cruce Christi, in sepultura, in resurrectione tertia die, in ascensione in caelum, et sede ad dexteram Patris, ita gestum est, ut his rebus non mystice tantum dictis sed etiam gestis configuraretur vita christiana, quae hic geritur": Alcuin, *De fide s. Trin.*, Bk. III, c. xvii (PL, CI, 49 D; following Augustine); he cites Gal. 5:24; Rom. 6:4; Col. 3:1. Leidrad, *De sacr. bapt.*, c. vii: "The Psalmist says, 'Just as ointment on the head. . . .' Hence that anointing about which we read in the Old Testament is a figure of the anointing which has truly been completed in Christ and is daily being fulfilled in his members" — "Psalmista ait: Sicut unguentum in capite. . . . Hujus ergo unctionis quae in Christo veraciter completa est, et in membris ejus quotidie impletur, figura exstitit unctio illa, de qua in V. T. legimus . . ." (XCIX, 864 A). Cf. K. Barth, *Dogmatik*, t. IV, 1, 608-13: The history of Jesus Christ, his death and his resurrection, is just like our most intimate history (summarized by H. Bouillard, *Karl Barth*, II, 1957, ch. 1).

52. "Ad interiora": Greg. *In Ez.*, Bk. II, h. 8, n. 3: "When they preach the mysteries of the heavenly kingdom to the already proficient, they lead us inside through the subtler meaning" — "Cum jam proficientibus caelestis regni mysteria praedicant, per subtiliorem sensum nos ad interiora perducunt" (PL, LXXVI, 1029 C).

53. "Secundum interiorem hominem": Or., *In Num.*, h. 11, n. 7 (89).

54. *Tr. de inter. homine*, c. i, n. 2: "For the soul that has God within it is God's temple, in which the divine mysteries are being celebrated" — "Anima enim Deum habens in se, templum Dei est, in quo divina mysteria celebrantur" (PL, CLXXXIV, 509 D).

55. "Quid est autem praeparatio nuptiarum, nisi sanctarum expositio Scripturarum?": Bruno of Segni, *In Matt.*, P. IV, c. xxii (PL, CLXV, 252 C). Rupert,

In Gen., Bk. VII, c. ii: to open the Scriptures is to accede to the nuptial union: "Isaac led Rebecca into this tent and took her to wife, that is, once their minds had been opened, Christ sent the spiritual understanding of the Scriptures and instituted a new Church for himself" — "in hoc tabernaculum introduxit Isaac Rebeccam, et accepit uxorem, id est, apertis illorum sensibus, immisit Christus spiritualem Scripturarum intellectum et novam sibi instituit Ecclesiam" (PL, CLXVII, 447 C). See above, Chapter 5.4 (on Cana).

56. "L'Écriture n'est qu'Écriture. Ma consolation est l'essence,
    Et que Dieu dise en moi sa Parole d'éternité."
    Le Pélerin chérubinique, II, 137.

Cf. Gerson, texts analyzed by A. Combes, *Essai sur la critique de Ruysbroeck par Gerson*, t. 3, 162-73.

57. *Création relig. et pensée contemplative* (1950), 162: "distique qu'un catholique n'accepterait point, mais qu'un protestant contemporain de Silesius ne pouvait regarder qu'avec une entière hostilité. Il est difficile de pousser plus loin, et d'ailleurs d'exprimer plus magnifiquement en si peu de mots, la doctrine de l'illumination intérieure." [This is a "distich that a Catholic would not at all accept, but which a Protestant contemporary of Silesius could only consider with complete hostility. It is difficult to push any further and yet to express more magnificently in so few words this doctrine of interior illumination."]

58. Bk. III, 227. J. Tarracó, "Angelus Silesius y la mistica española," *Anal. Sacra tarraconensia* 29 (1956), 95-114.

59. *In Amos*: "though according to tropology the divine word is born of the virginal soul every day" — "licet secundum tropologiam quotidie de anima virginali nascatur sermo divina" (PL, XXV, 1090 B).

60. "Nativitas aeternitatis," "nativitas temporalis," "nativitas mysterialis" — "toties enim nascitur Christus, quoties fit aliquis christianus": S. 5 (PL, CCXII, 523 A). This "always" of the Catholic tradition, this "etiam nunc," this "quotidie" could never be opposed as though favoring a contradiction to the "once and for all" of the Epistle to the Hebrews.

61. "Donec occurramus omnes in virum perfectum, in mensuram aetatis plenitudinis Christi": *De Jesu puero duod.*, I, c. iv (A. Hoste — J. Dubois, SC, 60, 56). [Trans. note: Cf. Vulgate Eph. 4:13.]

62. "Interioris hominis sacramentum": *Enchirid.*, c. xiv, n. 53 (J. Rivière, 98).

63. *C. Cels.*, Bk. IV, c. vi (278). *In Cant.*, h. 2: "Non solum autem in Maria ab umbra ejus nativitas coepit, sed et in te, si dignus fueris, nascitur sermo Dei" (SC, 37, 91).

64. *In Jer.*, h. 6: "I shall also speak of the daily birth of our Savior" — "etiam de Salvatoris nostri quotidiana nativitate dicam"; "Quid mihi enim prodest si descendat (Verbum) in mundum, et ego ipsum non habeam?" (PL, XXV, 637 A, 632 C). Same point, *In Jos.*, h. 26, n. 2: "What good would it be to have left Egypt by baptism, if this were merely to carry the opprobrium of Egypt with him? What good would it be even to have crossed the desert, i.e., to have rejected the world, if this meant to keep the stains of ancient vices?" (459). Cf. *In Num.*, h. 3, n. 1 (14).

65. "Si autem et in alicujus corde non cecidit civitas confusionis, huic Christus necdum advenit": *In Jer.*, h. 21, n. 11 (PG, XIII, 540 CD).

66. Or., *In Matt.*, ser. 38 (73-4).

67. "Sunt enim quibus nondum natus est Christus": *De div.*, s. 44, n. 1 (PL, CLXXXIII, 666 AB). Cf. *In vig. nat.*, s. 6, n. 10 (114 AC). Against a persistent misunderstanding, it is necessary to say once again: in speaking of this "birth" in the Christian soul, i.e., in developing the third sense of Scripture, mystical tropology, neither St. Bernard nor Origen, nor any of the spiritual authors cited here minimizes the unique fact of the Incarnation to even the slightest degree! None of them either says or lets one understand by anything that he says that the Incarnation might be "merely an important stage in the long process of God's strategy of making himself known to human beings, . . . followed by other more important stages of the process" (Hanson, *op. cit.*, 354-5)! It is exactly the other way around. The fact of the Incarnation is by so much the more magnified and shown to be unique above every other fact, that its fruit is shown off all the better. Only an anti-mystical (that is to say, anti-Catholic) prejudice explains such a misunderstanding.

68. *Paul Claudel interroge l'Apoc.*, 305: ". . . Alors . . . ce n'est plus nous qui agissons, ce sont ces paroles introduites qui agissent en nous, dégageant l'esprit dont elles sont faites, ce qui était inclus en elles de sens et de sonorité, et qui véritablement deviennent esprit et vie, et de mots motifs. Elles se font une place au travers de notre arrangement mental, il y a en elles une certaine force irrésistible d'autorité et d'ordre. Mais elles ont cessé d'être extérieures, elles sont devenues nous-mêmes. *Et le Verbe s'est fait chair, et Il a habité en nous: in nobis*, il faut comprendre toute la force happante, appropriatrice, de ces deux mots." Cf. Ps.-Ambrose, *s.* 52 (PL, XVII, 710 A).

69. Greg., *Ep.*, Bk. V, 46 (*Gr. Reg.*, I, 345-6).

70. Bernard, *De div.*, s. 5, n. 1: "Semel locutus est Deus, sed continua et perpetua locutio est" (PL, CLXXXIII, 554 C).

71. Philip of Harvengt, *De dignit. cler.*, c. 6: "While he enjoined them to do deeds in the flesh, he foretold those that were to be fulfilled spiritually in us, and the real history of that time has been made into our prophecy" — "Dum illis agere quae carnalia sunt indixit, quae spiritualiter in nobis implenda erant praedixit, et illius temporis realis historia, nostra facta est prophetia" (PL, CCIII, 675 A).

72. St. Benedict, *Reg. mon.*, 73. Later on, in Chapter 17, one will see how this ought rightly to be understood.

73. Greg., *In Ez.*, Bk. II, h. 5, n. 3 (PL, LXXVI, 986 B). Cf. *Mor.*, Bk. XXIII, c. xix, n. 34 (271-2).

74. Greg., *In Ez.*, Bk. I, h. 7, n. 17: "In the darkness of the present life this Scripture has become for us a light for the journey" — "Haec nobis Scriptura in tenebris vitae praesentis, facta est lumen itineris" (cites 2 Peter 1:19; Ps. 118:105; Ps. 17:29; PL, LXXVI, 848 C). Berengaud, *In Ap.*, v. 4: "Scripture . . . without whose light we are unable in the night of this age to traverse the paths of righteousness" — "Scripturam . . . sine cujus lumine in nocte hujus saeculi per vias rectitudinis incedere non valemus" (XVII, 875 B). Cf. 10th cent. catechesis: "Scripture, the light of the just" — "Scriptura, lumen justorum" (Wilmart, 42).

75. Alcuin, *Ep.* 232 (PL, C, 510 D).

76. Greg., *In Ez.*, Bk. I, h. 10, n. 5: "And since our weakness is not enough to grasp the words of heaven, he himself feeds us who proportions a measure of

wheat for us in time, [considering] to what extent we may be nourished by the food through the grace of divine dispensation: while today we understand in the sacred word what we did not know yesterday, we may also comprehend tomorrow what we do not know today" — "Et quia ad capienda verba caelestia idonea nostra infirmitas non est, ipse nos cibat, qui nobis in tempore mensuram tritici temperat, quatenus in sacro verbo dum hodie intelligimus quod hesterno die nesciebamus, cras quoque comprehendamus quod hodie nescimus, per divinae dispensationis gratiam alimento nutriamur" (PL, LXXVI, 887 C).

77. Angelome, *In Reg.*, Bk. II, c. ix (PL, CXV, 359-60).

78. Rabanus, *In I Mach.* (PL, CIX, 1160 B). Claudius, *In Reg.*, Bk. III (L, 1155 A). Odo, *Collat.*, Bk. III, c. xliii (CXXXIII, 627 D).

79. Rupert, *De div. off.*, Bk. VIII, c. viii (PL, CLXX, 225-6).

80. Gerhoh, *In ps.* (PL, CXCIV, 997 B): "therefore, since holy Scripture as a whole is the book of the wars of the Lord" — "cum ergo sacra Scriptura tota sit liber bellorum Domini." Cf. Jerome, *In Is.*, Bk. II, c. v, 13: "History reports . . . that these things have happened to the Jewish people literally, and that they are being experienced today spiritually, too" — "Haec juxta litteram accidisse populo Judaeorum . . . narrat historia, quod quidem et spiritualiter hodie quoque patiuntur" (XXIV, 83 A). Or., *In Jer.*, h. 6 (XXV, 633 C), etc.

81. Oger of Locedio, *s.* 1, n. 1 (PL, CLXXXIV, 880 D). Aelred, numerous passages (PL, CXCV). Rabanus, *In Gen.*: "Having been sufficiently instructed in moral understanding, consider, through the wandering of the patriarchs from place to place, our own pilgrimage in this world" — "Moralique intellectu sufficienter instructus, per patriarcharum de loco in locum transmigrationem, nostram in hoc mundo considera peregrinationem" (CVII, 442 C); etc.

82. Greg., *In Ez.*, Bk. II, h. 3, n. 20: "Our whole defense is contained in the sacred eloquence" — "Universa nostra munitio in sacro eloquio continetur" (PL, LXVI, 968 C). Goscelin, *L. conf.*, 3: "Set your heart to the understanding of the Scriptures, which also contain the mystery of the Church and of the spiritual wars in various dark sayings" — "Pone cor tuum ad intelligentiam Scripturarum, quae et Ecclesiae spiritualiumque bellorum in variis aenigmatibus continent mysterium" (Talbot, 80). Bruno of Segni, *In Ap.* (CLXV, 634 B).

83. Or., *In Jo.*, Bk. XX, c. x (337-9).

84. Cf. Or., *In Num.* Jerome, to Fabiola, on the forty-two stations of the Hebrews in the desert: *Ep.* 78 (4, 52-92). Irenaeus, *Adv. Haer.*, Bk. IV, c. xxx, n. 1: "The departure (from Egypt) is typical, ours is the true departure" — "Typica profectio (ex Aegypto), vera nostra profectio" (PG, VII, 1064 C). Peter Damian, *op.* 32, c. ii (PL, CXLV, 546-7).

85. Ambrose, *Ep.* 49, n. 3 (PL, XVI, 1154 B). Gerhoh, *Exp. sup. canonem*: Scripture, earthly paradise and kingdom of God (*Op. in.*, I, 23). [Trans. note: Here the word 'garden' recalls the Garden of Eden; de Lubac himself uses the French "le Paradise." This word, of Iranian origin (see *Oxford English Dictionary*, s.v. 'paradise'), means a pleasure garden. It was transliterated into Greek (Kittel, *Theological Dictionary of the New Testament*, V, 765-73, s.v. *paradeisos*) and Hebrew (Brown-Driver-Briggs, 825b, s.v. *pardês*). The modern Persian equivalent is *firdaus* (F. Steingass, *A Comprehensive Persian-English Dictionary*, 917b. De Lubac here

seems to be using the word with the full range of its semantic overtones, to express both earthly and heavenly delight.]

86. *De Isaac et an.*, c. iv, n. 29 (PL, XIV, 513 A).

87. "In eo quod in Scripturis intelligis caritas patet, et in eo quod non intelligis caritas latet": *S. de laude caritatis* (Eugippius, *Thes.*, c. ccclii: PL, LXII, 1086 AB); "so he who holds charity in his conduct grasps both what is plain and what is hidden in the divine words" — "ille itaque tenet et quod patet et quod latet in divinis sermonibus, qui caritatem tenet in moribus." *S.* May 14, n. 1: "Omnis enim pagina, quaecumque aperitur, hanc sonat" (Morin, 1930, 292). *In ps. CXXXVIII*, n. 31: "Conficit nobis potionem ad amorem suum quibusdam miris modis" (PL, XXXVII, 1803). Cf. Rabanus, *In Reg.*, Bk. III, c. vii (CIX, 169 A). Angelome, *In Reg.* (CXV, 440 C); etc. Cf. Pascal: "Tout ce qui ne va pas à la charité est figure."

88. "Nihil nobiscum agunt, nisi ut diligamus . . .": Aug., *De musica*, Bk. VI, c. xiv, n. 43 (Thonnard, 450); *In ps. CIII, s. 1*, n. 9 (CCL, 40, 1482-3). Cf. Or., *In Matt.* ser. 4 (7-9).

89. *In Ez.*, Bk. I, h. 10, n. 14 (PL, LXXVI, 891 B); *Mor.*, Bk. XX, c. ix, n. 20 (149 BC).

90. "Ad aedificationem caritatis": Aug., *In ps. CXL*, n. 2: "[Charity] is hidden wherever there is anything obscure in Scripture; it is revealed wherever there is anything plain" — "Quidquid obscurum est in Scriptura, haec (caritas) ibi occulta est; quidquid ibi planum est, haec ibi aperta est" (PL, XXXVII, 1816).

91. Rabanus, *In Ex.*, Bk. III, c. xiv: "the superior understanding, i.e., the one gleaming with gospel charity" — "superior intellectus, id est, evangelica caritate praefulgidus" (PL, CVIII, 173 C). Bede, *Hexaem.*, Bk. IV: "And let no one ever think he has understood Scripture rightly [in a passage] in which he was unable to find instruction in charity" — "Neque ullateneus se Scripturam recte intellexisse quisquam putet, in qua institutionem caritatis invenire non potuit" (XCI, 168 CD). Rabanus, *Cler. inst.*, Bk. III, c. iv (CVII, 381 A). Odorannus, *Opusc.* 3 (CXLII, 803 B). Bernard, *In Cant.*, s. 51, n. 4: "charity which the Scriptures must serve" — "caritas cui Scripturas servire oportet" (CLXXXIII, 1027 A). Honorius, *Scala caeli major*, c. ii (CLXXII, 1231 A). Adam Scotus, s. 3, n. 1 (CXCVIII, 107 A). John of Salisbury, *Polycr.*, Bk. VII, c. xi (CXCIX, 661 AD). Martin of Leon, s. 2 in dedic. (CCIX, 81 C). *Lib. de paenitentia*, c. xi (CCXIII, 875 AB); etc.

92. "Mira atque ineffabilis sacri eloquii virtus agnoscitur, cum supremo amore animus penetratur": *In Ez.*, Bk. I, c. vii, n. 8 (PL, LXXVI, 844 B).

93. James 1:23.

94. C. X (Cohn-Wendland, 6, 67).

95. *In ps. CIII, s. 1,* n. 4: "He set his Scripture before you as a mirror" — "Posuit tibi speculum Scripturam suam" (PL, XXXVII, 1338); *In ps. CXXIII,* n. 3: "you are studying yourselves as in the mirror of the Scriptures" — "tanquam in speculo Scripturarum vos ipsos attendatis" (1641); s. 49, n. 5: "Let Scripture be like a mirror for you" — "Scriptura sit tibi tanquam speculum" (XXXVIII, 322-3); etc.

96. *Mor.*, Bk. II, n. 1 (PL, LXXV, 553 D).

97. Bruno of Segni, *In Is.* (*Sp. cas.*, 3, 13). Abelard, *Ep.* 8 (PL, CLXXVIII, 306 A). Ps.-Hugo, *In reg. S. Aug.*, c. xii (CLXX, 924 AB). *Instr. sacerdotis*, P. II, c. xi, n. 28 (CLXXXIV, 788 BC). Petrus Cellensis, s. 13 (CCII, 677 C). Gaufrid of Sainte-Barbare, *Ep.* 43 (CCV, 875 C). Absalon, s. 22 (CCXI, 137 A). Peter Lombard, *s. in caena Dom.* (CLXXI, 515 BC). Adam of Perseigne, *Ep.* 30, 2 (Bouvet, 255-6). Alcuin,

L. de virt., c. v (PL, CI, 616 CD). John of Fecamp (Leclerq, L'amour des lettres, 59-60); etc. Cf. R. Bradley, "Backgrounds of the title Speculum in med." (Speculum, 1954, 110-5).

98. Ps.-Hugo, Spec., c. viii (PL, CLXXVII, 374 B).

99. Bernard, De div., s. 24, n. 2: "finally it is also our food, and sword, and medicine, and strength, and rest, as well as our resurrection and consummation. . . . For a living and effective word, an examiner of hearts and of thoughts, is tearing through and judging all the secrets of the heart" — "denique et cibus noster est, et gladius, et medicina, et confirmatio, et requies, resurrec[t]io quoque et consummatio nostra. . . . Omnia namque cordis secreta rimatur atque dijudicat sermo vivus et efficax, cordum atque cogitationum perscrutator" (PL, CLXXXIII, 604 A).

100. Bernard, In Cant., s. 3, n. 1: "Today we are reading in the book of experience; turn back to yourselves and let each one look to his own conscience upon the things that are to be said" — "Hodie legimus in libro experientiae; convertimini ad vos ipsos, et attendat unusquisque conscientiam suam super his quae dicenda sunt" (PL, CLXXXIII, 794 A). S. 1, n. 11 (789 C). S. 57, n. 5 (1052 B). S. 31, n. 5 appeals to the "propria experientia" (942 C); etc. De convers., c. iii, n. 4: "Apply your inner hearing, reflect the eyes of the heart, and you will learn by your own experience what may be done" — "Applica intus auditum, reflecte oculos cordis, et proprio disces experimento quid agatur" (CLXXXII, 836 C). "No one knows himself," Edmund Husserl will say, "if he does not read the Bible."

101. Jean Châtillon, Sermons et opusc. inédits de Richard de SV, I (1951), B: "Ce n'est point ici l'homme qui explique l'Écriture, mais l'homme qui se sert de l'Écriture pour s'expliquer, à lui-même afin de se dépasser."

102. "Animae caelesti sponso adhaerentes, in Scripturarum speculo sese percipere debent": Galland of Rigny, Lib. Prov., 135 (J. Châtillon, 87).

103. Bernard, In ps. Qui habitat, s. 7, n. 11: "The way of spiritual understanding . . . is not lacking to you so long as you consult your own experience about this" — "Non vobis deest . . . spiritualis intelligentiae via, dummodo propriam super hoc experientiam consulatis" (PL, CLXXXIII, 206 B).

104. "Experimentum de Verbo": Bernard, In Cant., s. 74, n. 7 (CLXXXIII, 1142 A).

105. *They do not yet understand through experience:* Godfrey of Admont, H. dom. 24: "He hears or reads the word of the Lord as many well instructed in literary studies coming from the world read and understand the Scriptures, but they do not yet understand through experience" — "Audit quidem vel legit verbum Domini, sicut multi de saeculo venientes, litterarum studiis bene instructi, legunt Scripturas et intelligunt, sed per experientiam nondum intelligunt" (PL, CLXXIV, 161 A).

106. Alexander Neckam, De nat. rer., Bk. II, c. cliv: Scripture is a mirror; "but, marvel to behold, take away the lead holding up the glass and no image of the beholder will be reflected; take away the foundation of faith, and you will no longer see yourself clearly in holy Scripture" — "sed, mira res, subtrahe plumbum suppositum vitro, jam nulla resultabit imago inspicientis; subtrahe fundamentum fidei, jam teipsum in sacra Scriptura non videbis dilucide" (239).

107. Greg., In Ez., Bk. II, h. 1, n. 14: "Holy Scripture can be understood as a

measuring rod inasmuch as anyone who reads it measures himself in it, either to the extent that he is advancing in spiritual virtue or inasmuch as he has remained far separated from the goods that have been enjoined" — "Potest etiam calamus mensurae Scriptura sacra pro eo intelligi, quod quisque hanc legit, in ea semetipsum metitur, vel quantum in spirituali virtute proficit, vel quantum a bonis quae praecepta sunt longe disjunctus remansit" (PL, LXXVI, 945 A).

108. Or., *In Gen.*, h. 12, n. 5: "When you take the book of the Scriptures, you may also begin to advance an understanding from the proper meaning, and try also to drink from the fountain of your own wit according to what you have learned in the Church" — "Cum apprehenderis librum Scripturarum, incipias etiam ex proprio sensu proferre aliquem intellectum, et secundum ea quae in Ecclesia didicisti, tenta et tu bibere de fonte ingenii tui" (112). *In Cant.*, Bk. III (206). This will become a commonplace. Cf. this "Prayer before the reading of holy Scripture," in the notebook of Sister Bonaventure Theresa of Saint John, in the year 1704: "O Jésus . . . , donnez-moi à boire; je vous demand à boire des sources de vos Écritures. . . . Seigneur, donnez-moi de cette eau, . . . qui devienne en moi une fontaine d'eau qui jaillisse jusque dans la vie éternelle."

109. "Bibe aquam de tuis vasis et de tuis puteis": Isidore, *L. de var. q.*, c. l, n. 1 (145). Cf. Or., *In Num.*, h. 12, n. 1 (94-6). Following a profound expression of St. Odo of Cluny, he who meditates upon Scripture not only makes a place for the Lord within himself: he discovers this place in it. *Vita Geraldi*, Bk. I, c. vi: "Ad amorem divinum, vel Scriptu[r]ae sanctae meditationem recurrens, internae mortis ruinam evadebat; illo nimirum Davidico spiritu jam, ut reor, affatus, quo ille fervens non dabat somnum oculis, donec, actionibus divinis exoccupatus, locum Domino in seipso inveniret" (PL, CXXXIII, 646 A). Greg., *Reg. past.*, P. III, c. xxiv, comments on the text in a purely moral sense (LXXVII, 95 C). For Honorius, *In Prov.*, it is an exhortation to avoid the exegeses of heretics (CLXXII, 315 C).

110. Peter of Riga, *Aurora, In Cant.* (Pitra, 2, 163):

"Fons est hic pia mens meditans caelestia: vivos
In se non cessat doctrinae gignere rivos.
Cuilibet ex istis, inquit Scriptura, fluentis,
Hinc erit in vitam fons vivus aquae salientis. . . ."

Notes to Chapter Nine
§3. Monastic Exegesis

1. *In Ez.*, h. 4, n. 4-8 (PG, XIII, 699-704). (Danel has become Daniel.) In their imitators these three men can be contemporaries; all three are one in Christ.

2. G. Folliet, AA, "Les trois catégories de chrétiens," *Augustinus magister* 2 (1954), 6312-44. Fr. Châtillon, "Tria genera hominum . . . ," RMAL 10 (1954), 169-75.

3. "alius est ordo praedicantium, alius continentium, atque alius bonorum conjugum": *In Ez.*, Bk. II, h. 4, n. 5 (PL, LXXVI, 976 AB).

4. *L. de var. q.*, c. lv (166-8).

5. Again, Hildegarde, *Ep.* 48 and 51 (PL, CXCVII, 248 B, 264 C).

Notes to Page 144

6. Cf. this other trio: Abraham designates those who obey faithfully, Isaac those who hope firmly, Jacob those who fight manfully; Adam Scotus, s. 18, c. ii (PL, CXCVIII, 195 B).

7. *L. carolini*, Bk. IV, c. xviii: "In quibus tribus sanctis omnes sanctorum multitudo signatur etc." (PL, XCVIII, 1223 C). *Anon. in Cant., prol.:* "Tres ordines sunt in Ecclesia: Noe, Job, Daniel; Noe doctores, Job conjugati, Daniel contemplativi" (CLXXII, 519 C). Alan of Lille, s. 4 (CCX, 209 AB). Cf. Bede, *In Cant.*, Bk. V (XCI, 1176 C).

8. "Tres bene vivendi distinctiones" or "tres credentium in Christum ordines": Rupert, *In Ez.*, Bk. II, c. xxiii (PL, CLXVII, 1483-4).

9. Fr. Châtillon, *loc. cit.*, 172: "Consacré par la Glose ordinaire," it will take on "chez saint Bonaventure d'imposantes proportions."

10. Paul E. Beichner, *Speculum*, 24, 244. Cf. PL, CLXXI, 1387.

11. 1 Sam. 19:16. Godfrey of Admont, *In Scr.*, h. 6 (PL, CLXXIV, 1095 A); h. 12 (112-3),

12. Bernard, *In vig. nat.*, s. 6, n. 8-9 (PL, CLXXXIII, 113 CD).

13. Isidore, *L. de var. q.*, c. lv: the three kinds of animals of Levit.; the sorts of wood of Lebanon in Isaiah 60:13 (167-8). Godfrey of Admont, *In Scr.*, h. 12: "Per altitudinem caeli vita continentium, per latitudinem terrae vita conjugatorum, per profundum abyssi ordo praelatorum non injuste valet intelligi" (PL, CLXXIV, 112 A). Richard, *L. except.:* the three tabernacles or the three decks of Noah's ark (J. Chatillon, 314, 229). Honorius, *In Cant.:* capilli, dentes, genae (CLXXII, 449 AC); *Sp. Eccl.:* tria tabernacula (853 B).

14. The "conjugati . . . per officium imo jacent": Rabanus, *In Ez.*, Bk. XV (PL, CX, 918-9); according to Greg., *In Ez.*, Bk. II, h. 5, n. 19 (LXXVI, 996 A).

15. "Inter laïcos et monachos medius, quantum est superior inferiore, tantum inferior superiore": Abbo of Fleury (PL, CXXXIX, 464 D).

16. (1) The "operantes in agro," the "ordo conjugatorum," is "infimus"; (2) the "molentes in mola," the "ordo eorum qui bene praesunt," is "medius"; (3) and the "quiescentes in lecto," the "ordo contemplationi vacantium," is "supremus": *In Reg.*, Bk. III, c. x (PL, CLXVII, 1150-1). *In Num.*, Bk. II, c. xxi, enumeration not hierarchized (901 D). Joachim of Flora, *Psalt.* l. 2 (f. 247-55).

17. "Conjugati . . . secundum indulgentiam": Sermon bénéd. (Leclercq, *St. ans.*, 31, 24-5). *Rép. clunis. à Cîteaux* (Leclercq, RB 67, 83 and 88-90). Abbo, *Apol.:* "Conjugii quidem ratio sola indulgentia permittitur" (PL, CXXXIX, 463 BC).

18. "In extremis": Godfrey of Admont, *In Scr.*, h. 12: "quamvis ea quae mundi sunt diligant, tamen, quia legaliter vivunt, et legali connubio utuntur, in extremo per misericordiam Dei salvabuntur" (PL, CLXXXIV, 463 BC).

19. "Conjugati et paenitentes": *L. carolini* (PL, XCVIII, 1223 C).

20. *Sent.*, Bk. VII, c. xix-xxiii (PL, CLXXXVI, 931-9).

21. *De tribus ord. Ecclesiae* (*De div.* 35), n. 1, def. of the conjugati: "fidelis populus terrena licite possidens" (PL, CLXXXIII, 634 BD). Cf. *In vig. nat.*, s. 6, n. 9: "Ecclesia praelatorum, fidelis populus, nostra professio" (113 D).

22. The "fons misericordiae": *In nat. Dom.*, s. 1, n. 7 (PL, CLXXXIII, 118-9). Meanwhile, *De div.*, s. 91, n. 1: "conjugati paenitentes in mundo" (710 D); it is a question of the voices of the heavenly Jerusalem — and the expression cannot be restrictive.

23. R. Puyllen, c. xiii-v (PL, CLXXXVI, 936-9).

24. "Conjugati — continentes — contempativi": Werner, *Defl.*, Bk. II: "Templum (Ecclesia) quod ex lapidibus et cedris et acro construitur (1 Kings 8), quia ex tribus ordinibus, sc. ex conjugatis, ex continentibus et ex contemplativis caeleste aedificium erigitur" (PL, CLVII, 1248 B).

25. "Conjugati — continentes — virgines": Richard, *L. except.*, P. 2, Bk. I, c. xiv (Châtillon, 229).

26. Noah signifies the "praelati"; Daniel signifies the "claustrales"; Job, the "officiales fratres": Bernard, *De div.*, s. 9, n. 3 (PL, CLXXXIII, 566 BC).

27. Odo of Canterbury (Leclercq, 126). Cf. Adam Scotus with regard to David in 1 Sam. 22:14: "Ingrediens prop[t]er novitios, egrediens propter obaedientiales, pergens propter claustrales" (PL, CXCVIII, 195 D). Henry of Marcy, *De per. civ. Dei*, tr. 12 (CCIV, 342-3).

28. The "praelati," the "paenitentes," and the "innocentes": Adam Scotus, *Ad viros rel.*, s. 8 (Petit, 194). Peter Comestor also expounds on the trio of Ez., which he assimilates to the trio of Ps. 79: Ephraim, Benjamin, Manasseh, or "conjugati, praelati, contemplativi," these last being either "claustrales" or "scholares": s. for the Epiph. (PL, CLXXI, 412-3).

29. Honorius, Aelred, *S. ined.* 21 (Talbot, 146-8). Adam Scotus, *De tripl. Eccl. statu* (PL, CXCVIII, 144-5); *De trip. tab.*, Bk. II, c. xix (see Chapter 11 below); etc.

30. Petrus Cellensis, *De disc. claustr.*: "Scripsit sanctus Augustinus . . . de disciplina christiana; scripsi ego . . . de claustrali disciplina" (PL, CCII, 1098).

31. Cf. Bruno of Querfurt (†1009), *V. s. Adalb.*, c. xxvii: "Philosophia Benedicti patris nutritus erat"; etc.

32. "Ad ultimum": Petrus Cellensis, *op. cit.*, c. viii: "Philosophi itaque suam statuerunt disciplinam, Judaei acceperunt suam, christiani suam, et ad ultimum eremitae et claustrales suam" (PL, CCII, 1113 C).

33. (1) The "lex naturae," (2) the "lex litterae," (3) the "lex gratiae," and (4) the "lex regulae": Hervaeus of Villepreux (v. 1180) (Leclercq, *R. Mab.*, 36, 10).

34. Peter Damian, *Op.* 15, c. xxix: "Si quando de saeculari habitu quis ad eremum converti voluerit" (PL, CXLV, 361 CD). *Lib. de modo bene viv.*, c. vi, n. 15: "Necesse est omni converso . . ." (CLXXXII, 1209 B). Aelred, *De temp.*, s. 21 (CXCV, 322 BC). At the time of Cassiodorus, 'conversus' did not yet, at least habitually, designate a monk: A. Van de Vyver, RB 53, 80-3. Cf. Et. Galtier, RHE, 1937.

35. "Saeculares facultates": Frater Boso: "Scriptum est quod monachum solummodo facit conversio vitae prioris et saecularium abjectio facultatum" (H. Rochais, *R. Mab.*, 43, 44).

36. "Conversio": Bernard, *Ep.* 108 (PL, CLXXXII, 249 B); *De div.*, s. 95, n. 2: "Cum aliqui simpli[e]s ad conversionem veniunt, severitatem regulae expavescunt" (CLXXXIII, 719 C). Geoffrey of Auxerre, *In f. S. Bern.*: "ad monasticam religionem conversus" (Leclercq, *Etudes*, 1953, 158). Sometimes the "laicorum conversio" is the taking of the cross for the crusade: Henry of Marcy, *Ep.* 31 (PL, CCIV, 204, 247 B). Cf. Congar, *St. ans.*, 43, 89.

37. "Morum conversio": Cf. Julian of Vézelay, s. 21: "Tria quae teste Deo juravimus observare, obedientiam regularem, morum conversionum, et in loco finetenus stabilitatem" (M. Lebreton, *St. ans.*, 37, 133). Anselm, *Ep.*, Bk. II, 52 (PL,

CLVIII, 1206-7). When Othloh wrote, *De tentat. suis.*, P. 2: "Postquam in sanctum Emmerani caenobium ad conversionem veni" (CXLVI, 57 B), the context indicated again a sense more moral than institutional. For other formulations: "emendation morum," "conversatio morum": see M. Rothenhausler, "Zur Aufnahmeordung der Re. S. Benedicti," in Hd. Herwegen, *B. zur Gesch. des alten Münschtums* . . . , III, 1, 20-82.

38. "Ad conversionem venire": Gilbert, *Ep.* 2, n. 2, to Adam, who was deferring his entry into religion: "Felix plane et bis felix, si conversionem tuam salutis occasionem aliis effeceris" (PL, CLXXXIV, 291 C). Bernard, *passim. L. de modo bene viv.*, c. vii, *de conversione* (1210-1); c. vi, n. 16 (1209 C). *De doctr. vitae agendae*, n. 2 (1187 B). *In nat. Jo. B.*, n. 6: "Mira rerum conversio, hominem vix mundum ingressum mundi fugere gloriam" (996 B). Odo of Canterbury, *s. on S. Benedict* (Leclercq, *St. ans.*, 31, 130, 134); etc.

39. *Reg. S. Aureliani*, c. I (Holst., 2, 149). *Reg. S. Caesarii* (*ibid.*, 145); etc.

40. "De acceleranda conversione": Gaufrid of Sainte Barbare, *Declam. ex Bern.*, c. xxvii, n. 32 (PL, CLXXXIV, 455 C).

41. Herrmann of Laon (PL, CLVI, 996-7).

42. We are speaking again of the "convert." Anselm of Havelberg, *L. de ord. can.*, c. xxxviii: "De conversis laicis. . . . Dum ex laicali conversione homines illiterati . . . jugum Christi suscepturi convertuntur" (PL, CLXXXVIII, 1118 A); etc.

43. "Superna vocatio" — "a saeculi vanitate": Prayer of the Cistercian profession: "Deus qui nos a saeculi vanitate conversos ad supernae vocationis amorem accendis" (*Rituale cist.*, Lérins, 1892).

44. "Domus conversionis": *De cl. animae*, Bk. II, c. xx: "Cum enim videt in domo conversionis bona contemplationis et recogitat in se ea quae audierat adhuc in saeculo positus de bonis activae vitae" (PL, CLXXVI, 1076 C); etc.

45. "Nisi conversi fueritis . . . non intrabitis in regnum caelorum" [Matt. 18: 3]: Bernard, *S. ad clericos et conv.* (ms of Engelberg): "vera nobis vita non nisi in conversione est, nec aliter ad eam patet ingressus, dicente Domino: nisi conversi . . ." (Leclercq, *R. Mab.*, 1947, 1-7). Cf. Eph. 4:4.

46. "Fuge mundum et homines, si vis salvari": Ps.-Bernard, *Letter from Oxford* (Leclercq, *St. ans.*, 37, 180).

47. Oger of Locedio, *De verbis Dom. in caena*, s. 11, n. 5-6 (PL, CLXXXIV, 932 BC).

48. *S. De Emmaüs*, n. 16: "Custodia monumenti, sc. observantiae regulares claustri. Monumentum istud Christus non deserit, qui nobiscum se promisit esse usque ad consummationem saeculi" (PL, CLXXXIV, 976 C).

49. Gilbert Crispin (Leclercq, *St. ans.*, 31, 120).

50. Geoffrey of Vendome, s. 11 (PL, CLVII, 276 C); *Ep.* (101 C, 147 B, 158 A). For such a Cistercian, the passage from Cluny to Cîteaux will be a "secunda conversio." *Dial. inter Clun. et Cist.* (M.D., 5, 1594 B).

51. (Monachus) "secundo ergo baptizatus est et emundatus ab omnibus peccatis" (*St. ans.*, 31, 137). Peter Damian, *Op.* 13, c. vi (PL, CXLV, 300 A); *Op.* 16, c. viii (377 A). Rupert, *De Sp. sancto*, Bk. VIII, c. viii (CLXVII, 1791 A). Bernard, *De praecept.*, c. xvii, n. 54 (CLXXXII, 889 BC); etc. Cf. R. Collette, *Religiosae professionis valor satisfactorius* (1887). G. Morin, *L'idéal monast.*, c. IV. Again, St. Thomas Aquinas, 2a 2ae, q. 189, a. 3, ad 3m. See p. 149.

52. "conversio spiritualis" — "adhuc in saeculo": Leclercq, RB, 1949, 186.

53. Aelred, *De temp., s.* 19: "tradidit se alicui sanctae congregationi . . . , intravit navim ut transeat saeculum" (PL, CXCV, 317 B).

54. Aelred, *De oner., s.* 11: "Hi qui sub uno ordine in unam coeunt societatem, quasi unam civitatem efficiunt" (PL, CXCV, 405 A).

55. Bernard, *Ep.* 107, n. 13 (PL, CLXXXII, 249 A); *In Cant., s.* 55, n. 2: Ego "qui videor monachus et Hierosolymita" (CLXXXIII, 1045 C).

56. The "genus clericorum regularium" and the "genus monachorum" he develops: "Genus clericorum regularium, genus Lemovicensium et Bellovacensium, genus quoque monachorum sanctorum, genus Carthusiensium et Cistercensium, genus Cluniacensium et Cyronensium; genus quoque caeterarum diversarum professionum, quarum singulae juxta genus suum unam eamdemque reginam a dextris Regis sui in vestitu deaurato aestantem circumdant quidem varietate, nec exspoliant unitate": *Trip. tab.,* P. II, c. xix, n. 136 (PL, CXCVIII, 740 AB).

57. Adam Scotus, *S.* 37, c. Ii (PL, CXCVIII, 334-5).

58. Adam Scotus, *De ord. et hab. can praem.,* s. 5, c. viii (PL, CXCVIII, 485 AB).

59. Aelred, *De temp., s.* 7 (CXCV, 247 D); *Spec. Carit.,* Bk. II, c. xv (560 A); *Orat. Pastor.,* n. 3 (Wilmart, *Auteurs sp.,* 292). Richard, *De exterm. mali* (CXCVI, 1073-1118). Or., *In Ex.,* h. 5, n. 2 (185). Cf. Francis de Sales to the community of the Filles-Dieu de Paris (Fontrevrault), 22 Nov. 1602: "You have passed from the Egypt of the world to the desert of religion, so as to make your way into the land of promise" — "Vous avez passé de l'Égypte du monde au désert de la religion, pour vous acheminer en la terre de promission."

60. *Rép. Bénédictine à Cîteaux* (Leclercq, RB 67, 85).

61. Honorius, *Gemma an.,* Bk. I, c. cxlix (PL, CLXXII, 590 BD). Geoffrey of Auxerre (Leclercq, *St. ans.,* 31, 175).

62. Gilbert Foliot, *Ep.* 112 (Giles, I, 148).

63. "'Et fluvius egrediebatur de loco voluptatis, ad irrigandum paradisum. . . .' Locus voluptatis Ecclesia est Praemonstratensis. . . . De hoc voluptatis loco fluvius egreditur, quo Paradisus irrigatur, cum in Ecclesia Praemonstratensi, quae mater est nostra, salubria instituuntur, ut ipse ordo reparetur. Cujus institutiones cum plures sint, hos quoque potissimum infirmat paenitentes, gubernantes, operantes, et contemplantes, et si qui alii sint; hi sunt novitii, obedientiarii, praelati, et claustrales. 'Egreditur,' ait Scriptura, 'fluvius de loco voluptatis ad irrigandum Paradisum, qui inde dividitur in quatuor capita . . .'": Adam Scotus, *Trip tab., proem.,* c. x (PL, CXCVIII, 616 AB).

64. *Exp. in Cant.* (PL, CLXXII, 367 BC, 384 D, 403 C).

65. Leclercq, *St. ans.,* 31, 176-7, 183-91.

66. *Dial. de clericis saec. et reg.:* "Apostolica vita est illa libera (Rachel) pro qua Christo conjungenda forma servi est ab illo accepta" (PL, CXCIV, 1387 C).

67. C. xxvi, *De vovo cant. virginibus cantando* (PL, CLXXXIV, 684 C).

68. *De afflict. et lect.:* "Leviticus specialiter tuus est, qui habitas in cella, in quo expiatione sacrificiorum mundantur omnia" (Leclercq, *Spir. de P. de Celle,* 237).

69. "Non sum liber? Non sum monachus? . . .": *De per. civ. Dei* (PL, CCIV, 251 D, 263 B, 400 D).

70. *Lib. de ord. can.,* c. xxxiv-v (PL, CLXXXVIII, 1113-6).

71. "In Christo Jesu per Evangelium ipse nos genuit": *De temp.*, s. 5 (PL, CXCV, 239 A).

72. *S. in.* (Talbot, 62). Walter Daniel, *Vita Aelredi:* "qui me genuit per evangelium Dei ad vitam S. Benedicti." Cf. A. Le Bail, "La paternité de S. Benoît sur l'Ordre de Cîteaux," COCR 9 (1947), 120-1.

73. "Extra Ecclesiam nulla salus" — "extra claustrum nulla salus": Thus Odo of Canterbury (Leclercq, *St. ans.*, 31, 127). *Quid sid monachatus:* "Nullus denique salvari potest, nisi vitam monachi sequatur in quantum potest" (R. W. Southern, *Med. and Ren. St.*, 3, 99). Whence the custom of "dying under the frock": L. Gougaud, *Dévotions et pratiques du moyen âge* (1925), 129-42. Leclercq, *St. ans.*, 37, 157-68.

74. Petrus Cellensis, *De disc. claustr.*, c. ii: "Quid dicam de monachis istis, vid. apostolis?" (PL, CCII, 1102 D).

75. *Rescriptum cujusdam pro monachis*, n. 13 (Foreville-Leclercq, *St. ans.*, 41, 62-3).

76. [On the *vita monastica* — *vita apostolica* identification]: Arno of Reichersberg (PL, CLXXXVIII, 1142 D, 1154 D). Gerhoh, *De aedif. Dei* (CXCIV, 1295 D, 1296 ACD). Ps.-Rupert (Honorius?), *De vita vere apost.*, Bk. IV, n. 4: "Si vis omnia Scripturae consulere testim[o]nia, nihil aliud videntur dicere quam Ecclesiam inchoasse a vita monastica" (CLXXVI, 611-64). On this work, see Ch. Dereine, RHE 46 (1951), 550; DHGE, 12 (1953), 394. M. D. Chenu, *La th. au XII s.*, 227-8. Leclercq, *St. ans.*, 41 (1957), 49, note 20.

77. "Cor unum et anima una" — ". . . Hic modus est monachis, quos vita ligat socialis": Odo of Cluny, *Occupatio*, Bk. VI, v. 583 (A. Swoboda, 136).

78. Fréculphe of Lisieux, *Chron.*, t. I, Bk. I, c. xi: "ex quo apparet talem primo credentium Christo fuisse Ecclesiam, quales nunc monachi imitantur et cupiunt. Tales eos asseruit (Philo), quales et Lucas refert . . ." (PL, CVI, 1127 A).

79. "Apostolicae institutionis formam": William of Saint Thierry, *De nat. et dign. am.*, c. ix, n. 24 (PL, CLXXXIV, 395 BD).

80. "Vita communis et apostolica," "vita regularis et apostolica," "regula apostolica": Gerhoh, *De aedif. Dei* (PL, CXCIV, 1203 C, 1205 C, 1206 D, 1209 B). Cf. Godfrey of Admont (CLXXIV, 154 C); etc.

81. "Professio apostolica": Geoffrey of Auxerre (Leclercq, *St. ans.*, 31, 175).

82. "Institutio apostolica": Gerhoh (PL, CXCIV, 1248).

83. "Apostolicae observationis disciplina": Cf. Ch. Dereine, art. "Chanoines": DHGE, 12, 377; "La spiritualité 'apostolique' . . ." (RHE 54, 41-65).

84. Rupert, *In reg. S. Ben.*, Bk. IV, c. viii (PL, CLXX, 531 A).

85. "Secundum imitationem apostolorum": Arno of Reichersberg (PL, CLXXXVIII, 1154 D).

86. "Ad instar primitivae Ecclesiae": Dereine, *loc. cit.* (11th century).

87. The "vita vere apostolica": The two disputes hit them right at the same time. Texts in J. Leclercq, *La vie parfaite* (1948), c. III; *id.*, "S. Antoine dans la tradit. monast. méd." (*St. ans.*, 38, 239-40). Already Peter Damian, *Op.* 28, *Apologeticus monachorum adv. canonicos, praef.:* "cum constet a monachis, non a canonicis universalem Ecclesiam fundatam, gubernatam et a diverso errore cribratam. . . . Apostolos certe et successores eorum . . . monachico non canonico more vivere

invenietis" (PL, CXLV, 511 D, 512 D). Bibliography in K. Fina, "Anselm von Havelberg," *Anal. praemonstr.* 32 (1956), 69-74.

88. *Lib. de ord. can. regul.*, c. iii and xxx-v (PL, CLXXXVIII, 1094 D, 1112-5). Cf. Gerhoh, *De aedif. Dei*, c. xxvii-ix (1267-70).

89. [Trans. note: The French word 'siècle', derived from the Latin *saeculum*, can refer either to a period of time (century or age) or to the temporal world as being involved with temporal affairs; here it is used in the latter sense.] *Rescriptum pro monachis*, against Thibaut d'Estampes, n. 28-37: symbol of Jacob and Esau (Foreville-Leclercq, *St. ans.*, 41). Cf. Rupert, *In reg. S. Ben.*, Bk. III-IV; *Alterc. monachi et clerici*; letter to Everard of Brauweiler (PL, CLXX, 511-38, 537-44).

90. Bernard of Monte Cassino, *In reg. S. Ben.* (Leclercq, *Vie parfaite*, 87).

91. Peter Comestor, s. 30: "Ipse (Aug.) vitam canonicam restauravit, non instauravit; ipsa est enim vita apostolorum et pauperum post mortem Salvatoris in Jerusalem communiter viventium" (PL, CXCVIII, 1790 D). S. 4: "Ad modum arboris tria considerantur in progressu religionis etc." (1734 D). S. 9 on the four actions accomplished at the Purification: "his enim quatuor, quatuor religionis status insinuantur: ortus, modus, progressus, exitus" (1746 A).

92. Gerhoh, *De aedif. Dei*, c. iv: "Augustinus ... sanctae socialis vitae regulam in Apostolorum Actibus breviter conscriptam sic elucidavit" (PL, CXCIV, 1206 C; cf. 1209 B).

93. Bernard of Monte Cassino, *loc. cit.*, 45.

94. Bernard, *Apol.*, c. x, n. 24 (PL, CLXXXII, 912-3).

95. Petrus Cellensis, *De disc. claustr.*, c. ii (PL, CCII, 1103-4). For the canons, Leibert of Saint Ruf, *Ep.* 1 (CLVII, 718 D).

96. *Ibid.*, c. i (1101 B).

97. *In Matt.*, t. XV, c. xv (392).

98. Eusebius, *Hist. eccl.*, Bk. VI, c. iii, n. 2 and 6 (Bardy, SC, 41, 87-8).

99. *Ep.* 125, n. 7: "J. Baptista vivebat in eremo. ... Filii prophetarum, quod monachi in V.T. legimus, aedificabant sibi casulas, etc." (PL, XXII, 1076 A). *Ep.* 58, n. 5 (2, 79).

100. "Monachorum institutor": *Prol. ad Gaudentium* (PL, LXVII, 417 D).

101. C. I, *de vita comm.* Cf. Yves M. J. Congar, *Quod omnes tangit, ab omnibus tractari et approbari debet*: "Les textes d'*Actes* IV, 32 et II, 42-7 dominent et inspirent toutes les institutions ou réformes de la vie religieuse," *Rev. hist. de droit fr. et étr.*, 1958, 228-30.

102. *Occupatio.* Cf. Dom Cassius Hallinger, "Le climat spir. des premiers temps de Cluny," *R. Mab.*, 46, 121. Teulfus of Morigny, *Chronicon*, Bk. II, *prol.* (PL, CLXXX, 133-5); etc.

103. *In Cant.*, Bk. III (PL, CLXVIII, 885 C). Peter Damian, *Op.* 28 (CXLV, 511-2). Other texts: Leclercq, *La vie parfaite*, 56-9.

104. *Coll.* 24, c. xxiv (701); *coll.* 18, c. iv.

105. *Verba seniorum* (PL, LXXIII, 994).

106. Smaragdus, *Diadema mon.*, c. lxxix (CII, 674 BC). Odo of Cluny, *Collect.*, Bk. II, c. vii (CXXXIII, 554 CD). Alcuin, *Lib. de virt.*, c. xviii (Leclercq, *St. ans.*, 31, 137); etc. To understand the analogy, one must think of a baptism of penitence.

107. Geoffrey of Vendôme, s. 11, *in f. b. Ben.*: "Gloriosus etenim iste sanctus nostrae secundae regenerationis inventor pariter exstitit et scriptor. Monastica,

inquam, religio, quam ipse instituit, secunda regeneratio jure nominatur, et etiam pontificali confirmationi non immerito comparatur. Hujus namque vitae observatione et praeterita peccata, sicut in baptismate, delentur, et contra futura, velut in confirmatione, christianus munitur. Hac beata vita, qui prius in seculari conversatione peccando mortui fuerant, vivificantur" (PL, CLVII, 276 C).

108. For other attestations, see Leclercq, *Vie parfaite*, 164-9.

109. Benedictine sermon of the perseverance of monks. Elmer of Canterbury, *Ep.* 1 (Leclercq, *St. ans.*, 31, 22-4, 62; cf. 72). Honorius, *Gemma*, Bk. I, c. cxlix (PL, CLXXII, 590 BD). Hugo of Bazelle (J. Morson, *St. ans.*, 41, 137).

110. Adam Scotus, *Trip. tab., proem.*, c. viii (PL, CXLVIII, 612-3); c. viii-xxi: paradisus = ecclesia praemonstratensis (612-24).

111. Rep. of the monk Raoul (Leclercq, *St. ans.*, 37, 164-5).

112. "Paradisus corporalis est quies claustralis": *S. ined.*, 88.

113. Parisius quidam, paradisus deliciarum,
    Est major cum sit maxima laude sua?
                De laud. div. sap., Bk. V, v. 563-4 (453).

114. Letter 8 (*ibid.*, 156).

115. *In Cant.*, n. 28 (Davy, 56).

116. Amédée Hallier, *Un éducateur monastique, Aelred de Rievaulx* (1959), p. 114. They "n'ont pas la même fonction dans l'Église, et une sensibilité nouvelle les inspire": The whole work should be read to give this remark its proper scope.

117. "Un sacré confidentiel": *La métamorphose des dieux*, I (1957).

118. One simple indication: "C'est presque uniquement par les moines que l'histoires arrive à prendre vie au moyen âge et par eux à atteindre sa pleine efflorescence," Ghellinck, *L'essor*, II, 90.

119. Among many other examples: *Vita S. Wolfelmi*, n. 19: "Vir Domini, novi ac veteris Testamenti paginas ex integro faciebat legendo revolvi" etc. (PL, CLIV, 419-20).

120. "Intégralement, selon l'ordre où ils se suivent": Leclercq, *S. Bernard mystique* (1948), 35; cf. 69.

121. "Quae est ista nova lex? Quae est ista nova doctrina? Unde ista nova doctrina? Unde ista nova regula? Unde ista, si auderem dicere, nova praesumptio et inaudita?": (A. Wilmart, "Une riposte de l'ancien monachisme au manifeste de S. Bernard," RB 46, 299). Cf. Celsus, in Origen, *C. Cels.*, Bk. VIII, c. cli (255), etc.

122. Nicolas of Clairvaux, *Ep.* 35: "In mea Clarevalle . . . frequens numerositas tam nobilium quam litteratorum novum hominem in novitate vitae parturiunt" (PL, CXCVI, 1627 A).

123. *Idem, Ep.* 45: "Effudi in me anima[m] meam, quoniam transibo in locum tabernaculi admirabilis usque ad domum Dei. Tabernaculum, Clarevallis domum non manufactam intelligo" (CXCVI, 1645 C).

124. *Idem, Ep.* 8: "De veteri Testamento et umbra Cluniacensium ad Cisterciensium evolavimus puritatem etc." (1603 CD).

125. Brocardus of Balerne to Nicholas (PL, CXCVI, 1605 D); cf. Jer. 13 and Ps. 76.

126. Robert of Torrinneio, *Tr. de immutatione ord. monachorum*, c. i (PL, CCII, 1311 CD).

127. Differences finely noted by J. Hourlier between William of St. Thierry, conservative and synthetic, and Bernard, analytic and modern: *St. Bernard th.*, 232-3.

128. Hugh Métel to Bernard: "Oleum nomen tuum. . . . Lingua tua, lingua nova; nova, inquam lingua loqueris, dum mysteria sacra insonas. . . . Introduces enim me in cellaria tua" (PL, CLXXXII, 687-8).

129. Placide Deseille, *Une initiation aux auteurs monast. du moyen âge* (1956), 3; "La liturgie des premiers cisterciens" (*La Maison Dieu*, LI, 1957, 84-5): "attachés surtout à contempler l'histoire du salut dans sa réalité objective, tel Rupert de Deutz dans son *De Trinitate*, tandis que les Cisterciens ont cherché Dieu surtout dans son image invisible, restaurée dans l'âme par la charité."

130. "Rectissima norma vitae humanae": *Reg. Monasteriorum*, c. lxxiii (Butler, 131).

131. "Infra domum conscientiae": Henry of Marcy, *De per. civ. Dei*, tr. 15 (PL, CCIV, 378 B).

132. Bernard, *In Cant.*, s. 80-5 (PL, CLXXXIII, 1165-94): ms of Engelberg (Leclercq, *R. Mab.*, 1947, 14). Aelred, *De anima* (Talbot, 1952). William of Saint Thierry, Isaac of Stella, Alcher of Clairvaux, etc. Cf. P. Michaud-Quantin, RMAL 5 (1949), 20-8. Ph. Delhaye, "Dans le sillage de S. Bernard, trois petits traités 'de conscientia'" (*Cîteaux in de Nederlanden*, V, 1954, 92-103). In these treatises, I. von Ivanka discerns two currents: *S. Bernard th.*, 208. On the doctrine of the image in Bernard: P. M. Standaert, ETL 23 (1947), 70-129.

133. "Haec ad Ecclesiae mysteria referantur; sed nos, moralem prosequentes intellectum . . .": Leclercq, *St. ans.*, 20, 223, note.

134. Bernard, *In Cant.*, s. 80, n. 3 (PL, CLXXXIII, 1167-8).

135. *In F. S. Andreae*, s. 2, n. 8: "Quatuor haec cornua sunt continentia, patientia, prudentia et humilitas" (PL, CLXXXIII, 513 A).

136. "Sex purgationes animae": *S.* 1-2, *Dom. prima post. oct. Epiph.* (CLXXXIII, 155-60); *De div.*, s. 55 (677-9); cf. *s.* 18 (587-8); *In Cant.*, s. 54, n. 4-5 (1039-40). The same, *De div.*, s. 106: the water changed to wine is fear changed into charity. Bruno of Segni, Cardinal Humbert, Rupert, Hildebert, Honorius, H. Losinga, Werner of St. Blaise . . . remained faithful to the six ages.

137. There is an analogous exegesis in Godfrey of Admont, who adds the explication in terms of the six ages: *H. Dom.* 16 (PL, CLXXIV, 110-1). Cf. Isaac of Stella, *s.* 10: "Sex autem hydriae durae et frigidae, quid sibi volunt? Talia fortasis erant hominum opera; nam senarius operationem . . . significat" (CXCIV, 1725 BC).

138. *S.* 47, c. xv-viii (PL, CXCVIII, 437-40); cf. *s.* 46, c. xiv-vi (427-9).

139. In *S. Bernard th.*, 24.

140. "Praeeunte spiritu libertatis": *In Cant.*, s. 14, n. 4 (PL, CLXXXIII, 841 C).

141. *Vita prima*, Bk. III, c. iii, n. 7: "Utebatur Scripturis tam libere commodeque ut non tam sequi illas quam praecedere crederetur et ducere ipse quo vellet, actorem earum ducem Spiritum sequens" (PL, CLXXXV, 307 B).

142. W. Losski, cited by P. Dumontier, *S. B. et la Bible*, 161: "un lien intime entre son esprit et l'esprit des Écritures." Compare the judgment of Rosenmüller, *Hist. interpretationis . . .*, P. 5 (1814), 209: "satis apparere arbitramur, Bernhardum artis interpretandi fuisse plane ignarum."

143. *Conf.*, Bk. XIII, c. xiii, n. 14. *De Trinit.*, Bk. XV, c. xxvii-viii, n. 50-1 (Agaësse, 561-7). Cf. the reflections of H. I. Marrou, *S. Aug. et la fin de la culture ant.*, 500-2.

144. Cf. Sixtus of Sienna, *Biblioth.* (2nd ed., 1576), 232: "universa scripta ejus, quae nihil aliud quam centones divinorum voluminum dici queunt." [Trans. note: According to Lewis and Short, *A Latin Dictionary*, 316, s.v. *cento*: "II. The title of a poem made up of various verses of another poem, a cento."

145. "Qu'y fait donc la Sainte Vierge, sinon de centoniser, de couler ses sentiments personnels dans les moules de la vielle langue scripturaire, et avec les mots et les versets qu'elle lui emprunte et entremêle à son propre langage, d'en former le plus somptueux, le plus majestueux portique ouvert sur le Nouveau Testament?": Dumontier, 115; 163, beautiful analysis of Bernard's language. On this work: P. Nober, S.J., "Lectio vere divina" (*Verbum Domini*, 31, 1953, 193-208). From many other passages still, one can say, as does Father H. Barré of the *De laudibus M. V.*, 2, 17 (PL, CLXXXIII, 70-1): "Elle est jaillie de source, et dérive cependant d'une longue tradition" (*S. Bernard th.*, 111).

Notes to Chapter Nine
§4. Bernard, Gregory, and Origen

1. "Voit tous les aspects de la vie spirituelle uniquement dans leur relation avec le grand mystère central, sans lequel ils n'auraient aucun sens": Thomas Merton, *Marthe, Marie et Lazare*, Fr. tr. (1957), 7. Leclercq, COCR 15, 88: "Dans les sermons de S. Bernard comme dans la liturgie et les Pères de l'Église, le mystère du Christ est toujours contemplé dans toute sa grandeur, selon toutes ses dimensions à la fois." ["In the sermons of St. Bernard, as in the liturgy and the Fathers of the Church, the mystery of Christ is always contemplated in all its greatness, in all its dimensions at once."]

2. *S.* 1 (PL, CIII, 155-6).

3. "Ecclesia, seu studiosa quaevis anima": *Parabola* 4, *De Christo et Eccl.* (PL, CLXXXIII, 767-70). *In Cant.*, s. 29, n. 9 (933C); s. 57, n. 3 (1051 B); s. 67, n. 11 (1107 CD); etc. From the beginning: s. 1, n. 8 (788 B). In the same way, Gilbert, *In Cant.*, s. 30, n. 5 (CLXXXIV, 157 C), and numerous other passages.

4. *In Cant.*, s. 12, n. 11 (PL, CLXXXIII, 833 D). Cf. the routine closing phrase: "in the name of the Bridegroom of the Church, our Lord Jesus Christ" — "in nomine sponsi Ecclesiae J.C.D. nostri."

5. C. Bodard, in *S. Bernard th.*, 43; Congar, *ibid.*, 142.

6. "En des termes semblables à ceux de saint Léon, de saint Ambroise et de saint Augustin, il insiste sur l'aspect social de la vie dans l'Église et sur la solidarité qui unit tous les membres dont le Christ est le chef": J. Leclercq, *S. Bernard mystique* (1948), 113.

7. William of Saint Thierry, *Vita prima Bernardi*, c. iv, n. 24: "Yet, humbly reading the Saints and the orthodox expositors of [Scriptures], he never deemed his own senses equal to theirs, but subjected them to be formed by theirs; and sticking closely to their footsteps, he himself often used to drink from the very well that they had." — "Sanctos tamen et orthodoxos earum expositores humiliter legens, n[e]quaquam eorum sensibus suos sensus aequabat, sed subjiciebat

formandos; et vestigiis eorum fideliter inhaerens, saepe de fonte unde illi hauserant et ipse bibebat" (PL, CLXXXV, 241 AB).

8. J. Mouroux, *Les critères* . . . , 256-7. Cf. Bernard, *In Cant., s.* 8, n. 2-3 (PL, CLXXXIII, 811 AD), etc.

9. He "tient toujours en sa mémoire la totalité des mystères": Dumontier, RMAL 3, 78.

10. "Praeter spem quoque meam diu nos discussio detinuit sacramentorum. Putavi, fateor, unum ad hoc sermonem sufficere, silvamque istam umbrosam latebrosamque allegoriarum pertransire nos cito, et ad planitiem moralium sensuum itinere diei quasi unius pervenire: sed secus contigit . . .": *In Cant., s.* 16, n. 1 (PL, CLXXXIII, 843 AB).

11. P. Dumontier, *S. Bernard et la Bible* (1953), 131-2: "une sorte d'humour à mine d'irrespect, mêlé d'ailleurs d'une grande poésie" — "à un enterrement de l'allégorie" — "non pas sans fleurs ni couronnes" — "loin, parmi ces buissons épineux, de l'allégorie grégorienne, aux fruits si doux à cueillir, *allegoriae fructus suaviter carpitur.*"

12. *In Ez.,* Bk. I, h. 5, n. 1: "O how marvelous is the depth of the eloquence of God! It is pleasing to be intent upon it; it is pleasing, under the guidance of grace, to penetrate its depths. As often as we discuss it with understanding, what else are we entering than the shade of the woods, so that we may be hidden from the heats of this age in its refreshment? There we gather the greenest grass of its sentences by reading; we chew them by treating them. . . ." — "O quam mira est profunditas eloquiorum Dei! Libet huic intendere, libet ejus intima, gratia duce, penetrare. Hanc quoties intelligendo discutimus, quid aliud quam silvarum opacitatem ingredimur, ut in ejus refrigerio ab hujus saeculi aestibus abscondamur? Ibi viridissimas sententiarum herbas legendo carpimus, tractando ruminamus . . ." (PL, LXXVI, 812 BC).

13. *In ps. XXVIII,* n. 9 (PL, XXXVI, 214).

14. "Mons umbrosus," "umbrosus per allegorias": *In Cant., proem.,* n. 5 (PL, LXXIX, 474 D).

15. "Initium libri in Ezechiel propheta magnis obscuritatibus clausum, et quibusdam mysteriorum nodis ligatum, in homiliis octo, Domino nostro Jesu Christo largiente, discussimus. — Jam nunc planiora sunt, et minus difficilia quae sequuntur. Caritati itaque vestrae colloquimur, eidem omnipotenti Deo gratias referentes, quia, post tot opaca silvarum, tandem laeti ad campos exivimus, in quibus liberis gressibus locutionis nostrae intrepidum pedem ponamus": *In Ez.,* Bk. I, h. 9, n. 1 (PL, LXXVI, 870 A). At Bk. II, h. 3, n. 17 it is only a question of the obscurity of the "allegoriarum umbrae" so long as the Old Testament endures (967-8).

16. "Sensus ergo allegoricos sub brevitate transcurrimus, ut ad moralitatis latitudinem citius venire valeamus. . . . Haec nos, fratres carissimi, pro indagandis allegoriae mysteriis succincte transcurrisse sufficiat; nunc ad intuendam latius rei gestae moralitatem animus recurrat": *In ev.,* h. 40, n. 2-3 (PL, LXXVI, 1303 B, 1304 C). Gregory himself designates his *Expositio in Job* as a "liber moralis": *Reg. Past.,* Bk. II, c. vi (LXXVII, 34 B); from his time onward they were called the *Moralia.*

17. Dumontier, 136-7: "la belle construction balancée" — "pâlir le latin de Grégoire" — "ne se trouve pas à l'aise dans l'allégorie" — "le garde-fou de la foi" — "comme une zone d'ombre."

18. "Transivimus allegoriarum umbras, ventum est ad indaganda moralia; aedificata est fides, instruatur vita; exercitatus est intellectus, doctetur vel ditetur actus": *In Cant.*, s. 17, n. 8 (PL, CLXXXIII, 859 A).

19. "Quidam vestrum, ut comperi, minus aequo animo ferunt, quod ecce jam per aliquot dies, dum stupori et admirationi sacramentorum inhaerere delectat, sermo quem ministramus, aut nullo fuerit, aut exiguo admodum moralium sale conditus. Id quidem praeter solitum . . .": *In Cant.*, s. 80, n. 1 (1166 BC).

20. Aelred, *De oner.*, s. 28 (PL, CXCV, 478 A); etc.

21. "Ad ortum rutilant superni luminis
 Legis mysteria plena caliginis."
    Abelard, *Hymn, dim. at Lauds* (PL, CLXXVIII, 1799 B).

22. "Nubes lucida": Petrus Cellensis, s. 66 (PL, CCXI, 847-8).

23. "Sicut Aurora terminum nocti imponit, sic et libellus iste tenebras umbrarum et veteris legis obscuritates discutiens veritatis fulgore . . . totus refulgeat": Manitius, III, 825.

24. So Irimbert, *In Jud.:* "The book of Samuel, which is all hidden in the darkness of the mysteries" — "Liber Samuelis, qui totus mysteriorum tenebris operitur" (Pez, 4, 164); "Abimelech is tending ambushes in the fields, while the Scripture of the Old Testament pretends hidden watchmen of allegory and morality in the deed described in the open letter" — "Abimelech insidias in agris tendit, cum veteris Testamenti Scriptura in exercitio litterae patentis latentes excubias allegoriae et moralitatis praetendit" (307); "He who dwells in the mountain regions, and to the south, and in the flatlands; by 'in the mountain regions' is meant the difficulty of the Old Testament literature; by 'the south', the high growth of allegories; by 'in the flatlands', the sweetness of the moral teachings." — "Qui in montanis et ad meridiem et in campestribus habitat: in montanis, litterarum veteris Testamenti difficultas; per meridiem, allegoriarum proceritas; in campestribus, morali[ta]t[u]m exprimitur suavitas" (151); etc.

25. *"Obscura allegoriae mysteria": Life of Saint Gertrude of Nivelles* (7th cent.), c. iii: "By the action of the Holy Spirit, she explained the obscure mysteries of allegory to her hearers" (MGH, *Scr. rer. merov.*, II, 458). Cf. Augustine, *In Job*, c. xxxviii (PL, XXXIV, 878). Gregory of Elvira, *Tr.* 16 (169). Paul Alvarus of Cordoba, *ep.* 5, n. 3 (Madoz, 152). Primasius, *In Ap.*, h. 4 (PL, XXXV, 3422). Aimon of Auxerre, *In Ap.* (CXVII, 1013 D); etc. See above, Chapter 5.2.

26. "*Caligo sacramenti; Scriptura mysteriis involuta . . .*": Aponius, *In Cant.*, Bk. IX (171); Bk. VII (129); Bk. XI (212).

27. "'Deus a Libano veniet, et sanctus de monte umbroso et condenso' (*Hab.* III). Mons enim Libanus umbrosus et condensus est altitudo divinarum Scripturarum adoperta figuris allegoriarum. Et Dominus noster a monte umbroso et condenso venit, quia sc. Scripturarum allegoricis sacramentis quando voluit revelatus apparuit, in quibus antequam appareret pronuntiatus ejusdem adventus latebat. Quasi enim de umbrosis et condensis silvarum opacitatibus exivit, qui, remotis figuris allegoriarum, in veritate lucis emicuit": *In Ap.*, Bk. III (470 AB). Cf. Aimon, *In Ap.* (PL, CXVII, 1013-4),

28. "Silva condensa": *C. Elip.*, c. iv (PL, XCIX, 158 A); *C. Fel. Urg.*, Bk. I, c. xix (371 B); *Conc. For.*, c. xiv (302 A); etc.

29. *In Ap.*, Bk. I, c. iii: "But since we are entering the deepest obscurities of the heavenly sacraments, let us briefly begin to explain whence the individual visions to follow may act, just as one who enters a misty and shadowy wood...." — "Quia vero profundissimas caelestium sacramentorum obscuritates intramus, ad declarationem sequentium unde singulae visiones agant breviter aperiamus, velut qui silvam condensam et umbrosam ingreditur etc." (PL, CXCVI, 701 AB). *Lib. except.*, P. 2, *prol.*: "we shall shed light on the deep obscurities of the allegories and tropologies" — "profundas allegoriarum et tropologiarum obscuritates ... elucidabimus" (Châtillon, 221). Cf. Absalon, *s.* 10 and 22 (PL, CCXI, 64 D, 134 C).

30. "Tantis obscuritatibus et futurorum typis obvoluta est": *Ep.* 121, *praef.* (PL, XXII, 1007).

31. "Allegoriae nubilum serena expositione discutitur": *Ep.* 84, n. 2 (4, 126).

32. "Abhinc tantum et dein[c]eps cura una fuit mihi, harum allegoriarum densa discussa caligine, ponere in lucem Christi et Ecclesiae secretas delicias. Igitur, redeamus ad indaganda moralia.... Atque in hoc ita congrue fiet, si quae dicta sunt in Christo et in Ecclesia, Verbo animaeque eadem nihilominus assignemus": *In Cant.*, *s.* 80, n. 1 (PL, CLXXXIII, 1166 CD). Cf. Peter Damian, *s.* 71: "once the clouds of allegory have been dissolved" — "dissolutis nebulis allegoriae" (CXLIV, 907 C).

33. "Ad mystica festinat intentio": *In annunt.*, *s.* 1, n. 5: "Vis nosse unde sit homini inhabitans gloria? Dico breviter, quoniam ad mystica festinat intentio. Nam et ea sola proposueram in verbis illis propheticis diligentius vestigare, sed reflexit ad moralia occurrens prima fronte apostolicus sermo de interna gloria et testimonio conscientiae" (PL, CLXXXIII, 384 CD).

34. "Ad opaca allegoriae et tropologiae jucunda transeamus": *In Joel*, c. iii (PL, CLXXV, 359 A).

35. "Gratius est enim quod Ecclesiae commune est": *In Cant.*, *s.* 30, n. 5 (PL, CLXXXIV, 157 C).

36. "Ignoscite mihi, fratres mei, quia qui morum vestrorum servire debueram instructioni, plus forsitan quam necesse erat demoratus sum in illius ineffabilis admiratione et praeconio mysterii.... Nescio tamen si ulla esse possit efficacior ac suavior morum aedificatio, quam hujus mysterii, id est Verbi incarnati, fidelis et pia consideratio": *In annunt.*, *s.* 2, n. 4 (PL, CLXXV, 122 C). Cf. *In verba Cant. Quae habitas*, n. 2: "There is need of investigation not only so that the mystic features may be dug up, but also so that the moral ones may be sucked out" — "Scrutinio quidem opus est, non solum ut eruantur mystica, sed etiam ut sugantur moralia"; but the two remain united in exactly this formula: "collect the spirit of the sermons from the sermons themselves" — "spiritum de sermonibus de sermonibus colligite" (211 BC).

37. "Tout moine qu'il est, se montre nettement soucieux de construction doctrinale": André Fracheboud, COCR, 1945, 143 (regarding Paré, 245).

38. *S.* 9 (PL, CXCIV, 1719 BC).

39. PL, CXCIV, 1690 D, 1719 B, 1729 CD, 1806 B.

40. "Non sic nos divinas Scripturas accipimus, sed nec Ecclesia Dei!": *In ps.* XC, 10 (PL, CLXXXIII, 205 D).

41. Cf. HE, 65.

42. *La théol. myst. de S. Bernard* (1934), 28, note.

43. *In Cant.*, Bk. I: "Where we cannot discover something about the divine senses by inquiry, then, once the passion of this speech has been taken in, let us ask God for a visitation of his Word, and say: 'Let him kiss me with the kiss of his mouth'" — "Ubi vero quaerentes aliquid de divinis sensibus invenire non possumus, tunc affectu hujus orationis assumpto petamus a Deo visitationem Verbi ejus, et dicamus: Osculetur me ab osculo oris sui" (PG, XIII, 86 B).

44. "Ad videndam gloriam Christi et regnum, hoc est Verbi perfectionem et regnum": *In Matt.*, ser. 38 (72): "If anyone is to see the glorious and kingly form of the Word and his glorious coming . . ." — "Si quis gloriosam et regalem formam verbi visurus est et adventum ipsius gloriosam . . ." (71).

45. The image of the hunt was already in Clement, *Strom.*, I, c. ix, 43-4: one must follow the truth on the track like a hunter.

46. *In Cant.*, Bk. III (216). Cf. Ambrose, *In ps. CXVIII, s.* 6, n. 10: "hunters of the Lord" — "venatores Domini" (PL, XV, 1271 B).

47. *In Cant.*, Bk. III (202). *In Jer.*, h. 18, n. 9. Origen compares himself no longer to the hunter but to a thirsty stag, who desires "to drink up the Christ Jesus" (PG, XIII, 482 AB).

48. *In Cant.*, h. 2, n. 10 (Rousseau, SC, 37, 97).

49. *Ipse Christi arcanus et reconditus sensus: In Cant.*, Bk. I (108). Honorius, *In Cant.*: "With its whole effort, the Church is seeking the Beloved in Scriptures" — "Ecclesia tota intentione dilectum in Scripturis quaerit" (PL, CLXXII, 447 D).

50. *In Jo.*, Bk. XIII, c. xxix (253-4).

51. "Quousque mihi sponsus meus mittit oscula per Moysen, mittit oscula per prophetas? Jam ipsius cupio ora contingere, ipse veniat, ipse descendat": *In Cant.*, h. 1, n. 2 (SC, 37, 63).

52. *In Matt.*, ser. 38: "he who is to be nourished on the perfection of the word" — "qui perfectione verbi est nutriendus . . ." (72).

53. *Animam Christus in intelligentiam sui inducit: In Cant.*, Bk. I (109).

54. *In Cant.*, h. 2, n. 11, (Rousseau, 98).

55. *In Jer.*, h. 18, n. 10 (PG, XIII, 484 B). Origen among those "who are held by a tender affection for Jesus" — "qui tenero erga Jesum tenentur affectu": *In Rom.*, Bk. V, c. x (XIV, 1049 C). For him it is not merely a question of "insatiable curiosity," as E. De Faye said, *Origen*, 3, 265.

56. "Et nous avons à subir cela jusqu'à ce que nous devenions tels que non seulement il nous visite fréquemment, mais qu'il demeure auprès de nous, suivant la réponse qu'il fit à son disciple: Si quelqu'un m'aime, il garde ma parole, et mon Père l'aime, et nous viendrons à lui, et nous établirons notre demeure auprès de lui!" — "l'hiver sera passé": *In Cant.*, Bk. III (203-4); *ibid.* (218); *C. Cels.*, Bk. II, c. lxvi (188); *In Cant.*, h. 1, n. 7 (SC, 37, 75).

57. *In Ez.*, Bk. XII: The people could not see the face of Moses coming down from Sinai; this is what occurred to me when I read Ezekiel's description of the temple, "wherever the eye of the heart is opened and I judge that I have seen something and got hold of the Bridegroom, and I say in joy: 'I have found the one whom my soul has sought' . . . , the divine word deserts me again, and the Bridegroom flees from the mountains and my eyes are shut up with blindness" — "ubicumque oculus cordis aperitur et me aliquid videre aestimavero, et tenere sponsum, et gaudens dixero: Inveni quem quaesivit anima mea . . . , rursum me

deserit sermo divinus, fugitque sponsus e montibus et clauduntur oculi caecitate . . ." (PL, XXV, 375 CD). This is hardly any more than a comparison. More than once Jerome "laicizes" Origen's themes in this way: see p. 386, n. 156, in Volume 1.

58. "Ecce iste advenit, saliens super montes": *In ps. CXVIII*, s. 6, n. 6-7 (PL, XV, 1269-70); n. 8: "If she [the soul] should desire, if she crave, if she pray and pray assiduously without any discussion and be entirely intent upon the Word, suddenly she seems to hear the voice of him whom she does not see, and comes to recognize the odor of his divinity in her innermost sense; those who believe well experience this often. The nostrils of the soul suddenly quiver with spiritual grace, and she senses that she is breathing the breath of the presence of him whom she is seeking and says: 'Behold it is he himself whom I am in quest of, he whom I desire." — "Hec (anima) si desideret, si cupiat, si oret et oret assidue, sine [u]lla disceptione, et tota intendat in Verbum, subito vocem sibi videtur ejus audire quem non videt, et intimo sensu odorem divinitatis ejus agnoscit; quod patiuntur plerumque qui bene credunt. Rept[a]ntur subito narres animae spiritali gratia, et sentit sibi praesentiae ejus flatum aspirare quem quaerit et dicit: Ecce iste ipse est quem requiro, ipse quem desidero" (1270 BC); n. 9: "When we think about some point of the Scriptures and are not able to find an explanation for it, while we hesitate, while we seek, do not the deepest dogmas seem to rise before us as upon the mountains: then, appearing to us as it were above the hills, does it not illuminate the mind, so as to pour upon the senses what seemed hard to be able to find? Hence, from being almost absent, the Word becomes present in our hearts. And again, etc. he went across, and he is leaving, and he is returning, etc." — "Nonne cum aliquid de Scripturis cogitamus et explanationem ejus invenire non possumus, dum dubitamus, dum quaerimus, subito nobis quasi super montes altissima dogmata videtur ascendere: deinde quasi super colles apparens nobis, illuminat mentem, ut infundat sensibus quod invenire posse difficile videbatur? Ergo quasi ex absente fit praesens Verbum in cordibus nostris. Et rursus, etc. Transiit, et exit, et revertitur etc." (1270 CD); n. 18-20, commenting on "behind the wall, through the windows" — "post parietem, per fenestras" (1273-4).

59. "Os ad os loqui, quasi osculari est, et internam intelligentiam mente tangere": *Sup. Cant.*, c. i, n. 3 (PL, LXXIX, 479 C).

60. "Quid est dilectum apprehendere, nisi Christi sensum in Scripturis invenire?": *In Zach.*, Bk. III (PL, CLXVIII, 749 D). *In Cant., prol.,* Origen's image of the hunt has been replaced by that of the fight (837). See Chapter 13.3 below.

61. *In Cant.*, s. 45, n. 5 (PL, CLXXXIII, 1001 C); 47, n. 2 (1008 D); 51, n. 2 (1025 BC); 52, n. 1 (1030 A); 53, n. 5 (1035 C); 56, n. 1 (1046 D); 57, n. 8 (1053 D); 58, n. 3 (1056 D); etc.

62. "Dialectique de la présence et de l'absence, de la possession et de la non-possession, de la certitude et de l'incertitude, de la lumière et de l'obscurité, de la foi et de la vie éternelle": Leclercq, *L'amour des lettres*, 30-1, speaking about Gregory; cf. Butler, *Western Mysticism*, 2nd. ed., 115.

63. The "vicissitudines euntis et redeuntis Verbi": *In Cant.*, s. 74, n. 4; cf. 3-7 (PL, CLXXXIII, 1140-2). The visits of the Word, always short and intermittent: s. 32, n. 2 (946 AB).

64. "Drame de la vicissitude" — "le critère authentique d'une expérience

réelle de Dieu": "Sur les critères de l'expérience spirit. d'après les sermons sur le Cant. des cant.," ASOC 9 (1953), 262.

65. *In Cant.*, s. 74, n. 1-7 (PL, CLXXXIII, 1149-52); etc. [Trans. note: Monks regularly sit or stand facing each other north and south across the aisle of the monastic choir and meditatively sing or recite the alternate stanzas of the Psalms back and forth in alternation like an invisible but audible slow-moving spiritual volleyball. This is "le Jeu divin," "the divine Game," or, to change the metaphor to that of a sung conversation, "the divine Play." Chant involves dialectical interplay.]

66. *Exp. alt. in Cant.* (PL, CLXXX, 533 C, 541 B).

67. *In Cant.*, s. 4, especially n. 8-9; a search for God in meditating upon Scripture (PL, CLXXXIV, 31-32), commenting on Cant. 3:2: "I shall rise and go around the city" — "surgam et circuibo civitatem." That day at least, Gilbert inherited Bernard's inspiration.

68. *De temp.*, s. 25: "But how does that man approach or go back who is everywhere and is missing from nowhere . . . ? But when . . . his grace visits our mind, it is as though he is present; when his grace is taken away, it is as though he is distant. . . . The heart of her husband confides in her. . . . Today on the contrary the situation is turned around: meditation is foul, prayer makes one bristle, reading seems worthless: in addition, lust is attacking, the flesh is being kindled, the mind is rattled with various rages: your husband is absent. . . ." — "Sed iste vir spiritualis quomodo accedit, vel quomodo recedit, qui ubique est, et numquam deest . . . ? Sed cum . . . gratia sua mentem nostram visitat, quasi praesens est; cum ipsa gratia subtrahitur, quasi procul est. . . . Confidit in ea cor viri sui. . . . Hodie in contrarium res versa est: sordet meditatio, horret oratio, lectio vilescit; insuper impugnat libido, succenditur caro, mens quasi quibusdam furiis agitatur: absens est vir tuus . . ." (PL, CXCV, 355-6).

69. *In Cant.*, Bk. V, *in fine:* "In them he practices his leaps which he raises on high through the grace of contemplation and instructs about celestial things through certain subtle contacts. And the grace of divine contemplation is beautifully compared with a leap, since the taste of internal contemplation is brief and quickly flies away, and when it suddenly raises the mind with a gleaming flash, on receding it more quickly puts it down. But by the very receding it kindles the mind more vehemently. The beloved leaps in the mountains while he illuminates readers in the more sublime sacraments of the Scriptures with rare insight. Therefore he leaps in the mountains, but leaps across the hills, since the grace of contemplation pours more frequently through sublime souls, but through lower ones, etc. But this taste of internal sweetness is so brief and flies away so quickly, that it can be called a leaping rather than a standing or a sitting." — "In illis saltus suos exercet quos per contemplationis gratiam ad alta sustollit et per quosdam subtiles contactus de caelestibus instruit. Et pulchre divinae contemplationis gratia saltatui comparatur, quia gustus contemplationis internae brevis est, et cito avolat, et cum subito quodam chorusco mentem perlustrando elevat, citius recedendo deponit. Ipso tamen recessu mentem vehementius accendit. Salit etiam dilectus in montibus, dum in sublimioribus Scripturarum sacramentis raro intellectu legentes illuminat. . . . Salit ergo in montibus, sed colles transilit, quia sublimes animas contemplationis gratia crebrius perfundit, inferiores vero etc.

Qui tamen suavitatis internae gustus tam brevis est et tam cito avolat, ut saltus potius quam status vel sessio vocari possit" (Leclercq, *St. ans.*, 20, 229, 230).

70. *Exhortatio in amorem claustri et desiderium lectionis divinae:* "Run off, hasten, roll, unroll, scrutinize the Scriptures, and, if need be, overturn the whole cabinet itself, until you find it [wisdom]. . . . You have gone a little through the books, as you have found what your soul delights in." — "Discurre, festina, volve, revolve, scrutare Scripturas, et everte, si necesse est, totum ipsum armarium, donec invenias eam (sapientiam). . . . Pertransisti paululum codices, ut invenisti quem diligit anima tua" (Leclercq, *Anal. mon.*, II, 36).

71. *In Eccl.*, h. 19: "So the beloved flees. But the beloved flees not so as to escape; he is hiding and concealing himself to provoke love, so that he may be sought for in desire, and not be found until he is loved most ardently, etc." — "Fugit igitur dilectus. Sed dilectus non fugit ut effugiat; sed abscondit se tantum et celat in irritationem dilectionis, ut quaeratur in desiderio, et non inveniatur, quoadusque ardentissime diligatur etc." (PL, CLXXV, 231 BC). Cf. *In Hier. cael.*, Bk. X: "when the spirit comes to the heart, he is sensed in what is perceived; whence he comes or where he goes is not investigated. The when he comes is the starting-point; the whither he goes, is consummation and end . . ." — "quando spiritus ad cor venit, sentitur quidem in eo quod percipitur; unde autem veniat aut quo vadat, non investigatur. Unde venit, principium est; quo vadit, consummatio et finis . . ." (1148 A). *De arca Noe morali,* Bk. IV, c. iii-iv (CLXXVI, 667-70); but the datum is objectivized in history and it is less a question of the Word than of God. In the same way, *De amore sponsi ad sponsam* (987-94), it is a question of "the word that God addresses to the soul."

72. *S.* 29: "Neither does the mind remain long fixed in contemplation, since, having been repelled by the very light, it is called back to itself" — "Neque enim in contemplatione mens diu figitur, quia ad se ipsam ipso lumine reverberata revocatur" (PL, CCV, 757 A).

73. This point has been recalled by Dom A. Le Bail and Dom J. Leclercq (RB 63, 829). The "new religious sensibility," which one sometimes explains by attributing it to Bernard, is later. This reputation of Bernard "rests in part on apocrypha issued from the 14th and 15th centuries" (Leclercq).

74. *In Cant.*, s. 6, n. 3: "Having had mercy upon their errors, God, stepping forth with dignity from the cloudy and misty mountain, pitched his tent in the sun; he took flesh as flesh for the wise, through which they learn also to taste the spirit." — "Quorum Deus miseratus errores, de monte umbroso et condenso dignanter egrediens, in sole posuit tabernaculum suum; obtulit carnem sapientibus carnem, per quam discerent sapere et spiritum" (PL, CLXXXIII, 804 A).

75. Cf. Congar, "L'ecclésiologie de S. Bernard," in *S. Bernard th.*, 124.

76. *In asc.*, s. 5, n. 10-2: "Not only before the passion, but also after the resurrection . . . , when it is read that even the sense was open for them so that they might understand the Scriptures, he rather informed their understanding than purged their affection" — "Nec modo ante passionem, sed et post resurrectionem . . . , quando et sensum eis ut Scripturas intelligerent legitur aperuisse, intellectum potius informabat, quam purgabat affectum . . ." (PL, CLXXXIII, 320

AB, 321). Cf. Leclercq, "Le mystère de l'ascension dans les sermons de S. B.," COCR 15, 81-8.

77. "Dissuesce huic seducibili sensui, innitere verbo, fidei assuesce": *In Cant.*, s. 28, n. 9 (CLXXXIII, 925 C). "Do not touch me, says Jesus; accustom yourself to the faith. For only faith contains within its own mysterious breast what is the length, the breadth, the height and the depth of Wisdom; what the eye has not seen, what the ear has not heard, that which has not entered into the heart of man, the faith carries him as enveloped in itself and preserves him under a sacred seal" — "Ne me touche pas, dit Jésus; accoutume-toi à la foi. Seule, en effet, la foi comprend dans son sein mystérieux ce qu'est la longueur, la largeur, la hauteur, et la profondeur de la Sagesse; ce que l'oeil n'a pas vu, ce que l'oreille n'a pas entendu, ce qui n'est pas entré dans la coeur de l'homme, la foi le porte comme enveloppé en elle-même et le conserve sous un sceau sacré" (tr. A. Béguin, 345).

78. *Dom. I post oct. Epiph.*, s. 2, n. 1 (PL, CLXXXIII, 158 A). *In asc.*, s. 5, n. 12 (321 AB).

79. *De divis. nat.*, Bk. V, c. xxxviii: "O Lord Jesus, I ask of you no other reward, no other happiness, no other joy than that I should understand your words, which have been inspired [through] your Holy Spirit, purely and without any error of fallacious theory. For this is the highest point of my felicity, and the end of perfect contemplation, since even the purest rational soul will find nothing further, since nothing further exists." — "O Domine Jesu, nullum aliud praemium, nullam aliam beatitudinem, nullum aliud gaudium a te postulo, nisi ut ad purum absque ullo errore fallacis theoriae verba tua, quae tuum sanctum Spiritum inspirata sunt, intelligam. Haec est enim summa felicitatis meae, finisque perfectae est contemplationis, quoniam nihil ultra rationabilis anima etiam purissima inveniet, quia nihil ultra est" (PL, CXXII, 1010 BC).

80. *De Sp. sancto*, Bk. I, c. vi: "For behold we are reading sacred Scripture. What do we believe sacred Scripture to be except the Word of God? Plainly many words have been distributed by the pen of the prophets, but the wholeness of the Scriptures is the one Word of God. One Word, I say, which souls faithful to God have conceived like the seed of a lawful husband, and bearing with eloquent mouth, have handed it on, with various signs, i.e., letters, so as to transmit it for us to understand. Therefore, when we read holy Scripture, we are handling the Word of God, we hold God's Son before our eyes through a mirror and in darkness. . . ." — "Ecce enim Scripturam sacram legimus. Quid autem Scripturam sacram nisi Verbum Dei esse credimus? Plane multa sunt verba digesta calamo prophetarum, sed unum est Dei Verbum universitas Scripturarum. Verbum, inquam, unum, quod velut semen de legitimo viro uno Deo fideles animae conceperunt, et ore facundo parientes, signis quibusdam, id est litteris, ut nobis cognoscendum transmitterent, tradiderunt. Cum igitur Scripturam sanctam legimus, Verbum Dei tractamus, Filium Dei per speculum et in aenigmate prae oculis habemus . . . (and from thence God's love, the Holy Spirit, proceeds within us)" (PL, CLXVII, 1575-6). "Yet in the poverty of our pilgrimage we have certain firstfruits of the understanding" — "Habemus tamen in hac nostrae peregrinationis paupertate quasdam primitias intelligentiae" to understand that the Spirit proceeds from the Father and from the Son (1575 C).

81. Rupert, *In Mich.*, Bk. I, unites Gregory's forest with Origen's hunt: "Wish-

ing to inquire into and investigate the sense, the true sense, of the Scriptures, we recall hunting trips in the woods, in the use of which are approved certain dogs that are truly hunters. If we are the dogs of the Lord, our hunt is for the sense of the truth in the thickest forest of holy Scriptures. We run so as to catch; and we are joyful and exult before it whenever, perseveringly intent amidst all the difficulties of the text, we bring back a good and useful sense that edifies the reader and so to speak pleases our fellow-reveler." — "Sensum Scripturarum sensum verum quaerere et indagere cupientes, silvaticarum venation[u]m recordamur, quarum in usu quinam canes veraciter venatici sint, comprobantur etc. Si canes Domini sumus, sensus veritatis in sanctarum Scripturarum silva densissima venatio nobis est. Currimus ut comprehendamus; et tunc laeti sumus, tunc coram illo laetari gestimus, si inter omnes litterae difficultates perseveranter intenti, sensum bonum et utilem, qui lectorem aedificet et velut convivam oblectet, reportamus" (PL, CLXVIII, 455 AB).

82. *In Cant.*, s. 69, n. 6: "If I feel the sense to understand Scriptures open up before me, or a speech as it were boil up with wisdom from deep inside, or mysteries be revealed with a light infused from on high, or indeed be spread out before me like a most abundant sprout of heaven, and pour the more fruitful rains of meditations upon my mind from above, then I have no doubt that the Bridegroom is at hand. These are the riches of the Word, and we receive them from his bounty." — "Si sensero aperiri mihi sensum ut intelligam Scripturas, aut sermonem sapientia quasi ebullire ex intimis, aut infuso lumine desuper revelari mysteria, aut certe expandi mihi quasi quoddam largissimum caeli germium, et uberiores desursum influere animo meditationum imbres: non ambigo sponsum adesse. Verbi siquidem hae copiae sunt, et de plenitudine ejus ista accipimus" (PL, CLXXXIII, 1115 B). Even the turn of phrase is from Origen. Cf. William of Saint Thierry, *De nat. et dign. amoris*, c. x, n. 31: "This is the taste that the spirit of understanding, i.e., the understanding of the Scriptures and sacraments of God, produces for us in Christ." — "Hic est gustus quem in Christo facit nobis spiritus intellectus, intellectus sc. Scripturarum et sacramentorum Dei etc." (CLXXXIV, 399 A).

83. *In Cant.*, s. 57, n. 7-8 (CLXXXIII, 1053-4). In *S. Bernard th.*, 512, Father Daniélou has noted "the deep kinship" between the mysticism of Bernard and that of Origen.

84. *In Cant.*, s. 62, n. 6: "Hence, in the perfect, who both dare by purity of conscience and are able by sharpness of understanding to penetrate the secrets of wisdom, she dwells in caves of rock." — "Ergo in perfectis quidem, qui mirari ac penetrare arcana sapientiae et puritate conscientiae audent, et intelligentiae acumine possunt, habitat in foraminibus petrae" (1078 D).

85. *In Cant.*, s. 23, n. 3: "And if you please, we may look for these three things in holy Scriptures: the garden, the storage room, the bedchamber. For in them the soul thirsting for God cheerfully occupies herself and stays, knowing that there she doubtless will find the one she is thirsting for. So let the garden be the simple, plain history; let the store room be the moral sense; let the bedchamber be the secret of the theory of contemplation." — "Et quaeramus, si placet, tria ista in Scripturis sanctis, hortum, cellarium, cubiculum. In ipsis nempe libenter Deum sitiens anima versatur et moratur, sciens se ibi absque dubio inventuram quem sitit. Sit itaque hortus, simplex ac plana historia; sit cellarium moralis sensus; sit

cubiculum arcanum theoriae contemplationis" (PL, CLXXXIII, 885 D). *De div.*, s. 92, n. 1: "The threefold entry is made for the rational soul by her Bride-groom, namely, the Word of God, according to the three-fold sense of the Scriptures — historical, moral, mystical. The historical is in the garden; the moral, in the store room; the mystical, in the bedchamber." — "Haec triplex introductio fit animae rationali a sponso suo, Verbo sc. Dei, secundum triplicem sensum Scripturarum, historicum, moralem, mysticum. In horto est historicus, in cellario moralis, in cubiculo mysticus..." (714 B). Cf. *In Cant. commentatio ex Bern.*, n. 31-2 (CLXXXIV, 431-3). Compare *Miscellanea*, Bk. IV, tit. 30: "panis sub cinere, — hordeum, — triticus" (CLXXVII, 712-3). Honorius, *In Cant.:* "The wine-cellar is holy Scripture; Christ introduced the Church into it when he gave her spiritual understanding." — "Cella vinaria est sacra Scriptura; in hanc Christus Ecclesiam introduxit, dum ei spiritualem intelligentiam dedit" (CLXXII, 386 A). Robert of Tombelaine, *Sup. Cant.*, c. ii, n. 5: "For what is more appropriate than to take the wine-cellar as the secret contemplation of eternity?" — "Quid enim per cellam vinariam congruentius quam ipsam arcanam aeternitatis contemplationem accipimus?" (LXXIX, 495 D).

86. Petit, *Prémontrés*, 127.

87. *H. dom.* 51: "The breast of Jesus is holy Scripture, since, just as the heart is in the breast, and life is in the heart, so too does the spiritual sense whereby man is vivified and revivified inside lie hidden within holy Scripture." — "Pectus Jesu, sacra Scriptura est, quia sicut in pectore cor, et in corde vita est, sic latet in sacra Scriptura spiritualis ille sensus, ex quo vivificatur homo et reviviscit intrinsecus" (PL, CLXXIV, 339 B).

88. *S.* 23: "But behold those following the Word himself who was made a lamp for our feet and holding firm wherever he goes, wherever he crosses, and wherever he turns, and not letting go whithersoever he penetrate and enter, till at last he has led us into the house of his father and into the bedchamber of his mother (*Cant.* III), i.e., of the unbegotten paternal essence, wisdom, and power, etc." — "Sed ecce sequentes ipsum Verbum lucernam factum pedibus nostris, tenentesque quocumque ierit, quaque transierit, et quocumque se verterit, nec dimittentes quocumque penetraverit, et introierit, tandem introduxit nos in domum patris sui et in cubiculum genitricis (*Cant.* III), id est, ingenitae paternae essentiae, sapientiae et potentiae etc." (PL, CXCIV, 1768 B).

89. *In annunt., s.* 3, n. 6: "That soul, conjoined in person to the Word himself, was fed with the Word.... You too, then, if you know how, will perform that act in your silence, so as to eat the bread of the divine word in the presence of the Lord, preserving and comparing in your heart, as did Mary, the things that are said of Christ. Christ will be delighted to chew this bread with you, and he who feeds you will himself be fed in you; and the more that bread is eaten, the more there will be left over to be eaten." — "Verbo pascebatur anima illa, Verbo ipsi in persona conjuncta.... Id igitur operis tu quoque, si sapis, in silentio tuo actitabis, ut panem verbi divini comedas coram Domino, conservans, sicut Maria, quae de Christo dicuntur, et conferens in corde tuo. Hunc panem tecum Christus manducare delectabitur, et qui te pascit, ipse in te pascetur; et panis iste quo plus editur, plus abundabit edendus..." (PL, CLXXV, 128 A).

90. *De per. civ. Dei*, tr. 15: "Now let God go forth unto his rest.... — For he

goes forth when he lifts us to higher things and reveals to us the secrets of evangelical wisdom, leading us into his bedchamber, no longer interpreting the Scriptures for us in pilgrim fashion on the road, but manifesting himself to us with open eyes under the house of consciousness through the breaking of the bread."
— "Exsurgat jam Deus in requiem suam. . . . — Tunc enim exsurgit, cum ad superiora nos elevat et arcana evangelicae sapientiae nobis revelat, introducens nos in cubiculum suum, non jam in specie peregrini per viam nobis Scripturas interpretans, sed revelatis oculis infra domum conscientiae per fractionem panis se nobis manifestans" (PL, CCIV, 378 B).

91. Cf. Leclercq, *Études*, 184-91. First attestation for the word of Bernard in a text of around 1185 (p. 186). His title itself of "Doctor mellifluus" seems less early. It is the explication of Scripture that Bernard calls his "ministry." *In Cant.*, s. 22, n. 2: "ministerium meum . . . , quotidie sc. exire et haurire etiam de manifestis rivulis Scripturarum, et ex eis singulorum necessitatibus inservire . . ." (CLXXXIII, 878 D).

Notes to Chapter Nine
§5. *Doctor mellifluus*

1. "Et forte subtiliores litterae favi erunt, mel vero est qui in his est intellectus": *In Is.*, h. 2, n. 2 (252).

2. "mel apum, contemplationes sunt ex prophetis et evangeliis": *In Ez.*, after the chains (PG, XIII, 722-3, note). Cf. *In Ez.*, h. 7, n. 5: "Behold, . . . the honeys of the bees, the prophets. . . . On the law's finest wheat-flour, the honey of the gospel, fed on which . . ." — "Ecce . . . mella apum prophetarum. . . . De simila legis, melle evangelii, e quibus cibati etc." (722-3); on Ezek. 16:19: "I have fed you on finest wheat-flour and honey and oil" — "simila et melle et oleo cibavi te."

3. *In Num.*, tr. 27, n. 12 (278). *In Is.*, h. 2, n. 2 (242).

4. *De prom.*, P. 2, c. xxi, n. 40: "Favum vero mellis quod in ore leonis hujus invenit, legem spiritalem populi ejus, auditor, intellige, quod apes patriarchae atque prophetae construentes, in eum mella infuderint divini eloquiii. . . . Dedit ex eo . . . parentibus suis, sive discipulis, cum aperuit sensum eorum ut intelligerent Scripturas . . ." (PL, LI, 791 AB).

5. *Ep.* 23, n. 16: "Puto et ipse nobis leo ille est, in cujus mortui ore cibum mellia invenimus. Quid enim dulcius Dei Verbo? Et quid fortius Dei dextera? Aut in cujus mortui favus et apes, nisi in cujus verbo salutis nostrae bonum et congregatio gentium? Quarum potius figuram plerique in hoc leone posuerunt, quia populus gentium qui credidit, corpus feritatis erat ante, nunc Christi est; in quo Apostoli velut apes a rore caeli et divinarum floribus gratiarum mella sapientiae condiderunt, ac si esca ab ore edentis exierit: quia prius efferae Deo nationes receptum Dei verbum fideli ab ore edentis exierit: quia prius efferae Deo nationes receptum Dei verbum fideli corde sumentes, fructum salutis ediderint. Qui vero Christum magis in eodem sibi leone proponunt etc." (Hartel, 173).

6. *In ps. CXVIII*, s. 22, n. 6 (PL, XXXVII, 1566).

7. *In ps. CXVIII*, v. 103 (PL, LXX, 871 A).

8. The "aperta doctrina sapientiae" — "dulcis et nutritoria": Aug., s. 25, n. 1 (PL, XXXVIII, 167).

9. *In Cant.*, Bk. VII (131); but also: 139; see p. 393, n. 128, below.

10. The "mellifluum examen": *Ep.* 3 (PL, LXXXIX, 93 C).

11. *In Ex.*, c. iii (PL, XCI, 294 D).

12. The "caelestis intellectus": *Sup. Par. Sal.*, Bk. III, (XCI, 1013 CD).

13. "eruditio parvulorum": *In Cant.*, Bk. IV (XCI, 1142 D).

14. *In Sam.*, Bk. II, c. ix: "Multo securius in apostolicis quam in Platonicis quaeritur consilium salubre pagellis. Nam et apes ipsae, quae hujusmodi mella faciunt ore quidem praetendunt dulcia dicta quae mulceant, sed in posterioribus servant venenata gesta quae feriant" (XCI, 590 A).

15. "favus distillans": *In Cant.*, Bk. IV (XCI, 1141-2). Cf. *In Sam.*, Bk. II, c. ix: the eyes of the mind have been clarified by the arguments of the master "mellito, ut ita dicam, ore, quasi favore compositione verborum" (589 C).

16. "multa spiritualium sensuum mella congessit": *In Ap., praef.* (153 B).

17. "Favus distillans labia tua, sponsa": Cant. 4:11. Cf. *In Cant.* 4, 11: "Favus mel in cera est; mel autem in cera spirtualis est divinorum eloquiorum sensus in littera. Mel stillans, quia multiplices sensus pene singulae sententiae habent. Labia sponsae sunt doctores, qui multifarios sensus sacris litteris ineese pandunt" (PL, C, 652 D).

["Mel et lac sub lingua tua": *ibid.* Interpreted as the "fortior doctrina" or the "doctrina perfectorum."]

18. "Quasi mel de petra" — "Cum sit lapis in fundamento Sion fundatus, mellifluo spiritalis vitae poculo credentium mentes satiat": Bk. I, c. xvii (PL, XCVIII, 1045 A). Cf. Psalms and Deut. 32.

19. "Mel, quod in promptu est ad comedendum, moralem litterae superficiem insinuat; favus autem, in quo mel de cera exprimitur, allegoricam locutionem figurate denuntiat, ubi, subducto litterae velamine, suavitas sensus spiritalis aliquando cum labore vel mora percipitur": *In Prov. Sal.*, Bk. II, c. xxiv (PL, CXI, 757-8).

20. Aimon, *In Cant.*: "Divine Scripture is therefore rightly called a trickling honeycomb, since it is understood in many ways and is explained in various senses." — "Recte ergo divina Scriptura favus distillans vocatur, quia multipliciter intelligitur et variis sensibus exponitur" (CXVII, 321 C).

21. "Per mel eliquatum patens doctrina sapientiae intelligitur, per favum vero occulta sapientia doctrinae, quae in abstrusioribus sacramentis sicut mel in favo clauditur": *In ps. CXVIII* (PL, XCIII, 1073 C).

22. "Favus est mel in cera; mel autem in cera est spiritalis intelligentia latens in littera; sed favus distillat, dum dulcis allegoria de littera manat": *In Cant.* (PL, CLXXII, 423 A).

23. "Historia, de qua quasi mel de favo veritas allegoriae exprimitur" — "Quasi favus mel continens in cera, veritas latens sub allegoria": *In ps. CXVIII* (PL, CXCVI, 351 B). The gold is the moral sense; the precious stones are anagogy; the "favus" [honeycomb] is the mysteries; the pure honey is the clear sense, history (351-2).

24. "refectio robustorum" — "consolatio parvulorum": *In Cant.*, c. xxviii (PL, CXCVI, 487 A).

25. "magnae virtutis et sapientiae mella": *De admon. cl. et laic.*, c. vii (PL, CXLVI, 257 B).

26. "mel Dei" — "spiritualis intelligentiae dapes": *Op.* 49, c. viii (PL, CXLV, 728 B).

27. "Placuit mihi doctrinae ipsius discretio, qui cum spiritualem intellectum in littera, hoc est, mel occultaret in cera, pro captu singulorum, vinum valentibus, lac infirmis noverat propinare": *S. in vitam S. Florentii*, Bk. I, c. x (PL, CLXXI, 1538 D).

28. "Mel in cera, devotio in littera est; alioquin littera occidit, si absque spiritus condimento glutieris": *In Cant.*, s. 7, n. 5 (PL, CLXXIII, 869 B).

29. "Scrutantes singula velut apes sedulae mel de floribus, spiritum de sermonibus colligite": *In verba Cant.*, II (PL, CLXXXV, 211 A).

30. "Frangite panem verbi, apponite favum mellis, quem distillaverunt manus vestrae": PL, XXXII, 692 B.

31. "Non ego ille sum cui dicebatur: Favus distillans labia tua": PL, CLXXXV, 1095 D.

32. *In Cant.*, s. 41, n. 3-4 (PL, CLXXXIV, 216 BC). Paschasius, *Vita Walae*, Bk. II, c. xiii: "He left the apiary of the monks honeyed with virtues." — "Reliquit monachorum alvearium virtutibus mellificatum" (MGH, *Scr.*, II, 559).

33. Cf. Bede, *Ad Accam, in Esdram:* "once the shell of the letter has been uncovered, to find something still deeper and more hallowed in the marrow of the spiritual sense" — "retecto cortice litterae, altius aliquid et sacratius in medulla sensus spiritualis invenire" (PL, XCI, 808 B). Berengaud, *In Ap.* (XVII, 832 AB). Bernard, *S. de David*, n. 2 (CLXXIII, 334 C). Alan of Lille, *s.* 4 (CCX, 207 A); etc.

34. Honorius, *In Cant.*: "The nut is sacred Scripture, whose bark or shell is the letter, and whose kernel is the spiritual understanding" — "Nux est sacra Scriptura, cujus cortex vel testa est littera, nucleus vero spiritualis intelligentia" (PL, CLXXII, 466 B). Werner, *Defl.*, Bk. II: "As honey in wax and kernel under the shell, so is the sweetness of morality under the bark of history." — "Sicut mel in cera, et nucleus sub testa, sic sub cortice historiae dulcedo moralitatis" (CLVII, 1137 B); etc.

35. Rupert, *In Deut.*, Bk. I, c. xxvii: "You will break the ear with your hand, says he, so that you may reach the hidden grains, i.e., discuss the letter that killeth, so that you may live by the spiritual sense deposited within." — "Franges, inquit, spicam manu, ut ad latentia grana pervenias, id est, discutias occidentem litteram, ut de reposito intrinsecus spirituali sensu vivas" (PL, CLXVII, 945 D). Ps.-Hugo, *s.* 27 (CLXXVII, 957 A); etc.

36. *Latens in littera spiritalis medulla: In Ez.*, Bk. II, h. 10, n. 2 (PL, LXXVI, 1058 C).

37. "Favus, proprie mel in cera, dicitur pagina Veteris Testamenti, quod in se, quasi mel, doctrinam evangelicam continebat": PL, CCX, 786-7.

38. "ut quasi ex diversis flosculis, nostri interventu laboris, mellita quaedam doctrina emergat": J. M. Parent, *Beiträge Bäumker* 3 (1935), 307.

39. Jerome attributes it to Nepotianus, *Ep.* 52, c. iii (PL, XXII, 529).

40. Bk. IV, v. 100-1, 169.

41. Bk. I, v. 430-4. Cf. Macrobius, *Sat.*, Bk. VII, c. vii (Eyssenhardt, 435-6). [Trans. note: De Lubac's citation on p. 603, note 10. Cf. our note 42.]

42. [Trans. note: Here de Lubac inserts another superscript 10 marking a du-

Notes to Page 166

plicate occurrence of note 10 on p. 603, which had already been given at our note 41. The citation is a dead end.]

43. "Quam dulcia faucibus meis eloquia tua, super mel et favum!": Ps. 118:103. Cf. Ecclus. 6:17. Sweetness of honey: Garnier, *s.* 26 (PL, CCV, 742 AB). Cf. Peregrinus: "Vir venerandus nomine Serlo, valde litteratus, et cujus eloquium audientibus erat acceptabile super mel et favum" (d'Achery, *Spic.*, II, 575).

44. Or., *In Is.*, h. 2, n. 2 (252); *In Jud.*, h. 5, n. 2 (493). Aug., *In ps. LXI*, n. 1 (CCL, 39, 772). The "doctrina melliflua" of St. John: Honorius (PL, CLXXII, 833 A).

45. Aug., *s.* 103, c. iv, n. 5 (PL, XXXVIII, 615).

46. Aug., *In ps. CXXXII*, n. 2 (CCL, 40, 1927).

47. Hilary, *In ps. CXVIII*, h. 13, n. 11 (PL, IX, 588 AB).

48. Greg., *Mor.*, Bk. XX, c. viii, n. 18 (PL, LXXVI, 148 AB). Bede, *In Cant.*, Bk. IV, c. v: "dulcedinem sensuum spirituali[t]um" (XCI, 1152 B). Ps.-Bede, *In Jo.* (XCII, 690 C). G. Foliot, *M. Cant.*, c. v (CCII, 1268 C). Cf. Aponius, *M. Cant.*, Bk. VII (CXL, 213).

49. "In cordis fauce sapit, in ore dulcescit": Peter Damian, *Op.* 49, c. viii (PL, CXLV, 728 A).

50. Adam Scotus, *s.* 36, c. ix (PL, CXCVIII, 333 C).

51. Greg., *Mor.*, Bk. XXIII, c. xvii, n. 31 (PL, LXXVI, 269 C). Cf. Jerome, *ep.* 58, c. ix (3, 83; according to Plautus). *Misc.*, Bk. IV, t. XVIII (CLXXVII, 708 A).

52. Jerome, *In ps. LXXX* (*An. mar.*, III, 2, 74).

53. "Miram et ineffabilem dulcedinem": Richard, *Exp. in Hab.* (PL, CXCVI, 402 D).

54. "Hunc cecinit Salomon mira dulcedine librum . . .": Alcuin, *In Cant.* (PL, C, 641).

55. "Palatum cordis": an expression of Augustine, taken up again by Gregory, John of Fecamp, Geoffrey of Auxerre . . . (Leclercq, *Jean de Fécamp*, 1946, 99; and *St. ans.*, 31, 184). Bede, *In Cant.*, Bk. I: "Multi enim legentes vel audientes possunt verba Domini dicere, possunt facillime mysteria fidei perscrutari, sed pauci admodum inveniuntur qui haec, quam dulciter sapiant, veraciter in cordis palato sentiant" (PL, XCI, 1170 D).

56. Ps.-Ambrose, *s.* 21, n. 6: "ille spiritualis favus a domino largiatur, qui in aeterna beatitudine in palato faucis animae nobis dulcescat" (PL, XVII, 646 C).

57. Greg., *Mor.*, Bk. XVI, c. v, n. 8: "Mel quippe invenire, est sancti intellectus dulcedinem degustare" (PL, LXXV, 112 C).

58. Greg., *In Ez.*, Bk. I, h. 10, n. 13 (PL, LXXVI, 890 C). Berengaud, *In Ap.* (XVII, 866 B); etc. Cf. Eph. 3:3.

59. Alvarus, *Vita S. Eulogii*, c. i, n. 2: "Rithmicis versibus nos laudibus mulcebamus; et hoc erat exercitium nobis melle suavior, favis jucundior" (*P. lat. aevi car.*, III, 122). Bernon of Reichenau, *Vita S. Udalr.*, c. iii (PL, CXLII, 1187 A).

60. "*Quid enim dulcius Dei Verbo?*": Paulinus of Nola, *ep.* 23, n. 16 (PL, LXI, 267 B).

61. Bruno of Segni, *In Gen.*, c. xxvi: "Christus cujus eloquentia super mel et favum sunt dulciora" (PL, CLXIV, 205 D); etc. Cf. Jerome, *ep.* 30, c. xiii (2, 34).

62. Evagrius, *Alterc. Sim. et Theophili:* "mel autem est dulcedo doctrinae ejus" (Bratke, 17).

63. St. Bruno (?), *In ps. LXXX:* "Et saturavit melle procedente de petra, sc. de dulcedine sapientiae, de Christo vid. qui petra firmissima est procedente" (PL,

CLII, 1073 C). Peter Lombard, *In ps. LXXX* (CXCI, 775 B). Cf. Cassiodorus (LXX, 591 C).

64. *Poema de nom. Jesu,* v. 5 (PL, LXI, 741 A): In ore Christus nectar, in lingua favus.

65. "fidelibus dulcedo mellis invenitur": *In Ex.,* h. 7, n. 8 (216). P. Damian, *s.* 6 (PL, CXLIV, 540 B). On this sweetness of the manna: Ps.-Eusebius of Emesa, *h. de Pascha:* "mellifluum pluviae illius donum" (LXVII, 1053 D).

66. *De Isaac,* c. v, n. 49 (PL, XIV, 519 B); *De bono mortis,* c. xx (550 BC).

67. [*"Sweet to taste and strong at nourishing"*:] *In Ex.,* c. xvi (PL, CLXIV, 269 AB). Adam Scotus, *s.* 43, c. ix (CXCVIII, 399 B).

68. *"adeps frumenti — mel de petra": In ps. LXXX* (Morin, 73-4).

69. *Ep.* 73, n. 8 (PL, XXXIII, 248). *In Jo.,* tr. 120, n. 8: "sanctae deliciae" (CCL, 35, 1955).

70. *Mor.,* Bk. XVI, c. xix, n. 24 (PL, LXXV, 1132-3). *In Ez.* (LXXV, 887 D). Cf. *In Cant.* (LXXIX, 513 AB). J. Châtillon, *Dulcedo, D. Sp.,* f. 23, 1777-95.

71. "cujus fuit tam amaena, tam lactea, tam dulcis oratio, ut mihi ex ore ipsius non tam verba quam mella quaedam fluxisse videantur": *Common.,* c. xvii, n. 23 (Rauschen, 39).

72. Bk. III, c. xx, n. 4: "Euphonia est suavitas vocis; haec et melos a suavitate et melle dicta" (PL, LXXXII, 165 B).

73. Qui leni jugo Christi colla submittere cupis,
Regulae sponte de mentem, dulcia ut capias mella.
Hic Testamenti veteris, novique cuncta doctrina,
Hic ordo divinus, hicque castissima vita.

The author could be Simplicius, abbot of Monte Cassino (RB 50, 91).

74. "melliflua suavitas": *Vita,* n. 7 (PL, LXXXIX, 1272 B).

75. "ubi angelorum melliflua indesinenter sonant organa": Ps.-Hildefonse, *s.* 1 (PL, XCVI, 341 B).

76. "melliflua sanctae Scripturae cognitio": *Ep. Gislae et Rectr. ad Alb.* (PL, C, 738 D).

77. "quasi duo deliciosi pisces" — "O mirabilis profunditas! O mella fluenta, Hybleo nectare dulciora! O novum saporem ex paradisiacis fontibus caelestis Hierosolymae terrigenis allatum!": *In Rom.* (PL, CIII, 34 BC).

78. *Vita S. Galli:* "virum Dei dulcifluis dogmatibus suis populum instruere flagitabant" (MGH, *Scr.,* II, 14). *V. Adalhredi,* n. 14: "dulcifluus affatu" (525). St. Gertrude, *Insinuat.* Bk. IV, c. iv: "dulcifluum pectus Domini" (1662 ed., 399). Cf. Adam Scotus, *Ad viros rel., s.* 4 (Petit, 162). Rupert: "mel in ore dulcifluum" (PL, CLVII, 501 D).

79. "Mellifluo dulces eructans pectore succos": *Versus de sanctis Euboricensis eccl.,* v. 1410 (*P. lat. aevi car.,* I, 200).

80. "Nec nos oblectant dulciflua dona Lici,
Mellifluusque medus domata nostra fugit."

Ibid., III, 177; cf. 166.

[Trans. note: I was unable to find a Latin dictionary entry for *medus.* The *Oxford English Dictionary,* s.v. 'mead' reports a Greek transcription in Priscus. Since mead is a drink made of honey, the present context seems to support the conjecture.]

Notes to Pages 167-68

81. *Ibid.,* 567; cf. 5, 9, 45 note, 246, 268, 270, 337.
82. "melliflua dicta": Poem 1 (*P. lat. m. aevi,* I, 127)
83. "melliflua dilectio": Adrian to Charlemagne: "Pro vestra melliflua regali dilectione" (MGH, *Ep.,* 5, 7); *ibid.:* "melliflua excellentia."
84. "mellifluus amor": Alcuin, Poem 88: "mellifluo Christi devotus amore" (*P. lat. m. aevi,* I, 309).
85. "sapor mellifluus": Alvarus, *Ep.* 4, c. x: "mellifluum libando saporem" (PL, CXXI, 433 AB).
86. "mellifluae voces": *Ecloga duarum sanctimonialium* (PL, CXX, 1556 C).
87. "melliflua verba": Pref. to the *Lib. scint.* of Defensor of Ligugé: "Legas animo et melliflua grate suscipias verba" (Rochais, RB 63, 262). M. sermo, melliflua locutio, m. lectio, mellifluae syllabae: MGH, *Ep.,* 5, 440, 358, 440, 621, 5.
88. "melliflua mandata": *Ibid.,* 142.
89. "mellifluis sensibus delibutae": Alcuin, *Ep.* 8 (PL, C, 149 A); *Ep.* 160: "omni melle dulciores nobis . . . litterae delatae sunt" (417 B).
90. "mellifluum nomen": MGH, *Ep.,* 5, 619, 326.
91. "Quicumque mellifluo caritatis jaculo vulnera omni favo dulciora in corde accipiet . . .": *Ep.* 40 (C, 200 C); "Ecce venit, ecce venit paternae pietatis pagina, quam diu desiderabam, omni melle palato meo dulcior" (200 B). [". . . that makes one think of the Précieuses" is an allusion to the style satirized in Molière's one-act comedy "Les Précieuses ridicules" (1659).]
92. "latissimus melliflui pectoris sinus": *Ep.* 216 (C, 490 C). Cf. Paschasius, *V. S. Adalhardi,* c. x: "mel et lac ex ejus lingua manasse . . . prae dulcore nimio" (CXX, 1514 AB).
93. "cuncta, flores, aromata, rosae, lilia suaveolentia melliflua sunt": *Adv. Claud.* (PL, CV, 510 B). Wipo, *Tetralogus* (MGH, *Scr.,* XI, 253):

Mellis dulcedo per Christum fluxit Olympo
Ut sapiant famuli delicias Domini. . . .

94. *In Deut.,* Bk. IV, c. ii: "quasi ergo in firma petra mel dedit, quando adhuc mortalis Dominus miraculorum suorum dulcedinem discipulis ostendit" (PL, CVIII, 975 D).
95. "mellifluae suavitates" — "dulcedo melliflua": *Coll. in V. T.* (PL, CXLV, 1108 C, 1119 A). *Rescript. Aribonis:* "Orationibus vestris et sancti examinis sub vestro regimine mellificantis recreari optamus, etc." (CXLII, 1086 B).
96. "Mellifluis omnem Paulus rigat imbribus orbem": *De S. Paulo* (PL, CXLV, 961 C).
97. "melliflui oris facundia": *V. Theodorici abb. Andag.,* c. viii (MGH, *Scr.,* XII, 41).
98. "melliflua atque salutifera scripta": *Vita,* by André of Strume, c. vii, n. 74 (PL, CXLVI, 792 D).
99. "Salve, confrater, mihi dulcis semper amore,
    Dulcior es mihi tu quam mellis gustus in ore:
    Nescit amare liquor, sed amor dulcescit et ad cor
    Intrat, et alterius conjungit faedere pectus."
        — Poem 7 (K. Strecker, MGH, *Ep. sel.,*
            III, 1925, 28); cf. *Ep.* 95 (100).

100. Sedis apostolicae regimen
Dogmate mellifluo moderans.

P. Gall-Morel (1868), 239.

101. "lactiflua patria, melliflui parentes, dulces cognati, frequentes amici, blandientes epistolae . . .": Bk. I (Talbot, 37).

102. *Chron. S. Vincentii Vulturn.* (Muratori, I, 2, 359).

103. *Prol.*: "Serenissimum vultum et mellifluum eloquium tuum"; "dulciora melle colloquia de labiis mellifluis distillantur": Abbey of St. Benedict of Acyel, "Les sermons inédits de J. de Ford sur le Cant." (COCR 5, 253, 259j). Arnulf, *ep.* 29: "litteras vestras dignationis accepi, quarum singula verba mihi visa sunt stillare dulcedinem et suavi sincerae caritatis melle manare" (J. A. Giles, 136).

104. *Gesta abbatum Gemblacensium*, c. xlii, on Abbot Olbert (MGH, *Scr.*, VIII, 541).

105. "Vox tua, o Jesu, plena est caritate melliflua": Leclercq, *St. ans.*, 31, 125. Baudry of Bourgueil, carmen 161:

Ad te currebant examina discipulorum
Et refovebantur mella parentis apis.

106. *Ep.* 196, n. 1 (PL, CLXXXII, 363 CD).

107. "dulcedo divini Verbi": *In Jud.* (Pez, 4).

108. *Planctus B. V. M.*: "hujus caelestis atque melliflui carminis" (Delhaye, ET, 254). The "mellea cantica" of the angels resound to the heaven: Adam of SV.

109. "quod non dulcissimi Jesu fuisset melle mellitum" — "favis aliquid caepit emanare dulcissimi et mellifluum Christi nomen sibi merum vindicavit affectum": *De spir. amicitia, prol.* (PL, CXCV, 660 A); Bk. I (662 A).

110. "Melli dulcedinem suam praestitisti, et dulcior melle tu es": *Med. Ans.* 13 (PL, CLVIII, 774 A).

111.   ". . . Et auris
Mellifluae vocis dulci seducta canore
Seducit mentem. . . ."

Bk. VII, c. iii (PL, CCX, 552 C).

112. "super mellifluum pectus Domini" — "melliflua Salvatoris praesentia" — "Vox tua, plena suavitate melliflua": *Insin.*, Bk. IV, c. iv (1622, pp. 399, 400, 408).

113. *in melle dulcedo*: Wazelin of Liège, *De concord. et esp. 4 ev.* (H. Silvestre, RB 63, 320).

114. "suavitas doctrinae Christi": *In Cant.*, Bk. III (PG, XIII, 152 A); "mela quidem suavia et dulcia esse dogmata ecclesiastica, quae in Christi Ecclesia praedicantur."

115. "mysteriorum suavitas": *In Zach.*, Bk. III (PL, CLXVIII, 759 C).

116. "sacramentorum caelestium deliciae": *In Cant.*, Bk. VI (PL, CLXVIII, 947 B). Again he says: "auro gravius, melle dulcius" (1958 B). *In reg. S. Ben.*, Bk. II, c. ix: "it is sweet to contemplate the conjunction of the prophets and the apostles" (CLXX, 506 B).

117. "amaenitas mysteriorum sacrae Scripturae": *In Hexaem.*, coll. 14, n. 6 (Q., 5, 394).

118. "dulcedo spiritalis intelligentiae" — "melliflua suavitas latentis mysterii" — "mel mysticae suavitatis" — "favus litterae": Irimbert, *In Cant.* (Pez, 2, 1, 401).

119. Guibert of Nogent, *Trop. in Os.* (PL, CLVI, 384 C). Martin of Leon, *serm. prol.* (CCVIII, 29 C).

120. Quodv., *De prom.*, P. II, c. xxi, n. 40 (PL, LI, 791 B).

121. "Tot sunt deliciae quot sunt diversitates spiritalis intelligentiae": *In Cant.*, c. viii (PL, CCII, 1298 C).

122. *Did.*, Bk. IV, c. i (PL, LCXXVI, 777 C); Bk. V, c. ii: "sic et mel in favo gratius" (790 B); Bk. VI, c. iii (807 C).

123. *In Joel:* "Aqua est conditio historialis; lac doctrina moralis; dulcedo aedificatio spiritualis" (PL, CLXXV, 368-9).

124. *De Emman.*, Bk. II, c. xxiii (PL, CXCVI, 656-7). *In Cant.*, c. xxviii: "Favus distillans sunt labia devotae animae, quia spiritualis dulcedinis liquore fluunt et aliis ad aedificationem hunc fundunt. Hunc favum congerit anima de diversis Scripturae floribus; hos perquirit, his insidet, de his suavitatem spirtualis dulcedinis extrahit et elicit. Ab his spirituale mel colligit" (486 CD). P. Lombard, *In ps. CXVIII*, 11: "Comparatio tamen ad mel vel favum fit, quia in Novo judicia aperta, et operta in Veteri Testamento, quae dulciora sapiunt, palato fidei, quam faucibus carnis mel vel favus" (CXCI, 212 B).

125. *In Jud.*, Bk. I (Pez, 4, 234-5).

126. *In Ez.*, c. xviii (PL, CLXVII, 1440 D). G. Foliot, *In Cant.:* "Totum vero Testamentum novum si consideres, nil nisi quod dulce est et desiderabile prorsus invenies" (CCII, 1281 D).

127. "Interdum, mea legens, sic delectabiliter afficior, quasi haec probatus aliqua composuerit auctor" (J. Seemüller, 2).

128. Dant tua labia favum per cerea mella liquatum.
    Sub linguaque tua lac et praedulcia mella,
    Vestibus aeque tuis redolet fragrantia thuris.
    Ut favus in cera latitat, sic littera plena
    Subtilis sensus mysteria continet intus:
    Quae cum doctores veluti capsae locupletes
    Ubere doctrina fundunt in vascula vina,
    Fortibus hinc verbi redolet dulcedo superni.
    Sub tamen hac lingua quae stillat dulcia mella,
    Sensibus infirmis non desit copia lactis.
    Illos historiis, hos pascat ut allegoriis.
    Dumque cohaerentes subjecti sive docentes
    Te vallent sponsa quasi vestimenta decora,
    Frag[r]a[n]t odor suavis mihi de vestris benefactis.
        J. Schilterus, *Thes. ant. teuton.*, I (1728), 31-2.

129. Aponius, *In Cant.*, Bk. VII (139). Bede, *In Cant.*, Bk. IV, c. v: "Favo comparantur hi qui in litteris sacris dulcedinem sensuum spiritualium investigare atque ad salutem audientium elucidare praedicando noverunt..." (PL, XCI, 1152 B). G. Foliot, *In Cant.* (CCII, 1268 C); etc.

130. "Liber qui viscera replevit, dulcis in ore sicut mel factus est, quia ipsi de

omnipotenti Deo sciunt suaviter loqui, qui hunc didicerint in cordis sui visceribus veraciter amare. In ejus quippe ore Scriptura sacra dulcis est, cujus vitae viscera mandatis illius replentur, quia ei suavis est ad loquendum, cui interius impressa ad vivendum fuerit": *In Ez.*, Bk. I, h. 10, n. 13 (PL, LXXVI, 890 C). Cf. *In Cant.* (LXXIX, 513 AB).

131. Mella cor obdulcantia
Tua distillant labia,
Fragrantum vim aromatum
Tuum vincit eloquium?

PL, CXLV, 957 C.

Peter the Venerable, *Ep.* 6, n. 4, on the virtues practiced at Cluny: "mellifluae aromatum ac pigmentorum fragrantiae" (Leclercq, p. 185).

132. *Ep.* 2 (MGH, *Ep.*, 5, 10, 22, 46, 51). Manegold, *Ad Gebeh.*, c. vii: "mellifluus papa Greg." (*L. de lite*, I, 323). Hymn to Greg.: "organum mellifluum (Spiritus)" (A. Poncelet, *Anal. boll.*, 1887, 45-6).

133. "verba Gregorii melliflua": Adam Scotus, *De trip. tab., ep.*, c. iv: "ut verbis Gregorii mellifluis utar" (PL, CLCVIII, 629 *).

134. "mellifluus papa Gregorius": *Ep.* 1 (MGH, *Ep.*, 1, 2, 159).

135. "doctrinae semina . . . quae post in populos mellitos declamaret gutture, congerebat": *Vita Greg.*, Bk. I, c. iii (PL, LXXV, 64 A).

136. "Nectaris Ambrosii redolentia carpito mella": Ekkehard Jun., *De casibus S. Galli*, c. xi (Goldast-Senckenberg, 1, 52). John of Salisbury, *H. Pont.*, c. xiii: "Ambrosius, mellifluus doctor Ecclesiae" (Chibnall, 30).

137. "Quam autem mellifluus in responsis fuerit et alloquiis, lacrymae eorum qui hominem viderant et post ipsum supererant, requirentibus eum liquido manifestabant": *Ekk. minimi decani S. Galli, L. de vita B. N. Balb.*, c. xxv (*ibid.*, 1, 2, 241).

138. "Lingua tua, favus est et distillans mel" — "Ipse osculetur me osculo oris sui: . . . osculo oris tui, mellito eloquio procedente ex ore tuo jocundo": *Ep.* 1 (*Sacrae antiq. monumenta* . . . , 2, 1731, 312, 313).

139. "sanctus Bernardus, cui Jesus mel in ore": *S. inéd.* (Leclercq, *Études*, 159). Bernard, *In Cant.*, s. 15, n. 6 (PL, CLXXXIII, 847 A). In a hymn that a MS probably prior to 1174 contains, the life of Bernard is called "favus in ore"; of his speech it is said: "mel sapiebat" (Leclercq, 175).

140. "mel et lac sub lingua": Geoffrey, *V. prima* (1155), Bk. IV, c. vii: "Mel et lac sub lingua ejus; nihilominus in ore ejus ignea lex" (PL, CLXXXV, 307).

141. "et ori mellifluo quo Salvatoris doctrina profluxit, fellea posita manus porrexerunt nefarie" (v. 1150; Talbot, ASOC 7, 227).

142. *De div.*, s. 18, n. 1: "Ipsa ergo procedant tanquam cellulae mellis, ut facile adhuc labilem liquorem suavitatis solidior possit materia continere" (PL, CLXXXIII, 587 C).

143. Bernard, *In asc.*, s. 5, n. 11 (PL, CLXXXIII, 320 B). Robert of Tombelaine, *In Cant.*, c. iv, n. 15: "Recte ergo labia sponsae favus vocantur, quia dum in carnis fragilitate sapientia magna habetur, quasi mel in cera absconditur" (LXXIX, 513 A). Sicard, *Mitr.*, Bk. VI, c. xiv (CCXIII, 323 C); etc. Or the soul and the body: Hervaeus (CLVIII, 594 C).

144. Werner, *Defl.*, Bk. II (PL, CLVII, 1174 AB). Adam Scotus, *De trip. tab.*, P. 3, c. xvi, n. 176 (CXCVIII, 783 AB). *Allegoriae*, s.v. favus et mel (CXII, 922 CD, 997 C). Cf. Greg., *In Cant.* (LXXIX, 513 AB).

145. Rupert, *In Cant.*, Bk. IV (PL, CLXVIII, 904 A). Bk. III (894 BC).

146. Or the triplet mel-butyrum-oleum: as in Petrus Cellensis, *s.* 94 (PL, CCII, 921 CD).

147. Jerome, *In Job* (PL, XXVI, 669 D). Greg., *Mor.*, Bk. XV, c. xvi, n. 20 (LXXV). *Misc.*, Bk. I, tit. II (CLXXVII, 477 C). Absalon, *s.* 7 (CCXI, 48-52). Hervaeus, *In Is.*, Bk. I (CLXXXI, 100-2). Irimbert, *In Jud.*, Bk. I (Pez, 4, 166).

148. Richard, *S. in die Paschae:* "Egrediamur per sensum carnis, et pascus inveniemus in lacte humanitatis Christi; ingrediamur per sensum rationis, et pascus inveniemus in melle divinitatis ejus" (PL, CXCVI, 1074 B).

149. Gerhoh, *Ep. ad quasdam sanctim.:* "Et ego vicissim a vobis exigo non tam mulieris fortis fortia opera quam mel et lac reconditum sub lingua vestra, et eructandum inter cantica spiritalia, dilectione Dei tanquam melle dulcorata et dilectione proximorum quasi lacte redundantia" (*Op. in.*, I, 371).

150. Cassiodorus, *In ps. CXVIII*, v. 18 (PL, LXX, 843 A).

151. Isidore, *Etym.*, Bk. XX, c. ii, n. 36-7 (PL, LXXXII, 711 AB).

152. Paschasius, *In Matt.*, Bk. II, c. iii (PL, CXX, 154 CD). Peter Comestor, *s.* 31 (CXCVIII, 1794 B). Garnier, *s.* 18 (CCV, 690 AB); etc.

153. Joachim of Flora, *Sup. 4 ev.* (Buonaiuti, 118).

154. Peter Comestor, *s.* 30 (PL, CXCVIII, 1791 BD). Absalon, *s.* 7: "est enim mel purgativum, conservativum et dulce" (CCXI, 50 D).

155. Aldhelm, *De virg.*, c. iv (MGH, *A. ant.*, XV, 232). Paschasius, *In ps. XXIV*, Bk. I (PL, CXX, 997 D). Bernard, *In adv.*, *s.* 2, n. 3 (CLXXXIII, 42 AC). Werner, *Defl.*, Bk. II (CLVII, 1148-9). Alexander Neckam, *De laud. div. sap.*, Bk. IX, n. 223-54 (491-2).

156. "quae mellifica naturaliter est": Hervaeus, *In Is.*, Bk. I (PL, CLXXXI, 102 D).

157. Irimbert, *In Jud.*, Bk. I (Pez, 4); etc.

158. Peter Comestor, *s.* 31 (PL, CLCVIII, 1793 AB). Cf. Tertullian, *De praescr.*, c. xlviii.

159. "mel in lingua" vs. "mel sub lingua": Greg., *Sup. Cant.*, c. iv, n. 15 (PL, LXXIX, 513 B). Bede, *In Cant.*, Bk. IV (XCI, 1143 A); etc. Cf. Hesychius, *In Lev.*, Bk. I: "Dixit sub lingua, ut ostenderet quia paganorum sapientia et Judaeorum littera linguae Ecclesiae, id est doctrinae subjecta est" (PG, XCIII, 810 D).

160. "dulcedo carnis": Or., *In Ez.*, h. 8, n. 2, on Prov., 5:2-3: "Distillat enim mel de labiis mulieris meretricis. Ingressa est ad Moysen, ad Isaiam, ad Jeremiam, et de scripturis eorum sibi mella collegit. Vade ad haereticos loquentes: haec dicit Moyses, haec Isaias, haec Jeremias; et videbis quomodo de labiis eorum non fluant mella, sed distillent decerpentium de Scripturis verba paucissima. Et ideo mel distillat de labiis mulieris meritricis" (PG, XIII, 730 BC). Jerome, *ep.* 128, n. 2 (PL, XXII, 1096-7).

161. "adulantium favores" — "blandimenta deceptionis": Isidore, *L. de var. q.*, c. lviii, n. 4 (181).

162. "philosophia mundanis" — "mel saecularis dulcedinis": Isidore, *Q. in Lev.*, c. iii (PL, LXXXIII, 322 C). Rabanus, *In Lev.*, Bk. I, c. iv (CVIII, 263 A). Walafrid Strabo, *Epit. Rab.*, c. ii (CXIV, 800 A). Rupert, *In Lev.*, Bk. I, c. x (CLXVII, 753 C).

Richard, *L'except.*, p. II, Bk. III, c. x (Châtillon, 257). Cf. the three wisdoms distinguished by Origen, *De princ.*, Bk. III, c. iii, n. 2 (257).

163. "mel dulcedo," "mel dulcedinis," "mel dulce," "mel dulcoratum": Absalon, *s.* 7 (PL, CCXI, 50-2).

164. John to Gaufrid of Saint Barbara: "Si tam dulcis est memoria, qualis erit praesentia! Si mel et lac est sub lingua, quid erit super linguam!" (PL, CCV, 849 D).

165. *S.* 30 and 31 (PL, CXCVIII, 1791-5).

166. *S.* 7 (PL, CCXI, 48-52).

167. *Ep.* 107, n. 13 (PL, CLXXXII, 248 C). *De div.*, *s.* 4, n. 3 (CLXXXVIII, 582 D, 583 A); *s.* 97, n. 1-2 (724 BC). *In dom. I post oct. Epiph.*, *s.* 2, n. 1-2 (157-8); etc.

168. "Quanta in his multitudo dulcedinis!": *In Cant.*, *s.* 61, n. 5 (PL, CLXXXIII, 1073 B).

169. "elicere suave quidpiam": *In Cant.*, *s.* 39, n. 1 (977 D).

170. *De Jesu duod.*, I, c. v (SC, 60, 56); etc.

171. *In Cant.*, *s.* 5, n. 1 (PL, CLXXXIV, 32 BC); *s.* 6, n. 5 (41 BD); *s.* 24, n. 2 (126 A). *Tract. asc.*, vi, n. 2 (272-3); etc.

172. *De verbis Dom. in caena*, *s.* 4, n. 1 (PL, CLXXXIV, 895 D); *s.* 9, n. 9 (917); *s.* 11, n. 2 (930 AB); *s.* 14, n. 1 (944 B).

173. N. 18 (PL, CLXXIV, 975 B); n. 5 (967 D).

174. *S.* 16 (PL, CCXI, 102 B).

175. "sermones mellifluos": *De Jesu duod.*, I, c. v (SC, 60, 56). Ogier of Locedio, *op. cit.*, *s.* 14, n. 1: "quae de ore mellifluo Christi profluxere dulcia eloquia vitae" (CLXXXIV, 944 B).

176. "distillabat dulcedinem sermonis divini": *In Cant.*, *s.* 41, n. 5-6 (PL, CLXXXIV, 217 AD).

177. "Qualia mella sacri favus distillat eloquii!": Gilbert, *In Cant.*, *s.* 34, n. 2 (178 CD).

178. *Sup. Cant.*, c. iv, n. 15: "sapientiae dulcedo" (PL, LXXIX, 513 B). *Mor.*, Bk. XVIII, c. xl, n. 62: "ut hanc sapientiam, quae Christus est, percipere mereamur" (LXXVI, 72 AB).

179. *In annunt.*, *s.* 2, n. 4: "Non enim in solo pane vivit homo, sed in omni verbo quod procedit de ore Dei. Verumtamen donec sapiat tibi veritas, non sine difficultate ad interiora trajicitur. Ubi vero caeperis in ea oblectari, jam non cibus sed potus est, et sine difficultate intrat in animam, quo vid. spiritualis cibus intelligentiae potu sapientiae digeratur" (PL, CLXXXIII, 392 B).

180. *In Jo.*, Bk. I, c. xix (24).

181. *In Cant.*, *s.* 28, n. 8 (CLXXXIII, 925 A). If he sees Wisdom *in the flesh*, in this flesh he sees *Wisdom*: "in carne aspicere Sapientiam": *In Cant.*, *s.* 78, n. 8 (1162 C). Cf. Or., *In Matt.*, ser. 38: "Qui videt gloriosum adventum, id est adventum sapientiae in animam suam" (72).

182. *In die Pasch.*, *s.*, n. 1 (PL, CLXXXIII, 273 D). Gilbert, *In Cant.*, *s.* 34, n. 1: "Verbum Dei quanto amplius ruminatur in ore, tanto dulcius sapere debet in corde" (CLXXXIV, 895 B). Robert of Tombelaine, *Sup. Cant.*, c. iv, n. 15: "Quando vero electus quisque praedicat . . . , tunc favus distillat, quia quanta dulcedo sapientiae in corde lateat, per oris fragilitatem audientibus manifestat" (LXXIX, 519 A); etc.

183. *In Cant.*, s. 75, n. 9 (1149 A); s. 80, n. 2 (1166 D); s. 85, n. 12-4 (1193-4); s. 69, n. 2: "Quid est venire in animam Verbum? Erudire in sapientia" (1113 A). Cf. s. 62, n. 3, regarding St. John and St. Paul (1076 D). William of Saint Thierry, *Exp. alt. in Cant.* (CLXXXIV, 482 B, 509 D).

184. *In Cant.*, s. 31, n. 6: "Vide autem tu ne quid nos in hac Verbi animaeque commistione corporeum seu imaginatorium sentire existimes.... In spiritu fit ista conjunctio, quia spiritus est Deus. . . . Verbum nempe est, non sonans sed penetrans. . . . Facies est non formata sed formans ..." (PL, CLXXXIII, 943 AC); n. 1: "Studiosis mentibus Verbum sponsus frequenter apparet, et non sub una specie ..." (940 C); n. 4: God is not made to be known "per imagines extrinsecus apparentes seu voces sonantes; sed est divina inspectio, eo differentior ab his quo interior etc." (942 AB).

185. "Sano palato, sapit jam bonum, sapit ipsa sapientia": *In Cant.*, s. 85, n. 8 (1192 A; cf. 1191 D).

186. "si quid in tam dulci historia dulcius lateat": *S. on Emmäus*, n. 2 (PL, CLXXXIV, 965 D).

187. Bernard, *In Cant.*, s. 22, n. 2: "In hujusmodi non capit intelligentia, nisi quantum experientia attingit" (PL, CLXXXIII, 878 C).

188. *S. on Emmäus*, n. 20: "Incipiens a Moyse etc. Beati qui noverunt gustu felicis experientiae, quam dulciter, quam mirabiliter in oratione et meditatione Scripturas dignatur Dominus revelare" (PL, CLXXXIV, 976 C); n. 34 (979-80). Aelred, *S. ined.*, 4: "Legite, quaeso, in libro experientiae" (Talbot, 49; following Bernard).

189. Bernard, *In Cant.*, s. 28, n. 9 (PL, CLXXXIII, 925 C).

190. "Hic est gustus, quem in Christo facit nobis spiritus intellectus, intellectus sc. Scripturarum et sacramentorum Dei. Unde, cum post resurrectionem suam Dominus discipulis apparuit, 'tunc, inquit evangelista, aperuit illis sensum ut intelligerent Scripturas.' Cum enim Scripturarum interiorem sensum et virtutem mysteriorum et sacramentorum Dei coeperimus non solum intelligere, sed etiam quadam, ut ita dicam, experientiae manu palpare et tractare . . . , unc demum Sapientia quod suum est exsequitur ...": William of Saint Thierry, *Liber de nat. et dign. am.*, c. x, n. 31 (PL, CLXXXIV, 399 AC). Cf. *Exp. alt. in Cant.* (531 D); *In Cant.*, c. xlv (Davy, 72).

191. "beata scientia, in qua continetur vita aeterna" — "gustare, hoc est intelligere" — "ex hoc gustu per hunc saporem in hac sapientia satiatus": *Ibid.* (399 CD). Cf. *In Cant.*, c. xxv (Davy, 54), with allusion to ps.-Vergil: "Sic vos non vobis mellificatis, apes."

192. "super omnia aromata" — "carmen mellifluum": Aelred, *S. ined.*, 19, on St. Paul: "Omnis pene sermo illius inchoatur a Christo, terminatur in Christo, et per totius melliflui carminis seriem, hujus suavissimi nominis salutare fragrascit unguentum" (Talbot, 131). Nicholas of Clairvaux, *In nat. Dom.*, s. 1-2 (PL, CLXXXIV, 829 A, 832 BC, 838 C). Gilbert, *In Cant.*, s. 11, n. 2 (59 A).

193. "mel dulce" — "Spiritus Domini": Aelred, *De temp.*, s. 91 (PL, CXCXV, 320 CD). Guerric: "Spiritus enim meus, inquit Jesus, super mel dulcis. . . . Ita probantes quid sapiat manna absconditum, etc." (CLXXXV, 211 C).

194. "non modo in Spiritu, sed de ipso quoque Spiritu" — *Spiritus ante faciem*

nostram Christus Dominus: Bernard, *De div.*, s. 18, n. 1 (PL, CLXXXIII, 587 C); *In Cant.*, s. 3, n. 5 (796 A).

195. "Decora et delectabilis est significatio mystica": Bernard, *In dom. I post oct. Epiph.*, s. 2, n. 1 (CLXXXIII, 158 B). Cf. *ep.* 106, n. 2 (CLXXXII, 242 AB).

196. "Plena quippe sunt omnia supernis mysteriis ac caelesti singula dulcedine redundantia, si tamen diligentem habeant inspectorem": Bernard, *In laud. V. M.*, s. 1, n. 1 (CLXXXIII, 56 C; cf. 57 A). Cf. Luke of Mont Cornillon, *Mor. in Cant.:* "Meliora sunt ubera tua vino, id est, dulcior est moralitas et allegoria, quam dura plerumque et irrationabilis historiae intelligentia" (CCIII, 505 A). Ps.-Isidore, *In Cant.:* "Dulcedo evangelicae doctrinae austeritate legali melior est" (LXXXIII, 1119 A).

197. "mellea sapientia": Gilbert, *In Cant.*, s. 41, n. 3: "Quando puram et plenam intelligentiam spiritualium sacramentorum? Quanto sapientiam melleam, quam Paulus loquitur inter perfectos? Nam, sicut cellulis favus mellis, ita purissimis figurarum sacramentis caelestis sapientia continetur" (CLXXXIV, 216 B).

198. *Suavitas spiritus:* Bernard, *In Cant.*, s. 3, n. 1 (PL, CLXXXIII, 794 B).

199. "quasi raptim et in transitu": *H. dom.* 27: "Hora illa supernae visitationis congrue tempori quod cito transit comparatur, eo quod brevis sit, quia quidquid ibi de interna dulcedine homo degustando percipit, totum quasi raptim et in transitu fit, quia diu haberi non poterit; sed quantumlibet brevis sit, numquam sine effectu sanitatis transit . . ." (PL, CLXXIV, 185 B). *H.* 15 *in Script.* (1129 B).

200. *H. fest.* 12: "Vera etenim sapientia imbuitur, collustratur, qui divini saporis aliquid in caena dominica percipere meretur . . . , caeno dico illa, quando Deus accedit ad cor hominis, et cor hominis illuminatur etc." (671 BC).

201. *H. dom.* 51: "qui imitatores sunt Joannis . . . cum Domino et in caena sunt et . . . supra pectus Jesu recumbunt. Pectus Jesu, sacra Scriptura est, quia sicut in pectore cor, et in corde vita est, sic latet in sacra Scriptura spiritualis ille sensus, ex quo vivificatur homo et reviviscit intrinsecus etc." (339 B).

202. *H. dom.* 14: "Cum enim invisibilis ejus unctio, quae est perfecta cordis compunctio, intrisecus nos docere caeperit, tanta latitudine sensum adaperit, ut profunda Scripturarum mysteria, quae clausa prius et latentia vix auditor capiebat, subtiliter sapere et investigare mens nostra valeat. Altiora quippe et subtiliora de absconditis Scripturae mysteriis virtus nobis compunctionis intimat, quam ulla doctorum diligentia edocere nos valeat" (99 B).

203. *Liber de* 10 *oner. Is.*, c. viii: "Si cibum nostrum sacram Scripturam per intelligentiam cordis et imitationem operis fecerimus" (1196 D).

204. *De ben. Jacob:* "a lacte litterae ad eliciendam spiritalis gratiae dulcedinem sensus nos spiritaliter converterit"; "spiritalis ille intellectus . . . , omni jucunditate pulchrior"; "lacte simplicis litterae remoto, non solum leviora sed et fortiora sacrae Scripturae secreta etc." (1142 CD).

205. "Licet sensus iste allegoricus sit, tamen et redolet moralitem, ipsaque allegoriarum mysteria non carent moralitatis dulcedine": *H. dom.* 15 (105 B).

206. PL, CLXXIV, *passim;* 212 A: "plene atque perfecte quae in illa (Scriptura) latet dulcedinem intelligendo."

207. Cf. Hervaeus, *In Is.*, Bk. I: "dulcedo divinae sapientiae ejus" (Christi);

"dulcedo caelestis doctrinae"; signified by the honey that "cadit ex aere" (PL, CLXXXI, 100 A, 101 A). Odo of Cluny, *V. Grealdi*, Bk. I, c. vi (CXXXIII, 646 A).

208. "Dulcedo Dei" (PL, CLXXIV, 196 B), etc. The similarities between Bernard and Godfrey are not at all a priori surprising: Already during Bernard's lifetime copies of his works were collected at Admont, doubtless by the intermediary of the Cistercian abbey of Ebrach, whose abbot Adam (†1161) was in communication with Bernard. Cf. Leclercq, *Études*, 19, 29, 139-40.

209. "latentem in Scripturis dulcedinem haurire": *In Ap.*, Bk. II, *prol.* (PL, CLXIX, 863).

210. "Mel est dulcis doctrina allegoriae": *Exp. in Cant.* (PL, CLXXII, 423 B); "dulcis allegoria" (423 A).

211. "aeternae jucunditatis, incorruptionis, suavitatis mysteria redolentes": *In Jud.* (Pez, 4, 168, 163).

212. *In Cant.*, c. viii (PL, CCII, 1298 C).

213. "doctrina moralis" — "dulcedo" — "aedificatio spiritualis": C. iii: "Capitulum hoc prius moraliter discutiamus; deinde ad opaca allegoriae et tropologiae jucunda transeamus" (PL, CLXXV, 359 A); etc.

214. See pp. 169-70 above.

215. "allegoricus sensus acutior, tropologicus est suavior": C. viii (PL, CLXXVII, 375 C).

216. "Mysticus sermo . . . sicut panis est, qui confirmat cor hominis, velut fortior cibus verbi; suasorius autem ethicus, dulcis et mollior": *In ps. CXVIII, s.* 13, n. 23 (PL, XV, 1388 A); cf. 1197 A).

217. "sacratior sensus" — "suavitas moralitatis": Rupert, *In Gen.*, Bk. V, c. xv-vi: "moraliter nihilominus suavitatem ex hoc loco capere possumus" (PL, CLXVII, 381 B). Gerhoh, *In ps. LXX* (194, 311 A). Irimbert, *In Jud.* (Pez, 4, 151); etc. — Rupert, nevertheless, knows that the "dulcedo" is found not in a separated moral sense, but in the "plenitudo Scripturarum": *In Deut.*, Bk. II, c. xvi (CLXVII, 990 D); *In Zach.* (CLXVIII, 759 C); *In Cant.*, Bk. VI (947 B); etc.

218. "moralitatis dulcedinem": *Dial.* 7, c. xi (PL, CXCII, 1243 CD).

219. "sapida refectio": PL, CXII, 849 AB.

220. *In Cant.*, viii, 5 (PL, CCII, 1298 CD).

221. "Valde dulcis potus est in historia; sed et dulcior in allegoria; dulcissimus vero in moralitate; longe autem incomparabiliter in anagogen, id est in contemplatione": *Ps.-Lib. de Ans. sim.*, c. cxciv (PL, CLIX, 707-8).

222. "lac historiae" — "mel tropologiae" — "solidus panis allegoriae": *S.* 4 (PL, CCX, 209 CD).

223. PL, CCX, 240 B.

224. "cibus grossior" — "cibus dulcior": *In Cant.*, Bk. IV (PL, CCVI, 495 A). Amédée of Lausanne (CLXXXVIII, 1333 C).

225. "lac et mel" — "facilitas historiae" — "dulcedo tropologiae": Gloss on the Sentences, prol. (RTAM, 1931, 355).

226. "Tropologia magis movet quam allegoria": *Hist. scol.* (PL, CXCVIII, 1055-6); "suavior" (1063-4).

227. See Chapters 1 and 2 above. Cf. anonymous saint *ad pastores, de praedic. verbi divini*: "Hinc agnoscetis historiarum simplicatem et intelligetis allegoriarum mysteria; hinc percipietis dulcedinem moralitatis" (PL, CLXXI, 818 D).

228. Petrus Riga, petra cujus rigat initia Christus
 Legem mellifluo texit utramque stilo.

HLF, 17, 30.

229. Doctores notat Ecclesia nomen labiorum,
 Per quos verborum stillat dulcedo sacrorum:
 In redolente favo latitat mel, cera videtur,
 Clausus in his verbis moralis sensus habetur.

Cited by Trochon, *op. cit.* (1878), 63.

Notes to Chapter Ten
§1. A Twofold Anagogy

1. Or., *In Jos.*, h. 8, n. 3 (343): *Adhuc excelsius amplitudinem mysterii dilatemus.*
2. Jerome, *In Is.* (PL, XXIV, 153 C): *Spiritalis intelligentiae culmina persequamur.*
3. Or., *In Ex.*, h. 7, n. 8 (214).
4. Bernard, *In adv.*, s. 4, n. 1 (PL, CLXXXIII, 47 C); s. 5, n. 1 (50-1). Henry of Marcy, *De per. civ. Dei*, tr. 1: "According to the spiritual sense, the whole of Old Testament Scripture extends out into the past looking forward to the future, predicting a threefold coming of the Christ: either the first, which was hidden and humble . . . ; or the second, which, present every day, is perceived by the saints as interior and sweet; or the third, which, conspicuous and terrifying, is expected at the end of time." — "Secundum sensum vero spiritualem tota ipsa Scriptura veteris Testamenti futura prospiciens in anteriora se extendit, triplicem Christi praenuntians adventum; vel primum, qui occultus fuit et humilis . . . ; vel secundum, qui praesens quotidie a sanctis intimus sentitur et dulcis; vel tertium, qui manifestus et terribilis in fine temporum expectatur" (CCIV, 259 C). Cf. Paschasius, *In Matt.*, Bk. XI, c. xxiv (CXX, 818-9).
5. Thus Salomon Glassius, *Philologia sacra* (1711), 161: "Anagogia rectius dicetur *anagōgē*, subvectio, elevatio; nam *anagōgia* proprie defectum disciplinae, juxta Budaeum, item dissolutam vitam, et animum juvenis indomitum notat, ab *anagōgos*, intractabilis, contumax, dissolutus vita." — "Anagogy will more rightly be called *anagōgē*, carrying, lifting; for *anagōgia* according to Budaeus properly expresses a lack of discipline, a dissolute life, and the unrestrained mind of youth, from *anagōgos*, unmanageable, stubborn, of dissolute life."
6. In both cases it was employed figuratively to designate death. Cf. P. Boyancé, *Le culte des Muses chez les philosophes grecs*, 138-40.
7. Garnier, s. 31 (PL, XXV, 766 B): "ab *ana*, quod est sursum, et *agōgē*, quod est ductio."
8. *Elem. Theol.* (Dodds, 281). *Hymns*, I, 36; II, 1; IV, 5.
9. *In Phaed.*, 171.
10. Cf. René Roques, *L'univers dionysien* (1953), 204, note 7; *Recherches de philosophie* 3-4 (1959), 216-20 (Dionysius and Hugo).
11. *Hier. Cael.*, c. ii. J. Scotus, *Sup. Hier. Cael.* (PL, CXXII, 146 AB).
12. M. D. Chenu, *La th. au XII s.*, 133; cf. 186-7. Hugo, *In Hist. Cael.*, Bk. II and IX (PL, CLXXV, 944 CD, 946 A, 1104 AC).
13. Aelred, s. 10 (PL, CXCV, 205 D): "sensus de superioribus." Cf. Heterius and Beatus, *Ad. Elip.*, Bk. I, c. civ: "But the spirit in the higher angelic understanding, which is called anagoge" — "spiritus vero, in superiori intellectu angelico, qui anagoge appellatur" (XCVI, 958 A).
14. *Spec. Eccl.*, c. viii (PL CLXXVII, 375 B).
15. Bede, *In Hex.*, Bk. IV: "according to *anagōgē*, i.e., the sense leading to higher things. . . . Whether it reveals an allegory or leads the eye of its explanation to contemplate the things above" — "juxta anagogen, id est, sensum ad superiora ducentem. . . . Sive allegoriam revelet, sive ad superna contemplanda oculum suae expositionis attollat" (PL, XCI, 168 B, C). Hugo, *Reportatio* of Laurent (RTAM 25, 276).

16. Raoul de S.-G., *In Lev.*, Bk. XV, *praef.*: "Figures . . . are also anagogic that lead us to higher things, i.e., imbue us with the divine" — "Figurae . . . anagogicae quoque sunt, quae ad superiora nos ducunt, id est, de divinis nos imbuunt" (185 H).

17. Robert of Melun, *Sent.*, Bk. I, p. I, c. vi (Martin, 175): "quae per visibilia ad invisibilia animi levat intelligentiam."

18. Cassian (PL, XLIX, 965 A). Cf. Rabanus, *In I Cor.* (CXII, 130 B): "per quam ad invisibilia ac futura sermo transfertur."

19. Aug., *Civ. Dei*, Bk. XV, c. ii (PL, XLI, 439): "pars enim quaedam terrenae civitatis imago caelestis civitatis effecta est."

20. Hervaeus, *In Is.*, Bk. I (PL, CLXXXI, 69 A): "Jerusalem nunc intellige illam supernam."

21. Bonav., *Brevil.*, *proem.*, n. 4 (Q., 5, 205): "quando per unum factum intelligendum est aliud, quod desiderandum est, scilicet, aeterna felicitas beatorum." Cf. *In Hex.*, c. xiii (390-1).

22. Richard, *Nonnullae all. Tab.* (PL, CXCVI, 200 CD): "Quid enim dicimus anagogen, nisi mysticam et sursum directivam supercaelestium intelligentiam? In praedictis duobus, quaeritur doctrina morum et mysteriorum. Ad anagogen spectat sperandarum praevidentia praemiorum."

23. The "impletio figurarum": Hugo de F., *De Claustro an.*, Bk. III, c. viii (PL, CLXXVI, 1098 A). Th. de Perseigne, *In Cant.*, Bk. VII (CCVI, 495 A). Cf. Aug., *In ps. LXII*, n. 1: "Modicum quod restat venturum esse credimus, quando jam videmus tanta quae tunc futura erant, modo compleri, etc." (CCL, 39, 794).

24. *Op. cit.* "Quartus (sensus) est anagogicus, sc. quando per res signatas in Scriptura volumus ulterius significare aliquid quod pertinet ad statum vitae futurae; et dicitur anagogicus, id est, sursum ducens, sc. ad caelestia."

25. "Altior sensus": Bede, *In Esdram*, Bk. I (PL, XCI, 821 A).

26. "Altior theoria": J. Scotus, *In Jo.*, fr. 1 (PL, CXXII, 304 BC); he also says "altior allegoria." *Gloss in Deut.* XXXI, 30: "so that thus we may be advanced to heavenly contemplation" — "ut sic ad caelestem theoriam provehamur" (CXIII, 487 D).

27. Cassiodorus, *In ps. CXVIII* (PL, LXX, 900 C): "futuri saeculi sacramenta *declarat*."

28. Bede, *De Tab.*, Bk. I, c. vi (PL, XCI, 410 D): "de vita futura *disputat*." Rabanus, *In Ex.*, Bk. III, c. xi (CVIII, 148 B).

29. Or., *In Jos.*, h. 25, n. 3 (455): "ad mysteria futuri saeculi *contuenda*."

30. Aimon, *In Ap.*, Bk. II (PL, CXVII, 410 A): "ad *contemplanda* mysteria caelestia." G. De Nogent, *Trop. in Os.*: "anagogen quae ad Dei contemplationem pertinet" (CLVI, 384 B); etc.

31. *Coll.* 14, c. viii (Pichery, SC, 54, 190): "Anagogia vero de spiritalibus mysteriis ad sublimiora quaedam et sacratiora caelorum secreta conscendens."

32. G. Durand, *Rationale*, Bk. VI, c. ii: "There is a fourfold coming of the Son of God: . . . the first is the coming into the flesh . . . ; the second, into the mind. . . . The third advent is in the death of each individual. . . . The fourth will be in majesty. . . ." — "Est quadruplex adventus Filii Dei: . . . primus adventus est in carnem . . . ; secundus, in mentem. . . . Tertius adventus est in morte cujuslibet. . . . Quartus erit in majestate . . ." (Lyon, 1551, f. 155, 1). There would have been an in-

termediate form. Hélinand, s. 1: "Four advents of the Savior to men . . . : in the flesh specifically to the Jews, on the mountain to the chosen, in death to individuals, at the end to all" — "Quatuor adventus Salvatoris ad homines . . . : in carne specialiter ad Judaeos, in monte ad electos, in morte ad singulos, in fine ad universos" (PL, CCXII, 481 C). The "mons" (of the tranfiguration) has become "mens," and the "mors" of Christ on Calvary has become the death of each individual.

33. G. de S.-Th., *In Cant.*, n. 125 (Davy, 156). Cf. Gunther., *De orat.*, Bk. V, c. i (PL, CCXII, 141 B); etc. Hesychius, *In Lev.*, Bk. II (PG, XCIII, 860 D). John Scotus, *Div. Nat.*, Bk. I, n. 12 (PL, CXXII, 452-3).

34. André Feuillet, *La Demeure céleste et la Destinées des chrétiens*, RSR 44 (1956), 361-4.

35. Acts 3:21. 2 Peter 3:3-4. Or., *In Jos.*, h. 16, n. 3: The true Joshua has conquered all the earth — and still there remains much more of the earth to conquer (397).

36. "Per speculum et in aenigmate." Jerome, *Ep.* 120, c. viii: "For now we see through a mirror in an enigma, and when the veil of history has been split, so that we may enter the fore-court of God, nevertheless we cannot know his secrets and all the mysteries that are kept enclosed within the heavenly Jerusalem" — "Nunc enim per speculum videmus in aenigmate, et cum historiae velum scissum sit, ut ingrediamur atrium Dei, tamen secreta ejus et universa mysteria, quae in caelesti Jerusalem clausa retinentur, scire non possumus" (PL, XXII, 992); etc.

37. Or., *In Matt.*, serm. 138 (285). *In Jo.*, Bk. X, c. v (185). Richard, *In Ap.*, Bk. II, c. x: "The opening of the seventh seal, then, is the explanation of the holy speech about what is going to happen at the end of the age" — "Apertio igitur septimi sigilli, manifestatio sacri eloquii de his quae fient circa finem saeculi" (PL, CXCVI, 776 A).

38. *Misc.*, Bk. IV, tit. 2: "Holy Scripture has exaltation, because it promises eternal joys; a terrible aspect, because it threatens the reprobate with the punishments of Gehenna" — "Scriptura sacra . . . habet altitudinem, quia aeterna gaudia promittit; horribilem aspectum, quia reprobis supplicia minatur gehennae" (PL, CLXXVII, 703 B).

39. Ambrose, *De Isaac et an.*, c. v, n. 42 (PL, XIV, 516 AB): "Per evangelium in terris videmus caelestia mysteria figurata."

40. Junilius, *De part. div. legis*, Bk. I, c. x: "It is the intention of the Old [Testament] to point out the New by means of figures and intimations; that of the New, to enkindle human minds for the glory of eternal happiness" — "Veteris intentio est, novum figuris denuntiationibusque monstrare; novi autem, ad aeternae beatitudinis gloriam humanas mentes accendere" (PL, LXVIII, 20 D).

41. Bernard, *In Cant.*, s. 33, n. 6 (PL, CLXXXIII, 953 D): "Erat aurora, et ipsa subobscura satis, tota illa Christi conversatio super terram."

42. Guerric, *De resurr. Dom.*, s. 2, n. 1: "He performed the first resurrection for us with the Sacrament of his own resurrection, and on the model of that same resurrection he will perform a second one for us" — "Sacramento suae resurrectionis operatus est nobis resurrectionem primam, et exemplo ejusdem suae resurrectionis operabitur nobis secundam" (PL, CLXXXV, 144-5).

43. Guerric, *De purif.*, s. 6, n. 5: "so that by means of the truth of the things

within us we may at some point rejoice in the completeness of what the Son of God willed to prefigure today within himself a little bit at a time" — "ut quod hodie figurare voluit in seipso Filius Dei quadam dispensatoria specie, completum quandoque gaudeamus in nobis ipsa rerum veritate" (PL, CLXXXV, 91-2). Cf. P. Lombard, *s. In caena Dom.* (CLXXI, 510 C).

44. Or., *De princ.*, Bk. IV, c. iii, n. 13: "Spiritus vultus nostri Christus Dominus, cujus diximus quia in umbra ejus vivemus in gentibus — cum sc. ab evangelio temporali dignius omnes sanctos ad aeternum evangelium transferet, secundum quod Joannes in Ap. de aeterno evangelio designavit" (344). *In Rom.*, Bk. I, c. iv (PG, XIV, 847 B). Cf. *In ps. XXXVIII*, h. 1, n. 2 (XII, 1402 AB).

45. Honorius, *Gemma animae*, Bk. III, c. xxxiii: "Just as the Hebrew people prefigured the festivity of the Christian people, so in its festivals did the Church presignify the solemnities of the age to come" — "Sicut Hebraicus populus praefiguravit festivitatem christiani populi, ita Ecclesia per sua festa praesignat solemnitates futuri saeculi" (PL, CLXXII, 651 CD). Chrys., *In Gal.*, c. iv, n. 4: "Hagar, then, is the figure of the lower Jerusalem . . . ; the Church, on the other hand, is the type of the supernal [Jerusalem]." — "Inferioris igitur Jerosolymae figura erat Agar. . . . Supernae vero typus est Ecclesia" (PG, LXI, 662).

46. *Ibid.*, c. cxxv (677 B). Cf. Congar, *Le myst. du Temple*, 248.

47. J. Châtillon, *Hoc, ibi, interim*, RAM 25 (1949), 194-9. [Trans. note: The colloquial secular meaning is "meanwhile," "in the mean time."]

48. Aug., *De sp. et litt.*, c. xxxiii-iv, etc. Cf. J. Plagnieux, *Le chrétien en face de la loi d'après le De sp. et littera de S. Aug.*, in *Theologie in Geschichte und Gegenwart* (*Mélanges Michael Schmaus*, 1957), 746.

49. Or., *In Lev.*, h. 13, n. 2 (470); *In Cant. fr.* (PG, XIII, 201 D), etc. P. Lombard, *In ps. XVII*, v. 13 (PL, CXCI, 191 A).

50. "Nox ut dies illuminatur"; "nox illuminatio in deliciis meis": Rupert, *In Ex.*, Bk. II, c. xxi (PL, CLXVII, 629 BC).

51. J. Gribomont, *Le lien des deux Testaments selon la théol. de S. Thomas*, ETL (1946), 87.

52. Gal. 4:26. Cf. Aelred, *s.* 10 (PL, CXCV, 205 CD).

53. Heb. 12:22. Cf. Apoc. 21–22. Cf. Chromatius, *In Matt.*, tr. 10, c. iii, n. 4 on Jerusalem: "the type of Christ's body, which is yon spiritual and heavenly Church" — "typus corporis christi, quod est spiritalis illa et caelestis Ecclesia" (CCL, 9, 421-2).

54. Or., *De princ.*, Bk. IV, c. ii, n. 2: "illam regulam disciplinamque, quam ab Jesu Christo traditam sibi apostoli per successionem posteris quoque suis caelestem Ecclesiam docentibus tradiderunt" — "tēs kanonos tēs Iēsou Christou kata diadochēn tōn apostolōn ouraniou ekklēsias" (308-9). Cf. Irenaeus, *Adv. Haer.*, Bk. IV, c. xxxii, n. 2: "pointing out the type of the heavenly things . . . and prefiguring the images of those that are in the Church" — "typum autem caelestium ostendens . . . et imagines eorum quae sunt in Ecclesia praefigurans" (PG, VII, 1071 B).

55. Phil. 3:20.

56. Isidore, *L. de var. q.*, c. xxvii (75).

57. "Caelestem patriam, quam Ecclesiam catholicam dicimus": Apringius, *In*

Ap. (3). Autpert [?], *In Ap., praef.* (407 G). Cf. Richard, *In Ap.,* Bk. I, c. (PL, CXCVL; comp. 736 D and 737 A).

58. "And that very city (namely the Holy Church) that is to reign in heaven still struggles on earth": *In Ez.,* Bk. II, h. 1, n. 5 (PL, LXXVI, 338 D). Cf. Aug., *Civ. Dei,* init. — but the word 'Ecclesia' is not present.

59. *Op.* 3, q. 10: "Erat namque Hierusalem urbs illa magna regalis, ubi templum famosissimum Deo fuerat constructum; postea vero quam venit illa, qui erat verum Templum Dei, et caelestis Hierusalem caepit aperire mysteria, deleta est illa terrena, ubi caelestis apparuit" (PL, CXLV, 66 D). Rupert, *In Zach.,* Bk. V: "Therefore here, as in many places in Scripture, Jerusalem signifies the Church on pilgrimage in this world, [a Church] which, while it is on pilgrimage, even though not completely is nevertheless in hope already the heavenly Jerusalem." — "Ergo Hierusalem hic, sicut est in plerisque Scripturarum locis, Ecclesiam significat in hoc mundo peregrinantem, quae, quamdiu peregrinatur, etsi nondum re, tamen spe jam est caelestis Hierusalem" (CLXVIII, 791 D). Bonizon, *Liber ad amicum,* I: "Mother the Church, which is above" — "Mater Ecclesia, quae sursum est" (Jaffé, II, 603).

60. Bk. IV, c. iii, n. 2 (326); b. 6-8: "The Jerusalem which is above, the one that is our mother, is free" — ". . . quae sursum est Jerusalem libera est, quae est mater nostra" (332-5). *In Jos.,* h. 13, n. 1, commenting on 1 Cor. 10:11: "All these things that occurred by way of figure for them, was written for our sake. . . . — He understands all these to be mysteries of the kingdom of heaven." — "Haec omnia quae figuraliter accidebant illis, scripta sunt propter nos. . . . — Haec omnia, mysteria intelligit esse regni caelorum" (371); h. 17, n. 1 (400 C).

61. *In Lam. Jer.,* Bk. I (PL, CXX, 1086, 1099-100, 1206-7, etc.).

62. *Trip. tab.,* P. III, c. ix, n. 155 (PL, CXCVIII, 760 CD).

63. "Umbrae et imagini deserviunt caelestium": Heb. 8:5; cf. 9:24; 12:25; 13:30. Or., *De princ.,* Bk. IV, c. ii, n. 16 (315-6); c. iii, n. 12 (341). Ambrose, *In ps. I,* n. 31: "Lex enim exemplar est et umbra caelestium" (26). Ps.-Atton (Claudius) [?], *In Hebr.:* "caelestium figuram ostendebant . . . id est novi Testamenti opera quae Ecclesiae caelestis nuncupantur opera, qui ex ea caelestia promerentur" (PL, CXXXIV, 771 D); which brings us back to the first notion or pretty close to it.

64. Col. 3:1-2. Cf. P. Lombard (PL, CXCI, 702 C). Honorius (CLXXII, 327 B).

65. "Per typica ad vera, et per temporalia ad aeterna, et per carnalia ad spiritualia, et per terrena ad caelestia." *Adv. Haer.,* Bk. IV, c. xiv, n. 3, citing Exod. 25:40 (PG, VII, 1012 A). C. xix, n. 1: everything in the O.T. is a "typus eorum quae sunt caelestia" (1030 A); cf. c. xxxii, n. 2: "pointing out the type of the heavenly things, . . . prefiguring the images of those that are in the Church, . . . and containing the prophecy of things to come" — "typum autem caelestium ostendens . . . et imagines eorum quae sunt in Ecclesia praefigurans . . . , et prophetiam futurorum continens" (1071 B). Cf. *Demonstr.,* c. ix (Froidevaux, SC, 62, 46).

66. *In Jo.,* Bk. X, c. xviii (189).

67. Father A. Vaccari, *Inst. Bibl.,* 1 (6th ed., 1951), 516, seems to disapprove of this text. In *Scritti di erudizione e di filologia* he comments on it three times (1, 90-1; 2, 158, 352) as if Or. opposed "ideas" or "speculative truths" to the historical realities in the manner of Philo's seeing in Adam the intellect or in Eve sensation. The immediate context, like the whole specifically Origenian synthesis, seems to us to

disconfirm an interpretation along these lines. Granting that this sort of "psychic" explanation was found in Philo, he cites them much too much for our taste; but this is scarcely the fellow whom he would want so emphatically to call upon the authority of St. Paul and the "sensus Christi." Mr. H.-Ch. Puech himself considers this text "disquieting": *La Gnose et le temps*. Eranos-Jahrbuch 20, *Mensch und Zeit* (1951-2), 75, note 19.

68. *In Lev.*, h. 5, n. 1; Heb. 8:5 (334).

69. *In Amos* (PL, XXV, 1000 B): "De littera debemus ascendere ad spiritum, de terrenis ad caelestia."

70. *Disc.* 45, c. xxxiii. A little earlier, before entering the analysis, he had said: "Let us partake of the Passover, now still in the fashion of an image *(typikōs)* though already more manifestly *(gymnoteron)* than in the past, — for, though I hate to say it, the Passover of the Law was the more obscure image of an image, — but a little later we shall take it more perfectly and more purely, when the Word will drink it up anew in the kingdom of his Father, revealing and teaching us what he has now uncovered for us in a certain measure *(metreōs)*" (PG, XXXVI, 635-6).

71. *Elegy of Caesarius*, c. i, n. 6: *apo tēs sarkos kai tōn proskairōn epi ta pneumatika kai aïdia* (Boulenger, 4).

72. *De vera rel.*, c. l, n. 98: to elevate ourselves to the eternal, "we use the steps that divine providence has deigned to shape for us" — "utamur gradibus quos nobis divina providentia fabricare dignata est . . ." (Pegon, 168); etc.

73. *In dom. palm.*: "Vetus quidem est lex, novum autem est Verbum; temporale exemplar, sed sempiterna est gratia" (PL, LIV, 493 B).

74. *In Ez.*, Bk. II, h. 2, n. 17: "While . . . the Patriarchs and the Prophets of the Old Testament . . . are preaching the heavenly mysteries to come" — "Patres Testamenti veteris et Prophetae . . . dum caelestia mysteria ventura praedicant" (PL, LXXVI, 967 B); h. 1, n. 16: "when we desire to cross over from the temporal sacraments to the eternal" — "dum a sacramentis temporalibus transire ad aeterna cupimus" (947 A).

75. *Ep.*, Bk. IV, 31: "What is holy Scripture but a letter of the omnipotent God to his creature? . . . Therefore, I beg of you, try to meditate upon the words of your creator every day. . . . Learn the heart of God in the words of God, so that you may the more ardently strive for things eternal" — "Quid est autem Scriptura sacra, nisi quaedam epistola omnipotentis Dei ad creaturam suam? . . . Stude ergo, quaeso, et quotidie creatoris tui verba meditare. . . . Disce cor Dei in verbis Dei, ut ardentius ad aeterna suspiras" (706 AB).

76. *De doctr. spir.*, c. xii (PL, CXXXIII, 273 A).

77. *In Hebr.*, VIII, 5: "Dominus enim voluit nos ad intelligibilia et spiritualia manuduci."

78. Or., *In Ex.*, h. 11, n. 6: the opposition between the "present age" and of the "age to come" (259). As archetype of our earth, the promised land is no less a land of promise for us. Eternal like God, our entry into it is no less "to come": *In Num.*, h. 7, h. 5, etc. The "protology" of Or. is at the same time eschatology, conforming to the Epistle to the Hebrews. Cf. H. Cornélis, RSPT (1959), 217, note 193.

79. *In Num.*, h. 9, n. 5: "the mystery to come" — "mysterium futurum" (60);

h. 16, n. 1: "the mysteries to come" — "mysteria futura" (138); h. 23, n. 5 (217); etc. See above, Chapter 8.2.

80. Or., *Sel. in ps. XXII*, 5 (PG, XII, 1264 A), etc. Cf. *In Rom.*, Bk. V, c. 1 (XIV, 1020-1).

81. Or., *In Gen.*, h. 12, n. 2 (108). Cf. 2 Cor. 4:18: "non ea quae videntur, sed quae non videntur, id est non carnalia sed spiritualia, non praesentia sed futura."

82. Cf. M. Harl, *Or. et la fonction révélatrice . . . ,* 144.

83. HE, 284-6. Cf. René Cadiou, *La jeunesse d'Or.* (1935), 142. Mr. O. Cullmann seems to us to overemphasize the contrast between Irenaeus and Origen, when he writes, *Christ et le Temps* (1947), 40: "Aucun théologien de l'antiquité n'a saisi aussi nettement qu'Irénée l'opposition fondamentale qui existe entre la conception grecque et la conception biblique du temps. Parmi les théologiens des premiers siècles, il est celui qui a le mieux compris l'essence de l'héllénisme et qui n'a commis à l'égard du message néo-testamentaire aucune de ces violences, aucune de ces mutilations ou de ces altérations dont se rendus coupables, non seulement les gnostiques, mais aussi, dans l'École d'Alexandrie, Clément et Origène." ("No theologian in antiquity has grasped the fundamental opposition that exists between the Greek and the biblical conceptions of time so well as Irenaeus. Among the theologians of the earliest centuries, it was he who best understood the essence of Hellenism and who did not commit against the New Testament message any of those acts of violence, those mutilations or those alterations that have rendered culpable not only the Gnostics but also, in the school of Alexandria, Clement and Origen.") The author adds in a note "L'opposition entre l'héllénisme et le christianisme est bien marquée par L. Laberthonière, *Le réalisme chrétien et l'idéalisme grec* (1904), etc." ("The opposition between Hellenism and Christianity is well delineated by L. Laberthonière. . . .") Now, if this latter work is inspired in its hermeneutics by any Father, it would be Origen as much as or even more than Irenaeus.

84. Or., *In Jo.*, Bk. XIII, c. xxxvi (262).

85. *In Luc.*, Bk. V, c. vi, n. 49 (Tissot, SC, 45, 201). See p. 202, herein.

86. *In Ez.*, Bk. XIII (PL, XXV, 416 D): "quotidie impletur in credentibus, et ad perfectum complebitur quando corruptivum hoc induerit incorruptionem." Cf. *In Is.*, Bk. XVII: "Though we see these things partially being unfolded daily in the Church, nevertheless they will be fulfilled more fully at the consummation of the world and at the Savior's second coming" — "quae licet ex parte in Ecclesia quotidie videamus expleri, tamen in mundi consummatione plenius complebuntur, et in secundo Salvatoris adventu" (XXIV, 598 C).

87. *In Ez.*, Bk. II, h. 10, n. 5 (PL, LXXVI, 1060 C): "secreta gaudia interioris vitae."

88. *Op. 9, de eleem. prol.* (PL, CXLV, 209 B): "rutilantium nitore gemmarum, sed spiritualium radiat decore virtutum."

89. Hildegard, *op. 10* (PL, CXCVII, 162 D).

90. *De nat. rer.*, Bk. I, c. xv: "Ad hoc ut perfectum redderet harmoniae caelestis consonantiam, opus erat octava sphaera. . . . Sic septenarius virtutum perfectam non reddit consonantiam, antequam ad octavam beatitudinis aeternae perveniatur" (54-5). Cf. Rupert, *In Matt.* IV (PL, CLXVIII, 1389 C). Gerhoh, *Libellus de ord. donorum* (*Op. in.*, I, 98).

91. Aug., *In ps. XXXII*, 2, *s.* 1, n. 8 (PL, XXXVI, 283): "novum testamentum, quod est regnum caelorum."

92. Cf. Eph. 4:3.

Notes to Chapter Ten
§2. Exegesis and Contemplation

1. *Prima Glossa sup. Gen.* (*Biblia sacra cum Gl. Ord.*, Anvers, 1634, 1): "spiritualis intellectus per quem de summis et caelestibus tractatur et ad superiora ducimur"; cited by the text "Girum celi" (Leclercq, AHDLMA 13, 321).

2. A "sermo mysticus, dogmaticus ac solidus": *In Num.*, Bk. IV, c. 1 (PL, CVIII, 784 D); *In Ez.*, Bk. XVIII (CX, 1033A).

3. Thus W. Strabo, having announced "four ways of understanding" Jerusalem, states only three: historical, allegorical, and finally "but through anagogy, the holy soul, which is always able to see the Lord through contemplation": "per anagogen vero, animam sanctam, quae Dominum per contemplationem mentis semper meretur videre" (PL, CXIV, 973 CD). *De subversione Jerusalem.* The last two senses, the one concerning the "anima" and the other "contemplation," are given under the single name anagogy.

4. Garnier, *s.* 31: "One sort of speculation is enigmatical, the other anagogical, depending on whether its name is derived from *speculum* (mirror) or from *specula* (watch-tower). For when one contemplates God through a glass darkly, this speculation is derived from *speculum* and is called enigmatic. . . . On the other hand, speculation is derived from *specula* when the mind is led so high that, with no preceding signs, with no subsisting causes, the mind, having been purged of every image, is brought back simply the same way to its infinite superessential origin . . . ; this sort of speculation belongs to very few indeed, and is called anagogical." — "Est autem speculatio alia aenigmatica, alia anagogica. Unde a speculo vel a specula nominatur. Quando enim per speculum in aenigmate, id est per similitudines et imagines rerum Deum quis contemplatur, a speculo speculatio dicitur et aenigmatica vocatur. . . . A specula vero speculatio dicitur, quando mens ita sursum ducitur, ut nullis signis praecedentibus, nullis causis subsistentibus, mens ab omni imagine defaecata, ad superessentialem et infinitivam originem simpliciter et reciproce refertur . . . , quae quidem admodum paucorum est, et anagogica dicitur" (PL, CCV, 765). See also the more compact explanations of Innocent III, *In sept. ps. paenit.*, 5: "For Zion is to be interpreted as a speculation, either as a watchtower, i.e., the universal Church, or else as the faithful soul which contemplates God now through faith and will ultimately look him in the face." — "Sion quippe interpretatur speculatio, sive specula, hoc est universalis Ecclesia, sive fidelis anima, quae nunc Deum speculatur per fidem et tandem contemplabitur ipsum per speciem" (CCXVII, 1096D). P. of Poitiers, *Allegoriae sup. tab. M., prol.:* "Ad aenigmaticam scientiam pertinet sensus allegoricus, qui per eum utrumque cognoscit Deum, ad comprehensionem pertinet sensus anagogicus, per quem cognoscitur quid in futuro nobis collaturus sit Deus" (M.-C., 1). See pp. 194-5.

5. *Osculum aeternitatis:* Cf. G. de S. Th., *In Cant.*, n. 33 (Davy, 60).

Notes to Pages 189-90

6. *In Jo.*, tr. 22, n. 2 (CCL, 36, 223): "Fidei fructus, intellectus, ut perveniamus ad vitam aeternam, ubi non nobis legatur evangelium, sed Ille qui nobis modo evangelium dispensavit, remotis omnibus lectionis paginis, et voce lectoris et tractatoris, appareat."

7. *In ps. LXXXIII*, n. 8 (CCL, 39, 1153): ". . . Numquid enim in domo tua talis disputatio erit, quasi quae doceat ignaros, quasi quae commemoret obliviosos? Aut vero in illa patria evangelium recitabitur, ubi ipsum Dei Verbum contemplabitur?"

8. *In ps. CXIX*, n. 6 (40, 1783): "sine lectione, sine litteris."

9. *In ps. XCIII*, n. 6 (39, 1305-6).

10. In Jo., Bk. XIII, c. v-vii (230-1). The Samaritan woman asked not to have to draw water from the well anymore, i.e., from the Scripture.

11. HE, c. viii.

12. *De div. nat.*, Bk. V, c. xxxviii (PL, CXXII, 1010 BC).

13. Cf. Paul Vignaux, *Philosophie au moyen âge* (1958), 18-9.

14. *In Ap.*, Bk. XII, c. xxi (PL, CLXIX, 1203 BD): "in semetipso et in corde Patris."

15. *In Ap.*, Bk. III, on Apoc. 4:1 (PL, CLXIX, 904 B). Gerhoh, *Exp. sup. can.*: "The kingdom of God, i.e., holy Scripture" — "Regnum Dei, sanctam vid. Scripturam" (*Op. in.*, I, 23); etc. See above, Chapter 5.5. But inversely, Rupert, *De Sp. sancto*, Bk. I, n. 6: "While we are reading holy Scripture, we are treating the Word of God, and have the Son of God before our eyes through a mirror and in obscurity." — "Cum Scripturam sanctam legimus, Verbum Dei tractamus Filium Dei per speculum et in aenigmate prae oculis habemus" (PL, CLXVII, 1575 D).

16. "Quid autem sacra nobis Scrptura, nisi vera repromissionis est terra?" Rupert, *In Ap., ad Frid.* (PL, CLXIX, 826); but a little later: "to enter upon the knowledge of God through the truth of the Scriptures. . . . We do not yet see the Lord face to face when we are reading or understanding the Scriptures; nevertheless the very vision of God which is at some point to be perfected, already begins here through the Scriptures." — "ad notitiam Dei per Scripturarum veritatem introire. . . . Nondum quidem dum Scripturas legimus, aut intelligimus, facie ad faciem Dominum videmus; verumtamen ipsa Dei visio quae quandoque perficienda est hic jam per Scripturas inchoatur."

17. J. J. Olier, *Explication des cérém. de la grand'messe de paroisse* (1687), 407-8.

18. *In Matt.*, Bk. XI (PL, CXX, 852 D).

19. S. 18, in f. Jo. Bapt. (PL, CCXVII, 540 C): "Violenti diripiunt regnum caelorum, id est, intelligunt mysteria Scripturarum."

20. Cf. Or., *In Jo.*, Bk. XIII, c. x (234); *In Jos.*, h. 6, n. 1 (323).

21. *Gen. litt.*, Bk. XII, c. vi-xiv (PL, XXXIV, 458-65). Alcuin, *In Ap. praef.* (C, 1089). Others, subdividing the first, distinguish four visions: Richard, *In Ap.*, Bk. I, c. i (PL, CXCVI, 686-7).

22. *Hom. fest.* 73 (PL, CLXXIV, 999 AB). Autpert, *In Ap.*, Bk. II (429-30). Aimon, *In Ap., praef.* (PL, CXVII, 738-40). Potho of Prüm, *De st. domus Dei*, Bk. II (495 H). Honorius, *Scala caeli major* (PL, CLXXII, 1231 B). Hervaeus, *In Is.*, Bk. I (CLXXXI, 19-20); *In II Cor.* (1113-4). Garnier of R., s. 3: "Through the testimony of the sacred speech we have learned three kinds of visions: bodily, spiritual, intellectual." — "Tria siquidem visionum genera, teste sacro eloquio, didicimus: corporale, spirituale, intellectuale" (CCV, 583 C); etc.

23. Hervaeus (PL, CLXXXI, 20 A): not "per aliquam spiritaliter vel corporaliter figuratam significationem," but "puro et acuto intellectu mentis"; this he names, using an Augustinian expression: "contuitus mentis" (19 B) [Trans.: i.e., a connatural "intuition of the mind"].

24. *In Ap.*, Bk. I (429 D): "ad divina mysteria rimanda."

25. *Exiit edictum*, c. iv (Châtillon — Tulloch, 100).

26. Roger Baron, *op. cit.*, 116.

27. *Allegoriae, prol.* (PL, CXII, 849 AB). There was thus a remedy for the excessively extrinsic character of tropology noted in the preceding chapter.

28. B. Hauréau, *Notices et extraits*, 32 (1888), 122: (1) "intellectus alitur"; (2) "mentem super se effundit, ut . . . usque ad domum Dei rapiatur."

29. Cf. Or., *In I Thess. fr.* (PG, XIV, 1297 D). Jerome, *Ep.* 119, c. x (6, 117-8).

30. Serlon de Savigny, *s.* 5 *in Pent.* (Tissier, 6, 111): "Habent (perfecti) altitudinem intelligentiae in contemplatione spiritualium."

31. Rabanus, *In Ez.*, Bk. VI, c. x (PL, CX, 640 A).

32. PL, CLXI, 707-8: ". . . In hac cella quatuor habentur dolia mellifluae dulcedinis plena, quorum ista sunt nomina: simplex historia, allegoria, moralitas, anagogen, id est intellectus tendens ad superiora. Ista quidem dolia modo quo superius diximus sunt ordinata: primo namque loco in Scriptura sacra, tanquam juxta ostium, est simplex historia; deinde allegoria, postea moralitas; novissime vero quasi in angulo est anagogen, id est contemplatio. Valde dulcis potus est historia; sed et dulcior in allegoria; dulcissimus vero in moralitate; longe autem incomparabiliter dulcior in anagogen. . . .

"Potus qui continetur in primo dolio, id est in historia, sunt simplicia gesta sanctorum et exempla, quibus dum intendimus, animas nostras magna dul-[c]edine quodammodo potamus. In secundo autem dolio, id est in allegoria, est fidei instructio; per allegoriam namque ad fidem instruimur et in interiore homine admirandae suavitatis sapore imbuimur. In tertio vero dolio, id est in moralitate, est morum compositio; per moralitatem enim mores nostros componimus, et quasi mirae dulcedinis potu refecti, hilares et amabiles proximis nostris apparemus. Potus qui continetur in quarto dolio, illo vid. qui stat in angulo, id est in anagogen, est quidam suavissimus divini amoris affectus, cujus ineffabili dulcedine, cum anima nostra reficitur, ipsi summae divinitati quodammodo unitur.

"Cum igitur cellarius iste aliquos in cellarium suum, sanctam vid. Scripturam, introducit, modo quo superius diximus, eis ad potandum tribuit; simpliciores namque et rudes in fide ac ejus amore, de prio dolio solet potare, id est de historia; capaciores vero de allegoria, perfectiores autem de moralitate, perfectissimos autem de anagogen, id est de contemplatione. Sciendum vero quod quisquis de quarto dolio, de illo vid. quod stat in angulo, id est, de anagogen biberit, quantulumcumque inde gustaverit, statim, ob miram ipsius potus dulcedinem, ebrius erit: illa vid. ebrietate ad quam sponsus electos suos invitat in Canticis: 'Comedite, amici, et bibite et inebriamini, carissimi,' etc.

". . . Habet autem istud cellarium in se quoddam ostium; in isto vero ostio, quaedam clavis habetur, per quam infidelibus clauditur et fidelibus aperitur. Ostium hujus cellarii, id est sanctae Scripturae, est recta fides; clavis autem, humilitas. . . ."

Accordingly, the profane can indeed "tanquam fur" and "quadam vi saecularis scientiae," "de primis doliis quasi quasdam guttas lumbere"; but he is absolutely unable to penetrate as far as "ad ultimum dolium, in quo continetur illud vinum quod laetificat cor hominis, id est in anagogen" (708 D). See above, Chapter 9.4.

33. Joachim of Flora expresses it in proper terms, *Sup. 4 ev.*: "the anagogical understanding belongs to those who, once the burden of flesh has been laid aside, are resting in yon blessed fatherland" — "anagogicus intellectus illorum est qui, deposito carnis onere, in illa beata patria requiescunt" (288).

34. *In Ap.*, v. 7 (PL, XVII, 961 AC): "Torrentemque non potuit transvadare, qui profunditatem divinorum caelestiumque mysteriorum nullus, sicut est, perscrutari potest. . . . Ecce angelus prophetam usque ad locum praefinitum ducit, et non eum transduxit, quia omnipotens Deus suos sanctos usque ad contemplanda secreta et arcana mysteria suae divinitatis perducit, sed nequaquam eos transducit; quia fragilitas humana perfecte non potest comprehendere illa inscrutabilia et divina mysteria."

35. *In Ap.*, Bk. IV, c. viii (496 EF): "nequaquam contemplatio perficitur, quamvis ardentissime inchoetur."

36. *In Num.*, Bk. I, c. xxxvii: "Hanc requiem (Domini), hanc terram viventium ad explorandum missi sumus, quicumque Scripturas sacras in manibus habemus etc." (PL, CLXVII, 874-5).

37. According to Bernard, *In Sept., s.* 1, n. 3 (PL, CLXXXIII, 164-5).

38. *In ps. CIV*, n. 3 (CCL, 40, 1537): "*Quaerite faciem ejus semper;* ut non huic inquisitioni, qua significatur amor, finem praestet inventio, sed, amore crescente, inquisitio crescat inventi." *In ps. XVII*, n. 12: "Nec propterea quisquam in illa luce, quae futura est cum ex fide ad speciem venerimus, jam se esse arbitratur, si Scripturas recte intelligit; in prophetis enim atque in omnibus divini Verbi praedicatoribus obscura doctrina est" (38, 96).

39. *In Ez.*, Bk. I, h. 3, n. 1 (PL, LXXVI, 806 A): "Quid enim per faciem nisi notitia, et quid per pennas nisi volatus exprimitur?" The image of the wings and of flight was already found in Vict. of Pettau, following Apoc. 4:8; but there it expressed merely the superior knowledge that "the preaching of the N.T." has of Scripture: *In Ap.* (Hausleiter, 55-6).

40. *Ibid.*, n. 1, 2, 6, 11, 13, 15 (LXXVI, 806 ABC, 810 C, 812 AC).

41. "The flight of allegory": *In I Reg., proem.* (PL, LXXIX, 17 B).

42. *In Ez.*, Bk. I, h. 3, n. 14: "Unless the all-powerful Word became man for the sake of men, human hearts would not fly to contemplate the excellence of the Word." — "Nisi . . . omnipotens Verbum propter homines homo fieret, humana corda ad contemplandam Verbi excellentiam non volarent" (PL, LXXXI, 812 B).

43. *Ibid.*, n. 1: "But because we are carried above ourselves, since we are lifted in the air." — "Per contemplationem vero quia super nosmetipsos tollimur, quia in aere levamur" (806 B).

44. *Ibid.*, n. 15: "they transcend other men by the flight of their contemplation" — "caeteros homines contemplationis suae volatu transcendunt" (812 C); n. 9: "through the hovering of the heart in the Word" — "per suspensionem cordis in Verbum" (809 C). Berengaud, *In Ap.*, V, 2: "These seats have been converted into wings for the fathers of the new Testament" — "Haec sedilia patribus

novi Testamenti in alas conversa sunt" (XVII, 803 B). Rupert (CLXVII, 1427 D). *Rép. clun. à Cîteaux:* "contemplationis volatus" (RB 67, 86). Richard, *Benj. major*, Bk. I, c. iii (CXCVI, 66 I); *In Ap.* (1304 A). Still another image in Greg., *In Ez.*, Bk. II, h. 5, n. 3: "The door has a cover, since Scripture as a whole has been written for our sake, but it is not understood by us as a whole" — "Habet . . . porta tectum, quia Scriptura tota quidem propter nos scripta est, sed non tota intelligitur a nobis" (LXXVI, 986 BC).

45. *In Cant.,* s. 81, n. 1 (PL, CLXXXIII, 1171 B): "affinitas animae ad Verbum." [Trans. note: *affinitas* is a relationship or an alliance by marriage.]

46. *In Gen.*, h. 11, 13, 14 (tr. Doutreleau, SC, 7); *In Num.*, h. 12 (tr. A. Méhat, SC, 29).

47. *Mor.,* Bk. II, c. xx, n. 35: "Causarum verborumque incrementis, quasi quibusdam ad aeternitatem passibus ducimur" (SC, 32, 207-8).

48. Cf. Richard, *In Ap.,* Bk. I (PL, CXCVI, 687 AB, 688 A and C).

49. Cf. Hugo, *In Hier. cael.*, Bk. IX: "anagogies . . . through each [order] of the hierarchic illuminations" — "anagogas . . . per unumquodque sc. ordinem hierarchicarum illuminationum" (PL, CLXXV, 1104 C).

50. *Ibid.,* Bk. II, c. 1: "he says 'anagogic' because it leads those cast down back to the higher things. . . . For the ascension or lifting up of the mind to the contemplation of the things above is called anagoge" — "anagogicam dicit, quia dejectos ad superiora reducit. . . . Anagoge enim, ascensio mentis sive elevatio vocatur in contemplationem supernorum" (944 D, 946 A).

51. *Coll.* 14, c. viii (Pichery, SC, 54, 191): "ad invisibilia ac futura sermo transfertur."

52. Cf. Bede, *In Esdram*, Bk. I: "By means of the anagogic, i.e., the higher sense, he implies the building up of the holy Church" — "Anagogico, id est altiori sensu, aedificationem insinuat sanctae Ecclesiae" (PL, XCI, 321A).

53. *S.* 31 (PL, CCV, 765-6); *s.* 35 (715). Cf. the description of anagogy that Dionysius the Carthusian will give, *De donis Sp. sancti*, Bk. III, c. xxxi (XXXV, 232).

54. Leclercq, *L'amour des lettres,* 210. [Trans. note: cf. English translation *The Love of Learning and the Desire for God.*]

55. Yves Congar, "Le Purgatoire," in *Le myst. de la mort et sa célébration* (1951), 312.

56. *S.* 60 (PL, CLXXI, 635 D): "agit de Deo et supercaelestibus." John Sarrasin to J. de Sal. on the *Hier. Cael.:* "This book brings together a lot for understanding all of the divine Scriptures in which the deeds or words of the angels are dealt with" — "Confert autem liber iste pluriu[m]um ad intelligentiam omnium divinarum Scripturarum, in quibus de factis aut dictis agitur angelorum" (CXCIX, 144 AB). Adam of Pers., *ep.* 30: "The fourth [sense] is anagogy, which leads the mind upwards to the understanding or contemplation of heavenly things" — "Quartus (sensus) est anagoge, quae sursum animum ducit, ad intelligentiam vel contemplationem caelestium rerum" (J. Bouvet, 213).

57. *Comp. errorum papae* (Goldast, 2, 957): "Anagogia est expositio, qua[e] invisibilia Dei per ea quae facta sunt intellecta conspiciuntur."

58. *In Ap.*, XII, 21 (PL, CLXIX, 203): "ut in ipsa vel per ipsam utcumque perpendere quaeamus, non jam quid vel quomodo sit Deus, sed quid non sit, et quod nulli creaturae assimilandus sit Deus."

59. *S.* 21 (PL, CXCIV, 1760 CD). Cf. M. A. Fracheboud, "Le Pseudo-Denys l'Ar. parmi les sources du cistercien Is. de l'Ét." (COCR, 1947).

60. *S.* 23 (PL, CCV, 730 AB): ". . . Mens humana, certae contemplationis gradibus ad summa conscendens, sacra divini eloquii inspectione caelestia secreta etiam anagogice contemplatur; et sic ex duobus generibus visionum ad omnem perfectionem ascendit, quae per gratiam divinae revelationis theologorum et prophetarum mentibus fuit infusa; quod (primum) genus visionis graece theophanias, id est, divinas apparitiones appellant; alterum, quo ascensu mentis et excessu nude et pure et absque integumento, sicut est, illum caelestem sacratissimum nititur contemplari, quod anagogicum nuncupatur.

"Sed in hoc ultimo genere visionis ita tremit et palpitat mens humana, ut tenebris ignorantiae suae obvoluta, ad illam claritatem et veritatis lumen, nisi dirigatur, exire non potest; sed quasi caeca et manuductione utens, quo non videt incedit; et incipit liquefieri per visionem et visitationem Dilecti; ut nec illud de Deo concipiat quod debet, aut velit, nec loqui possit quod concipit, cum caelestis regni circumvelatum ultra, et divini luminis incircumscriptum adhuc investigare nititur, et deficit investigans. Haeret in contemplatione mens attonita, obstupescit trepida, loquens penitus obmutescit, et inopem reddit copia, quam fecerat inopia copiosam; miroque modo proficiendo deficit, et tunc magis proficit, cum venerit ad defectum. . . ."

Notes to Chapter Ten
§3. The Unity of the Fourfold Sense

1. *In Gal.*, c. v, lect. 7: "Per hoc enim quod dico 'fiat lux' ad litteram de luce corporali, pertinet ad sensum litteralem. Si intelligatur 'fiat lux,' id est, nascatur Christus in Ecclesia, pertinet ad sensum allegoricum. Si vero dicatur 'fiat lux,' id est, ut per Christum introducamur ad gloriam, pertinet ad sensum anagogicum. Si autem dicatur 'fiat lux,' id est, per Christum illuminemur in intellectu et inflammemur in affectu, pertinet ad sensum moralem."

2. T. III, 21: "Historice intentum, (hoc) intelligitur de occisione Goliath proprio suo ense per puerum David. Allegorice, significat Christum vincentem daemonem eadem cruce, quam illi paravit. Tropologice, denotat bellum justorum contra daemonem de carne tentantem, qua compressa atque coercita, caput ejus absciditur, cum primi illius insultus vincti inanesque redduntur. Et anagogice importatur victoria Christi in die judicii, quando novissime inimica mors destruetur."

3. *De annunc.*, s. 4 (Q., 9, 671): "Secundum intellectum litteralem convenit virgini Mariae, in cujus tabernaculo requievit Dominus corporaliter. Secundum allegoricum convenit militanti Ecclesiae, in cujus tabernaculo requiescit Dominus sacramentaliter. Secundum moralem convenit fideli animae, in cujus tabernaculo requiscit Dominus spiritualiter. Secundum anagogicum convenit caelesti curiae, in cujus tabernaculo requiescit sempiternaliter." On the fourfold house where Christ is found: *In Epiph.*, s. 2 (9, 151). On the fourfold altar: text ed. by Wilmart, *Mém. Lagrange*, 312.

4. *Exp. in Cant.*, prol. (PL, CLXXII, 349 AC): "Hic liber agit de nuptiis, quae

fiunt quatuor modis, sc., historice, allegorice, tropologice, anagogice. . . . Juxta historiam fiunt nuptiae duobus modis, aut carnis commixtione, aut sola desponsatione. . . . Juxta allegoriam quoque fiunt nuptiae duobus modis. Uno, quo Verbum Dei carnem sibi conjunxit, id est, quo Deus humanam naturam sumpsit, quam in dextera Patris exaltatam in solio gloriae collocavit. Alio, quo Christus Deus homo universam Ecclesiam, id est, totam fidelium multitudinem, per commixtionem corporis sui sibi sociavit. . . . Juxta tropologiam etiam fiunt nuptiae duobus modis. Uno, quo anima Christo per dilectionem copulatur; alio, quo anima, quod est inferior vis interioris hominis spiritui, qui est superior vir[?] ejus per consensum divinae legis conjungitur. . . .

"Juxta anagogen nihilominus fiunt nuptiae duobus modis: uno, quo Christus resurgens a morte novus homo caelos ascendit, et multitudinem angelorum sibi sociavit; alio, quo adhuc post resurrectionem totam Ecclesiam in visione deitatis suae gloriae copulavit."

5. Peter Cellensis, *s.* 13: "Zion is sometimes taken for the heavenly fatherland, sometimes for the matchless virgin, sometimes for the Church universal, sometimes for the faithful soul" — "Sion aliquando accipitur patria caelestis, aliquando virgo singularis, aliquando Ecclesia universalis, aliquando anima fidelis" (PL, CCII, 674 C).

6. Bk. II, c. vii. Already in the *Ap.* Jerusalem "symbolizes not only the Church triumphant, but also the Church on earth, since she is represented as breathing with the Spirit which lives in her after the return of the Spouse (*Ap.* xxii, 17)": Henri Crouzel, BLE (1957), 71.

7. E.g., *In Ez.*, h. 5, n. 4: "And we all who have studied the divine Scriptures are Jerusalem, whether we live well or badly" — "Et omnes quidem, qui didicimus divinas Scripturas, sive bene sive male vivamus, Hierusalem sumus"; h. 6, n. 4; n. 8: "The Lord Jesus Christ our God again visits wretched Jerusalem, i.e., our sinful soul" — "Dominus Jesus Christus Deus noster rursum visitat miseram Hierusalem, id est, peccatricem animam nostram" (374, 383, 387). *In Lev.*, h. 10, n. 2: "'If you have risen again with Christ, etc.': does this not clearly tell you: Do not search for Jerusalem on earth, neither for the observances of the Law nor the fast of the Jews, but for the fasting of Christ; for you ought with fasting to approach your high priest the Christ who is at all events to be sought not on earth but in the heavens." — "Si resurrexistis cum Christo, etc.: nonne aperte tibi dicit: noli quaerere in terris Jerusalem, nec observantias legis nec jejunium Judaeorum, sed jejunium Christi, jejunans enim debes adire pontificem tuum Christum, qui utique non in terris requirendus est sed in caelis" (444). *In Jo.*, t. X, 18 (Jerusalem = the soul: PG, XIV, 357 B); t. X, 23-5 (= the city of living stones). *In Jer.*, h. 21 (= the holy soul: XIII, 515 C, etc.). *Sel. In Jer.*, c. xxix (= the Church; 518 AD). *Sel. In Thren.*, c. i (= the perfect soul: 609 B; the heavenly city: 607 D, 610 B), etc.

8. Especially in his commentary on Ezekiel. He criticizes those who, rejecting the "Jewish fables" and the carnal sense, look too high by way of reaction and see figurations of the heavenly Jerusalem, angelic combats or the action of demons where in fact it is a question of the Church here below and heretics. But Origen does not in fact make such a dissociation. See n. 53 below. Rabanus picks up these passages from Jerome: *In Ez.*, Bk. VII, c. xvi (PL, CX, 666 AB); Bk. XIII, c. xxxviii (867 D).

9. *In ps. CXXXI*, n. 21 (PL, XXXVII, 1725): "illa Jerusalem ad cujus pacem currimus. . . ." *In ps. CXXXIV*, n. 22 (CCL, 40, 1562); n. 28: this is the "kingdom of God's grace" — "regnum graciae Dei" (1654), etc. Jerome, *In Is.*, Bk. III, c. xlix (PL, XXIV, 470-2).

10. *Coll.* 14, c. viii (SC, 54, 190-1). Eucherius, *L. formul.*, c. ix (Wotke, 51).

11. *In Cant.*, Bk. IV (PL, XCI, 1142 AB).

12. *In Gal.* (PL, CXII, 331 C).

13. *In Gal.*, IV (PL, CIII, 191 A).

14. *Lib. quo ordine* (PL, CLVI, 26 A).

15. *De animae exsilio*, c. xii (PL, CLXXII, 1245 CD).

16. *Spec. Eccl.*, c. viii (PL, CLXXVII, 374-5).

17. Bk. III, tit. LIV, 62 (PL, CLXXVII, 670 BC, 674 A).

18. *Rat. div. off.*, c. cxiii (PL, CCII, 118 D).

19. *Glose in Hist. scol.*, in 1193 (RTAM, 1931, 361).

20. PL, CXIII, 28 D. Robert of Basevorn, *Forma praed.* (Charland, 294). Wyclif, *Serm.*, P. III, s. 22 (Loserth, 170; cf. 269).

21. PL, CLXXVI, 1131-2.

22. Aug., *In ps. IX*, n. 12 (PL, XXXVI, 122); *L*, n. 22 (598); *LXI*, n. 7 (734); *XCVIII, LXXIV*, n. 10 (1656); *CXXXIV*, n. 26 (1755). Greg., *In Ez.* (LXXVI, 857 A). John Scotus, *In Jo.*, fr. 1 (CXXII, 308 A). Rupert, *De div. off.*, Bk. IX, c. xi (CLXX, 262 A), Godrey of Admont (CLXXIV, 22 A, 26 A, 159 A). Hervaeus, *In Is.* (CLXXXI, 238 D, 291-2, 302-3). P. Cellensis, *s.* 90 (CCII, 914 A). Adam Scotus, *s.* 8, c. vi (CXCVIII, 144 A); *Ad viros rel.*, *s.* 1 and 6 (Petit, 129, 1273). Th. De Perseigne, *In Cant.*, Bk. VIII (CCVI, 548 B). Durandus of Mende, *Rat. div. off.*, Bk. I, c. 1 (Lyon, 1568, 4); etc. Cf. Prosper, *In ps. CXV*, v. 19 (PL, LI, 322 A). A. Gelin, *Vie spir.*, 86, 366: "We owe to St. Jerome the rabbinically flavored interpretation 'vision of peace.'"

23. Aug., *s.* 252, n. 7: "Illam Ecclesiam beatam, mysticam, magnam" (PL, XXXIX, 1175). *Ench.*, c. xv-xvi (Rivière, 204-14); etc.

24. *Ps. CXXI*, 3. Aug., *In ps. CXXI* (PL, XXXVII, 1618-29).

25. *Occupatio*, Bk. VII (A. Swoboda, 169-71).

26. *Prosa ecclesiae Silvanectensis* (tropes of St. Martial and Nevers; Misset-Weale, I, 376):

> Haec est magna Hierusalem, civitas scilicet illa superna,
> Ex auro mundo circumtexta, gemmis quae rutilat muri per ampla.
> Haec est illa caelestis aula, angelorum patria,
> Ecclesia, firmaque petra, aeternaque regia,
> Dicta est quae pacis visio, urbs celsa Hierusalem
> Ex vivisque petris struitur, beatorum animis. . . .

More celebrated yet is the finale of Hillebert's *Alpha et Omega* (PL, CLXXI, 1411-2), "one of the master-pieces of medieval poetry," says Mlle C. Mohrmann (CCM 1, 292).

27. Bk. I, v. 14, 103, 265, 269-72, 301, 309 (H. C. Hoskier, 1929):

> Patria luminis inscia turbinis, inscia litis . . .
> Patria splendida, terraque florida, libera spinis . . . .

> Urbs Sion, cus bona, patria consona, patria lucis, ...
> Urbs Sion aurea, patria lactea, cive decora,
> Omne cor obruis, omnibus ostruis et cor et ora,
> Nescio, nescio quae jubilatio, lux tibi qualis,
> Quam socialia gaudia, gloria quam specialis. ...
>
> Urbs Sion unica, mansio mystica, condita caelo ...
> Opprimit omne cor ille tuus decor, o Sion, o pax!

28. Leclercq, *L'amour des lettres*, 63-7. Cf. S. A. Hurlbut, "The Picture of the Heavenly Jerusalem in the Writing of Johannes of Fécamp, *De contemplativa vita*, and in the Elisabethan Hymns" (1943; cf. BTAM 7, 18).

29. *De duodecim lapidibus et civitate cael. Hierus.*, 12th cent. (*De viris inl. Cassin.*, 30; Manitius, 3, 450). Cf. *Commendatio cael. Hier.* (PL, CLIX, 624).

30. 2nd *s. for All Saints' Day* (Delhaye, ET, 233-43).

31. *Glossa in Ex.* XX, 2: "The heavenly Jerusalem, which is the mother of freedom, the chorus of freedom" — "Caelestis Hierusalem, quae est mater libertatis, chorus libertatis" (PL, CXIII, 249 D). Our spiritual exegetes at least are therefore an exception to the sometime too real forgetfulness that Gilson speaks of in *Les métamorphoses de la Cité de Dieu* (1952), p. 73: "Forgetting the grand apocalyptic vision of the heavenly Jerusalem, the City of God has been reduced to the Church, which, in the authentically Augustinian perspective, is merely the pilgrim portion." — "Oubliant la grande vision apocalyptique de la Jérusalem céleste, on a réduit la Cité de Dieu à l'Église qui, dans la perspective augustinienne authentique, n'en était que la partie pérégrine. ..."

32. Cf. *In ps. XCIII, XXIV,* and *XXX* (CCL, 39, 1325-6, 1330).

33. "They have been linked to each other": Guigo the Carthusian, *Scala claustr.*, c. xii, n. 13 (PL, CLXXXIV, 482 C).

34. Greg., *In Ez.*, Bk. I, h. 10, n. 1 (PL, LXXVI, 886 C). *Mor., ep. miss.*, c. i: "so that I would not only shake loose the words of history through the senses of the allegories, but I would bend the senses of the allegories still further toward the exercise of morality" — "ut non solum verba historiae per allegoriarum sensus excuterem, sed allegoriarum sensus protinus in exercitium moralitatis inclinarem" (PL, LXXV, 512 A).

35. Luke of M. C., *In Cant. mor.* (PL, CCIII, 550 D): "de historia ad allegoriam, et de allegoria ad moralitatem."

36. Gaudentius, *Tr.* 10: "For we know that through the grace of the Son of God the law of the whole old observance has been completed in the truth of the New Testament" — "Nam totius observantiae veteris legem per gratiam Filii Dei in ver[i]tate Novi Te[s]tamenti cognovimus esse completam" (100). Rabanus, *In Ex.*, Bk. I, c. viii: "For the sacrament of circumcision is truly brought to an end when it is no longer possible to sin. ..." — "Tunc enim veraciter circumcisionis sacramentum finitur, quando jam ultra non licet peccare ..." (PL, CVIII, 27 A).

37. Alcuin, *Div. off.*, c. xxvi: "For the day of Pentecost took its beginning when the voice of God thundering from above was heard on Mount Sinai. ... But Pentecost began in the New Testament when he revealed the coming of the Holy Spirit that Christ foretold" — "Pentecostes enim dies coepit exordium quando Dei vo[x]

in Sina monte desuper intonantis audita est.... In Novo autem Testamento Pentecostes cæpit, quando adventum sancti Spiritus, quem Christus prædixit, exhibuit" (PL, CI, 1226 D).

38. Basil, *Treatise on the Holy Spirit*, c. xv: "To prepare us for the life of the resurrection, the Lord proposes to us the kind of evangelical life by proposing to us to be gentle, resigned, to keep ourselves pure from the love of pleasure, to have a life detached from riches, of such a sort that from now on we may realize by deliberated will that which the life to come will possess naturally, so to speak" — "Le Seigneur, pour nous préparer à la vie de la résurrection, nous propose le genre de vie évangélique en nous proposant d'être doux, résignés, de nous garder purs de l'amour du plaisir, d'avoir une vie détachée des richesses, de sorte que nous réalisions dès maintenant par volonté délibérée ce que la vie future possédera comme naturellement" (B. Pruche, SC, 17, 171).

39. Hilary, *Tr. myst.*, Bk. I, c. xxii (SC, 19, 112): "Numquid non corporaliter gestis spiritualiter gerenda succedunt?"; etc.

40. Cf. E. Molland, *The Conception of the Gospel in the Alexandrian Theology* (Oslo, 1938), 152: "The spiritual world (of Origen) is the world above, but it is also the world to come." — "Le monde spirituel (d'Or.) est le monde d'en haut mais il est aussi le monde futur." See our discussion of Origen in Volume 1.

41. *S.* 54 (PL, CXCIV, 1873 B): "... Ubique quod mirabiliter dictum vel factum est, mirabilius in sacramento recapitulatur et commemoratur. *A capite ergo cuncta revolvuntur.* Omnia enim priora, posteriorum sunt figurae, quae nunc suis incipiunt revelari temporibus; et haec ipsa involucra quaedam sunt, et exemplaria futurorum. Et sicut ista prioribus magis vera et manifesta, sic et istis illa futura, ut semper in imagine et quadam vanitate pertranseat universa vanitas, omnis homo vivens, donec ad nudam et manifestam et stabilem veritatis faciem perveniat." Bede, *In Sam.*, Bk. II, c. ix: "Quicumque spiritualiter universa in Christo et Ecclesia recapitulari dignoscimus" (XCI, 592 A).

42. Heterius and Beatus, *Ad Elip.*, Bk. I, c. xcviii (PL, XCVI, 955 B): "nullum granum potest ad maturitatem venire, nisi intra paleam latitaverit." [Trans. note: An *involucrum* is "that in which something is wrapped, a wrapper, a covering, case," or "envelope" — Lewis and Short, *A Latin Dictionary* (997); it is etymologically connected with the verb *involvo,* to roll into. Accordingly, one can roll something into its wrapper or covering until the appropriate later time, when the wrapper can be rolled away to reveal the something inside.]

43. *Ibid.*, Bk. I, c. cv: the history of the Christ "is not allegory; it did not signify another Christ, as the Patriarchs and the Prophets signified and foretold that he was to come" — "non est allegoria; non significavit alterum Christum, sicut Patriarchae et Prophetae hunc significaverunt et praedicaverunt esse venturum" (PL, XCVI, 958 D).

44. *Christus substantialiter semper idem; Christus seipsum significat:* Cf. Guimond. d'Aversa, *De corp. et sang. Dom. ver. in euch.*, Bk. II: "In all these, then, Christ encounters us as a sign of his Church." — "In his igitur omnibus suae sanctae Ecclesiae signum nobis Christus occurrit." "In this way, then, Christ is always substantially the same, but in performing visible deeds he signifies himself acting invisibly" — "Ita ergo Christus substantialiter semper idem, tamen

visibilia, operans, seipsum significat invisibiliter operantem" (PL, CXLIX, 1459 A, 1461 C).

45. William of St. Thierry, *Spec. fidei*: "Hence the temporal works of the Lord become marvelous sacraments of eternity within the faithful heart" — "Ex quo fiunt temporalia Domini opera in corde fideli aeternitatis mira quaedam sacramenta" (PL, CLXXX, 387 D). Langton, *In Gen.*, III, 19: "The Word of God must be converted into deed" — "Verbum Dei debet converti in opus" (Smalley, 249, note 1). Cf. L. Cerfaux, *Le Christ dans la théol. de S. Paul*, 215: "soteriology is extended in the experience of Christian life and in ecclesiology" — "la sotériologie se prolonge dans l'expérience de la vie chrétienne et dans l'ecclésiologie."

46. Paschasius, *In Lam.*, Bk. II (PL, CXX, 119 A): *Translatus est Christus ad Ecclesiam.* . . .

47. Greg., *Mor.*, Bk. VI, c. i, n. 2: "Spiritales fructus allegoria germinet, quos tamen ex radice historiae veritas producit" (PL, LXXV, 730 C).

48. P. Grelot, in *Intr. à la Bible* by A. Robert and A. Feuillet, I, 208: "tout un jeu de correspondances relie entre eux les aspects et les étapes du Dessein de Salut qui se déploie ici-bas pour se consommer au-delà de l'histoire."

49. Greg., *In Ez.*, Bk. II, h. 3, n. 18: "per litteram ad allegoriam tendimus" (PL, LXXVI, 968 A).

50. *Benj. major*, Bk. IV, c. xiv (PL, CXCVI, 151 C): *Scriptura multa nobis in unum loquitur.*

51. *Itin.*, c. iv, n. 4 (Q., 5, 306): "intrando in seipsam, intrat in supernam Jerusalem."

52. *In Lev.*, Bk. XVI, c. i (198 H): "Jerusalem vero, id est visio pacis, debet esse anima nostra, civitas utique quam Deus inhabitare dignetur." Cf. Or., *In Num.*, h. 26, n. 7 (254-5), etc.

53. Dom O. Rousseau, *La Jérusalem céleste, Vie sp.*, 86 (1951), 380: "In our view it is wrong to have blamed Origen for having applied the notion of motherhood sometimes to the Jerusalem above, sometimes to the Church on earth, as though there were some sort of non sequitur arising from an imperfect ecclesiology (Plumpe)." — "C'est à tort, croyons-nous, qu'on a reproché à Or. d'avoir appliqué la notion de maternité tantôt à la Jérusalem d'en haut, tantôt à l'Église de la terre, comme s'il y avait là une inconséquence due à une ecclésiologie imparfaite (Plumpe)." Cf. Or., *In Jer.*, h. 6 (Jerome's tr.): ". . . those who dwell in the Church; this is the city of the great King, this is the vision of peace" — "eos qui in Ecclesia habitant; haec est civitas magni Regis, haec est visio pacis . . ." (PL, XXV, 634 A); *In Jos.*, h. 21, n. 2 (431-2); etc.

54. Rupert, *In Zach.* (PL, CLXVIII, 791 D): "nondum re, tamen spe . . ."; according to Augustine. See p. 184 above.

55. Richard, *In Ap.*, Bk. II, c. i (PL, CXCVI, 744 AB): "Caelum est sancta Ecclesia."

56. *In Jo.*, Bk. II (PL, CLXIX, 284-5): "sicut Pater aeternus sine Filio coaeterno nihil operatur, ita nihil eorum, quae ad salutem hominum sive in lege sive in evangelio corporaliter acta sunt, a spirituali intelligentia vacare patiuntur."

57. Guerric, *De annunt.*, s. 2, n. 4: "what the sacrament is to redemption, the exemplar is also for your imitation" — "quod sacramentum est ad redemptionem, exemplum quoque tibi est ad imitationem" (PL, CLXXXV, 122 D).

58. Aug., *C. Adim. man.*, c. xvi, n. 2: "when there is no longer a shadow to be prefigured in the body, but the thing itself is to be borne in the heart" — "cum jam non esset umbra in corpore figuranda, sed res ipsa in corde gestanda" (PL, XLIII, 156).

59. F. Nogues, *Rev. des. q. liturg. et paroiss.* (1937), 240: "est quelque chose d'invisible."

60. M. Merleau-Ponty, *Éloge de la philosophie* (1953), 17: "jonction de l'événement et du sens."

61. Cf. Albert the Great, *In I Sent.*, d. 1, a. 5. L. Bouyer, *Le sens de la vie monast.* (1950), 270-1.

62. Rupert, *In Ez.*, Bk. II, c. xvii: "Una sancta Scriptura est, in qua thesaurus noster est, . . . si in litterae theca aurum spiritus et sacramentorum Christi pretiosos novimus possidere lapides" (PL, CLXVII, 1479 A).

63. *Mor.*, Bk. XXIX, c. xxxi, n. 69: all the pages of the Bible "unum praedicant" — "preach one thing"; "They have to be sure been divided in time, but not in preaching" — "divisi quidem fuerunt tempore, sed non praedicatione" (PL, LXXVI, 515 CD). See Chapter 8 above.

64. Cf. Rabanus, *In Ruth*, c. xiii: "Corrigia ergo calceamenti est ligatura mysterii, Joannes itaque solvere corrigiam calceamenti ejus non valet, quia incarnationis ejus mysterium nec ipse investigare suficit, qui hanc per prophetiae spiritum agnovit" (PL, CVIII, 1218 D).

65. Cf. *Sur les chemins de Dieu* (1956), ch. VI.

66. Aelred, *De oner.*, s. 12 (PL, CXCV, 405 C): "cum (Deus) maxim[u]m nobis sacramentorum abyssum quasi de novo jam incipiat aperire."

67. 2 Cor. 3:18.

68. *Coll.* 14, c. xi (Pichery, SC, 54, 197).

69. *Mor.*, Bk. VI, c. xvi, n. 22 (PL, LXXV, 741 BC).

70. *Sent.*, Bk. I, c. xviii, n. 5 (PL, LXXXIII, 576 B): "Scriptura sacra pro uniuscujusque lectoris intelligentia variatur, sicut manna. . . . Et cum sit pro uniuscujusque intellectu diversus (sermo dominicus), in se tamen permanet unus"; n. 3: "in Scripturis sanctis quasi in montibus excelsis, et viri perfecti sublimia intelligentiae, quibus gressus contemplationis quasi cervi erigant, et simplices quasi parva animalia inveniunt modicos intellectus, ad quos humiles ipsi refugiant." This theme is the one familiar to Augustine and to Gregory.

71. *Esquisse de Rome chrét.*, I, 409: "Le symbole a une signification en quelque sorte expansive, qui s'étend avec l'intelligence du lecteur."

72. Henry Duméry, *Critique et religion* (1957), 247, note 3: "Selon le niveau d'intelligence qu'on prend, l'Écriture différencie ses réponses; et celles-ci, on s'en doute, valent ce que vaut la qualité de l'interrogation." Cf. Greg., *Mor.*, Bk. XXIII, c. xix, n. 34: "God has designed the holy books to be written so as to answer the many secret questions of every man. . . . He has composed one Scripture by which he might satisfy everyone's questions" (PL, LXXVI, 271 B). See Chapter 16 below.

73. *In Ez.*, Bk. II (PL, CX, 534 D): "In quantum quisque ad alta profecerit, in tantum ei sacra eloquia de altioribus loquuntur."

74. *Diad. mon.*, c. iii: "Plerumque fit ut sacrae Scripturae verba esse mystica quisque sentiat, si, accensus supernae contemplationis gratia, semetipsum ad caelestia suspendat. . . . Scriptura sacra aliquo modo cum legentibus crescit, a

rudibus lectoribus quasi recognoscitur, et tamen a doctis semper nova reperitur, etc." (PL, CII, 598 AB).

75. *In ev.*, Bk. II, h. 23, n. 1 (PL, LXXVI, 1182 C): "Nihil ergo simplex Veritas per duplicitatem facit, sed talem se eis exhibuit in corpore, qualis apud illos erat in mente." On the idea of a "constant progress" in Gregory, see Leclercq, *L'amour des lettres*, 36-7.

76. Bede, *In Luc.* (PL, XCII, 627 A). Werner, *Defl., s. de resurr.* (CLVII, 931 C).

77. *In Matt.*, c. xxxii and xxxv (58, 65). *C. Cels.*, Bk. VI, c. lxxvii (2, 146-9). *In Luc.*, h. 3 (20-3), etc. Cf. H. de Lubac, *Aspects du bouddhisme*, I (1951), ch. III. See Chapter 2.1 above.

78. One may compare *In I Reg.*, Bk. III, c. v, n. 30: "Contemplatio enim virtus est, per quam, non solum ipsa Scriptura condita recognoscitur, sed per quam nondum condita conderetur, et per quam condita ad Dei voluntatem quotidie disponatur" (PL, LXXIX, 216 C).

79. Dom Butler, *Western Mysticism*, 124, note 1, has noted the frequency in Gregory of such formulas as the following: "animus dilatatus," "mentis laxatur sinus," "cum in Dei lumine rapitur (animus) super se, in interioribus ampliatur," etc.

80. *In Jer.*, h. 5 (PL, XXV, 627 C): "extenditur anima nostra, quae prius fuerat contracta, ut possit capax esse sapientiae Dei."

81. "The Gregory, whom they (i.e. the Catholics) call the Great, I call the public dancer *and torch-bearer* for the theology of perdition" — "Gregorius, quem isti Magnum, ego praesultorem *kai dadoukhon* theologiae pereuntis voco" (*Corp. Ref.*, 11, 16).

82. *Dogmeng.*, III (4th ed., 1910), 257-69. Cf. R. Seeberg, *Lehrbuch der Dogmeng.*, III (4th ed., 1930), 37-46.

83. *Hist. critica philosophiae*, III (1743), 560-3: "doctorem exigui judicii"; "superstitio, judicii paupertas," etc. The author devotes the practice of the fourfold sense to the same censure, *ibid*. The absence of deep metaphysical speculation in Gregory leads Brücker to deny him "high spirituality"; but when this deep speculation is found among other Fathers, they are readily blamed for betraying the simplicity of the Gospel.

84. Fr. B. Arbz, *The Mind of the Middle Ages* (3rd ed., 1958), 192. See p. 343, n. 5, above.

85. French translation, I, 590.

86. On the tragic circumstances in which these homilies were uttered, see John the Deacon, Bk. IV, c. lxvi-vii (PL, LXXV, 215-9).

87. *De consid.*, Bk. I, c. ix: "Obsidio urbi et barbaricus ensis civium cervicibus imminebat: numquid tamen terruit beatam papam Gregorium, quominus sapientiam scriberet in otio? Eo nempe temporis . . . obscurissimam et extremeam partem Exechielis tam diligenter quam eleganter exposuit" (PL, CLXXXII, 739 BC).

88. Cf. Denys de Sainte-Marthe, *Hist. de S. Gr. le Grand* (1697), 230: "Cette fidélité soit du Pasteur à prêcher la parole de Dieu, soit des peuples à venir l'entendre malgré toutes les inquiétudes que leur causaient les affaires présentes, me paraît un aussi grand miracle que celui qu'on dit être arrivé en ce même temps" (namely the miracle of the dove).

89. *In Ez.*, Bk. II, h. 5; n. 17 (PL, LXXVI, 995 B): "Mentes . . . inde apud se amplae fiunt, unde ad se veritatis lumen quasi per angustias admittunt."

90. But, *In Ez.*, h. 1, n. 16, Origen explained the prophet's vision in another way: "If you consider how the universe is dissolved through contrary events, whether in those that are thought to stray or in those that are thought to be alien to straying about, you will see how the wheel is in the middle of the wheel" — "Si consideras quomodo per contrarios eventus solvatur universitas rerum, sive in his qui putantur errare, sive in his qui ab errore dicuntur alieni, videbis quomodo rota in medio rotae sit" (PG, XIII, 681 C). Cf. Jerome, *ep.* 64, c. 18: "The wheel is in the wheel, i.e., time is in time and the year turns round again into itself." — "Rota in rota est, id est tempus in tempore, et annus in semetipsum rovolvitur etc." (3, 134).

91. *In ps. CXVIII, s.* 4, n. 28: "O great contest of reasonable horses! O marvelous mystery! Wheel was running within wheel and was not suffering impediment; New Testament was within the Old Testament, it was running within that through which it was being announced." — "O rationabilium equorum grande certamen! O mirandum mysterium! Rota intra rotam currebat, et non impediebatur; novum Testamentum in veteri Testamento erat, intra illud currebat per quod annuntiabatur" (PL, XV, 1250 AB). See above, Chapter 5.4.

92. Here comes the example of the burning bush, etc.

93. It should be noted that here "sacra lectio" does not mean the act of reading, but the Book itself. Cf. Cassiodorus: *Inst. div. lectionum* (var.: litterarum).

94. *In Ez.*, Bk. I, h. 7 (PL, LXXVI, 844-8): "*Quocumque ibat spiritus, illuc eunte spiritu, et rotae pariter levabantur, sequentes eum. Spiritus enim vitae erat in rotis.*

"Quo enim spiritus legentis tendit, illuc et divina eloquia levantur, quia sic[ut] in eis altum quid videndo et sentiendo quaesieris, haec eadem sacra eloquia tecum crescunt, tecum in altiora ascendunt. In una enim eademque Scripturae sententia, alius sola historia pascitur, alius typicam, alius vero intelligentiam per typum contemplativam quaerit. Et fit plerumque ut in una eademque sententia cuncta simul tria valeant inveniri.

"Dicta igitur sacri eloquii cum legentium spiritu crescunt. . . .

"Videamus quomodo sequuntur rotae spiritum, qui vitae spiritus dicitur et rotis inesse perhibetur. . . . In quantum quisque ad alta profecerit, in tantum ei sacra eloquia de altioribus loquuntur. . . . Rotae vadunt, stant, elevantur, quia quaesita sacra lectio talis invenitur, qualis et fit ipse a quo quaeritur. Ad activam enim vitam profecisti: stat tecum. Ad contemplativam vitam per Dei gratiam pervenisti: volat tecum. . . .

"Haec nobis Scriptura in tenebris vitae praesentis facta est lumen itineris. . . . Scimus tamen quia et ipsa . . . nobis obscura est, nisi hanc nostris mentibus Veritas illustrat. . . . Lumen enim creatum nobis non lucet, nisi illuminetur a Lumine non creato. Quia ergo omnipotens Deus ad salutem nostram sanctorum Testamentorum dicta et ipse creavit, et ipse aperuit, spiritus vitae erat in rotis."

Cardinal Humbert will apply the text of Ezekiel not only to the Scriptures, but also to the writings of the Fathers and to conciliar texts: *Adv. Simoniacos*, Bk. III, c. xxviii (*L. de lite*, I, 234). For St. Maximus, *Mystagogy*, the wheel within the wheel was the two worlds, sensible and intelligible, or reality and knowledge of reality (PG, XCI, 670).

Notes to Chapter Ten
§4. Questions of Method

1. We are no less aware of the limitation that it entails and that require complementary studies conducted according to other methods. Our third and fourth volumes, however, will fill this gap to some extent.

2. M. D. Chenu, "Naturalisme et théol. au XII s.," RSR 37, 5. Certain cases of this kind have been studied in *Corpus mysticum* (2nd ed., 1949).

3. *In Is.:* "ut et experimentum caperem ingenioli mei" (PL, XXIV, 91 D); "pro tenuitate ingenioli" (377 C). *In Abd.:* "ingenioli mei primam temeritatem" (XXV, 1097 C). *In Zach.:* "ingeniolo meo aliquod offerre munusculum" (1417 B).

4. "Secundum capacitatem ingenioli sui" or "pro tenuitate, pro modulo, pro captu, pro simplicatate ingenioli sui": Bede, *Ep.* 13 and 16 (PL, XCIV, 698 A, 702 B). Sed. Sc., *In Eph.* (CIII, 207 CD). J. Scot., *Ep.* 14 (MGH, *Ep.*, 6, 158). W. Strabo, *Epit. in Lev.* (PL, CXIV, 795 A). Anastas., *Ep.* I (MGH, *Ep. aevi car.*, V, 396). Humbert to Rabanus (*ibid.*, III, 439). Helperic of St.-Gall, *L. de computo*, c. xxxviii (PL, CXXXVII, 48 B). Letald de Micy, *L. de mirac. S. Maximini*, c. xvi, n. 45 (CXXXVII, 818 C). Oderann., *op.* 7 (CXLII, 814 D). Thiorfr., *Flores epitaph. sanct.*, Bk. IV, c. vii, goes one better: "intentatae materiae tenuissimi ingenioli mei ausus sim manum inserere" (CLVII, 400 A). Sigebert, *De script. eccl.*, c. clxxi: "cautelam ingenioli mei aequa lance libravi" (CLX, 587 B). Honorius, *Sel. ps. exp., dedic.*: "Studium tuum . . . cymbam ingenioli mei impellit in pelagus intransnavigabile" (CLXXII, 769-70). Aelred, *De sp. amic.*, Bk. I (CXCV, 670 A). John of Salisbury, Bk. II, c. x (CXCIX, 867 B); *Ep.* 175 (170 B). Al. Neckam, *De nat. rer.*, Bk. I, c. v (36). Robert Canutus (12th c.; Manitius, 3, 241). B. de Morval, *De cont. mundi, prol.*: "in ingeniolis suis gloriantes" (Hoskier, XXXV); etc.

5. "Scientiolae suae": Cf. Hucbald of St.-Amand, *V. S. Rictrudae*, c. i (ASS, May, 3, 81 D).

6. *In Cant., s.* 1, n. 1: "Vobis, fratres, alia quam aliis de saeculo, aut certe aliter dicenda sunt" (PL, CLXXXIII, 785 C).

7. "De qua re non est hic disserendi locus": *In ps. IV*, n. 1 (CCL, 38, 14).

8. St. Basil.

9. *Mutatis mutandis,* consider the analogous observation by Father Teilhard de Chardin speaking about "l'acquis human," [the human achievement] "lentement déposé par l'expérience des siècles" [slowly deposited through the experience of centuries]: "It is noteworthy that each individual participates and collaborates in these diverse products of shared reflection without possessing them completely. The modern idea of the atom, for example, belongs at this moment *in common* to a certain number of thousands of physicists *without being totally possessed by any one of them.*" — "A ces divers produits de la co-réflexion il est notable que chacun participe et collabore, sans les posséder complètement. L'idée moderne d'Atome, par exemple, appartient en ce moment, *en commun*, à un certain nombre de milliers de physiciens, *sans être possédée totalement par aucune.*" *L'apparition de l'homme* (1956), 337. (The author's own italics.)

10. Cf. M. D. Chenu, *La th. au XII s.*, xi: "To be worthy of its object, especially if this object is the thought and the life of the Christian people," history has "to disengage the internal laws that determine the climate of the age and the faith of

the faithful; thus, within this climate and within this faith, it reveals, through the most disparate encounters, the collective points of clarity that constitute the unity and the tensions of generations at work." — "Pour être digne de son objet, surtout si cet objet est la pensée et la vie du peuple chrétien," l'histoire doit "dégager les lois internes qui déterminent le climat du siècle et la foi des fidèles; elle manifest alors, dans ce climat et dans cette foi, les lucidités collectives qui composent à travers les plus disparates conjonctures, l'unité et les tensions des générations au travail."

11. Cf. Mircea Eliade, *Traité d'h. des rel.* (1949), 22, 34, 383-4.

12. The words 'hermeneutics' and 'exegesis' have the same original sense: but usage applies the first rather to the principles of interpretation and the second to the practice of it.

13. Father Pontien Polman, *L'élément histor. dans la controv. relig. du XVI s.* (1932), 7 and 48: regarding Erasmus, Pico della Mirandola, Lefèvre d'Étaples, Zwingli. But one would have to distinguish between one sort of allegory and another. See Chapter 18 below.

14. Some have found it "piquant" ["rough"] that Origen "has collaborated so actively to establish the text of the Scriptures, the indispensable basis for a good understanding of the 'literal' sense" — "ait collaboré si activement à la fixation du texte des Écritures, base indispensable pour la bonne intelligence du sens 'littéral.'" *Sciences ecclés.*, V (1953), 21, note 1. The fact seems "rough" only for one suffering from the prejudice just pointed out.

15. Cf. Keble, 46: "In fact, we find that few authors have done more for elucidation of the historical sense"; 55: "Origen did not only receive the letter, but acknowledge the historical meaning of the Holy Book"; etc.

16. P. Antin, *Essai sur S. Jérôme*, 84.

17. It is known that when Pope Damasus charged him with revising the translation of the Bible, he continued to want to translate at least all the homilies of Origen. At the beginning of the Origenist crisis he continued to use Origen in his own commentaries massively. P. Courcelle, 88-100. Antin, 156: in his commentaries "as Jerome advanced, he increased the portion of spirituality" — "Jérôme, à mesure qu'il avance, grandit la part de la spiritualité." See above, Chapter 4.2.

18. Antin, 160: "Allegorical and mystical exegesis interested Jerome above all." — "C'est l'exégèse allégorique et mystique qui intéresse surtout Jérôme."

19. Cited by Sanders, *Etudes sur S. Jérôme*, 84.

20. *In Is.*, Bk. V, *init.* (PL, XXIV, 153 C); Bk. V: "That I stick to the letter and eat earth like a serpent is owing to your will, who were willing to hear only the historical interpretation." — "Quod haereo litterae et in more serpentis terram comedo, tuae est voluntatis, qui historicam tantum interpretationem audire voluisti" (160 C).

21. ". . . Quia juxta historiam . . . interpretati sumus et inter confragosos scopulos naviculam reximus, spiritalis intelligentiae vela pandamus, ut, flante Domino et sua reserante mysteria, laeti perveniamus ad portum": *In Abd.*, 20-1 (PL, XXV, 1116 A). *Ep.* 64, c. xviii: "Juxta morem nostrum spiritali postea intellegentiae vela pandamus" (3, 132).

22. *In Is.*, Bk. VI (XXIV, 865 CD); Bk. I (34 BC), etc.

23. Thus "juxta occidentem litteram" and "juxta spiritum vivificantem": *In Jer.* (XXIV, 727 B).

24. "Nec studium tam esse mihi ut exponam verba, quam ut imbuam corda": *In Cant.*, s. 16, n. 1 (PL, CLXXXIII, 849 A).

25. Leclercq, *Etudes*, 56: "Deprehendi nos, dum moralibus adinveniendis sensibus nimis intenti essemus, nonnullis in locis a veritate litterae per errorem exorbitasse. . . . Caetera, quantum arbitror, recta sunt, et ista facile corrigi possunt."

26. *Ep. an. ad Hugonem:* "The whole series of the sacred page ought first to be scrutinized three or four times thoroughly at the historical level, and then quite transcended." — "Universa autem sacrae paginae series secundum historiam primo, ter aut quatuor perscrutanda est et pertranseunda" (PL, CCXIII, 715 A).

27. PL, XXXIV, 485-546.

28. John of Salisbury, *Metal.*, Bk. III, c. i; first it is necessary to explicate Porphyry's *Isagoge* "in superficie," without metaphysical investigation (PL, CXCIX, 890-2).

29. "The truth of history": PL, CVI, 917ff. Still he cannot keep himself from expressing a few mystic views in the passage (920, 931 B, etc.).

30. PL, CXCVIII, 871 ff.

31. "Nemo autem a nobis sententias aut moralitates expectet: historiam enim, . . . non disputantis more, sed disserentis ordine prosequi intendimus": Bk. II, *prol.* (MGH, *Scr.*, XX, 144). Like Fréculphe, Otto allows himself a few infractions of the rule he sketched out for himself; he says of Joshua, Bk. I, c. xx: "He, the first bearing the form of the Savior in office and in name, was able to lead the people of God into the land of promise, which is the prototype of the city we are dealing with" — "Hic primus officio nomineque formam gerens salvatoris, in terram promissionis quae hujus, unde agimus, typus civitatis est, populum Dei inducere meruit" (138). In this we recognize a sign of the profound impression made by Origen's exegesis of this book. [Trans. note: Joshua in Hebrew is Yehoshua', which (a) is transliterated into Greek and Latin as 'Jesus' and which (b) probably means 'YHWH is salvation'; see *The Jewish Encyclopedia*, VII, 282, s.v. 'Joshua (Jehoshua)' at 'The Change in His Name' and *The Catholic Encyclopedia*, VIII, 524, s.v. 'Josue. VIII.']

32. Cf. K. Haid, *op. cit.*, 165-81: *Otto von Freising und Bernhard von Cl.*

33. PL, LXXX, 327-42 (ed. Flemming, incomplete). Cf. Gaar-Dekkers, *Clavis Patrum lat.*, n. 1120. B. Bischoff, *Wendepunkte in der Geschichte der laiernischen Exegese im Frühmittelalter, S. Er.*, 6 (1954), 255.

34. *Trop. in Os. et Am.*, proem. (PL, CLVI, 339-40).

35. *De vita sua*, Bk. I, c. xvii (CLVI, 875-6). In another domain, cf. the declaration of Alexander Neckam, *De nat. rer.*, Bk. I: "Nolo tamen ut ominetur lector me naturas rerum fugere volentes investigare velle philosophice aut physice; moralem enim libet instituere tractatum" (2-3).

36. M. Th. D'Alverny, "Pierre le Vén. et la légende de Mahomet," in *A Cluny* (1950), 161.

37. "On the ten plagues of Egypt according to the spiritual sense": PL, CLXXII, 266 C.

38. PL, CXCVIII, 1054-6.

39. Hugo of Rouen, *In Hex.:* "In this booklet of ours we are trying to investigate history rather than attain the allegorical or moral senses" — "In hoc opusculo nostro magis historiam exqu[i]rendo tractamus, quam sensus allegoricos seu morales attingamus" (Lecomte, 236).

40. This explanation of ch. xiii-xxiii, dedicated to Amabilis, dates from 397; it will form Book V of the commentary dedicated to Eustochius; Books VI-VII will complete it with allegorical explanation. Bk. V, *init.:* "Amabili episcopo rogatus ut in decem Isaeiae scriberem visiones . . . , historiam tantum quod petebat edisserens. . . . Sexti voluminis juxta tropologiam arripiemus exordium et . . . spiritalis intelligentiae culmina persequemur" (PL, XXIV, 153 C). See pp. 46 and 50-51 in Volume 1

41. Bardy, DTC, 13, 1612-3. Cf. PL, CX, 495-6.

42. "Moraliter tantum, intermissis mysteriis scripturae illius." "Quia sic volebam, et sic petieram ab eo": *V. Prima Bernardi*, Bk. I, c. xv, n. 59 (PL, CLXXXV, 259 B). This is doubtless the *Brevis commentatio*, which belongs to Bernard "pour le fond et la forme" but from which William "n'est pas absent": Dom J. Hourlier, ASOC 12 (1956), 105-14.

43. "Cohibentes nos intra nos, et in nobismetipsis nosmetipsos metientes": PL, CLXXX, 476 A. William does not understand the moral sense entirely as does Bernard; but that is without importance here. Even today, a dogmatician can openly value the works of his colleague the exegete, and vice versa; although the fact be rarer, the same man can show himself, in certain cases, both an excellent exegete and an excellent dogmatician.

Notes to Chapter Ten
§5. The Apostolic Preaching

1. "Novi et Veteris Testamenti veritate patefacta": PL, LXX, 1322 C. Cf. A. Souter, *Pelagius' Exposition of Thirteen Epistles of St. Paul*, I, 15, 318-20. There is thus nothing surprising any more if Jerome abandons all allegorical exegesis to comment on the Epistle to Titus.

2. "Duodecim apostolos, per quos Scriptura Novi Testamenti condita est, et Veteris revelata mysteria": Martin de Léon, *In dedic. eccl.*, s. 2 (PL, CCIX, 87 D). Honorius: "expositores Scripturarum" (CXCIV, 674 D).

3. Rabanus, *De laud.*, Bk. II, c. xx (PL, CVII, 285 A).

4. Greg., *In Ez.*, Bk. II, h. 3, n. 17: "Argentum sonat et lucet, aes vero sonat et non lucet; quia praedicatores Novi Testamenti aperte locuti sunt quae etiam monstrare potuerunt. Praedicatores vero Testamenti veteris, quia per allegoriarum umbras de caelesti mysterio obscura dicta protulerunt, quasi sine luce sonitum dederunt" (PL, LXXVI, 967-8).

5. Thus Gerhoh, *In ps.:* "Qui ergo secreta Scripturae sacrae mysteria cum apostolis intelligunt et diligunt" (PL, CXCIV, 318 B); etc.

6. "Solent enim cervi, inter condensa nemorum ingredientes, ramos ipsis cornibus separare, et campum ubi pascantur sibi et aliis animalibus aperire, sicut sancti Apostoli opacitates et occulta mysteria Scripturarum in quibus et ipsi

pascerentur, et alios pascerent aperuerunt": Manegold, *In ps. XXVIII* (PL, XCIII, 624 D).

7. "Qui non potest intelligere vocem prophetantis, audiat vel sensum exponentis; qui non intelligit sensum vaticinantis prophetae, credat vel sententiae exponentis evangelistae": *De Emm.*, Bk. I, c. i (PL, CXCVI, 606 D). See Chapter 8 above.

8. Apringius, *In Ap.*, c. vi (Vega, 34).

9. Peter Damian: "qui . . . praedicationis gratiam . . . divinitus acceperunt" (PL, CXLV, 1152 A). Nervaeus, *In Rom.*: "nobiles in apostolis dicuntur, id est inter praedicatores qui discipuli erant apostolorum" (CLXXXI, 807 D).

10. Cf. DBS, 3, 472-5: "L'Écriture sainte et la prédication" (H. Höpfl); DB, 2, 191 (H. Lesêtre).

11. Prosper, *In ps. CIII*, 3 (PL, LI, 289 A); 12: "Montes enim sunt prophetae, montes, apostoli, montes omnes praedicatores veritatis et sublimes quippe doctores, a quibus qui spiritalis est non aberrat" (292 AB).

12. "Verbum fidei, quod praedicamus": Rom. 10:8. Or., *In Num.*, h. 9, n. 1: "Ubi vera fides est integra Verbi Dei praedicatio," "ubi vera Dei praedicatio" (54).

13. Isidore, *L. de var. q.*, c. lix: "fermento fidei et evangelicae praedicationis" (182).

14. Autpert, *In Ap.*, Bk. V (523 C); cf. 564 C, 569 G, 570 B: "divina praedicatio."

15. "Sonus apostolicae praedicationis": "omnis praedicatorum ordo in apostolorum colligitur unione." Paschasius, *In Matt.*, Bk. XI (PL, CXX, 803-4). Cf. Arnulf, lexov., *s. 3 in synodo* (J. A. Giles, 1844, 17).

16. Berengoz: "Dominus noster Jesus Christus per praedicatores Ecclesiae nomen suum . . . voluit ubique distendi" (PL, CLX, 1028 B); etc. Gregory (LXXVI, 1284 B).

17. Irimbert, *In Jud.*: "Sancta Scriptura ordini praedicatorum divinitus datur" (Pez, 4, 157).

18. Cf. Greg., *In Ez.*, Bk. I, h. 6, n. 16 (PL, LXXVI, 836 C).

19. Sed. Sc., *In I Cor.* II (PL, CIII, 131 C); *In II Cor.* II: "Odor notitiae Dei antequam Deus ipse videatur per praedicationem apostolorum sentitur" (165 B). Serlon de Sav., *s. I in assumpt.*: "Est Ecclesia mater ejus (Christi); verbi praedicatione ipsum generando" (Tissier, 6, 115).

20. Manegold, *In ps. LXXX*: "Quando . . . Christus per praedicatores suos petivit sibi sponsam Ecclesiam de gentibus" (PL, XCIII, 923 C). Aug., *In ps. VIII*, n. 3: "Tuncenim misit Spiritum sanctum quo impleti discipuli cum fiducia praedicaverunt verbum Dei, ut Ecclesiae congregarentur" (CCL, 38, 50).

21. *Exp. in cant.* (Anon., 12th cent.): "Praedicatores tui . . . ligantes praedicatione fideles Christi Capiti suo" (PL, CLXXII, 530 D).

22. Hilary, *Instr. ps.*, n. 12; n. 13: "secundum ogdoadem evangelicam" (11, 12).

23. Aimo, *In Ap.*, Bk. VII (PL, CXVII, 1210 D).

24. *Mor.*, Bk. XXIX, c. xxiv, n. 49 (PL, LXXVI, 503-4). Br. of Segni, *In Ap.*, Bk. II, c. iv (CLXVII, 627 B).

25. The "ministerium praedicationis" or the "officium praedicationis": *In ev.*, Bk. I, h. 17, n. 1 (LXXVI, 1139 B). *In I Reg.*, Bk. II, c. ii, n. 19 (LXXIX, 153-4); n. 29 (158 C); Sed. Sc. (CIII, 162 B). Atfrid., *V. s. Liudgeri*, Bk. II (MGH, Scr., II, 411).

26. "Successores apostolorum, sancti praedicatores": Honorius (PL, CLXXII,

Notes to Pages 218-19

320 D). Bede, *In Marc.*: "praedicantibus apostolis apostolorumque successoribus" (XCII, 159 B). Rupert, on Greg.: "doctrina praedicationis (Ecclesiam) illuminavit" (CLXX, 636 B). The name of preachers given to the Apostles, Fathers, and Doctors became part of the language of ancient exegesis. Greg.: "(Patrum) quippe actio nobis aperit, hoc quod in suis praedicationibus pagina Testamentorum dicit" (LXXVI, 901 D; cf. 198 C, etc.). Hincmar (CXXV, 497 B); etc. Pseudo-preachers are also spoken of as pseudo-prophets or pseudo-apostles: Hervaeus (PL, CLXXXI, 1298-9); *Vita Amedei*, c. v (M. A. Dimier, *St. Ans.*, 40, 91); etc. Cassiodorus, *In I Jo.*: to the verus praedicator is opposed the verus Antichristus (LXX, 1372 BC).

27. "Doctores apostolici": *V. s. Ethelwoldi, praef.*: The Savior "diffused many lights of apostolic doctors throughout the world" — "multa per universum orbem (Salvator) diffudit apostolicorum luminaria doctorum" (PL, CXXXVII, 81 C).

28. "Et gladius triumphalis potentiae vibrat in dextera, et catholicae praedicationis tuba resonat in lingua": Alcuin, *Ep.* 171, 178 (MGH, *Ep.*, 4, 281, 194).

29. "Praedicatio est quoddam instrumentum quo Ecclesia Dei fabricata est": Leclercq, AHDLMA 15, 113. Cf. H. Urs von Balthasar, *La prière contemplative* (tr. R. Givord, 1959), 220: "La mission de prédication de l'Église, à laquelle est ordonée et subordonée la mission théologique elle-même." ["The mission of the Church's preaching, to which the theological mission itself is ordered and subordinated."]

30. "Sagena apostolica, ex duplici textura Novi et veteris Testamenti contexta": P. Lombard (PL, CLXXI, 491 C).

31. A "new preaching," the "true preaching," of "new preachers" or a "new order of preachers": *In I Reg.* (PL, LXXIX, 103 B, 146 D); *ibid.* (96 AB, 145 A, 147 C, 149 A, 155 C); "the preacher of a new grace" — "novae grati[a]e praedicator" (147 C); "the calling of the new preachers" — "novorum praedicatorum vocatio" (152 A), etc.

32. Br. of Segni, *In ps. XXVII*: "The Lord prepared them to preach the Gospel and to reveal and explain the Scriptures" — "Hos autem praeparavit Dominus ad evangelium praedicandum et Scripturas revelandas et exponendas" (PL, CLXIV, 789 D); *In ps. XVI* (745 B); *In Ex.*: "You explain the Scriptures, you preach the gospels" — "Scripturas exponitis, evangelia praedicatis" (364 C); etc.

33. Hervaeus, *In Ep.* (PL, CLXXXI, 1248 D). On the equivalence of the prophets and preachers: Greg., *In I Reg.*, l, IV, c. I, n. 13 (LXXIX, 290 AC), etc.

34. Garnier, s. 1: "Patriarchae et Prophetae antiqui . . . absconderunt ignem id est lumen fidei, in puteo, id est in obscura Scripturarum profunditate. Quem ignem . . . nepotes eorum, id est Apostoli, quaerentes etc." (PL, CCV, 564 CD).

35. Richard, *In Ap.*: "perfecti doctores evangelici" (PL, CXCVI, 770 D).

36. Gaudentius, *Tr.* 15 (135).

37. Berengaud, *In Ap.*: "quamvis novum Testamentum apertio sit veteris Testamenti, tamen multa in eo obscure ponuntur, quae necesse est ut exponantur" (PL, XVII, 838 D); v. 4: "septimum sigillum Christus aperuit, cum ea quae per significationem gesta sunt, doctoribus Ecclesiae per inspirationem Spiritus sancti manifestavit" (848 A). Anselm of Havelberg, *Dial.*, Bk. II, c. xxiii: "Per catholicos doctores, quasi per organum suum, sacras Scripturas vet. et n. Test¬ menti nobvis . . . aperuit . . ." (CLXXXVIII, 1201 D).

38. "In tota veteris Testamenti littera, Christi mysteria resplendent": Irimbert, *In Jud.* (Pez, 4, 160): "per Spiritum sanctum scientia et intelligentia doctorum in scriptura veteris Testamenti sublimatur" (168).

39. "Quoniam et intellectu Scripturarum adimpleta sunt corda eorum intrinsecus, et variae linguae audiebantur extrinsecus": Gerhoh, *Lib. de ord. donorum* (*Op. in.*, I, 127).

40. Claudius, *In Reg.*, Bk. IV (PL, L, 1170 A).

41. *"Virtus et potestas evangelicae praedicationis"*: Prosper, *In ps. CIX* (PL, LI, 318 D). Cf. Joachim of Flora, *Sup. quat. ev.*: "splendescere praedicationem evangelii, quae est facies Christi Jesu" (Buon., 138).

42. *Adv. Haer.*, Bk. II, c. xxxv, n. 4; Bk. III, xxi, 5; Bk. IV, x, 1; xxxiv, 2; xxvi, 1; Bk. V, xvii, 1; xxxiv, 3. H. Holstein, "La Tradition des Apôtres chez S. Irénée," RSR 36 (1948), 233, 259, 269-70. H. D. Simonin, RSPT (1939), 357: the origin of the ecclesiastical notion of tradition is perhaps an interpretation of the Old Testament Scriptures based upon the teaching of Christ and the Apostles and opposed to rabbinic traditions" — "une interprétation des Écritures de l'A.T. fondée sur l'enseignement du Christ et des Apôtres, et s'opposant aux traditions rabbiniques." For an analogous doctrine of Tertullian: R. F. Refoulé, *Tert., De la prescription* (SC, 46), introd., 56-7.

43. "sanctis apostolis removentibus superficiem litterae": *In Jos.*, h. 20, n. 5; the same for the "doctores ecclesiarum" (424).

44. *Per.*, Bk. II, c. xi, n. 3 (186).

45. *C. Cels.*, Bk. II, c. vi (1, 132). Hilary, *Instr. ps.*, n. 5: "Non est vero ambigendum, ea quae in psalmis dicta sunt, secundum evangelicam praedicationem intelligi oportere etc." (6).

46. PL, XCIX, 451 C.

47. "Evangelistae revelant arcana secretorum, et quae prophetae operuerunt, ipsi aperuerunt": *S. in ramis palm.* (Talbot, COCR 7, 1940, 37).

48. "Praedicatores . . . arcana Scripturarum discunt in occulto, quae loquantur in aperto, unde filios nutriant Ecclesiae": *In Cant.*, Bk. X (PL, CCVI, 711 D). Florus, *De tenenda*, c. vii: "Absconditum quidem a saeculis in Deo, sed inter Scripturas prophetarum Ecclesiae ejus, inter caetera quae ad mysterium Salvatoris pertinent, praedicatione patefactum apostolica" (CXXI, 1101 CD). Claudius of Turin, *In Hebr.*: "Non autem oportebat umbram auferri priusquam illud, quod significabatur, confirmatum esset contestatione apostolorum praedicantium de fide credentium populorum" (CXXXIV, 771 C). Richard, *In Ap.*, Bk. VII, c. x: "Sanctis etenim doctoribus ea quae in sacra pagina continentur occulta, primum per divinam gratiam aperiuntur, quae postmodum sive per ipsos sive per ...os populis manifeste praedicantur" (CXCVI, 886 B); *In ps. XXVIII* (306 B). ...d of Cremona, *Mitrale*, Bk. II, c. v (CCXII, 73 A); etc.

"Verus Isaac, sc. Dominus Jesus Christus, Matrem omnium nostrum, ...cripturam, secundum quam Deo renascimur, in conjugium suum, id ...cae praedicationis usum, assumpsit": *In Gen.*, Bk. VII, c. iv (PL,

..., 70 B.

... est evangelica praedicatio, quae de Domino Jesu Christo ...tae, in cujus lumine videbimus lumen, a quo generaliter omnis vera voluptas emanat. . . . Quae (aqua) tam longe lateque defluxit, ut mundum repleverit universum. . . . Haec irrigat paradisum, id est fecundat Ecclesiam . . .": *In comm. de ev., s.* 3 (PL, CCXVII, 605 CD).

52. Or., *De princ.*, Bk. I, *praef.*, c. ii: "servetur vero ecclesiastica praedicatio per successionis ordinem ab apostolis tradita et usque ad praesens in ecclesia permanens" (8). Robert of Tombelaine, *In Cant.*, c. viii, n. 2 (PL, LXXIX, 529 B); n. 13: "sanctae Ecclesiae fidem praedicans" (544 D). Cf. Greg., *In I Reg.*, Bk. II, c. ii, n. 17: "praedicator sanctae Ecclesiae" (153 A); n. 26 (157 C). Autpert, *In Ap.* (573 F); etc.

53. "Mysterium Salvatoris, praedicatione patefactum apostolica": Florus, *De tenenda*, c. vii (PL, CXXI, 1101 CD). Paulinus, *C. Elip.*, c. vii (XCIX, 158 A).

54. *C. Faust.*, Bk. XXII, c. lxxix: "Dispensatores N.T., idemque expositores V. T." (PL, XLII, 451). Abelard on Jacob's ladder: "Hujus scalae, hoc est sacrae Scripturae, quasi duo latera duo sunt Testamenta, quae quidem ad invicem quasi quibusdam gradibus insertis connectuntur, dum per expositiones doctorum rota rotae applicatur, et quod in veteri fuerat praedictum, in novo monstratur exhibitum. Angeli per hanc scalam ascendentes et descendentes, sancti sunt praedicatores" (CLXXVIII, 553 B).

55. Maximus of Turin, *s.* 80, on Cyprian (PL, LVII, 426 C).

56. "Ubi veteris obscuritas revelatur": Aug., *C. Faust.*, Bk. XXII, c. lxxvii (PL, XLII, 450).

57. Thus in the explication of Ps. 7:13: "arcum suum tetendit et paravit illum," those who make the O.T. intelligible by the New are sometimes named "expositores" (Gerhoh, PL, CXCIII, 735 B), sometimes "doctores" (Aimo, CXVI, 219 A). Bede, *In Cant.*: "Doctores . . . Idem sancti praedicatores" (XCI, 1192 CD).

58. "Quia sacramenta prophetiae sanctis doctoribus, qui haec toto orbe praedicent, patefecit": Jerome, *In Is.*, Bk. XVI, c. lviii (PL, XXIV, 567 B). Bede, *In Marc.* 6 (XCII, 194 B). Ps.-Bede, *In Matt.* 14 (72 C).

59. Br. of Segni, *In Ap.*, Bk. II, c. iv (PL, CLXV, 626 A). Rabanus, *In Paral.*, Bk. IV, c. xxvii (CIX, 514 B).

60. Hélinand, *s.* 24: "Os autem Domini recte appellari potest quilibet catholicus praedicator, qui divini verbi est prolator" (PL, CCXII, 679 D).

61. Jerome, *h. in Matt.* (*An. mar.*, III, 2, 374).

62. Aponius, *In Cant.*, Bk. VII (131). Honorius, *In Cant.* (PL, CLXXII, 384 C); etc.

63. Greg., *In Ez.*, Peter of Riga, *Aurora, In Cant.* (Pitra, II, 217):

Christi qui spargunt sacra verba, duces animarum,
Signari possunt roseo splendore genarum:
Per quos Ecclesiae facies jucunda nitescit,
Dum per eos credens populorum gloria crescit.

64. Greg., *In Cant.* (PL, LXXIX, 485 A). Honorius, *In Cant.*: "ubera Ecclesiae, magistri in utraque lege docti" (PL, CLXXII, 422 B); etc. Cf. above, Chapter 6.4.

65. Aponius, *In Cant.*, Bk. III (47); Bk. VI (110-1). Alan of Lille, *Distinctiones* (PL, CCX, 746 C); etc.

66. Bede, *In Cant.* (PL, XCI, 1130-1, 1133 CD, 1140A). Robert of Tambelaine, *I Cant.* (PL, LXXIX, 494 B, 508 C, 509 C, 512 A); etc.

67. "Praedicatores Ecclesiae bene labia sponsae esse dicuntur, quia per

populis loquitur, et per eos ad fidem parvuli quique erudiuntur, dum per eos occulta divinae Scripturae quasi cordis latentia manifestantur": Robert of Tambelaine, *In Cant.*, c. iv, n. 15 (512 D).

68. "Ut de dentibus esca subigitur, ita et verbum Dei, qui est panis vitae apostolica traditione tractatus, quae dentibus comparatur, ad omnia viscera ecclesiastici corporis videtur esse submissus": Gr. of Elvira, *Tr.* 4 (75). Beregoz (PL, CLX, 996 D). Werner, *Defl.* Bk. I (CLVII, 973 C). Peter of Riga, *Aurora* (Pitra, II, 13, 214):

> Christi sunt oculi qui sensu mystica cernunt;
> Dentes, qui frangunt fortia dicta patrum.

> Possunt et dentes quadam ratione vocari
> Doctores qui comminuunt, quasi dente molari,
> Panem Scripturae. . . .

69. "In populo fidelium lumen praedicationis fundunt": Alan of Lille, *Dist.* (PL, XXC, 747 D).

70. Cf. *L. de modo bene viv.*, c. v, n. 12 (PL, CLXXXIV, 1200 D): Joachim of Flora, *Sup. 4 ev.*: "spiritales doctores . . . qui claritatem anagogicae intelligentiae primi hominibus ostenderunt" (54).

71. P. of Riga, *Aurora, In Gen.* (Pitra, II, 165):

> Per servos Abrahae doctores accipe sanctos
> Qui de Scripturis mystica verba trahunt.

72. J. of Flora, *op. cit.* (30, 38).

73. S. 22: "apertionem (Scripturae) in intelligentia evangelica vel apostolica doctrina" (PL, CLXXVIII, 521 C). Rabanus, *In Mach.*, Bk. II (CIX, 1243 A).

74. "In voce cataractarum": Rabanus, *De univ.*, Bk. XI, c. vi (PL, CXI, 314-5).

75. "Propter spiritum": Aug., *In ps. CXXXIV*, n. 17 (CCL, 40, 1949-50).

76. Wilmart, *Mém. Lagrange*, 317: "Caelum, sacra Scriptura, ut ibi: 'Caelum sicut liber plicabitur' et iterum: 'Extendens caelum sicut pellem.' Libri plicatio est mysteriorum sacrae Scripturae occultatio, sive praedicationis substractio. Libri vel caeli extensio est sacrae Scripturae seu mysteriorum ejus revelatio."

77. This is not the place to distinguish more kinds of preaching, e.g., kerygma and catechesis. Already in Origen there are no more specialized terms. Let us add that true allegorical exegesis is "spiritual": besides "eruditio," it presupposes "contemplatio." The "doctor perfectus," says St. Gregory, the one who is "in line praedicationis vir perfectus," who possesses the "perfectio praedi is," is he who joins "revelatio contemplationis" to "eruditio sacrae ae"; he whose "doctrina sacri eloquii" is made fruitful by the "revelatio ntemplationis": *In I Reg.*, Bk. III, c. v, n. 30 (PL, LXXIX, 216 BD). s sapientiae praedicator": PL, LXXVI, 309 B.
V, 1036 D; LXXVI, 211 B, 503 D, 606 B; LXXVII, 325 D.
5 (CCL, 122, 289). Autpert, *S. in transf.*, n. 13 (PL, LXXXIX, 314 H); Bk. IX (611 H). Paulinus (XCIX, 154 B, 368 C). L. Carol. , 1116 B). Alcuin, *Ep.* 123 (C, 358 C). *Orationes ad Deum et* ian (CXLV, 592 C, 1119 B). Isaac, s. 10 (CXCIV, 1750 B).

Notes to Pages 222-23

John of Salisbury, *Polycr.*, Bk. IV, c. iii (CXCIX, 518 A). Hervaeus (CLXXXI, 1115). Otto of Fr., *Chr.*, Bk. VIII, *prol.* (278); etc.

81. "Tantus praedicator": Bk. II, c. xxviii (PL, XCVIII, 1097 C). Cf. 1 Tim. 2:7; 2 Tim. 1:11, etc.

82. The "egregius doctor": Greg., *In I Reg.* (PL, LXXIX, 71 B, 177 B). *V. s. Maioli*, Bk. II, c. xvii (CXXXVII, 762 C). H. of Losinga (G.-S., 2, 310). Gerhoh (CXCIV, 1246 B). Bede, *Ep.* 9 (XCIV, 689 B). The title was nevertheless applied to others; it had been even to Ovid!

83. The "mirabilis doctor": Hervaeus, *In I Cor.* (PL, CLXXXI, 815 A): "cui nullus comparari potest in scientia."

84. The "specialis doctor": Irimbert of Admont, *In Jud.*, Bk. V (Pez, 4, 176).

85. The "perfectus doctor evangelii," the "magnus et mirabilis catechizator orbis terrarum": Rupert, *Div. off.*, Bk. IV, c. xxi (PL, CLXX, 116 D, 117 A).

86. The "egregius explanator": Or., *In Rom.*, Bk. III, c. vii (PG, XIV, 942 A).

87. "Profunda et obscura sacrae Scripturae penetravit": Peter Comestor (Martin, RTAM, 1931, 64).

88. "Ipse enim sacramenta legis et evangelii caeteris apostolis manifestius exposuit": Aelred, *S. ined.* 19 (134). Bede, *In Cant.*, Bk. III: "Juxta expositionem Apostoli petra erat Christus" (PL, XCI, 1111 C).

89. "Profunditatem propheticam explanat Apostolus": Arnold of Bonneval, *Hexaem.* (PL, CLXXXIX, 1525 B).

90. Sed. Sc., *In Rom.*: "Certum est in omnibus pene locis Apostoli sensum ex legis et prophetarum manare thesauris" (PL, CIII, 43 B); according to Origen, *In Rom.*, Bk. III, c. viii (PG, XIV, 946 C).

91. "De veteri structa est Instrumento": *Ibid.* (39 B). Cf. Aug., *In ps. CIII, s.* 1, n. 5 (CCL, 40). Already in Clement, *Strom.*, 4, c. xxi, 134: "L'Ecriture de Paul, encore qu'il soit récent dans le temps, est suspendue à l'A.T., d'où elle tire son inspiration et son langage, et la foi du Christ et la connaissance de l'Evangile est l'interprétation et l'accomplissement de la Loi" (Tr. J. Moingt, RSR 47, 543-4).

92. "Spiritualem intelligentiam persequebatur": Herbert of Losinga, *In s. Paul* (G.-S., 2, 300, 310).

93. Prose du Bec, Conv. de s. Paul (ms de 1105; M.W. 1, 529):

Lux aetherea quem circumfulgens visu privat,
   Spiritalem ei intuitum donat.

94. Rupert, *Div. off.*, Bk. VIII, c. viii (PL, CLXX, 225 B). Werner, *Defl.*, Bk. I, *idem*, on the "sancti doctores" (CLVII, 890 D).

95. "Moyses dixit quod Abraham duos filios habuit . . . ; Paulus dixit: Haec sunt duo Testamenta. Divisit hoc verbum, et invenit mysterium. Beatus ergo qui colligit, quod divisit Christus": Ambrose, *In Luc.*, Bk. VI, n. 91 (Tissot, SC, 45, 262).

96. Quodv., *De prom.*, P. II, c. xxi, n. 40: "Hoc ex ore leonis mortui abstulit, qui repulsis Judaeis legem ipsam etiam gentibus ministravit" (PL, LI, 791 A).

97. Joachim of Flora, *Sup. 4 ev.* (99).

98. Or., *Sel. In Ez.*, c. xx (PG, XIII, 819-20 B).

99. Raoul Ardent, *H. in dom. 12 post Trin.* (PL, CLV, 2035 D).

100. Bede, *In Act.*: "Paulus non modo Christi mysteria praedicabat, sed h etiam in Christo Jesu consummata docebat" (PL, XCII, 979 B).

101. PL, CXI.

102. Ps-Hugo (PL, CLXXV, 879-924).

103. Richard, *Nonn. alleg.*: "Ad mensuram (evangelistarum) allegorica doctrina se format" (PL, CXCVI, 220 C). Godfrey of Admont, *H. dom.* 7: "Quia docuit nos Apostolus, sequamur doctrinam illius" (= let us look for the spiritual sense everywhere) (CLXXIV, 60 C).

104. Atto depends a lot on Augustine and Jerome; he copies from the copyists (Rabanus, Claudius, Remi); he borrows a passage of the Ambrosiaster from Claudius (PL, CIV, 837-40).

105. *Exp. ep. S. Pauli* (PL, CXXXIV). *In I Cor.*: "in eo quod Paulus, loquens de N.T., de V.T. sumens exemplum, confirmat, idipsum ostendit concordinam legis et evangelii; ostendit etiam allegorizandum esse" (367 C).

106. *In I Cor.*: "His verbis ostendit nobis exemplum allegorizandi" (372 D). *In Gal.*: "Hoc loco ostendit allegorizandi et figuras requirendi exemplum" (531 A). Cf. Irenaeus, *Adv. Haer.*, Bk. IV, c. xli, n. 4: "Apostolum vero praedicatorem esse veritatis et omnia consonantia veritatis praeconio docuisse" (PG, VII, 1118 A).

107. Paul Bellet, OSB, "Oracio de Claudi de Tori en el comentari a Hebreus del Pseudo Atto de Vercelli," *Colligere Fragmenta*, Festschrift Alban Dold (Beuron, 1952), 140-3. Cf. Stegmüller, s.v. Claudius.

108. "De figuris et de veritate Christi": *In Hebr.*: "Voluit tacito nomine de figuris legis et veritate Christi reddere rationem" (727 B). It is for having neglected this that Miss Smalley, 88, speaks of the "confused Alexandrian terminology" which would relate the word "allegory" equally "to the subject-matter of Scripture and to the method of exposition"; indeed she adds: "'Allegory,' for instance, equals 'doctrine,' whether it be the teaching of St. Paul in his Epistles or the commentator's allegorical exposition of the Law." In the eyes of the whole ancient tradition, Paul was precisely par excellence the commentator or the allegorical exegete of the Law. From the traditional point of view, which ought to be that of the historian, the duality therefore does not exist, at least in this case.

109. *In Hebr.*: "Astruit siquidem omnia, quae ille populus acceperat, significativo modo data sunt" (767 AB). "Omnia siquidem, sive sacerdotium, sive tabernaculum, sive sacrificia, umbrae fuerunt et exemplaria etc." (771 B). Atto himself on occasion develops some classic allegories: *In I Cor.* (367 CD, 368 D), etc. Jerome, *In Is.*, Bk. XVIII, c. lxv: "B. Apostolus Paulus, Christo in eo loquente, Scripturam veterem edisserens, Abraham patriarcham non solum circumcisionis sed praeputii asserit patrem" (PL, XXIV, 646 C); *In Jer.*, Bk. VI: "Nos autem sequentes auctoritatem apostolorum et evangelistarum et maxime apostoli Pauli, [qu]idquid populo Israel carnaliter repromittitur, in nobis spiritualiter completum [de]monstramus" (866 CD). Abelard, *In Rom.*, Bk. IV, c. x (CLXXVIII, 925 AC).

De tenenda, c. vii (PL, CXXI, 1101-2).

x (PL, XCIX, 292 B): "Beatus Apostolus . . . legis aenigmata per [d]isputationum disseruit verba."

[s]ensus apostolicus": *C. Fel. Urg.* (PL, XCIX, 451 C).

[q]uae protulit, allegorice protulit, et mystice cuncta intelligendo 16 (PL, CXXI, 436 C).

[e] vetustas litterae et novitas spiritus": *In Rom.* (PL, CIII,

115. We correct the printed text, which has "utilitatem" [instead of "vilitatem"].

116. "Scyphus argenteus, splendor divinorum eloquiorum. . . . Habebat scyphum argenteum, id est divinam scientiam, sed latebat intra saccum, hoc est intra legalis litterae vilitatem. Sed venit dispensator, disrupit saccum; venit Ananias, missus a Christo, dissolvit legalis litterae grossitudinem, id est caecitatem. Mox scyphus resplenduit, quia Paulus continuo fiducialiter in synagogis agere caepit, praedicans Christum et occidentem litteram ad spiritalem transferens intellectum": *In Gen.*, c. xliv (PL, CXXXI, 120 CD). Cf. 1 Cor. 15:9. In an unedited homily, Gilbert Foliot develops "a very complicated allegory on the cup found in Joseph's brother's sack of wheat" in the same direction: Ch. Dumont, "Autour des sermons *De oneribus* d'Aelred de R.," (COCR, 1957, 118). The same for Honorius, *In s. Pauli die* (CCXXII, 860 C), but without precisions. Notker calls Paul Benjamin (CXXXI, 1014 B).

117. C. vi: "Per architriclinum fortissimum praedicatorem Paulum intelligimus" (PL, CI, 1182 A). Aelred will also say that Paul and his followers "legem intelligunt spiritualem carnalesque observantias evangelicis praeceptis commutant": *S. ined.* 19 (130).

118. "Audi doctorem gentium, audi de ministris unum, qui sciunt unde sit et quomodo factum sit bonum vinum": *S.* 10 (PL, CXCIV, 1724 B).

119. "Cui Redemptor duplicis scientiae, sive duorum Testamentorum pecuniam concedit": Bk. II, c. xxv (PL, XCVIII, 1090 CD). Ambrose, *In Luc.*, Bk. VII, 82 (SC, 52, 35).

120. "Cum alteri concesserit Dei Filius claves regni caelorum, alteri clavem aperiendorum legalium verborum": Bk. I, c. vi (1020 CD). Honorius, *De ss. Petro et Paulo:* "Paulus aperit sua clave januas Scripturae" (CLXXII, 969 D).

121. "[C]ujus rei mysterium ipse Paulus postquam mentionem historiae fecit, statim subsecutus aperuit": Leclercq, *St. ans.*, 31, 125.

122. "Pandit nunc eloquio mystica sereno": *Fons philosophiae*, v. 662 (58).

123. "O quam bonum et quam jucundum sedere ad mensam Pauli! *Et haec refectio, allegorica*": *L. de panibus*, c. ii (PL, CCII, 937 C).

124. *L. div. operum*, P. 3, 10, 9 (PL, CXCVII, 1010 A): ". . . Sicut rota currum, currus vero omne pondus portat: ita doctrina Pauli legem Christ fert, quoniam nova lex de veteri lege texta est, in qua Moyses circumcisionem et oblationes conclusit, quae omnia Spiritus sanctus in novam sanctitatem renovavit, et quae Paulus cum novo igne in submista c[a]tenula monilis justitiae conglutinavit." [Trans. note: "cetenula" — probably a slip for "catenula."]

125. "Recte . . . Ecclesia . . . de Epistolis beati Pauli apostoli non amplius quam quatuordecim tenet, ut etiam ex ipso Epistolarum numero ostenderet quod Doctor egregius Legis et Evangelii secreta rimasset": *Alulfi praefaciuncula in Ep. b. Pauli* (PL, LXXIX, 1202 BC). Hervaeus, *In Ep. s. Pauli, praef.* (CLXXXI, 593 C).

126. Lanfranc, *In omnes ep. s. Pauli, praef.* (PL, CL, 101-2). Hervaeus (CLXXI, 593-4). Cf. Rabanus (CXI, 1275 D).

127. *L. de rebus in adm. sua gestis* (PL, CLXXXVI, 1237 B):

Tollis agendo molam de furfure, Paule, farinam,
    Mosaicae legis intima nota facis;

Fit de tot granis verus sine furfure panis,
   Perpetuusque cibus noster et angelicus.

128. E. Male, *L'art. rel. en Fr. au XII s.*, 2nd ed., 167-8:

Lex Moysis celat quae sermo Pauli revelat:
Nunc data grana Sinaï per eum sunt facta farina.

129. "In culmo sacrae litterae est germen, sive granum spiritalis intelligentiae"; "de culmo litterae illius"; "spiritalis intelligentiae farinam": *In Os.*, Bk. III (PL, CLXVIII, 128 CD).

130. "Sacrificia talis evangelii religione mutasti": *In ps. XXXIX* (An. mar., III, 1, 45).

131. "Paulus, vas electionis, vas aromaticum": *In Cant.*, s. 12, n. 2 (PL, CLXXXIII, 828 D).

132. "Os Pauli, fons magnus et indeficiens": *In Cant.*, s. 10, n. 1 (CLXXXIII, 819 C).

133. "S. Paul et l'exégèse juive de son temps," *Mél. Robert*, 497. Cf. Jean Levie, "Les limites de la preuve d'Écrit. sainte en théologie," NRT 71, 1009-29.

134. "Il faut toujours répéter que le génie de saint Paul, les lumières qu'il reçut de Dieu ne parurent jamais mieux que dans l'accord qu'il perçut entre les deux Testaments." *Ep. aux Romains*, 81; cited by St. Lyonnet, 505.

populis loquitur, et per eos ad fidem parvuli quique erudiuntur, dum per eos occulta divinae Scripturae quasi cordis latentia manifestantur": Robert of Tambelaine, *In Cant.*, c. iv, n. 15 (512 D).

68. "Ut de dentibus esca subigitur, ita et verbum Dei, qui est panis vitae apostolica traditione tractatus, quae dentibus comparatur, ad omnia viscera ecclesiastici corporis videtur esse submissus": Gr. of Elvira, *Tr.* 4 (75). Beregoz (PL, CLX, 996 D). Werner, *Defl.* Bk. I (CLVII, 973 C). Peter of Riga, *Aurora* (Pitra, II, 13, 214):

> Christi sunt oculi qui sensu mystica cernunt;
> Dentes, qui frangunt fortia dicta patrum.
>
> Possunt et dentes quadam ratione vocari
> Doctores qui comminuunt, quasi dente molari,
> Panem Scripturae. . . .

69. "In populo fidelium lumen praedicationis fundunt": Alan of Lille, *Dist.* (PL, XXC, 747 D).

70. Cf. *L. de modo bene viv.*, c. v, n. 12 (PL, CLXXXIV, 1200 D): Joachim of Flora, *Sup. 4 ev.*: "spiritales doctores . . . qui claritatem anagogicae intelligentiae primi hominibus ostenderunt" (54).

71. P. of Riga, *Aurora, In Gen.* (Pitra, II, 165):

> Per servos Abrahae doctores accipe sanctos
> Qui de Scripturis mystica verba trahunt.

72. J. of Flora, *op. cit.* (30, 38).

73. *S.* 22: "apertionem (Scripturae) in intelligentia evangelica vel apostolica doctrina" (PL, CLXXVIII, 521 C). Rabanus, *In Mach.*, Bk. II (CIX, 1243 A).

74. "In voce cataractarum": Rabanus, *De univ.*, Bk. XI, c. vi (PL, CXI, 314-5).

75. "Propter spiritum": Aug., *In ps. CXXXIV*, n. 17 (CCL, 40, 1949-50).

76. Wilmart, *Mém. Lagrange*, 317: "Caelum, sacra Scriptura, ut ibi: 'Caelum sicut liber plicabitur' et iterum: 'Extendens caelum sicut pellem.' Libri plicatio est mysteriorum sacrae Scripturae occultatio, sive praedicationis substractio. Libri vel caeli extensio est sacrae Scripturae seu mysteriorum ejus revelatio."

77. This is not the place to distinguish more kinds of preaching, e.g., kerygma and catechesis. Already in Origen there are no more specialized terms. Let us add that true allegorical exegesis is "spiritual": besides "eruditio," it presupposes "contemplatio." The "doctor perfectus," says St. Gregory, the one who is "in ordine praedicationis vir perfectus," who possesses the "perfectio praedicationis," is he who joins "revelatio contemplationis" to "eruditio sacrae Scripturae"; he whose "doctrina sacri eloquii" is made fruitful by the "revelatio internae contemplationis": *In I Reg.*, Bk. III, c. v, n. 30 (PL, LXXIX, 216 BD).

78. "Verus sapientiae praedicator": PL, LXXVI, 309 B.

79. PL, LXXV, 1036 D; LXXVI, 211 B, 503 D, 606 B; LXXVII, 325 D.

80. Bede, *H.* 35 (CCL, 122, 289). Autpert, *S. in transf.*, n. 13 (PL, LXXXIX, 314 C); *In Ap.* Bk. I (412 H); Bk. IX (611 H). Paulinus (XCIX, 154 B, 368 C). *L. Carol.* (XCVIII, 1091 D, 1098 A, 1116 B). Alcuin, *Ep.* 123 (C, 358 C). *Orationes ad Deum et apost.* (CI, 1168 A). P. Damian (CXLV, 592 C, 1119 B). Isaac, *s.* 10 (CXCIV, 1750 B).

omnis vera voluptas emanat. . . . Quae (aqua) tam longe lateque defluxit, ut mundum repleverit universum. . . . Haec irrigat paradisum, id est fecundat Ecclesiam . . .": *In comm. de ev., s.* 3 (PL, CCXVII, 605 CD).

52. Or., *De princ.*, Bk. I, *praef.*, c. ii: "servetur vero ecclesiastica praedicatio per successionis ordinem ab apostolis tradita et usque ad praesens in ecclesia permanens" (8). Robert of Tombelaine, *In Cant.*, c. viii, n. 2 (PL, LXXIX, 529 B); n. 13: "sanctae Ecclesiae fidem praedicans" (544 D). Cf. Greg., *In I Reg.*, Bk. II, c. ii, n. 17: "praedicator sanctae Ecclesiae" (153 A); n. 26 (157 C). Autpert, *In Ap.* (573 F); etc.

53. "Mysterium Salvatoris, praedicatione patefactum apostolica": Florus, *De tenenda*, c. vii (PL, CXXI, 1101 CD). Paulinus, *C. Elip.*, c. vii (XCIX, 158 A).

54. *C. Faust.*, Bk. XXII, c. lxxix: "Dispensatores N.T., idemque expositores V. T." (PL, XLII, 451). Abelard on Jacob's ladder: "Hujus scalae, hoc est sacrae Scripturae, quasi duo latera duo sunt Testamenta, quae quidem ad invicem quasi quibusdam gradibus insertis connectuntur, dum per expositiones doctorum rota rotae applicatur, et quod in veteri fuerat praedictum, in novo monstratur exhibitum. Angeli per hanc scalam ascendentes et descendentes, sancti sunt praedicatores" (CLXXVIII, 553 B).

55. Maximus of Turin, *s.* 80, on Cyprian (PL, LVII, 426 C).

56. "Ubi veteris obscuritas revelatur": Aug., *C. Faust.*, Bk. XXII, c. lxxvii (PL, XLII, 450).

57. Thus in the explication of Ps. 7:13: "arcum suum tetendit et paravit illum," those who make the O.T. intelligible by the New are sometimes named "expositores" (Gerhoh, PL, CXCIII, 735 B), sometimes "doctores" (Aimo, CXVI, 219 A). Bede, *In Cant.:* "Doctores . . . Idem sancti praedicatores" (XCI, 1192 CD).

58. "Quia sacramenta prophetiae sanctis doctoribus, qui haec toto orbe praedicent, patefecit": Jerome, *In Is.*, Bk. XVI, c. lviii (PL, XXIV, 567 B). Bede, *In Marc.* 6 (XCII, 194 B). Ps.-Bede, *In Matt.* 14 (72 C).

59. Br. of Segni, *In Ap.*, Bk. II, c. iv (PL, CLXV, 626 A). Rabanus, *In Paral.*, Bk. IV, c. xxvii (CIX, 514 B).

60. Hélinand, *s.* 24: "Os autem Domini recte appellari potest quilibet catholicus praedicator, qui divini verbi est prolator" (PL, CCXII, 679 D).

61. Jerome, *h. in Matt.* (*An. mar.*, III, 2, 374).

62. Aponius, *In Cant.*, Bk. VII (131). Honorius, *In Cant.* (PL, CLXXII, 384 C); etc.

63. Greg., *In Ez.*, Peter of Riga, *Aurora, In Cant.* (Pitra, II, 217):

Christi qui spargunt sacra verba, duces animarum,
Signari possunt roseo splendore genarum:
Per quos Ecclesiae facies jucunda nitescit,
Dum per eos credens populorum gloria crescit.

64. Greg., *In Cant.* (PL, LXXIX, 485 A). Honorius, *In Cant.:* "ubera Ecclesiae, magistri in utraque lege docti" (PL, CLXXII, 422 B); etc. Cf. above, Chapter 6.4.

65. Aponius, *In Cant.*, Bk. III (47); Bk. VI (110-1). Alan of Lille, *Distinctiones* (PL, CCX, 746 C); etc.

66. Bede, *In Cant.* (PL, XCI, 1130-1, 1133 CD, 1140A). Robert of Tambelaine, *In Cant.* (PL, LXXIX, 494 B, 508 C, 509 C, 512 A); etc.

67. "Praedicatores Ecclesiae bene labia sponsae esse dicuntur, quia per eos

Index

Abbo, 70
Abbo of Fleury, 144
Abelard, 49, 94, 195, 215, 221
Absalon, 31, 173
Adalberon of Reims, 120
Adam of Perseigne, 88
Adam of Saint Victor, 85
Adam Scotus, 38, 49, 79, 88, 113, 119, 135, 137, 138, 146, 152, 176, 184, 190
Adrevald of Fleury-sur-Loire, 48
Aelfric the Englishman, 120
Aelred of Rievaulx, 107, 113, 140, 147, 149, 160, 165, 169, 173
Aileran the Wise, 215
Aimé of Monte-Cassino, 201
Aimon of Auxerre, 9, 53, 74, 91, 92, 164
Aimon of Bazoches, 164, 165
Alan of Lille, 30, 49, 165, 169, 177
Albert the Great, 38
Alcuin, 48, 68, 119, 164, 167, 218, 224
Aldhelm, 94, 119, 163
Aldhelm of Sherborne, 37
Alexander Neckam, 31, 149, 187
Alexander of Canterbury, 112, 114, 176, 191
Alvarus, Paul, 9
Alvarus of Cordoba, 25, 223
Amalarius, 37
Ambrose, 7, 8, 22, 23, 28, 29, 30, 52, 59, 64, 65, 74, 83, 86, 87, 90, 93, 107, 141, 160, 171, 176, 187, 203, 206
Ambrose Autpert, 8, 57, 74, 91, 122, 156, 163, 167, 168, 190, 192
Anaxagoras, 2
Angelome of Luxeuil, 48, 57, 91, 113
Angelus Silesius, 139, 140
Anselm, 149
Antisthenes, 2, 102
Aponius, 57, 136, 163
Arator, 44
Aristides Quintilian, 2
Aristophanes, 3
Aristotle, 3, 59
Ariulphe, 70
Arnold of Bonneval, 49
Arnold of Brescia, 169
Arno of Reichersberg, 147, 148
Aspringius, 112
Atto of Vercelli, 223
Augustine, 3, 7, 8, 17, 20, 21, 22, 42, 45, 46, 47, 50, 51, 52, 57, 62, 63, 64, 65, 66, 68, 76, 77, 78, 83, 86, 87, 88, 90, 92, 93, 95, 96, 98, 102, 107, 114-17, 120, 123, 124, 136, 140, 141, 142, 143, 149, 152, 154, 163, 166, 184, 185, 188, 189, 190, 193, 195, 209, 213, 214-15, 220, 221
Avitus, 109

Bachiarius, 107

Index

Baron, S. W., 19
Barth, Karl, 96
Baruzi, Jean, 139
Bauer, G. L., 18
Beatus of Liebana, 24, 42, 80, 84, 107
Becket, Thomas, 121
Bede, 37, 38, 48, 51, 59, 61, 68, 70, 73, 74, 84, 87, 90, 91, 114, 119, 163, 199, 213
Béleth, John, 199
Benedict, 147, 148, 149, 151
Berengaud, 75, 87, 110, 111, 114, 192
Bernard, 20, 22, 34, 57, 62, 78, 107, 113, 120, 122, 135, 136, 137, 140, 144, 150, 151-58, 160, 161-62, 165, 169, 172, 173, 175, 194, 196, 206, 208, 213, 215, 216, 226
Bernard de Morval, 200
Bernard of Cluny, 123
Bischoff, Berhard, 212
Bloch, Marc, 72
Bodard, Claude, 152
Boethius, 215
Bonaventure, 25, 37, 144, 169, 198, 203
Bossuet, 26, 107
Braulio of Saragossa, 8
Brücker, J., 206
Bruno, 84, 87, 223
Bruno of Segni, 61, 85, 166

Cassian, John, 8, 26, 87, 149, 180, 181, 194, 204
Cassiodorus, 73, 101, 163, 213, 216-17, 223
Celsus, 64
Christian of Stavelot, 48, 78
Chrysostom, John, 9, 14, 15, 17, 69, 86
Cicero, 17, 70, 101
Claudel, Paul, 47, 140
Claudius of Turin, 8, 24, 36, 54, 68, 74, 84, 87, 107, 223
Clement of Alexandria, 3, 29, 35, 87, 103, 104
Columban, 171
Conrad of Hirschau, 42
Cornutus, 3, 12, 104

Cunibert, 168
Curtius, E. R., 19
Cyprian, 52
Cyril of Alexandria, 36, 93

Damasus, 163
David of Augsbourg, 49
Democritus, 2
Denis the Little, 149
Didymus the Blind, 36, 180, 199
Diogenes of Apollonia, 2
Dionysius, 66, 120, 180, 194-96
Dionysius of Halicarnassus, 3
Dionysius the Carthusian, 37, 50
Dorsch, E., 18
Doutreleau, 199
Dumontier, 152
Dungal, 168
Durandus of Mende, 23

Eadmer, 119
Ebert, 206
Egbert of Schönau, 169
Elmer of Canterbury, 119
Epicurus, 2
Eucher, 32, 88
Eusebius, 3, 149
Everard of Bethune, 177
Ewald, H., 18

Faustus, 63
Febvre, Lucien, 67
Felix of Urgel, 223
Florentius of Worcester, 165
Florus of Lyon, 223
Foliot, Gilbert, 97, 170, 175, 176
Fréculphe of Lisieux, 42, 68, 215
Fulbert of Chartres, 168

Garnier of Rochefort, 66, 88, 113, 160, 195, 196
Garnier of Saint Victor, 121
Gaudentius of Brescia, 30, 45, 51
Geoffrey of Auxerre, 120, 147, 152, 165, 172
Gerbet, 204
Gerhoh of Reichersberg, 22, 30, 53, 54, 61, 62, 87, 113, 130, 147, 161

Index

Gertrude, 169
Gilbert Foliot, 173
Gilbert of Hoyland, 157, 160, 165
Gilbert of Stanford, 160
Giles of Paris, 94, 177
Gilson, Etienne, 158
Glaber, Raoul, 70, 73
Godfrey of Admont, 28, 46, 87, 119, 162, 175, 190
Godfrey of Saint Victor, 130, 169, 201, 224
Godfrey of Viterbo, 215
Goscelin, 168
Gratian, 121
Gregory, 8, 17, 23, 24-25, 31, 33, 45, 46, 48, 52, 54, 62, 65, 66, 70, 73, 74, 76, 79, 80, 82, 83, 87, 88, 99, 106, 109, 110-11, 114, 117, 118-23, 128, 134, 135, 137, 142, 143, 144, 154, 155, 158, 160, 167, 170-71, 173, 184, 185, 187, 193, 194, 195, 196, 201, 204, 205-206, 217, 218, 222
Gregory of Elvira, 22, 29, 53
Gregory of Nazianzus, 102, 185
Gregory of Nyssa, 23, 35, 86, 180, 204
Gregory of Tours, 109
Grelot, P., 7
Grimaldus, 119
Guerric of Igny, 157, 162, 165, 173
Guibert of Nogent, 28, 30, 31, 38, 58, 73, 74, 91, 113, 177, 199, 215

Hadrian I, 171
Harnack, 206
Hatch, Edwin, 11-12
Hélinand of Froidmont, 28, 119, 122, 139
Henry of Marcy, 49, 162
Heraclitus, 2, 15
Herbert of Losinga, 21
Herrad of Landsberg, 169
Hervaeus of Bourg Dieu, 30, 48, 66, 85, 113, 138, 190
Heterius, 107
Hilary, 7, 20, 29, 86, 90, 96
Hildebert, 26
Hildegard, 224
Hippolytus, 136

Honorius, 38, 54, 91, 95, 120, 132, 147, 164, 175, 198, 199, 215
Hugh Métel, 78, 171
Hugh of Fleury, 70
Hugh of Rouen, 78, 176
Hugh of Saint Victor, 25, 30, 38, 43, 49, 56, 61, 77, 85, 88, 98, 113, 119, 129, 157, 160, 170, 176, 194
Hugo, 164, 190
Hugo de Fouilloy, 199
Humbert, 48, 107

Innocent III, 38, 66, 190, 220
Irenaeus, 17, 53, 64, 104, 184, 219
Irimbert of Admont, 91, 96, 114, 169, 170, 175
Isaac of Stella, 62, 78, 107, 158, 162, 196, 202, 224
Isidore of Seville, 24, 42, 43, 48, 57, 66, 74, 84, 86, 90, 91, 113, 114, 120, 143, 167, 172, 204, 205

Jerome, 9, 14, 25, 35, 36, 46, 47, 49, 51, 53, 55, 58, 59, 61, 65, 70, 74, 77, 80, 83, 87, 91, 137, 139, 149, 157, 160, 166, 180, 185, 187, 190, 199, 208, 213, 216, 226
Joachim of Flora, 110
John Gualbert, 168
John of Ford, 168, 219
John of Gorze, 122
John of Kelso, 49, 113
John of Saint Vincent, 168
John of Salisbury, 38, 49, 66, 79, 88, 113, 119, 121
John the Deacon, 72, 171
John Scotus Erigena, 33, 89, 113, 161, 189, 194, 196
Josephus, 28
Julian the Apostate, 13, 100
Junilius the African, 73-74, 87

Keble, John, 12

Lactantius, 3
Lagrange, 226
Laidcend, 121
Laistner, L. W., 212

Index

Langton, Stephen, 37, 44, 49, 88, 199
Leander of Seville, 72
Leclercq, Jean, 214
Leo, 116-17, 158, 185
Letald of Micy, 73
Letbert of Saint Ruf, 137
Longinus, 2
Louis of Leon, 58
Lucian, 2
Lupus of Ferrières, 120
Lyonnet, Stanislas, 226

McNally, Robert, 212
Maimonides, 59
Malraux, André, 150
Manegold, 97, 120, 164, 171
Marbodius, 165
Marcion, 123
Martianus Capella, 90
Melanchthon, 206
Mercury Quadratus, 100
Metrodorus of Lampsacus, 2
Milburn, R. L. P., 7
Milo of Saint Amand, 167
Mohrmann, Christine, 22
Morus, Nathan, 11
Mosheim, 47
Mouroux, Jean, 160

Newman, J. H., 12
Nicholas of Lyra, 10, 34, 37, 58, 173, 199
Nöldeke, Th., 18
Notker Labeo, 121
Notker the Stammerer, 48, 119, 121, 171

Ockham, 195
Odo of Cambrai, 169
Odo of Canterbury, 224
Odo of Cluny, 118, 123, 200
Odo of Ourscamp, 150
Odorannus, 137
Oger, 173
Olympiadorus, 3, 180
Ordericus Vitalis, 42-43
Origen, 5-7, 9, 10, 12, 13, 14-15, 17, 18, 23, 24, 25, 27, 28, 29, 32, 35, 45, 46, 47, 51, 52, 53, 55, 56, 57, 60, 61, 63, 64, 67-68, 74, 75, 80, 86, 87, 90, 95, 101, 102, 104-5, 107, 109, 114, 117, 124, 127, 134, 136, 140, 143, 146, 149, 154, 158, 159-63, 169, 173, 175, 180, 184-85, 189, 199, 204, 205, 206, 209, 212, 214, 219
Othloh of Saint Emmeran, 73, 85, 88, 91, 112, 164, 185
Otto of Freising, 43, 70, 117, 215

Pachomius, 149
Pascal, Blaise, 135
Paschasius Radbertus, 24, 28, 36, 87, 111, 184, 189
Paterius, 119, 121
Paul, 1, 6-9, 11, 183, 222-23, 225
Paul the Deacon, 74
Paula, 47
Paulinus of Aquilaea, 25, 85, 131, 157, 167, 219, 223
Paulinus of Nola, 163, 166, 168, 172
Paul of Nisibis, 87
Peter Cellensis, 224
Peter Comestor, 28, 48, 49, 73, 78, 88, 173, 177, 195, 215
Peter Damian, 25, 87, 93, 119, 149, 164-65, 168, 171, 184, 187
Peter Lombard, 30, 92, 177, 190
Peter of Cornwall, 109
Peter of Poitiers, 49, 88, 91
Peter of Riga, 144, 156, 177
Peter the Venerable, 110, 121
Petrus Cellensis, 147
Philodemus of Gadara, 1
Philo of Alexandria, 3-4, 7, 28, 33, 142, 148
Plato, 2, 3
Plotinus, 15-16
Plutarch, 2, 10, 13, 18
Porphyry, 2-3, 4, 12, 18, 215
Potho of Prüm, 94, 137
Preiss, Th., 19
Proclus, 3, 180
Prodicus of Ceos, 2
Pseudo-Bede, 28
Pseudo-Dionysius, 65, 180
Pseudo-Eloi, 84

Index

Pseudo-Heraclitus of Pontus, 1, 15
Pseudo-Hugo, 88
Pseudo-Plutarch, 2
Pseudo-Primasius, 8
Pseudo-Remigius of Auxerre, 23

Quintilian, 89
Quodvultdeus, 91, 163

Rabanus Maurus, 9, 21, 22, 24, 30, 36, 37, 38, 46, 48, 53, 68, 74, 75, 78, 84, 87, 98, 109, 114, 119, 120, 142, 144, 152, 188, 199, 204-5, 216, 223
Raoul of Saint Germer, 48, 203
Remi of Auxerre, 36, 67, 87, 94, 224
Richard of Cirencestria, 70
Richard of Middleton, 50
Richard of Saint Victor, 24, 34, 49, 57-58, 66, 81, 88, 91, 98, 112, 131, 153, 157, 164, 170, 190, 203, 217, 223
Robert of Melun, 42, 85, 92, 129
Robert of Mont Saint Michel, 70
Robert Puyllen, 144
Rodolphe of Saint Trond, 73
Roger of Wendover, 70, 172
Rosenmüller, I. G., 11, 37
Rufinus, 20, 23, 24, 25, 79
Rupert of Deutz, 24, 25, 28, 32, 34, 36, 48, 51, 53, 57, 59, 62, 74, 87, 93, 94, 98, 107, 112, 114, 119, 137, 144, 149, 151, 160, 161, 169, 170, 175, 189, 192, 195, 203, 219, 225

Sallust, 3, 13, 15-16, 100
Sandaeus, 139
Schrader, Ed., 18
Sedulius Scotus, 9, 114, 167, 199, 223
Seneca, 29
Serlon of Savigny, 95
Sigebert of Gembloux, 43, 117
Simon, Richard, 10
Sixtus of Sienna, 37, 38
Smalley, Beryl, 59, 212

Smaragdus, 167, 205
Spicq, C., 212
Stephen of Tournai, 120
Stesimbrotus, of Thasos, 2
Strabo, 2
Strauss, D. Fr., 18
Stücken, E., 18
Suger, 225

Tajón of Saragossa, 121
Tertullian, 3, 4-5, 8, 9, 10, 21, 86
Theagenes of Rhegium, 2
Theodemir, 107
Thomas Aquinas, 35, 185, 197
Thomas of Perseigne, 219
Thomas of Vercelli, 177
Titus Livy, 70
Tostado, Alonso, 181
Turre, J. M. de, 197
Tyconius the African, 93, 115

Ulrich of Strasbourg, 49
Urban II, 148

Vaccari, A., 18, 212
Victor, 214
Vincent of Lerins, 167

Walafrid Strabo, 96
Wellhausen, J., 18
Wette, Lebrecht de, 18
William Firmat, 160
William of Malmsbury, 43
William of Saint Thierry, 20, 32, 57, 82, 150, 160, 216
Williram of Ebersberg, 170
Winckler, H.

Xenophon, 3

Zeno, 102
Zöckler, 213